FOLKWAYS

A STUDY OF
MORES, MANNERS,
CUSTOMS AND MORALS

WILLIAM GRAHAM SUMNER

DOVER PUBLICATIONS, INC.
MINEOLA, NEW YORK

Published in the United Kingdom by David & Charles, Brunel House, Forde Close, Newton Abbot, Devon TQ12 4PU.

Bibliographical Note

This Dover edition, first published in 2002, is an unabridged republication of the last Ginn and Company edition of the work originally published in 1907 by Ginn and Company under the title *Folkways: A Study of the Sociological Importance of Usages, Manners, Customs, Mores, and Morals* and first republished by Dover Publications, Inc. in 1959.

Library of Congress Cataloging-in-Publication Data

Sumner, William Graham, 1840–1910.
    Folkways : a study of mores, manners, customs and morals / William Graham Sumner.
        p. cm.
    Originally published: Boston : Ginn, 1907.
    Includes bibliographical references and index.
    ISBN 0-486-42496-0 (pbk.)
      1. Manners and customs. I. Title.

GT75 .S8 2002
390—dc21

                                     2002025911

Manufactured in the United States of America
Dover Publications, Inc., 31 East 2nd Street, Mineola, N.Y. 11501

PREFACE

In 1899 I began to write out a text-book of sociology from material which I had used in lectures during the previous ten or fifteen years. At a certain point in that undertaking I found that I wanted to introduce my own treatment of the "mores." I could not refer to it anywhere in print, and I could not do justice to it in a chapter of another book. I therefore turned aside to write a treatise on the "Folkways," which I now offer. For definitions of "folkways" and "mores" see secs. 1, 2, 34, 39, 43, and 66. I formed the word "folkways" on the analogy of words already in use in sociology. I also took up again the Latin word "mores" as the best I could find for my purpose. I mean by it the popular usages and traditions, when they include a judgment that they are conducive to societal welfare, and when they exert a coercion on the individual to conform to them, although they are not coördinated by any authority (cf. sec. 42). I have also tried to bring the word "Ethos" into familiarity again (secs. 76, 79). "Ethica," or "Ethology," or "The Mores" seemed good titles for the book (secs. 42, 43), but Ethics is already employed otherwise, and the other words were very unfamiliar. Perhaps "folkways" is not less unfamiliar, but its meaning is more obvious. I must add that if any one is liable to be shocked by *any* folkways, he ought not to read about folkways at all. "Nature her custom holds, let shame say what it will" (*Hamlet*, IV, 7, *ad fin.*). I have tried to treat all folkways, including those which are most opposite to our own, with truthfulness, but with dignity and due respect to our own conventions.

Chapter I contains elaborate definitions and expositions of the folkways and the mores, with an analysis of their play in human society. Chapter II shows the bearing of the folkways on human interests, and the way in which they act or are acted on. The thesis which is expounded in these two chapters is : that the folkways are habits of the individual and customs of the society which arise from efforts to satisfy needs ; they are intertwined with goblinism and demonism and primitive notions of luck (sec. 6), and so they win traditional authority. Then they become regulative for succeeding generations and take on the character of a social force. They arise no one knows whence or how. They grow as if by the play of internal life energy. They can be modified, but only to a limited extent, by the purposeful efforts of men. In time they lose power, decline, and die, or are transformed. While they are in vigor they very largely control individual and social undertakings, and they produce and nourish ideas of world philosophy and life policy. Yet they are not organic or material. They belong to a superorganic system of relations, conventions, and institutional arrangements. The study of them is called for by their *social* character, by virtue of which they are leading factors in the science of society.

When the analysis of the folkways has been concluded it is necessary that it should be justified by a series of illustrations, or by a setting forth of cases in which the operation of the mores is shown to be what is affirmed in the analysis. Any such exposition of the mores in cases, in order to be successful, must go into details. It is in details that all the graphic force and argumentative value of the cases are to be found. It has not been easy to do justice to the details and to observe the necessary limits of space. The ethnographical facts which I present are not subsequent justification of generalizations otherwise obtained. They are selections from a great array of facts from which the generalizations were deduced. A number of other very important cases which I included in my plan of proofs and illustrations I have been obliged to leave out for lack of space. Such are : Demonism, Primitive Religion, and Witchcraft ; The Status of Women; War ; Evolution and the Mores ; Usury ; Gambling ; Societal

Organization and Classes; Mortuary Usages; Oaths; Taboos; Ethics; Æsthetics; and Democracy. The first four of these are written. I may be able to publish them soon, separately. My next task is to finish the sociology.

W. G. SUMNER

YALE UNIVERSITY

With the reprinting of *Folkways* it seems in place to inform the admirers of this book and of its author concerning the progress of Professor Sumner's work between 1907 and his death, in his seventieth year, in April, 1910. Several articles bearing on the mores, and realizing in part the programme outlined in the last paragraph of the foregoing Preface, have been published: "The Family and Social Change," in the *American Journal of Sociology* for March, 1909 (14: 577–591); "Witchcraft," in the *Forum* for May, 1909 (41: 410–423); "The Status of Women in Chaldea, Egypt, India, Judea, and Greece to the time of Christ," in the *Forum* for August, 1909 (42: 113–136); "Mores of the Present and the Future," in the *Yale Review* for November, 1909 (18: 233–245); and "Religion and the Mores," in the *American Journal of Sociology* for March, 1910 (15: 577–591). Of these the first and last were presidential addresses before the American Sociological Society. All are included in Volume I (War and Other Essays) of a four-volume set of Sumner's writings, published since his death by the Yale University Press.

Regarding the treatise on the "science of society" (for he had decided to call it that instead of "sociology") mentioned in the Preface, it should be said that Professor Sumner left a considerable amount of manuscript in the rather rough form of a first draft, together with a great mass of classified materials. He wrote very little on this treatise after the completion of *Folkways*, and not infrequently spoke of the latter to the present writer as "my last book." It is intended, however, that the *Science of Society* shall be, at some time in the future, completed, and in such form as shall give to the world the fruits of Professor Sumner's intellectual power, clarity of vision, and truly herculean industry.

The present revision of *Folkways* incorporates but few and unimportant corrections. Certain of these are from the hand of the author, and others from that of the present writer.

A photograph of Professor Sumner has been chosen for insertion in the present edition.* It was taken April 18, 1902, and is regarded by many as being the most faithful representation in existence of Sumner's expression and pose, as he appeared in later years. This is the Sumner of the " mores," with mental powers at ripe maturity and bodily vigor as yet unimpaired by age. The Yale commencement orator of 1909 said of Sumner, in presenting him for the Doctorate of Laws : " His intellect has broadened, his heart has mellowed, as he has descended into the vale of years." While advancing age weakened in no respect the sheer power and the steady-eyed fearlessness of mind and character which made Sumner a compelling force in the university and in the wider world, it seems to some of us that the essential kindliness of his nature came out with especial clearness in his later years. And it is the suggestion of this quality which lends a distinctive charm, in our eyes, to the portrait chosen to head this volume.

A. G. KELLER

YALE UNIVERSITY

*Editor's Note to the 2002 Dover Edition: The photograph is not reproduced in this edition.

CONTENTS

FOLKWAYS

CHAPTER I

FUNDAMENTAL NOTIONS OF THE FOLKWAYS AND OF THE MORES

Definition and mode of origin of the folkways. — The folkways are a societal force. — Folkways are made unconsciously. — Impulse and instinct; primeval stupidity; magic. — The strain of improvement and consistency. — The aleatory element. — All origins are lost in mystery. — Spencer on primitive custom. — Good and bad luck; ills of life; goodness and happiness. — Illustrations. — Immortality and compensation. — Tradition and its restraints. — The concepts of "primitive society"; "we-groups" and "others-groups." — Sentiments in the in-group towards out-groups. — Ethnocentrism. — Illustrations. — Patriotism. — Chauvinism. — The struggle for existence and the competition of life; antagonistic coöperation. — Four motives: hunger, love, vanity, fear. — The process of making folkways. — Suggestion and suggestibility. — Suggestion in education. — Manias. — Suggestion in politics. — Suggestion and criticism — Folkways based on false inferences. — Harmful folkways. — How "true" and "right" are found. — The folkways are right; rights; morals. — The folkways are true. — Relations of world philosophy to folkways. — Definition of the mores. — Taboos. — No primitive philosophizing; myths; fables; notion of social welfare. — The imaginative element. — The ethical policy and the success policy. — Recapitulation. — Scope and method of the mores. — Integration of the mores of a group or age. — Purpose of the present work. — Why use the word "mores." — The mores are a directive force. — Consistency in the mores. — The mores of subgroups. — What are classes? — Classes rated by societal value. — Class; race; group solidarity. — The masses and the mores. — Fallacies about the classes and the masses. — Action of the masses on ideas. — Organization of the masses. — Institutions of civil liberty. — The common man. — The "people"; popular impulses. — Agitation. — The ruling element in the masses. — The mores and institutions. — Laws. — How laws and institutions differ from mores. — Difference between mores and some cognate things. — Goodness or badness of the mores. — More exact definition of the mores. — Ritual. — The ritual of the mores. — Group interests and policy. — Group interests and folkways. — Force in the folkways. — Might and right. — Status. — Conventionalization. — Conventions indispensable. — The "ethos" or group character; Japan. — Chinese ethos. — Hindoo ethos. — European ethos.

1. Definition and mode of origin of the folkways. If we put together all that we have learned from anthropology and ethnography about primitive men and primitive society, we perceive that the first task of life is to live. Men begin with acts, not with thoughts. Every moment brings necessities which must be satisfied at once. Need was the first experience, and it was followed at once by a blundering effort to satisfy it. It is generally taken for granted that men inherited some guiding instincts from their beast ancestry, and it may be true, although it has never been proved. If there were such inheritances, they controlled and aided the first efforts to satisfy needs. Analogy makes it easy to assume that the ways of beasts had produced channels of habit and predisposition along which dexterities and other psychophysical activities would run easily. Experiments with newborn animals show that in the absence of any experience of the relation of means to ends, efforts to satisfy needs are clumsy and blundering. The method is that of trial and failure, which produces repeated pain, loss, and disappointments. Nevertheless, it is a method of rude experiment and selection. The earliest efforts of men were of this kind. Need was the impelling force. Pleasure and pain, on the one side and the other, were the rude constraints which defined the line on which efforts must proceed. The ability to distinguish between pleasure and pain is the only psychical power which is to be assumed. Thus ways of doing things were selected, which were expedient. They answered the purpose better than other ways, or with less toil and pain. Along the course on which efforts were compelled to go, habit, routine, and skill were developed. The struggle to maintain existence was carried on, not individually, but in groups. Each profited by the other's experience; hence there was concurrence towards that which proved to be most expedient. All at last adopted the same way for the same purpose; hence the ways turned into customs and became mass phenomena. Instincts were developed in connection with them. In this way folkways arise. The young learn them by tradition, imitation, and authority. The folkways, at a time, provide for all the needs of life then and there. They are uniform, universal in the group, imperative, and invariable. As time goes on, the folkways become more and more arbitrary, positive, and imperative. If asked why they act in a certain way in certain cases, primitive people always answer that it is because they and their ancestors always have done so. A sanction also arises from ghost fear. The ghosts of ancestors would be angry if the living should change the ancient folkways (see sec. 6).

2. The folkways are a societal force. The operation by which folkways are produced consists in the frequent repetition of petty acts, often by great numbers acting in concert or, at least, acting in the same way when face to face with the same need. The immediate motive is interest. It produces habit in the individual and custom in the group. It is, therefore, in the highest degree original and primitive. By habit and custom it exerts a strain on every individual within its range; therefore it rises to a societal force to which great classes of societal phenomena are due. Its earliest stages, its course, and laws may be studied; also its influence on individuals and their reaction on it. It is our present purpose so to study it. We have to recognize it as one of the chief forces by which a society is made to be what it is. Out of the unconscious experiment which every repetition of the ways includes, there issues pleasure or pain, and then, so far as the men are capable of reflection, convictions that the ways are conducive to societal welfare. These two experiences are not the same. The most uncivilized men, both in the food quest and in war, do things which are painful, but which have been found to be expedient. Perhaps these cases teach the sense of social welfare better than those which are pleasurable and favorable to welfare. The former cases call for some intelligent reflection on experience. When this conviction as to the relation to welfare is added to the folkways they are converted into mores, and, by virtue of the philosophical and ethical element added to them, they win utility and importance and become the source of the science and the art of living.

3. Folkways are made unconsciously. It is of the first importance to notice that, from the first acts by which men try to satisfy needs, each act stands by itself, and looks no further than the immediate satisfaction. From recurrent needs arise habits for the individual and customs for the group, but these results are consequences which were never conscious, and never foreseen or intended. They are not noticed until they have long existed, and it is still longer before they are appreciated. Another long time must pass, and a higher stage of mental development must be reached, before they can be used as a basis from which to deduce rules for meeting, in the future, problems whose pressure can be foreseen. The folkways, therefore, are not creations of human purpose and wit. They are like products of natural forces which men unconsciously set in operation, or they are like the instinctive ways of animals, which are developed out of experience, which reach a final form of maximum adaptation to an interest, which are handed down by tradition and admit of no exception or variation, yet change to meet new conditions, still within the same limited methods, and without rational reflection or purpose. From this it results that all the life of human beings, in all ages and stages of culture, is primarily controlled by a vast mass of folkways handed down from the earliest existence of the race, having the nature of the ways of other animals, only the topmost layers of which are subject to change and control, and have been somewhat modified by human philosophy, ethics, and religion, or by other acts of intelligent reflection. We are told of savages that "It is difficult to exhaust the customs and small ceremonial usages of a savage people. Custom regulates the whole of a man's actions, — his bathing, washing, cutting his hair, eating, drinking, and fasting. From his cradle to his grave he is the slave of ancient usage. In his life there is nothing free, nothing original, nothing spontaneous, no progress towards a higher and better life, and no attempt to improve his condition, mentally, morally, or spiritually." [1] All men act in this way with only a little wider margin of voluntary variation.

4. Impulse and instinct. Primeval stupidity. Magic. "The mores (*Sitten*) rest on feelings of pleasure or pain, which either directly produce actions or call out desires which become causes of action." [2] "Impulse is not an attribute of living creatures,

[1] JAI, XX, 140.
[2] Lazarus in *Ztsft. für Völkerpsy.*, I, 452.

like instinct. The only phenomenon to which impulse applies is that men and other animals imitate what they see others, especially of their own species, do, and that they accomplish this imitation the more easily, the more their forefathers practiced the same act. The thing imitated, therefore, must already exist, and cannot be explained as an impulse." "As soon as instinct ceased to be sole ruler of living creatures, including inchoate man, the latter must have made mistakes in the struggle for existence which would soon have finished his career, but that he had instinct and the imitation of what existed to guide him. This human primeval stupidity is the ultimate ground of religion and art, for both come without any interval, out of the magic which is the immediate consequence of the struggle for existence when it goes beyond instinct." "If we want to determine the origin of dress, if we want to define social relations and achievements, e.g. the origin of marriage, war, agriculture, cattle breeding, etc., if we want to make studies in the psyche of nature peoples, — we must always pass through magic and belief in magic. One who is weak in magic, e.g. a ritually unclean man, has a 'bad body,' and reaches no success. Primitive men, on the other hand, win their success by means of their magical power and their magical preparations, and hence become 'the noble and good.' For them there is no other morality [than this success]. Even the technical dexterities have certainly not been free from the influence of belief in magic." [1]

5. The strain of improvement and consistency. The folkways, being ways of satisfying needs, have succeeded more or less well, and therefore have produced more or less pleasure or pain. Their quality always consisted in their adaptation to the purpose. If they were imperfectly adapted and unsuccessful, they produced pain, which drove men on to learn better. The folkways are, therefore, (1) subject to a strain of improvement towards better adaptation of means to ends, as long as the adaptation is so imperfect that pain is produced. They are also (2) subject to a strain of consistency with each other, because they all answer their several purposes with less friction and antagonism when

[1] Preuss in *Globus*, LXXXVII, 419.

they coöperate and support each other. The forms of industry, the forms of the family, the notions of property, the constructions of rights, and the types of religion show the strain of consistency with each other through the whole history of civilization. The two great cultural divisions of the human race are the oriental and the occidental. Each is consistent throughout; each has its own philosophy and spirit; they are separated from top to bottom by different mores, different standpoints, different ways, and different notions of what societal arrangements are advantageous. In their contrast they keep before our minds the possible range of divergence in the solution of the great problems of human life, and in the views of earthly existence by which life policy may be controlled. If two planets were joined in one, their inhabitants could not differ more widely as to what things are best worth seeking, or what ways are most expedient for well living.

6. The aleatory interest. If we should try to find a specimen society in which expedient ways of satisfying needs and interests were found by trial and failure, and by long selection from experience, as broadly described in sec. 1 above, it might be impossible to find one. Such a practical and utilitarian mode of procedure, even when mixed with ghost sanction, is rationalistic. It would not be suited to the ways and temper of primitive men. There was an element in the most elementary experience which was irrational and defied all expedient methods. One might use the best known means with the greatest care, yet fail of the result. On the other hand, one might get a great result with no effort at all. One might also incur a calamity without any fault of his own. This was the aleatory element in life, the element of risk and loss, good or bad fortune. This element is never absent from the affairs of men. It has greatly influenced their life philosophy and policy. On one side, good luck may mean something for nothing, the extreme case of prosperity and felicity. On the other side, ill luck may mean failure, loss, calamity, and disappointment, in spite of the most earnest and well-planned endeavor. The minds of men always dwell more on bad luck. They accept ordinary prosperity as a matter of course. Misfortunes arrest their attention and remain in their memory.

Hence the ills of life are the mode of manifestation of the aleatory element which has most affected life policy. Primitive men ascribed all incidents to the agency of men or of ghosts and spirits. Good and ill luck were attributed to the superior powers, and were supposed to be due to their pleasure or displeasure at the conduct of men. This group of notions constitutes goblinism. It furnishes a complete world philosophy. The element of luck is always present in the struggle for existence. That is why primitive men never could carry on the struggle for existence, disregarding the aleatory element and employing a utilitarian method only. The aleatory element has always been the connecting link between the struggle for existence and religion. It was only by religious rites that the aleatory element in the struggle for existence could be controlled. The notions of ghosts, demons, another world, etc., were all fantastic. They lacked all connection with facts, and were arbitrary constructions put upon experience. They were poetic and developed by poetic construction and imaginative deduction. The nexus between them and events was not cause and effect, but magic. They therefore led to delusive deductions in regard to life and its meaning, which entered into subsequent action as guiding faiths, and imperative notions about the conditions of success. The authority of religion and that of custom coalesced into one indivisible obligation. Therefore the simple statement of experiment and expediency in the first paragraph above is not derived directly from actual cases, but is a product of analysis and infer ence. It must also be added that vanity and ghost fear produced needs which man was as eager to satisfy as those of hunger or the family. Folkways resulted for the former as well as for the latter (see sec. 9).

7. All origins are lost in mystery. No objection can lie against this postulate about the way in which folkways began, on account of the element of inference in it. All origins are lost in mystery, and it seems vain to hope that from any origin the veil of mystery will ever be raised. We go up the stream of history to the utmost point for which we have evidence of its course. Then we are forced to reach out into the darkness upon the line of direction marked by the remotest course of the historic stream. This is the way in which we have to act in regard to the origin of capital, language, the family, the state, religion, and rights. We never can hope to see the beginning of any one of these things. Use and wont are products and results. They had antecedents. We never can find or see the first member of the series. It is only by analysis and inference that we can form any conception of the "beginning" which we are always so eager to find.

8. Spencer on primitive custom. Spencer[1] says that "guidance by custom, which we everywhere find amongst rude peoples, is the sole conceivable guidance at the outset." Custom is the product of concurrent action through time. We find it existent and in control at the extreme reach of our investigations. Whence does it begin, and how does it come to be? How can it give guidance "at the outset"? All mass actions seem to begin because the mass wants to act together. The less they know what it is right and best to do, the more open they are to suggestion from an incident in nature, or from a chance act of one, or from the current doctrines of ghost fear. A concurrent drift begins which is subject to later correction. That being so, it is evident that instinctive action, under the guidance of traditional folkways, is an operation of the first importance in all societal matters. Since the custom never can be antecedent to all action, what we should desire most is to see it arise out of the first actions, but, inasmuch as that is impossible, the course of the action after it is started is our field of study. The origin of primitive customs is always lost in mystery, because when the action begins the men are never conscious of historical action, or of the historical importance of what they are doing. When they become conscious of the historical importance of their acts, the origin is already far behind.

9. Good and bad luck; ills of life; goodness and happiness. There are in nature numerous antagonistic forces of growth or production and destruction. The interests of man are between the two and may be favored or ruined by either. Correct knowledge of both is required to get the advantages

[1] *Princ. of Sociology*, sec. 529.

and escape the injuries. Until the knowledge becomes adequate the effects which are encountered appear to be accidents or cases of luck. There is no thrift in nature. There is rather waste. Human interests require thrift, selection, and preservation. Capital is the condition precedent of all gain in security and power, and capital is produced by selection and thrift. It is threatened by all which destroys material goods. Capital is therefore the essential means of man's power over nature, and it implies the purest concept of the power of intelligence to select and dispose of the processes of nature for human welfare. All the earliest efforts in this direction were blundering failures. Men selected things to be desired and preserved under impulses of vanity and superstition, and misconceived utility and interest. The errors entered into the folkways, formed a part of them, and were protected by them. Error, accident, and luck seem to be the only sense there is in primitive life. Knowledge alone limits their sway, and at least changes the range and form of their dominion. Primitive folkways are marked by improvidence, waste, and carelessness, out of which prudence, foresight, patience, and perseverance are developed slowly, by pain and loss, as experience is accumulated, and knowledge increases also, as better methods seem worth while. The consequences of error and the effects of luck were always mixed. As we have seen, the ills of life were connected with the displeasure of the ghosts. *Per contra*, conduct which conformed to the will of the ghosts was goodness, and was supposed to bring blessing and prosperity. Thus a correlation was established, in the faith of men, between goodness and happiness, and on that correlation an art of happiness was built. It consisted in a faithful performance of rites of respect towards superior powers and in the use of lucky times, places, words, etc., with avoidance of unlucky ones. All uncivilized men demand and expect a specific response. Inasmuch as they did not get it, and indeed the art of happiness always failed of results, the great question of world philosophy always has been, What is the real relation between happiness and goodness? It is only within a few generations that men have found courage to say that there is none. The whole strength of the notion that they are correlated is in the opposite experience which proves that no evil thing brings happiness. The oldest religious literature consists of formulas of worship and prayer by which devotion and obedience were to produce satisfaction of the gods, and win favor and prosperity for men.[1] The words "ill" and "evil" have never yet thrown off the ambiguity between wickedness and calamity. The two ideas come down to us allied or combined. It was the rites which were the object of tradition, not the ideas which they embodied.[2]

10. Illustrations. The notions of blessing and curse are subsequent explanations by men of great cases of prosperity or calamity which came to

---

[1] Rogers, *Babyl. and Assyria*, I, 304; Jastrow, in Hastings, *Dict. Bible*, Supp. vol., 554.

[2] Pietschmann, *Phoenizier*, 154.

their knowledge. Then the myth-building. imagination invented stories of great virtue or guilt to account for the prosperity or calamity.[1] The Greek notion of the Nemesis was an inference from observation of good and ill fortune in life. Great popular interest attached to the stories of Crœsus and Polycrates. The latter, after all his glory and prosperity, was crucified by the satrap of Lydia. Crœsus had done all that man could do, according to the current religion, to conciliate the gods and escape ill fortune. He was very pious and lived by the rules of religion. The story is told in different forms. "The people could not make up their minds that a prince who had been so liberal to the gods during his prosperity had been abandoned by them at the moment when he had the greatest need of their aid."[2] They said that he expiated the crime of his ancestor Gyges, who usurped the throne; that is, they found it necessary to adduce some guilt to account for the facts, and they introduced the notion of hereditary responsibility. Another story was that he determined to sacrifice all his wealth to the gods. He built a funeral pyre of it all and mounted it himself, but rain extinguished it. The gods were satisfied. Crœsus afterwards enjoyed the friendship of Cyros, which was good fortune. Still others rejected the doctrines of correlation between goodness and happiness on account of the fate of Crœsus. In ancient religion "the benefits which were expected from the gods were of a public character, affecting the whole community, especially fruitful seasons, increase of flocks and herds, and success in war. So long as the community flourished, the fact that an individual was miserable reflected no discredit on divine providence, but was rather taken to prove that the sufferer was an evil-doer, justly hateful to the gods."[3] Jehu and his house were blamed for the blood spilt at Israel, although Jehu was commissioned by Elisha to destroy the house of Ahab.[4] This is like the case of Œdipus, who obeyed an oracle, but suffered for his act as for a crime. Jehovah caused the ruin of those who had displeased him, by putting false oracles in the mouths of prophets.[5] Hezekiah expostulated with God because, although he had walked before God with a perfect heart and had done what was right in His sight, he suffered calamity.[6] In the seventy-third Psalm, the author is perplexed by the prosperity of the wicked, and the contrast of his own fortunes. "Surely in vain have I cleansed my heart and washed my hands in innocency, for all day long have I been plagued, and chastened every morning." He says that at last the wicked were cast down. He was brutish and ignorant not to see the solution. It is that the wicked prosper for a time only. He will cleave unto God. The book of Job is a discussion of the relation between goodness and happiness. The crusaders

[1] Pietschmann, *Phoenizier*, 115.	[2] Maspero, *Peuples de l'Orient*, III, 618.
[3] W. R. Smith, *Religion of the Semites*, 259.
[4] Hosea i. 4; 2 Kings ix. 8.
[5] 1 Kings xxii. 22; Judges ix. 23; Ezek. xiv. 9; 2 Thess. ii. 11.
[6] 2 Kings xv. 3.

were greatly perplexed by the victories of the Mohammedans. It seemed to be proved untrue that God would defend His own Name or the true and holy cause. Louis XIV, when his armies were defeated, said that God must have forgotten all which he had done for Him.

11. Immortality and compensation. The notion of immortality has been interwoven with the notion of luck, of justice, and of the relation of goodness and happiness. The case was reopened in another world, and compensations could be assumed to take place there. In the folk drama of the ancient Greeks luck ruled. It was either envious of human prosperity or beneficent.[1] Grimm[2] gives more than a thousand ancient German apothegms, dicta, and proverbs about "luck." The Italians of the fifteenth century saw grand problems in the correlation of goodness and happiness. Alexander VI was the wickedest man known in history, but he had great and unbroken prosperity in all his undertakings. The only conceivable explanation was that he had made a pact with the devil. Some of the American Indians believed that there was an hour at which all wishes uttered by men were fulfilled.[3] It is amongst half-civilized peoples that the notion of luck is given the greatest influence in human affairs. They seek devices for operating on luck, since luck controls all interests. Hence words, times, names, places, gestures, and other acts or relations are held to control luck. Inasmuch as marriage is a relationship in which happiness is sought and not always found, wedding ceremonies are connected with acts "for luck." Some of these still survive amongst us as jests. The fact of the aleatory element in human life, the human interpretations of it, and the efforts of men to deal with it constitute a large part of the history of culture. They have produced groups of folkways, and have entered as an element into folkways for other purposes.

12. Tradition and its restraints. It is evident that the "ways" of the older and more experienced members of a society deserve great authority in any primitive group. We find that this rational authority leads to customs of deference and to etiquette in favor of the old. The old in turn cling stubbornly to tradition and to the example of their own predecessors. Thus tradition and custom become intertwined and are a strong coercion which directs the society upon fixed lines, and strangles liberty. Children see their parents always yield to the same custom and obey the same persons. They see that the elders are allowed to do all the talking, and that if an outsider enters, he is saluted by those who are at home according to rank and in fixed order

---

[1] Reich, *Mimus*, 718.   [2] *Teuton. Mythol.*, 1777.
[3] Leland and Prince, *Kuloskap*, 150.

All this becomes rule for children, and helps to give to all primitive customs their stereotyped formality. "The fixed ways of looking at things which are inculcated by education and tribal discipline, are the precipitate of an old cultural development, and in their continued operation they are the moral anchor of the Indian, although they are also the fetters which restrain his individual will."[1]

13. The concept of " primitive society " ; we-group and others-group. The conception of "primitive society" which we ought to form is that of small groups scattered over a territory. The size of the groups is determined by the conditions of the struggle for existence. The internal organization of each group corresponds to its size. A group of groups may have some relation to each other (kin, neighborhood, alliance, connubium and commercium) which draws them together and differentiates them from others. Thus a differentiation arises between ourselves, the we-group, or in-group, and everybody else, or the others-groups, out-groups. The insiders in a we-group are in a relation of peace, order, law, government, and industry, to each other. Their relation to all outsiders, or others-groups, is one of war and plunder, except so far as agreements have modified it. If a group is exogamic, the women in it were born abroad somewhere. Other foreigners who might be found in it are adopted persons, guest friends, and slaves.

14. Sentiments in the in-group and towards the out-group. The relation of comradeship and peace in the we-group and that of hostility and war towards others-groups are correlative to each other. The exigencies of war with outsiders are what make peace inside, lest internal discord should weaken the we-group for war. These exigencies also make government and law in the in-group, in order to prevent quarrels and enforce discipline. Thus war and peace have reacted on each other and developed each other, one within the group, the other in the intergroup relation. The closer the neighbors, and the stronger they are, the intenser is the warfare, and then the intenser is the internal organization and discipline of each. Sentiments are produced to

[1] *Globus*, LXXXVII, 128.

correspond. Loyalty to the group, sacrifice for it, hatred and contempt for outsiders, brotherhood within, warlikeness without, — all grow together, common products of the same situation. These relations and sentiments constitute a social philosophy. It is sanctified by connection with religion. Men of an others-group are outsiders with whose ancestors the ancestors of the we-group waged war. The ghosts of the latter will see with pleasure their descendants keep up the fight, and will help them. Virtue consists in killing, plundering, and enslaving outsiders.

15. Ethnocentrism is the technical name for this view of things in which one's own group is the center of everything, and all others are scaled and rated with reference to it. Folkways correspond to it to cover both the inner and the outer relation. Each group nourishes its own pride and vanity, boasts itself superior, exalts its own divinities, and looks with contempt on outsiders. Each group thinks its own folkways the only right ones, and if it observes that other groups have other folkways, these excite its scorn. Opprobrious epithets are derived from these differences. " Pig-eater," " cow-eater," " uncircumcised," " jabberers," are epithets of contempt and abomination. The Tupis called the Portuguese by a derisive epithet descriptive of birds which have feathers around their feet, on account of trousers.[1] For our present purpose the most important fact is that ethnocentrism leads a people to exaggerate and intensify everything in their own folkways which is peculiar and which differentiates them from others. It therefore strengthens the folkways.

16. Illustrations of ethnocentrism. The Papuans on New Guinea are broken up into village units which are kept separate by hostility, cannibalism, head hunting, and divergences of language and religion. Each village is integrated by its own language, religion, and interests. A group of villages is sometimes united into a limited unity by connubium. A wife taken inside of this group unit has full status; one taken outside of it has not. The petty group units are peace groups within and are hostile to all outsiders.[2] The Mbayas of South America believed that their deity had bidden them live by making war on others, taking their wives and property, and killing their men.[3]

[1] Martius, *Ethnog. Brasil.*, 51.   [2] Krieger, *New Guinea*, 192.
[3] Tylor, *Anthropology*, 225.

17. When Caribs were asked whence they came, they answered, "We alone are people." [1] The meaning of the name Kiowa is " real or principal people." [2] The Lapps call themselves "men," or "human beings." [3] The Greenland Eskimo think that Europeans have been sent to Greenland to learn virtue and good manners from the Greenlanders. Their highest form of praise for a European is that he is, or soon will be, as good as a Greenlander. [4] The Tunguses call themselves "men." [5] As a rule it is found that nature peoples call themselves "men." Others are something else — perhaps not defined — but not real men. In myths the origin of their own tribe is that of the real human race. They do not account for the others. The Ainos derive their name from that of the first man, whom they worship as a god. Evidently the name of the god is derived from the tribe name. [6] When the tribal name has another sense, it is always boastful or proud. The Ovambo name is a corruption of the name of the tribe for themselves, which means "the wealthy." [7] Amongst the most remarkable people in the world for ethnocentrism are the Seri of Lower California. They observe an attitude of suspicion and hostility to all outsiders, and strictly forbid marriage with outsiders. [8]

18. The Jews divided all mankind into themselves and Gentiles. They were the "chosen people." The Greeks and Romans called all outsiders "barbarians." In Euripides' tragedy of *Iphigenia in Aulis* Iphigenia says that it is fitting that Greeks should rule over barbarians, but not contrariwise, because Greeks are free, and barbarians are slaves. The Arabs regarded themselves as the noblest nation and all others as more or less barbarous. [9] In 1896, the Chinese minister of education and his counselors edited a manual in which this statement occurs: "How grand and glorious is the Empire of China, the middle kingdom! She is the largest and richest in the world. The grandest men in the world have all come from the middle empire." [10] In all the literature of all the states equivalent statements occur, although they are not so naïvely expressed. In Russian books and newspapers the civilizing mission of Russia is talked about, just as, in the books and journals of France, Germany, and the United States, the civilizing mission of those countries is assumed and referred to as well understood. Each state now regards itself as the leader of civilization, the best, the freest, and the wisest, and all others as inferior. Within a few years our own man-on-the-curbstone has learned to class all foreigners of the Latin

---

[1] Martius, *Ethnog. Brasil.*, 51.
[2] *Bur. Eth.*, XIV, 1078.
[5] Hiekisch, *Tungusen*, 48.
[6] Hitchcock in *U. S. Nat. Mus.*, 1890, 432.
[7] Ratzel, *Hist. Mankind*, II, 539.
[8] *Bur. Eth.*, XVII (Part I), 154.
[9] Von Kremer, *Kulturgesch. d. Orients*, II, 236.
[10] Bishop, *Korea*, 438.

[3] Wiklund, *Om Lapparna i Sverige*, 5.
[4] Fries, *Grönland*, 139.

peoples as "dagos," and "dago" has become an epithet of contempt. These are all cases of ethnocentrism.

19. Patriotism is a sentiment which belongs to modern states. It stands in antithesis to the mediæval notion of catholicity. Patriotism is loyalty to the civic group to which one belongs by birth or other group bond. It is a sentiment of fellowship and coöperation in all the hopes, work, and suffering of the group. Mediæval catholicity would have made all Christians an in-group and would have set them in hostility to all Mohammedans and other non-Christians. It never could be realized. When the great modern states took form and assumed control of societal interests, group sentiment was produced in connection with those states. Men responded willingly to a demand for support and help from an institution which could and did serve interests. The state drew to itself the loyalty which had been given to men (lords), and it became the object of that group vanity and antagonism which had been ethnocentric. For the modern man patriotism has become one of the first of duties and one of the noblest sentiments. It is what he owes to the state for what the state does for him, and the state is, for the modern man, a cluster of civic institutions from which he draws security and conditions of welfare. The masses are always patriotic. For them the old ethnocentric jealousy, vanity, truculency, and ambition are the strongest elements in patriotism. Such sentiments are easily awakened in a crowd. They are sure to be popular. Wider knowledge always proves that they are not based on facts. That we are good and others are bad is never true. By history, literature, travel, and science men are made cosmopolitan. The selected classes of all states become associated; they intermarry. The differentiation by states loses importance. All states give the same security and conditions of welfare to all. The standards of civic institutions are the same, or tend to become such, and it is a matter of pride in each state to offer civic status and opportunities equal to the best. Every group of any kind whatsoever demands that each of its members shall help defend group interests. Every group stigmatizes any one who fails in zeal, labor, and sacrifices for group interests. Thus the sentiment of loyalty to the group, or the group head, which was so strong in the Middle Ages, is kept up, as far as possible, in regard to modern states and governments. The group force is also employed to enforce the obligations of devotion to group interests. It follows that judgments are precluded and criticism is silenced.

20. Chauvinism. That patriotism may degenerate into a vice is shown by the invention of a name for the vice: chauvinism. It is a name for boastful and truculent group self-assertion. It overrules personal judgment and character, and puts the whole group at the mercy of the clique which is ruling at the moment. It produces the dominance of watchwords and phrases which take the place of reason and conscience in determining conduct. The patriotic bias is a recognized perversion of thought and judgment against which our education should guard us.

21. The struggle for existence and the competition of life; antagonistic coöperation. The struggle for existence must be carried on under life conditions and in connection with the competition of life. The life conditions consist in variable elements of the environment, the supply of materials necessary to support life, the difficulty of exploiting them, the state of the arts, and the circumstances of physiography, climate, meteorology, etc., which favor life or the contrary. The struggle for existence is a process in which an individual and nature are the parties. The individual is engaged in a process by which he wins from his environment what he needs to support his existence. In the competition of life the parties are men and other organisms. The men strive with each other, or with the flora and fauna with which they are associated. The competition of life is the rivalry, antagonism, and mutual displacement in which the individual is involved with other organisms by his efforts to carry on the struggle for existence for himself. It is, therefore, the competition of life which is the societal element, and which produces societal organization. The number present and in competition is another of the life conditions. At a time and place the life conditions are the same for a number of human beings who are present, and the problems of life policy are the same. This is another reason why the attempts to satisfy interest become mass phenomena and result in folkways. The individual and social elements are always in interplay with each other if there are a number present. If one is trying to carry on the struggle for existence with nature, the fact that others are doing the same in the same environment is an essential condition for him. Then arises an alternative. He and the others may so interfere with each other that all shall fail, or they may combine, and by coöperation raise their efforts against nature to a higher power. This latter method is industrial organization. The crisis which produces it is constantly renewed, and men are forced to raise the organization to greater complexity and more comprehensive power, without limit. Interests are the relations of action and reaction between the individual and the life conditions, through which relations the evolution of the individual is produced. That evolution, so long as it goes on prosperously, is well living, and it results in the self-realization of the individual, for we may think of each one as capable of fulfilling some career and attaining to some character and state of power by the developing of predispositions which he possesses. It would be an error, however, to suppose that all nature is a chaos of warfare and competition. Combination and coöperation are so fundamentally necessary that even very low life forms are found in symbiosis for mutual dependence and assistance. A combination can exist where each of its members would perish. Competition and combination are two forms of life association which alternate through the whole organic and superorganic domains. The neglect of this fact leads to many socialistic fallacies. Combination is of the essence of organization, and organization is the great device for increased power by a number of unequal and dissimilar units brought into association for a common purpose. McGee[1] says of the desert of Papagueria, in southwestern Arizona, that "a large part of the plants and animals of the desert dwell together in harmony and mutual helpfulness [which he shows in detail]; for their energies are directed not so much against one another as against the rigorous environmental conditions growing out of dearth of water This communality does not involve loss of individuality, . . . indeed the plants and animals are characterized by an individuality greater than that displayed in regions in which perpetuity of the species depends less closely on the persistence of individuals." Hence he speaks of the "solidarity of life" in the desert. "The saguaro is a monstrosity in fact as well as in appearance, — a product of miscegenation between plant and animal, probably depending for its form of life history, if not for its very existence, on its commensals."[2] The Seri protect pelicans from themselves by a partial taboo, which is not understood. It seems that they could not respect a breeding time, or establish a closed season, yet they have such an appetite for the birds and their eggs that they would speedily exterminate them if there were no restraint. This combination has been well called antagonistic coöperation.

[1] *Amer. Anthrop.*, VIII, 365.
[2] Cf. also *Bur. Eth.*, XVII (Part I), 190 *.

It consists in the combination of two persons or groups to satisfy a great common interest while minor antagonisms of interest which exist between them are suppressed. The plants and animals of the desert are rivals for what water there is, but they combine as if with an intelligent purpose to attain to a maximum of life under the conditions. There are many cases of animals who coöperate in the same way. Our farmers put crows and robins under a protective taboo because the birds destroy insects. The birds also destroy grain and fruits, but this is tolerated on account of their services. Madame Pommerol says of the inhabitants of Sahara that the people of the towns and the nomads are enemies by caste and race, but allies in interest. The nomads need refuge and shelter. The townspeople need messengers and transportation. Hence ties of contract, quarrels, fights, raids, vengeances, and reconciliations for the sake of common enterprises of plunder.[1] Antagonistic coöperation is the most productive form of combination in high civilization. It is a high action of the reason to overlook lesser antagonisms in order to work together for great interests. Political parties are constantly forced to do it. In the art of the statesman it is a constant policy. The difference between great parties and factions in any parliamentary system is of the first importance ; that difference consists in the fact that parties can suppress minor differences, and combine for what they think most essential to public welfare, while factions divide and subdivide on petty differences. Inasmuch as the suppression of minor differences means a suppression of the emotional element, while the other policy encourages the narrow issues in regard to which feeling is always most intense, the former policy allows far less play to feeling and passion.

22. Hunger, love, vanity, and fear. There are four great motives of human action which come into play when some number of human beings are in juxtaposition under the same life conditions. These are hunger, sex passion, vanity, and fear (of ghosts and spirits). Under each of these motives there are interests. Life consists in satisfying interests, for "life," in a society, is a career of action and effort expended on both the

---

[1] *Une Femme chez les Sahariennes*, 105.

material and social environment. However great the errors and misconceptions may be which are included in the efforts, the purpose always is advantage and expediency. The efforts fall into parallel lines, because the conditions and the interests are the same. It is now the accepted opinion, and it may be correct, that men inherited from their beast ancestors psychophysical traits, instincts, and dexterities, or at least predispositions, which give them aid in solving the problems of food supply, sex commerce, and vanity. The result is mass phenomena ; currents of similarity, concurrence, and mutual contribution ; and these produce folkways. The folkways are unconscious, spontaneous, uncoördinated. It is never known who led in devising them, although we must believe that talent exerted its leadership at all times. Folkways come into existence now all the time. There were folkways in stage coach times, which were fitted to that mode of travel. Street cars have produced ways which are suited to that mode of transportation in cities. The telephone has produced ways which have not been invented and imposed by anybody, but which are devised to satisfy conveniently the interests which are at stake in the use of that instrument.

23. Process of making folkways. Although we may see the process of making folkways going on all the time, the analysis of the process is very difficult. It appears as if there was a "mind " in the crowd which was different from the minds of the individuals which compose it. Indeed some have adopted such a doctrine. By autosuggestion the stronger minds produce ideas which when set afloat pass by suggestion from mind to mind. Acts which are consonant with the ideas are imitated. There is a give and take between man and man. This process is one of development. New suggestions come in at point after point. They are carried out. They combine with what existed already. Every new step increases the number of points upon which other minds may seize. It seems to be by this process that great inventions are produced. Knowledge has been won and extended by it. It seems as if the crowd had a mystic power in it greater than the sum of the powers of its members. It is sufficient, however, to explain this, to notice that there is a coöperation and constant suggestion which is highly productive when it operates in a crowd, because it draws out latent power, concentrates what would otherwise be scattered, verifies and corrects what has been taken up, eliminates error, and constructs by combination. Hence the gain from the collective operation is fully accounted for, and the theories of *Völkerpsychologie* are to be rejected as superfluous. Out of the process which has been described have come the folkways during the whole history of civilization.

The phenomena of suggestion and suggestibility demand some attention because the members of a group are continually affecting each other by them, and great mass phenomena very often are to be explained by them.

24. Suggestion ; suggestibility. What has been called the psychology of crowds consists of certain phenomena of suggestion. A number of persons assembled together, especially if they are enthused by the same sentiment or stimulated by the same interest, transmit impulses to each other with the result that all the impulses are increased in a very high ratio. In other words, it is an undisputed fact that all mental states and emotions are greatly increased in force by transmission from man to man, especially if they are attended by a sense of the concurrence and coöperation of a great number who have a common sentiment or interest. "The element of psychic coercion to which our thought process is subject is the characteristic of the operations which we call suggestive."[1] What we have done or heard occupies our minds so that we cannot turn from it to something else. The consensus of a number promises triumph for the impulse, whatever it is. *Ça ira.* There is a thrill of enthusiasm in the sense of moving with a great number. There is no deliberation or reason. Therefore a crowd may do things which are either better or worse than what individuals in it would do. Cases of lynching show how a crowd can do things which it is extremely improbable that the individuals would do or consent to, if they were taken separately. The crowd has no greater guarantee of wisdom and virtue than an individual would have. In fact, the participants in a crowd almost always throw away

[1] Stoll, *Suggestion und Hypnotismus*, 702.

all the powers of wise judgment which have been acquired by education, and submit to the control of enthusiasm, passion, animal impulse, or brute appetite. A crowd always has a common stock of elementary faiths, prejudices, loves and hates, and pet notions. The common stock is acted on by the same stimuli, in all the persons, at the same time. The response, as an aggregate, is a great storm of feeling, and a great impulse to the will. Hence the great influence of omens and of all popular superstitions on a crowd. Omens are a case of "egoistic reference."[1] An army desists from a battle on account of an eclipse. A man starting out on the food quest returns home because a lizard crosses his path. In each case an incident in nature is interpreted as a warning or direction to the army or the man. Thus momentous results for men and nations may be produced without cause. The power of watchwords consists in the cluster of suggestions which has become fastened upon them. In the Middle Ages the word "heretic" won a frightful suggestion of base wickedness. In the seventeenth century the same suggestions were connected with the words "witch" and "traitor." "Nature" acquired great suggestion of purity and correctness in the eighteenth century, which it has not yet lost. "Progress" now bears amongst us a very undue weight of suggestion. Suggestibility is the quality of liability to suggestive influence.[2] "Suggestibility is the natural faculty of the brain to admit any ideas whatsoever, without motive, to assimilate them, and eventually to transform them rapidly into movements, sensations, and inhibitions."[3] It differs greatly in degree, and is present in different grades in different crowds. Crowds of different nationalities would differ both in degree of suggestibility and in the kinds of suggestive stimuli to which they would respond. Imitation is due to suggestibility. Even suicide is rendered epidemic by suggestion and imitation.[4] In a crisis, like a shipwreck, when no one knows what to do, one, by acting, may lead them all

---

[1] Friedmann, *Wahnideen im Völkerleben*, 222.
[2] Binet, *La Suggestibilité*, treats of its use in education.
[3] Lefevre, *La Suggestion*, 102.
[4] Funck-Brentano, *Le Suicide*, 117.

through imitative suggestibility. People who are very suggestible can be led into states of mind which preclude criticism or reflection. Any one who acquires skill in the primary processes of association, analogy, reiteration, and continuity, can play tricks on others by stimulating these processes and then giving them selected data to work upon. A directive idea may be suggested by a series of ideas which lead the recipient of them to expect that the series will be continued. Then he will not perceive if the series is broken. In the Renaissance period no degree of illumination sufficed to resist the delusion of astrology, because it was supported by a passionate fantasy and a vehement desire to know the future, and because it was confirmed by antiquity, the authority of whose opinions was overwhelmingly suggested by all the faiths and prejudices of the time.[1]

25. Suggestion in education. Manias. Parents and teachers use suggestion in rearing children. Persons who enjoy social preëminence operate suggestion all the time, whether intentionally or unintentionally. Whatever they do is imitated. Folkways operate on individuals by suggestion; when they are elevated to mores they do so still more, for then they carry the suggestion of societal welfare. Ways and notions may be rejected by an individual at first upon his judgment of their merits, but repeated suggestion produces familiarity and dulls the effect upon him of the features which at first repelled him. Familiar cases of this are furnished by fashions of dress and by slang. A new fashion of dress seems at first to be absurd, ungraceful, or indecent. After a time this first impression of it is so dulled that all conform to the fashion. New slang seems vulgar. It makes its way into use. In India the lingam symbol is so common that no one pays any heed to its sense.[2] This power of familiarity to reduce the suggestion to zero furnishes a negative proof of the power of the suggestion. Conventionalization also reduces suggestion, perhaps to zero. It is a mischievous thing to read descriptions of crime, vice, horrors, excessive adventures, etc., because familiarity lessens the abhorrent suggestions which those things ought to produce. Swindlers and all others who have an interest to lead the minds of their fellow-men in a certain direction employ suggestion. They often develop great practical skill in the operation, although they do not understand the science of it. It is one of the arts of the demagogue and stump orator. A man who wanted to be nominated for an office went before the convention to make a speech. A great and difficult question agitated the party. He began by saying that he would state his position

---

[1] Burckhardt, *Renaissance*, 512.   [2] Nivedita, *Web of Indian Life*, 212.

on that question frankly and fully. "But first," said he, "let me say that I am a Democrat." This brought out a storm of applause. Then he went on to boast of his services to the party, and then he stopped without having said a word on the great question. He was easily nominated. The witch persecutions rested on suggestion. "Everybody knew" that there were witches. If not, what were the people who were burned? Philip IV of France wanted to make the people believe that the templars were heretics. The people were not ready to believe this. The king caused the corpse of a templar to be dug up and burned, as the corpses of heretics were burned. This convinced the people by suggestion.[1] What "they say," what "everybody does," and what "everybody knows" are controlling suggestions. Religious revivals are carried on by suggestion. Mediæval flagellations and dances were cases of suggestion. In fact, all popular manias are to be explained by it. Religious bodies practice suggestion on themselves, especially on their children or less enthusiastic members, by symbols, pictures, images, processions, dramatic representations, festivals, relics, legends of their heroes. In the Middle Ages the crucifix was an instrument of religious suggestion to produce vivid apprehension of the death of Jesus. In very many well-known cases the passions of the crowd were raised to the point of very violent action. The symbols and images also, by suggestion, stimulate religious fervor. If numbers act together, as in convents, mass phenomena are produced, and such results follow as the hysterical epidemics in convents and the extravagances of communistic sects.[2] Learned societies and numbers of persons who are interested in the same subject, by meeting and imparting suggestions, make all the ideas of each the common stock of all. Hyperboreans have a mental disease which renders them liable to suggestion. The women are afflicted by hysteria before puberty. Later they show the phenomena of "possession," — dancing and singing, — and still later catalepsy.[3]

26. Suggestion in politics. The great field for the use of the devices and apparatus of suggestion at the present time is politics. Within fifty years all states have become largely popular. Suggestion is easy when it falls in with popular ideas, the pet notions of groups of people, the popular commonplaces, and the current habits of thought and feeling. Newspapers, popular literature, and popular oratory show the effort to operate suggestion along these lines. They rarely correct; they usually flatter the accepted notions. The art of adroit suggestion is one of the great arts of politics. Antony's speech over the body of Cæsar is a classical example of it. In politics, especially at elections, the old apparatus of suggestion is employed again, — flags, symbols, ceremonies, and celebrations. Patriotism is systematically cultivated by anniversaries, pilgrimages, symbols, songs, recitations, etc.

[1] Schotmüller, *Untergang des Templer-Ordens*, I, 136.
[2] Regnard, *Les Maladies Épidemiques de l'Esprit.*
[3] *Globus*, LXXXV, 262.

Another very remarkable case of suggestion is furnished by modern advertisements. They are adroitly planned to touch the mind of the reader in a way to get the reaction which the advertiser wants. The advertising pages of our popular magazines furnish evidence of the faiths and ideas which prevail in the masses.

27. Suggestion and criticism. Suggestion is a legitimate device, if it is honestly used, for inculcating knowledge or principles of conduct; that is, for education in the broadest sense of the word. Criticism is the operation by which suggestion is limited and corrected. It is by criticism that the person is protected against credulity, emotion, and fallacy. The power of criticism is the one which education should chiefly train. It is difficult to resist the suggestion that one who is accused of crime is guilty. Lynchers generally succumb to this suggestion, especially if the crime was a heinous one which has strongly excited their emotions against the unknown somebody who perpetrated it. It requires criticism to resist this suggestion. Our judicial institutions are devised to hold this suggestion aloof until the evidence is examined. An educated man ought to be beyond the reach of suggestions from advertisements, newspapers, speeches, and stories. If he is wise, just when a crowd is filled with enthusiasm and emotion, he will leave it and will go off by himself to form his judgment. In short, individuality and personality of character are the opposites of suggestibility. Autosuggestion properly includes all the cases in which a man is "struck by an idea," or "takes a notion," but it is more strictly applied to fixed ideas and habits of thought. An irritation suggests parasites, and parasites suggest an irritation. The fear of stammering causes stammering. A sleeping man drives away a fly without waking. If we are in a pose or rôle, we act as we have heard that people act in that pose or rôle.[1] A highly trained judgment is required to correct or select one's own ideas and to resist fixed ideas. The supreme criticism is criticism of one's self.

28. Folkways due to false inference. Furthermore, folkways have been formed by accident, that is, by irrational and incongruous action, based on pseudo-knowledge. In Molembo a pestilence broke out soon after a Portuguese had died there. After that the natives took all possible measures not to allow any white man to die in their country.[2] On the Nicobar islands some natives who had just begun to make pottery died. The art was given up and never again attempted.[3] White men gave to one Bushman in a kraal a stick ornamented with buttons as a symbol of authority. The recipient died leaving the stick to

---

[1] Lefèvre, *Suggestion*, 98.   [2] Bastian, *San Salvador*, 104.
[3] Ratzel, *Anthropogeog.*, II, 699.

his son. The son soon died. Then the Bushmen brought back the stick lest all should die.[1] Until recently no building of incombustible materials could be built in any big town of the central province of Madagascar, on account of some ancient prejudice.[2] A party of Eskimos met with no game. One of them returned to their sledges and got the ham of a dog to eat. As he returned with the ham bone in his hand he met and killed a seal. Ever afterwards he carried a ham bone in his hand when hunting.[3] The Belenda women (peninsula of Malacca) stay as near to the house as possible during the period. Many keep the door closed. They know no reason for this custom. "It must be due to some now forgotten superstition."[4] Soon after the Yakuts saw a camel for the first time smallpox broke out amongst them. They thought the camel to be the agent of the disease.[5] A woman amongst the same people contracted an endogamous marriage. She soon afterwards became blind. This was thought to be on account of the violation of ancient customs.[6] A very great number of such cases could be collected. In fact they represent the current mode of reasoning of nature people. It is their custom to reason that, if one thing follows another, it is due to it. A great number of customs are traceable to the notion of the evil eye, many more to ritual notions of uncleanness.[7] No scientific investigation could discover the origin of the folkways mentioned, if the origin had not chanced to become known to civilized men. We must believe that the known cases illustrate the irrational and incongruous origin of many folkways. In civilized history also we know that customs have owed their origin to "historical accident," — the vanity of a princess, the deformity of a king, the whim of a democracy, the love intrigue of a statesman or prelate. By the institutions of another age it may be provided that no one of these things can affect decisions, acts, or interests, but then the power to decide the ways may have passed to clubs,

[1] Lichtenstein, *South Africa*, II, 61.
[2] Sibree, *Great African Island*, 301.
[3] *Bur. Eth.*, XVIII (Part I), 325.
[4] *Ztsft. f. Eth.*, XXVIII, 170.
[5] Wilken, *Volkenkunde*, 546.
[6] Sieroshevski, *Yakuty*, 558.
[7] See Chapter XIV.

trades unions, trusts, commercial rivals, wire-pullers, politicians, and political fanatics. In these cases also the causes and origins may escape investigation.

29. Harmful folkways. There are folkways which are positively harmful. Very often these are just the ones for which a definite reason can be given. The destruction of a man's goods at his death is a direct deduction from other-worldliness; the dead man is supposed to want in the other world just what he wanted here. The destruction of a man's goods at his death was a great waste of capital, and it must have had a disastrous effect on the interests of the living, and must have very seriously hindered the development of civilization. With this custom we must class all the expenditure of labor and capital on graves, temples, pyramids, rites, sacrifices, and support of priests, so far as these were supposed to benefit the dead. The faith in goblinism produced other-worldly interests which overruled ordinary worldly interests. Foods have often been forbidden which were plentiful, the prohibition of which injuriously lessened the food supply. There is a tribe of Bushmen who will eat no goat's flesh, although goats are the most numerous domestic animals in the district.[1] Where totemism exists it is regularly accompanied by a taboo on eating the totem animal. Whatever may be the real principle in totemism, it overrules the interest in an abundant food supply. " The origin of the sacred regard paid to the cow must be sought in the primitive nomadic life of the Indo-European race," because it is common to Iranians and Indians of Hindostan.[2] The Libyans ate oxen but not cows.[3] The same was true of the Phœnicians and Egyptians.[4] In some cases the sense of a food taboo is not to be learned. It may have been entirely capricious. Mohammed would not eat lizards, because he thought them the offspring of a metamorphosed clan of Israelites.[5] On the other hand, the protective taboo which forbade killing crocodiles, pythons, cobras, and other animals enemies of man was harmful

---

[1] Ratzel, *Hist. Mankind*, II, 276.
[2] W. R. Smith, *Religion of the Semites*, 299.
[3] Herodotus, IV, 186.
[4] Porphyry, *De Abstin.*, II, 11 ; Herodotus, II, 41.
[5] W. R. Smith, *Religion of the Semites*, 88.

to his interests, whatever the motive. " It seems to be a fixed
article of belief throughout southern India, that all who have
willfully or accidentally killed a snake, especially a cobra, will
certainly be punished, either in this life or the next, in one of
three ways : either by childlessness, or by leprosy, or by ophthal-
mia." [1] Where this faith exists man has a greater interest to
spare a cobra than to kill it. India furnishes a great number of
cases of harmful mores. " In India every tendency of humanity
seems intensified and exaggerated. No country in the world is
so conservative in its traditions, yet no country has undergone
so many religious changes and vicissitudes." [2] " Every year thousands perish of disease that might recover if they would take
proper nourishment, and drink the medicine that science prescribes, but which they imagine that their religion forbids them
to touch." " Men who can scarcely count beyond twenty, and
know not the letters of the alphabet, would rather die than eat
food which had been prepared by men of lower caste, unless it
had been sanctified by being offered to an idol ; and would kill
their daughters rather than endure the disgrace of having unmarried girls at home beyond twelve or thirteen years of age." [3]
In the last case the rule of obligation and duty is set by the
mores. The interest comes under vanity. The sanction of the
caste rules is in a boycott by all members of the caste. The
rules are often very harmful. " The authority of caste rests
partly on written laws, partly on legendary fables or narratives,
partly on the injunctions of instructors and priests, partly on
custom and usage, and partly on the caprice and convenience of
its votaries." [4] The harm of caste rules is so great that of late
they have been broken in some cases, especially in regard to
travel over sea, which is a great advantage to Hindoos.[5] The
Hindoo folkways in regard to widows and child marriages must
also be recognized as socially harmful.

30. How " true " and " right " are found. If a savage puts his
hand too near the fire, he suffers pain and draws it back. He

---

[1] Monier-Williams, *Brahmanism and Hinduism*, 324.
[2] *Ibid.*, 101.   [4] *Ibid.*, 125.
[3] Wilkins, *Hinduism*, 299.   [5] JASB, IV, 353.

knows nothing of the laws of the radiation of heat, but his instinctive action conforms to that law as if he did know it. If he wants to catch an animal for food, he must study its habits and prepare a device adjusted to those habits. If it fails, he must try again, until his observation is "true" and his device is "right." All the practical and direct element in the folkways seems to be due to common sense, natural reason, intuition, or some other original mental endowment. It seems rational (or rationalistic) and utilitarian. Often in the mythologies this ultimate rational element was ascribed to the teaching of a god or a culture hero. In modern mythology it is accounted for as "natural."

Although the ways adopted must always be really "true" and "right" in relation to facts, for otherwise they could not answer their purpose, such is not the primitive notion of true and right.

31. The folkways are "right." Rights. Morals. The folkways are the "right" ways to satisfy all interests, because they are traditional, and exist in fact. They extend over the whole of life. There is a right way to catch game, to win a wife, to make one's self appear, to cure disease, to honor ghosts, to treat comrades or strangers, to behave when a child is born, on the warpath, in council, and so on in all cases which can arise. The ways are defined on the negative side, that is, by taboos. The "right" way is the way which the ancestors used and which has been handed down. The tradition is its own warrant. It is not held subject to verification by experience. The notion of right is in the folkways. It is not outside of them, of independent origin, and brought to them to test them. In the folkways, whatever is, is right. This is because they are traditional, and therefore contain in themselves the authority of the ancestral ghosts. When we come to the folkways we are at the end of our analysis. The notion of right and ought is the same in regard to all the folkways, but the degree of it varies with the importance of the interest at stake. The obligation of conformable and coöperative action is far greater under ghost fear and war than in other matters, and the social sanctions are severer, because group interests are supposed to be at stake. Some usages contain only a slight element of right and ought. It may well be believed that notions

of right and duty, and of social welfare, were first developed in connection with ghost fear and other-worldliness, and therefore that,
in that field also, folkways were first raised to mores. "Rights"
are the rules of mutual give and take in the competition of life
which are imposed on comrades in the in-group, in order that the
peace may prevail there which is essential to the group strength.
Therefore rights can never be "natural" or "God-given," or
absolute in any sense. The morality of a group at a time is the
sum of the taboos and prescriptions in the folkways by which
right conduct is defined. Therefore morals can never be intuitive.
They are historical, institutional, and empirical.

World philosophy, life policy, right, rights, and morality are
all products of the folkways. They are reflections on, and generalizations from, the experience of pleasure and pain which is won
in efforts to carry on the struggle for existence under actual life
conditions. The generalizations are very crude and vague in their
germinal forms. They are all embodied in folklore, and all our
philosophy and science have been developed out of them.

32. The folkways are "true." The folkways are necessarily
"true" with respect to some world philosophy. Pain forced men
to think. The ills of life imposed reflection and taught fore-
thought. Mental processes were irksome and were not undertaken until painful experience made them unavoidable.[1] With
great unanimity all over the globe primitive men followed the
same line of thought. The dead were believed to live on as ghosts
in another world just like this one. The ghosts had just the same
needs, tastes, passions, etc., as the living men had had. These
transcendental notions were the beginning of the mental outfit of
mankind. They are articles of faith, not rational convictions.
The living had duties to the ghosts, and the ghosts had rights;
they also had power to enforce their rights. It behooved the
living therefore to learn how to deal with ghosts. Here we have
a complete world philosophy and a life policy deduced from it.
When pain, loss, and ill were experienced and the question was
provoked, Who did this to us? the world philosophy furnished
the answer. When the painful experience forced the question,

---

[1] Fritsch, *Eingeborenen Südafr.*, 57.

Why are the ghosts angry and what must we do to appease them? the "right" answer was the one which fitted into the philosophy of ghost fear. All acts were therefore constrained and trained into the forms of the world philosophy by ghost fear, ancestral authority, taboos, and habit. The habits and customs created a practical philosophy of welfare, and they confirmed and developed the religious theories of goblinism.

33. Relation of world philosophy and folkways. It is quite impossible for us to disentangle the elements of philosophy and custom, so as to determine priority and the causative position of either. Our best judgment is that the mystic philosophy is regulative, not creative, in its relation to the folkways. They reacted upon each other. The faith in the world philosophy drew lines outside of which the folkways must not go. Crude and vague notions of societal welfare were formed from the notion of pleasing the ghosts, and from such notions of expediency as the opinion that, if there were not children enough, there would not be warriors enough, or that, if there were too many children, the food supply would not be adequate. The notion of welfare was an inference and resultant from these mystic and utilitarian generalizations.

34. Definition of the mores. When the elements of truth and right are developed into doctrines of welfare, the folkways are raised to another plane. They then become capable of producing inferences, developing into new forms, and extending their constructive influence over men and society. Then we call them the mores. The mores are the folkways, including the philosophical and ethical generalizations as to societal welfare which are suggested by them, and inherent in them, as they grow.

35. Taboos. The mores necessarily consist, in a large part, of taboos, which indicate the things which must not be done. In part these are dictated by mystic dread of ghosts who might be offended by certain acts, but they also include such acts as have been found by experience to produce unwelcome results, especially in the food quest, in war, in health, or in increase or decrease of population. These taboos always contain a greater element of philosophy than the positive rules, because the taboos contain reference to a reason, as, for instance, that the act would displease the ghosts. The primitive taboos correspond to the fact that the life of man is environed by perils. His food quest must be limited by shunning poisonous plants. His appetite must be restrained from excess. His physical strength and health must be guarded from dangers. The taboos carry on the accumulated wisdom of generations, which has almost always been purchased by pain, loss, disease, and death. Other taboos contain inhibitions of what will be injurious to the group. The laws about the sexes, about property, about war, and about ghosts, have this character. They always include some social philosophy. They are both mystic and utilitarian, or compounded of the two.

Taboos may be divided into two classes, (1) protective and (2) destructive. Some of them aim to protect and secure, while others aim to repress or exterminate. Women are subject to some taboos which are directed against them as sources of possible harm or danger to men, and they are subject to other taboos which put them outside of the duties or risks of men. On account of this difference in taboos, taboos act selectively, and thus affect the course of civilization. They contain judgments as to societal welfare.

36. No primitive philosophizing; myths; fables; notion of societal welfare. It is not to be understood that primitive men philosophize about their experience of life. That is our way; it was not theirs. They did not formulate any propositions about the causes, significance, or ultimate relations of things. They made myths, however, in which they often presented conceptions which are deeply philosophical, but they represented them in concrete, personal, dramatic and graphic ways. They feared pain and ill, and they produced folkways by their devices for warding off pain and ill. Those devices were acts of ritual which were planned upon their vague and crude faiths about ghosts and the other world. We develop the connection between the devices and the faiths, and we reduce it to propositions of a philosophic form, but the primitive men never did that. Their myths, fables, proverbs, and maxims show that the subtler relations of things did not escape them, and that reflection was not wanting, but the method of it was very different from ours. The notion of societal welfare was not wanting, although it was never consciously put before themselves as their purpose. It was pestilence, as a visitation of the wrath of ghosts on all, or war, which first taught this idea, because war was connected with victory over a neighboring group. The Bataks have a legend that men once married their fathers' sisters' daughters, but calamities followed and so those marriages were tabooed.[1] This inference and the cases mentioned in sec. 28 show a conception of societal welfare and of its relation to states and acts as conditions.

37. The imaginative element. The correct apprehension of facts and events by the mind, and the correct inferences as to the relations between them, constitute knowledge, and it is chiefly by knowledge that men have become better able to live well on earth. Therefore the alternation between experience or observation and the intellectual processes by which the sense, sequence, interdependence, and rational consequences of facts are ascertained, is undoubtedly the most important process for winning increased power to live well. Yet we find that this process has been liable to most pernicious errors. The imagination has interfered with the reason and furnished objects of pursuit to men, which have wasted and dissipated their energies. Especially the alternations of observation and deduction have been traversed by vanity and superstition which have introduced delusions. As a consequence, men have turned their backs on welfare and reality, in order to pursue beauty, glory, poetry, and dithyrambic rhetoric, pleasure, fame, adventure, and phantasms. Every group, in every age, has had its "ideals" for which it has striven, as if men had blown bubbles into the air, and then, entranced by their beautiful colors, had leaped to catch them. In the very processes of analysis and deduction the most pernicious errors find entrance. We note our experience in every action or event. We study the significance from experience. We deduce a conviction as to what we may best do when the case arises again. Undoubtedly this is just what we ought to do in order to live well. The process presents us a constant reiteration

---

[1] *Bijdragen tot T. L. en V.-kunde*, XLI, 203.

of the sequence, — act, thought, act. The error is made if we allow suggestions of vanity, superstition, speculation, or imagination to become confused with the second stage and to enter into our conviction of what it is best to do in such a case. This is what was done when goblinism was taken as the explanation of experience and the rule of right living, and it is what has been done over and over again ever since. Speculative and transcendental notions have furnished the world philosophy, and the rules of life policy and duty have been deduced from this and introduced at the second stage of the process, — act, thought, act. All the errors and fallacies of the mental processes enter into the mores of the age. The logic of one age is not that of another. It is one of the chief useful purposes of a study of the mores to learn to discern in them the operation of traditional error, prevailing dogmas, logical fallacy, delusion, and current false estimates of goods worth striving for.

38. The ethical policy of the schools and the success policy. Although speculative assumptions and dogmatic deductions have produced the mischief here described, our present world philosophy has come out of them by rude methods of correction and purification, and "great principles" have been deduced which now control our life philosophy; also ethical principles have been determined which no civilized man would now repudiate (truthfulness, love, honor, altruism). The traditional doctrines of philosophy and ethics are not by any means adjusted smoothly to each other or to modern notions. We live in a war of two antagonistic ethical philosophies : the ethical policy taught in the books and the schools, and the success policy. The same man acts at one time by the school ethics, disregarding consequences, at another time by the success policy, in which the consequences dictate the conduct ; or we talk the former and act by the latter [1]

39. Recapitulation. We may sum up this preliminary analysis as follows : men in groups are under life conditions ; they have needs which are similar under the state of the life conditions ; the relations of the needs to the conditions are interests under the heads of hunger, love, vanity, and fear ; efforts of numbers

[1] See Chapter XX

at the same time to satisfy interests produce mass phenomena which are folkways by virtue of uniformity, repetition, and wide concurrence. The folkways are attended by pleasure or pain according as they are well fitted for the purpose. Pain forces reflection and observation of some relation between acts and welfare. At this point the prevailing world philosophy (beginning with goblinism) suggests explanations and inferences, which become entangled with judgments of expediency. However, the folkways take on a philosophy of right living and a life policy for welfare. Then they become mores, and they may be developed by inferences from the philosophy or the rules in the endeavor to satisfy needs without pain. Hence they undergo improvement and are made consistent with each other.

40. The scope and method of the mores. In the present work the proposition to be maintained is that the folkways are the widest, most fundamental, and most important operation by which the interests of men in groups are served, and that the process by which folkways are made is the chief one to which elementary societal or group phenomena are due. The life of society consists in making folkways and applying them. The science of society might be construed as the study of them. The relations of men to each other, when they are carrying on the struggle for existence near each other, consist in mutual reactions (antagonisms, rivalries, alliances, coercions, and coöperations), from which result societal concatenations and concretions, that is, more or less fixed positions of individuals and subgroups towards each other, and more or less established sequences and methods of interaction between them, by which the interests of all members of the group are served. The same might be said of all animals. The social insects especially show us highly developed results of the adjustment of adjacent interests and life acts into concatenations and concretions. The societal concretions are due to the folkways in this way, — that the men, each struggling to carry on existence, unconsciously coöperate to build up associations, organization, customs, and institutions which, after a time, appear full grown and actual, although no one intended, or planned, or understood them in advance. They stand there as produced by "ancestors." These concretions of relation and act in war, labor, religion, amusement, family life, and civil institutions are attended by faiths, doctrines of philosophy (myths, folklore), and by precepts of right conduct and duty (taboos). The making of folkways is not trivial, although the acts are minute. Every act of each man fixes an atom in a structure, both fulfilling a duty derived from what preceded and conditioning what is to come afterwards by the authority of traditional custom. The structure thus built up is not physical, but societal and institutional, that is to say, it belongs to a category which must be defined and studied by itself. It is a category in which custom produces continuity, coherence, and consistency, so that the word "structure" may properly be applied to the fabric of relations and prescribed positions with which societal functions are permanently connected. The process of making folkways is never superseded or changed. It goes on now just as it did at the beginning of civilization. "Use and wont" exert their force on all men always. They produce familiarity, and mass acts become unconscious. The same effect is produced by customary acts repeated at all recurring occasions. The range of societal activity may be greatly enlarged, interests may be extended and multiplied, the materials by which needs can be supplied may become far more numerous, the processes of societal coöperation may become more complicated, and contract or artifice may take the place of custom for many interests ; but, if the case is one which touches the ways or interests of the masses, folkways will develop on and around it by the same process as that which has been described as taking place from the beginning of civilization. The ways of carrying on war have changed with all new inventions of weapons or armor, and have grown into folkways of commanding range and importance. The factory system of handicrafts has produced a body of folkways in which artisans live, and which distinguish factory towns from commercial cities or agricultural villages. The use of cotton instead of linen has greatly affected modern folkways. The applications of power and machinery have changed the standards of comfort of all classes. The folkways, however, have kept their character and authority through all the changes of form which they have undergone.

41. Integration of the mores of a group or age. In further development of the same interpretation of the phenomena we find that changes in history are primarily due to changes in life conditions. Then the folkways change. Then new philosophies and ethical rules are invented to try to justify the new ways. The whole vast body of modern mores has thus been developed out of the philosophy and ethics of the Middle Ages. So the mores which have been developed to suit the system of great secular states, world commerce, credit institutions, contract wages and rent, emigration to outlying continents, etc., have become the norm for the whole body of usages, manners, ideas, faiths, customs, and institutions which embrace the whole life of a society and characterize an historical epoch. Thus India, Chaldea, Assyria, Egypt, Greece, Rome, the Middle Ages, Modern Times, are cases in which the integration of the mores upon different life conditions produced societal states of complete and distinct individuality (ethos). Within any such societal status the great reason for any phenomenon is that it conforms to the mores of the time and place. Historians have always recognized incidentally the operation of such a determining force. What is now maintained is that it is not incidental or subordinate. It is supreme and controlling. Therefore the scientific discussion of a usage, custom, or institution consists in tracing its relation to the mores, and the discussion of societal crises and changes consists in showing their connection with changes in the life conditions, or with the readjustment of the mores to changes in those conditions.

42. Purpose of the present work. "Ethology" would be a convenient term for the study of manners, customs, usages, and mores, including the study of the way in which they are formed, how they grow or decay, and how they affect the interests which it is their purpose to serve. The Greeks applied the term "ethos" to the sum of the characteristic usages, ideas, standards, and codes by which a group was differentiated and individualized in character from other groups. "Ethics" were things which pertained to the ethos and therefore the things which were the standard of right. The Romans used "mores" for customs in the broadest and richest sense of the word, including the notion that customs served welfare, and had traditional and mystic sanction, so that they were properly authoritative and sacred. It is a very surprising fact that modern nations should have lost these words and the significant suggestions which inhere in them. The English language has no derivative noun from "mores," and no equivalent for it. The French *mœurs* is trivial compared with "mores." The German *Sitte* renders "mores" but very imperfectly. The modern peoples have made morals and morality a separate domain, by the side of religion, philosophy, and politics. In that sense, morals is an impossible and unreal category. It has no existence, and can have none. The word "moral" means what belongs or appertains to the mores. Therefore the category of morals can never be defined without reference to something outside of itself. Ethics, having lost connection with the ethos of a people, is an attempt to systematize the current notions of right and wrong upon some basic principle, generally with the purpose of establishing morals on an absolute doctrine, so that it shall be universal, absolute, and everlasting. In a general way also, whenever a thing can be called moral, or connected with some ethical generality, it is thought to be "raised," and disputants whose method is to employ ethical generalities assume especial authority for themselves and their views. These methods of discussion are most employed in treating of social topics, and they are disastrous to sound study of facts. They help to hold the social sciences under the dominion of metaphysics. The abuse has been most developed in connection with political economy, which has been almost robbed of the character of a serious discipline by converting its discussions into ethical disquisitions.

43. Why use the word mores. "Ethica," in the Greek sense, or "ethology," as above defined, would be good names for our present work. We aim to study the ethos of groups, in order to see how it arises, its power and influence, the modes of its operation on members of the group, and the various attributes of it (ethica). "Ethology" is a very unfamiliar word. It has been used for the mode of setting forth manners, customs, and mores in satirical comedy. The Latin word "mores" seems to be, on the whole, more practically convenient and available than any other for our purpose, as a name for the folkways with the connotations of right and truth in respect to welfare, embodied in them. The analysis and definition above given show that in the mores we must recognize a dominating force in history, constituting a condition as to what can be done, and as to the methods which can be employed.

44. Mores are a directive force. Of course the view which has been stated is antagonistic to the view that philosophy and ethics furnish creative and determining forces in society and history. That view comes down to us from the Greek philosophy and it has now prevailed so long that all current discussion conforms to it. Philosophy and ethics are pursued as independent disciplines, and the results are brought to the science of society and to statesmanship and legislation as authoritative dicta. We also have *Völkerpsychologie, Sozialpolitik,* and other intermediate forms which show the struggle of metaphysics to retain control of the science of society. The "historic sense," the *Zeitgeist,* and other terms of similar import are partial recognitions of the mores and their importance in the science of society. It can be seen also that philosophy and ethics are products of the folkways. They are taken out of the mores, but are never original and creative; they are secondary and derived. They often interfere in the second stage of the sequence, — act, thought, act. Then they produce harm, but some ground is furnished for the claim that they are creative or at least regulative. In fact, the real process in great bodies of men is not one of deduction from any great principle of philosophy or ethics. It is one of minute efforts to live well under existing conditions, which efforts are repeated indefinitely by great numbers, getting strength from habit and from the fellowship of united action. The resultant folkways become coercive. All are forced to conform, and the folkways dominate the societal life. Then they seem true and right, and arise into mores as the norm of welfare. Thence are produced faiths, ideas, doctrines, religions, and philosophies, according to the stage of civilization and the fashions of reflection and generalization.

45. Consistency in the mores. The tendency of the mores of a period to consistency has been noticed (sec. 5). No doubt this tendency is greatly strengthened when people are able to generalize "principles" from acts. This explains the modern belief that principles are causative. The passion for equality, the universal use of contract, and the sentiments of humanitarianism are informing elements in modern society. Whence did they come? Undoubtedly they came out of the mores into which they return again as a principle of consistency. Respect for human life, horror at cruelty and bloodshed, sympathy with pain, suffering, and poverty (humanitarianism), have acted as "causes" in connection with the abolition of slavery, the reform of the criminal law and of prisons, and sympathy with the oppressed, but humanitarianism was a generalization from remoter mores which were due to changes in life conditions. The ultimate explanation of the rise of humanitarianism is the increased power of man over nature by the acquisition of new land, and by advance in the arts. When men ceased to crowd on each other, they were all willing to adopt ideas and institutions which made the competition of life easy and kindly.

46. The mores of subgroups. Each class or group in a society has its own mores. This is true of ranks, professions, industrial classes, religious and philosophical sects, and all other subdivisions of society. Individuals are in two or more of these groups at the same time, so that there is compromise and neutralization. Other mores are common to the whole society. Mores are also transmitted from one class to another. It is necessary to give precision to the notion of classes.

47. What are classes? Galton[1] made a classification of society by a standard which he did not strictly define. He called it "their natural gifts." It might be understood to be mental power, reputation, social success, income from societal work, or societal value. Ammon took up the idea and developed it, making a diagrammatic representation of it, which is reproduced on the following page.[2]

[1] *Hereditary Genius*, 34.
[2] Ammon, *Gesellschaftsordnung*, 53.

48. If we measure and classify a number of persons by any physical characteristic (stature, weight) we find that the results always fall under a curve of probable error. That they should do so is, in fact, a truism. If a number of persons with different degrees of power and resistance are acted on by the same influences, it is most probable that the greatest number of them will reach the same and a mean degree of self-realization, and

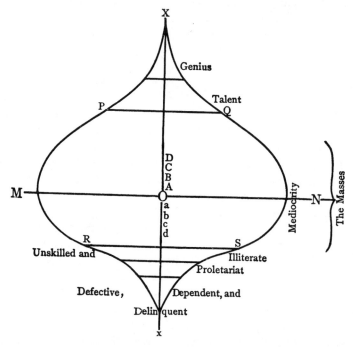

others in proportion to their power and resistance. The fact has been statistically verified so often, and for such a great variety of physical traits, that we may infer its truth for all traits of mind and character for which we have no units, and which we cannot therefore measure or statistically classify.

49. Classes rated by societal value. If we take societal value as the criterion of the classification of society, it has the advantage of being germane to the interests which are most important in connection with classification, but it is complex. There is no unit of it. Therefore we could never verify it statistically. It conforms, in the main, to mental power, but it must contain also a large element of practical sense, health, and opportunity (luck). On the simplest analysis, there are four elements, — intellectual, moral, economic, and physical; but each of these is composite. If one of them is present in a high degree, and the others in a low degree, the whole is inharmonic, and not highly advantageous. The highest societal value seems to go with a harmonious combination, although it may be of lower grades. A man of talent, practical sense, industry, perseverance, and moral principle is worth more to society than a genius, who is not morally responsible, or not industrious. Societal value also conforms, in a general way, to worldly success and to income from work contributed to the industrial organization, for genius which was not effective would have no societal value. On the other hand, however, so long as scientific work and books of the highest value to science and art pay the authors nothing, the returns of the market, and income, only imperfectly measure societal value. All these limitations being allowed for, nevertheless societal value is a concrete idea, especially on its negative side (paupers, tramps, social failures, and incompetents). The defective, dependent, and delinquent classes are already fully differentiated, and are made objects of statistical enumeration. The rest only differ in degree. If, therefore, all were rated and scaled by this value, the results would fall under a curve of probable error. In the diagram the axis Xx is set perpendicular and the ordinates are divided equally upon it in order to make the divisions correspond to " up " and " down " as we use those words in social discussion. Then MN is the line of the greatest number. From O upwards we may cut off equal sections, OA, AB, etc., to indicate grades of societal value above that of the greatest number, and from O downwards we may cut off equal sections of the same magnitude to indicate grades of societal value less than that of the greatest number. At the top we have a small number of men of genius. Below these we may cut off another section which includes the men of talent.

At the bottom we find the dependent, defective, and delinquent classes which are a burden on society. Above them is another stratum, the proletariat, which serves society only by its children. Persons of this class have no regular mode of earning a living, but are not, at the moment at which the classification is made, dependent. These are the only ones to whom the term "proletarian" could with any propriety be applied. Next above these is another well-defined stratum, — the self-supporting, but unskilled and illiterate. Then all who fall between PQ and RS are characterized by mediocrity, and they constitute "the masses." In all new countries, and as it would seem at the present time also in central Europe, there is a very strong current upwards from the lower to the upper strata of $PQRS$. Universal education tends to produce such a current. Talented men of the period are very often born in humble circumstances, but succeed in taking their true place in the societal scale. It is true, of course, that there is a counter-current of degenerate sons and grandsons. The present diagram is made unsymmetrical with respect to MN to express the opinion that the upper strata of $PQRS$ (the lower professional and the semiprofessional classes) are now, in any civilized society, larger in proportion than symmetry would indicate.[1] The line MN is therefore a mode, and the class upon it is the modal class of the society, by means of which one society might be compared with another.

50. Galton estimated the number of men of genius in all history at four hundred. An important fraction of these were related by blood. The "men of the time" he rates at four hundred and fifty in a million, and the more distinguished of them at two hundred and fifty in a million. These latter he defines by saying that a man, to be included amongst them, "should have distinguished himself pretty frequently, either by purely original work, or as a leader of opinion." He finds that illustrious men are only one in a million. On the other hand, idiots and imbeciles in England and Wales are one in four hundred, of whom thirty per cent can be educated so as to be equal to one

[1] Ammon made the diagram symmetrical.

third of a normal man each ; forty per cent can be made worth two thirds of a man ; twenty-five or thirty per cent pass muster in a crowd. Above these are silly persons whose relatives shield them from public knowledge. Then above these come the Dundreary type.[1]

51. Class ; race ; group solidarity. If the group which is classified is a large one, and especially if it is a genetic unit (race, tribe, or nation), there are no gaps in the series. Each individual falls into his place by virtue of his characteristic differences. Just as no two are anthropologically alike, so we may believe that no two are alike or equal in societal value. That all men should be alike or equal, by any standard whatever, is contrary to all the facts of human nature and all the conditions of human life. Any group falls into subdivisions, the members of each of which are approximately equal, when measured by any standard, because the classification is imperfect. If we make it more refined, the subdivisions must be subdivided again. We are in a dilemma : we cannot describe mankind at all without categories, and if we go on to make our categories more and more exact, each one of them would at last contain only one person. Two things result which are practically important, and which furnish us with scientific concepts which we can employ in further study : (1) The classification gives us the notion of the relative position of one, or a subdivision, in the entire group. This is the sense of "class."[2] (2) The characteristic differences furnish the notion of individuality and personality. The concept of a race, as the term is now used, is that of a group clustered around a mean with respect to some characteristic, and great confusion in the use of the word "race" arises from the attempt to define races by their boundaries, when we really think of them by the mean or mode, e.g. as to skin color. The

---

[1] *Hereditary Genius*, 25, 47.

[2] Lapouge affirms that "in different historical periods, and over the whole earth, racial differences between classes of the same people are far greater than between analogous classes of different peoples," and that "between different classes of the same population there may be greater racial differences than between different populations" (*Pol. Anth. Rev.*, III, 220, 228). He does not give his definition of class.

coherence, unity, and solidarity of a genetic group is a very striking fact. It seems to conceal a play of mystic forces. It is, in fact, no more mysterious than the run of dice. The propositions about it would all become, in the last analysis, identical propositions; e.g. it is most probable that we shall meet with the thing which is present in the greatest number; or, it is most probable that the most probable thing will happen. In the middle of the nineteenth century, when attention was first called to the solidarity and internal correlations of groups, especially if they were large and genetic, it was believed that occult and far-reaching laws had been discovered. That opinion has long been abandoned. If there are four dice in a box, each having from one to six dots on its faces, the chance of throwing four sixes is just the same as that of throwing four ones. The mean of the sums of the dots which may fall uppermost is fourteen, which can be produced by one hundred and forty-six throws. Suppose that the components of social value are four, — intellectual, moral, physical, economic, — represented by the four dice, and that the degrees are represented by the dots. We should get four sixes once in twelve hundred and ninety-six throws. Of the one hundred and forty-six throws which give the mean fourteen, seventy-two show one six up. That might be a Hercules fit only for a dime museum. Seventy-eight of the combinations are inharmonious, but have one strong element.[1] In societal matters it is by no means indifferent whether the equal sums of societal value are made up of very unequal, or of harmonious, components. So in a group of a million persons the chance of a great genius, who would stand alone towards X is just the same as that of an utter idiot who would stand alone towards x, and the reason why the number at the mode is so great is that the societal value is the sum of components, of which many sums may be equal, although the components are very unequal. Two strata at equal distances above and below O are equal in number, so far as their useful powers and resistances go, but education introduces a new component which destroys their equality and forces a redistribution

---

[1] Ammon, *Gesellschaftsordnung*, 49.

Galton [1] suggests that, if people who would when adults fall in classes V, W, or X in our diagram could be recognized in infancy, and could be bought for money, it would be a great bargain for a nation, England for instance, to buy them for much money and rear them as Englishmen. Farr estimated the baby of an agricultural laborer as worth £5, capital value. A baby who could be reared to take a place in the class X would have a capital value of thousands of pounds. The capital value would be like that of land of different degrees of natural advantage, but none of it yet exploited.

52. The masses and the mores. In connection with the mores the masses are of very great importance. The historical or selected classes are those which, in history, have controlled the activities and policy of generations. They have been differentiated at one time by one standard, at another time by another. The position which they held by inheritance from early society has given them prestige and authority. Merit and societal value, according to the standards of their time, have entered into their status only slightly and incidentally. Those classes have had their own mores. They had the power to regulate their lives to some extent according to their own choice, a power which modern civilized men eagerly desire and strive for primarily by the acquisition of wealth. The historical classes have, therefore, selected purposes, and have invented ways of fulfilling them. Their ways have been imitated by the masses. The classes have led the way in luxury, frivolity, and vice, and also in refinement, culture, and the art of living. They have introduced variation. The masses are not large classes at the base of a social pyramid; they are the core of the society. They are conservative. They accept life as they find it, and live on by tradition and habit. In other words, the great mass of any society lives a purely instinctive life just like animals. We must not be misled by the conservatism of castes and aristocracies, who resist change of customs and institutions by virtue of which they hold social power. The conservatism of the masses is of a different kind. It is not produced by interests, but it is instinctive. It is due

[1] PSM, LX, 218.

to inertia. Change would make new effort necessary to win routine and habit. It is therefore irksome. The masses, moreover, have not the power to reach out after " improvements," or to plan steps of change by which needs might be better satisfied. The mores of any society, at a period, may be characterized by the promptness or reluctance of the masses to imitate the ways of the classes. It is a question of the first importance for the historian whether the mores of the historical classes of which he finds evidence in documentary remains penetrated the masses or not. The masses are the real bearers of the mores of the society. They carry tradition. The folkways are their ways. They accept influence or leadership, and they imitate, but they do so as they see fit, being controlled by their notions and tastes previously acquired. They may accept standards of character and action from the classes, or from foreigners, or from literature, or from a new religion, but whatever they take up they assimilate and make it a part of their own mores, which they then transmit by tradition, defend in its integrity, and refuse to discard again. Consequently the writings of the literary class may not represent the faiths, notions, tastes, standards, etc., of the masses at all. The literature of the first Christian centuries shows us scarcely anything of the mores of the time, as they existed in the faith and practice of the masses. Every group takes out of a new religion which is offered to it just what it can assimilate with its own traditional mores. Christianity was a very different thing amongst Jews, Egyptians, Greeks, Germans, and Slavs. It would be a great mistake to suppose that any people ever accepted and held philosophical or religious teaching as it was offered to them, and as we find it recorded in the books of the teachers. The mores of the masses admit of no such sudden and massive modification by doctrinal teaching. The process of assimilation is slow, and it is attended by modifying influences at every stage. What the classes adopt, be it good or ill, may be found pervading the mass after generations, but it will appear as a resultant of all the vicissitudes of the folkways in the interval. " It was the most frightful feature of the corruption of ancient Rome, that it extended through every class in the community." [1] "As in the Renaissance, so now [in the Catholic reaction] vice trickled downward from above, infiltrating the mass of the people with its virus." [2] It is the classes who produce variation ; it is the masses who carry forward the traditional mores.

53. Fallacies about the masses and classes. It is a fallacy to infer that the masses have some occult wisdom or inspiration by virtue of which they select what is wise, right, and good from what the classes offer. There is, also, no device by which it is possible to obtain from the masses, in advance or on demand, a judgment on any proposed changes or innovations. The masses are not an oracle. If any answers can be obtained on the problems of life, such answers will come rather from the classes. The two sections of society are such that they may coöperate with advantage to the good of all. Neither one has a right or a better claim to rule the society.

54. Action of the masses on thoughts. Fifty years ago Darwin put some knowledge into the common stock. The peasants and artisans of his time did nothing of the kind. What the masses do with thoughts is that they rub them down into counters just as they take coins from the mint and smooth them down by wear until they are only disks of metal. The masses understand, for instance, that Darwin said that " men are descended from monkeys." Only summary and glib propositions of that kind can ever get currency. The learned men are all the time trying to recoin them and give them at least partial reality. Ruskin set afloat some notions of art criticism, which have penetrated all our cultivated classes. They are not lost, but see what has become of them in fifty years by popularization. A little later a new gospel of furniture and house decoration was published. The masses have absorbed it. See what they have made of it. Eastlake wanted no machine work, but machinery was not to be defeated. It can make lopsided things if those are the fashion, and it can make all the construction show if Eastlake has got the notion into the crowd that the pegs ought to be on the outside. Thinking and understanding are too hard work. If any one

[1] Lecky, *Morals*, I, 262.　　　[2] Symonds, *Catholic Reaction*, I, 455.

wants to blame the masses let him turn to his own case. He will find that he thinks about and understands only his own intellectual pursuit. He could not give the effort to every other department of knowledge. In other matters he is one of the masses and does as they do. He uses routine, set formulæ, current phrases, caught up from magazines and newspapers of the better class.

55. Organization of the masses. Masses of men who are on a substantial equality with each other never can be anything but hopeless savages. The eighteenth-century notion that men in a state of nature were all equal is wrong-side up. Men who were equal would be in a state of nature such as was imagined. They could not form a society. They would be forced to scatter and wander, at most two or three together. They never could advance in the arts of civilization. The popular belief that out of some such horde there has come by the spontaneous develop-ment of innate forces all the civilization which we possess is entirely unfounded. Masses of men who are approximately equal are in time exterminated or enslaved. Only when enslaved or subjugated are some of them carried up with their conquerors by organization and discipline (negroes and Indians amongst us). A horde in which the only differences are those of age and sex is not capable of maintaining existence. It fights because only by conquering or being conquered can it endure. When it is subjugated and disciplined it consists of workers to belabor the ground for others, or tax payers to fill a treasury from which others may spend, or food for gunpowder, or voting material for demagogues. It is an object of exploitation   At one moment, in spite of its aggregate muscle, it is helpless and imbecile; the next moment it is swept away into folly and mischief by a sug-gestion or an impulse. Organization, leadership, and discipline are indispensable to any beneficial action by masses of men. If we ignore this fact, we see the machine and the boss evolved out of the situation which we create.

56. Institutions of civil liberty. Institutions also must be pro-duced which will hold the activities of society in channels of order, deliberation, peace, regulated antagonism of interests, and justice, according to the mores of the time. These institutions put an end to exploitation and bring interests into harmony under civil liberty. But where do the institutions come from? The masses have never made them. They are produced out of the mores by the selection of the leading men and classes who get control of the collective power of the society and direct it to the activities which will (as they think) serve the interests which they regard as most important. If changes in life conditions occur, the interests to be served change. Great inventions and discoveries, the opening of new continents, new methods of agriculture and commerce, the introduction of money and financial devices, improved state organization, increase the economic power of the society and the force at the disposal of the state. Industrial interests displace military and monarchical interests as the ones which the state chiefly aims to serve, not because of any tide of "progress," but because industrialism gives greater and more varied satisfactions to the rulers. The increase of *power* is the primary condition. The classes strive with each other for the new power. Peace is necessary, for without peace none of them can enjoy power. Compromise, adjustment of interests, antagonistic coöperation (sec. 21), harmony, are produced, and institutions are the regulative processes and apparatus by which warfare is replaced by system. The historical process has been full of error, folly, selfishness, violence, and craft. It is so still. The point which is now important for us is that the masses have never carried on the struggles and processes by which civilized society has been made into an arena, within which exploitation of man by man is to some extent repressed, and where individual self-realization has a large scope, under the institutions of civil liberty. It is the historical and selected classes which have done this, often enough without intending or foreseeing the results of actions which they inaugurated with quite other, perhaps selfish, class purposes in view. A society is a whole made up of parts. All the parts have a legitimate share in the acts and sufferings of the society. All the parts contribute to the life and work of the society. We inherit all the consequences of all their acts. Some of the consequences are good and some are bad.

It is utterly impossible to name the classes which have done useful work and made beneficial sacrifices only, and the other classes which have been idle burdens and mischief makers only. All that has been done has been done by all. It is evident that no other view than this can be rational and true, for one reason because the will and intention of the men of to-day in what they do has so little to do with the consequences to-morrow of what they do. The notion that religion, or marriage, or property, or monarchy, as we have inherited them, can be proved evil, or worthy of condemnation and contempt on account of the selfishness and violence interwoven with their history, is one of the idlest of all the vagaries of the social philosophers.

57. The common man. Every civilized society has to carry below the lowest sections of the masses a dead weight of ignorance, poverty, crime, and disease. Every such society has, in the great central section of the masses, a great body which is neutral in all the policy of society. It lives by routine and tradition. It is not brutal, but it is shallow, narrow-minded, and prejudiced. Nevertheless it is harmless. It lacks initiative and cannot give an impulse for good or bad. It produces few criminals. It can sometimes be moved by appeals to its fixed ideas and prejudices. It is affected in its mores by contagion from the classes above it. The work of "popularization" consists in bringing about this contagion. The middle section is formed around the mathematical mean of the society, or around the mathematical mode, if the distribution of the subdivisions is not symmetrical. The man on the mode is the "common man," the "average man," or the "man in the street." Between him and the democratic political institutions — the pulpit, the newspapers, and the public library — there is a constant reaction by which mores are modified and preserved. The aim of all the institutions and literature in a modern state is to please him. His aim is to get out of them what suits him. The yellow newspapers thrive and displace all the others because he likes them. The trashy novels pay well because his wife and daughters like them. The advertisements in the popular magazines are addressed to him. They show what he wants. The "funny items" are adjusted to his sense of humor. Hence all these things are symptoms. They show what he "believes in," and they strengthen his prejudices. If all art, literature, legislation, and political power are to be cast at his feet, it makes some difference who and what he is. His section of society determines the mores of the whole.

58. " The people." Popular impulses. In a democratic state the great middle section would rule if it was organized independently of the rest. It is that section which constitutes "the people" in the special technical sense in which that expression is current in political use. It is to it that the Jeffersonian doctrines about the "wisdom" of the people would apply. That section, however, is never organized independently; that is to say, "the people" never exist as a body exercising political power. The middle section of a group may be enthused by an impulse which is adapted to its ways and notions. It clings to persons, loves anecdotes, is fond of light emotions, and prides itself on its morality. If a man wins popularity in that section, the impulse which his name can give to it may be irresistible (Jefferson, Jackson). The middle section is greatly affected by symbolism. "The flag" can be developed into a fetich. A cult can be nourished around it. Group vanity is very strong in it. Patriotic emotions and faiths are its favorite psychological exercises, if the conjuncture is favorable and the material well-being is high. When the middle section is stirred by any spontaneous and consentaneous impulses which arise from its nature and ways, it may produce incredible results with only a minimum of organization. "A little prosperity and some ideas, as Aristotle saw, are the ferment which sets the masses in ebullition. This offers an opportunity. A beginning is made. The further development is unavoidable." [1]

59. Agitation. Every impulse given to the masses is, in its nature, spasmodic and transitory. No systematic enterprise to enlighten the masses ever can be carried out. Campaigns of education contain a fallacy. Education takes time. It cannot be treated as subsidiary for a lifetime and then be made the

[1] Gumplowicz, *Soziologie*, 126.

chief business for six months with the desired result. A campaign of education is undemocratic. It implies that some one is teacher and somebody else pupil. It can only result in the elucidation of popular interests and the firmer establishment of popular prejudice. On the other hand, an agitation which appeals skillfully to pet notions and to latent fanaticism may stampede the masses. The Middle Ages furnished a number of cases. The Mahdis who have arisen in Mohammedan Africa, and other Moslem prophets, have produced wonderful phenomena of this kind. The silver agitation was begun, in 1878, by a systematic effort of three or four newspapers in the middle West, addressed to currency notions which the greenback proposition had popularized. What is the limit to the possibilities of fanaticism and frenzy which might be produced in any society by agitation skillfully addressed to the fallacies and passions of the masses? The answer lies in the mores, which determine the degree of reserved common sense, and the habit of observing measure and method, to which the masses have been accustomed. It follows that popular agitation is a desperate and doubtful method. The masses, as the great popular jury which, at last, by adoption or rejection, decides the fate of all proposed changes in the mores, needs stability and moderation. Popular agitation introduces into the masses initiative and creative functions which destroy its judgment and call for quite other qualities.

60. The ruling element in the masses. The masses are liable to controlling influences from elements which they contain. When crises arise in a democratic state attention is concentrated on the most numerous strata nearest to MN (see the diagram, p. 40), but they rarely possess self-determination unless the question at issue appeals directly to popular interest or popular vanity. Moreover, those strata cannot rule unless they combine with those next above and below. So the critical question always is, in regard to the masses $PQRS$, which parts of it will move the whole of it. Generally the question is, more specifically, What is the character of the strata above a line through A or B, and what is their relation to the rest of $PQRS$? If the upper part of the section $PQRS$ consists of employers and the lower part of employés, and if they hate and fight each other, coherence and sympathy in the society will cease, the mores will be characterized by discord, passion, and quarrelsomeness, and political crises will arise which may reach any degree of severity, for the political parties will soon coincide with the class sections. The upper part of $PQRS$ is made up of the strata which possess comfort without luxury, but also culture, intelligence, and the best family mores. They are generally disciplined classes, with strong moral sense, public spirit, and sense of responsibility. If we are not in error as to the movement in civilized states of the present time from the lower into the upper strata of $PQRS$, by virtue of ambition and education, then it follows that the upper strata are being constantly reënforced by all the elements in the society which have societal value, after those elements have been developed and disciplined by labor and self-denial. The share which the upper strata of the masses have in determining the policy of the masses is therefore often decisive of public welfare. On the other hand, it is when the masses are controlled by the strata next above RS that there is most violent impulsiveness in societal movements. The movements and policies which are characterized as revolutionary have their rise in these classes, although, in other cases, these classes also adhere most stubbornly to popular traditions in spite of reason and fact. Trade unionism is, at the present time, a social philosophy and a programme of policy which has its origin in the sections of the masses next above RS.

The French Revolution began with the highest strata of the masses, and the control of it passed on down from one to another of the lower strata, until it reached the lowest, — the mob gathered in the slums of a great city.

61. The mores and institutions. Institutions and laws are produced out of mores. An institution consists of a concept (idea, notion, doctrine, interest) and a structure. The structure is a framework, or apparatus, or perhaps only a number of functionaries set to coöperate in prescribed ways at a certain conjuncture. The structure holds the concept and furnishes instrumentalities for bringing it into the world of facts and action in a way to serve the interests of men in society. Institutions are either crescive or enacted. They are crescive when they take shape in the mores, growing by the instinctive efforts by which the mores are produced. Then the efforts, through long use, become definite and specific. Property, marriage, and religion are the most primary institutions. They began in folkways. They became customs. They developed into mores by the addition of some philosophy of welfare, however crude. Then they were made more definite and specific as regards the rules, the prescribed acts, and the apparatus to be employed. This produced a structure and the institution was complete. Enacted institutions are products of rational invention and intention. They belong to high civilization. Banks are institutions of credit founded on usages which can be traced back to barbarism. There came a time when, guided by rational reflection on experience, men systematized and regulated the usages which had become current, and thus created positive institutions of credit, defined by law and sanctioned by the force of the state. Pure enacted institutions which are strong and prosperous are hard to find. It is too difficult to invent and create an institution, for a purpose, out of nothing. The electoral college in the constitution of the United States is an example. In that case the democratic mores of the people have seized upon the device and made of it something quite different from what the inventors planned. All institutions have come out of mores, although the rational element in them is sometimes so large that their origin in the mores is not to be ascertained except by an historical investigation (legislatures, courts, juries, joint stock companies, the stock exchange). Property, marriage, and religion are still almost entirely in the mores. Amongst nature men any man might capture and hold a woman at any time, if he could. He did it by superior force which was its own supreme justification. But his act brought his group and her group into war, and produced harm to his comrades. They forbade capture, or set conditions for it. Beyond the limits, the individual might still use force, but his comrades were no longer responsible. The glory to him, if he succeeded, might be all the greater. His control over his captive was absolute.

Within the prescribed conditions, " capture " became technical and institutional, and rights grew out of it. The woman had a status which was defined by custom, and was very different from the status of a real captive. Marriage was the institutional relation, in the society and under its sanction, of a woman to a man, where the woman had been obtained in the prescribed way. She was then a " wife." What her rights and duties were was defined by the mores, as they are to-day in all civilized society.

62. Laws. Acts of legislation come out of the mores. In low civilization all societal regulations are customs and taboos, the origin of which is unknown. Positive laws are impossible until the stage of verification, reflection, and criticism is reached. Until that point is reached there is only customary law, or common law. The customary law may be codified and systematized with respect to some philosophical principles, and yet remain customary. The codes of Manu and Justinian are examples. Enactment is not possible until reverence for ancestors has been so much weakened that it is no longer thought wrong to interfere with traditional customs by positive enactment. Even then there is reluctance to make enactments, and there is a stage of transition during which traditional customs are extended by interpretation to cover new cases and to prevent evils. Legislation, however, has to seek standing ground on the existing mores, and it soon becomes apparent that legislation, to be strong, must be consistent with the mores.[1] Things which have been in the mores are put under police regulation and later under positive law. It is sometimes said that " public opinion " must ratify and approve police regulations, but this statement rests on an imperfect analysis. The regulations must conform to the mores, so that the public will not think them too lax or too strict. The mores of our urban and rural populations are not the same ; consequently legislation about intoxicants which is made by one of these sections of the population does not succeed when applied to the other. The regulation of drinking places, gambling places,

---

[1] " In the reigns of Theodosius and Honorius, imperial edicts and rescripts were paralyzed by the impalpable, quietly irresistible force of a universal social need or sentiment." — Dill, *Rome from Nero to M. Aurel.*, 255.

and disorderly houses has passed through the above-mentioned stages. It is always a question of expediency whether to leave a subject under the mores, or to make a police regulation for it, or to put it into the criminal law. Betting, horse racing, dangerous sports, electric cars, and vehicles are cases now of things which seem to be passing under positive enactment and out of the unformulated control of the mores. When an enactment is made there is a sacrifice of the elasticity and automatic self-adaptation of custom, but an enactment is specific and is provided with sanctions. Enactments come into use when conscious purposes are formed, and it is believed that specific devices can be framed by which to realize such purposes in the society. Then also prohibitions take the place of taboos, and punishments are planned to be deterrent rather than revengeful. The mores of different societies, or of different ages, are characterized by greater or less readiness and confidence in regard to the use of positive enactments for the realization of societal purposes.

63. How laws and institutions differ from mores. When folkways have become institutions or laws they have changed their character and are to be distinguished from the mores. The element of sentiment and faith inheres in the mores. Laws and institutions have a rational and practical character, and are more mechanical and utilitarian. The great difference is that institutions and laws have a positive character, while mores are unformulated and undefined. There is a philosophy implicit in the folkways; when it is made explicit it becomes technical philosophy. Objectively regarded, the mores are the customs which actually conduce to welfare under existing life conditions. Acts under the laws and institutions are conscious and voluntary; under the folkways they are always unconscious and involuntary, so that they have the character of natural necessity. Educated reflection and skepticism can disturb this spontaneous relation. The laws, being positive prescriptions, supersede the mores so far as they are adopted. It follows that the mores come into operation where laws and tribunals fail. The mores cover the great field of common life where there are no laws or police regulations. They cover an immense and undefined domain, and they break the way in new domains, not yet controlled at all. The mores, therefore, build up new laws and police regulations in time.

64. Difference between mores and some cognate things. Products of intentional investigation or of rational and conscious reflection, projects formally adopted by voluntary associations, rational methods consciously selected, injunctions and prohibitions by authority, and all specific conventional arrangements are not in the mores. They are differentiated by the rational and conscious element in them. We may also make a distinction between usages and mores. Usages are folkways which contain no principle of welfare, but serve convenience so long as all know what they are expected to do. For instance, Orientals, to show respect, cover the head and uncover the feet; Occidentals do the opposite. There is no inherent and necessary connection between respect and either usage, but it is an advantage that there should be a usage and that all should know and observe it. One way is as good as another, if it is understood and established. The folkways as to public decency belong to the mores, because they have real connection with welfare which determines the only tenor which they can have. The folkways about propriety and modesty are sometimes purely conventional and sometimes inherently real. Fashions, fads, affectations, poses, ideals, manias, popular delusions, follies, and vices must be included in the mores. They have characteral qualities and characteral effect. However frivolous or foolish they may appear to people of another age, they have the form of attempts to live well, to satisfy some interest, or to win some good. The ways of advertisers who exaggerate, use tricks to win attention, and appeal to popular weakness and folly; the ways of journalism; electioneering devices; oratorical and dithyrambic extravagances in politics; current methods of humbug and sensationalism, — are not properly part of the mores but symptoms of them. They are not products of the concurrent and coöperative effort of all members of the society to live well. They are devices made with conscious ingenuity to exert suggestion on the minds of others. The mores are rather the underlying facts in regard to the faiths, notions, tastes, desires, etc., of that society at that time, to which all these modes of action appeal and of whose existence they are evidence.

65. What is goodness or badness of the mores. It is most important to notice that, for the people of a time and place, their own mores are always good, or rather that for them there can be no question of the goodness or badness of their mores. The reason is because the standards of good and right are in the mores. If the life conditions change, the traditional folkways may produce pain and loss, or fail to produce the same good as formerly. Then the loss of comfort and ease brings doubt into the judgment of welfare (causing doubt of the pleasure of the gods, or of war power, or of health), and thus disturbs the unconscious philosophy of the mores. Then a later time will pass judgment on the mores. Another society may also pass judgment on the mores. In our literary and historical study of the mores we want to get from them their educational value, which consists in the stimulus or warning as to what is, in its effects, societally good or bad. This may lead us to reject or neglect a phenomenon like infanticide, slavery, or witchcraft, as an old "abuse" and "evil," or to pass by the crusades as a folly which cannot recur. Such a course would be a great error. Everything in the mores of a time and place must be regarded as justified with regard to that time and place. "Good" mores are those which are well adapted to the situation. "Bad" mores are those which are not so adapted. The mores are not so stereotyped and changeless as might appear, because they are forever moving towards more complete adaptation to conditions and interests, and also towards more complete adjustment to each other. People in mass have never made or kept up a custom in order to hurt their own interests. They have made innumerable errors as to what their interests were and how to satisfy them, but they have always aimed to serve their interests as well as they could. This gives the standpoint for the student of the mores. All things in them come before him on the same plane. They all bring instruction and warning. They all have the same relation to power and welfare. The mistakes in them are component parts of them. We do not study them in order to approve some of them and condemn others. They are all equally worthy of attention from the fact that they existed and were used. The chief object of study in them is their adjustment to interests, their relation to welfare, and their coördination in a harmonious system of life policy. For the men of the time there are no "bad" mores. What is traditional and current is the standard of what ought to be. The masses never raise any question about such things. If a few raise doubts and questions, this proves that the folkways have already begun to lose firmness and the regulative element in the mores has begun to lose authority. This indicates that the folkways are on their way to a new adjustment. The extreme of folly, wickedness, and absurdity in the mores is witch persecutions, but the best men of the seventeenth century had no doubt that witches existed, and that they ought to be burned. The religion, statecraft, jurisprudence, philosophy, and social system of that age all contributed to maintain that belief. It was rather a culmination than a contradiction of the current faiths and convictions, just as the dogma that all men are equal and that one ought to have as much political power in the state as another was the culmination of the political dogmatism and social philosophy of the nineteenth century. Hence our judgments of the good or evil consequences of folkways are to be kept separate from our study of the historical phenomena of them, and of their strength and the reasons for it. The judgments have their place in plans and doctrines for the future, not in a retrospect.

66. More exact definition of the mores. We may now formulate a more complete definition of the mores. They are the ways of doing things which are current in a society to satisfy human needs and desires, together with the faiths, notions, codes, and standards of well living which inhere in those ways, having a genetic connection with them. By virtue of the latter element the mores are traits in the specific character (ethos) of a society or a period. They pervade and control the ways of thinking in all the exigencies of life, returning from the world of abstractions to the world of action, to give guidance and to win revivification. "The mores [*Sitten*] are, before any beginning of reflection, the regulators of the political, social, and religious behavior of the individual. Conscious reflection is the worst enemy of the mores, because mores begin unconsciously and pursue unconscious purposes, which are recognized by reflection often only after long and circuitous processes, and because their expediency often depends on the assumption that they will have general acceptance and currency, uninterfered with by reflection." [1] " The mores are usage in any group, in so far as it, on the one hand, is not the expression or fulfillment of an absolute natural necessity [e.g. eating or sleeping], and, on the other hand, is independent of the arbitrary will of the individual, and is generally accepted as good and proper, appropriate and worthy." [2]

67. Ritual. The process by which mores are developed and established is ritual. Ritual is so foreign to our mores that we do not recognize its power. In primitive society it is the prevailing method of activity, and primitive religion is entirely a matter of ritual. Ritual is the perfect form of drill and of the regulated habit which comes from drill. Acts which are ordained by authority and are repeated mechanically without intelligence run into ritual. If infants and children are subjected to ritual they never escape from its effects through life. Galton [3] says that he was, in early youth, in contact with the Mohammedan ritual idea that the left hand is less worthy than the right, and that he never overcame it. We see the effect of ritual in breeding, courtesy, politeness, and all forms of prescribed behavior. Etiquette is social ritual. Ritual is not easy compliance with usage ; it is strict compliance with detailed and punctilious rule. It admits of no exception or deviation. The stricter the discipline, the greater the power of ritual over action and character. In the training of animals and the education of children it is the perfection, inevitableness, invariableness, and relentlessness of routine which tells. They should never experience any exception or irregularity. Ritual is connected with words, gestures, symbols, and signs. Associations result, and, upon a repetition

---

[1] v. Hartmann, *Phänom. des Sittl. Bewusztseins*, 73.

[2] Lazarus in *Ztsft. für Völkerpsy.*, I, 439.

[3] *Human Faculty*, 216.

of the signal, the act is repeated, whether the will assents or not. Association and habit account for the phenomena. Ritual gains further strength when it is rhythmical, and is connected with music, verse, or other rhythmical arts. Acts are ritually repeated at the recurrence of the rhythmical points. The alternation of night and day produces rhythms of waking and sleeping, of labor and rest, for great numbers at the same time, in their struggle for existence. The seasons also produce rhythms in work. Ritual may embody an idea of utility, expediency, or welfare, but it always tends to become perfunctory, and the idea is only subconscious. There is ritual in primitive therapeutics, and it was not eliminated until very recent times. The patient was directed, not only to apply remedies, but also to perform rites. The rites introduced mystic elements. This illustrates the connection of ritual with notions of magical effects produced by rites. All ritual is ceremonious and solemn. It tends to become sacred, or to make sacred the subject-matter with which it is connected. Therefore, in primitive society, it is by ritual that sentiments of awe, deference to authority, submission to tradition, and disciplinary coöperation are inculcated. Ritual operates a constant suggestion, and the suggestion is at once put in operation in acts. Ritual, therefore, suggests sentiments, but it never inculcates doctrines. Ritual is strongest when it is most perfunctory and excites no thought. By familiarity with ritual any doctrinal reference which it once had is lost by familiarity, but the habits persist. Primitive religion is ritualistic, not because religion makes ritual, but because ritual makes religion. Ritual is something to be done, not something to be thought or felt. Men can always perform the prescribed act, although they cannot always think or feel prescribed thoughts or emotions. The acts may bring up again, by association, states of the mind and sentiments which have been connected with them, especially in childhood, when the fantasy was easily affected by rites, music, singing, dramas, etc. No creed, no moral code, and no scientific demonstration can ever win the same hold upon men and women as habits of action, with associated sentiments and states of mind, drilled in from childhood. Mohammedanism shows the power of ritual. Any occupation is interrupted for the prayers and prescribed genuflections. The Brahmins also observe an elaborate daily ritual. They devote to it two hours in the morning, two in the evening, and one at midday.[1] Monks and nuns have won the extreme satisfaction of religious sentiment from the unbroken habit of repeated ritual, with undisturbed opportunity to develop the emotional effects of it.

68. The ritual of the mores. The mores are social ritual in which we all participate unconsciously. The current habits as to hours of labor, meal hours, family life, the social intercourse of the sexes, propriety, amusements, travel, holidays, education, the use of periodicals and libraries, and innumerable other details of life fall under this ritual. Each does as everybody does. For the great mass of mankind as to all things, and for all of us for a great many things, the rule to do as all do suffices. We are led by suggestion and association to believe that there must be wisdom and utility in what all do. The great mass of the folkways give us discipline and the support of routine and habit. If we had to form judgments as to all these cases before we could act in them, and were forced always to act rationally, the burden would be unendurable. Beneficent use and wont save us this trouble.

69. Group interests and policy. Groups select, consciously and unconsciously, standards of group well living. They plan group careers, and adopt purposes through which they hope to attain to group self-realization. The historical classes adopt the decisions which constitute these group plans and acts, and they impose them on the group. The Greeks were enthused at one time by a national purpose to destroy Troy, at another time by a national necessity to ward off Persian conquest. The Romans conceived of their rivalry with Carthage as a struggle from which only one state could survive. Spain, through an effort to overthrow the political power of the Moors in the peninsula and to make it all Christian, was educated up to a national purpose to make Spain a pure "Christian" state, in the dogmatic and ecclesiastical sense of the word. Moors and Jews were expelled at

[1] Wilkins, *Mod. Hinduism*, 195.

great cost and loss. Germany and Italy cherished for generations a national hope and desire to become unified states. Some attempts to formulate or interpret the Monroe doctrine would make it a national policy and programme for the United States. In lower civilization group interests and purposes are less definite. We must believe that barbarous tribes often form notions of their group interests, and adopt group policies, especially in their relations with neighboring groups. The Iroquois, after forming their confederation, made war on neighboring tribes in order either to subjugate them or to force them to come into the peace pact. Pontiac and Tecumseh united the red men in a race effort to drive the whites out of North America.

70. Group interests and folkways. Whenever a group has a group purpose that purpose produces group interests, and those interests overrule individual interests in the development of folkways. A group might adopt a pacific and industrial purpose, but historical cases of this kind are very few. It used to be asserted that the United States had as its great social purpose to create a social environment which should favor that development of the illiterate and unskilled classes into an independent status for which the economic conditions of a new country give opportunity, and it was asserted that nothing could cause a variation from this policy, which was said to be secured in the political institutions and political ideas of the people. Within a few years the United States has been affected by an ambition to be a world power. (A world power is a state which expects to have a share in the settlement of every clash of interests and collision of state policies which occurs anywhere on the globe.) There is no reason to wonder at this action of a democracy, for a democracy is sure to resent any suggestion that it is limited in its functions, as compared with other political forms. At the same time that the United States has moved towards the character of a world power it has become militant. Other states in the past which have had group purposes have been militant. Even when they arrived at commerce and industry they have pursued policies which involved them in war (Venice, Hansa, Holland). Since the group interests override the individual interests, the selection and determination of group purposes is a function of the greatest importance and an act of the greatest effect on individual welfare. The interests of the society or nation furnish an easy phrase, but such phrases are to be regarded with suspicion. Such interests are apt to be the interests of a ruling clique which the rest are to be compelled to serve. On the other hand, a really great and intelligent group purpose, founded on correct knowledge and really sound judgment, can infuse into the mores a vigor and consistent character which will reach every individual with educative effect. The essential condition is that the group purpose shall be "founded on correct knowledge and really sound judgment." The interests must be real, and they must be interests of the whole, and the judgment as to means of satisfying them must be correct.

71. Force in the folkways. Here we notice also the intervention of force. There is always a large element of force in the folkways. It constitutes another modification of the theory of the folkways as expedient devices, developed in experience, to meet the exigencies of life. The organization of society under chiefs and medicine men greatly increased the power of the society to serve its own interests. The same is true of higher political organizations. If Gian Galeazzo Visconti or Cesare Borgia could have united Italy into a despotic state, it is an admissible opinion that the history of the peninsula in the following four or five hundred years would have been happy and prosperous, and that, at the present time, it would have had the same political system which it has now. However, chiefs, kings, priests, warriors, statesmen, and other functionaries have put their own interests in the place of group interests, and have used the authority they possessed to force the societal organization to work and fight for their interests. The force is that of the society itself. It is directed by the ruling class or persons. The force enters into the mores and becomes a component in them. Despotism is in the mores of negro tribes, and of all Mohammedan peoples. There is an element of force in all forms of property, marriage, and religion. Slavery, however, is the grandest case of force in the mores, employed to make some serve the interests of others, in the societal organization. The historical classes, having selected the group purposes and decided the group policy, use the force of the society itself to coerce all to acquiesce and to work and fight in the determined way without regard to their individual interests. This they do by means of discipline and ritual. In different kinds of mores the force is screened by different devices. It is always present, and brutal, cruel force has entered largely into the development of all our mores, even those which we think most noble and excellent.

72. Might and right. Modern civilized states of the best form are often called jural states because the concept of rights enters so largely into all their constitutions and regulations. Our political philosophy centers around that concept, and all our social discussions fall into the form of propositions and disputes about rights. The history of the dogma of rights has been such that rights have been believed to be self-evident and self-existent, and as having prevailed especially in primitive society. Rights are also regarded as the opposite of force. These notions only prove the antagonism between our mores and those of earlier generations. In fact, it is a characteristic of our mores that the form of our thinking about all points of political philosophy is set for us by the concept of rights. Nothing but might has ever made right, and if we include in might (as we ought to) elections and the decisions of courts, nothing but might makes right now. We must distinguish between the anterior and the posterior view of the matter in question. If we are about to take some action, and are debating the right of it, the might which can be brought to support one view of it has nothing to do with the right of it. If a thing has been done and is established by force (that is, no force can reverse it), it is right in the only sense we know, and rights will follow from it which are not vitiated at all by the force in it. There would be no security at all for rights if this were not so. We find men and parties protesting, declaiming, complaining of what is done, and which they say is not "right," but only force. An election decides that those shall have power who will execute an act of policy. The defeated party denounces the wrong and wickedness of the act. It is done. It may be a war, a conquest, a spoliation; every one must help to do it by paying taxes and doing military service or other duty which may be demanded of him. The decision of a lawsuit leaves one party protesting and complaining. He always speaks of "right" and "rights." He is forced to acquiesce. The result is right in the only sense which is real and true. It is more to the purpose to note that an indefinite series of consequences follow, and that they create or condition rights which are real and just. Many persons now argue against property that it began in force and therefore has no existence in right and justice. They might say the same of marriage or religion. Some do say the same of the state. The war of the United States with Mexico in 1845 is now generally regarded as unjustified. That cannot affect the rights of all kinds which have been contracted in the territory then ceded by Mexico or under the status created on the land obtained by the treaty of peace with that country. The whole history of mankind is a series of acts which are open to doubt, dispute, and criticism, as to their right and justice, but all subsequent history has been forced to take up the consequences of those acts and go on. The disputants about "rights" often lose sight of the fact that the world has to go on day by day and dispute must end. It always ends in force. The end always leaves some complaining in terms of right and rights. They are overborne by force of some kind. Therefore might has made all the right which ever has existed or exists now. If it is proposed to reverse, reform, or change anything which ever was done because we now think that it was wrong, that is a new question and a new case, in which the anterior view alone is in place. It is for the new and future cases that we study historical cases and form judgments on them which will enable us to act more wisely. If we recognize the great extent to which force now enters into all which happens in society, we shall cease to be shocked to learn the extent to which it has been active in the entire history of civilization. The habit of using jural concepts, which is now so characteristic of our mores, leads us into vague and impossible dreams of social affairs, in which metaphysical concepts are supposed to realize themselves, or are assumed to be real.

73. Status in the folkways. If now we form a conception of the folkways as a great mass of usages, of all degrees of importance, covering all the interests of life, constituting an outfit of instruction for the young, embodying a life policy, forming character, containing a world philosophy, albeit most vague and unformulated, and sanctioned by ghost fear so that variation is impossible, we see with what coercive and inhibitive force the folkways have always grasped the members of a society. The folkways create status. Membership in the group, kin, family, neighborhood, rank, or class are cases of status. The rights and duties of every man and woman were defined by status. No one could choose whether he would enter into the status or not. For instance, at puberty every one was married. What marriage meant, and what a husband or wife was (the rights and duties of each), were fixed by status. No one could alter the customary relations. Status, as distinguished from institutions and contract, is a direct product of the mores. Each case of status is a nucleus of leading interest with the folkways which cluster around it. Status is determined by birth. Therefore it is a help and a hindrance, but it is not liberty. In modern times status has become unpopular and our mores have grown into the forms of contract under liberty. The conception of status has been lost by the masses in modern civilized states. Nevertheless we live under status which has been defined and guaranteed by law and institutions, and it would be a great gain to recognize and appreciate the element of status which historically underlies the positive institutions and which is still subject to the action of the mores. Marriage (matrimony or wedlock) is a status. It is really controlled by the mores. The law defines it and gives sanctions to it, but the law always expresses the mores. A man and a woman make a contract to enter into it   The mode of entering into it (wedding) is fixed by custom. The law only ratifies it. No man and woman can by contract make wedlock different for themselves from the status defined by law, so far as social rights and duties are concerned. The same conception of marriage as a status in the mores is injured by the intervention of the ecclesiastical and civil formalities connected with it. An individual is born into a kin group, a tribe, a nation, or a state, and he has a status accordingly which determines rights and duties for him. Civil liberty must be defined in accordance with this fact ; not outside of it, or according to vague metaphysical abstractions above it. The body of the folkways constitutes a societal environment. Every one born into it must enter into relations of give and take with it. He is subjected to influences from it, and it is one of the life conditions under which he must work out his career of self-realization. Whatever liberty may be taken to mean, it is certain that liberty never can mean emancipation from the influence of the societal environment, or of the mores into which one was born.

74. Conventionalization. If traditional folkways are subjected to rational or ethical examination they are no longer naïve and unconscious. It may then be found that they are gross, absurd, or inexpedient. They may still be preserved by conventionalization. Conventionalization creates a set of conditions under which a thing may be tolerated which would otherwise be disapproved and tabooed. The special conditions may be created in fact, or they may be only a fiction which all agree to respect and to treat as true. When children, in play, "make believe" that something exists, or exists in a certain way, they employ conventionalization. Special conditions are created in fact when some fact is regarded as making the usual taboo inoperative. Such is the case with all archaic usages which are perpetuated on account of their antiquity, although they are not accordant with modern standards. The language of Shakespeare and the Bible contains words which are now tabooed. In this case, as in very many others, the conventionalization consists in ignoring the violation of current standards of propriety. Natural functions and toilet operations are put under conventionalization, even in low civilization. The conventionalization consists in ignoring breaches of the ordinary taboo. On account of accidents which may occur, wellbred people are always ready to apply conventionalization to mishaps of speech, dress, manner, etc. In fairy stories, fables, romances, and dramas all are expected to comply with certain conventional understandings without which the entertainment is impossible ; for instance, when beasts are supposed to speak. In the mythologies this kind of conventionalization was essential. One of us, in studying mythologies, has to acquire a knowledge of the conventional assumptions with which the people who believed in them approached them. Modern Hindoos conventionalize the stories of their mythology.[1] What the gods are said to have done is put under other standards than those now applied to men. Everything in the mythology is on a plane by itself. It follows that none of the rational or ethical judgments are formed about the acts of the gods which would be formed about similar acts of men, and the corruption of morals which would be expected as a consequence of the stories and dramas is prevented by the conventionalization. There is no deduction from what gods do to what men may do. The Greeks of the fifth century B.C. rationalized on their mythology and thereby destroyed it. The mediæval church claimed to be under a conventionalization which would prevent judgment on the church and ecclesiastics according to current standards. Very many people heeded this conventionalization, so that they were not scandalized by vice and crime in the church. This intervention of conventionalization to remove cases from the usual domain of the mores into a special field, where they can be protected and tolerated by codes and standards modified in their favor, is of very great importance. It accounts for many inconsistencies in the mores. In this way there may be nakedness without indecency, and tales of adultery without lewdness. We observe a conventionalization in regard to the Bible, especially in regard to some of the Old Testament stories. The theater presents numerous cases of conventionalization. The asides, entrances and exits, and stage artifices, require that the spectators shall concede their assent to conventionalities. The dresses of the stage would not be tolerated elsewhere. It is by conventionalization that the literature and pictorial representations of science avoid collision with the mores of propriety, decency, etc. In all artistic work there is more or less conventionalization. Uncivilized people, and to some extent uneducated people amongst ourselves, cannot tell what a picture represents or

[1] Wilkins, *Mod. Hinduism*, 317.

means because they are not used to the conventionalities of pictorial art. The ancient Saturnalia and the carnival have been special times of license at which the ordinary social restrictions have been relaxed for a time by conventionalization. Our own Fourth of July is a day of noise, risk, and annoyance, on which things are allowed which would not be allowed at any other time. We consent to it because "it is Fourth of July." The history of wedding ceremonies presents very many instances of conventionalization. Jests and buffoonery have been tolerated for the occasion. They became such an annoyance that people revolted against them, and invented means to escape them. Dress used in bathing, sport, the drama, or work is protected by conventionalization. The occasion calls for a variation from current usage, and the conventionalization, while granting toleration, defines it also, and makes a new law for the exceptional case. It is like taboo, and is, in fact, the form of taboo in high civilization. Like taboo, it has two aspects, — it is either destructive or protective. The conventionalization bars out what might be offensive (i.e. when a thing may be done only under the conditions set by conventionalization), or it secures toleration for what would otherwise be forbidden. Respect, reverence, sacredness, and holiness, which are taboos in low civilization, become conventionalities in high civilization.

75. Conventions indispensable. Conventionality is often denounced as untrue and hypocritical. It is said that we ought to be natural. Respectability is often sneered at because it is a sum of conventionalities. The conventionalizations which persist are the resultant of experiments and experience as to the devices by which to soften and smoothen the details of life. They are indispensable. We might as well renounce clothes as to try to abolish them.

76. The ethos or group character. All that has been said in this chapter about the folkways and the mores leads up to the idea of the group character which the Greeks called the ethos, that is, the totality of characteristic traits by which a group is individualized and differentiated from others. The great nations of southeastern Asia were long removed from familiar contact with the rest of mankind and isolated from each other, while they were each subjected to the discipline and invariable rule of traditional folkways which covered all social interests except the interferences of a central political authority, which perpetrated tyranny in its own interest. The consequence has been that Japan, China, and India have each been molded into a firm, stable, and well-defined unit group, having a character strongly marked both actively and passively. The governing classes of Japan have, within fifty years, voluntarily abandoned their traditional mores, and have adopted those of the Occident, while it does not appear that they have lost their inherited ethos. The case stands alone in history and is a cause of amazement. In the war with Russia, in 1904, this people showed what a group is capable of when it has a strong ethos. They understand each other; they act as one man; they are capable of discipline to the death. Our western tacticians have had rules for the percentage of loss which troops would endure, standing under fire, before breaking and running. The rule failed for the Japanese. They stood to the last man. Their prowess at Port Arthur against the strongest fortifications, and on the battlefields of Manchuria, surpassed all record. They showed what can be done in the way of concealing military and naval movements when every soul in the population is in a voluntary conspiracy not to reveal anything. These traits belong to a people which has been trained by generations of invariable mores. It is apparently what the mediæval church wanted to introduce in Europe, but the Japanese have got it without selfish tyranny of the ruling persons and classes. Of course, it admits of no personal liberty, and the consequences of introducing occidental notions of liberty into it have yet to be seen. "The blacksmith squats at his anvil wielding a hammer such as no western smith could use without long practice. The carpenter pulls instead of pushing his extraordinary plane and saw. Always the left is the right side, and the right side the wrong. Keys must be turned, to open or close a lock, in what we are accustomed to think the wrong direction." "The swordsman, delivering his blow with both hands, does not pull the blade towards him in the moment of striking, but pushes it from him.

He uses it indeed, as other Asiatics do, not on the principle of
the wedge, but of the saw." [1] In family manners the Japanese
are gentle. Cruelty even to animals appears to be unknown.
"One sees farmers coming to town, trudging patiently beside their
horses or oxen, aiding their dumb companions to bear the burden, and using no whips or goads. Drivers or pullers of carts
will turn out of their way, under the most provoking circumstances, rather than overrun a lazy dog or a stupid chicken." [2]
Etiquette is refined, elaborate, and vigorous. Politeness has been
diffused through all ranks from ancient times.[3] "The discipline
of the race was self-imposed. The people have gradually created
their own social conditions." [4] "Demeanor was [in ancient times]
most elaborately and mercilessly regulated, not merely as to
obeisances, of which there were countless grades, varying according to sex as well as class, but even in regard to facial expression,
the manner of smiling, the conduct of the breath, the way of sitting, standing, walking, rising." [5] "With the same merciless
exactitude which prescribed rules for dress, diet, and manner of
life, all utterance was regulated both positively and negatively,
but positively much more than negatively. . . . Education cultivated a system of verbal etiquette so multiform that only the
training of years could enable any one to master it. The astonishment evoked by Japanese sumptuary laws, particularly as inflicted
upon the peasantry, is justified, less by their general character than
by their implacable minuteness, — their ferocity of detail." "That
a man's house is his castle cannot be asserted in Japan, except in
the case of some high potentate. No ordinary person can shut
his door to lock out the rest of the world. Everybody's house
must be open to visitors ; to close its gates by day would be
regarded as an insult to the community, sickness affording no
excuse. Only persons in very great authority have the right of
making themselves inaccessible. . . . By a single serious mistake
a man may find himself suddenly placed in solitary opposition to
the common will, — isolated, and most effectively ostracized."
"The events of the [modern] reconstruction strangely illustrate

[1] Hearn, *Japan*, 11. [3] *Ibid.*, 391. [5] *Ibid.*, 191.
[2] *Ibid.*, 16. [4] *Ibid.*, 199.

the action of such instinct [of adaptation] in the face of peril, —
the readjustment of internal relations to sudden changes of environment. The nation had found its old political system powerless
before the new conditions, and it transformed that system. It had
found its military organization incapable of defending it, and it
reconstructed that organization. It had found its educational
system useless in the presence of unforeseen necessities, and
it had replaced that system, simultaneously crippling the power
of Buddhism, which might otherwise have offered serious opposition to the new developments required."[1] To this it must be
added that people who have had commercial and financial dealings
with Japanese report that they are untruthful and tricky in transactions of that kind. If they cannot "reform" these traits there
will be important consequences of them in the developments of
the near future.

77. Chinese ethos. It is evident that we have in the Japanese
a case of an ethos, from the habits of artisans to the manners
of nobles and the military system, which is complete, consistent,
authoritative, and very different from our own. A similar picture
of the Chinese might be drawn, from which it would appear that
they also have a complete and firm ethos, which resembles in general the Japanese, but has its individual traits and characteristic
differences.[2] The ethos of the Japanese, from the most ancient
times, has been fundamentally militant. That of the Chinese is
industrial and materialistic.

78. Hindoo ethos. The Hindoos, again, have a strongly marked
ethos. They have a name for it — *kharma*, which Nivedita says
might be translated "national righteousness." It "applies to that
whole system of complex action and interaction on planes moral,
intellectual, economic, industrial, political, and domestic, which we
know as India, or the national habit. . . . By their attitude to it,
Pathan, Mogul, and Englishman are judged, each in his turn, by
the Indian peasantry."[3] The ethos of one group always furnishes
the standpoint from which it criticises the ways of any other group.

---

[1] Hearn, *Japan*, 107, 187, 411.

[2] Williams, *Middle Kingdom*; Smith, *Chinese Characteristics*.

[3] Nivedita, *Web of Indian Life*, 150.

79. European ethos. We are familiar with the notion of "national character" as applied to the nations of Europe, but these nations do not have each an ethos. There is a European ethos, for the nations have so influenced each other for the last two thousand years that there is a mixed ethos which includes local variations. The European *kharma* is currently called Christian. In the ancient world Egypt and Sparta were the two cases of groups with the firmest and best-defined ethos. In modern European history the most marked case is that of Venice. In no one of these cases did the elements of moral strength and societal health preponderate, but the history of each showed the great stability produced by a strong ethos. Russia has a more complete and defined ethos than any other state in Europe, although the efforts which have been made since Peter the Great to break down the traditions and limitations of the national ethos, and to adopt the ethos of western Europe, have produced weakness and confusion. It is clear what is the great power of a strong ethos. The ethos of any group deserves close study and criticism. It is an overruling power for good or ill. Modern scholars have made the mistake of attributing to *race* much which belongs to the ethos, with a resulting controversy as to the relative importance of nature and nurture. Others have sought a "soul of the people" and have tried to construct a "collective psychology," repeating for groups processes which are now abandoned for individuals. Historians, groping for the ethos, have tried to write the history of "the people" of such and such a state. The ethos individualizes groups and keeps them apart. Its opposite is cosmopolitanism. It degenerates into patriotic vanity and chauvinism. Industrialism weakens it, by extending relations of commerce with outside groups. It coincides better with militancy. It has held the Japanese people like a single mailed fist for war. What religion they have has lost all character except that of a cohesive agent to hold the whole close organization tight together.

CHAPTER II

CHARACTERISTICS OF THE MORES

Introduction.—The mores have the authority of facts.—Whites and blacks in southern society. — The mores are unrecorded. — Inertia and rigidity of the mores. — Persistency of the mores. — Persistency against new religion. — Roman law. — Effects of Roman law on later mores. — Variability of the mores. — The mores of New England. — Revolution. — The possibility of modifying the mores. — Russia. — Emancipation in Russia and in the United States. — Arbitrary change in the mores. — The case of Japan. — The case of India. — The reforms of Joseph II. — Adoption of the mores of another age. — What changes are possible. — Dissent from the mores. Group orthodoxy. — Retreat and isolation to start new mores. — Social policy. — Degenerate and evil mores. — The correction of aberrations in the mores. — The mores of advance and decline; cases. — The Greek temper in prosperity. — Greek pessimism. — Greek degeneracy. — Sparta. — The optimism of advance and prosperity. — Antagonism between an individual and the mores of the group. — Antagonism of earlier and later mores. — Antagonism between groups in respect to mores. — Missions and mores. — Missions and antagonistic mores. — Modification of the mores by agitation. — Capricious interest of the masses. — How the group becomes homogeneous. — Syncretism. — The art of administering society.

In this chapter we have to study the persistency of the mores with their inertia and rigidity, even against a new religion or a new "law," i.e. a new social system (secs. 80–87); then their variability under changed life conditions or under revolution (secs. 88–90); then the possibility of making them change by intelligent effort, considering the cases of Japan, India, and the reforms of Joseph II (secs. 91–97); or the possibility of changing one's self to adopt the mores of another group or another age (secs. 98–99). We shall then consider the dissent of an individual or a sect from the current mores, with judgment of disapproval on them (secs. 100–104), and the chance of correcting them (sec. 105). Next we shall consider the great movements of the mores, optimism and pessimism, which correspond to a rising or falling economic conjuncture (secs. 106–111). Then come the antagonisms between an individual and the mores, between the mores of an earlier and a later time, and between the groups in respect to mores, with a notice of the problem of missions (secs. 112–118). Finally, we come to consider agitation to produce changes in the mores, and we endeavor to study the ways in which the changes in the mores do come about, especially syncretism (secs. 119–121).

80. The mores have the authority of facts. The mores come down to us from the past. Each individual is born into them as he is born into the atmosphere, and he does not reflect on them, or criticise them any more than a baby analyzes the atmosphere before he begins to breathe it. Each one is subjected to the influence of the mores, and formed by them, before he is capable of reasoning about them. It may be objected that nowadays, at least, we criticise all traditions, and accept none just because they are handed down to us. If we take up cases of things which are still entirely or almost entirely in the mores, we shall see that this is not so. There are sects of free-lovers amongst us who want to discuss pair marriage (sec. 374). They are not simply people of evil life. They invite us to discuss rationally our inherited customs and ideas as to marriage, which, they say, are by no means so excellent and elevated as we believe. They have never won any serious attention. Some others want to argue in favor of polygamy on grounds of expediency. They fail to obtain a hearing. Others want to discuss property. In spite of some literary activity on their part, no discussion of property, bequest, and inheritance has ever been opened. Property and marriage are in the mores. Nothing can ever change them but the unconscious and imperceptible movement of the mores. Religion was originally a matter of the mores. It became a societal institution and a function of the state. It has now to a great extent been put back into the mores. Since laws with penalties to enforce religious creeds or practices have gone out of use any one may think and act as he pleases about religion. Therefore it is not now " good form " to attack religion. Infidel publications are now tabooed by the mores, and are more effectually repressed than ever before. They produce no controversy. Democracy is in our American mores. It is a product of our physical and economic conditions. It is impossible to discuss or criticise it. It is glorified for popularity, and is a subject of dithyrambic rhetoric. No one treats it with complete candor and sincerity. No one dares to analyze it as he would aristocracy or autocracy. He would get no hearing and would only incur abuse. The thing to be noticed in all these cases is that the masses oppose a deaf ear to every argument against the mores. It is only in so far as things have been transferred from the mores into laws and positive institutions that there is discussion about them or rationalizing upon them. The mores contain the norm by which, if we should discuss the mores, we should have to judge the mores. We learn the mores as unconsciously as we learn to walk and eat and breathe. The masses never learn how we walk, and eat, and breathe, and they never know any reason why the mores are what they are. The justification of them is that when we wake to consciousness of life we find them facts which already hold us in the bonds of tradition, custom, and habit. The mores contain embodied in them notions, doctrines, and maxims, but they are facts. They are in the present tense. They have nothing to do with what ought to be, will be, may be, or once was, if it is not now.

81. Blacks and whites in southern society. In our southern states, before the civil war, whites and blacks had formed habits of action and feeling towards each other. They lived in peace and concord, and each one grew up in the ways which were traditional and customary. The civil war abolished legal rights and left the two races to learn how to live together under other relations than before. The whites have never been converted from the old mores. Those who still survive look back with regret and affection to the old social usages and customary sentiments and feelings. The two races have not yet made new mores. Vain attempts have been made to control the new order by legislation. The only result is the proof that legislation cannot make mores. We see also that mores do not form under social convulsion and discord. It is only just now that the new society seems to be taking shape. There is a trend in the mores now as they begin to form under the new state of things. It is not at all what the humanitarians hoped and expected. The two races are separating more than ever before. The strongest point in the new code seems to be that any white man is boycotted and despised if he "associates with negroes" (sec. 114, at the end). Some are anxious to interfere and try to control. They take their stand on ethical views of what is going on. It is evidently impossible for any one to interfere. We are like spectators at a great natural convulsion. The results will be such as the facts and forces call for. We cannot foresee them. They do not depend on ethical views any more than the volcanic eruption on Martinique contained an ethical element. All the faiths, hopes, energies, and sacrifices of both whites and blacks are components in the new construction of folkways by which the two races will learn how to live together. As we go along with the constructive process it is very plain that what once was, or what any one thinks ought to be, but slightly affects what, at any moment, is. The mores which once were are a memory. Those which any one thinks ought to be are a dream. The only thing with which we can deal are those which are.

82. The mores are unrecorded. A society is never conscious of its mores until it comes in contact with some other society which has different mores, or until, in higher civilization, it gets information by literature. The latter operation, however, affects only the literary classes, not the masses, and society never consciously sets about the task of making mores. In the early stages mores are elastic and plastic ; later they become rigid and fixed. They seem to grow up, gain strength, become corrupt, decline, and die, as if they were organisms. The phases seem to follow each other by an inherent necessity, and as if independent of the reason and will of the men affected, but the changes are always produced by a strain towards better adjustment of the mores to conditions and interests of the society, or of the controlling elements in it. A society does not record its mores in its annals, because they are to it unnoticed and unconscious. When we try to learn the mores of any age or people we have to seek our information in incidental references, allusions, observations of travelers, etc. Generally works of fiction, drama, etc., give us more information about the mores than historical records. It is very difficult to construct from the Old Testament a description of the mores of the Jews before the captivity. It is also very difficult to make a complete and accurate picture of the mores of the English colonies in North America in the seventeenth century. The mores are not recorded for the same reason that meals, going to bed, sunrise, etc., are not recorded, unless the regular course of things is broken.

83. Inertia and rigidity of the mores. We see that we must conceive of the mores as a vast system of usages, covering the whole of life, and serving all its interests ; also containing in themselves their own justification by tradition and use and wont, and approved by mystic sanctions until, by rational reflection, they develop their own philosophical and ethical generalizations, which are elevated into " principles " of truth and right. They coerce and restrict the newborn generation. They do not stimulate to thought, but the contrary. The thinking is already done and is embodied in the mores. They never contain any provision for their own amendment. They are not questions, but answers, to the problem of life. They present themselves as final and unchangeable, because they present answers which are offered as "the truth." No world philosophy, until the modern scientific world philosophy, and that only within a generation or two, has ever presented itself as perhaps transitory, certainly incomplete, and liable to be set aside to-morrow by more knowledge. No popular world philosophy or life policy ever can present itself in that light. It would cost too great a mental strain. All the groups whose mores we consider far inferior to our own are quite as well satisfied with theirs as we are with ours. The goodness or badness of mores consists entirely in their adjustment to the life conditions and the interests of the time and place (sec. 65). Therefore it is a sign of ease and welfare when no thought is given to the mores, but all coöperate in them instinctively. The nations of southeastern Asia show us the persistency of the mores, when the element of stability and rigidity in them becomes predominant. Ghost fear and ancestor worship tend to establish the persistency of the mores by dogmatic authority, strict taboo, and weighty sanctions. The mores then lose their naturalness and vitality. They are stereotyped. They lose all relation to expediency. They become an end in themselves. They are imposed by imperative authority without regard to interests or conditions (caste, child marriage, widows). When any society falls under the dominion of this disease in the mores it must disintegrate before it can live again. In that diseased state of the mores all learning consists in committing to memory the words of the sages of the past who established the formulæ of the mores. Such words are "sacred writings," a sentence of which is a rule of conduct to be obeyed quite independently of present interests, or of any rational considerations.

84. Persistency. Asiatic fixity of the mores is extreme, but the element of persistency in the mores is always characteristic of them. They are elastic and tough, but when once established in familiar and continued use they resist change. They give stability to the social order when they are well understood, regular, and undisputed. In a new colony, with a sparse population, the mores are never fixed and stringent. There is great "liberty." As the colony always has traditions of the mores of the mother country, which are cherished with respect but are never applicable to the conditions of a colony, the mores of a colony are heterogeneous and are always in flux. That is because the colonists are all the time learning to live in a new country and have no traditions to guide them, the traditions of the old country being a hindrance. Any one bred in a new country, if he goes to an old country, feels the "conservatism" in its mores. He thinks the people stiff, set in their ways, stupid, and unwilling to learn. They think him raw, brusque, and uncultivated. He does not know the ritual, which can be written in no books, but knowledge of which, acquired by long experience, is the mark of fit membership in the society.

85. Persistency in spite of change of religion. Matthews saw votive effigies in Mandan villages just like those which Catlin had seen and put into his pictures seventy years before.[1] In the meantime the Mandans had been nearly exterminated by war

---

[1] *N. S. Amer. Anthrop.*, IV, 3.

and disease, and the remnant of them had been civilized and Christianized. The mores of the Central American Indians inculcate moderation and restraint. Their ancient religion contained prescriptions of that character, and those prescriptions are still followed after centuries of life under Christianity.[1] In the Bible we may see the strife between old mores and a new religious system two or three times repeated. The so-called Mosaic system superseded an older system of mores common, as it appears, to all the Semites of western Asia. The prophets preached a reform of the Jahveh religion and we find them at war with the inherited mores.[2] The most striking feature of the story of the prophets is their antagonism to the mores which the people would not give up. Monotheism was not established until after the captivity.[3] The recurrence, vitality, popularity, and pervasiveness of traditional mores are well shown in the Bible story. The result was a combination of ritual monotheism with survivals of ancient mores and a popular religion in which demonism was one of the predominant elements. The New Testament represents a new revival and reform of the religion. The Jews to this day show the persistency of ancient mores. Christianity was a new adjustment of both heathen and Jewish mores to a new religious system. The popular religion once more turned out to be a grand revival of demonism. The masses retained their mores with little change. The mores overruled the religion. Therefore Jewish Christians and heathen Christians remained distinguishable for centuries. The Romans never could stamp out the child sacrifices of the Carthaginians.[4] The Roman law was an embodiment of all the art of living and the mores of the Roman people. It differed from the mores of the German peoples, and when by the religion the Roman system was brought to German people conflict was produced. In fact, it may be said that the process of remolding German mores by the Roman law never was completed,[5] and that now the German

---

[1] *Globus*, LXXXVII, 130.
[2] "Religion of Israel," Hastings, *Dict.*, Supp. vol.
[3] Tiele, *Relig. in Alterthum*, I, 295.
[4] *Ibid.*, 242.
[5] Stammler, *Stellung der Frauen*, 3.

mores have risen against the Roman law and have accepted out
of it only what has been freely and rationally selected. Marriage
amongst the German nations was a domestic and family function.
Even after the hierocratic system was firmly established, it was
centuries before the ecclesiastics could make marriage a clerical
function.[1] In the usages of German peasants to-day may be
found numerous survivals of heathen notions and customs.[2] In
England the German mores accepted only a limited influence
from the Roman law. The English have adopted the policy of
the Romans in dealing with subject peoples. They do not
meddle with local customs if they can avoid it. This is wise,
since nothing nurses discontent like interference with folkways.
The persistency of the mores is often shown in survivals, — senseless ceremonies whose meaning is forgotten, jests, play, parody,
and caricature, or stereotyped words and phrases, or even in
cakes of a prescribed form or prescribed foods at certain festivals.

86. Roman law. In the Roman law everything proceeds
from the emperor. He is the possessor of all authority, the
fountain of honor, the author of all legislation, and the referee
in all disputes. Lawyers trained by the study of this code
learned to conceive of all the functions of the state as acts,
powers, and rights of a monarchical sovereign. They stood
beside the kings and princes of the later Middle Ages ready
to construe the institutions of suzerainty into this monarchical
form. They broke down feudalism and helped to build the absolutist dynastic state, wherever the Roman law was in force, and
wherever it had greatly influenced the legal system. The church
also had great interest to employ the Roman law, because it
included the ecclesiastical legislation of the Christian emperors
of the fourth and fifth centuries, and because the canon law was
imitated from it in spirit and form. In all matters of private
rights the provisions of the Justinian code were good and beneficial, so that those provisions won their own way by their own
merit.[3] In the *Sachsenspiegel* there was no distinction of property

---

[1] Friedberg, *Recht der Eheschliessung.*
[2] *Ztsft. f. Volkskunde*, XI, 272.
[3] Scherr, *Deutsche Kultur- und Sittengesch.*, 171.

between man and wife, but this meant that all which both had was a joint capital for use in their domestic economy. When the marriage was dissolved the property returned to the side from which it came. Later, in many districts, this arrangement developed into a real community of goods under various forms. " It was in regard to these adjustments of property rights that the jurists of the Middle Ages did most harm by introducing the Roman law, for it was especially in regard to this matter that the Roman law stood in strongest contrast to the German notions, and the resistance of the German people is to be seen in the numerous local systems of law, which remained in use in most of Germany; unfortunately not everywhere, nor uniformly." [1]

87. The Roman law: its effect on later mores. Throughout the north of Europe, upon conversion to Christianity, tithes were the stumbling-block between the old mores and the new system.[2] The authority for the tithe system came from the Roman system. It was included in the Roman jurisprudence which the church adopted and carried wherever it extended. After the civil code was revived it helped powerfully to make states. This was a work, however, which was hostile to the church. The royal lawyers found in the civil code a system which referred everything in society to the emperor as the origin of power, rights, and honor. They adopted this standpoint for the kings of the new dynastic states and, in the might of the Roman law, they established royal absolutism, which was unfavorable to the church and the feudal nobles. They found their allies in the cities which loved written law, institutions, and defined powers. Stubbs[3] regards the form of the Statute of Westminster (1275) as a proof that the lawyers, who "were at this time getting a firm grasp on the law of England," were introducing the principle that the king could enact by his own authority. The spirit of the Roman law was pitiless to peasants and artisans, that is, to all who were, or were to be made, unfree. The Norman laws depressed the Saxon ceorl to a slave.[4] In similar manner they came into war with all Teutonic mores which contained popular rights and primary freedom. Stammler[5] denies that the Roman law, in spite of lawyers and ecclesiastics, ever entered into the flesh and blood of the German people. That is to say, it never displaced completely their national mores. The case of the

---

[1] Stammler, *Stellung der Frauen*, 8.
[2] Wachsmuth, *Bauernkriege*, in Raumer, *Taschenbuch*, V.
[3] *Charters*, 449.
[4] Stubbs, *History*, II, 453.
[5] *Stellung der Frauen*, 3.

property of married persons is offered as a case in which the German mores were never overcome.[1] A compromise was struck between the ancient mores and the new ways, which the Roman Catholic religion approved.

88. Variability. No less remarkable than the persistency of the mores is their changeableness and variation. There is here an interesting parallel to heredity and variation in the organic world, even though the parallel has no significance. Variation in the mores is due to the fact that children do not perpetuate the mores just as they received them. The father dies, and the son whom he has educated, even if he continues the ritual and repeats the formulæ, does not think and feel the same ideas and sentiments as his father. The observance of Sunday ; the mode of treating parents, children, servants, and wives or husbands ; holidays ; amusements ; arts of luxury ; marriage and divorce ; wine drinking, — are matters in regard to which it is easy to note changes in the mores from generation to generation, in our own times. Even in Asia, when a long period of time is taken into account, changes in the mores are perceptible. The mores change because conditions and interests change. It is found that dogmas and maxims which have been current do not verify ; that established taboos are useless or mischievous restraints ; that usages which are suitable for a village or a colony are not suitable for a great city or state ; that many things are fitting when the community is rich which were not so when it was poor ; that new inventions have made new ways of living more economical and healthful. It is necessary to prosperity that the mores should have a due degree of firmness, but also that they should be sufficiently elastic and flexible to conform to changes in interests and life conditions. A herding or an agricultural people, if it moves into a new country, rich in game, may revert to a hunting life. The Tunguses and Yakuts did so as they moved northwards.[2] In the early days of the settlement of North America many whites " Indianized " ; they took to the mode of life of Indians. The Iranians separated from the Indians of Hindostan and became agriculturists. They adopted a new

[1] Sec. 86.
[2] Hiekisch, *Tungusen*, 31 ; Sieroshevski, *Yakuty*, I, 415.

religion and new mores. Men who were afraid of powerful enemies have taken to living in trees, lake dwellings, caves, and joint houses. Mediæval serfdom was due to the need of force to keep the peasant on his holding, when the holding was really a burden to him in view of the dues which he must pay. He would have run away if he had not been kept by force. In the later Middle Ages the villain had a valuable right and property in his holding. Then he wanted security of tenure so that he could not be driven away from it. In the early period it was the duty of the lord to kill the game and protect the peasant's crops. In the later period it became the monopoly right of the lord to kill game. Thus the life conditions vary. The economic conjuncture varies. The competition of life varies. The interests vary with them. The mores all conform, unless they have been fixed by dogma with mystic sanctions so that they are ritual obligations, as is, in general, the case now in southeastern Asia. The rights of the parties, and the right and wrong of conduct, after the mores have conformed to new life conditions, are new deductions. The philosophers follow with their systems by which they try to construe the whole new order of acts and thoughts with reference to some thought fabric which they put before the mores, although it was found out after the mores had established the relations. In the case in which the fixed mores do not conform to new interests and needs crises arise. Moses, Zoroaster, Manu, Solon, Lycurgus, and Numa are either mythical or historical culture heroes, who are said to have solved such crises by new "laws," and set the society in motion again. The fiction of the intervention of a god or a hero is necessary to account for a reconstruction of the mores of the ancestors without crime.

89. Mores of New England. The Puritan code of early New England has been almost entirely abandoned, so far as its positive details are concerned, while at the same time some new restrictions on conduct have been introduced, especially as to the use of spirituous liquors, so that not all the changes have been in the way of relaxation. The mores of New England, however, still show deep traces of the Puritan temper and world philosophy. Perhaps nowhere else in the world can so strong an illustration be·seen both of the persistency of the spirit of the mores and of their variability and adaptability. The mores of New England have extended to a large immigrant population and have won large control over them. They have also been carried to the new states by immigrants, and their perpetuation there is an often-noticed phenomenon. The extravagances in doctrine and behavior of the seventeenth-century Puritans have been thrown off and their code of morals has been shorn of its angularity, but their life policy and standards have become to a very large extent those of the civilized world.

90. Revolution. In higher civilization crises produced by the persistency of old mores after conditions have changed are solved by revolution or reform. In revolutions the mores are broken up. Such was the case in the sixteenth century, in the French Revolution of 1789, and in minor revolutions. A period follows the outburst of a revolution in which there are no mores. The old are broken up; the new are not formed. The social ritual is interrupted. The old taboos are suspended. New taboos cannot be enacted or promulgated. They require time to become established and known. The masses in a revolution are uncertain what they ought to do. In France, under the old régime, the social ritual was very complete and thoroughly established. In the revolution, the destruction of this ritual produced social anarchy. In the best case every revolution must be attended by this temporary chaos of the mores. It was produced in the American colonies. Revolutionary leaders expect to carry the people over to new mores by the might of two or three dogmas of political or social philosophy. The history of every such attempt shows that dogmas do not make mores. Every revolution suffers a collapse at the point where reconstruction should begin. Then the old ruling classes resume control, and by the use of force set the society in its old grooves again. The ecclesiastical revolution of the sixteenth century resulted in a wreck whose discordant fragments we have inherited. It left us a Christendom, half of which is obscurantist and half scientific; half is ruled by the Jesuits and half is split up into wrangling sects. The English Revolution of the seventeenth century was reversed when it undertook to reconstruct the mores of the English people. The French revolutionists tried to abolish all the old mores and to replace them by products of speculative philosophy. The revolution was, in fact, due to a great change in conditions, which called for new mores, and so far as the innovations met this demand they became permanent and helped to create a conviction of the beneficence of revolution. Napoleon abolished many innovations and put many things in the old train again. Many other things have changed name and face, but not character. Many innovations have been half assimilated. Some interests have never yet been provided for (see sec. 165).

91. Possibility of modifying mores. The combination in the mores of persistency and variability determines the extent to which it is possible to modify them by arbitrary action. It is not possible to change them, by any artifice or device, to a great extent, or suddenly, or in any essential element; it is possible to modify them by slow and long-continued effort if the ritual is changed by minute variations. The German emperor Frederick II was the most enlightened ruler of the Middle Ages. He was a modern man in temper and ideas. He was a statesman and he wanted to make the empire into a real state of the absolutist type. All the mores of his time were ecclesiastical and hierocratic. He dashed himself to pieces against them. Those whom he wanted to serve took the side of the papacy against him. He became the author of the laws by which the civil institutions of the time were made to serve ecclesiastical domination. He carried the purpose of the crusades to a higher degree of fulfillment than they ever reached otherwise, but this brought him no credit or peace. The same drift in the mores of the time bore down the Albigenses when they denounced the church corporation, the hierarchy, and the papacy. The pope easily stirred up all Europe against them. The current opinion was that every state must be a Christian state according to the mores of the time. The people could not conceive of a state which could answer its purpose if it was not such. But a " Christian state " meant one which was in harmony with the pope and the ecclesiastical organization. This demand was not affected by the faults of the organization, or the corruption and venality of the hierarchy. The popes of the thirteenth century rode upon this tide, overwhelming opposition and consolidating their power. In our time the state is charged with the service of a great number of interests which were then intrusted to the church. It is against our mores that ecclesiastics should interfere with those interests. There is no war on religion. Religion is recognized as an interest by itself, and is treated with more universal respect than ever before, but it is regarded as occupying a field of its own, and if there should be an attempt in its name to encroach on any other domain, it would fail, because it would be against the mores of our time.

92. Russia. When Napoleon said : " If you scratch a Russian you find a Tartar," what he had perceived was that, although the Russian court and the capital city have been westernized by the will of the tsars, nevertheless the people still cling to the strongly marked national mores of their ancestors. The tsars, since Peter the Great, have, by their policing and dragooning, spoilt one thing without making another, and socially Russia is in the agonies of the resulting confusion. Russia ought to be a democracy by virtue of its sparse population and wide area of unoccupied land in Siberia. In fact all the indigenous and most ancient usages of the villages are democratic. The autocracy is exotic and military. It is, however, the only institution which holds Russia together as a unit. On account of this political interest the small intelligent class acquiesce in the autocracy. The autocracy imposes force on the people to crush out their inherited mores, and to force on them western institutions. The policy is, moreover, vacillating. At one time the party which favored westernizing has prevailed at court ; at another time the old Russian or pan-Slavic party. There is internal discord and repression. The ultimate result of such an attempt to control mores by force is an interesting question of the future. It also is a question which affects most seriously the interests of western civilization. The motive for the westernizing policy is to get influence in European politics. All the interference of Russia in European politics is harmful, menacing, and unjustifiable. She is not, in character, a European power, and she brings no contribution to European civilization, but the contrary. She has neither the capital nor the character to enable her to execute the share in the world's affairs which she is assuming. Her territorial extensions for two hundred years have been made at the cost of her internal strength. The latter has never been at all proportioned to the former. Consequently the debt and taxes due to her policy of expansion and territorial greatness have crushed her peasant class, and by their effect on agriculture have choked the sources of national strength. The people are peaceful and industrious, and their traditional mores are such that they would develop great productive power and in time rise to a strong civilization of a truly indigenous type, if they were free to use their powers in their own way to satisfy their interests as they experience them from the life conditions which they have to meet.

93. Emancipation in Russia and the United States. In the time of Peter the Great the ancient national mores of Russia were very strong and firmly established. They remain to this day, in the mass of the population, unchanged in their essential integrity. There is, amongst the upper classes, an imitation of French ways, but it is unimportant for the nation. The autocracy is what makes " Russia," as a political unit. The autocracy is the apex of a military system, by which a great territory has been gathered under one control. That operation has not affected the old mores of the people. The tsar Alexander II was convinced by reading the writings of the great literary coterie of the middle of the nineteenth century that serfdom ought to be abolished, and he determined that it should be done.[1] It is not in the system of autocracy that the autocrat shall have original opinions and adopt an independent initiative. The men whom he ordered to abolish serfdom had to devise a method, and they devised one which was to appear satisfactory to the tsar, but was to protect the interests which they cared for. One is reminded of the devices of American politicians to satisfy the clamor of the moment, but to change nothing. The reform had but slight root in public

[1] Simkhovitsch, *Feldgemeinschaft in Russland,* Chap. XXIX.

opinion, and no sanction in the interests of the influential classes ; quite the contrary. The consequence is that the abolition of serfdom has thrown Russian society into chaos, and as yet reconstruction upon the new system has made little growth. In the United States the abolition of slavery was accomplished by the North, which had no slaves and enforced emancipation by war on the South, which had them. The mores of the South were those of slavery in full and satisfactory operation, including social, religious, and philosophical notions adapted to slavery. The abolition of slavery in the northern states had been brought about by changes in conditions and interests. Emancipation in the South was produced by outside force against the mores of the whites there. The consequence has been forty years of economic, social, and political discord. In this case free institutions and mores in which free individual initiative is a leading element allow efforts towards social readjustment out of which a solution of the difficulties will come. New mores will be developed which will cover the situation with customs, habits, mutual concessions, and coöperation of interests, and these will produce a social philosophy consistent with the facts. The process is long, painful, and discouraging, but it contains its own guarantees.

94. Arbitrary change. We often meet with references to Abraham Lincoln and Alexander II as political heroes who set free millions of slaves or serfs " by a stroke of the pen." Such references are only flights of rhetoric. They entirely miss the apprehension of what it is to set men free, or to tear out of a society mores of long growth and wide reach. Circumstances may be such that a change which is imperative can be accomplished in no other way, but then the period of disorder and confusion is unavoidable. The stroke of the pen never does anything but order that this period shall begin.

95. Case of Japan. Japan offers a case of the voluntary resolution of the ruling class of a nation to abandon their mores and adopt those of other nations. The case is unique in history. Humbert says that the Japanese were in the first throes of internal revolution when foreigners intervened.[1] Schallmeyer infers that

[1] *Japan and the Japanese*, 360.

the " adaptability of an intelligent and disciplined people is far greater than we, judging from other cases, have been wont to believe." [1] Le Bon absolutely denies that culture can be transmitted from people to people. He says that the ruin of Japan is yet to come, from the attempt to adopt foreign ways.[2] The best information is that the mores of the Japanese masses have not been touched. The changes are all superficial with respect to the life of the people and their character.[3] " Iyéyasu was careful to qualify the meaning of ' rude.' He said that the Japanese term for a rude fellow signified 'an other-than-expected person' — so that to commit an offense worthy of death it was only necessary to act in an ' unexpected manner,' that is to say, contrary to prescribed etiquette." [4] " Even now the only safe rule of conduct in a Japanese settlement is to act in all things according to local custom ; for the slightest divergence from rule will be observed with disfavor. Privacy does not exist ; nothing can be hidden ; everybody's vices or virtues are known to everybody else. Unusual behavior is judged as a departure from the traditional standard of conduct ; all oddities are condemned as departures from custom, and tradition and custom still have the force of religious obligations. Indeed, they really *are* religious and obligatory, not only by reason of their origin, but by reason of their relation also to the public cult, which signifies the worship of the past. The ethics of Shinto were all included in conformity to custom. The traditional rules of the commune — these were the morals of Shinto : to obey them was religion; to disobey them impiety." [5] Evidently this is a description of a society in which tradition and current usage exert complete control. It is idle to imagine that the masses of an oriental society of that kind could, in a thousand years, assimilate the mores of the Occident.

96. Case of the Hindoos. Nivedita [6] thinks that the Hindoos have adopted foreign culture easily. " One of the most striking features of Hindoo society during the past fifty years has been the readiness of the people to adopt a foreign form of culture,

[1] *Vererbung und Auslese*, 282.
[2] *Pol. Anth. Revue*, III, 416.
[3] Brandt in *Umschau*, VIII, 722.
[4] Hearn, *Japan*, 193.
[5] *Ibid.*, 112. Cf. sec. 76.
[6] *Web of Indian Life*, 125.

and to compete with those who are native to that culture on
equal terms." Monier-Williams tells us, however, that each
Hindoo "finds himself cribbed and confined in all his movements,
bound and fettered in all he does by minute traditional regulations. He sleeps and wakes, dresses and undresses, sits down and
stands up, goes out and comes in, eats and drinks, speaks and is
silent, acts and refrains from acting, according to ancient rule." [1]
As yet, therefore, this people assumes competition with the English without giving up its ancient burdensome social ritual. It
accepts the handicap.

97. Reforms of Joseph II. The most remarkable case of
reform attempted by authority, and arbitrary in its method, is
that of the reforms attempted by Joseph II, emperor of Germany. His kingdoms were suffering from the persistence of old
institutions and mores. They needed modernizing. This he
knew and, as an absolute monarch, he ordained changes, nearly
all of which were either the abolition of abuses or the introduction of real improvements. He put an end to survivals of mediæval
clericalism, established freedom of worship, made marriage a civil
contract, abolished class privilege, made taxation uniform, and replaced serfdom in Bohemia by the form of villanage which existed
in Austria. In Hungary he ordered the use of the German language instead of Latin, as the civil language. Interferences with
language act as counter suggestion. Common sense and expediency were in favor of the use of the German language, but the
order to use it provoked a great outburst of national enthusiasm
which sought demonstration in dress, ceremonies, and old usages.
Many of the other changes made by the emperor antagonized
vested interests of nobles and ecclesiastics, and he was forced to
revoke them. He promulgated orders which affected the mores,
and the mental or moral discipline of his subjects. If a man
came to enroll himself as a deist a second time, he was to receive
twenty-four blows with the rod, not because he was a deist, but
because he called himself something about which he could not
know what it is. No coffins were to be used, corpses were to be
put in sacks and buried in quicklime. Probably this law was wise

[1] *Brahmanism and Hinduism*, 352.

from a purely rational point of view, but it touched upon a matter in regard to which popular sentiment is very tender even when the usage is most irrational. "Many a usage and superstition was so closely interwoven with the life of the people that it could not be torn away by regulation, but only by education." Non-Catholics were given full civil rights. None were to be excluded from the cemeteries. The unilluminated Jews would have preferred that there should be no change in the laws. Frederick of Prussia said that Joseph always took the second step without having taken the first. In the end the emperor revoked all his changes and innovations except the abolition of serfdom and religious toleration.[1] Some of his measures were gradually realized through the nineteenth century. Others are now an object of political effort.

98. Adoption of mores of another age. The Renaissance was a period in which an attempt was made by one age to adopt the mores of another, as the latter were known through literature and art. The knowledge was very imperfect and mistaken, as indeed it necessarily must be, and the conceptions which were formed of the model were almost as fantastic as if they had been pure creations of the imagination. The learning of the Renaissance was necessarily restricted to the selected classes, and the masses either remained untouched by the faiths and fads of the learned, or accepted the same in grotesquely distorted forms. A phrase of a classical writer, or a fanciful conception of some hero of Plutarch, sufficed to enthuse a criminal, or to upset the mental equilibrium of a political speculator. The jumble of heterogeneous mores, and of ideas conformable to different mores, caused numbers to lose their mental equilibrium and to become victims either of enthusiasm or of melancholy.[2] The phenomena of suggestion were astounding and incalculable.[3] The period was marked by the dominion of dogmatic ideas, accepted as regulative principles for the mores. The result was the dominion of the phrase and the prevalence of hollow affectation. The men who were most thoroughly interested in the new learning, and had

---

[1] Mayer, *Oesterreich*, II, 454–465.   [2] Gauthiez, *Lorenzaccio*, 230.
[3] *Ibid.*, 227.

lost faith in the church and the religion of the Middle Ages, kept
up the ritual of the traditional system. The Renaissance never
made any new ritual. That is why it had no strong root and
passed away as a temporary fashion. Hearn [1] is led from his
study of Japan to say that "We could no more mingle with the
old Greek life, if it were resurrected for us, no more become a
part of it, than we could change our mental identities." The
modern classicists have tried to resuscitate Greek standards,
faiths, and ways. Individuals have met with a measure of success in themselves, and university graduates have to some extent
reached common views of life and well living, but they have
necessarily selected what features they would imitate, and so
they have arbitrarily overruled their chosen authority. They have
never won wide respect for it in modern society. The New England Puritans, in the seventeenth century, tried to build a society
on the Bible, especially the books of Moses. The attempt was
in every way a failure. It may well be doubted if any society
ever existed of which the books referred to were a description,
and the prescriptions were found ill adapted to seventeenth-century facts. The mores made by any age for itself are good and
right for that age, but it follows that they can suit another age
only to a very limited extent.

99. What changes are possible. All these cases go to show
that changes which run with the mores are easily brought about,
but that changes which are opposed to the mores require long
and patient effort, if they are possible at all. The ruling clique
can use force to warp the mores towards some result which they
have selected, especially if they bring their effort to bear on the
ritual, not on the dogmas, and if they are contented to go slowly.
The church has won great results in this way, and by so doing
has created a belief that religion, or ideas, or institutions, make
mores. The leading classes, no matter by what standard they
are selected, can lead by example, which always affects ritual.
An aristocracy acts in this way. It suggests standards of elegance, refinement, and nobility, and the usages of good manners,
from generation to generation, are such as have spread from the

[1] *Japan*, 20.

aristocracy to other classes. Such influences are unspoken, unconscious, unintentional. If we admit that it is possible and right for some to undertake to mold the mores of others, of set purpose, we see that the limits within which any such effort can succeed are very narrow, and the methods by which it can operate are strictly defined. The favorite methods of our time are legislation and preaching. These methods fail because they do not affect ritual, and because they always aim at great results in a short time. Above all, we can judge of the amount of serious attention which is due to plans for "reorganizing society," to get rid of alleged errors and inconveniences in it. We might as well plan to reorganize our globe by redistributing the elements in it.

100. Dissent from the mores; group orthodoxy. Since it appears that the old mores are mischievous if they last beyond the duration of the conditions and needs to which they were adapted, and that constant, gradual, smooth, and easy readjustment is the course of things which is conducive to healthful life, it follows that free and rational criticism of traditional mores is essential to societal welfare. We have seen that the inherited mores exert a coercion on every one born in the group. It follows that only the greatest and best can react against the mores so as to modify them. It is by no means to be inferred that every one who sets himself at war with the traditional mores is a hero of social correction and amelioration. The trained reason and conscience never have heavier tasks laid upon them than where questions of conformity to, or dissent from, the mores are raised. It is by the dissent and free judgment of the best reason and conscience that the mores win flexibility and automatic readjustment. Dissent is always unpopular in the group. Groups form standards of orthodoxy as to the "principles" which each member must profess and the ritual which each must practice. Dissent seems to imply a claim of superiority. It evokes hatred and persecution. Dissenters are rebels, traitors, and heretics. We see this in all kinds of subgroups. Noble and patrician classes, merchants, artisans, religious and philosophical sects, political parties, academies and learned societies, punish by social penalties dissent from, or disobedience to, their code of group conduct.

The modern trades union, in its treatment of a "scab," only presents another example. The group also, by a majority, adopts a programme of policy and then demands of each member that he shall work and make sacrifices for what has been resolved upon for the group interest. He who refuses is a renegade or apostate with respect to the group doctrines and interests. He who adopts the mores of another group is a still more heinous criminal. The mediæval definition of a heretic was one who varied in life and conversation, dress, speech, or manner (that is, the social ritual) from the ordinary members of the Christian community. The first meaning of "Catholic" in the fourth century was a summary of the features which were common to all Christians in social and ecclesiastical behavior; those were Catholic who conformed to the mores which were characteristic of Christians.[1] If a heretic was better than the Catholics, they hated him more. That never excused him before the church authorities. They wanted loyalty to the ecclesiastical corporation. Persecution of a dissenter is always popular in the group which he has abandoned. Toleration of dissent is no sentiment of the masses.

101. Retreat and isolation to make new mores. Quakers. In the stage of half-civilization and above there have been many cases of sects which have "withdrawn from the world" and lived an isolated life. They were dissenters from the world philosophy or the life policy current in the society to which they belonged. The real issue was that they were at war with its mores. In that war they could not prevail so as to change the mores. They could not even realize their own plan of life in the midst of uncongenial mores. The English Puritans of the sixteenth and seventeenth centuries tried to transform the mores of their age. Many of them emigrated to uninhabited territory in order to make a society in which their ideal mores should be realized. Very many sects and parties emigrated to North America in the seventeenth century with the same purpose. The Quakers went to the greatest extreme in adopting dress, language, manners, etc., which should be different from the current usages. In all this they were multiplying ritual means of isolation and of

---

[1] Harnack, *Dogmengesch.* (3d ed.), I, 319.

cultivation of their chosen ways of life. They were not strenuous about theological dogmas. Their leading notions were really about the mores and bore on social policy. In the Netherlands, in 1657, they appeared as a militant sect of revolutionary communists and levelers.[1] In New England they courted persecution. They wanted to cultivate states of mind and traits of social character which they had selected as good, and their ritual was devised to that end (humility, simplicity, peacefulness, friendliness, truth). They are now being overpowered and absorbed by the mores of the society which surrounds them. The same is true of Shakers, Moravians, and other sects of dissenters from the mores of the time and place.

102. Social policy. In Germany an attempt has been made to develop social policy into an art (*Socialpolitik*). Systematic attempts are made to study demographical facts in order to deduce from them conclusions as to the things which need to be done to make society better. The scheme is captivating. It is one of the greatest needs of modern states, which have gone so far in the way of experimental devices for social amelioration and rectification, at the expense of tax payers, that those devices should be tested and that the notions on which they are based should be verified. So far as demographical information furnishes these tests it is of the highest value. When, however, the statesmen and social philosophers stand ready to undertake any manipulation of institutions and mores, and proceed on the assumption that they can obtain data upon which to proceed with confidence in that undertaking, as an architect or engineer would obtain data and apply his devices to a task in his art, a fallacy is included which is radical and mischievous beyond measure. We have, as yet, no calculus for the variable elements which enter into social problems and no analysis which can unravel their complications. The discussions always reveal the dominion of the prepossessions in the minds of the disputants which are in the mores. We know that an observer of nature always has to know his own personal equation. The mores are a societal equation. When the mores are the thing studied in

---

[1] Van Duyl, *Beschavingsgeschiedenis van het Nederl. Volk*, 237.

one's own society, there is an operation like begging the question. Moreover, the convictions which are in the mores are "faiths." They are not affected by scientific facts or demonstration. We "believe in" democracy, as we have been brought up in it, or we do not. If we do, we accept its mythology. The reason is because we have grown up in it, are familiar with it, and like it. Argument would not touch this faith. In like manner the people of one state believe in "the state," or in militarism, or in commercialism, or in individualism. Those of another state are sentimental, nervous, fond of rhetorical phrases, full of group vanity. It is vain to imagine that any man can lift himself out of these characteristic features in the mores of the group to which he belongs, especially when he is dealing with the nearest and most familiar phenomena of everyday life. It is vain to imagine that a "scientific man" can divest himself of prejudice or previous opinion, and put himself in an attitude of neutral independence towards the mores. He might as well try to get out of gravity or the pressure of the atmosphere. The most learned scholar reveals all the philistinism and prejudice of the man-on-the-curbstone when mores are in discussion. The most elaborate discussion only consists in revolving on one's own axis. One only finds again the prepossessions which he brought to the consideration of the subject, returned to him with a little more intense faith. The philosophical drift in the mores of our time is towards state regulation, militarism, imperialism, towards petting and flattering the poor and laboring classes, and in favor of whatever is altruistic and humanitarian. What man of us ever gets out of his adopted attitude, for or against these now ruling tendencies, so that he forms judgments, not by his ruling interest or conviction, but by the supposed impact of demographic data on an empty brain. We have no grounds for confidence in these ruling tendencies of our time. They are only the present phases in the endless shifting of our philosophical generalizations, and it is only proposed, by the application of social policy, to subject society to another set of arbitrary interferences, dictated by a new set of dogmatic prepossessions that would only be a continuation of old methods and errors.

103. Degenerate and evil mores. Mores of advance and decline. The case is somewhat different when attempts are made by positive efforts to prevent the operation of bad mores, or to abolish them. The historians have familiarized us with the notion of corrupt or degenerate mores. Such periods as the later Roman empire, the Byzantine empire, the Merovingian kingdom, and the Renaissance offer us examples of evil mores. We need to give more exactitude to this idea. Bad mores are those which are not well fitted to the conditions and needs of the society at the time. But, as we have seen, the mores produce a philosophy of welfare, more or less complete, and they produce taboos which are concentrated inhibitions directed against conduct which the philosophy regards as harmful, or positive injunctions to do what is judged expedient and beneficial. The taboos constitute morality or a moral system which, in higher civilization, restrains passion and appetite, and curbs the will. Various conjunctures arise in which the taboos are weakened or the sanctions on them are withdrawn. Faith in the current religion may be lost. Then its mystic sanctions cease to operate. The political institutions may be weak or unfit, and the civil sanctions may fail. There may not be the necessary harmony between economic conditions and political institutions, or the classes which hold the social forces in their hands may misuse them for their selfish interest at the expense of others. The philosophical and ethical generalizations which are produced by the mores rise into a realm of intellect and reason which is proud, noble, and grand. The power of the intelligence is a human prerogative. If the power is correctly used the scope of achievement in the satisfaction of needs is enormously extended. The penalty of error in that domain is correspondingly great. When the mores go wrong it is, above all, on account of error in the attempt to employ the philosophical and ethical generalizations in order to impose upon mores and institutions a movement towards selected and "ideal" results which the ruling powers of the society have determined to aim at. Then the energy of the society may be diverted from its interests. Such a drift of the mores is exactly analogous to a vice of an individual, i.e. energy is expended on acts which are

contrary to welfare. The result is a confusion of all the functions of the society, and a falseness in all its mores. Any of the
aberrations which have been mentioned will produce evil mores,
that is, mores which are not adapted to welfare, so that a group may
fall into vicious mores just as an individual falls into vicious habits.

104. Illustrations. This was well illustrated at Byzantium.
The development of courtesans and prostitutes into a great and
flourishing institution; the political rule, by palace intrigues, of
favorites, women, and eunuchs; the decisive interference of royal
guards; the vices of public amusements and baths; the miseries and calamities of talented men and the consequent elimination of that class from the society; the sycophancy of clients;
the servitude of peasants and artisans, with economic exhaustion
as a consequence; demonism, fanaticism, and superstition in religion, combined with extravagant controversies over pedantic
trifles, — such are some of the phenomena of mores disordered
by divorce from sober interests, and complicated by arbitrary
dogmas of politics and religion, not forgetting the brutal and
ignorant measures of selfish rulers. In the Merovingian kingdom
barbaric and corrupt Roman mores were intermingled in a period
of turmoil. In the Renaissance in Italy all the taboos were
broken down, or had lost their sanctions, and vice and crime ran
riot through social disorder. As to the degeneracy of mores, we
meet with a current opinion that in time the mores tend to "run
down," by the side of another current opinion that there is, in
time, a tendency of the mores to become more refined and purer.
If the life conditions do not change, there is no reason at all
why the mores should change. Some barbarian peoples have
brought their mores into true adjustment to their life conditions,
and have gone on for centuries without change. What is true,
however, is that there are periods of social advance and periods
of social decline, that is, advance or decline in economic power,
material prosperity, and group strength for war. In either case
all the mores fall into a character, temper, and spirit which conform to the situation. The early centuries of the Christian
era were a period of decline. Tertullian[1] has a passage in

---

[1] *De Anima*, 30.

which he describes in enthusiastic terms the prosperity and progress of his time (end of the second century). He did not perceive that society was in a conjuncture of decline. Many, however, from the time of Augustus saw evil coming. The splendors of the empire did not delude them. Tacitus feared evil from the Germans ; others from the Parthians.[1] The population of the Roman empire felt its inferiority to its ancestors. One thing after another gave way. Nothing could serve as a fulcrum for resisting decline, or producing recovery. In such a period despair wins control. The philosophy is pessimistic. The world is supposed to be coming to an end. Life is not valued. Ascetic practices fall in with the prevailing temper. Martyrdom has no great terrors ; such as it has can be overcome by a little enthusiasm. Inroads of barbarians only add a little to the other woes, or hasten an end which is inevitable and is expected with resignation. At such a time a religion of demonism, other-worldliness, resignation, retirement from the world, and renunciation appeals both to those who want a dream of escape and to those who despair. Our own time, on the other hand, is one of advance on account of great unoccupied territories now opened at little or no cost to those who have nothing. Such a period is one of hope, power, and gain for the masses. Optimism is the philosophy. All the mores get their spirit from it. "Progress" is an object of faith. A philosophy of resignation and renunciation is unpopular. There is nothing which we cannot do, and will not do, if we choose. No mistake will cost much. It can be easily rectified. In the Renaissance in Italy, besides the rejection of religion and the disorder of the state, there was a great movement of new power derived from the knowledge which was changing the life conditions. Great social forces were set loose. Men of heroic dimensions, both in good and ill, appeared in great numbers. They had astounding ability to accomplish achievements, and appeared to be possessed by devils, so superhuman was their energy in vice and crime as well as in war, art, discovery, and literature. No doubt this phenomenon of heroic men belongs to an age of advance with a great upbursting of new power under more

[1] Boissier, *Relig. Rom.*, I, 239.

favorable conditions. It is to be noticed also that reproduction responds to conditions of advance or decline. In decline marriage and family become irksome. Celibacy arises in the mores. In times of advance sex vice and excess reach a degree, as in the Renaissance, which seems to constitute a social paroxysm. The sex passion rises to a frenzy to which everything else is sacrificed. The notion that mores grow either better or worse by virtue of some inherent tendency is to be rejected. Goodness or badness of the mores is always relative only. Their purpose is to serve needs, and their quality is to be defined by the degree to which they do it. We have noticed that there is in them a strain towards consistency, due to the fact that they are more efficient when consistent. They are consistent also in aberration and error when they fall under the dominion of any one of the false tendencies above described. Hence we may have the phenomena of degenerate mores characterizing a period; being a case of change in the mores not due to any external and determinable cause, and analogous either to vice or disease.

105. The correction of aberrations. It is possible to arrest or avert such an aberration in the mores at its beginning or in its early stages. It is, however, very difficult to do so, and it would be very difficult to find a case in which it has been done. Necessarily the effort to do it consists in a prophecy of consequences. Such prophecy does not appeal to any one who does not himself foresee error and harm. Prophets have always fared ill, because their predictions were unwelcome and they were unpopular. The pension system which has grown up in the United States since the civil war has often been criticised. It is an abuse of extreme peril in a democracy. Demagogues easily use it to corrupt the voters with their own money. It is believed that it will soon die out by its own limitations. There is, however, great doubt of this. It is more likely to cause other evil measures, in order that it may not die out. If we notice the way in which, in this case, people let a thing go on in order to avoid trouble, we may see how aberrant mores come in and grow strong.

106. Mores of advance or decline. Seeck thinks that a general weariness of life in the Greco-Roman world caused indifference to procreation. It accounts for the readiness to commit suicide and for the indifference to martyrdom. Life was hardly worth having. He says that during the whole period of the empire there was no improvement in the useful arts, no new invention, and no new device to facilitate production. Neither was there any improvement in the art of war, in literature, or the fine arts. As to transportation and commerce there seems to have been gain in the first centuries of the Christian era.[1] Such inventions as were made required a very long time to work their way into general use. This sluggishness is most apparent in mental labor. After the time of Hadrian science cannot be said to have existed. The learned only cited their predecessors. Philosophy consisted in interpreting old texts. The only gains were in religion, and those all were won by Semites or other peoples of western Asia.[2] Both Greeks and Romans exterminated the *élite* of their societies, and pursued a policy which really was a selection of the less worthy.[3] Men fled from the world. They wanted to get out of human society. They especially wanted to escape the state. The reason was that they suffered pain in society, especially from the political institutions. The Christian church gave to this renunciation of social rights and duties the character of a religious virtue. "Pessimism took possession of the old peoples at the beginning of the Christian era. This world is regarded as delivered over to destruction. Men long for a better life and the immortality of the gods, outside of this transitory existence. To this sentiment corresponds the division of the universe into a world of light above, the realm of the good, and a world of darkness below, where the evil powers dwell. Men live in a middle space. Myths explained how our world arose as a mixture of good and evil, between the two realms of good and evil. Man belongs to both ; to the world of light by his soul, to the world of darkness by his body. Men struggle for redemption from this world and from carnality, and long to soar through the series of the heavens, so as to come before the face of the highest God, there

[1] Pöhlmann, *Die Uebervölkerung d. Antiq. Grossstädte*, 12.
[2] Seeck, *Untergang der Antiq. Welt*, I, 258 ff., 278.
[3] *Ibid.*, Chap. III.

to live forever. This one can do after death, if he has during life undergone the necessary consecration, and has learned the words which can open heaven for him. In order to impart the consecration, and break the powers of darkness, one of the higher gods, the Redeemer-God, himself descended to earth. This religious theory is held by secret sects. The folk religions are dead. They can no longer satisfy the wants of men. Those of the same faiths and sentiments meet in secret brotherhood. The East must have been full of such secret sects, which corresponded to the petty states of the earlier period." [1] There was a very widespread opinion that the world was old and used up so that it could produce no more, just as a woman beyond her prime could no longer bear children.[2] "Whenever in any people, consciousness of its decline becomes vivid, a strange tendency to self-destruction arises in it. This is not to be explained scientifically, although it has been often observed." The best commit suicide first, for they do not fear death.[3] Romans of wealth and rank committed suicide in the first and second century with astonishing levity; Christians, of the masses, went to martyrdom in the same way. Pliny expresses the feeling that life had little or no value.[4]

107. The Greek temper in prosperity. The Greeks, until the fourth century before Christ, were characterized by the joy of life. They lived in close touch with nature, and the human body was to them not a clog or a curse, but a model of beauty and a means of participating in the activities of nature. Their mores were full of youthful exuberance. Their life philosophy was egoistic and materialistic. They wanted to enjoy all which their powers could win, yet their notion of *olbos* was so elevated that our modern languages have no word for it. It meant opulence, with generous liberality of sentiment and public spirit. "I do not call him who lives in prosperity, and has great possessions, a man of *olbos*, but only a well-to-do treasure keeper." [5] Such were the mores of the age of advance in wealth, population, military art, knowledge, mental achievement, and fine arts, — all of which evidently

---

[1] Gunkel, *Zum Religions-gesch. Verständniss d. N. T.*, 19.
[2] Seeck, I, 353.
[3] *Ibid.*, 364 ff.
[4] *Hist. Nat.*, VII, 41, 44, 46, 51, 56.
[5] Euripides, *Antiope*, frag. 32.

were correlative and coherent parts of an expanding prosperity and group life.

108. Greek pessimism. It is true that this light-hearted, gay, and artistic temper was boyish. Behind it there always was a pessimistic world philosophy. The gods envied men any happiness and success, and would cast down any one who was successful. The joyous temper always was that of the man who has made up his mind to enjoy himself and forget, since to take thought and care would do no good. This philosophy embittered all prosperity. The epic heroes suffered painful ends, and when the tragedians took up the stories again they heaped up crime and woe.[1] Pessimism was in the myths. While things went well the life policy of joyous carelessness overbore the pessimism, but when things began to go ill the conviction arose that life is not worth living. The abuses of democracy in the cities took away all the joy of success. It was wisdom just to take things as they came. Life was not worth having, for itself. If circumstances turned the balance of joy and pain so that the latter predominated a little, suicide was a rational relief. Religion did not cause this pessimism, but also it did not oppose it. Suicide was no offense to the gods, because they did not give life.[2] The Greeks held their doctrine of pessimism, the envy of the gods, etc., to be a correct induction from observation of life. Herodotus brought back a conviction of it from his travels.[3] Tradition ascribed to Solon the saying that "there is not a single happy mortal to be found amongst all the sun shines on."[4]

109. Greek degeneracy. The decline of the Greeks in the three centuries before our era is so great and sudden that it is very difficult to understand it. The best estimate of the population of the Peloponnesus in the second century B.C. puts it at one hundred and nine per square mile.[5] Yet the population was emigrating, and population was restricted. A pair would have but one or two children. The cities were empty and the land was uncultivated.[6]

[1] Burckhardt, *Griech. Kulturgesch.*, II, 375 ff.   [3] *Ibid.*, 395.
[2] *Ibid.*, 391.   [4] *Ibid.*, 397.
[5] Beloch, *Bevölkerung d. Griech.-Röm. Welt*, 157.
[6] Polybius, XXVII, 9, 5; Seeck, *Untergang d. Antiq. Welt*, I, 325, 360.

There was neither war nor pestilence to account for this. It may be that the land was exhausted. There must have been a loss of economic power so that labor was unrewarded. The mores all sank together. There can be no achievement in the struggle for existence without an adequate force. Our civilization is built on steam. The Greek and Roman civilization was built on slavery, that is, on an aggregation of human power. The result produced was, at first, very great, but the exploitation of men entailed other consequences besides quantities of useful products. It was these consequences which issued in the mores, for, in a society built on slavery as the form of productive industry, all the mores, obeying the strain of consistency, must conform to that as the chief of the folkways. It was at the beginning of the empire that the Romans began to breed slaves because wars no longer brought in new supplies.[1] Sex vice, laziness, decline of energy and enterprise, cowardice, and contempt for labor were consequences of slavery, for the free.[2] The system operated, in both the classical states, as a selection against the superior elements in the population. This effect was intensified by the political system. The city became an arena of political struggle for the goods of life which it was a shame to work for. Tyrannies and democracies alternated with each other, but both alike used massacre and proscription, and both thought it policy to get rid of troublesome persons, that is, of those who had convictions and had courage to avow them. Every able man became a victim of terrorism, exerted by idle market-place loafers. The abuse of democratic methods by those-who-had-not to plunder those-who-had must also have had much to do with the decline of economic power, and with the general decline of joy in life and creative energy. It would also make marriage and children a great and hopeless burden. Abortion and sex vice both directly and indirectly lessened population, by undermining the power of reproduction, while their effect to destroy all virile virtues could not fail to be exerted.[3] It was another symptom of disease in the mores that the number

[1] Seeck, I, 355.
[2] Seeck, II, Chap. IV; Beloch, *Griech. Gesch.*, I, 226.
[3] Burckhardt, *Griech. Kulturgesch.*, I, 222, 237, 259, 273; II, 355, 367, 370.

of males in the Roman empire greatly exceeded the number of females.[1] The Roman system used up women.

110. Sparta. The case of Sparta is especially interesting because the Spartan mores were generally admired and envied in the fourth century B.C. They were very artificial and arbitrary. They developed into a catastrophe. The population declined to such a point that it was like group suicide. The nation incased itself in fossilized mores and extremest conservatism, by which its own energies were crushed. The institutions produced consequences which were grotesque compared with what had been expected from them.[2]

111. Optimism of prosperity. "I apprehend that the key to the joyful character of the antique religions known to us [in western Asia] lies in the fact that they took their shape in communities that were progressive and, on the whole, prosperous." Weak groups were exterminated. Those which survived "had all the self-confidence and elasticity that are engendered by success in the struggle of life." "The religious gladness of the Semites tended to assume an orgiastic character and become a sort of intoxication of the senses, in which anxiety and sorrow were drowned for the moment."[3]

112. Antagonism between an individual and the mores. The case of dissent from the mores, which was considered above (sec. 100), is the case in which the individual voluntarily sets himself in antagonism to the mores of the society. There are cases in which the individual finds himself in involuntary antagonism to the mores of the society, or of some subgroup to which he belongs. If a man passes from one class to another, his acts show the contrast between the mores in which he was bred and those in which he finds himself. The satirists have made fun of the *parvenu* for centuries. His mistakes and misfortunes reveal the nature of the mores, their power over the individual, their pertinacity against later influences, the confusion in character produced by changing them, and the grip of habit which appears

---

[1] Seeck, I, 337.

[2] Burckhardt, I, 139 ff. ; Beloch, *Griech. Gesch.*, I, 283, 570 ; II, 362.

[3] W. Rob. Smith, *Relig. of the Semites*, 260.

both in the persistence of old mores and the weakness of new ones. Every emigrant is forced to change his mores. He loses the sustaining help of use and wont. He has to acquire a new outfit of it. The traveler also experiences the change from life in one set of mores to life in another. The experience gives him the best power to criticise his native mores from a standpoint outside of them. In the North American colonies white children were often stolen by Indians and brought up by them in their ways. Whether they would later, if opportunity offered, return to white society and white mores, or would prefer to remain with the Indians, seems to have depended on the age at which they were captured. Missionaries have often taken men of low civilization out of the society in which they were born, have educated them, and taught them white men's mores. If a single clear and indisputable case could be adduced in which such a person was restored to his own people and did not revert to their mode of life, it would be a very important contribution to ethnology. We are forced to believe that, if a baby born in New England was taken to China and given to a Chinese family to rear and educate, he would become a Chinaman in all which belongs to the mores, that is to say, in his character, conduct, and code of life.

113. Antagonism of earlier and later mores. When, in the course of time, changes occur in the mores, the men of a later generation find themselves in antagonism to the mores of their ancestors. In the Homeric poems cases are to be found of disapproval by a later generation of the mores of a former one. The same is true of the tragedies of the fifth century in respect to the mythology and heroism in Homer. The punishment of Melantheus, the unfaithful goatherd, was savage in the extreme, but when Eurykleia exulted over the dead suitors, Ulysses told her that it was a cruel sin to rejoice over slain enemies.[1] In the *Iliad* boastful shouts over the dead are frequent. In the *Odyssey* such shouts are forbidden.[2] Homer thinks that it was unseemly for Achilles to drag the corpse of Hector behind his chariot.[3] He says that the gods disapproved, which is the mystic

[1] *Od.*, XXII, 474 ff.   [2] *Ibid.*, 412.   [3] *Iliad*, XXII, 395.

way of describing a change in the mores.[1] He also disapproves
of the sacrifice of Trojan youths on the pyre of Patroclus.[2] It
was proposed to Pausanias that he should repay on the corpse of
Mardonius the insults which Xerxes had practiced on the corpse
of Leonidas at Thermopylæ, but he indignantly refused.[3] In
the *Eumenides* of Æschylus the story of Orestes is represented
as a struggle between the mores of the father family and those
of the mother family. In the *Herakleidæ* there is a struggle
between old and new mores as to the killing of captives. Many
such contrasts are drawn between Greek and barbarian mores, the
latter being old and abandoned customs which have become
abominable to the Greeks (incest, murder of strangers). In the
fourth century the Greeks were so humbled by their own base
treatment of each other that this contrast ceased to be drawn.[4]
Similar contrasts between earlier and later mores appear in the
Bible. Our own mores set us in antagonism to much which we
find in the Bible (slavery, polygamy, extirpation of aborigines).
The mores always bring down in tradition a code which is old.
Infanticide, slavery, murder of the old, human sacrifices, etc., are
in it. Later conditions force a new judgment, which is in revolt
and antagonism to what always has been done and what everybody does. Slavery is an example of this in recent history.

114. Antagonism between groups in respect to mores. When
different groups come in contact with each other their mores are
brought into contrast and antagonism. Some Australian girls
consider that their honor requires that they shall be knocked
senseless and carried off by the men who thereby become their
husbands. If they are the victims of violence, they need not be
ashamed. Eskimo girls would be ashamed to go away with
husbands without crying and lamenting, glad as they are to go.
They are shocked to hear that European women publicly consent in church to be wives, and then go with their husbands
without pretending to regret it. In Homer girls are proud to
be bought and to bring to their fathers a bride price of many
cows. In India *gandharva* marriage is one of the not-honorable

---

[1] *Iliad*, XXIV, 51.   [2] *Ibid.*, XXIII, 164.   [3] Herodotus, IX, 78.
[4] Burckhardt, *Griech. Kulturgesch.*, I, 327.

forms. It is love marriage. It rests on passion and is considered sensual; moreover, it is due to a transitory emotion. If property is involved in marriage the institution rests on a permanent interest and is guaranteed. Kaffirs also ridicule Christian love marriage. They say that it puts a woman on a level with a cat, the only animal which, amongst them, has no value.[1] Where polygamy prevails women are ashamed to be wives of men who can afford only one each; under monogamy they think it a disgrace to be wives of men who have other wives. The Japanese think the tie to one's father the most sacred. A man who should leave father and mother and cleave to his wife would become an outcast. Therefore the Japanese think the Bible immoral and irreligious.[2] Such a view in the mores of the masses will long outlast the "adoption of western civilization." The Egyptians thought the Greeks unclean. Herodotus says that the reason was because they ate cow's flesh.[3] The Greeks, as wine drinkers, thought themselves superior to the Egyptians, who drank beer. A Greek people was considered inferior if it had no city life, no agora, no athletics, no share in the games, no group character, and if it kept on a robber life.[4] The real reason for the hatred of Jews by Christians has always been the strange and foreign mores of the former. When Jews conform to the mores of the people amongst whom they live prejudice and hatred are greatly diminished, and in time will probably disappear. The dislike of the colored people in the old slave states of the United States and the hostility to whites who "associate with negroes" is to be attributed to the difference in the mores of whites and blacks. Under slavery the blacks were forced to conform to white ways, as indeed they are now if they are servants. In the North, also, where they are in a small minority, they conform to white ways. It is when they are free and form a large community that they live by their own mores. The civil war in the United States was due to a great divergence in the

[1] *Globus*, LXXV, 271.
[2] Hubbard, *Smithson. Rep.*, 1895, 673.
[3] Herodotus, II, 41.
[4] Burckhardt, *Griech. Kulturgesch.*, I, 314.

mores of the North and the South, produced by the presence or absence of slavery. The passionate dislike and contempt of the people of one section for those of the other was due to the conception each had formed of the other's character and ways. Since the abolition of slavery the mores of the two sections have become similar and the sectional dislike has disappeared. The contrast between the mores of English America and Spanish America is very great. It would long outlast any political combination of parts of the two, if such should be brought about.

115. Missions and mores. The contrasts and antagonisms of the mores of different groups are the stumbling-blocks in the way of all missionary enterprise, and they explain many of the phenomena which missions present. We think that our "ways" are the best, and that their superiority is so obvious that all heathen, Mohammedans, Buddhists, etc., will, as soon as they learn what our ways are, eagerly embrace them. Nothing could be further from the truth. "It is difficult to an untraveled Englishman, who has not had an opportunity of throwing himself into the spirit of the East, to credit the disgust and detestation that numerous everyday acts, which appear perfectly harmless to his countrymen, excite in many Orientals."[1] If our women are shocked at polygamy and the harem, Mohammedan women are equally shocked at the ball and dinner dresses of our ladies, at our dances, and at the manners of social intercourse between the sexes. Negroes in East Africa are as much disgusted to see white men eat fowl or eggs as we are at any of their messes. Missions always offer something from above downwards. They contain an assumption of superiority and beneficence. Half-civilized people never admit the assumption. They meet it just as we would meet a mission of Mohammedans or Buddhists to us. Savages and barbarians dismiss "white man's ways" with indifference. The virtues and arts of civilization are almost as disastrous to the uncivilized as its vices. It is really the great tragedy of civilization that the contact of lower and higher is disastrous to the former, no matter what may be the point of contact, or how little the civilized may desire to do harm.

[1] Galton, *Inquiries into Human Faculty*, 216.

116. Missions and antagonistic mores. Missionaries always
have to try to act on the mores. The ritual and creed of a religion, and reading and writing, would not fulfill the purpose.
The attempt is to teach the social ritual of civilized people.
Missionaries almost always first insist on the use of clothing
and monogamy. The first of these has, in a great number of
cases, produced disease and hastened the extinction of the aborigines. The second very often causes a revolution in the societal
organization, either in the family form, the productive industry,
or the political discipline. The Hawaiians were a people of a
very cheerful and playful disposition. The missionaries trained
the children in the schools to serious manners and decorum.
Such was the method in fashion in our own schools at the time.
The missionary society refused the petition of the Hawaiians
for teachers who would teach them the mechanic arts.[1] This is
like the refusal of the English missionary society to support
Livingstone's policy in South Africa because it was not religious.
Until very recent times no white men have understood the
difference between the mother family and the father family.
Missionaries have all grown up in the latter. Miss Kingsley
describes the antagonism which arises in the mind of a West
African negro, brought up in the mother family, against the
teaching of the missionary. The negro husband and wife have
separate property. Neither likes the white man's doctrine of
the community of goods. The woman knows that that would
mean that she would have none. The man would not take her
goods if he must take her children too. "White culture expects
a man to think more of his wife and children than he does
of his mother and sisters, which to the uncultured African is
absurd."[2] Evidently it is these collisions and antagonisms of the
mores which constitute the problems of missions. We can quote
but a single bit of evidence that an aboriginal people has gained
benefit from contact with the civilized. Of the Bantu negroes
it is said that such contact has increased their vigor and vitality.[3]
The "missionary-made man" is not a good type, according to

[1] *Amer. Jo. Sociol.*, VIII, 408. [2] Kingsley, *West African Studies*, 377.
[3] *B. & M. Soc. d'Anthrop.*, 1901, 362.

the military, travelers, and ethnographers.[1] Of the Basutos it is said that the converted ones are the worst. They are dishonest and dirty.[2] In Central America it is said that the judgment is often expressed that "an Indian who can read and write is a good-for-nothing." The teachers in the schools teach the Indian children to despise the ways of their race. Then they lose the virtues of trustworthiness and honesty, for which the Indians were noteworthy.[3] There is no such thing as "benevolent assimilation." To one who knows the facts such a phrase sounds like flippant ignorance or a cruel jest. Even if one group is reduced to a small remnant in the midst of a great nation, assimilation of the residue does not follow. Black and white, in the United States, are now tending to more strict segregation. The remnants of our Indians partly retain Indian mores, partly adopt white mores. They languish in moral isolation and homelessness. They have no adjustment to any social environment. Gypsies have never adopted the mores of civilized life. They are morally and physically afloat in the world. There are in India and in the Russian empire great numbers of remnants of aboriginal tribes, and there are, all over the world, groups of pariahs, or *races maudites*, which the great groups will not assimilate. The Jews, although more numerous, and economically far stronger, are in the same attitude to the peoples amongst which they live.

117. Modification of the mores by agitation. To this point all projects of missions and reform must come. It must be recognized that what is proposed is an arbitrary action on the mores. Therefore nothing sudden or big is possible. The enterprise is possible only if the mores are ready for it. The conditions of success lie in the mores. The methods must conform to the mores. That is why the agitator, reformer, prophet, reorganizer of society, who has found out "the truth" and wants to "get a law passed" to realize it right away, is only a mischief-maker. He has won considerable prestige in the last hundred years, but

[1] Portman, *Station Studies*, 78.
[2] *Amer. Anthrop.*, VI, 353, citing *Jo. Afr. Soc.*, 1903, 208.
[3] *Globus*, LXXXVII, 129.

if the cases are examined it will be found that when he had success it was because he took up something for which the mores were ready. Wilberforce did not overthrow slavery. Natural forces reduced to the service of man and the discovery of new land set men "free" from great labor, and new ways suggested new sentiments of humanity and ethics. The mores changed and all the wider deductions in them were repugnant to slavery. The free-trade agitators did not abolish the corn laws. The interests of the English population had undergone a new distribution. It was the redistribution of population and political power in the United States which made the civil war. Witchcraft and trial by torture were not abolished by argument. Critical knowledge and thirst for reality made them absurd. In Queen Anne's reign prisons in England were frightful sinks of vice, misery, disease, and cruel extortion. "So the prisons continued until the time of Howard,"[1] seventy-five years later. The mores had then become humanitarian. Howard was able to get a response.

118. Capricious interest of the masses. Whether the masses will think certain things wrong, cruel, base, unjust, and disgusting; whether they will think certain pleas and demands reasonable; whether they will regard certain projects as sensible, ridiculous, or fantastic, and will give attention to certain topics, depends on the convictions and feelings which at the time are dominant in the mores. No one can predict with confidence what the response will be to any stimulus which may be applied. The fact that certain American products of protected industries are sold abroad cheaper than at home, so that the protective tariff taxes us to make presents to foreigners, has been published scores of times. It might be expected to produce a storm of popular indignation. It does not do so. The abuses of the pension system have been exposed again and again. There is no popular response in condemnation of the abuse, or demand for reform. The error and folly of protection have been very fully exposed, but the free-trade agitation has not won ground. In truth, however, that agitation has never been carried on sincerely

---

[1] Ashton, *Social Life in the Time of Queen Anne*, Chap. XLI.

and persistently. Many of those who have taken part in it have not aimed to put an end to the steal, but to be taken into it. The notion of "making something out of the government" in one way or another has got into the mores. It is the vice of modern representative government. Civil-service reform has won but little popular support because the masses have learned that the successful party has a right to distribute the offices amongst its members. That has become accepted doctrine in the mores. A local boss said: "There is but one issue in the Fifth Maryland district. It is this, Can any man get more from Uncle Sam for the hard-working Republicans of the district than I can?"[1] This sentiment wins wide sympathy. Prohibitory legislation accords with the mores of the rural, but not of the urban, population. It therefore produces in cities deceit and blackmail, and we meet with the strange phenomenon, in a constitutional state, that publicists argue that administrative officers in cities ought to ignore the law. Antipolygamy is in the mores; antidivorce is not. Any injustice or arbitrary action against polygamy is possible. Reform of divorce legislation is slow and difficult. We are told that "respect for law" is in our mores, but the frequency of lynching disproves it. Let those who believe in the psychology of crowds write for us a logic of crowds and tell how the corporate mind operates.

119. How the group becomes homogeneous. The only way in which, in the course of time, remnants of foreign groups are apparently absorbed and the group becomes homogeneous, is that the foreign element dies out. In like manner people who live by aberrant mores die. The aberrant forms then cease to be, and the mores become uniform. In the meantime, there is a selection which determines which mores shall survive and which perish. This is accomplished by syncretism.

120. Syncretism. Although folkways for the same purpose have a great similarity in all groups, yet they present variations and characteristic differences from group to group. These variations are sometimes due to differences in the life conditions, but generally causes for them are unascertainable, or the

[1] *N. Y. Times,* September 19, 1904.

variations appear capricious. Therefore each in-group forms its own ways, and looks with contempt and abhorrence upon the ways of any out-group (sec. 13). Dialectical differences in language or pronunciation are a sufficient instance. They cannot be accounted for, but they call out contempt and ridicule, and are taken to be signs of barbarism and inferiority. When groups are compounded by intermarriage, intercourse, conquest, immigration, or slavery, syncretism of the folkways takes place. One of the component groups takes precedence and sets the standards. The inferior groups or classes imitate the ways of the dominant group, and eradicate from their children the traditions of their own ancestors. Amongst Englishmen the correct or incorrect placing of the *h* is a mark of caste. It is a matter of education to put an end to the incorrect use. Contiguity, neighborhood, or even literature may suffice to bring about syncretism of the mores. One group learns that the people of another group regard some one of its ways or notions as base. This knowledge may produce shame and an effort to breed out the custom. Thus whenever two groups are brought into contact and contagion, there is, by syncretism, a selection of the folkways which is destructive to some of them. This is the process by which folkways are rendered obsolete. The notion of a gradual refinement of the mores in time, which is assumed to go on of itself, or by virtue of some inherent tendency in that direction, is entirely unfounded. Christian mores in the western empire were formed by syncretism of Jewish and pagan mores. Christian mores therefore contain war, slavery, concubinage, demonism, and base amusements, together with some abstract ascetic doctrines with which these things are inconsistent. The strain of the mores towards consistency produced elimination of some of these customs. The church embraced in its fold Latin, Teutonic, Greek, and Slavonic nations, and it produced a grand syncretism of their mores, while it favored those which were Latin. The Teutonic mores suffered elimination. Those which were Greek and Slavonic were saved by the division of the church. Those which now pass for Christian in western Europe are the result of the syncretism of two thousand years. When now western Christians come in contact with heathen, Mohammedans, Buddhists, or alien forms of Christianity, they endeavor to put an end to polygamy, slavery, infanticide, idolatry, etc., which have been extruded from western Christian mores. In Egypt at the present time the political power and economic prosperity of the English causes the Mohammedans to envy, emulate, and imitate them in all those peculiarities which are supposed to be causes of their success. Hence we hear of movements to educate children, change the status of women, and otherwise modify traditional mores. It is another case of the operation by which inferior mores are rendered obsolete.

121. The art of societal administration. It is not to be inferred that reform and correction are hopeless. Inasmuch as the mores are a phenomenon of the society and not of the state, and inasmuch as the machinery of administration belongs to the state and not to the society, the administration of the mores presents peculiar difficulties. Strictly speaking, there is no administration of the mores, or it is left to voluntary organs acting by moral suasion. The state administration fails if it tries to deal with the mores, because it goes out of its province. The voluntary organs which try to administer the mores (literature, moral teachers, schools, churches, etc.) have no set method and no persistent effort. They very often make great errors in their methods. In regard to divorce, for instance, it is idle to set up stringent rules in an ecclesiastical body, and to try to establish them by extravagant and false interpretation of the Bible, hoping in that way to lead opinion; but the observation and consideration of cases which occur affect opinion and form convictions. The statesman and social philosopher can act with such influences, sum up the forces which make them, and greatly help the result. The inference is that intelligent art can be introduced here as elsewhere, but that it is necessary to understand the mores and to be able to discern the elements in them, just as it is always necessary for good art to understand the facts of nature with which it will have to deal. It belongs to the work of publicists and statesmen to gauge the forces in the mores and to perceive their tendencies. The great men of a great epoch are those who have understood new currents in the mores. The great reformers of the sixteenth century, the great leaders of modern revolutions, were, as we can easily see, produced out of a protest or revulsion which had long been forming under and within the existing system. The leaders are such because they voice the convictions which have become established and because they propose measures which will realize interests of which the society has become conscious. A hero is not needed. Often a mediocre, commonplace man suffices to give the critical turn to thought or interest. "A Gian Angelo Medici, agreeable, diplomatic, benevolent, and pleasure-loving, sufficed to initiate a series of events which kept the occidental races in perturbation through two centuries."[1] Great crises come when great new forces are at work changing fundamental conditions, while powerful institutions and traditions still hold old systems intact. The fifteenth century was such a period. It is in such crises that great men find their opportunity. The man and the age react on each other. The measures of policy which are adopted and upon which energy is expended become components in the evolution. The evolution, although it has the character of a nature process, always must issue by and through men whose passions, follies, and wills are a part of it but are also always dominated by it. The interaction defies our analysis, but it does not discourage our reason and conscience from their play on the situation, if we are content to know that their function must be humble. Stoll boldly declares that if one of us had been a judge in the times of the witch trials he would have reasoned as the witch judges did, and would have tortured like them.[2] If that is so, then it behooves us by education and will, with intelligent purpose, to criticise and judge even the most established ways of our time, and to put courage and labor into resistance to the current mores where we judge them wrong. It would be a mighty achievement of the science of society if it could lead up to an art of societal administration which should be intelligent, effective, and scientific.

[1] Symonds, *Catholic Reaction*, I, 144.
[2] Stoll, *Suggestion und Hypnotismus*, 248.

CHAPTER III

THE STRUGGLE FOR EXISTENCE

Tools, Arts, Language, Money

Processes and artifacts of the food supply. — Fishing. — Methods of fishing. — The mystic element. — Religion and industry. — Artifacts and freaks of nature. — Forms of stone axes. — How stone implements are made. — How arrowheads are made. — How stone axes are used. — Acculturation or parallelism. — Fire-making tools. — Psychophysical traits of primitive man. — Language. — Language and magic. — Language is a case of folkways. — Primitive dialects. — Taking up and dropping language. — Pigeon dialects. — How languages grow. — Money. — Intergroup and intragroup money. — Predominant wares. — Intragroup money from property; intergroup money from trade. — Shell and bead money. — Token money. — Selection of a predominant ware. — Stone money in Melanesia. — Plutocratic effects of money. — Money on the northwest coast of North America. — Wampumpeag and roanoke. — Ring money. Use of metal. — The evolution of money. — The ethical functions of money.

122. Processes and artifacts of the food supply. The processes and the artifacts which are connected with food supply offer us the purest and simplest illustrations of the development of folkways. They are not free from the admixture of superstition and vanity, but the element of expediency predominates in them. It is reported of the natives of New South Wales that a man will lie on a rock with a piece of fish in his hand, feigning sleep. A hawk or crow darts at the fish, but is caught by the man. It is also reported of Australians that a man swims under water, breathing through a reed, approaches ducks, pulls one under water by the legs, wrings its neck, and so secures a number of them.[1] If these stories can be accepted with confidence, they may well furnish us a starting point for a study of the art of catching animals. The man really has no tool, but must rely entirely on his own quickness and dexterity. Birdlime is a device

---

[1] Smyth, *Aborig. of Victoria*, I, 194, 197.

for which many plants furnish material,[1] and which is available even against large game, which is fretted and worn out by it until it becomes the prey of man. A Botocudo hunter grates the eggs of an alligator together, when he finds them on the bank, and so entices the mother.[2] The Yuroks of California sprinkled berries on the shallow bottom of a river and stretched a net a few inches below the surface of the water. Ducks diving for the berries were caught by the neck in the meshes and drowned. As they hung quiet they did not frighten away others.[3] The Tarahumari catch birds by stringing corn kernels on a fiber which is buried underground. The bird swallows the corn and cannot eject it.[4] Various animals were trained to help man in the food quest and were thus drawn into the industrial organization. The animals furnished materials (skin, bone, teeth, hair, horns) and also tools, so that the food quest broadened beyond the immediate supply of food into mechanical industrial forms. The Shingu Indians, although they lived on the product of the ground, were obliged to continue the chase because of the materials and implements which they got from the animals. They used the jaw of a fish, with the teeth in it, as a knife; the arm and leg bones of apes as arrow points; the tail spike of a skate for the same; the two front claws of the armadillo to dig the ground (a process which the animal taught them by the same use of his claws); the shell of a river mussel as a scraper to finish wooden tools. " These people were hunters without dogs, fishers without hooks, and tillers without plow or spade. They show how much development life was capable of in the time before metals." [5] The palometa is a fish which weighs two or three pounds. It has fourteen teeth in each jaw so sharp that the Abipones shear sheep with the jaw.[6] Such cases might be pursued into great detail. They show acute observation, great ingenuity, clever adaptation, and teachableness. The lasso, bola, boomerang, and throw knife,

---

[1] Mason, *Origin of Invention*, 252.

[2] Tylor, *Anthrop.*, 208.

[3] Powers, *California Indians*, 50.

[4] Lumholtz, *Scribner's*, October, 1894, 448.

[5] Von den Steinen, *Berl. Mus.*, 1888, 205.

[6] Southey, *Brazil*, I, 131.

as well as the throw stick, are products of persistent and open-minded experience. The selection and adaptation of things in nature to a special operation in the arts often show ingenuity as great as that manifested in any of our devices.[1] This ingenuity is of the same kind as that shown by many animals. Intelligent experiment, however, is not wanting. It is reported of Eskimo that they invent imaginary hard cases, such as might occur to them, and, by way of sport, discuss the proper way to deal with the case.[2] Operations similar to this in play show a mode in which ingenuity must have been developed and inventions produced. In the higher grades of the hunting stage, such as are presented by the North American Indians, buffalo hunting, for instance, calls for the highest organization and skill, and establishes inflexible discipline.[3]

123. Fishing. Fishing furnishes a parallel case. A Thlinkit fisherman puts on a cap which resembles the head of a seal, and hiding his body between the rocks makes a noise like a seal. This entices seals towards him and gives him opportunity to kill them.[4] The Australians had a fish spear and a net made of fibers, which were chewed by the women to make them soft. They had no hooks until they got them from the whites.[5] Weirs for fishing were built of stone. One is described which was a labyrinth of stone circles, of which some were connected with each other. The walls are three or four feet high. The fish get confused and are caught by hand.[6] Remains of weirs, consisting of wattled work of reeds or saplings, are found in the rivers of northern Europe. The device of putting into the water some poisonous or narcotic substance in order to stupefy the fish is met with all over the globe. It was employed by the aborigines on Lanzarote (Canary Islands). There the fish were freshened in unpoisoned waters.[7] It is quite impossible that this device should have spread only by contact. It must have been independently invented. It secured a large amount of fish with very little

---

[1] E.g. a rasp made from the skin of the palate of a kind of ray, by Tahitians, Vienna Museum.

[2] Mason, *Origin of Invention*, 23.

[3] Grinnell, *Folk Tales*, 295.

[4] Dall, *Bur. Eth.*, III, 122.

[5] Ratzel, *Völkerkunde*, II, 52.

[6] Smyth, *Aborig. of Victoria*, I, 202

[7] *N. S. Amer. Anthrop.*, II, 466.

trouble. The Ainos dam the stream, leaving only a few openings, opposite each of which, below, they build a platform. The fish jump at the opening, but some miss it and fall on the platform where they are caught.[1] The Polynesians depend largely on fish for their food supply. They had nets a thousand ells long, which could be handled only by a hundred men. They made hooks of shell, bone, and hard wood.[2] The first fishhooks of prehistoric men in Europe and North America were made of pieces of bone pointed at both ends, the cord being attached in the middle.[3] The Shingu Indians fished with bow and arrow, nets, scoop baskets, and weirs. Bait was used to make the fish rise. Then they were shot with an arrow. The people had no hooks, but eagerly adopted them when they became acquainted with them.[4] They and other Brazilians set a long cylindrical basket in a stream in such a way that when the fish enters it and seizes the bait, it tilts up into a perpendicular position. The fish cannot then get out.[5]

124. Methods of fishing. Nilsson remarks on the astonishing resemblance between all the fishing apparatus of Scandinavians, Eskimo, and North Americans.[6] The problem is solved in the same way, but the materials within reach impose limiting conditions. The rod and hook yield to the net when the fish are plentiful. Then, however, the spear also is used. It is sometimes made so that the head will come off when the fish is struck. By its buoyancy the spearhead, sticking in the body of the fish, compels it to rise, when it is caught.[7] A peculiar device is reported from Dobu, New Guinea. A string long enough to reach to the ground is fastened to a kite. At the end of the string is a tassel of spider's web. The kite is held at such a height that the tassel just skims the water. The fish catching at it entangles its teeth in the spider's-web tassel and is caught.[8] The Chinese have trained cormorants to do their fishing for them.

[1] *U. S. Nat. Mus.*, 1890, 471.   [2] Ratzel, *Völkerkunde*, II, 163.

[3] Smithson, *Contrib. to Knowledge*, XXV ; Rau, *Prehist. Fishing.*

[4] Von den Steinen, *Berl. Mus.*, 1888, 209, 231, 235.

[5] Ehrenreich, *Völkerkunde Brasiliens ; Berl. Mus.*, 1891, 57.

[6] *Prim. Inhab. of Scandinavia*, 35.

[7] JAI, XXIII, 160.   [8] *Ibid.*, XXVIII, 343.

125. The mystic element. Although the food quest is the most utilitarian and matter-of-fact branch of the struggle for existence, the mystic element does not fail to present itself. No doubt it would be found interwoven with many of the cases mentioned above, if the question was raised and the investigation made. In the Caroline archipelago fishing is combined with various rites and religious notions. The chief medicine man owes the authority of his position, not to his knowledge of the art of fishing, but to his knowledge of the formulæ of incantation and exorcism employed in fishing. There must be abstinence from the sex relation before a fishing expedition. The men start in silence. Especially, the hoped-for success must not be mentioned. The boat must have a formula of luck pronounced over it. Sacrifices of taro are offered to win the favor of the god, lest the lines be broken by sharks or become entangled in rocks. If the expedition fails to get a good catch, the fault is laid to the men. Some one of them is thought to have done something amiss.[1]

126. Religion and industry. Here we meet with a familiar cycle of notions and usages. We must assume them in all cases, whether they are reported or not, for the element of supernatural intervention, or magic, seems never to be wanting. At higher stages it gives way to religious ritual or to priestly blessing. The Japanese sword maker formerly wore a priestly garb when making a sword, which was a sacred craft. He also practiced a purificatory ritual. The sacred rope of rice straw, the oldest symbol of Shinto, was suspended before the smithy. The workman's food was all cooked with holy fire, and none of his family might enter the workshop or speak to him while he was at work.[2] There were also ascetic practices in the Shinto religion, which an elected representative of the community undertook each year for the prosperity of the whole.[3] There is never a case of authority in human society which does not go back, for its origin and explanation, to the influence of the other world (ghosts, etc.) over this world.

127. Artifacts and freaks of nature. In the Oxford University museum may be seen a case full of natural stones, flints,

---

[1] Kubary, *Karolinenarchipel.*, 123–130. [2] Hearn, *Japan*, 139. [3] *Ibid.*, 165.

etc., so like the artifacts of the Chellean type that it would require a skilled observer to determine whether they are artificial or not. The collection includes apparent celts, rings, perforated stones, borers, scrapers, and flint flakes, so that the objects are by no means such as would lie at the beginning of the series of artifacts, in regard to which the doubt whether they were artificial would arise from their rudeness and consequent resemblance to stones broken by natural conjunctures. In the museum at Dresden may be seen a collection of stones, natural products, which might serve as models for artificial axes, celts, etc. One object shows the possibility of freaks of nature of this class. It is a water-worn stone which might be taken for a skull. In the Copenhagen museum is a great collection of stone tools arranged in sequence of perfection, beginning with the coarsest and rudest and advancing to the highest products of art of this kind. That collection is arranged solely with reference to the development of the flint and stone implements as tools for a certain use. The sequence is very convincing as to the interpretation put on the objects, and also as to the strain towards improvement. Time and place are disregarded in the arrangement. The earliest specimens in the series are very rude, and only expert opinion could justify their place amongst artifacts. It reminds us of what we are told about specimens of Australian " tomahawks." It is said of such a weapon from West Australia that if it was "found anywhere divested of the gum and handle, it is doubtful whether it could be recognized by any one as a work of art. It is ruder in its fashioning, owing principally to the material of which it is composed, than even the rude, unrubbed, chipped cutting-stones of the Tasmanians." [1] With regard to these stone implements of the Tasmanians Tylor said that some of them are "ruder in make than those of the mammoth period, inasmuch as their edges are formed by chipping only one surface of the stone, instead of both, as in the European examples." The Tasmanians, when they needed a cutting implement, caught up a suitable flat stone, knocked off chips from one side, partly or all around the edge, and used it without more ado. This they did under the

[1] Smyth, *Aborig. of Victoria*, I, 340.

eyes of modern Europeans. Tylor showed, " from among flint instruments and flakes from the cave of le Moustier in Dordogne, specimens corresponding in make with such curious exactness to those of the Tasmanians that, were they not chipped from different stones, it would hardly be possible to distinguish those of recent savages from those of European cavemen. It is not strange that experienced archæologists should have been at first inclined to consider a large portion of the Tasmanian stone implements exhibited as wasters and flakes, or chips, struck off in shaping implements." These stones had no handle. They were grasped in the hand.[1] In the Oxford museum may be seen side by side flint shapes from St. Acheul, Tasmania, India, and the Cape of Good Hope. All the paleolithic implements which we possess, even the oldest and rudest, belong far on in a series of which the antecedent members are wanting, for the art, if recognized, is seen to be advanced and artistic.[2] The Seri of southern California use a natural cobblestone, which is shaped only by the wear of use, and is discarded when sharp edges are produced by use or fracture. They use their teeth and claws like beasts. They have not a knife-sense and need training before they can use a knife. The stone selected is of an ovoid form somewhat flattened. By use it is battered on the ends and ground on the sides so that it becomes personal property and acquires fetishistic import. It is buried with the corpse of the woman who owned and used it.[3] Holmes, after experimenting with the manufacture of stone implements, declared that "every implement resembling the final forms and every blade-shaped projectile point made from a bowlder, or similar bit of rock, not already approximate in shape, must pass through the same or very nearly the same, stages of development, leaving the same wasters, whether shaped to-day, yesterday, or a million years ago; whether in the hands of the civilized, the barbarous, or the savage man."[4] This conclusion is very important, for it

[1] Tylor, JAI, XXII, 137 ; JAI, XXIV, 336 ; *Early Hist. of Mankind*, 195; Ling Roth, *Tasmania*, 158.
[2] JAI, XXIII, 276.
[3] *Bur. Eth.*, XVII (Part I), 153,* 245.*   [4] *Ibid.*, XV, 61.

recognizes a certain constant determination of the art of stone-implement making by the qualities of the material and the muscular activities of man. It has been disputed whether the form called "turtle-backs" were one form in the series of artifacts, or a misform produced by errors in manufacture. "The American archæologists, who have labored long to repeat the processes of the aborigines in stone work, find themselves unavoidably making 'turtle-backs,' when they are really trying to make the leaf-shaped blade."[1] The handicraftsmen of the Smithsonian Institute have not been able to make a leaf-shaped blade such as may be seen in the museums, and no Indian has been found who could make one. "This is one of the lost arts."[2] Other pieces of rude form have been set aside as chips, or rejects, but such are found in use as scrapers, or in handles, and are to be recognized as products which belong to the series.[3] Some rude implements found in the hill gravels of Berkshire, England, have been offered as anterior to the paleolithic implements as usually classified.[4] Lubbock said that he could not find in the large Scandinavian collections "a single specimen of a true paleolithic type."[5]

128. Forms of stone axes. Stone axes are found all over the globe. Chipped, sharpened, polished, grooved, pierced, handled, are different kinds which may be set in a series of advancing improvement, and under each grade local varieties may be distinguished, but the art is essentially the same everywhere. "Probably no discovery is older than the fact that friction would wear away wood or bone, or even stone."[6] It was also learned that rawhide and sinew shrank in drying, and this fact was very ingeniously used to attach handles, the sinew or membrane being put on while fresh and wet. American stone axes are grooved to receive a handle made by an ingenious adaptation of roots and branches with pitch or bitumen. "Bored stone axes are found in the tropical regions of America. Although they are very rare, they are well executed."[7] The device of boring stone axes appears

---

[1] Mason, *Origin of Invention*, 132.
[2] *Ibid.*, 123, 136.
[3] *Intern. Cong. Anthrop.*, 1893, 67.
[4] JAI, XXIV, 44.
[5] *Ibid.*, X, 316.
[6] Mason, *Origin of Invention*, 148.
[7] Ratzel, *Völkerkunde*, II, 586.

at the end of the stone age in the lake dwellings of Switzerland. Perhaps they were only decorative.[1] The Polynesians used stone axes which were polished but not bored or grooved, and the edge was not curved.[2] The Pacific islanders clung to the type of the adze, so that even when they got iron and steel implements from the whites they preferred the knife of a plane to an ax, because the former could be used adze-fashion.[3] In the stone graves of Tennessee have been found implements superior to all others found in the United States in size, variety, and workmanship. Amongst these are a flint sickle-shaped tool, axes a foot long or more, a flint sword twenty-two inches long, a flint needle eight inches long; also objects supposed to be for ceremonial or decorative use. Stone axes with handles all in one piece have been found in Tennessee, Arkansas, and South Carolina.[4]

129. How stone implements are made. What was the process by which these stone implements were made? The artifacts bear witness directly to two or three different operations, separate or combined, and to a great development of the process. As above stated, Tasmanians, after they became known to Europeans, made stone implements as they needed them, giving to a stone a rude adaptation to the purpose by chipping off a few flakes. Short sharp blows were struck by one stone upon another. The blow must, however, fall upon just the right spot or it would not produce the desired result. Therefore the flakes were often thrown off by pressure. A stick or horn was set against the spot where the force should be applied, and braced against the breast of the operator, while he held the stone between his feet. This latter operation is described as used by the Mexicans to get flakes of obsidian.[5] By carrying further the process of chipping or pressing the stone could be shaped more perfectly, and by rubbing it on another stone it could be given a cutting edge.

[1] Ranke, *Der Mensch*, II, 519.
[2] Ratzel, *Völkerkunde*, II, 149.
[3] Hagen, *Unter den Papuas*, 214; Pfeil, *Aus der Südsee*, 97.
[4] Thurston, *Antiq. of Tenn., etc.*, 218, 230–240, 259; JAI, XIII, XVI; *Bur. Ethnol.*, XIII; *Smithson. Rep.*, 1874, 1877, 1886, Parts I, II, III; *Peabody Mus.*, No. 7.
[5] Lubbock, *Prehist. Times*, 90.

The rubbing process could also be applied to the surface to make it smooth instead of leaving it as it was after the flaking process. The processes of striking and pressing were also combined. The pebble was broken by blows and the pieces were further reduced to shape by the pressing process. Different devices were also invented for holding the stone securely and in the proper position. Skill and judgment in perceiving how and for what purpose each pebble could best be treated was developed by the workers, and division of labor arose amongst them as some acquired greater skill in one operation and others in another. The operations of pressing and striking were also made complex in order to accomplish what was desired. A sapling was cut off so that the stump of a limb was left at the bottom of it. It was set against the spot where the force was needed, and a blow struck in the crotch of the limb caused the chip to fly. This apparatus was improved and refined by putting a horn tip on the end point of contact. Another device was to cut a notch in a tree trunk, which could be used as a fulcrum. A long lever was used to apply the pressure to the stone laid at the root of the tree, or on the horizontal space at the bottom of the notch.[1] These variations show persistent endeavor to get control of the necessary force and to apply it at the proper point with the least chance for error and loss. Buckley reported about the "tomahawks" of the aborigines of Victoria, that the stone was split into pieces, without regard to their shape, but of convenient thickness. A piece was rubbed on rough granite until "it is brought to a very fine thin edge, and so hard and sharp as to enable them to fell a very large tree with it." The handles are "thick pieces of wood, split and then doubled up, the stone being in the bend and fixed with gum, very carefully prepared for the purpose, so as to make it perfectly secure when bound round with sinews."[2] The natives of the Admiralty Islands use obsidian which is dug from layers in the ground. Only a few know the art of making axes, and they prosecute it as a means of livelihood. Skill is required especially to judge of the way in which the stone will split. The only tool is a stone

---

[1] *Smithson. Rep.*, 1885, Part I, 874, 882; *Ibid.*, 1887, Part I, 601.
[2] Smyth, *Aborig. of Victoria*, I, 359.

with which light, sharp blows are struck.[1] The axes of the Swiss lake dwellings were made from bowlders of any hard stone. By means of a saw of flint set in wood, with sand and water, a groove was cut on one side and then on the other. With a single blow from another stone the bowlder was made to fall in two. By means of a hard stone the piece was rudely shaped and then finished by friction. A modern student has made such an ax in this way in five hours. Sometimes the stone was set in a handle of wood or horn.[2] It will be noticed that this process was not possible until an auxiliary tool, the flint saw, had already been made. The tools and processes were all rude and great skill and dexterity were required in the operator. " Lafitau says the polishing of a stone ax requires generations to complete. Mr. Joseph D. McGuire fabricates a grooved jade ax from an entirely rough spall in less than a hundred hours." [3]

130. How arrowheads are made. As to arrowheads, " there are a dozen or more authentic reports by eye-witnesses of the manufacture of arrowheads in as many different ways." [4] The California Indians broke up a piece of flint or obsidian to the proper-sized pieces. A piece was held in the left hand, which was protected by a piece of buckskin. Pressure was put upon the edge by a piece of a deer's antler, four to six inches long, held in the right hand. In this way little pieces were chipped off until the arrowhead was formed. Only the most expert do this successfully.[5] Sometimes the stone to be operated on is heated in the fire, and slowly cooled, which causes it to split in flakes. A flake is then shaped with buck-horn pincers, tied together at the point with a thong.[6] In another report it is the stone with which the operation is performed which is said to be heated.[7] In a pit several hundred flint implements were found stored away in regular layers with alternate layers of sand between. Perhaps the purpose was to render them more easy to work to the desired finish.[8] Catlin describes another process of making

---

[1] *Globus*, LXXXVII, 238.

[2] Ranke, *Der Mensch*, II, 517.

[3] Mason, *Origin of Invention*, 26.

[4] *U. S. Nat. Mus.*, 1894, 658.

[5] Powers, *Calif. Indians*, 374.

[6] *Ibid.*, 104 ; *Smithson. Rep.*, 1886, Part I, 225.

[7] *Smithson. Rep.*, 1887, Part I, 601.

[8] *Bur. Eth.*, XII, 561.

arrowheads which required two workmen. One held the stone in his left hand and placed a chisel-like instrument at the proper point. The second man struck the blow. Both sang during the operation. The blows were in the rhythm of the music, and a quick "rebounding" stroke was said to be essential to good success.[1] A "lad" in Michigan made arrowheads in imitation of Indian work, from flint, glass, and obsidian, with a piece of oak stick five inches long as a tool.[2] Sophus Müller[3] says of modern attempts to imitate stone-implement making that an average workman can learn in fourteen days to make five hundred to eight hundred arrowheads per day, but that no one of the best workmen has been able to equal the fine chipping on the neolithic stone weapons, although many have made the small implements on the types of the old stone age.

131. How stone axes were used. After stone axes were made it required no little independent sense to use them for the desired result. A modern archæologist used a stone ax of gray flint, with an edge six and a half centimeters long, set in a handle after the prehistoric fashion, to cut sticks of green fir, in order to test the ax. He held the stick upright and chopped into it notchwise until he could break it in two. He cut in two a stick eighteen centimeters in diameter in eighteen minutes. He struck fifteen hundred and seventy-eight cuts. At the fourteen hundred and eighty-fifth cut a piece flew from his ax.[4] A modern investigator made a polished ax in eleven hours and forty-five minutes. He cut down an oak tree 0.73 meter in circumference, with twenty-two hundred blows of the ax, in an hour and thirteen minutes.[5] When primitive men desired to cut down a tree, fire was applied to it and the ax was used only to chop off the charred wood so that the fire would attack the wood again. Canoes were hollowed out of tree trunks by the same process. These processes are reported from different parts of the world remote from each other.[6] Without these auxiliary devices the stone

[1] *Smithson. Rep.*, 1885, Part II, 743.   [2] *Scient. Amer.*, March 10, 1906.
[3] *Vor Oldtid*, 169.   [4] *Aarbøger f. Oldkyndighed*, 1891.
[5] *L'Anthropologie*, XIV, 417.
[6] JAI, XXVIII, 296; *Bur. Ethnol.*, II, 205; Horn, *Mennesket i den forhistoriske Tid*, 168.

ax can really be used only as a hammer, for, by means of it, the wood is beaten into a fibrous condition and is not properly cut.[1] Nevertheless, the Shingu Indians cleared forests, built houses and canoes, and made furniture with the stone ax alone.[2] The Indians of Guiana, with stone and bone implements, cut down big trees, cut out the core of them, and made weapons and tools of great perfection and beauty.[3] The same may be said of very many other peoples. Some Australians value stone axes so much that they except them from the custom to bury all a man's property with him. Axes are inherited by the next of kin.[4]

132. Acculturation versus parallelism. The facts in regard to making and using stone implements bring up the question whether such arts have a single origin and are spread by contagion (acculturation), or are invented independently by many people who have the same tasks to perform, and the same or similar materials at hand (parallelism). Lippert[5] says that " the different modes of fashioning flint arrowheads show us that we must not think of the earliest art as all tied to a single tradition, and carried away from this. On the contrary, human ingenuity has set about accomplishing the acts which are necessary for the struggle for existence in different places, with the elements there at hand." We have seen above that the materials may, from their character, so limit and condition the operations of manufacture as to set lines for the development of the art. If the processes of the men are also limited and conditioned by the nature of human nerves and muscles so that they must run on certain lines, it would follow that the human mind also, in face of a certain problem, will fall into conditioned modes of activity, and we should approach the doctrine that men must think the same thoughts by way of mental reaction on the same experiences and observations.

The facts, however, show that an art, beginning in the rudest way, is produced along lines of concurrent effort, and is the

---

[1] *Globus*, LXXVI, 79.

[2] Von den Steinen, *Berl. Mus.*, 1888. 203.

[3] Schomburgk, *Britisch Guiana*, I, 424.

[4] Howitt, *S. E. Australians*, 455.

[5] *Kulturgesch.*, I, 289.

common property of the group. All practice it as it is, and all are unconsciously coöperating to improve it. The processes are folkways. The artifacts are tools and weapons which, by their utility, modify the folkways and become components in them. The skill, dexterity, patience, ingenuity, and power of combination which result are wider and higher possessions which also modify the folkways at later stages of effort. The generalizations of truth and right widen at every stage, and produce a theory of welfare, which must be recognized as such, no matter how rude it may be. It consists in the application of the notions of goblinism as they are prevalent at the time in the group. The art itself is built up by folkways according to their character as everywhere exhibited, for arts are modes of providing for human necessities by processes and devices which can be universally taught, and can be handed down forever. The arts of an isolated group run against limits, even if the group has great ingenuity, as we see in the case of China. It is when arts are developed by give and take between groups that they reach their highest development. The wider the area over which the coöperation and combination are active, the higher will be the achievements. " Every art is born out of the intelligence of its age." [1] It has been mentioned above that Polynesians cannot use an ax. They want to set the blade transverse to the handle. The negroes of the Niger Protectorate are very clumsy at going up or down stairs. It is a dexterity, not to say an art, which they have had no chance to acquire. They also find it very difficult to understand or interpret a picture, even of the least conventional kind.[2] The Seri of Tiburon Island have not the knife habit. They draw a knife towards the body instead of pushing it away.[3] Hence we see that the lack of a habit, or lack of opportunity to see a dexterity practiced, constitutes a narrowing of the mental horizon.

133. Fire-making tools. Another art which would offer us parallel phenomena to that of stone working is that of fire making. It must have had several independent centers of origin. It

---

[1] *Umschau*, VII, 184. [2] JAI, XXVIII, 108.
[3] *Bur. Ethnol.*, XVII, Part I, 152.

existed all over the globe. Its ultimate origin is unknown to us. It may have originated in different ways at different centers. The simplest instruments for making fire can be classified according to the mode of movement employed in them as drilling, plowing, and sawing instruments. The fire drills have also undergone very important development and improvement, so that they have become very complicated machines. The ingenuity and inventive skill which were required to make a fire drill which was driven by a bow were as great as the same powers when manifested by an Edison or a Bessemer.

134. Psychophysical traits of primitive men. All the artifacts were made and all the arts were produced by the concurrent efforts of men to serve their interests. We find that primitive men put patient effort and astonishing ingenuity into their tools. They also attained to great skill in the use of clumsy tools. It is true, in general, of primitive men that they shirk all prolonged effort or patient application, but they do use great patience and perseverance when they expect to accomplish something of great importance to their interests. The same is true if they expect to gratify their vanity. In hair dressing or tattooing they submit to very irksome restraint prolonged through a long time. Also in feather work, partly useful and partly ornamental, they assorted feathers piece by piece, and enlaced the feathers in the meshes of their hats and caps, or fastened them into scepters with pitch. They could make houses, etc., with their axes only by long-continued industry.[1] South American Indians made tools for printing tattoo patterns on the body. They were blocks, on each face of which a pattern was raised, perhaps a different one on each side.[2] It should be noticed what prodigious power a large body of men can put forth when they all work at the same task and are greatly interested in it. They begin by the same process, but the process differentiates and improves in their hands. Each gains skill and dexterity. They learn from each other, and the product is multiplied.

135. Language. Language is a product of the folkways which illustrates their operation in a number of most important details.

---

[1] Martius, *Ethnog. Brasil.*, 405. [2] Boggiani, *I Caduvei*, I, 168.

Language is a product of the need of coöperative understanding in all the work, and in connection with all the interests, of life. It is a societal phenomenon. It was necessary in war, the chase, and industry so soon as these interests were pursued coöperatively. Each group produced its own language which held that group together and sundered it from others.[1] All are now agreed that, whatever may have been the origin of language, it owes its form and development to usage. "Men's usage makes language." "The maxim that 'usage is the rule of speech' is of supreme and uncontrolled validity in every part and parcel of every human tongue."[2] "Language is only the imperfect means of men to find their bearings in the world of their memories; to make use of their memory, that is, their own experience and that of their ancestors, with all probability that this world of memory will be like the world of reality."[3] The origin of language is one of those origins which must ever remain enveloped in mystery. "How can a child understand the combinations of sound and sense when it must know language in order to learn them? It must learn to speak without previously knowing how to speak, without any previous suspicion that the words of its mother mean more than the buzzing of a fly. The child learns to speak from an absolute beginning, just as, not the original man, but the original beast, learned to speak before any creature could speak."[4] The beasts evidently did not learn to speak. They only learned to use the beast cries, by which they transmitted warnings, sex invitations, calls to united struggles, etc. The cries answered the purpose and went no further. Men, by virtue of the expanding power in them which enthused their zeal and their play, broke through the limitations of beast language, and went on to use the sounds of the human speech instrument for ever richer communications. Poetic power in blossom guides the development of a child's language as it guided that of the men who made the first languages.[5] "The original languages must

[1] Gumplowicz, *Sociol. und Politik*, 93.
[2] Whitney, *Language and the Study of Language*, 37, 40.
[3] Mauthner, *Kritik der Sprache*, III, 2.
[4] *Ibid.*, II, 403.   [5] *Ibid.*, II, 426, 427.

be, in comparison with our languages, like the wildest love-passion compared with marital custom." [1] Every word has a history of accidents which have befallen it, the beginnings of which are lost in the abyss of time.[2] In the Middle Ages the word " Word " came to mean the Word of God with such distinctness that the romance languages adopted parabola, or derivatives from it, for "word." [3] The students of linguistics recognize metaphor as another great mode of modifying the signification of words. By metaphor they mean the assembling of like things, and the selection and extirpation of unlike things.

136. Language and magic. Preuss offers an explanation of the origin of language which is interesting on account of its connection with the vast operation of magic : " Language owes its origin to the magic of tones and words. The difficulty of winning any notion about the beginnings of human speech lies in the fact that we cannot think of any cause which should give occasion for speech utterances. Such occasions are products of education, after language already existed. They are effects of language, not causes of it. . . . Language belongs, like play, dances, and fine arts, to the things which do not come on a direct line of development out of the instinctive satisfaction of life-needs and the other activities which create things of positive value, but it is the result of belief in magic, which prompted men to imitate noises made in labor, and other natural sounds, through a wide range, in order thereby to produce operations." [4]

137. Language is a case of mores. Whitney said that language is an institution. He meant that it is in the folkways, or in the mores, since welfare is connected with the folkways of language, albeit by some superstition. He adds : " In whatever aspect the general facts of language are viewed, they exhibit the same absence of reflection and intention." [5] " No one ever set himself deliberately at work to invent or improve language, — or did so, at least, with any valuable and abiding result. The work is all accomplished by a continual satisfaction of the needs of the moment, by ever yielding to an impulse and

[1] Mauthner, 278.   [2] *Ibid.*, 186.   [3] *Ibid.*, 184.
[4] *Globus*, LXXXVII, 397.   [5] *Language*, 48, 51.

grasping a possibility, which the already acquired treasure of
words and forms, and the habit of their use, suggest and put
within reach." [1] "Every single item of alteration, of whatever
kind, and of whatever degree of importance, goes back to some
individual or individuals who set it in circulation, from whose
example it gained a wider and wider currency, until it finally won
that general assent, which is alone required in order to make
anything in language proper and authoritative." [2] These statements might be applied to any of the folkways. The statements
on page 46 of Whitney's book would serve to describe and
define the mores. This shows to what an extent language is a
case of the operation by which mores are produced. They are
always devices to meet a need, which are imperceptibly modified
and unconsciously handed down through the generations. The
ways, like the language, are incorporeal things. They are borne
by everybody and nobody, and are developed by everybody and
nobody. Everybody has his little peculiarities of language. Each
one has his peculiarities of accent or pronunciation and his pet
words or phrases. Each one is suggesting all the time the use of
the tricks of language which he has adopted. "Nothing less than
the combined effort of a whole community, with all its classes
and orders, in all its variety of characters, circumstances, and
necessities, is capable of keeping in life a whole language." [3]
"Every vocable was to us [children] an arbitrary and conventional sign; arbitrary, because any one of a thousand other
vocables could have been just as easily learned by us and associated with the same idea; conventional, because the one we
acquired had its sole ground and sanction in the consenting use
of the community of which we formed a part." [4] "We do not,
as children, make our language for ourselves. We get it by
tradition, all complete. We think in sentences. As our language forms sentences, that is, as our mother-tongue thinks, so
we learn to think. Our brain, our entire thought-status, forms
itself by the mother-tongue, and we transmit the same to our
children." [5] Nature men have only petty coins of speech. They

---

[1] Whitney, *Language*, 46.   [2] *Ibid.*, 44.   [3] *Ibid.*, 23.   [4] *Ibid.*, 14.
[5] Schultze, *Psychologie der Naturvölker*, 96.

can express nothing great. They cannot compare, analyze, and combine. They are overwhelmed by a flood of details, in which they cannot discern the ruling idea. The material and sensual constitute their limits. If they move they have to get a new language. The American languages are a soft mass which changes easily if tribes separate, or as time goes on, or if they move their habitat.[1] Sometimes measures are adopted in order to make the language unintelligible, as the Bushmen insert a syllable in a word to that end.[2] "The language of nature peoples offers a faithful picture of their mental status. All is in flux. Nothing is fixed or crystallized. No fundamental thoughts, ideas, or ideals are present. There is no regularity, logic, principles, ethics, or moral character. Lack of logic in thinking, lack of purpose in willing or acting, put the mind of a nature man on a plane with that of our children. Lack of memory, antilogic, paradox, fantasy in mental action, correspond to capriciousness, levity, irresponsibility, and the rule of emotions and passions in practical action."[3] "Man's language developed because he could make, not merely passive and mechanical associative and reproductive combinations of notions, like a beast, but because he had active, free, and productive apperceptions, which appear in creative fantasy and logical reflection."[4] "Man does not speak because he thinks. He speaks because the mouth and larynx communicate with the third frontal convolution of the brain. This material connection is the immediate cause of articulate speech."[5] This is true in the sense that speech is not possible until the vocal organs are present, and are duly connected with the brain. "The specific cry, somewhat modified by the vocal resources of man, may have been sufficient for the humble vocabulary of the earliest ages, and there exists no gulf, no impassable barrier, between the language of birds, dogs, anthropoid apes, and human speech."[6] "The warning or summoning cry, the germ of the demonstrative roots, is the parent of the names of number, sex, and distance ; the emotional cry of which

[1] Schultze, 86.
[2] *Ibid.*, 89; *Am Urquell*, II, 22, 48.
[3] Schultze, 91.
[4] *Ibid.*, 99.
[5] Lefevre, *Race and Language*, 3.
[6] *Ibid.*, 27.

our interjections are but the relics, in combination with the
demonstratives, prepares the outlines of the sentence, and already
represents the verb and the names of states or actions. Imitation, direct or symbolical, and necessarily only approximative to
the sounds of external nature, i.e. onomatopœia, furnished the
elements of the attributive roots, from which arose the names
of objects, special verbs, and their derivatives. Analogy and
metaphor complete the vocabulary, applying to the objects, dis-
cerned by touch, sight, smell, and taste, qualifying adjectives
derived from onomatopœia. Reason, then coming into play,
rejects the greater part of this unmanageable wealth, and adopts
a certain number of sounds which have already been reduced
to a vague and generic sense, and by derivation, combination,
and affixes, which are the root sounds, produces those endless families of words, related to each other in every degree
of kindred, from the closest to the most doubtful, which gram-
mar finally ranges in the categories known as the parts of
speech." [1] " That metaphor makes language grow is evident.
It brings about connection between place, time, and sound
ideas." [2]

138. Primitive dialects. The *cebus azarae,* a monkey of Paraguay, makes six distinct sounds when excited, which causes its
comrades to emit similar sounds.[3] The island Caribs have two
distinct vocabularies, one of which is used by men and by women
when speaking to each other, and by men when repeating, in
oratio obliqua, some saying of the women. Their councils of war
are held in a secret jargon into which women are never initiated.[4]
The men and women have separate languages, a custom which
is noted also amongst the Guycurus and other peoples of Brazil.[5]
Amongst the Arawaks the difference between the languages of
the sexes is not in regard to the use of words only, but also
in regard to their inflection.[6] The two languages are sometimes differentiated by a constant change, e.g. where in the
man's language two vowels come together the woman's lan-

---

[1] Lefevre, 42.   [4] JAI, XXIV, 234.
[2] Mauthner, II, 468.   [5] Martius, *Ethnog. Bras.,* 106.
[3] Darwin, *Descent of Man,* 53.   [6] *Ibid.,* 704.

guage intercalates a k.[1] The Arawaks have words which only men may speak, and others which only women may speak.[2] Dialectical variations are illustrated for us by facts which come under observation and report. Christian [3] mentions an American negro castaway, who settled on Raven's Island with a native wife and children and a few relatives and servants. In forty years they had produced " a new and peculiar dialect of their own, broadening the softer vowels and substituting *th* or *f* for the original *t* sound in the parent ponapeian." Martius mentions that native boatmen in Brazil, who had grown up together, had each some little peculiarity of pronunciation. Such a difference would produce a dialect in case of isolation. On the other hand, the ecclesiastics adopted the Tupi language and made it a general language for the province of Gram Para, so that it was used in the pulpit until 1757 and is now necessary for intercourse in the interior.[4] The Gauchos of central Uruguay speak Spanish with harsh rough accents. They change *y* and *ll* into the French *j*.[5] Whitney and Waitz thought that all American languages proceeded from a single original one. Powell thought that they were "many languages, belonging to distinct families, which have no apparent unity of origin."[6] Evidence is adduced, however, that "the same aboriginal peoples who named the waters of North America coined also the prehistoric geographical titles in South America."[7] The Finns and Samoyeds are, from the standpoint of language, practically the same race. The two tongues present the highest development of the agglutinative process of the Ural-Altaic languages.[8]

139. Taking up and dropping languages. The way in which languages are taken up or dropped is also perplexing. Keane [9] gives a list of peoples who have dropped one language and taken up another; he also gives a list of those who have changed physical type but have retained the same language. Holub [10] mentions the Makololo, who have almost entirely disappeared, but

[1] Ehrenreich, *Berl. Mus.* (1891), II, 9.
[2] Schomburgk, *Brit. Guiana*, I, 227.
[3] *Caroline Isl.*, 175.
[4] Spix and Martius, *Brasilien*, 927.
[5] JAI, XI, 41.
[6] *Bur. Ethnol.*, VII, 44.
[7] PSM, XLIV, 81.
[8] JAI, XXIV, 393.
[9] *Ethnology*, 202.
[10] *Sieben Jahre in Süd-Afrika*, II, 173.

their language has passed to their conquerors. It became necessary to the latter from the spread of their dominion and from
their closer intercourse with the peoples south of the Zambesi,
on account of which, "without any intentional interference by
the rulers, a common and easily understood language showed
itself indispensable." Almost every village in New Guinea has
its own language, and it is said that in New Britain people who
live thirty miles apart cannot understand each other.[1]

140. Pigeon dialects. The Germans find themselves at a disadvantage in dealing with aborigines because they have no
dialect like pigeon English or the Coast Malay used by the
Dutch.[2] Many examples are given, from the Baltic region, of
peasant dialects made in sport by subjecting all words to the
same modification.[3] Our own children often do this to English
in order to make a secret language.

141. How languages grow. What we see in these cases is that,
if we suppose men to have joined in coöperative effort with only
the sounds used by apes and monkeys, the requirement of their
interests would push them on to develop languages such as we
now know. The isolating, agglutinative, incorporative, and inflectional languages can be put in a series according to the convenience and correctness of the logical processes which they embody
and teach. The Semitic languages evidently teach a logic different from that of the Indo-European. It is a different way of
thinking which is inculcated in each great family of languages.
They represent stages in the evolution of thought or ways of thinking. The instance is one of those which best show us how folkways are built up and how they are pulled down. The agglutination
of words and forms sometimes seems like a steady building process;
again, the process will not go forward at all. "In the agglutinative languages speech is berry jam. In the inflectional languages
each word is like a soldier in his place with his outfit."[4] The
"gooing" of a baby is a case of the poetic power in its blossoming exuberance. The accidental errors of pronunciation which
are due to very slight individual variations in the form of the

[1] Ratzel, *Völkerkunde*, II, 230.
[2] Krieger, *New Guinea*, 208.
[3] *Am Urquell*, II, 22, 48.
[4] Schultze, *Psychol. d. Naturvölker*, 93.

vocal organs are cases of individual contribution to the development of language. The baby words and individual mispronunciations which are taken up by a family and its friends, but never get further, show us how dialects grow. There are changes in language which are, "in their inception, inaccuracies of speech. They attest the influence of that immense numerical majority among the speakers of English who do not take sufficient pains to speak correctly, but whose blunders become finally the norm of the language."[1] In analogy things which are alike are embraced in a single term; in metaphor two or more things which seem alike, but may not be so, are grouped together and are embraced in a single term. All these modes of change in language attest the work of individuals on language. Sometimes there is extension of influence to a group. Sometimes the influence is only temporary and is rejected again. Sometimes it falls in with a drift of taste or habit, when it is taken up and colors the pronunciation or usage of the population of a great district, and becomes fixed in the language. All this is true also on the negative side, since usage of words, accent, timbre of the voice, and pronunciation (drawling, nasal tones) expel older usages. Language therefore illustrates well all the great changes of folkways under the heads of coöperation and antagonism. We have an excellent chance to study the operation in the case of slang. A people who are prosperous and happy, optimistic and progressive, will produce much slang. It is a case of play. They amuse themselves with the language. We may think the new words and phrases vulgar and in bad taste, or senseless and ridiculous. We may reject them, but the masses will decide whether they shall be permanently rejected or not. The vote is informal. The most confirmed purist will by and by utter a new slang word when he needs it. One's objections are broken down. One's taste is spoiled by what he hears. We are right in the midst of the operation of making folkways and can perceive it close at hand.

142. Money. Money is another primitive device which is produced in the folkways. Money was not called into existence

[1] Whitney, *Language*, 28.

by any need universally experienced and which all tried to satisfy as well as they could. It was produced by developing other devices, due to other motives, until money was reached as a result. Property can be traced to portable objects which were amulets, trophies, and ornaments all at once. These could be accumulated, and if they were thought to be the abodes of powerful spirits, they were gifts which were eagerly sought, or valuable objects for exchange. They led to hoarding (since the owner did not like to part with them), and they served as marks of personal distinction.[1] The interplay of vanity and religion with the love of property demands attention. Religion also caused the aborigines of the northwest provinces of South America to go to the rivers for gold only in sufficient amount to buy what they needed. Any surplus they returned to the stream. "They say that if they borrow more than they really need the river-god will not lend them any more." [2] In later times and higher civilization coins have been used as amulets to ward off or to cure disease.[3] The Greenland Eskimo laughed when they were offered gold and silver coins. They wanted objects of steel, for which they would give anything which they had and which was desired.[4] The Tarahumari of Sonora do not care for silver money. Their Crœsus raises three hundred or four hundred bushels of corn per annum. The largest herd of cattle contains thirty or forty head. They generally prefer cotton cloth to dollars.[5] "A Dyak has no conception of the use of a circulating medium. He may be seen wandering in the Bazaar with a ball of bee's wax in his hand for days together, because he cannot find anybody willing to take it for the exact article which he requires." [6] We meet with a case in which people have gold but live on a system of barter. It is a people in Laos, north of Siam. They weigh gold alone in scales against seeds of grain.[7] In the British

[1] Schurz, *Entstehungsgesch. des Geldes*, *Deutsch. Geogr. Blätter*, XX, 22.
[2] JAI, XIII, 245.
[3] JASB, I, 390.
[4] *Amer. Anthrop.*, IX, 192.
[5] *Scribner's*, September, 1894, 298.
[6] Ling Roth, *Sarawak*, II, 231.
[7] Ridgeway, *Origin of Currency and Weight Standards*, 166.

Museum (Case F, Ireland) may be seen bronze rings, to be sewn on garments as armor or to be used as money, or both. The people along the west coast of Hindostan, from the Persian Gulf to Ceylon, used as money the fishhook which was their most important tool. It became degraded into a piece of doubled wire of silver or bronze. If the degradation had gone on, doubtless it would have resulted in a lump of metal, just as the Siamese silver coins are the result of doubling up silver rings.[1] The play of custom and convention is well shown by the use of the Macedonian coins in England. The coins of Philip bore on the obverse a head with a wreath, and on the reverse a chariot driver drawn by two horses. In Britain this coin became a sign of value and lost its reference to the sovereign. It is possible to show the order of the reigns of the kings by the successive omissions of parts of the figures, until only the wreath was left and four perpendicular strokes and two circles for the legs of one horse and two chariot wheels. Each change was a mark of value and then it was further changed to save trouble.[2] On the Palau Islands there were seven grades of money, determined by the size. Only three or four pieces exist of the first grade. The second grade is of jasper. The third consists of agate cylinders. These three grades are used only by nobles. They have the same rank as gems amongst us. The people think of the money as coming from an island where it lives a divine life, the lower ranks serving the upper. They have myths of the coming of the money to Palau.[3] These examples show to what a great extent other ideas than those of value come into play in money.

143. Intergroup and intragroup money. When money is used to overcome the difficulties of barter two cases are to be distinguished, — the intergroup and the intragroup uses, which are primarily distinguished by a space relation. The intragroup use is here, in the we-group, close at hand. The intergroup use is between our group and some out-group. It will be found that all money problems include these two cases. " At least we shall

[1] Ridgeway, 27.
[2] Evans, *Ancient British Coins.*
[3] Semper, *Palau Ins.*, 61.

find that the current commonplace of the economists about the succession of natural economy, money economy, and credit economy, is not even remotely apt to the real problems." [1] What is true is that, on a money economy, it is found that there is, or may be, a constant exchange of money for goods and goods for money, from which gain or loss may result; and furthermore that the risk (aleatory element) in this exchange is intensified, if time is allowed to intervene. Inside the we-group the first need for money is for fees, fines, amercements, and bride price. In Melanesia pigs are not called money and there is shell, feather, and mat money, but pigs are paid for fines, penalties, contributions to feasts, fees in the secret society, pay for wives, and in other societal relations. What is needed is a mobile form of wealth, with which social dues can be paid. This is the function of money which the paper-money projectors have in mind when they propose to issue paper which the state shall take for taxes. It is evident that it is to be distinguished from the economic function of money as a circulating medium. The intragroup money needs to be especially a measure and store of value, while the intergroup money needs to be a medium of exchange. In the former case barter is easy; in the latter case it is regular. In the former case a multiple standard is available; in the latter case what is needed to discharge balances is a commodity of universal demand. When credit is introduced its sphere is intragroup. The debtors would like the money to be what every one can get. The creditors would like it to be what every one wants.

144. Various predominant wares. In the northeastern horn of Africa the units of value which are used as money are salt, metal, skins, cotton, glass, tobacco, wax, coffee beans, and korarima. Cattle and slaves are also used as units of value from time to time amongst the Oromo. Salt is used as money in prismatic pieces, twenty-two centimeters long and three centimeters to five millimeters broad at the bottom, which weigh from seven hundred and fifty grams to one and one half kilograms each. It is carried in bundles of twenty to thirty pieces, wound

[1] Schurz, 3.

in leaves.[1] The Galla use rods of iron six to twelve centimeters long, somewhat thicker in the middle, well available for lance ends, one hundred and thirty of which are worth one thaler in Schoa; also pieces of copper, tin, and zinc; calf-skins; black, printed, and unprinted cotton cloth; pieces of cloth; coarse red cotton yarn (for knitting); and strings of beads. The universal and intergroup money is the Maria Theresa thaler weighing 571.5 to 576 English grains.[2] Cameron mentions the exchange of intergroup money for intragroup money at a fair at Kawile, on the eastern shore of Lake Tanganyika. At the opening of the fair the money changers gave out the local money of bugle beads, which they took in again when the fair closed.[3] On the French Congo the boatmen were paid with paper bons, which were superseded by metal ones in 1887. When the recipient takes his bon to the station he obtains at first a number of nails, beads, or other articles for it, which he can then exchange for what he wants. Tokens of copper are issued at Franceville, stamped " F," of different shapes and sizes, but always of the same shape and size for the same value in French money.[4] At Grand Bassam in West Africa the manilla (bracelet) serves as money. For six months the natives give oil for these bracelets of metal mixed of copper, lead, zinc, antimony, and iron, which can be closed around the arm or leg of a slave by a blow of the hammer. Then for six months they exchange the bracelets for the European goods which they want.[5] These bracelets were a store of wealth for the black men.[6] The Kru have few cattle, which pass from one to another in bride purchases, since these can be made with nothing else. It is impossible to have wives and cattle too until one's daughters grow up.[7] Since the seventeenth century cylindrical (bugle) green-blue beads have been money on the ivory and gold coasts. They

---

[1] Paulitschke, *Ethnog. N.O. Afrikas*, I, 317; Vannutelli e Citerni, *L'Omo*, 463.
[2] Paulitschke, I, 318, 320.
[3] *Across Africa*, 176.
[4] Zay, *Hist. Monetaire des Colon. Franç.*, 249.
[5] *Ibid.*, 246.
[6] Kingsley, *West African Studies*, 82.
[7] Schurz, *Entstehungsgesch. des Geldes, Deutsch. Geogr. Blätter*, XX, 14.

come from an ancient cemetery on the Bokabo Mountains and
are of Egyptian origin. They were buried with the dead.[1] A
local money of stone is reported also from Avetime in Ehve-
land. It is said to have been used as ornament. Pieces of quartz
and sandstone, rudely square but with broken corners, from
four to five centimeters in diameter and one and a half to two
centimeters thick, rubbed down by friction, have been found.[2]

**145. Intragroup money from property; intergroup money
from trade.** These cases already show us the distinction between
intragroup money and intergroup money. The effect of trade is
to develop one or more predominant wares. In the intragroup
exchanges this is an object of high desire to individuals for use.
It may be an amulet ornament, or a thing of great use in the
struggle for existence, e.g. cattle, or a thing of universal acceptance by which anything can be obtained. In intergroup trade
it is the chief object of export, the thing for which the trade is
carried on, e.g. salt, metal, fur. If this commodity is not easily
divisible, the money is something which can be given "to boot,"
e.g. tobacco, sugar, opium, tea, betel.[3] That is money which will
"pass." This does not mean that which can be forced to pass
("legal tender"), but that which will go without force. Amulet
ornaments may be either a whim which does not take, or fashion
may seize upon something of this kind and make it a tribe mark.
Then it becomes group money, because it is universally desired.
The articles admit of accumulation, and ostentation is a new joy;
they also admit of change and variety. They are available for
gifts to the medicine man (to satisfy ghosts, get rain, or thwart
disease). They may be used to buy a wife, or to buy a step in
the secret society of the men, or to pay a fine or penalty to the
chief. The differentiation of goods starts emotion on the line of
least resistance, and the predominant goods are the ones of
widest demand. Often the predominant ware has a gain from
taboo, probably on account of relation to the dead.[4] A thing

[1] *Anthropologie* (1900), XI, 677, 680.
[2] *Globus*, LXXXI, 12.
[3] Schurz, *Entstehungsgesch. des Geldes*, 38.
[4] *Ibid.*, 25.

which is rare and hard to get may become intragroup money. In Fiji the teeth of the spermaceti whale are taken as a measure of value and sign of peace. In German New Guinea the bent tusks of a boar are used as money. In California red birds' heads are used in the same way. Trophy skulls of birds and beasts become a store of wealth, and money with which trade can be carried on with neighbors.[1] The first step seems to be to use the predominant article as the third term of reference in barter. Intergroup money is really a ware and so remains, as gold is now; but groups widen as communication improves, and group money gets a very wide range. In intergroup affairs, therefore, the relations sooner become impersonal and mechanical. The things which are best for this purpose become mobile. Some are better as stores of value, others as means of power, others as measures of value. The last are on the way to become money. The others are more like gems. Thus group money arose from property; intergroup money from trade.

146. Shell and beads. Shells had very great convenience for money and their value was increased by the fact that ghosts dwelt in them. Cowries were early used as money, 2200 of them equaling in value one franc.[2] They are now losing currency. On Fernando Po bits of achatectonia shells are made into belts and used as currency.[3] A far less widespread shell of a sea snail was used in northern Transvaal.[4] Other cases of the use of shells will be given below. A dress pattern of cotton cloth, seven ells, called a "tobe," is a unit of monetary reference through the Sudan.[5] Another money in the same region is the iron spade, with which tribute is paid to the petty rulers of eastern Equatoria. The spades are made of native iron and are used upon occasion to cut down the grass.[6] Expeditions into the Niam Niam territories always have a smith with them whose duty it is to make rings of copper and iron wire, with a square section, for minor purchases.[7] The currency of beads has greatly lessened wherever more useful objects of European manufacture have become known.[8] Forms of the lance head are used to buy a

---

[1] Schurz, 22.

[2] Foureau, *D'Alger au Congo*, 539.

[3] Kingsley, *Travels in West Africa*, 59.

[4] *Globus*, LXXVIII, 203; *Ibid.*, LXXXII, 243.

[5] Peel, *Somaliland*, 102.

[6] Junker, *Afrika*, III, 52; *Ibid.*, I, 341.

[7] Schweinfurth, *Heart of Africa*, I, 502.

[8] Junker, II, 245; *Ibid.*, I, 295.

wife, who costs twenty or thirty of them.[1] Further south von Götzen found brass wire, in pieces fifteen to thirty-five centimeters long, in use as money, not being an article of use, but a real money used to store value, to buy what is wanted, and to pay taxes for protection against one's forest neighbors.[2] Formerly, when beads were still used as money, each district had its own preferred size, shape, and color. Travelers found that the fashion in a district had changed since the information was obtained, relying on which they had provided themselves. This is, however, evidently a part of the operation of differentiating the predominant ware.[8]

147. Token money. Token money demands treatment by itself, as a special development of the money-producing movement. If different groups adopt different kinds of amulet ornaments as money, such intragroup money may be token money. If one such group conquers another, the conquerors may throw the money of the conquered out of use (whites and Indians as to wampum). In Burma Chinese gambling counters are used as money.[4] Gutta-percha tokens issued by street-car companies in South America are said to be used in the same way. Postage stamps, milk tickets, etc., have been so used by us. In Massachusetts, in the eighteenth century, pieces of paper were circulated which had no redemption whatever. They bore the names of coins of silver which did not exist, but which had a definition in a certain amount of silver of a certain fineness. At Carthage pieces of leather which inclosed an unknown object, probably one of the holy moneys, were circulated.[5] The same is reported of bits of leather cut, like samples, from a skin and circulated in place of it. The device succeeded for the in-group money, but it led to the attempt to put copper tokens in the place of silver coins, which resulted in disaster.[6] The cacao beans of Mexico were wares, if of good quality. Larger ones of poorer quality were money. A part of the value was imaginary. Cloth was formerly money in Bohemia. A loosely woven variety of cloth was used for this purpose, the cloth utilities as a textile fabric and as money being separated. On the west coast of Africa little mats were used as money. They were stamped by the Portuguese government. Mat

---

[1] Junker, I, 415.
[2] von Götzen, *Durch Afr.*, 339.
[8] Schurz, 28; Volkens, *Kilimanjaro*, 221.
[4] Schurz, 17.
[5] Meltzer, *Carthage*, II, 106.
[6] Schurz, 19.

money was also used on the New Hebrides, especially to buy
grades in the great secret society. The mats are long and narrow and are more esteemed when they are old and black from
the smoke of the huts. They are kept in little houses where
they are smoked. "When they hang with soot they are particularly valued." [1] Useless broken rice is used as money in Burma
and elsewhere in the East.[2] The use of token money, in which
a part of the value is imaginary, always implies the inclosure of
a group and the exclusion of foreign trade. Then, within the
group, the value may be said to be real and not imaginary. It
depends on the monopoly law of value and varies with the quantity but not proportionately to the quantity. Kublai-Khan, using
a Chinese device, got possession of all the gold and silver and
issued paper. His empire was so great that all trade was intragroup trade, and his power made his paper money pass.[3] The
Andamanese made inferior pots to be used as a medium in barter.[4] They have very little trade; are on a stage of mutual gift
making.[5] Token money is an aberration of the folkways, due to
misapprehension of the peculiarity of group money. At the same
time it has been used with advantage for subsidiary silver coinage.

148. Selection of a predominant ware. Crawfurd, in his history of the
Indian Archipelago, mentions a number of different articles used there as
money, — cakes of beeswax, salt, gold dust, cattle, and tin.[6] The tin coins
are small irregular laminæ with a hole in the center, 5600 of them being worth
a dollar. Brass coins which come down from the Buddhist sovereigns of Java
are still met with; also other brass coins introduced by the Mohammedan
sovereigns. In the museum at Vienna copper rings, bound into a circle,
inclosed in a fibrous envelope, are another form of money. The selection of
a predominant ware is shown in such cases as the one described in Ling
Roth.[7] When Low was at Kiau, in 1851, beads and brass wire were wanted.
When others were there some years later the people all had their hearts set
on brass wire. The Englishmen "distributed a good deal of cloth, at
reasonable rates, in exchange for food and services rendered." In 1858 they
found that even brass wire, unless of very great size, was despised, and cloth
was eagerly desired.

[1] Codrington, *Melanesians*, 323.
[2] *Amer. Anthrop.*, XI, 285.
[3] Marco Polo, II, 18.
[4] JAI, XII, 373.
[5] *Ibid.*, 339.
[6] *Indian Archipelago*, 280.
[7] *Sarawak*, II, 234.

One thing which helped the selection of a predominant ware was that only a specified article would make peace, atone for a wrong, compose a quarrel, or ransom a captive. Also various articles obtained such prestige, on account of age and the glory of ancestors, that the possession of them conferred authority and social importance on their owners. Such are porcelain jars in Borneo, bronze drums in Burma, bronze cannon in the East-Indian Archipelago. Many African chiefs stored up ivory tusks for social prestige long before the white men came and gave them value in world commerce.[1]

149. Stone money in Melanesia. We must, however, turn our attention to Melanesia where the shell and stone money have been pushed to a most remarkable development, quite out of line with the rest of the Melanesian civilization. On the Solomon Islands there are some petty reef communities which occupy themselves solely with fishing and making shell-bead money.[2] On New Britain divarra is made by boring and stringing fathoms of shell money. A fathom is worth two shillings sterling, and two hundred and fifty fathoms coiled up together looks like a life buoy.[3] In the northwestern Solomon Islands the currency consists of beasts' teeth of two kinds, — those of a kind of flying dog and of a kind of dolphin. Each tooth is bored at the root and they are strung on thin cords. These people also use the small disks of shell, five millimeters in diameter and from one to one and a half millimeters thick.[4] The shell money of New Britain has very great influence on the lives of the people. It minimizes the evil and fatality of war, in which every life and every wound must be paid for. It establishes the right of property. It makes the people frugal and industrious, and makes them a commercial people. To it may also be attributed their selfishness and ingratitude. " Its influence is supposed to extend even to the next life. There is not a custom connected with life or death in which this money does not play a great and leading part. . . . Take away their money and their secret societies sink at once into nothing, and most of their customs become nothing."[5] Evidently the missionary testifies that the money stimulates commercialism with all its good and ill. Coils of feathers which are spoken of as money are also reported from the New Hebrides and Santa Cruz. Feathers are attached with resin to the outside of coils, inside of which are charms, each possessing a protective property. This money is very rare and, if shown, may be handled only by the owner.[6] Our information as to the commercial uses and effects of these island shell moneys is very imperfect. The money seems to be still on the stage of gems. It is used to buy steps of rank in the secret society, which cost pigs and money and mark social importance, which is, like

[1] Schurz, 13.
[2] Woodford, *Naturalist amongst Head-Hunters*, 16.
[3] Cayley-Webster, *New Guinea and Cannibal Countries*, 93.
[4] Parkinson, *Ethnog. d. Nordwestl. Salomo Ins.*, 22.
[5] JAI, XVII, 314, 316.
[6] JAI, XXVIII. 164.

other forms of force, regarded as supernatural. Rank can be gained only by the consent of those who already have it.[1]

150. Plutocratic effects of money. It must not be understood that the money, on the barbaric stage, enters into the struggle for existence, at least for food. There is only slight organization of labor. Each one produces what he needs. There is little luxury. "Nevertheless, money plays the chief rôle in the life of the people. The man, regarded as an animal, has enough to do to support life. If he wants a wife, wants to found a family, wants to be a member of the state, he must have money."[2] It is evident that the circulation of this money must produce phenomena which are unfamiliar to us.

The estimate placed by the Solomon Islanders on great stones of aragonite, obtained in the southern Palau islands, is such that they incur great risks in going to get them in their frail boats.[3] The pieces have the appearance of our own grindstones. They are set in rows by the men's clubhouses, and are in care of the chiefs. Christian mentions two of the Big Houses on Yap with stone money piled against the foundations. One piece was twelve feet in diameter and one and a half feet thick, and had a hole in the center two and a half feet in diameter.[4] A certain Captain O'Keefe, in 1882, fitted out a Chinese vessel and brought thousands of pieces of money from Palau to Yap. He brought the whole island in debt to himself. Nowadays they want big stones. Such six feet in diameter are not rare. This kind of money is the money of the men; that of the women is of mussel shells strung on strings. The exchange of a big piece for smaller kinds of money involves considerations of rank. Two of equal rank, and well disposed, exchange by dignity; if one is inferior, the good will of the other is requisite. The glass and porcelain money on Yap must have come from China or Japan. It has controlled the social development of the islands. It is also noticeable that other things of high utility, e.g. the wooden vessels in which yellow powder is prepared, or in which food is set forth at feasts, are made the objects of exchange, and, at the making of peace after a fight, or at other negotiations, affect the relations of tribes.[5] At the present time bags of dried cocoanut are employed as a medium of exchange, probably in intergroup trade.[6] What Kubary[7] says about the use of the money shows that it has no proper circulation. It accumulates in the

[1] JAI, X, 287.
[2] Kubary, *Karolinenarchipel.*, 2.
[3] Semper, *Palau Inseln*, 167.
[4] *Caroline Isl.*, 259.
[5] Kubary, *Karolinenarchipel.*
[6] Christian, *Caroline Isl.*, 237.
[7] *Die Soc. Einrichtungen d. Pelauer.*

hands of the great men, since it is used to pay fees, fines, gifts, tribute, etc. The armengol women, marriages, and public festivals start it out again, and on its way back it performs many social services. It is also reasonable to suppose that, having got a footing on these islands, it spread to others by social contagion. This explains the presence of a general medium of exchange amongst people who are otherwise barely out of the stone age.[1] The tales about the crimes which have been connected with the history of great pieces of the aragonite stone [2] remind us of the stories about the greatest diamonds yet found.

151. Money in northwestern North America. In South America nothing served the purposes of money. There was none in Peru. Metal, if they had any, was used by all for ornament.[3] Martius, however, says of the Mauhes that they used seeds of *paullinia sorbilis* as money. They obtained from the seeds a remedy for skin disease and diarrhœa.[4] The Nishinam of California had two kinds of shell money, ullo and hawok. The former consists of pieces, one or two inches long and one third of that in width, strung on a fiber. The pieces of shell take a high polish and make a fine necklace. The hawok is small money by comparison. A string of the large kind was worth ten dollars. It consisted of ten pieces. A string of one hundred and seventy-seven pieces of the small kind sold for seven dollars. In early days every Indian in California had, on an average, one hundred dollars' worth of the shell money, the value of two women (although they did not buy wives) or three average ponies.[5] The Hupa of California will not sell to an American the flakes of jasper or obsidian which they parade at their dances. They are not knives, but jewelry and money amongst themselves. Nearly every man has ten lines tattooed across the inside of his left arm. A string of five shells is the standard unit. It is drawn over the left thumb nail. If it reaches the uppermost tattooed line it is worth five dollars per shell.[6] They also grind down pieces of stone which looks like meershaum into cylinders one to three inches long, which they wear as jewelry and use as money.[7] The Eskimo of Alaska used skins as money. Here the effect of intergroup trade has been to change the skin which was taken as the unit. It is now the beaver. Other skins are rated as multiples or submultiples of this.[8] In Washington Territory dentalium and abelone shells were the money, also slaves, skins, and blankets, until the closer contact with whites produced changes.[9] The Karok use as money the red scalps of woodpeckers which are rated at from $2.50 to $5.00 each, and also dentalium shells of which they grind off the tip. The shortest pieces are worth twenty-five cents, the longest about two dollars. The strings are generally about the

[1] Pfeil, *Aus der Südsee*, 112.
[2] Semper, *Palau Ins.*, 118.
[3] Martius, *Ethnog. Brasil.*, 91.
[4] *Ibid.*, 402.
[5] Powers, *Calif. Indians*, 335.

[6] *Ibid.*, 76, 79.
[7] *Smithson. Rep.*, 1886, Part I, 232.
[8] *Bur. Eth.*, XVIII, Part I, 232.
[9] *Smithson. Rep.*, 1887, Part I, 647.

length of a man's arm. They were worth forty or fifty dollars a string, but have fallen in value, especially amongst the young.[1] The copper plates which are so highly valued on the northwestern coast may be esteemed holy on account of the ring in them. Slaves are killed and their flesh is used as bait in catching the dentalium snails, perhaps in order to get a mystic idea into the shells of the snails.[2]

152. Wampumpeag and roanoke. On the Atlantic coast shell money was made on Long Island Sound and at Narragansett from the shell of the round clam, in two colors, white and purple, the latter from the dark spot in the shell. These were bugles, the hole running in the thickness of the shell. They were called wampumpeag, were sewed on deer or other fine skins, and the belts thus made·were used to emphasize points in negotiation or in treaties, or in speeches. Farther down the coast beads were made like flat button molds, with holes bored through them perpendicularly to the plane of the shell, and called roanoke. These beads, of both kinds, but especially of the former kind, spread by exchange into the Mississippi Valley, and in the middle of the nineteenth century they had reached the upper waters of the Missouri River.

153. Ring money; use of metal. The standpoint of the Vedic hymns is that the cow is the real measure of value, but metal, especially gold, is used for money in the payment of penalties and weregild. The objects at stake in formulæ of oaths and of duels were estimated in gold.[3] There was therefore a pure gold currency. In ancient India, however, silver and copper were also used and locally some coins of lead and mixed metals occurred. In value one of gold equaled ten of silver, and one of silver forty of copper.[4] The most ancient money of China consisted of shells,[5] also of knives and dress patterns of silk.[6] The knives had rings at the end of the handle and were gradually reduced to rings of metal as money.[7] The same ancient king who established measures of length and capacity is the legendary author of money (2697 B.C.). He fixed the five objects of exchange, — beads, jade, gold, knives, textiles. The sign for money was combined of the signs for "shell" and "to exchange."[8] We hear that the Chinese emperor, 119 B.C., gave to his vassals squares of white deerskin, about one foot on a side, embroidered on the hem. He who had one of these could get an audience of the emperor.[9] We are inclined to connect with that usage the use of a scarf of bluish-white silk in central Asia, which was used in all greetings and ceremonies. A certain quality of this scarf was used in places as the unit of value.[10] Przewalsky mentions the chadak

[1] Powers, 21.
[2] Schurz, 25.
[3] Jolly, *Recht und Sitte*, 96.
[4] JASB, II, 214.
[5] Ridgeway, 21.
[6] Vissering, *Chinese Currency*.
[7] Ridgeway, 156.
[8] Puini, *Le Origine della Civiltà*, 64; *Century Dict.*, s.v. "Knife-money."
[9] Vissering, *Chinese Currency*, 38.
[10] *U. S. Nat. Mus.*, 1893, 723.

which is given to every guest in southern Mongolia, for which another must be given in return. In Chalcha chadaks are used as money, not as gifts.[1] An intragroup money of copper or brass rings is also reported from Korintji on Sumatra. They are cast of three sizes, so that one hundred and twenty, three hundred and sixty, and four hundred and eighty are required to equal a Dutch gulden.[2] In the Old Testament the bride price and penalties were to be paid in money.[3] Gifts and fees to the sanctuary were to be paid in kind.[4] If the sacrificer wished to redeem his animal, etc., he must pay twenty per cent more than the priest's assessment of it.[5] Until the Exile the precious metals were paid by weight.[6] The rings represented on the Egyptian monuments were of wire with a round section. Those found by Schliemann at Mykenæ are similar, or they are spirals of wire.[7] In Homer cattle are the unit of value, but metals are used as media. The talent is mentioned only in reference to gold.[8] Possibly Schurz is right in supposing that fluctuations in the value of cattle and sheep forced the classical nations to use metal.[9] The metals were in the shape of caldrons or tripods, in which fines were imposed. They may have been accumulated because used as money, or a great man who had many clients may have needed many for meals.[10] "The transition from the old simple mode of exchange to the use of currency can nowhere be better traced than amongst the Romans." Fines were set in cattle or sheep, but copper was used as well, weighed when sold. Then the state set the shape and fineness of the bars and stamped them with the mark of a sheep or ox. Later the copper was marked to indicate its value, and so money was reached.[11] Amongst Germans and Scandinavians the cow was the primitive unit of value.[12] It was superseded by metals used in rings to make out the fractions.[13]

154. The evolution of money. It is evident that money was developed out of trade by instinctive operations of interest, and that money existed long before the idea of it was formed. The separate operations were stimulated only by the most immediate

[1] *First Journey* (Germ.), 61.
[2] *Globus*, LXXVI, 372.
[3] Exod. xxii. 16; xxi. 36.
[4] Deut. xiv. 24.
[5] Levit. xxvii. 13, 15, 19.
[6] Buhl, *Soc. Verhält. der Isr.*, 95.
[7] Ridgeway, *Origin of Currency and Weight Standards*, 36.
[8] Ridgeway, 3.
[9] Schurz, 15.
[10] Babelon, *Origines de la Monnaie*, 72.
[11] Schrader, *Prehist. Antiq. of Aryans*, 153; Ridgeway, 31.
[12] Weinhold, *D. F.*, II, 52.
[13] Geijer, *Sveriges Historie*, I, 327; Sophus Müller, *Vor Oldtid*, 409.

and superficial desires, but they set supply and demand in motion and produced economic value thousands of years before any man conceived of value. The rational analysis of value and money is not yet satisfactorily made. There are, therefore, points of view in which money is the most marvelous product of the folkways. The unconsciousness of the operation and the secondary results of it are here in the strongest contrast. Inside of the we-group useful property was shared or exchanged in an infinite variety of ways, according to variations of circumstances. We cannot follow the customs which thence arose, because the phenomena have been reported to us without distinction between intragroup and intergroup transactions. We see groups of predominant wares set out in intergroup trade, and only slowly is a smaller number segregated to be the general terms of every trade. The inconvenience of barter was only slowly felt, and could not have been a motive until trade was customary and familiar. In intragroup exchanges the predominant ware was more easily differentiated. It was the thing greatly desired. Here the amulet-trophy-ornament was important for the elements of superstition, vanity, and magic which it bore. In intergroup trade the utility of the object predominated. It was sought in journeys only for its utility, and in that trade the transactions first became impersonal. In the selection of leading wares individuals could not experiment for their own risk. By taking what each wanted at a time selection at last resulted, and when we are told that a certain group uses this or that group of articles for money, we are told only what articles predominate in their desires or transactions; in other words, what stage in the selection of a money they have reached. It is evident that this entire operation was an impersonal and unregulated play of custom, which went through a long and varying evolution, but kept its authority all the time and at every stage. The persistence of the word "shilling" in our language is a striking proof of the power of custom — above all, popular custom — in connection with money. The metric system was invented to be a rational system, but the populace has insisted on dividing kilograms and liters into halves and quarters. Language, money, and weights

and measures are things which show the power of popular custom more than any others. The selection of predominant wares
reached its acme in the selection of *one*, not necessarily the commodity most desired, but, after the function of money is perceived, the one which performs it best. To return and take up
a greater number is to go backward on the path of civilization.

155. The ethical functions of money. From shells to gold the
ethics of social relations has clung to money. There is more pure
plutocracy in Melanesia than in New York. The differentiation
of men by wealth is greatly aided by money, because money adds
immensely to the mobility of wealth and lets all forces reach
their full effect in transactions. The social effect of debt is best
seen in barbarous societies which have money. Debt and war
together made slavery.[1] It is, however, an entire mistake to
regard a money-system as in itself a mischief-working system.
The effect of money is exhausted when we notice that it makes
wealth mobile and lets forces work out their full result by
removing friction. So soon as there is a money there is a
chance for exchanges of money for goods and goods for money,
also for the loan and repayment of money at different times,
under which transactions interests may change and speculation
can arise. These facts have always interested the ethical philosophers. " Naught hath grown current amongst mankind so
mischievous as money. This brings cities to their fall. This
drives men homeless, and moves honest minds to base contrivings.
This hath taught mankind the use of villainies, and how to give
an impious turn to every kind of act." [2] In such diatribes
" money " stands for wealth in general. Money, properly speaking, has no more character than axes of stone, bronze, iron, or
steel. It only does its own work impersonally and mechanically.
The ethical functions and character ascribed to it are entirely
false. There can be no such thing as " tainted money." Money
bears no taint. It serves the murderer and the saint with equal
indifference. It is a tool. It can be used one day for a crime,
the next day for the most beneficent purpose. No use leaves

---

[1] See Chapter VI.
[2] Sophokles, *Antigone*, 292 (Campbell's trans.).

any mark on it. The Solomon Islanders are expert merchants and "are fully the equal of white men in cheating." [1] They do it with shell money as whites do it with gold, silver, and banknotes. That is to say, the "money" is indifferent because it has no ethical function at all and absolutely no character.

156. There are other topics which might be brought under the struggle for existence as a cluster of folkways, with great advantage. The struggle for existence takes on many different forms and produces phenomena which are cases of folkways. It speedily develops industrial organization, which, in one point of view, is only the interaction of folkways. Weights and measures, the measurement of time, the communication of intelligence, and trade are primary folkways in their earliest forms and deserve careful study as such.

[1] JAI, XXVI, 405.

CHAPTER IV

LABOR, WEALTH

Introduction. — Notions of labor. — Classical and mediæval notions. — Labor has always existed. — Modern view of labor. — Movable capital in modern society; conditions of equality; present temporary status of the demand for men. — Effect of the facility of winning wealth. — Chances of acquiring wealth in modern times; effect on modern mores; speculation involved in any change. — Mores conform to changes in life conditions; great principles; their value and fate. — The French revolution. — Ruling classes; special privileges; corruption of the mores. — The standard of living.

157. The topics treated in Chapter III — tools, language, and money — belong almost entirely in the folkways. The element of esteem for tools is sometimes very great. They are made divine and receive worship. Nevertheless, there is little reflection stimulated to produce a sense of their importance to welfare. Therefore the moral element pertaining to the mores is not prominent in them. When the moral element exists at all in regard to tools, language, or money, it is independent and rises to the conception of prosperity, its sense and conditions. There are notions at all stages of civilization about productive labor and wealth, as parts of the fate of man on earth and of the conditions of his happiness and welfare. At this point they take the character of a philosophy, and are turned back on the work, as regulative notions of how, and how much, to work. The mores of the struggle for existence are in those notions. From the time when men had any accumulated wealth they seem to have been struck by its effect on the character of the possessor. The creature seemed to be stronger than the creator. Here ethical reflections began. They have been more actively produced since it has been possible for men to acquire wealth in a lifetime by their own efforts. Envy has been awakened, and has been gratified by theoretical discussions of the power, rights, and duties of wealth. When wealth was due to the possession of land or to the possession of rank and political power, the facts about its distribution seemed to be like the differences in health, strength, beauty, etc. It now appears that the ethics of poverty are as well worth studying as those of wealth, and that, in short, every man's case brings its own ethics, or that there are no ethics at all in the matter. The ideas, however, which are current in the society at the time are conditions for the individual, and they are a part of the mores of the environment in which the struggle for existence must be carried on.

158. Notions of labor. Nature peoples generally regard productive labor as the business of women, unworthy of men. The Jews believed in a God who worked six days and rested on the seventh. He differed from the Olympian gods of Greece, who were revelers, and from Buddha who tried to do nothing, or from Brahma who was only Thought. The Sabbath of rest implied other days of labor. In the book of Proverbs idleness is denounced as the cause of poverty and want.[1] Many passages are cited from the rabbinical literature in honor of productive labor and in disapproval of idleness.[2] In Book II, Chapter 62, of the Apostolic Constitutions, the basis of which is a Jewish work, it is taught that gainful occupations should be incidental and that the worship of God should be the main work of life. Hellenic shows and theaters are to be avoided. To this the Christian editor added heathen shows and sports of any kind. Young men ought to work to earn their own support. The Zoroastrian religion was a developed form of the strife between good forces and evil forces. The good men must enlist on the side of the good forces. This religion especially approved all the economic virtues, and productive efforts, like the clearing of waste land, or other labor to increase favorable conditions and to overcome harmful or obstructive influences, were religious, and were counted as help to the good forces.

[1] Prov. xxiv. 30.
[2] *Jewish Encyc.*, s.v. " Labor." The same view is found in 2 Thess. iii. 10, and Eph. iv. 28.

159. Classical and mediæval notions of labor. The Greeks and Romans regarded all labor for gain as degrading. The Greeks seem to have reached this opinion through a great esteem for intellectual pursuits, which they thought means of cultivation. The gainful occupations, or any occupations pursued for gain, were " banausic," which meant that they had an effect opposite to that of cultivation. The Romans seem to have adopted the Greek view, but they were prepared for it by militarism. The Middle Ages got the notion of labor from the Roman tradition. They mixed this with the biblical view. Labor was a necessity, as a consequence and penalty of sin, and directly connected, as a curse, with the " Fall." It was correlative to a curse on the ground, by which, also as a curse for sin, it was made hard to win subsistence by agriculture. The mediæval philosophers, being clerics, held a life of contemplation to be far superior to one of labor or fighting. Labor was at best an evil necessity, a hardship, a symptom of the case of man, alienated from God and toiling to get back, if there was a way to get back, to the kingdom of God. The church offered a way to get back, namely, by sacraments, devotion, ritual, etc., that is, by a technically religious life, which could be lived successfully only if practiced exclusively. It occupied all the time of the " religious," technically so called. Labor was used for penance and for ascetic purposes. Often it was employed for useful results and with beneficial effect on useful arts. The purpose, however, was to ward off the vices of leisure. The ascetic temper and taste made labor sweet, so long as asceticism ruled the mores of the age.[1] Labor for economic production was not appreciated by the church. The production of wealth was not a religious purpose. It was even discouraged, since disapproval of wealth and luxury was one of the deep controlling principles of mediæval Christianity. The unreality of mediæval world philosophy appeared most distinctly in the views of marriage and labor, the two chief interests of everyday life. Marriage was a concession, a compromise with human weakness. There was something better, viz. celibacy. Labor was a base necessity. Contemplation was better.

[1] Thomas Aquinas, *Summa*, II, 2, qu. 82, 1, 2; qu. 187, 3.

160. Labor has always existed. Wealth became possible. Land.
In all these cases the view of labor was dogmatic. It was
enjoined by religion. There was some sense and truth in each
view, but each was incomplete. The pursuit of gainful effort is
as old as the existence of man on earth. The development of
trade and transportation, slavery, political security, and the invention of money and credit are steps in it which have made possible
large operations, great gains, and wealth. Some men have
seized these chances and have made a powerful class. Rulers,
chiefs, and medicine men have observed this power which might
either enhance or supplant their own, and have sought to win it.
In all primitive agricultural societies land is the only possession
which can yield a large annual revenue for comfort and power.
The mediæval people of all classes got as much of it as they
could. It would be very difficult indeed to mention any time
when there were no rich men, and still harder to mention a time
when the power of wealth was not admired and envied, and given
its sway (sec. 150). Thus the religions and philosophies may have
preached various doctrines about wealth, and may have found
obedience, but the production of wealth, the love of wealth, and
the power of wealth have run through all human history. The
religions and philosophies have not lacked their effect, but they
have always had to compromise with facts, just as we see them
do to-day. The compromise has been in the mores. In so far as
it was imperfect and only partly effected there have been contradictions in the mores. Such was the case in the Middle Ages.
Wealth had great power. It at last won the day. In the fifteenth
century all wanted it, and were ready to do anything to get it.
Venality became the leading trait of the mores of the age. It
affected the interpretation of the traditional doctrines of labor,
wealth, the highest good, and of virtue, so that men of high purpose and honest hearts were carried away while professing disregard of wealth and luxury.

161. Modern view of labor. It is only in the most recent
times, and imperfectly as yet, that labor has been recognized as
a blessing, or, at worst, as a necessity which has great moral
and social compensations, and which, if rightly understood and

wisely used, brings joy and satisfaction. This can only be true, however, when labor is crowned by achievement, and that is when it is productive of wealth. Labor for the sake of labor is sport. It has its limits, and lies outside of the struggle for existence, which is real, and is not play. Labor in the struggle for existence is irksome and painful, and is never happy or reasonably attractive except when it produces results. To glorify labor and decry wealth is to multiply absurdities. The modern man is set in a new dilemma. The father labors, wins, and saves that his son may have wealth and leisure. Only too often the son finds his inheritance a curse. Where is the error ? Shall the fathers renounce their labors ?

162. Movable capital in modern society. Conditions of equality. Present temporary status of the demand for men. In modern times movable capital has been immensely developed and even fixed capital has been made mobile by the joint-stock device. It has disputed and largely defeated the social power of land property. It has become the social power. While land owners possessed the great social advantage, they could form a class of hereditary nobles. The nobles now disappear because their social advantage is gone. The modern financiers, masters of industry, merchants, and transporters now hold control of movable capital. They hold social and political power. They have not yet formed a caste of nobles, but they may do so. They may, by intermarriages, absorb the remnants of the old nobility and limit their marriages further to their own set. It is thus that classes form and reform, as new groups in the society get possession of new elements of social power, because power produces results. The dogmas of philosophers deal with what ought to be. What is and shall be is determined by the forces at work. No forces appear which make men equal. Temporary conditions occur under which no forces are at work which any one can seize upon. Then no superiority tells, and all are approximately equal. Such conditions exist in a new colony or state, or whenever the ratio of population to land is small. If we take into account the reflex effect of the new countries on Europe, it is easy to see that the whole civilized world has been under these conditions for the last two hundred or three hundred years. The effect of the creation of an immense stock of movable capital, of the opportunities in commerce and industry offered to men of talent, of the immense aid of science to industry, of the opening of new continents and the peopling of them by the poorest and worst in Europe, has been to produce modern mores. All our popular faiths, hopes, enjoyments, and powers are due to these great changes in the conditions of life. The new status makes us believe in all kinds of rosy doctrines about human welfare, and about the struggle for existence and the competition of life ; it also gives us all our contempt for old-fashioned kings and nobles, creates democracies, and brings forth new social classes and gives them power. For the time being things are so turned about that numbers are a source of power. Men are in demand, and an increase in their number increases their value. Why then should we not join in dithyrambic oratory, and set all our mores to optimism ? The reason is because the existing status is temporary and the conditions in it are evanescent. That men should be in demand on the earth is a temporary and passing status of the conjuncture which makes things now true which in a wider view are delusive. These facts, however, will not arrest the optimism, the self-confidence, the joy in life, and the eagerness for the future, of the masses of to-day.

163. Effect of the facility of winning wealth. All the changes in conditions of life in the last four hundred years have refashioned the mores and given modern society new ideas, standards, codes, philosophies, and religions. Nothing acts more directly on the mores than the facility with which great numbers of people can accumulate wealth by industry. If it is difficult to do so, classes become fixed and stable. Then there will be an old and stiff aristocracy which will tolerate no upstarts, and other classes will settle into established gradations of dependence. The old Russian boyars were an example of such an aristocracy. Certain mediæval cities ran into this form. In it the mores of conservatism are developed, -- unchangeable manners, fixed usages and ideas, unenlightenment, refusal of new ideas, subserviency of the lower classes, and sycophancy. The government is suspicious and cruel. If it is easily possible to gain wealth, a class of upstart rich men arises who, in a few years, must be recognized by the aristocracy, because they possess financial power and are needed. Struggles and civil wars may occur, as in the Italian cities, during this change, and the old aristocracy may long hold aloof from the new. In time, the new men win their way. The history of every state in Europe proves it. Old fortunes decay and old families die out. The result is inevitable. Laws and institutions cannot prevent it. Certain mores may have been recognized as aristocratic and there may be lamentations over their decline. They are poetic, romantic, and adventurous. Therefore they call out regret for their loss from those who do not think what would come back with them if they were recalled. Ethical philosophers may see ample reason to doubt the benefit of new mores and the vulgarization of everything. Society cannot stand still, and its movement will run the course set by the forces which produce it. It must be accepted and profit must be drawn from it, as best possible.

164. Chances of acquiring wealth in modern times; effect on modern mores; speculation involved in any change. The effect of the opening of new continents, the application of new inventions, and the expansion of commerce has been to make it easy for men with suitable talent to increase wealth. These changes have cheapened all luxuries, that is, have reduced them to common necessities. They have made land easily accessible to all, even the poorest, in the new countries, while lowering rent in old countries. They have raised wages and raised the standard of living and comfort. They have lessened the competition of life throughout civilized nations, and have made the struggle for existence far less severe. It is the changes in life conditions which have made slavery impossible and extended humanitarian sympathy. They have lessened social differentiation (that is, they have democratized), and they have intensified the industrial organization. In detail, and for individuals, this has often caused hardship. For the petty professional and semiprofessional classes it has been made harder to keep up the externals of a certain social position. For those classes the standard of living has risen faster than steam has cheapened luxuries. Discontent, anxiety, care for appearances, desire to impose by display, envy, and mean social ambition characterize the mores, together with energy and enterprise. Envy and discontent are amongst the very strongest traits of modern society. Very often they are only manifestations of irritated vanity. It is in the nature of things that classes of men and forms of property shall go through endless vicissitudes of advantage and disadvantage. Nobody can foresee these and speculate upon them with success. When it is proposed to "reorganize society" on any socialistic theory, or on no theory, it should be noticed that such an enterprise involves a blind speculation on the vicissitudes of classes and forms of property in the future. "Wealth, whether in land or money, has been increased by marriages and inheritances, reduced to fragments by divisions, even in noble families [in spite of settlements and entails], dissipated by prodigals, reconstituted by men of economical habits, centupled by industrious and competent men of enterprise, scattered by the indolent, the unfortunate, and the men of bad judgment, who have risked it unwisely. Political events have affected it as well as the favor of princes, advantageous offices in the state, popular revolts, wars, confiscations, from the abolition of serfdom in the fourteenth century until the abolition, in 1790, of the dues known as feudal, although they were, for the most part, owned by members of the bourgeoisie."[1] So it will be in the future, in spite of all that men can do. If two men had the same sum of money in 1200, and one bought land while the other became a money lender, anywhere in western Europe, the former would to-day be more or less rich according to the position of his land. He might be a great millionaire. The other would have scarcely anything left.[2] Shall we then all buy land now? Let those do so who can foresee the course of values in the next seven hundred years. The popular notion is that nobles have always owned land. The truth is that men who have acquired wealth have bought land and got themselves ennobled. In France, "in the seventeenth and eighteenth centuries, nineteen twentieths of those who were

[1] D'Avenel. *Hist. Econ.*, 142.   [2] D'Avenel, 397.

called nobles were middle-class men enriched, decorated, and possessed of land."[1] The middle class in western Europe has been formed out of the labor class within seven hundred years. The whole middle class, therefore, represents the successful rise of the serfs, but, since a labor class still remains, it is asserted that there has been no change. On the other hand, there has been a movement of nobles and middle-class grandees downward into the labor class and the proletariat. It was said, a few years ago, that a Plantagenet was a butcher in a suburb of London. It is also asserted that representatives of great mediæval families are now to be found as small farmers, farm laborers, or tramps in modern England.[2]

165. Mores conform to changes in life conditions; great principles; their value and fate. For our purpose it suffices here to notice how the mores have followed the changes in life conditions, how they have reacted on the current faiths and philosophies, and how they have produced ethical notions to justify the mores themselves. They have produced notions of natural rights and of political philosophy to support the new institutions. There are thousands in the United States who believe that every adult male has a natural right to vote, and that the vote makes the citizen. The doctrine of natural rights has received some judicial recognition, and it has been more or less accepted and applied in the constitutions of various states which were established in the nineteenth century. The American doctrines of 1776 and the French doctrines of 1789 are carried on and used in stump oratory until they get in the way of some new popular purpose, but what produced both was the fact that some new classes had won wealth and economic power and they wanted political recognition. To get it they had to invent some new " great principles " to justify their revolt against tradition. That is the way in which all " great principles " are produced. They are always made for an exigency. Their usefulness passes with the occasion. The mores are forever adjusting efforts to circumstances. Sooner or later they need new great principles. Then

---

[1] D'Avenel, 144.
[2] Hardy used this fact in *Tess of the D'Urbervilles*.

they obliterate the old ones. The old jingle of words no longer wins a response. The doctrine is dead. In 1776 it seemed to every Whig in America that it was a pure axiom to say that governments derive their just powers from the consent of the governed. They clung to this as a sacred dogma for over a hundred years, because it did not affect unfavorably any interest. It is untrue. Governments get their powers from the historical fact of their existence. They are all ephemeral, subject to change. When a change takes place it is controlled by the ideas and interests of the time of change, when the popular element in self-government may be much greater than when the constitution was last previously established. In 1898 the popular will, in the United States, was to take possession of the Philippine Islands and to become rulers there, not ruled, as the fathers were in the colonies of 1776. The great doctrine of tne source of due power was quickly trampled under foot. The same fate awaits all the rest of the " great principles." The doctrine that all men are equal is being gradually dropped, from its inherent absurdity, and we may at any time find it expedient to drop the jingle about a government of the people, by the people, and for the people. It was only good historically to destroy the doctrine, " Everything for the people ; nothing by them."

166. The French Revolution. The French Revolution was due to the fact that a great change had come about in the distribution of economic power between classes and in the class mores which correspond to economic power. All the political institutions of a modern state are conservative in the sense that they retain and sustain what is and has been, and resist interference or change. The historical picture is often such that abuses are maintained and reform seems hopeless, on account of the power of existing institutions and customs and the depth of convictions of social welfare which have become traditional. The student of the history is led to believe that any reform or revolution, as a dissolution of the inherited system of repression and retention, is worth all that it may cost. Hence some students of history become believers in " revolution " as a beneficent social force or engine. In the case of the French Revolution, the passions which were set loose destroyed the whole social order, swept away all the institutions, and even destroyed all the inherited mores. It is evident that this last is what the revolutionists finally aimed at. The *ancien régime* came to mean the whole fabric of the old society, with its codes, standards, and ideas of right, wrong, the desirable, etc. The revolutionists also undertook to invent new mores, that is, new codes and standards, new conceptions of things socially desirable, a new religion, and new notions of civil duty and responsibility. During the Directory and the Consulate there was a gulf between the ancient and the new in which there was anarchy of the mores, even after the civil machinery was repaired and set in operation again. Napoleon brought back institutions and forms of social order so far as seemed desirable for his own interest. The historical continuity was broken and has remained so. Of the *ancien régime* there can be found to-day only ruins and relics. Nevertheless, the ancient mores of social faith and morality, of social well living, of religious duty and family virtue, are substantially what they were before the great explosion. This is the last and greatest lesson of the revolution : it is impossible to abolish the mores and to replace them by new ones rationally invented. To change a monarchy into a republic is trifling. Individuals and classes can be guillotined. Institutions can be overturned. Religion can be abolished or put out of fashion. The mores are in the habits of the people, and are needed and practiced every day. The revolutionists ordered changes in the social ritual, and they brought about a disuse of " monsieur " and " madame." All their innovations in the ritual have fallen into disuse, and the old fashions have returned, in obedience to common sense. The new classes have not enjoyed their victory over the old as to courtesy, social comity, and civil good-fellowship. They have abandoned it, and have recognized the fact that the old aristocracy had well solved all matters of this kind. As wealth has increased and artisans and peasants have gained new powers of production and acquisition, they have learned to laugh at the civil philosophy and enthusiasm of the eighteenth-century philosophers, and have ordered their lives, as far as possible or convenient, on the old aristocratic models. Sans-culottism is inconsistent with respect for productive labor, or with the accumulation of wealth. No one who can earn great wages or who possesses wealth will, out of zeal for philosophical doctrines, prefer to live in squalor and want. The relation of modern mores to new feelings in respect to labor and trade, and to the accumulation of wealth, are to be easily perceived from the course of modern revolutions.

167. Ruling classes. Special privileges. Corruption of the mores. In every societal system or order there must be a ruling class or classes ; in other words, a class gets control of any society and determines its political form or system. The ruling class, therefore, has the power. Will it not use the power to divert social effort to its own service and gain ? It must be expected to do so, unless it is checked by institutions which call into action opposing interests and forces. There is no class which can be trusted to rule society with due justice to all, not abusing its power for its own interest. The task of constitutional government is to devise institutions which shall come into play at the critical periods to prevent the abusive control of the powers of a state by the controlling classes in it. The ruling classes in mediæval society were warriors and ecclesiastics, and they used all their power to aggrandize themselves at the expense of other classes. Modern society is ruled by the middle class. In honor of the bourgeoisie it must be said that they have invented institutions of civil liberty which secure to all safety of person and property. They have not, therefore, made a state for themselves alone or chiefly, and their state is the only one in which no class has had to fear oppressive use of political power. The history of the nineteenth century, however, plainly showed the power of capital in the modern state. Special legislation, charters, and franchises proved to be easy legislative means of using the powers of the state for the pecuniary benefit of the few. In the first half of the century, in the United States, banks of issue were used to an extravagant pitch for private interest. The history is disgraceful, and it is a permanent degradation of popular government that power could not be found, or did not exist, in the system to subjugate this abuse and repress this corruption of state power. The protective-tariff system is simply an elaborate system by which certain interests inside of a country get control of legislation in order to tax their fellow-citizens for their own benefit. Some of the victims claim to be taken "into the steal," and if they can make enough trouble for the clique in power, they can force their own admission. That only teaches all that the great way to succeed in the pursuit of wealth is to organize a steal of some kind and get inside of it. The pension system in the United States is an abuse which has escaped from control. There is no longer any attempt to cope with it. It is the share of the "common man" in the great system of public plunder. "Graft" is only a proof of the wide extent to which this lesson to get into the steal is learned. It only shows that the corrupt use of legislation and political power has affected the mores. Every one must have his little sphere of plunder and especial advantage. This conviction and taste becomes so current that it affects all new legislation. The legislators do not doubt that it is reasonable and right to enact laws which provide favor for special interests, or to practice legislative strikes on insurance companies, railroads, telephone companies, etc. They laugh at remonstrance as out of date and "unpractical." The administrators of life-insurance companies, savings banks, trusts, etc., proceed on the belief that men in positions of power and control will use their positions for their own advantage. They think that that is only common sense. "What else are we here for?" It is the supreme test of a system of government whether its machinery is adequate for repressing the selfish undertakings of cliques formed on special interests and saving the public from raids of plunderers. The modern democratic states fail under this test. There is not a great state in the world which was not democratized in the nineteenth century. There is not one of them which did not have great financial scandals before the century closed. Financial scandal is the curse of all the modern parliamentary states with a wide suffrage. They give liberty and security, with open chances for individual enterprise, from which results great individual satisfaction and happiness, but the political machinery offers opportunities for manipulation and corrupt abuse. They educate their citizens to seek advantages in the industrial organization by legislative devices, and to use them to the uttermost. The effect is seen in the mores. We hear of plutocracy and tainted money, of the power of wealth, and the wickedness of corporations. The disease is less specific. It is constitutional. The critics are as subject to it as the criticised. A disease of the mores is a disease of public opinion as to standards, codes, ideas of truth and right, and of things worth working for and means of success. Such a disease affects everybody. It penetrates and spoils every institution. It spreads from generation to generation, and at last it destroys in the masses the power of ethical judgment.

168. The standard of living. One of the purest of all the products of current mores is the standard of living. It belongs to a subgroup and is a product of the mores of a subgroup. It has been called a psychological or ethical product, which view plainly is due to an imperfect analysis or classification. The standard of living is the measure of decency and suitability in material comfort (diet, dress, dwelling, etc.) which is traditional and habitual in a subgroup. It is often wise and necessary to disregard the social standard of comfort, because it imposes foolish expenses and contemptible ostentation, but it is very difficult to disregard the social standard of comfort. The standard is upheld by fear of social disapproval, if one derogates from class "respectability." The disapproval or contempt of one's nearest associates is the sanction. The standards and code of respectability are in the class mores. They get inside of the mind and heart of members of the class, and betray each to the class demands.

169. If, however, the standard of living which one has inherited from his class is adopted as an individual standard, and is made the object of effort and self-denial, the individual and social results are of high value. One man said, " Live like a hog and you will behave like one " ; to which another replied, " Behave like a hog and you will live like one." Both were right in about equal measure. The social standard of a class acts like honor. It sustains self-respect and duty to self and family. The pain which is produced by derogation produces effort and self-denial. The social standard may well call out and concentrate all there is in a man to work for his social welfare. Evidently the standard of living never can do more than that. It never can add anything to the forces in a man's own character and attainments.

CHAPTER V

SOCIETAL SELECTION

170. Social selection by the mores. The most important fact about the mores is their dominion over the individual. Arising he knows not whence or how, they meet his opening mind in earliest childhood, give him his outfit of ideas, faiths, and tastes, and lead him into prescribed mental processes. They bring to him codes of action, standards, and rules of ethics. They have a model of the man-as-he-should-be to which they mold him, in spite of himself and without his knowledge. If he submits and consents, he is taken up and may attain great social success. If he resists and dissents, he is thrown out and may be trodden under foot. The mores are therefore an engine of social selection. Their coercion of the individual is the mode in which they operate the selection, and the details of the process deserve study. Some folkways exercise an unknown and unintelligent selection. Infanticide does this (Chapter VII). Slavery always exerts a very powerful selection, both physical and social (Chapter VI).

171. Instrumentalities of suggestion. Suggestion is exerted in the mores by a number of instrumentalities, all of which have their origin in the mores, and may only extend to all what some have thought and felt, or may (at a later stage) be used with set intention to act suggestively in extending certain mores.

Myths, legends, fables, and mythology spread notions through a group, and from generation to generation, until the notions become components of the mores, being interwoven with the folkways. Epic poems have powerfully influenced the mores. They present types of heroic actions and character which serve as models to the young. The *Iliad* and *Odyssey* became text-books for the instruction of Greek youth. They set notions of heroism and duty, and furnished all Greeks with a common stock of narratives, ideas, and ideals, and with sentiments which everybody knew and which could be rearoused by an allusion. Everybody was expected to produce the same reaction under the allusion. Perhaps that was a conventional assumption, and the reaction in thought and feeling may have been only conventional in many cases, but the suggestion did not fail of its effect even then. Later, when the ideals of epic heroism and of the old respect for the gods were popularly rejected and derided, this renunciation of the old stock of common ideas and faiths marked a decline in the morale of the nation. It is a very important question : What is the effect of conventional humbug in the mores of a people, which is suggested to the young as solemn and sacred, and which they have to find out and reject later in life? The *Mahabharata*, the *Kalevala*, the *Edda*, the *Nibelungen Noth*, are other examples of popular epics which had great influence on the mores for centuries. Such poems present models of action and principle, but it is inevitable that a later time will not appreciate them and will turn them to ridicule, or will make of them only poses and affectations. The former is the effect most likely to be produced on the masses, the latter on the cultured classes. In the Greco-Roman world, at the beginning of the Christian era, various philosophic sects tried to restore and renew the ideals of Greek heroism, virtue, and religious faith, so far as they seemed to have permanent ethical value. The popular mores were never touched by this effort. In fact, it is impossible for us to know whether the writings of Seneca, Plutarch, Marcus Aurelius, Epictetus, and Pliny represent to us the real rules of life of those men, or are only a literary pose. In the Renaissance, and since then, men educated in the classics have been influenced by them in regard to their standards of noble and praiseworthy character, and of what should be cultivated in thought and conduct. Such men have had a common stock of quotations, of accepted views in life philosophy, and of current ethical opinions. This stock, however, has been common to the members of the technical guild of the learned. It has never affected the masses. Amongst Protestants the Bible has, in the last four hundred years, furnished a common stock of history and anecdote, and has also furnished phrases and current quotations familiar to all classes. It has furnished codes and standards which none dared to disavow, and the suggestion of which has been overpowering. The effect on popular mores has been very great.

172. Symbols, pictures. Before the ability to read became general art was employed in the form of symbols to carry suggestion. Symbolic acts were employed in trade and contracts, in marriage and religion. For us writing has taken the place of

symbols as a means of suggestion. Symbols do not appeal to
us. They are not in our habits. Illustrative pictures influence us.
The introduction of them into daily newspapers is an important
development of the arts of suggestion. Mediæval art in colored
glass, carving, sculpture, and pictures reveals the grossness and
crass simplicity of the mediæval imagination, but also its child-
ish originality and directness. No doubt it was on account of
these latter characteristics that it had such suggestive power.
It was graphic. It stimulated and inflamed the kind of imagination which produced it. It found its subjects in heaven, hell,
demons, torture, and the scriptural incidents which contained
any horrible, fantastic, or grotesque elements. The crucifix
represented a man dying in the agony of torture, and it was the
chief symbol of the religion. The suggestion in all this art produced barbaric passion and sensuality. Any one who, in childhood, had in his hands one of the old Bibles illustrated by wood
cuts knows what power the cuts had to determine the concept
which was formed from the text, and which has persisted through
life, in spite of later instruction.

173. Apparatus of suggestion. In modern times the apparatus of suggestion is in language, not in pictures, carvings
morality plays, or other visible products of art. Watchwords
catchwords, phrases, and epithets are the modern instrumentalities. There are words which are used currently as if their meaning was perfectly simple, clear, and unambiguous, which are not
defined at all. "Democracy," the "People," "Wall Street,"
"Slave," "Americanism," are examples. These words have
been called "symbols." They might better be called "tokens."
They are like token coins. They "pass"; that is their most
noteworthy characteristic. They are familiar, unquestioned,
popular, and they are always current above their value. They
always reveal the invincible tendency of the masses to mythologize. They are personified and a superhuman energy is attributed to them. "Democracy" is not treated as a parallel word
to aristocracy, theocracy, autocracy, etc., but as a Power from
some outside origin, which brings into human affairs an inspiration and energy of its own. The "People" is not the population,

but a creation of mythology, to which inherent faculties and capacities are ascribed beyond what can be verified within experience. " Wall Street " takes the place which used to be assigned to the devil. What is that " Wall Street " which is currently spoken of by editors and public men as thinking, wanting, working for, certain things ? There is a collective interest which is so designated which is real, but the popular notion under " Wall Street " is unanalyzed. It is a phantasm or a myth. In all these cases there is a tyranny in the term. Who dare criticise democracy or the people ? Who dare put himself on the side of Wall Street ? The tyranny is greatest in regard to " American" and " Americanism." Who dare say that he is not " American " ? Who dare repudiate what is declared to be " Americanism " ? It follows that if anything is base and bogus it is always labeled " American." If a thing is to be recommended which cannot be justified, it is put under "Americanism." Who does not shudder at the fear of being called " unpatriotic " ? and to repudiate what any one chooses to call " American " is to be unpatriotic. If there is any document of Americanism, it is the Declaration of Independence. Those who have Americanism especially in charge have repudiated the doctrine that " governments derive their just powers from the consent of the governed," because it stood in the way of what they wanted to do. They denounce those who cling to the doctrine as un-American. Then we see what Americanism and patriotism are. They are the duty laid upon us all to applaud, follow, and obey whatever a ruling clique of newspapers and politicians chooses to say or wants to do. " England " has always been, amongst us, a kind of counter token, or token of things to be resisted and repudiated. The " symbols," or " tokens," always have this utility for suggestion. They carry a coercion with them and overwhelm people who are not trained to verify assertions and dissect fallacies.

174. Watchwords, catchwords. A watchword sums up one policy, doctrine, view, or phase of a subject. It may be legitimate and useful, but a watchword easily changes its meaning and takes up foreign connotations or fallacious suggestions.

Critical analysis is required to detect and exclude the fallacy. Catchwords are acutely adapted to stimulate desires. In the presidential campaign of 1900 we saw a catchword deliberately invented, — "the full dinner pail." Such an invention turns suggestion into an art. Socialism, as a subject of popular agitation, consists almost altogether of watchwords, catchwords, and phrases of suggestion : "the boon of nature," "the banquet of life," "the disinherited," "the submerged tenth," "the mine to the miner," "restore the land to the landless." Trades unionism consists almost entirely, on its philosophical side, of suggestive watchwords and phrases. It is said that "labor" creates all value. This is not true, but the fallacy is complete when labor is taken in the sense of "laborers," collectively and technically so called, — an abuse of language which is now current. To say that wage-earners create all value is to assert a proposition from which numerous and weighty consequences follow as to rights and interests. "The interest of one is the interest of all" is a principle which is as good for a band of robbers as for a union of any other kind. "Making work" by not producing is the greatest industrial fallacy possible.

175. Slave, democracy. Since "democratic" is now a word to conjure with, we hear of democracy in industry, banking, education, science, etc., where the word is destitute of meaning or is fallacious. It is used to prejudice the discussion. Since the abolition of slavery the word "slave" has become a token. In current discussions we hear of "rent slaves," "wages slavery," "debt slavery," "marriage slavery," etc. These words bear witness to great confusion and error in the popular notions of what freedom is and can be. For negroes emancipation contained a great disillusion. They had to learn what being "free" did not mean. Debt slavery is the oldest kind of slavery except war captivity. A man in debt is not free. A man who has made a contract is not free. A man who has contracted duties and obligations as husband and father, or has been born into them as citizen, son, brother, etc., is not free. Can we imagine ourselves "free" from the conditions of human life? Does it do any good to stigmatize the case as "wages slavery," when what it means is that a man is under a necessity to earn his living? It would be a grand reform in the mores if the masses should learn to turn away in contempt from all this rhetoric.

176. Epithets. Works of fiction have furnished the language with epithets for types of individuals (sec. 622). Don Quixote, Faust, Punch, Reinecke Fuchs, Br'er Rabbit, Falstaff, Bottom, and many from Dickens (Pickwick, Pecksniff, Podsnap, Turveydrop, Uriah Heep) are examples. The words are like coins. They condense ideas and produce classes. They economize language. They also produce summary criticisms and definition of types by societal selection. All the reading classes get the use of common epithets, and the usage passes to other classes in time. The coercion of an epithet of contempt or disapproval is something which it requires great moral courage to endure.

177. Phrases. The educated classes are victims of the phrase. Phrases are rhetorical flourishes adapted to the pet notions of the time. They are artifices of suggestion. They are the same old tricks of the medicine man adapted to an age of literature and common schools. Instead of a rattle or a drum the operator talks about "destiny" and "duty," or molds into easy phrases the sentiments which are popular. It is only a difference of method. Solemnity, unction, and rhetorical skill are needed. Often the phrases embody only visionary generalities. "Citizenship," "publicity," "public policy," "restraint of trade," "he who holds the sea will hold the land," "trade follows the flag," "the dollar of the fathers," "the key of the Pacific," "peace with honor," are some of the recent coinages or recoinages. Phrases have great power when they are antithetical or alliterative. Some opponents of the silver proposition were quite perplexed by the saying: "The white man with the yellow metal is beaten by the yellow man with the white metal." In 1844 the alliterative watchword "Fifty-four forty or fight" nearly provoked a war. If it had been "Forty-nine thirty or fight," that would not have had nearly so great effect. The "Cape to Cairo" railroad is another case of alliteration. Humanitarianism has permeated our mores and has been a fountain of phrases

Forty years ago the phrase "enthusiasm of humanity" was invented. It inspired a school of sentimental philosophizing about social relations, which has been carried on by phrase making : "the dignity of labor," "the nobility of humanity," "a man is not a ware," "an existence worthy of humanity," "a living wage." "Humanity" in modern languages is generally used in two senses: (a) the human race, (b) the sympathetic sentiment between man and man. This ambiguity enters into all the phrases which are humanitarian.

178. Pathos. Suggestion is powerfully aided by *pathos*, in the original Greek sense of the word. Pathos is the glamour of sentiment which grows up around the pet notion of an age and people, and which protects it from criticism. The Greeks, in the fourth century before Christ, cherished pathos in regard to tyrannicide. Tyrants were bosses, produced by democracy in towns, but hated by democrats. Tyrannicides were surrounded with a halo of heroism and popular admiration.[1] Something of the same sentiment was revived in the sixteenth century, when it appeared that a tyrant was any ruler whose politics one did not like. It cost several rulers their lives. Pathos was a large element in the notions of woman and knighthood (twelfth and thirteenth centuries), of the church (thirteenth century), of the Holy Sepulcher (eleventh and twelfth centuries). In the thirteenth century there was a large element of pathos in the glorification of poverty. A great deal of pathos has been expended on the history and institutions of Greece and Rome in modern times. Classical studies still depend largely on it for their prestige. There is a pathos of democracy in the United States. In all English-speaking countries marriage is an object of pathos. The pathos is cultivated by poetry and novels. Humanitarianism is nourished by pathos and it stimulates pathos. The "poor" and the "laborers" are objects of pathos, on account of which these terms, in literature, refer to a conventional and unreal concept. Consequently there is no honest discussion of any topic which concerns the poor or laborers. Some people make opposition to alcohol an object of pathos.

[1] Burckhardt, *Kulturgesch. Griechenlands*, I, 211.

179. Pathos is unfavorable to truth. Whenever pathos is in play the subject is privileged. It is regarded with a kind of affection, and is protected from severe examination. It is made holy or sacred. The thing is cherished with such a preëstablished preference and faith that it is thought wrong to verify it. Pathos, therefore, is unfavorable to truth. It has always been an element in religion. It is an element now in patriotism, and in regard to the history of one's own country. The coercion of pathos on the individual comes in popular disapproval of truth-telling about the matter in question. The toleration for forgery and fraud in the Christian church until modern times, which to modern people seems so shocking and inexplicable, was chiefly due to pathos about religion and the church. If a forgery would help the church or religion, any one who opposed it would seem to be an enemy of religion and the church and willing to violate the pathos which surrounded them.

180. The value of analysis and verification as tests. In all the cases of the use of catchwords, watchwords, and phrases, the stereotyped forms of language seem to convey thought, especially ascertained truth, and they do it in a way to preclude verification. It is absolutely essential to correct thinking and successful discussion to reject stereotyped forms, and to insist on analysis and verification. Evidently all forms of suggestion tend to create an atmosphere of delusion. Pathos increases the atmosphere of delusion. It introduces elements which corrupt the judgment. In effect, it continues the old notion that there are edifying falsehoods and useful deceits. The masses always infuse a large emotional element into all their likes and dislikes, approval and disapproval. Hence, in time, they surround what they accept with pathos which it is hard to break through.

181. Humanity. The standard of humanity or of decent behavior, especially towards the weak or those persons who may be at one's mercy, or animals, is entirely in the mores of the group and time. To the Gauchos of Uruguay "inhumanity and love of bloodshed become second nature." Their customs of treating beasts habituate them to bloodshed. "They are callous to the sight of blood and suffering and come to positively enjoy it." They have no affection for their horses and dogs. They murder for plunder.[1] It is very rarely that we meet with such a description as that of any people. Polynesians were blood-thirsty and cruel, perhaps because they had no chase of wild animals in which to expend their energies.[2] North American Indians could invent frightful tortures, but they were not blood-thirsty. They were not humane. Suffering did not revolt them. Schomburgk[3] tells a story of an Indian who became enraged at his wife because she groaned with toothache. He cut down her hammock and caused her to fall so that she suffered a dislocation of the arm. A European witness went to the chief with a report and remonstrance, but the chief was astonished that any one should take any notice of such an incident. The Assyrians cut in stone representations of flaying, impaling, etc., and of a king with his own royal hands putting out the eyes of prisoners. The Egyptians represented kings slaying men (national enemies) in masses. The Romans enjoyed bloodshed and the sight of suffer-ing.[4] The Middle Ages reveled in cruelty to men and beasts. It is in the Middle Ages that we could find the nearest parallels to the Gauchos above. None of these people felt that repulsive revolt of the whole nature at inhumanity which characterizes modern cultivated people. The horrors have all receded out of our experience, and almost out of our knowledge. The line of familiarity is set far off. Therefore a little thing in the way of inhumanity is strange and exerts its full repulsive effect. Things happen, however, which show us that human nature is not changed, and that the brute in it may awake again at any time. It is all a question of time, custom, and occasion, and the indi-vidual is coerced to adopt the mores as to these matters which are then and there current.

182. Selection by distinction. One of the leading modes by which the group exercises selection of its adopted type on the individual is by distinction. Distinction is selection. It appeals to vanity. It acts in two ways and has two opposite effects. One likes to be separated from the crowd by what is admired, and dislikes to be distinguished for what is not admired. Cases

[1] JAI, XI, 44.   [2] Ratzel, *Völkerkunde*, II, 163.   [3] *Britisch Guiana*, II, 428.
[4] Grupp, *Kulturgesch. der Röm. Kaiserzeit*, I, 32.

occur in which the noteworthy person is not sure whether he ought to be proud or ashamed of that for which he is distinguished. When a society gives titles, decorations, and rewards for acts, it stimulates what it rewards and causes new cases of it. The operation of selection is direct and rational. The cases in which the application of distinction is irrational show most clearly its selective effect. School-teachers are familiar with the fact that children will imitate a peculiarity of one which marks him out from all the rest, even if it is a deformity or defect. Why then wonder that barbarian mothers try to deform their babies towards an adopted type of bodily perfection which is not rationally preferable? A lady of my acquaintance showed me one of her dolls which had wire attachments on its legs in imitation of those worn by children for orthopedic effect. She explained that when she was a child, another child who had soft bones or weak ankles, and who wore irons for them, was brought into her group of playmates. They all admired and envied her, and all wished that they had weak bones so that they could wear irons. This lady made wire attachments for her doll that it might reach the highest standard.

183. Aristocracies. All aristocracies are groups of those who are distinguished, at the time, for the possession of those things which are admired or approved, and which give superiority in the struggle for existence or in social power. In the higher civilization, until modern times, the possession of land was the only social power which would raise a man above sordid cares and enable him to plan his life as he chose. By talent an income could be won which would give the same advantage, but not with the same security of permanence and independence. The fields for talent were war, civil administration, and religion, the last including all mental activity. Men of talent had to win their place by craft and charlatanism (sorcery, astrology, therapeutics). Their position never was independent, except in church establishments. They had to win recognition from warriors and landowners, and they became comrades and allies of the latter. Merchants and bankers were the aristocracy at Carthage, Venice, Florence, and Genoa, and in the Hansa.

Talented military men were aristocrats under Napoleon, courtiers were such under Louis XIV, and ecclesiastics at Rome. Since the fourteenth century capital has become a new and the greatest and indispensable social power. Those who, at any time, have the then most important social power in their hands are courted and flattered, envied and served, by the rest. They make an aristocracy. The aristocrats are the distinguished ones, and their existence and recognition give direction to social ambition. Of course this acts selectively to call out what is most advantageous and most valued in the society.

184. There are a number of mass phenomena which are on a lower grade than the mores, lacking the elements of truth and right with respect to welfare, which illustrate still further and more obviously the coercion of all mass movements over the individual. These are fashion, poses, fads, and affectations.

185. Fashion. Fashion in dress has covered both absurdities and indecencies with the ægis of custom. From the beginning of the fourteenth century laws appear against indecent dress. What nobles invented, generally in order to give especial zest to the costume of a special occasion, that burghers and later peasants imitated and made common.[1] In the fifteenth century the man's hose fitted the legs and hips tightly. The latchet was of a different color, and was decorated and stuffed as if to exaggerate still further the indecent obtrusiveness of it.[2] Schultz[3] says that the pictures which we have do not show the full indecency of the dress against which the clergy and moralists of the fifteenth century uttered denunciations, but only those forms which were considered decent, that is, those which were within the limits which custom at the time had established At the same time women began to uncover the neck and bosom. The extent to which this may be carried is always controlled by fashion and the mores. Puritans and Quakers attempted to restrict it entirely, and to so construct the dress, by a neckerchief or attachment to the bodice, that the shape of the bust should be entirely concealed. The mores rejected this rule as

---

[1] Scherr, *Kulturgesch.*, 109.   [2] Rudeck, *Oeffentl. Sittlichkeit*, 45.
[3] *Deutsches Leben*, 285, 297, 332.

excessive. In spite of all the eloquence of the moral preachers, that form of dress which shows neck and bosom has become established, only that it is specialized for full dress and covered by conventionalization.

186. Conventionalization. Conventionalization also comes into play to cover the dress of the ballet or burlesque opera and the bathing dress. Conventionalization always includes strict specification and limits of time, place, and occasion, beyond which the same dress would become vicious. Amongst Moslems and Orientals this conventionalization as to dress has never been introduced. We are familiar with the fact that when a fashion has been introduced and has become common our eye is formed to it, and no one looks "right" or stylish who does not conform to it. We also know that after the fashion has changed things in the discarded fashion look dowdy and rustic. No one can resist these impressions, try as he may. This fact, in the experience of everybody, gives us an example of the power of current custom over the individual. While a fashion reigns its tendency is to greater and greater extravagance in order to produce the desired and admired effect. Then the toleration for any questionable element in the fashion is extended and the extension is unnoticed. If a woman of 1860, in the dress of her time, were to meet a woman of 1906, in the dress of her time, each would be amazed at the indecency of the dress of the other. No dress ever was more, or more justly, denounced for ugliness, inconvenience, and indecency than the crinoline, but all the women from 1855 to 1865, including some of the sweetest who ever lived, wore it. No inference whatever as to their taste or character would be justified. There never is any rational judgment in the fashion of dress. No criticism can reach it. In a few cases we know what actress or princess started a certain fashion, but in the great majority of cases we do not know whence it came or who was responsible for it. We all have to obey it. We hardly ever have any chance to answer back. Its all-sufficient sanction is that "everybody wears it," or wears it *so*. Evidently this is only a special application to dress of a general usage — conventionalization.

187. Uncivilized fashions. Those "good old times" of simplicity and common sense in dress must be sought in the time anterior to waistband and apron. All the barbarians and savages were guilty of folly, frivolity, and self-deformation in the service of fashion. They found an ideal somewhere which they wanted to attain, or they wanted to be distinguished, that is, raised out of the commonplace and universal. At one stage distinction comes from being in the fashion in a high and marked degree. Also each one flees the distinction of being out of the fashion, which would not draw admiration. At another stage distinction comes from starting a new fashion. This may be done by an ornament, if it is well selected so that it will "take."[1] Beads have been a fashionable ornament from the days of savagery until to-day. An Indian woman in Florida "had six quarts (probably a peck) of the beads gathered about her neck, hanging down her back, down upon her breasts, filling the space under her chin, and covering her neck up to her ears. It was an effort for her to move her head. She, however, was only a little, if any, better off in her possessions than most of the others. Others were about equally burdened. Even girl babies are favored by their proud mammas with a varying quantity of the coveted neckwear. The cumbersome beads are said to be worn by night as well as by day."[2] "A woman sometimes hangs a weight of over five pounds around her neck, for besides the ordinary necklaces the northern women wear one or more large white, polished shells, which are brought from the western coast and which weigh from half a pound upward."[3] "Fashions change in Bechuanaland; one year the women all wear blue beads, but perhaps the next (and just when a trader has laid in a supply of blue beads) they refuse to wear any color but yellow. At the time of writing [1886] the men wore small black pot hats, but several years ago they had used huge felt hats, like that of Rip Van Winkle, and as a consequence the stores are full of those unsalable ones."[4]

[1] Lippert, *Kulturgesch.*, I, 370.
[2] *Bur. Ethnol.*, V, 488.
[3] Cary and Tuck, *Chin Hills*, I, 173.
[4] JAI, XVI, 87; cf. Fritsch, *Eingeb. Süd-Afr.*, 170.

188. Fashion in ethnography. The Carib women in Surinam think that large calves of the leg are a beauty. Therefore they bind the leg above the ankle to make the calves larger. They begin the treatment on children.[1] Some Australian mothers press down their babies' noses. "They laugh at the sharp noses of Europeans, and call them tomahawk noses, preferring their own style."[2] The presence of two races side by side calls attention to the characteristic differences. Race vanity then produces an effort to emphasize the race characteristics. Samoan mothers want the noses and foreheads of their babies to be flat, and they squeeze them with their hands accordingly.[3] The "Papuan ideal of female beauty has a big nose, big breasts, and a dark-brown, smooth skin."[4] To-day the Papuans all smoke white clay pipes. Four weeks later no one will smoke a white pipe. All want brown ones. Still four weeks later no one wants any pipe at all. All run around with red umbrellas [5] On the Solomon Islands sometimes they want plain pipes; then again, pipes with a ship or anchor carved on them; again, pipes with a knob. Women wear great weights of metal as rings for ornament.[6] The Galla women wear rings to the weight of four or six pounds.[7] Tylor[8] says that an African belle wears big copper rings which become hot in the sun, so that the lady has to have an attendant, whose duty it is to cool them down by wetting them. The queen of the Wavunias on the Congo wore a brass collar around her neck, which weighed from sixteen to twenty pounds. She had to lie down once in a while to rest.[9] The Herero wear iron which in the dry climate retains luster. The women wear bracelets and leglets, and iron beads from the size of a pea to that of a potato. They carry weights up to thirty-five

[1] *Bijdragen tot T. L. en V.-kunde*, XXXV, 67.
[2] JAI, XIII, 280.
[3] *Austral. Assoc. Adv. Sci.*, 1892, 622.
[4] Hagen, *Unter den Papuas*, 241.
[5] *Ibid.*, 213.
[6] Woodford, *Naturalist among Headhunters*, 178.
[7] Paulitschke, *Ethnog. N.O. Afrikas*, I, 93.
[8] *Anthropology*, 243.
[9] JAI, XVII, 235.

pounds and are forced to walk with a slow, dragging step which is considered aristocratic. Iron is rare and worth more than silver.[1] Livingstone says that in Balonda poorer people imitate the step of those who carry big weights of ornament, although they are wearing but a few ounces.[2] Some women of the Dinka carry fifty pounds of iron. The rings on legs and arms clank like the fetters of slaves. The men wear massive ivory rings on the upper arm. The rich cover the whole arm. The men also wear leather bracelets and necklaces.[3] In Behar, Hindostan, the women wear brass rings on their legs. "One of these is heavy, nearly a foot broad, and serrated all around the edges. It can only be put on the legs by a blacksmith, who fits it on the legs of the women with his hammer, while they writhe upon the ground in pain." Women of the milkman caste wear bangles of bell metal, often up to the elbow. "The greater the number of bangles, the more beautiful the wearer is considered."[4] The satirist could easily show that all these details are shown now in our fashions.

189. Ideals of beauty. In Melanesia a girdle ten centimeters wide is worn, drawn as tight as possible. One cut from the body of a man twenty-seven years old measured only sixty-five centimeters.[5] The women of the Barito valley wear the *sarong* around the thighs so tight that it restricts the steps and produces a mincing gait which they think beautiful.[6] The Ruku-yenn of Guiana have an ideal of female beauty which is marked by a large abdomen. They wind the abdomen with many girdles to make it appear large. "The women of the Payaguas, in Paraguay, from youth up, elongate the breasts, and they continue this after they are mothers by means of bandages."[7] The southern Arabs drop hot grease from a candle on a bride's fingers, and then plaster the fingers with henna. Then the grease is taken off, and light-colored spots (if possible, regular) are left where it was, while the rest of the skin is colored brown by the henna.

---

[1] Büttner, *Das Hinterland von Walfischbai*, 235.
[2] *South Africa*, I, 298.
[3] Schweinfurth, *Heart of Afr.*, I, 153.
[4] JASB, III, 370.

[5] Finsch, *Samoafahrten*, 90.
[6] Schwaner, *Borneo*, I, 221.
[7] Ratzel, *Völkerkunde*, II, 570.

They put on the bride seventeen garments, a silk one and a muslin one alternately; then a mantle over all, and a rug on the mantle, and all possible ornaments.[1] Flinders Petrie thinks that we must recognize a principle of " racial taste," " which belongs to each people as much as their language, which may be borrowed like languages from one race by another, but which survives changes and long eclipses even more than language." [2] The cases given show that ideals of beauty are somehow formed, which call for a deformation of the human body. The foreheads are flattened, the lips enlarged, the ears drawn down, the skull forced into a sugar-loaf shape, the nose flattened, etc., to try to reach a form approved by fashion. There is an ideal of beauty behind the fashion, a selected type of superiority, which must be assumed as the purpose of the fashion.

190. Fashion in other things than dress. As will appear below, fashion controls many things besides dress. It governs the forms of utensils, weapons, canoes and boats, tools, etc., amongst savages. In the fifteenth and sixteenth centuries there was a fashionable attitude or pose in standing for women, in which the abdomen was thrown forward. It is often seen in pictures and portraits.[3] It is inelegant and destitute of meaning. The Venetians were luxurious and frivolous, jealous and distrustful of women, and fond of pleasure and fashion. From the end of the sixteenth century a shopkeeper in the Merceria adopted a custom of showing the new fashions of Paris on Ascension Day by means of a life-size doll dressed in them.[4] The Venetian women of that period wore patins, shoes with blocks underneath, some of which were two feet high. The women were unable to walk without a maid on each side to support them.[5] Yriarte thinks that these patins were due to the policy of the husbands. When an ambassador, in conversation with the doge and his counselors, said that shoes would be far more convenient, a counselor replied, " Only too convenient!

---

[1] Pommerol, *Une Femme chez les Sahariennes*, 243.
[2] *Smithson. Rep.*, 1895, 594.
[3] *Umschau*, IV, 789.
[4] Yriarte, *La Vie d'un Patricien de Venise*, 58.
[5] *Ibid.*, 53.

Only too much so!" Under the French Directory, a *demi-terme* was the name of a framework worn by women to look as if they would soon be mothers.[1] Thirty years ago "poufs" were worn to enlarge the dress on the hips at the side. The "Grecian bend," stooping forward, was an attitude both in walking and standing. Then followed the bustle. Later, the contour was closely fitted by the dress. No one thought that the human figure would be improved if changed as the dress made it appear to be. No fashion was adopted because it would have an indecent effect. The point for our purpose is that women wore dresses of the appointed shape because everybody did so, and for no other reason, being unconscious of the effect.

Erasmus, in his colloquy on the Franciscans, makes one of the characters say: "I think that the whole matter of dress depends upon custom and the opinions which are current." He refers to some unnamed place where adulterers, after conviction, are never allowed to uncover the private parts, and says, "Custom has made it, for them, the greatest of all punishments." "The fact is that nothing is so ridiculous that usage may not make it pass."

Fashion has controlled the mode of dressing the hair and deforming the body. It has determined what animals, or what special race of an animal species, should be petted. It controls music and literature, so that a composer, poet, or novelist is the rage or is forgotten. In mediæval literature the modes of allegory were highly esteemed and very commonly used. The writers described war and battles over and over again, and paid little attention to nature. In fact, natural background, geography, and meteorology were made as conventional as stage scenery, and were treated as of no interest and little importance. Modern taste for reality and for the natural details throws this mediæval characteristic by contrast into strong relief.

191. Miscellaneous fashions. Fashion rules in architecture. In the seventeenth and eighteenth centuries in England, English Renaissance and Gothic were regarded as barbaric, and palladian was admired. In France the preference was for rococo and

[1] Du Camp, *Paris*, VI, 388.

Mansard forms. At the present time the English Renaissance and Gothic are in favor again, and palladian is regarded with disfavor. Painting and sculpture undergo variations of fashion as to standards and methods. The same is true of literature. Poetry and novels follow phases of fashion. A successful novel makes imitations and sets a fashion for a time. Types of heroes and ideals of character come and go by fashion. The type of the man-as-he-should-be varies by fashion, and this type exerts a great selection in the education of the young. Educational methods run through fashions. Fads in methods of teaching arise, are advocated with great emphasis, have their run, decline, and disappear. There are fashions of standing, walking, sitting, gesture, language (slang, expletives), pronunciation, key of the voice, inflection, and sentence accent; fashions in shaking hands, dancing, eating and drinking, showing respect, visiting, foods, hours of meals, and deportment. When snuff was taken attitudes and gestures in taking it were cultivated which were thought stylish. Fashion determines what type of female beauty is at a time preferred, — plump or *svelte*, blond or brunette, large or petite, red-haired or black-haired. When was that "simple time of our fathers" when people were too sensible to care for fashions? It certainly was before the Pharaohs and perhaps before the glacial epoch. Isaiah (iii. 16) rebukes the follies of fashion. Chrysostom preached to the early church against tricks and manners of gesture and walk which had been learned in the theater. Since literature has existed moralists have satirized fashion. Galton has noticed what any one may verify, — that old portraits show "indisputable signs of one predominant type of face supplanting another." " If we may believe caricaturists, the fleshiness and obesity of many English men and women in the earlier years of this century [nineteenth] must have been prodigious."[1] Part of this phenomenon may be due to the fashion of painting. The portrait painter warps all his subjects toward the current standard of "good looks," but it is more probable that there is a true play of variation. Platycnemism and the pierced olecranon run in groups for a time. Then

[1] Galton, *Human Faculty*, 6, 8.

they run out. There are fashions in disease, as if fashion were really in nature. This goes beyond the limits of our definition, but the rise and passing away of variations in breeding plants and animals, and perhaps in men, suggests that fashion may be an analogous play of experiment, half caprice, half earnest, whose utility lies in selection. If there was no reaching out after novelty except upon rational determination, the case would be very different from what it is when variation brings spontaneous suggestions. Our present modes of dress (aside from the variations imposed by fashion) are the resultant of all the fashions of the last two thousand years.

192. All deformations by fashion are irrational. There is no guarantee that fashions will serve expediency. Deformations of the skull may not be harmful; they are not useful. The block inserted in the lip interferes with eating and speaking. It alters the language. Saliva cannot be retained, and flows over it. To those who are outside the fashion it is extremely ugly and disgusting. To those inside the fashion it is a standard of beauty and a badge of dignity and tribal position. All fashions tend to extravagance because the senses become accustomed to them, and it is necessary, in order to renew the impression of distinction, to exaggerate. The extravagances of fashion run through all grades of civilization. They show that fashion, coming from the whole to the individual, adds nothing to the sense, judgment, or taste of the latter, but imposes on him a coercion to conform. He who dissents is thought rustic and boorish. He is more or less severely boycotted, which means not only that he is made to suffer, but that he loses important advantages and hurts his interests.

193. Satires on fashion. Forty years ago a lady who swung her arms as she walked was considered strong-minded. A lady who was young when the present queen of England introduced the fashion of brushing up the hair and uncovering the ears says that it seemed indecent. Fashion is stronger than autocracy. Nicholas I of Russia disapproved of late hours and ordered that court balls should be commenced early that they might be finished early. He found himself almost alone until eleven o'clock, and had to give up his reform.[1] In the height of the crinoline fashion Leech published in *Punch* a picture of two maiden ladies who " think crinoline a preposterous and extravagant invention and appear at a party in a simple and elegant attire." The shocked horror of the bystanders is perfect, but the two ladies would to-day be quite in the fashion. Du Maurier published in *Punch* a skit in which a little girl asked her mother how Eve knew, the first time that she saw Cain as a baby, that he was not ugly. This is a very clever hit at the origin of conventions. There was when Cain was born no established convention that all babies are pretty.

194. Fashion in faiths and ideals. There are also fashions in trading, banking, political devices, traveling, inn keeping, book making, shows, amusements, flowers, fancywork, carriages, gardens, and games. There seem to be fashions in logic and reasoning. Arguments which are accepted as convincing at one time have no effect at another (sec. 227, n. 4). For centuries western Europe accepted the argument for the necessity of torture in the administration of justice as convincing. At different periods the satisfaction in allegory as a valid method of interpretation has been manifested and the taste for allegory in the arts has appeared. Philosophy goes through a cycle of forms by fashion. Even mathematics and science do the same, both as to method and as to concepts. That is why " methodology " is eternal. Mediæval " realism " ruled all thought for centuries, and its dominion is yet by no means broken. It prevails in political philosophy now. Nominalism is the philosophy of modern thought. Scholasticism held all the mental outfit of the learned. Thomas Aquinas summed up all that man knows or needs to know. A modern man finds it hard to hold his own attention throughout a page of it, even for historical purposes. " Phlogiston" and " vortices " had their day and are forgotten. Eighteenth-century deism and nineteenth-century rationalism interest nobody any more. Eighteenth-century economists argued in favor of stimulating population in order to make wages low, and thereby win in international competition. They never had a

[1] *Century Magazine*, XLII, 89.

compunction or a doubt about this argument. No wonder it has been asserted that all truth, except that which is mathematically demonstrable, is only a function of the age. When the earth is underpopulated and there is an economic demand for men, democracy is inevitable. That state of things cannot be permanent. Therefore democracy cannot last. It contains no absolute and "eternal" truth. While it lasts a certain set of political notions and devices are in fashion. Certain moral standards go with them. Evolution is now accepted as a final fact in regard to organic phenomena. A philosophy of nature is derived from it. Is it only a fashion, — a phase of thought? For to all but a very few such a philosophy has no guarantee except that it is current. All accept it because all accept it, and for no other reason. Narrower philosophies become the fashion in classes, coteries, and cliques. They are really affectations of something which wins prestige and comes to be a badge of culture or other superiority. A few are distinguished because they know Greek, or because they are "freethinkers," or because they are ritualists, or because they profess a certain cultus in art, or because they are disciples of Ruskin, Eastlake, Carlyle, Emerson, Browning, Tolstoi, or Nietsche, and cultivate the ideas and practices which these men have advocated as true and wise. Often such fashions of thought or art pass from a narrow coterie to a wider class, and sometimes they permeate the mores and influence an age. When men believed in witches they did so because everybody did. When the belief in witches was given up it was because a few men set the fashion, and it was no longer "enlightened" to believe in them.

195. Fashion not trivial; not subject to argument. Fashion is by no means trivial. It is a form of the dominance of the group over the individual, and it is quite as often harmful as beneficial. There is no arguing with the fashion. In the case of dress we can sometimes tell what princess or actress started the fashion, and we sometimes know, in the case of ideas, who set them afloat. Generally, however, it is not known who started a fashion in dress. The authority of fashion is imperative as to everything which it touches. The sanctions are ridicule and powerlessness. The dissenter hurts himself ; he never affects the fashion. No woman, whatever her age or position or her opinion about the crinoline fashion, could avoid wearing one. No effort to introduce a fashion of "rational dress" for women has ever yet succeeded. An artist, novelist, poet, or playwright of a school which is out of fashion fails and is lost. An opponent of the notions which are current can get no hearing. The fashion, therefore, operates a selection in which success and merit are often divorced from each other, but the selection is pitiless. The canons of criticism are set by fashion. It follows that there is no rational effect of fashion. There was a rule in goblinism : Say naught but good of the dead. The rule was dictated by fear that the ghost would be angry and return to avenge the dead. The rule has come down to us and is an imperative one. Eulogies on the dead are, therefore, conventional falsehoods. It is quite impossible for any one to depart from the fashion. The principle is in fashion that one should take the side of the weaker party in a contest. This principle has no rational ground at all. There is simply a slight probability that the stronger will be in the wrong. Fashion requires that we should all affect nonpartisanship in discussion, although it is absurd to do so. Of course these weighty rules on important matters go over into the mores, but they are fashions because they are arbitrary, have no rational grounds, cannot be put to any test, and have no sanction except that everybody submits to them.

196. Remoter effects of fashion. The selective effect of fashion, in spite of its irrationality and independently of the goodness or badness of its effect on interests, is a reflection on the intelligence of men. It accounts for many heterogeneous phenomena in society. The fashions influence the mores. They can make a thing modest or immodest, proper or improper, and, if they last long enough, they affect the sense and the standards of modesty and propriety. Fashions of banking and trading affect standards of honesty, or definitions of cheating and gambling. Public shows, dances, punishments, and executions affect, in time, standards of decency, taste in amusement, sentiments of humanity, views as to what is interesting and attractive.

Methods of argument which are fashionable may train people to flippancy, sophistry, levity of mind, and may destroy the power to think and reason correctly. Scherr[1] says that fashion served as a means to transfer to Germany the depravation of morals which had corrupted the Latin nations in the sixteenth century. Fashions now spread through all civilized nations by contact and contagion. They are spread by literature.

197. Slang and expletives. Slang and expletives are fashions in language. Expletives are of all grades from simple interjections to the strongest profanity. Many expletives are ancient religious formulas of objurgation, obsecration, asseveration, anathema, etc. They express a desire to curse or bless, invite or repel. Where the original sense is lost they sink into interjections, the whole sense of which is in the accent. Their use rises and falls with fashion in nations, classes, groups, and families, and it controls the habits of individuals. Whether certain persons use a pious dialect, a learned (pedantic) dialect, a gambler's slang, a phraseology of excessive adjectives and silly expletives, or profane expressions, oaths, and phrases which abuse sacred things, depends on birth and training. In this sense each dialect is the language for each group and corresponds to the mores of the group. There may be some psychology of expletives,[2] but they seem to be accounted for, like slang, by the expediency of expression, which is the purpose of all language. There is a need for expression which will win attention and impress the memory. A strong expletive shocks an opponent, or it is an instinctive reaction on a situation which threatens the well-being of the speaker. It is a vent to emotion which gives relief from it when other relief is not possible. This last is one of the chief useful reasons for expletives. However, even then they are a vicious habit, for stronger and stronger expressions are required to win the same subjective effects. Old expressions lose force. Slang is the new coinage. The mintage is often graphic and droll; it is also often stupid and vulgar. A selection goes on. Some of it is rejected and

---

[1] *Deutsche Frauenwelt*, II, 65.
[2] Patrick in *Psych. Rev.*, VIII, 113.

some enters into the language. Expletives also go out of fashion. The strain for effect can be satisfied only by constantly greater and greater excess. It becomes a bad personal habit to use grotesque and extravagant expressions. Slang and expletives destroy the power of clear and cogent expression in speech or writing; and they must affect powers of thinking. Although slang is a new coinage which reinvigorates the language, the fashion of slang and expletives must be rated, like the fashion of using tobacco and alcohol, as at best a form of play, a habit and custom which springs from no need and conduces to no interest. The acts result in an idle satisfaction of the doer, and the good or ill effects all fall within his own organism. The prevalence of such fashions in a society becomes a fact of its mores, for there will be rational effects on interests. The selective effect of them is in the resistance to the fashions or subjection to them. They are only to a limited extent enforced by social sanctions. There is personal liberty in regard to them. Resistance depends on independent judgment and self-control, and produces independence and self-control; that is, it affects character. Groups are differentiated inside the society of those who resist and those who do not, and the effect on the mores (character of the group) results. The selective effects appear in the competition of life between the two groups.

198. Poses, fads, and cant. When fashion seizes upon an idea or usage and elevates it to a feature of a society at a period, it is, as was said above, affected by those who cannot attain to the real type and who exaggerate its external forms. The humanism of the Renaissance produced an affectation of learning, dilettante interest in collecting manuscripts, and zeal for style which was genuine in scholars, but was an affectation of the followers. There was also an affectation of pagan philosophy and of alienation from Christianity. The euphuists in England in the sixteenth century, the *précieuses* of Molière's time, the *illuminati* of the eighteenth century, are instances of groups of people who took up a whim and exaggerated conduct of a certain type, practicing an affectation. There are poses which are practiced as a fashion for a time. Fads get currency.

Dandyism, athleticism, pedantry of various kinds, reforms of various kinds, movements, causes, and questions are phenomena of fads around which groups cluster, formed of persons who have a common taste and sentiment. Poses go with them. Poses are also affected by those who select a type of character which is approved. The dandy has had a score of slang names within two centuries corresponding to varieties of the pose and dress which he affected. He has now given way to the athlete, who is quite a different type. The Byronic pose prevailed for a generation. Goethe's Werther inspired a pose. They would both now be ridiculed. Favorite heroes in novels have often set a pose. Carlyle inspired a literary pose ("hatred of shams," etc.). He and Ruskin set a certain cant afloat, for every fad and pose which pretends to be sober and earnest must have a cant. Zola, D'Annunzio, Wagner, Ibsen, Gorky, Tolstoi, Sudermann, are men who have operated suggestion on the public mind of our time. They get a response from a certain number who thus cluster into a self-selected union of sympathy and propagate the cult of a view of life. Gloom and savagery, passion and crime, luxury and lust, romance and adventure, adultery and divorce, self-indulgence and cynicism, the reality of foulness and decay, are so suggested as to become centers on which receptive minds will organize and congenial ones will combine in sympathy. It is the effect of a great and active literature of belles-lettres, which is practically current throughout the civilized world, to multiply these sects of sentimental philosophy, with the fads and poses which correspond, and to provide them with appropriate cant. The cant of the voluptuary, the cynical egoist, the friend of humanity, and all the rest is just as distinct as that of the religious sectarian. Each of the little groups operates its own selection, but each is small. They interfere with and neutralize each other, but a general drift may be imparted by them to the mores. Our age is optimistic by virtue of the economic opportunities, power, and prosperity which it enjoys. The writers above mentioned are all pessimistic. They do not affect the age except upon the surface, by entertaining it, but they disturb its moral philosophy, they confuse its standards and codes, and they corrupt its tastes. They set fashions in literature which the writers of the second class imitate. In general, they relax the inhibitions which have come down to us in our mores without giving by suggestion an independence of character which would replace the traditions by sound judgments. Their influence will be greater when it has been diluted so as to reach the great mass. It hardly can be worse than that of the literature which is now used by that class.

199. Illustrations. In the later days of Greece the study of Homer became an affectation. Dio Chrysostom tells of a visit he made to a colony on the Borysthenes, in which nearly all could read the *Iliad*, and heard it more willingly than anything else.[1] The Athenians, especially the gilded youth, affected Spartan manners and ways. The dandies went about with uncut hair, unwashed hands, and they practiced fist-fights. They were as proud of torn ears as German students are of cuts on their faces.[2] The religious and social reforms of Augustus were a pose. They lacked sincerity and were adopted for a political purpose. Men took them up who did not conform their own conduct to them. Hence a "general social falsehood" was the result.[3] In the fourth and fifth centuries all the well-to-do classes spent their time in making imitations of the ancient literature and philosophy. They tried to imitate Seneca and Pliny, writing compositions and letters, and pursuing a mode of life which they supposed the men of the period of glory had lived.[4] The French of the fifteenth century had the greatest fear of ridicule; the Italians feared most that they might appear to be simpletons.[5] In the fifteenth and sixteenth centuries the "chevaliers transis" wore furs in summer and summer mantles in winter. They meant to prove that "love suffices for everything."[6] Old pictures of the sixteenth century show that it was considered modest to squint. A Spaniard thought

[1] *Orat.*, XXXVI.
[2] Beloch, *Griech. Gesch.*, II, 29.
[3] Boissier, *Relig. Rom.*, I, 211.
[4] Dill, *Last Century of the Western Empire.*
[5] Gregorovius, *Lucretia Borgia*, 99.
[6] De Maulde la Clavière, *Les Femmes de la Renaissance*, 457.

that it showed friendship for any one to squint at him. It was also considered a sign of probity to have the lips primly closed and drawn.[1] The Italian *cicisbeo* in the seventeenth century was a *cavalier servente*, who attended a married lady. Such men practiced extravagances and affectations, and are generally described as effeminate.[2]

200. Heroes, scapegoats and butts, caricature. Fashion sets, for any group at any time, its pet likes and dislikes. The mass must have its heroes, but also its victims and scapegoats and the butts of its ridicule. Caricature is futile when it is destitute of point. The test of it lies in the popular response which shows whether it has touched the core of the thing or not. When it can do this it reveals the real truth about the thing better than a volume of argument could do it. Sometimes a popular conviction is produced by a single incident which is a very important societal fact. The voyage of the Oregon from the Pacific (1898) convinced the American people that they must cut a canal through the isthmus. Probably this conviction was a *non sequitur*, but argument cannot overcome it, and it will control action with all the financial and other consequences which must ensue. A satire, an epigram, or a caricature may suffice to produce such a conviction.

201. Caricature. The mere rhetorical form may have the greatest importance. A caricature often stings national vanity. A state may be represented as afraid, as having " backed down,' as having appeared ridiculous. Group vanity is often a stronger motive than personal vanity, and the desire to gratify it will prove stronger than any rational conviction.

202. Relation of fads, etc., to mores. Thus the vanities, desires, prejudices, faiths, likes, and dislikes, which pervade a society, coerce dissenters and become stronger and stronger mass phenomena. They then affect interests. Then they wind strands of influence and control around individuals and demand sacrifices. In their combination they weave webs of action which constitute life and history. The selection which they

---

[1] Erasmus, *De Civil. Morum Pueril.*, I, i, 1.
[2] De Maulde, 470.

exert, drawing in some and repelling others, produces results on the societal fabric of a later time. The consequences react on character, moral tone, life philosophy, ethical principles, and ruling sentiments. Thus they affect the mores, or even enter into them. The whole is handed on to the rising generation to be their outfit of knowledge, faith, and policy, and their rules of duty and well living.

203. Ideals. An ideal is entirely unscientific. It is a phantasm which has little or no connection with fact. Ideals are very often formed in the effort to escape from the hard task of dealing with facts, which is the function of science and art. There is no process by which to reach an ideal. There are no tests by which to verify it. It is therefore impossible to frame a proposition about an ideal which can be proved or disproved. It follows that the use of ideals is to be strictly limited to proper cases, and that the attempt to use ideals in social discussion does not deserve serious consideration. An ideal differs from a model in that the model is deduced from reality but within the bounds of reality. It is subject to approved methods of attainment and realization. An ideal also differs from a standard, for a standard must be real.

204. When ideals may be used. What are the proper cases for the use of ideals? Ideals can be useful when they are formed in the imagination of the person who is to realize them by his own exertions, for then the ideal and the programme of action are in the same consciousness, and therefore the defects of an ideal are reduced or removed. Ideals are useful (*a*) in homiletics, which are chiefly occupied with attempts at sugges-tion. In limited cases a preacher or teacher can suggest ideals which, if apprehended and adopted, become types toward which young persons may train themselves. Even then these cases merge in the next class. (*b*) Ideals are useful in self-education. The idea is then taken up from books or from admired persons by suggestion and imitation, or from autosuggestion, but gen-erally from a combination of the two. An ideal from autosug-gestion produces enthusiasm. The fantastic character of the ideal, if the person is young, is unimportant. His will is enlisted to work for it. He can constantly compare the ideal with his experience. The ideal is at last shorn down to reality and merges in sober plans of effort. (c) A far larger field for ideals is afforded by vanity. As vanity is itself a subjective affection, but one which can be awakened only in society, it uses the imagination to suppose cases, plan unlimited schemes, devise types of self-decoration and dreams of superiority, distinction, power, success, and glory. The creations are all phantasms. The ends are all ideals. These ideals may not be extravagant. Vanity generally creates them by raising to a higher pitch some treatment of the body or dress, some admired trait of character, some action which has won glory, or given pleasure and won applause. This whole field for ideals is largely influenced by suggestion from the current tastes and fashionable standards in the group, but autosuggestion is also very active in it. (d) Ideals also find a great field in marriage. In this case ideals of happiness have powerfully affected the institution at all its stages. Experience of marriage has been partly pleasant and partly the contrary. The experience has stimulated the reflection: How blessed it would be if only this or that unpleasant detail could be corrected! This has led to idealization or the imaginative conception of a modified institution. Our novels now sometimes aid in this idealization. Men loved their daughters with zealous and protective affection long before they loved their wives. The father's love reached out to follow his daughter into matrimony and to secure for her some stipulations which should free wedlock for her from pain or care which other wives had to endure. These stipulations were always guided by idealization. The rich and great were first able to realize the modifications. These then passed into fashion, custom, and the mores, and the institution was perfected and refined by them.

205. Ideals of beauty. The educated ideals under the second and third of the above heads become mass phenomena under the influence of fashion, when they control many or all. Ideal types of beauty are adopted by a group. Uncivilized people adopt such types of bodily beauty (sec. 189). The origin of them is unknown. A Samoan mother presses her thumb on the

nose of her baby to flatten it.[1] An Indian mother puts a board
on the forehead of her baby to make it recede. Teeth are
knocked out, or filed into prescribed shapes, or blackened. The
skin is painted, cut into scars, or tattooed. Goblinism may have
furnished the original motives for some deformations, but the
natural physical features of the group which distinguish it from
others, or the features produced by goblinistic usages, come to
be the standard of beauty for the group. Those features are
accentuated and exaggerated by the deformations which are
practiced. The aim is at an ideal perfection of physical beauty.
All fashion in dress has the same philosophy. In other cases,
also, it seems that fashion is pursuing a fleeting and impossible
ideal of perfect beauty, style, grace, dexterity, etc., which shall
give distinction and superiority or impose subjection.

206. The man-as-he-should-be. Group ideals may be types of
character. In the Old Testament the ideal type is the "just
man," who conformed to ritual standards at all points. A Moslem is a man who is "faithful" to Islam, which is self-surrender
to the Omnipotent One.[2] The type of the perfect man-as-he-
should-be in the Mahabharata is one who will give his all to a
Brahmin. The god Siva, disguised as a Brahmin, came to a hero.
He ordered the hero to kill his own son and serve his corpse
for the Brahmin to eat. The hero obeyed at once. The Brahmin
set the hero's buildings on fire, but the latter served the dish
without heeding the fire. The Brahmin ordered him to eat of
the dish. He prepared to obey, but was excused from this trial.
He had triumphantly stood the test. There was nothing he
would not do for a Brahmin.[3] The poem also contains a type of
female perfection in person and character, — Savitri.[4] The
Greeks had many standards of personal excellence and social
worth which entered to some extent into their mores. The ideal
types were noble and refined. They have affected the mores of
the class educated in the "humanities" since the Renaissance.

[1] *Austr. Ass. Adv. Sci.*, 1892, 62; JAI, XIII, 280.
[2] Pischon, *Einfluss d. Islam*, 1.
[3] *Das Freie Wort*, II, 312.
[4] Holtzmann, *Indische Sagen*, I, 247.

They have never been truly incorporated in the mores of any society. *Olbos* was wealth, with grace, opulence, elegance, and generosity, and so wealth when not sordid or arrogant, the opposite of plutocratic. *Arete* was capacity, capability, and practical efficiency, — executive ability. *Aidos* was the opposite of "cheek." *Sophrosyne* was continence, self-control. *Kalokagathie* contained notions of economic, æsthetic, and moral good, fused into a single concept.[1] The *eleutheros* was the gentleman endowed with all admirable qualities.[2] The Greeks proved that people could sink very low while talking very nobly. The ideals were in the literature, not in the mores. "Their predisposition, their will, and their fate formed a consistent whole, and their decline was a consequence of the social and political life which they lived."[3] In the sixth and seventh centuries A.D. the man-as-he-should-be was religious, — a hermit or a monk. In any case he was an ascetic. In Charlemagne's time the preferred type was changed. It became the warrior and knight, and led up to chivalry. A new poetry flourished to develop and propagate the new ideal. In mediæval society there were strongly defined ideals of the man-as-he-should-be. *Milte* was generosity of heart and mind. In the twelfth and thirteenth centuries it was the noble desire of the lord to share all he had with his retainers, which desire called out their devotion to him.[4] The minstrels meant by it lavishness of gifts to themselves. *Maze* was the cardinal virtue. It meant observation of the limits in all actions and manifestations of feeling, the opposite of excess and extravagance.[5] The church taught admiration of arbitrary ideals of ecclesiastical virtues. The ideals were ascetic. They seem to have been derived from the fathers of the fourth and fifth centuries, but they offer an example of borrowed and adopted ideals which were fully incorporated in the popular mores. The age accepted ascetic standards of goodness and character. The religious classes and the lay classes did not fall under the same

[1] Burckhardt, *Griech. Kulturgeschichte*, I, 171; II, 365.
[2] Becker-Hermann, *Charikles*, III, 318.
[3] Burckhardt, II, 365.
[4] Uhlhand, *Dichtung und Sage*, 232.
[5] Weinhold, *Deutsche Frauen*, I, 162.

standards of conduct and duty. It was the business of the former to live by the full standard. All classes, however, accepted the standards as valid, and the layman conformed to them at times, or as far as worldly life would permit. Elizabeth of Thuringia seems to be the ideal of the married woman, but her saintliness interfered with her other duties, and even her own time does not seem to have been sure in its judgment of her. That she was flogged is a fact which has many relations to her character and her age.[1] All admired men who practiced asceticism and self-discipline. The types of the age were knightliness and saintliness. They were both highly elaborated. The knightly type began to develop in the time of Charlemagne and ran through the crusades. It contained grotesque and absurd elements. The story of the crusades is a criticism upon it. The knight was a fantastic person, who might do isolated deeds of valor, but who could not make a plan, work persistently to a purpose, coöperate with others, or either enforce or submit to discipline. Both the knight and the saint were ideal types which exerted a controlling power of selection through centuries.

207. The standard type of man. Is the ideal of the man-as-he-should-be to be found, for us, in the " common man," or in the highest product of our culture ? That is a most vital question for any society. It includes the question whether the society has a discord in itself as to its own ideal of the type of men it wants to produce. In the upper strata of the masses, amongst the educated, industrious, sober-minded people of good incomes, there exists the best family life. The children live constantly with their parents, and the latter watch over the health, manners, and morals of the children unceasingly from birth to maturity. The same parents make great sacrifices for the education of their children, although the class, as a class, has means to secure what is necessary without hard sacrifice. The point is that they value education highly and get it. We also multiply educational institutions. We feel sure that all this is good work. The churches and all good literature constantly inculcate good manners and morals according to the standards in the present

[1] Michael, *Gesch. d. Deutschen Volkes*, II, 209–214.

mores. Here is a set of objects to be prized and worked for in families, schools, self-education, literature, and art, which go to the production of a type of men as the highest product of our civilization. Then suddenly we are told that the common man is wise beyond all the philosophers. The man on the curbstone is the arbiter of our destinies, and the standard man. "Culture" is derided and sneered at. This latter view has great popularity. It brings up a serious question: whether we are spoiling our children by educating them. Are we spoiling them for political power? Are we putting them under disabilities for public influence? It is related of an English statesman, that when asked by an American mother whether she should send her son to Oxford, he replied: "Why send him to Oxford? Send him to Washington, where he will learn democracy. That is what he will need to know." Certainly it behooves us to know whether we are spoiling our sons by sending them to the universities, and whether we ought not rather to send them to Tammany Hall. Either on one side or the other there is a great mass of empty phrases and false but inflated rhetoric.

208. Who does the thinking? The notion that "the group thinks" deserves to be put by the side of the great freaks of philosophy which have been put forth from age to age. Only the élite of any society, in any age, think, and the world's thinking is carried on by them by the transplanting of ideas from mind to mind, under the stress and strain of clashing argument and tugging debate. If the group thinks, then thought costs nothing, but in truth thought costs beyond everything else, for thousands search and talk while only one finds; when he finds something, a step is won and all begins over again. If this is so, it ought to be universally known and recognized. All the mores would then conform to it.

209. The gentleman. In modern English-speaking society the "gentleman" is the name for the man-as-he-should-be. The type is not fixed and the definition is not established. It is a collective and social ideal. Gentlemen are a group in society who have selected a code and standard of conduct as most conducive to prosperous and pleasant social relations. Therefore manners are an essential element in the type. A gentleman is one who has been educated to conform to the type, and that he has the *cachet* is indicated by his admission to the group. Novels develop and transmit the ideal; clubs are the tribunal of it. It is a floating notion which varies with the mores. The modern reader finds very few cases in Greek literature of what he can recognize as gentlemen. Orestes in the *Electra* of Euripides opens the discussion of what makes the worth of a man, but after saying that it is not wealth or poverty, and not valor in war, he flinches the question and says that it is better to leave it untouched. The peasant, married to Electra, certainly acts the gentleman. He also says of Orestes and Pylades, that if they really are as noble as they seem, they will be as well satisfied with humble fare as with grand fare. A gentleman of a century ago would not be approved now. A gentleman of to-day in the society of a century ago would be thought to have rowdy manners. Artificial manners are not in the taste of our time; athletics are. The "gentleman" always tends to an arbitrary definition. It appears now that he must have some skill at sports and games. The selective force of the social type of the gentleman is obvious in our own society. The sentiment *noblesse oblige* was once the name for the coercive force exerted on a noble by the code of his class. Now that fixed classes are gone and the gentleman is only defined by the usage and taste of an informal class, it is a term for the duties which go with social superiority of any kind, so far as those duties are prescribed and sanctioned by public opinion.

210. Social standard set by taboos. It may be still more important to notice that the standard social type is defined by taboos with only social sanctions. The negative side of *noblesse oblige* is more important than the positive. A gentleman is under more restraints than a non-gentleman. In the eighteenth century he patronized cockfights and prize fights, and he could get drunk, gamble, tell falsehoods, and deceive women without losing caste. He now finds that *noblesse oblige* forbids all these things, and that it puts him under disabilities in politics and business.

A society exerts a positive selection on individuals by its definition of crimes and by its criminal jurisprudence. The taboos
are turned into laws and are enforced by positive penalties.

211. Crimes. The number and variety of crimes depends on
the positive action of the state. What things are crimes in a
state, therefore, indicates what the ruling authority desires to
prevent. The motives have often been entirely selfish on the
part of a king or a ruling caste, or they were dictated by a desire
to further the vanity of such persons. By judicial precedent at
Rome it was made a crime to beat a slave, or to undress near
a statue of the emperor, or to carry a coin bearing his image
into a latrine or a lupanar.[1] Xiphilin, in his epitome of the
history of Dio Cassius, inserts a story that, in the reign of
Domitian, a woman was executed for undressing near the statue
of that emperor.[2] The notions in the mores of what ought to
be prevented have been very variable and arbitrary. Juvenal
denounces a consul who while in office drove his own chariot,
although by night.[3] Seneca was shocked at the criminal luxury
of putting snow in wine.[4] Pliny is equally shocked at the fashion
of wearing gold rings.[5] Lecky, after citing these cases, refers
to the denunciations uttered by the church fathers against women
who wore false hair. Painting the face is an old fault of women,
against which moral teachers of all ages have thundered. Very
recently, amongst us, clergymen have denounced women for not
wearing bonnets in church, because Paul said that she " dishon-
oreth her head, for that is even all one as if she were shaven." [6]
These were not indeed cases of crimes, but of alleged vices or
sins. In sumptuary laws we have cases of legislation which made
fashions crimes. In the eighteenth century there was little legislation against brothels, drinking places, or gambling houses. We
make it a crime to sell rum, but not to drink it. On the other
hand, until recently commercial transactions and the lending of

---

[1] Suetonius, *Tiberius*, 58.
[2] Manning, *Trans. of Xiphilin*, II, 83; *Xiphilin's Epitome*, published in 1551.
[3] *Satires*, VIII, 146.
[4] *Nat. Quaest.*, IV, 13; *Ep.*, 78.
[5] *Hist. Nat.*, XXXIII, 4.
[6] *N. Y. Times*, August 18, 1903. (Cf. sec. 483.)

money for interest were so restricted in accordance with ethical and economic faiths that they were environed by crimes which are now obsolete. Heresy and sorcery were once very great crimes. Witchcraft and usury were abominable crimes.

212. Criminal law. In the original administration of justice it appears that there was only one punishment for the violation of taboo, sin and crime being coincident: that was death. Then, in cases, banishment was substituted for death, although this was only a change in form, since a banished man could not exist alone. In either case the selection was of the simplest kind. The society extruded from itself one who violated its rules. This is the fundamental sense of all punishments, like execution, transportation, or imprisonment, which remove the culprit from the society, permanently or for a time. Other punishments contained originally a large element of vengeance, vengeance being a primary impulse of great force to satisfy those whom the crimes injured and to deter others from the same crime. The administration of justice, therefore, bore witness to the judgment of the society as to what conduct and character should be selected for preservation or caused to cease. In all modern states the power to make acts crimes has been abused, and the motive of punishment has been so lost that we wrangle as to what it is. The ruling coterie uses the power to make things crimes to serve its own interests. Protectionists make it criminal to import goods. Governments do the same to further their fiscal purposes. They also make it criminal to immigrate or emigrate, or to coin money, even of full weight and fineness, or to carry letters and parcels. In England it is made a crime to violate railroad regulations. In some cases regulations for barber shops are enforced by making violations crimes. Generally, sanitary rules are so enforced. In the latest case it has been made a crime to spit in public places. The criminal law expresses the mores of the time when they have reached very concrete and definite formulæ of prohibition. Perhaps the administration of it expresses the mores still more clearly. It is now recognized as true that frightful penalties do not exert a proportionately deterrent effect. Our mores do not permit us to inflict pain in order to compel men to confess, or to put them in solitary confinement in dark and loathsome dungeons, or to let our prisons become sinks of vice and misery or schools of crime. The selective effect of punishment is the one which we seem to aim at, although not very intelligently.

213. Mass phenomena of fear and hope. Manias and delusions are mental phenomena, but they are social. They are diseases of the mind, but they are epidemic. They are contagious, not as cholera is contagious, but contact with others is essential to them. They are mass phenomena.[1] Some great hope (the good to be obtained by taking the heads of murdered men or from appeasing the gods by sacrificing one's children) or some great fear (drought, failure of food, purgatory), if common to the whole, makes them adopt any suggestion of a means to realize the hope or avert the feared calamity. Often there is no such quasi-rational reason for common action. Hysteria, especially amongst women and children, produces manias of falsehood, deceit (fasting women), trances, and witchcraft. In mediæval convents sometimes half the inmates were afflicted at the same time. Nervous depression and irritation produced physical acts of relief. One irritated another, and one surpassed another, until there was a catastrophe for the group.[2] Religious enthusiasm has produced innumerable manias and delusions. Mediæval Christianity, Mohammedanism, Persia, and modern Russia furnish cases. Martyrdom proves nothing with regard to the truth or value of a religion. All the sects have had martyrs. Martyrdom, even under torture, has been sought, under the influence of religious enthusiasm, not only by Christians[3] but by Donatists,[4] Manichæans, and other most abominated heretics. Even the Adamites produced martyrs who went joyously to death.[5] Quakers really provoked their own martyrdom in early New England.

214. Manias, delusions. The phenomena of manias, popular delusions, group hallucinations, self-immolation, etc., show the possibilities of mental contagion in a group. They are responses to hope or fear which affect large numbers at the same time.

---

[1] Achelis, *Die Ekstase*, 113.
[2] Regnard, *Sorcellerie*, 45.
[3] Lecky, *Eur. Morals*, I, 391.
[4] Gibbon, Chap. XXI.
[5] Lea, *Inquis.*, II, 518

They are often·produced by public calamities, or other ills of life. Those who suffer feel themselves selected as victims, and they ask, Who has done this to us, and why? Often people who are not victims interpret a natural incident by egoistic reference. This is done not on account of the destruction wrought by an earthquake or a tornado, but from pure terror at what is not understood, e.g. an eclipse.[1] Pilgrimages and crusades were cases of mania and delusion. The element of delusion was in the notion of high merit which could be won in pursuing the crusades. Very often manias and delusions are pure products of fashion, as in the case of the children's crusades, when the children caught the infection of the crusades, but did not know what they were doing, or why, and rushed on their own destruction. Often manias are logical deductions from notions (especially religious notions) which have been suggested, as in the case of the flagellants. It is the ills of life which drive people to such deductions, and they bear witness to excessive nervous excitement. The mediæval dancing mania was more purely nervous. The demonism and demonology of the Middle Ages was a fertile source for such deductions, which went far to produce the witchcraft mania. The demonistic notions taught by the church furnished popular deductions, which the church took up and reduced to dogmatic form, and returned as such to the masses. Thus the notions of sorcery, heresy, and witchcraft were developed.

215. Monstrous mass phenomena of mediæval society. There must have been a deep and strong anthropological reason for the development of monstrous social phenomena in mediæval society. The Latin world was disintegrated to its first elements between the sixth century and the tenth. Such a dissolution of society abolished the inherited mores with all their restraints and inhibitions, and left society to the control of fierce barbaric, that is physical, forces. At the same period the Latin world absorbed hordes of barbarians who were still on a low nomadic warrior stage of civilization, and who adopted the ruins of Roman culture without assimilating them. The Christian church contributed crass superstitions about the other world and the relations of this world to

[1] Friedmann, *Wahnideen im Völkerleben*, 224.

it. The product was the Merovingian and Carlovingian history. Passion, sensuality, ferocity, superstitious ignorance, and fear characterized the age. It is supposed that western Europe was overpopulated and that the crusades operated a beneficial reduction of numbers.[1] These facts may account for the gigantic mass phenomena in the early Middle Ages. Every sentiment was extravagant. Men were under some mighty gregarious instinct which drove them to act in masses, and they passed from one great passion or enthusiastic impulse to another at very short intervals. The passions of hatred and revenge were manifested, upon occasion, to the extremity of fiendishness. Nothing which the mind could conceive of seemed to be renounced as excessive (Clement V, John XXII). Gregory IX pursued the heretics and the emperor with an absorption of his whole being and a rancor which we cannot understand. Poverty was elevated into a noble virtue and a transcendent merit.[2] This was the height of ascetic absurdity, since poverty is only want, and the next step would be a cult of suicide. The mendicant orders fought each other malignantly. Every difference of opinion made a war of extermination. Civil contests were carried on with extravagant ferocity as to the means used and as to the exultation of success or the penalty of failure. What was lacking was discipline. There was no authority or doctrine which could set limits to private passion. Life was held cheap. The gallows and the pit were in use all the time. The most marked product of invention was instruments of torture. Men and women were burned to death for frivolous reasons. Punishments taught people to gloat over suffering. Torture was inflicted as idly as we take testimony. With all this went deep faith in the efficacy of ritual and great other-worldliness, that is, immediate apprehension of the other world in this one. All the mores were adjusted to these features of faith and practice. It all proceeded out of the masses of the people. The church was borne along like a chip on the tide. The church hung back from the crusades until the depth of the popular interest had been tested. Then the crusades were declared to be the "will of God." This

---

[1] Kugler, *Kreuzzüge*, 7.
[2] Michael, *Gesch. d. Deutschen Volkes*, II, 80.

gave their own idea back again to the masses with the approval
of the societal authority. The masses insisted on having acts and
apparatus provided by which to satisfy their application of dogma.
The power of the keys and the treasure of salvation were provided
accordingly. The souls of the people were torn by the antagonism between the wild passions of the age and the ecclesiastical
restraints on conduct. They feared the wrath of God and hell to
come. The ritual and sacramental system furnished a remedy.
The flagellants were a phenomenon of seething, popular passion,
outside of the church and unapproved by its authority. Antony
of Padua († 1231) started the movement by his sermons on
repentance and the wrath of God. Processions of weeping, praying, self-scourging, and half-naked penitents appeared in the
streets of all the towns of Christendom. "Nearly all enemies
made friends. Usurers and robbers made haste to restore ill-
gotten goods, and other vicious men confessed and renounced vanity. Prisons were opened. Prisoners were released. Exiles were
allowed to return. Men and women accomplished works of pity
and holiness, as if they feared the all-powerful God would consume them with fire from heaven."[1] This movement was altogether popular. It broke out again in 1349, in connection with
the Black Death. Flagellation for thirty-three and a half days
was held to purge from all sin. This was heresy and the flagellants were persecuted. The theory was a purely popular application by the masses of the church doctrine of penance, outside
of the church system. It reappeared from time to time. The
dancing mania began at Aix-la-Chapelle in 1373 and lasted for
several years.[2] It was an outlet for high nervous tension under
which the population was suffering on account of great calamities,
social distress, and superstitious interpretations of the same. In
short, the period was one of monstrous phenomena, extravagant
passions, and unreasonable acts.

216. Gregariousness of the Middle Ages. "To estimate fully
the force of these popular ebullitions in the Middle Ages, we
must bear in mind the susceptibility of the people to contagious

[1] Michael, *Gesch. d. Deutschen Volkes*, II, 255–258.
[2] Lea, *Inquis.*, II, 381, 393.

emotions and enthusiasms of which we know little in our colder
day. A trifle might start a movement which the wisest could not
explain nor the most powerful restrain. It was during the preaching of this crusade [of 1208, against the Albigenses] that
villages and towns in Germany were filled with women who,
unable to expend their religious ardor in taking the cross,
stripped themselves naked and ran silently through the roads
and streets. Still more symptomatic of the diseased spirituality
of the time was the crusade of the children, which desolated
thousands of homes. From vast districts of territory, incited
apparently by a simultaneous and spontaneous impulse, crowds
of children set forth, without leaders or guides, in search of the
Holy Land ; and their only answer, when questioned as to their
object, was that they were going to Jerusalem. Vainly did
parents lock their children up ; they would break loose and disappear ; and the few who eventually found their way home again
could give no reason for the overmastering longing which had
carried them away. Nor must we lose sight of other and less
creditable springs of action which brought to all crusades the
vile, who came for license and spoil, and the base, who sought
the immunity conferred by the quality of crusader." [1] "To com-
prehend fully the magnitude and influence of these movements we
must bear in mind the impressionable character of the populations
and their readiness to yield to contagious emotion. When we
are told that the Franciscan Berthold of Ratisbon frequently
preached to crowds of sixty thousand souls, we realize what power
was lodged in the hands of those who could reach masses so
easily swayed and so full of blind yearnings to escape from the
ignoble life to which they were condemned. How the slumber-
ing souls were awakened is shown by the successive waves of
excitement which swept over one portion of Europe after another
about the middle of the thirteenth century. The dumb, untutored
minds began to ask whether an existence of hopeless and brutal
misery was all that was to be realized from the promises of the
gospel. The church had made no real effort at internal reform ;
it was still grasping, covetous, licentious, and a strange desire

[1] Lea, *Inquis.*, I, 147.

for something — they knew not exactly what — began to take possession of men's hearts and spread like an epidemic from village to village and from land to land." [1]

What we see here is the power of mere gregariousness, the impulse of acting in a crowd, without knowledge or purpose. The mere sense of being in the current movement, or "in the fashion," is a pleasure. When the movement is great in its compass and the numbers involved there is an exhilaration about being in it. If the notions by which it is enthused are great, or holy and noble, in form and pretense, even if not really so, it may become demonic, and it may accomplish incredible things. We had a grand illustration of this at the outbreak of the Civil War, in 1861, both in the North and South. Dissent on both sides was overwhelmed and all were swept away into the prevailing current.

217. The mendicant orders. The mendicant orders responded to the deepest popular faiths and highest standards of the thirteenth century. Francis of Assisi († 1226) took up the notion that it was wrong to own property, or at least meritorious to renounce it, and affirmed that Christ and his apostles repudiated all property and lived on alms. The Timotheists of the fifth century had held this notion, but were rated as heretics.[2] Poverty, for Francis, did not mean a little property, but absolute rejection of all property. This was necessarily only a pose. He had to use other men's property, the use being right. Therefore he could only renounce productive labor. The popular religious temper of the time revered simplicity, humility, self-denial, and renunciation of "the world" as especially evangelical virtues. They were thought to be summed up in poverty. That Francis was a hero of this type of religion has been universally admitted. The virtues were just the ones which the Roman court did not show. Jacques de Vitry, an enthusiastic preacher against the Albigenses, went through Italy to Palestine in 1216. He left a journal[3] in which he recorded his sadness at observing that, at the papal court, all were busy with secular affairs, kings and kingdoms, quarrels and lawsuits, so that it was almost impossible to speak

---

[1] Lea, *Inquis.*, I, 268.   [2] Lea, *Sacerd. Celib.*, 377.
[3] *Nouv. Mem. de l'Acad. des Sciences, Lettres, et Beaux Arts de Belgique*, XXIII, 30.

about spiritual matters. He greatly admired the Franciscans, who were trying to renew primitive Christianity and save souls, thus shaming the prelates, who were "dogs who do not bark." The Count of Chiusi gave to Francis the mountain La Verna for retirement and meditation. Armed men were necessary to take possession of it against the beasts and robbers who had possession of it.[1] Carmichael believes that Francis received the stigmata, which he describes in detail. The Francis of tradition is a fabulous person, created out of the pet ideas of his time.[2] The historical person was a visionary. Dominic was a zealot. He wanted to convert all heretics by preaching or other means.

218. Other mendicant orders. De Vitry found Humiliati in Lombardy, who were living by ideas like those of Francis. The Augustinian hermits were founded in 1256, the Carmelites in 1245, and the Servites, or Servants of Mary, about 1275.[3] These were all mendicants, and they bear witness to the character of the notions of the time about poverty. It was a mania, and is fully expressed in the *Romaunt de la Rose*. Perhaps Francis did not mean to "found an order." He wanted to live in a certain way with a few friends. The spontaneous and very rapid spread of his order proves that it was concordant with a great popular taste. Francis was a dreamer and enthusiast, not a politician or organizer at all. In his testament he says: "After the Lord had given me care of the brethren, no one showed me what I ought to do, but the Highest Himself revealed to me that I ought to live according to the mode of the Holy Gospel." He was not thwarted and subjugated by the curia during his life, but his ideals were not maintained by the men in the order. The man who was later pope Gregory IX aided him to organize the order and to make it practically efficient, that is, to take the enthusiasm out of it and make it practical.[4] The popes of the thirteenth century approved. There was in the principles of the order an antagonism to the church as it was, and also an antagonism to common sense. The church authorities wanted to bring the order into practical use, and suspected it of the heresies of Florus. It therefore split into "conventuals," who conformed to the methods of conventual life, and the "spirituals," who clung to the doctrines and rules of the founder. The latter became "observantines" (1368) and "recollects" (1487).[5] The two branches hated each other and fought on all occasions. In 1275 the spirituals were treated as heretics, imprisoned in

[1] Carmichael, *In Tuscany*, 224.
[2] See the *Fioretti de Francisco*.
[3] Michael, *Gesch. d. Deutschen Volkes*, II, 97.
[4] Goetz, in *Hist. Vierteljahrschrift*, VI, 19.
[5] Lea, *Inquis.*, III, 172, 179.

chains, and forbidden the sacrament.[1] John XXII condemned their doctrine as heretical. This put the observantines in the same position as other heretical sects. They must be rebels and heretics or give up ideas which seemed to them the sum of all truth and wisdom. Generally they clung to their ideas like the heretics.[2] One of their heroes was Bernard Delicieux († 1320), who is celebrated as the only man who ever dared to resist the Inquisition. He was tortured twice, and condemned to imprisonment in chains on bread and water. He lived only a few months under this punishment.[3] Out of admiration immense sums were given to the mendicants, and they became notorious for avarice and worldly self-seeking.[4] As early as 1257 Bonaventura, the head of the order, reproached them with these faults.[5] " Some of the venomous hatred expressed by the Italian satirists for the two great orders of St. Francis and St. Dominic may perhaps be due to an ancient grudge against them as a papal police founded in the interests of orthodoxy, but the chief point aimed at is the mixture of hypocrisy with immorality, which rendered them odious to all classes of society." [6] " In general the Franciscans seem to us far less orthodox than the Dominicans. They issued from a popular movement which was irregular, unecclesiastical, very little conformed to the ideas of the hierarchy about discipline." " The followers of St. Francis continued to contain ardent-minded men who maintained that the Franciscan reform had not produced all its due results; that that reform was superior to popes and to the dispensations issued at Rome; that the appearance of the seraphic Francis was neither more nor less than the advent of a new Christianity and a new Christ, like in all respects to the first, but superior to it by poverty. Therefore all the democratic and communistic movements of later times, — the third order of St. Francis, the Beghards, Lollards, Bisocs, Fraticelli, Spiritual Brethren, Humiliati, and Poor Men of Lyons [Waldenses], who were exterminated by the state and the prisons of the Dominicans, have their origin in the old leaven of Katharism, Joachimism, and the eternal gospel." [7]

219. Popular mania for poverty and beggary. The strength of the mendicant orders was in their popularity. They reconquered for the church the respect of the masses. Then they became the inquisitors, and the abusers of power for their own interests, and fell into great disfavor. Their history shows well the course of interaction between the masses and the rulers, and the course of institutions born in popular mores but abused to serve private interests. The mendicant orders furnished the

[1] Lea, *Inquis.*, III, 33.
[2] *Ibid.*, 51, 59.
[3] Hauréau, *Bernard Delicieux*, 142.
[4] Lea, *Inquis.*, III, 34.
[5] *Ibid.*, 29.
[6] Symonds, *Renaissance*, I, 394.
[7] Renan, *Averroes*, 259 ff.

army of papal absolutism. The Roman Catholic writers say that the popes saved the world from the despotism of emperors. What is true is that the pope and the emperor contendeu for the mastery, and the masses gave it to the pope. What the popes did with it we know. That is history. What the emperors would have done with it is matter for conjecture. It is very probable that they would have abused the power as badly as the popes did, but conjectural history is idle.

220. Delusions. Of popular delusions one of the most striking and recurrent examples is the belief that new and despised religious sects, which are forced to meet in private, practice obscene and abominable orgies. The early Christians were accused of such rites, and they charged dissenting sects with the same.[1] The Manichæans, Waldenses, Huguenots, Puritans, Luciferans, Brothers of the Free Spirit, and so on through the whole list of heretical sects, have been so charged. Lea, in his History of the Inquisition, mentions over a dozen cases of such charges, some of which were true. Nowadays the same assertions are made against freemasons by Roman Catholics.[2] Jews are believed by the peasants of eastern Europe to practice abominable rites in secret. The idea that secret sects use the blood of people not of their sect, especially of babies, in base rites is only a variant of the broad idea about secret rites. It is sometimes said that the charges were invented to make sects unpopular, but it is more probable that they arose from the secrecy of the meetings only. Christians are so charged now in China.[3] The story of the discovery of such misbehavior always contains the same explanation — a husband followed his wife to the meeting and saw the proceedings.[4]

221. Manias need suggestion. Manias and delusions are like fashions and fads in that they always seem to need a suggestion from some outside source, and often it is impossible to find such a source. A strong popular belief, like the belief in Satan and demons, furnishes a ground for a general disposition to hold some other people responsible for all the ills which befall one's

---

[1] Lecky, *Eur. Morals*, I, 414, 417.
[2] Hansen, *Zauberwahn*, etc., 227.
[3] *N. Y. Times*, January 9, 1898.
[4] Lea, *Inquis.*, II, 373.

self. Then the disposition to act cruelly against the suspected person arises to a mental disease, and by coöperation of others under the same aberration makes a mania.[1] The explanation lies in autosuggestion or fixed ideas with the development loosely ranged under hysteria, which is the contagious form of nervous affection. The term "epidemic" can be applied only figuratively. "Mental disease occurs only on the ground of a specific constitutional and generally hereditary predisposition. It cannot therefore be spread epidemically, any more than diabetes or gout."[2] The epidemic element is due to hysterical imitation. In like manner, epidemics or manias of suicide occur by imitation, e.g. amongst the Circumcellions, a subdivision of the Donatists, in Africa, in the middle of the fourth century A.D.[3] Cognate with this was the mania for martyrdom which it required all the authority of the church to restrain.[4] Josephus[5] says of the Galileans, followers of Judas of Galilee, that they were famous for their indifference to death. Convents were often seats of frightful epidemics of hysteria. The accepted religious notions furnished a fruitful soil for it. To be possessed by devils was a distinction, and vanity was drawn into play.[6] Autosuggestion was shown by actions which were, or were supposed to be, the actions proper for "possessed" people. Ascetic practices prepared the person to fall a victim to the contagion of hysteria. The predisposition was also cultivated by the religious ecstasies, the miracle and wonder faiths, and the current superstitions. Then there was the fact which nearly any one may have experienced, that an old and familiar story becomes mixed with memory, so that he thinks that what he heard of happened to himself. Untrained people also form strong convictions from notions which have been long and firmly held without evidence, and they offer to others the firmness of their own convictions as grounds for accepting the same faith without proof. Ritual acts and ascetic observances which others can see, also conduct and zeal

---

[1] Friedmann, *Wahnideen im Völkerleben*, 207.
[2] *Ibid.*, 209.   [4] Lecky, *Eur. Morals*, I, 391.
[3] Gibbon, Chap. XXI.   [5] *Antiq.*, XVIII, 1.
[6] Regnard, *Sorcellerie*, etc.

in prayer or singing, and the odors of incense, help this transfer of faith without or against proof. These appeals to suggestibility all come under the head of drama. Nowadays the novels with a tendency operate the same suggestion. A favorite field for it is sociological doctrine. In this field it is a favorite process to proceed by ideals, but ideals, as above shown (secs. 203, 204), are fantastic and easily degenerate into manias when they become mass phenomena. Mariolatry, the near end of the world, the coming of the Paraclete, are subjects of repeated manias, especially for minds unsettled by excessive ascetic observances. It follows from all these cases of mental aberration that the minds of the masses of a society cannot be acted on by deliberation and critical investigation, or by the weight of sound reasoning. There is a mysticism of democracy and a transcendentalism of political philosophy in the masses to-day, which can be operated on by the old methods of suggestion. The stock exchange shows the possibility of suggestion. What one ought to do is to perceive and hold fast to the truth, but also to know the delusion which the mass are about to adopt ; but it is only the most exceptional men who can hold to a personal opinion against the opinion of the surrounding crowd.

222. Power of the crowd over the individual. The manias and delusions therefore dominate the individual like the fashions, fads, and affectations. It is the power of the crowd over the individual which is constant. The truth and justice of the popular opinion is of very inferior importance. The manias and delusions also operate selection, but not always in the same way, or in any way which can be defined. He who resists a mania may be trodden under foot like any other heretic. There occur cases, however, in which he wins by dissent. If he can outlive the mania, he will probably gain at a later time, when its folly is proved to all.

223. Discipline by pain. He who wants to make another do something, or to prevent him from doing something, may, if the former is the stronger, connect act or omission with the infliction of pain. This is only an imitation of nature, in which pain is a sanction and a deterrent. Family and school discipline have always rested on this artificial use of pain. It is, apparently, the most primary application of force or coercion. It combines directly with vengeance, which is a primary passion of human nature. Punishment is of this philosophy, for by punishment we furnish, or add, a painful consequence to acts which we desire to restrain, in the hope that the consequence will cause reflection and make the victim desist. The punishment may be imprisonment (i.e. temporary exclusion from the society), or fine, or scourging, or other painful treatment. The sense of punishment is the same whether the punishment be physical pain or other disagreeable experience. Although we have come to adopt modern ideas about the infliction of physical pain in punishment, we cannot depart far from its fundamental theory and motive. In the past, physical pain has been employed also, in lynching and in regular proceedings, to enforce conformity, and to suppress dissent from the current mores of the society. The physical proceedings are measures to produce conformity which differ from boycotting and other methods of manifesting disapproval and inflicting unpopularity in that they are positive and physical. Then the selection is positive and is pursued by external and physical sanctions.

224. The mediæval church operated societal selection. It is evident that the mediæval church was a machine to exert societal selection. The great reason for its strength as such is that it never made the mores of the age ; it proceeded out of them. It contributed, through a thousand previous years, phantasms about the other world and dogmas about the relation of this world to that one. These dogmas became mixed with all the experience of life in the days of civic decline and misery, and produced the mores of the tenth and eleventh centuries. All the great doctrines then took on the form of manias or delusions. In the early centuries of the Christian era " catholic " meant Christendom in its entirety, in contrast with the separate congregations, so that the concepts "all congregations " and the "universal church " are identical. However, the church over the whole world was thought to have been founded by the apostles, so that that only could be true which was found everywhere in Christendom. So " catholic " came to have a pregnant meaning, and got dogmatic and political connotations.[1] In the eleventh century all Christendom was reduced to civic fragments in which tyranny, oppression, and strife prevailed. It was not strange that "catholicity" was revived as an idea of a peace pact by means of which the church might unite Christendom into a peace group for the welfare of mankind (sec. 14). This was a grand idea. If the Christian church had devoted itself to the realization of it, by forms of constitutional liberty, the history of the world would have been different. The church, however, used "catholicity" as a name for universal submission to the bishop of Rome and for hierarchical discipline, and used all means to try to realize that conception. By the Inquisition and other apparatus it attempted to enforce conformity to this idea, and exercised a societal selection against all dissenters from it. The ecclesiastics of Cluny, in the eleventh century, gave form to this high-church doctrine, and they combined with it a rational effort to raise the clergy to honor for learning and piety, as a necessary step for the success of their church policy. The circumstances and ideas of the time gave to these efforts the form of a struggle for a monarchical constitution of the church. In the thirteenth century this monarchy came into collision with the empire as the other aspirant to the rule of Christendom. Already the papacy was losing moral hold on its subjects. The clergy were criticised for worldliness, arrogance, and tyranny, and the antagonism of the dynastic states, so far as they existed, found expression in popular literature. Walter von der Vogelweide is regarded as a forerunner of the Reformation on account of his bitter criticisms of the hierarchy.[2] It is, however, very noteworthy that, in spite of the popular language of the writers and their appeals to common experience, they did not break the people away from their ecclesiastical allegiance, and also that the church authorities paid little heed to the criticisms of these persons. The miracle and moral plays were in the taste of the age entirely. Besides being gross, they were irreligious and blasphemous. Ecclesiastics tolerated them nevertheless.[3] The

---

[1] Harnack, *Dogmengesch.* (3d ed.), I, 319.

[2] Jastrow and Winter, *Gesch. d. Hohenstaufen*, II, 241.

[3] Scherr, *Deutsche Kultur und Sittengesch.*, 183.

authorities moved only when "the faith" was brought in question. "The faith," therefore, acquired a technical signification of great importance. It was elevated to the domain of sentiment and duty and surrounded with pathos (sec. 178), while its meaning was undefined. In time it came to mean obedience to papal authority. Thus all the circumstances and streams of faith and sentiment of the eleventh and twelfth centuries concentrated in the hands of the hierarchy the control of society, because there was no other organ to accept the deposit. The Cluny programme was a programme of reform in the church such as everybody wanted. It gathered all "the good men" in a common will and purpose. The ideals and the means were selected, and the advocates of the same became the selected classes in society. They remained such long after the movement was spent and lost, but the notion remained that every good man, or would-be good man, ought to stand with the church.

225. The mediæval church. In the crusades the church went to war with Islam, another aspirant to rule mankind. It undoubtedly drilled and disciplined its own adherents by the crusades and thus confirmed its power. It is also certain that the crusades were popular and only put into effect the wish of the great body of Christians. It was the masses, therefore, who made the mediæval church. It possessed a corporate organization and hierarchy which was a body of personal interests, in which ambition, cupidity, and love of power were awakened. The church was venal, sensual, gross, and inhuman, because the mores of the age were such. How could the church be other than the age was? Where was it to find inspiration or illumination from without which should make ecclesiastics anything but men of their age? The men of that age left on record their testimony that the church was in no way better than the society.[1] From the end of the twelfth century man after man and sect after sect arose, whose inspiration was moral indignation at the vices and abuses in the church. Wycliffe denied transubstantiation on rationalistic grounds, but his work all consisted in criticism of hierarchical abuses and of the principles which made the abuses

[1] Mayer, *Oesterreich*, I, 156.

possible. The church never was on the level of the better mores of any time. Every investigation which we make leads us not to the church as the inspirer and leader, but to the dissenting apostles of righteousness, to the great fluctuations in the mores (chivalry, woman service, city growth, arts, and inventions), to the momentum of interests, to the variations in the folkways which travel (crusades and pilgrimages), commerce, industrial arts, money, credit, gunpowder, the printing press, etc., produced.

226. Sacerdotal celibacy. The church rode upon the tide and tried to keep possession of the social power and use it for the interest of ecclesiastics. Asceticism was in the mores. Everybody accepted the ascetic standard of merit and holiness as correct and just, whether he lived by it or not. Sacerdotal celibacy was a case of asceticism. Every one knew that it had come about in church history and was not scriptural or primitive. It was in the notions of the age that there were stages in righteousness, and that religious persons were bound to live by higher stages than persons not technically religious. Renunciation of sex was higher righteousness than realization of sex, as is taught in the seventh chapter of First Corinthians. This notion existed amongst heathen and pagans. The priests in the Melkart temple at Gades (Cadiz) were bound to celibacy.[1]

The merit of celibacy is a very old religious idea in Hindostan. The Todas have a celibate priesthood.[2] " It is one of the inconsistencies of the Hindu religion that it enjoins the duty of marriage on all, yet honors celibacy as a condition of great sanctity, and a means of acquiring extraordinary religious merit and influence." [3] " All the ascetic sects of the Saivas are celibates." [4] Lamas at Shang (98° E. 36° N.) are allowed to marry, but not in Tibet.[5] The Christian notion of the third century was that clerics ought to come up to the higher standard. This was the purest and highest reason for celibacy. It had been a standard of perfection in the Christian church for six hundred years before

---

[1] Pietschmann, *Phoenizier*, 223 note.
[2] Hopkins, *Religions of India*, 537.
[3] Monier-Williams, *Brahmanism and Hinduism*, 55.
[4] Wilkins, *Modern Hinduism*, 90.
[5] Rockhill, *Through Mongolia and Tibet*, 135.

Hildebrand. Whatever motives of policy or ecclesiastical ambition may have been mixed with it in the eleventh century, it had the merit of bringing doctrine and practice into accord.

227. The masses wanted clerical celibacy. It is to be noticed that clerical celibacy was a demand of the masses amongst church members, and that the demand came directly out of Christian mores. In the fourth century this doctrine was derived from sacramentarianism. The notion became fixed that there was an inherent and necessary incongruity between marriage and the celebration of the sacrament of the mass. " In the course of the fourth century it was a recognized principle that clerical marriages were criminal. They were celebrated, however, habitually, and usually with the greatest openness." [1] That means that they were in antagonism with church opinion and its tendency at that time. Sacerdotalism triumphed in the fifth century. " Throughout the struggle the papacy had a most efficient ally in the people." Preachers exhorted the people to holiness, and the people required this of the clergy, and enforced it by riots and mob violence. Cases are cited which " bring before us the popular tendencies and modes of thought, and show us how powerful an instrument the passions of the people became, when skilfully aroused and directed by those in authority." [2] The fundamental notion which underlies all asceticism was here at work, viz., that virtue has stages, that a man can be more than good, or worse than bad. The council of Constantinople, in 680, made new rules against the marriage of the clergy, because the old ones were neglected and forgotten. The motive stated was the welfare of the people, who regarded such marriages as scandalous. The excess in temper and doctrine was a mark of the period. The learned would have held the doctrine as a metaphysical truth only, but the masses turned it into a practical rule. The share of the masses in the establishment of the rule is a very important fact. Lea thinks that they were manipulated by the ecclesiastics.[3] In the religious revival of the eleventh century the marriage of the clergy was " popularly regarded as a heresy and a scandal."

---

[1] Lecky, *Eur. Morals*, II, 329.   [2] Lea, *Sacerd. Celibacy*, 81.
[3] *Ibid.*

There was no defense of it.[1] It was an undisputed fact that celibacy was not scriptural or primitive.[2] At that time "all orders, from bishops down, without shame or concealment, were publicly married and lived with their wives as laymen, leaving their children fully provided for in their wills. . . . This laxity prevailed throughout the whole of Latin Christendom, sacerdotal marriage being everywhere so common that it was no longer punished as unlawful and scarcely even reprehended."[3] "Not a thought of the worldly advantages consequent on the reform appears to have crossed the mind of Damiani. To him it was simply a matter of conscience that the ministers of Christ should be adorned with the austere purity through which alone lay the path to salvation. Accordingly, the arguments which he employs in his endless disputations carefully avoid the practical reasons which were the principal motive for enforcing celibacy. His main reliance was on the assumption that, as Christ was born of a virgin, so he should be served and the eucharist be handled only by virgins."[4] This took up again the fifth-century doctrine in its popular form, but it evidently led directly up to the heresy that the validity or benefit of the sacrament depended on the purity of the priest. In his zeal for celibacy Hildebrand fell into this heresy, although a man was burned for it at Cambrai in 1077.[5] Hildebrand also gave civil authorities power over ecclesiastics in order to carry out his reform.[6] In the middle of the twelfth century the "reform" was directed against the women (wives), for fear of the resistance of the men. In Rome the women were enslaved and given to the church of the Lateran. All bishops were ordered to seize the women for the benefit of their churches.[7] In 1095 the sacrament of marriage was declared by the lateran council less potent than the religious vow, although the contrary had been the church doctrine.[8] Thus what came out of the popular mores underwent the growth

---

[1] *Sac. Celib.*, 250, 252.

[2] *Canon Law*, can. XIII, dist. lvi.; Aquinas, *Sum.*, II, 2, qu. 186, art. 4, sec. 3.

[3] Lea, *Sac. Celib.*, 187.

[4] *Ibid.*, 213. This is a good example of the change in notions of good arguments (sec. 194).   [5] *Ibid.*, 244, 249.

[6] *Ibid.*, 235.   [7] *Ibid.*, 198.

[8] *Ibid.*, 326; *Canon Law*, Gratian's Com. on can. I, dist. xxvii.

of formulated dogma and deduction. In the thirteenth century marriage of the clergy ceased, but concubinage continued, concubines being a legitimate but inferior order of wives, whose existence was tolerated on payment of a fee known as *cullagium*.[1] "Scarcely had the efforts of Nicholas and Gregory put an end to sacerdotal marriage at Rome when the morals of the Roman clergy became a disgrace to Christendom."[2] "Those women [clerical concubines] came to be invested with a quasi-ecclesiastical character, and to enjoy the dearly prized immunities attached to that position."[3] Gerson (1363–1429) paid admiration to virginity and celibacy, but he "saw and appreciated its practical evils, and had no scruple in recommending concubinage as a preventive, which, though scandalous in itself, might serve to prevent greater scandals." In districts it became customary to require a new parish priest to take a concubine.[4] "This was the inversion which the popular opinion had undergone in four centuries."[5] "The principles of the church led irrevocably to the conclusion, paradoxical as it may seem, that he who was guilty of immorality, knowing it to be wrong, was far less criminal than he who married, believing it to be right."[6] At Avignon, when it was the seat of the papacy, sex license and vice became proverbial. A speech of the most shameless cynicism is attributed to Cardinal Hugo, in which he described the effect, in 1251, of the residence of the papal court there for eight years. In the fourteenth century that city became the most wicked, and especially the most licentious, in Christendom.[7] The first case of the presence of women at a feast in the Vatican is said to have been at the marriage of Teodorina, daughter of Innocent VIII, in 1488. Comedies were played before the mixed company.[8]

228. Abelard. A cleric who married flinched from the standard of his calling, in the view of the church. Hildebrand's decrees were like the other crowning acts of great men, — they came at the culmination of a great movement in the mores. They accorded

---

1 Lea, *Sac. Celib.*, 271.

2 *Ibid.*, 356.

3 *Ibid.*, 350.

4 *Ibid.*, 355.

5 *Ibid.*, 416.

6 *Ibid.*, 209.

7 *Ibid.*, 356 ff.

8 D'Ancona, *Orig. del teatro Ital.*, II, 73.

with the will and wish of the masses. In all ages acts are due to mixed motives, but in the Middle Ages the good motives were kept for show and the bad ones controlled. Clerics did not cease to have concubines until after the Council of Trent, and the difference between law and practice (bridged over by pecuniary penalties) called for special ethics and casuistry. The case of Abelard (1079–1142) shows what tragedies were caused. He claimed to be, and to some extent he was, a champion of reason and common sense, and he was a skeptic as to the current philosophy. He was vain, weak, and ambitious. He selected the loveliest woman he knew, and won her love, which he used to persuade her to be his concubine, that she might not hinder him in his career.[1] The treatment accorded to Heloise shows that a woman could be a concubine of an ecclesiastic, but not his wife, without condemnation. That was the allowance for human despair under the ecclesiastical rules.[2] Thus the church first suggested views of life and dogmas of religion, with which the masses combined their mores and returned them to the church as a gift of societal power. The church then formulated the mores and created disciplinary systems to use the power and make it institutional and perpetual. Then the mores revolted against the authority and the religion, and the ethics which it taught. A Roman Catholic writer says that a study of the Middle Ages will produce this result : " We shall have recognized in the church the professional peacemaker between states and factions, as well as between man and man, the equitable mediator between rulers and their subjects, the consistent champion of constitutional liberty, the alleviator of the inequalities of birth, the uninterested and industrious disseminator of letters, the refiner of habits and manners, the well-meaning guardian of the national wealth, health, and intellect, and the fearless censor of public and private morality."[3] These are, indeed, the functions which the church ought to have fulfilled, and about which ecclesiastics said something from time to time. Also, the church did do something for these

---

[1] Deutsch, *Abelard*, 44, 106, 111.
[2] Hausrath, *Abelard*, 28, 32.
[3] Hall, *Elizabethan Age*, 103.

interests when no great interest of the church was at stake on the other side. No unbiased student of the Middle Ages has been convinced that, in truth and justice, the work of the mediæval church could be thus summed up. The one consistent effort of the church was to establish papal authority. Its greatest crime was obscurantism, which was war on knowledge and civilization. This nothing can palliate or offset.

229. The English church and the mores. The church, however, from 1000 A.D. on was a machine of societal selection, and it pursued its work, suggesting and administering a work of that kind, grand results of which have come down to us in the civilization we have inherited. Our work largely consists in rational efforts to eliminate the elements which the church introduced. In some respects the history of clerical celibacy in England best illustrates the mores. In the sixteenth century the rule and usage of the church had inculcated, as a deep popular prejudice, the notion that a priest could not be married. Cranmer, in ordering a visitation, directed investigation " whether any do contemn married priests, and for that they be married will not receive the communion or other sacrament at their hands." [1] This prejudice very slowly died out, but it did die out and the popular judgment favored and required clerical marriage. In the nineteenth century popular judgment rose in condemnation of fox-hunting parsons, and also of pluralists, and it has caused reforms and the disappearance of those classes.

230. The selection of sacerdotal celibacy. If it had not been for sacerdotal celibacy, there would have been ecclesiastical feudalization and the ecclesiastical benefices would have become hereditary. The children of priests inherited benefices and intermarried so long as the marriage of priests was allowed. There would have been a priestly caste.[2] The church as an institution would have been greatly modified. The consequences we cannot imagine. If Hildebrand and the other eleventh-century leaders foresaw the effect, it was statesmanship on their part to establish the celibacy of the clergy. That institution has molded the priesthood and the mores of all who have adhered to the mediæval church. The

---

[1] Lea, *Sac. Celib.*, 488.   [2] *Ibid.*, 150.

Latin people of southern Europe are now horrified at the notion of a married priest. The concubine of a priest is a wicked woman, but she is not a social abomination. All protest and resistance seems to have passed away and, since the sixteenth century, sacerdotal celibacy has been accepted as a feature of the Romish Church, which all its members are expected to accept. It is a grand triumph of social selection.

231. How the church operated selection. The church was a great hierarchical organization for social power and control, which inherited part of the intense integration of the Roman empire. Fra Paolo Sarpi said of it, in the seventeenth century: "The interests of Rome demand that there shall be no change by which the power of the pontiff would be diminished, or by which the curia would lose any of the profits which it wins from the states, but the novelties by which the profits of the curia would be increased, or by which the authority of the states would be diminished and that of the curia increased, are not abhorred, but are favored. This we see every day." [1] The church decided all recognition and promotion, and disposed of all rewards of ambition. The monarchical and autocratic tendency in it was the correct process for attaining the purposes by which it was animated. Its legitimacy as an organization for realizing faiths and desires which prevailed in society is beyond question. It drew towards itself all the talent of the age except what was military. It crushed all dissenters and silenced all critics for centuries. Its enginery was all planned for selection. It disposed of the greatest prizes and the most dreadful penalties. All its methods were positive and realistic, and whatever can be accomplished by authority, tyranny, penalty, and repression it accomplished. In modern times political parties offer the nearest parallels. They are organizations for societal control, which distribute rewards and penalties and coerce dissenters. The history of the papacy in the fifteenth century reminds one of the history of Tammany Hall in the nineteenth century. The strength of Tammany is due to the fact that it fits the tastes and needs of a great modern city under democracy. When Tammany won an

---

[1] *Della Inquisizione di Venezia*, Opere IV, 51.

election it was said that the people had put the city in their hands and that they ought to profit by it. When Leo X was elected pope he said, "God has given us the papacy; now let us enjoy it." [1]

232. Mores and morals; social code. For every one the mores give the notion of what ought to be. This includes the notion of what ought to be done, for all should coöperate to bring to pass, in the order of life, what ought to be. All notions of propriety, decency, chastity, politeness, order, duty, right, rights, discipline, respect, reverence, coöperation, and fellowship, especially all things in regard to which good and ill depend entirely on the point at which the line is drawn, are in the mores. The mores can make things seem right and good to one group or one age which to another seem antagonistic to every instinct of human nature. The thirteenth century bred in every heart such a sentiment in regard to heretics that inquisitors had no more misgivings in their proceedings than men would have now if they should attempt to exterminate rattlesnakes. The sixteenth century gave to all such notions about witches that witch persecutors thought they were waging war on enemies of God and man. Of course the inquisitors and witch persecutors constantly developed the notions of heretics and witches. They exaggerated the notions and then gave them back again to the mores, in their expanded form, to inflame the hearts of men with terror and hate and to become, in the next stage, so much more fantastic and ferocious motives. Such is the reaction between the mores and the acts of the living generation. The world philosophy of the age is never anything but the reflection on the mental horizon, which is formed out of the mores, of the ruling ideas which are in the mores themselves. It is from a failure to recognize the to and fro in this reaction that the current notion arises that mores are produced by doctrines. The "morals" of an age are never anything but the consonance between what is done and what the mores of the age require. The whole revolves on itself, in the relation of the specific to the general, within the horizon formed by the mores. Every attempt to win an outside standpoint from which to reduce the whole to an absolute

1 Symonds, *Renaissance*, I, 372.

philosophy of truth and right, based on an unalterable principle, is
a delusion. New elements are brought in only by new conquests
of nature through science and art. The new conquests change
the conditions of life and the interests of the members of the
society. Then the mores change by adaptation to new conditions
and interests. The philosophy and ethics then follow to account
for and justify the changes in the mores ; often, also, to claim
that they have caused the changes. They never do anything but
draw new lines of bearing between the parts of the mores and
the horizon of thought within which they are inclosed, and which
is a deduction from the mores. The horizon is widened by more
knowledge, but for one age it is just as much a generalization
from the mores as for another. It is always unreal. It is only a
product of thought. The ethical philosophers select points on
this horizon from which to take their bearings, and they think
that they have won some authority for their systems when they
travel back again from the generalization to the specific custom
out of which it was deduced. The cases of the inquisitors and
witch persecutors who toiled arduously and continually for their
chosen ends, for little or no reward, show us the relation between
mores on the one side and philosophy, ethics, and religion on
the other. (See Chapters IX, XIV, and XV.)

**233. Orthodoxy in the mores. Treatment of dissent. Selec-
tion by torture.** It has been observed above (sec. 100) that the
masses always enforce conformity to the mores. Primitive taboos
are absolute. There is no right of private judgment. Renegades,
apostates, deserters, rebels, traitors, and heretics are but varieties
of dissenters who are all subject to disapproval, hatred, banishment, and death. In higher stages of civilization this popular
temper becomes a societal force which combines with civil
arrangements, religious observances, literature, education, and
philosophy. Toleration is no sentiment of the masses for anything
which they care about. What they believe they believe, and
they want it accepted and respected. Illustrations are furnished
by zeal for political parties and for accepted political philosophy.
The first punishment for dissent less than death is extrusion from
the society. Next come bodily pains and penalties, that is, torture.

Torture is also applied in connection with the death penalty, or modes of death are devised which are as painful as they can be made. The motive is to deter any one from the class of acts which is especially abominated. In the cases above cited (sec. 211), under criminal law, it will be observed that death by burning was applied in the case of incest, or other very abominable crime, in the laws of Hammurabi and other ancient codes (sec. 234). Such extreme penalties are first devised to satisfy public temper. The ruler is sure of popularity if he shows rigor and ferocity. His act will be regarded as just. It is now the popular temper, when any one commits a crime which is regarded as very horrible, to think and say what frightful punishment he deserves. It is a primary outpouring of savage vengeance. When precedents have been established for frightful punishments, the rulers apply the same in cases of disobedience against themselves or their authority. Now torture and ferocious penalties have reached another stage. They were invented by the masses, or in order to appeal to the masses. They have now become the means of authority and discipline. The history of torture is a long development of knowledge of pain, and of devices to cause it. Then it becomes a means which is at the disposal of those who have the power. The Dominican Izarn, in a chant of triumph over the Albigenses, represents himself as arguing with one of them to whom he says, " Believe as we do or thou shalt be burned." [1] This is the voice of a victorious party. It is the enforcement of uniformity against dissent. Systematic and legal torture then becomes an engine of uniformity and it acts selectively as it crushes out originality and independent suggestion. It is at the disposal of any party in power. Like every other system of policy it loses its effect on the imagination by familiarity, and that effect can be regained only by intensifying it. Therefore where torture has been long applied we find that it is developed to grades of incredible horror.

234. Execution by burning. In the ancient world execution by burning was applied only when some religious abomination was included in the crime, or when it seemed politically outrageous. In the laws of Hammurabi an hierodule who opened

[1] Lenient, *La satire au M. A.*, 41.

a dramshop or entered one to get a drink was to be burned.[1] One who committed incest with his mother was to meet the same punishment,[2] also one who married a mother and her daughter at the same time.[3] In Levit. xx. 14 if a man marries a mother and her daughter together, all are to be burned, and in Levit. xxi. 9 the daughter of a priest, if she becomes a harlot, is to be burned. At the end of the seventh century B.C. some priestly families connected with the temple of Amon at Napata, Egypt, by way of reform, introduced the custom of eating the meat of sacrifices uncooked. They were burned for heresy.[4] In the year 5 B.C., upon a rumor of the death of Herod I, some Jews tore down the Roman eagle from the gate of the temple. Herod caused forty-two of them to be burned.[5] Caligula caused an atellan composer to be burned in the arena for a sarcasm on the emperor.[6] Constantine ordered that if a free woman had intercourse with a slave man, the man should be burned.[7] In all the ancient and classical period, burning was reserved as a most painful form of death for the most abominable criminals and the most extravagant and rare crimes. By another law of Constantine it was ordered that if Jews and heaven worshipers should stone those who were converted from their sects to the Catholic faith, they should be burned.[8] In the Theodosian Code, also, any slave who accused his master of any crime except high treason was to be burned alive without investigation.[9] Thus burning became the penalty for criminals of a despised class or race.

235. Burning in North American colonies. In the colonial laws of Massachusetts, New Jersey, New York, South Carolina, and Virginia it was provided that negroes should be executed by burning. Here we have a recrudescence of the idea that great penalties are deterrent. Modern penologists do not believe that that is true. It is, however, the belief of the masses, which they have recently shown in methods of lynching. It might have been believed ten years ago that it would be impossible to get a

[1] Winckler, *Gesetze Hammurabis*, 19.
[2] *Ibid.*, 26.
[3] Müller, *Hammurabi*, 131.
[4] Maspero, *Peuples de l'Orient*, III, 666.
[5] *Jewish Encyc.*, VI, s.v. " Herod I."
[6] Suetonius, *Caligula*, 27.
[7] *Cod. Theod.*, IX, 9.
[8] *Cod. Justin.*, I, 9.
[9] *Cod. Theod.*, VI, 2.

crowd of Americans to burn a man at the stake, but there have
been many cases of it.[1]

236. Solidarity of group in penalty incurred by one. In
primitive society any one who departed from the ways of ancestors
was supposed to offend their ghosts ; furthermore, he was supposed to bring down their avenging wrath on the whole group of
which he was a member. This idea has prevailed until modern
times. It aroused the sentiment of vengeance against the dissenter, and united all the rest in a common interest against him.
Especially, if any misfortune befell the group, they turned against
any one who had broken the taboos. Thus goblinism was united
to the other reasons for disliking dissenters and gave it definite
direction and motive. At Rome, "in the days of the republic,
every famine, pestilence, or drought was followed by a searching
investigation of the sacred rites, to ascertain what irregularity
or neglect had caused the divine anger, and two instances are
recorded in which vestal virgins were put to death because their
unchastity was believed to have provoked a national calamity."[2]
In the Roman law is found a proposition which was often quoted
in the Middle Ages : "That which is done against divine religion
is done to the harm of all."[3] Hale[4] explains the tortures inflicted
by the Iroquois, by their desire to mark some kinds of Indian
warfare as very abominable, and so to drive them out of use.
Torture always flatters vanity. He who inflicts it has power.
To reduce, plunder, and torment an enemy is a great luxury.
The lust of blood is a frightful demon when once it is aroused.
A Hungarian woman of noble birth, at the beginning of the
seventeenth century, tortured to death thirty or forty of her
maidservants. She began by inflicting severe punishments and
developed a fiendish passion for the sight of suffering and blood.[5]
It is the combinations of the other elements, religion, ambition,
sex, vanity, and the lust of blood, with the dislike of dissenters,

---

[1] In 1899 a German officer was condemned to death by a court martial for
killing a half-breed subordinate with great torture. The emperor reduced the
punishment to fifteen years' imprisonment, and in May, 1902, granted the prisoner
a full pardon. — *Assoc. Press*, December 24, 1899; *N. Y. Times*, May 24, 1903.

[2] Lecky, *Morals*, I, 407.

[3] *Cod. Justin.*, I, 5, sec. 4.

[4] *Iroquois Book of Rites*, 97.

[5] Elsberg, *Elizabeth Bathory*.

which has caused the most frightful developments of torture and persecution. This brings us to the case of the mediæval inquisition. It is not to be expected that a phenomenon of high civilization will be simple and uniform. So the motives of Christian persecution to enforce conformity are numerous and mixed. It was directly against some of the leading principles of Christianity, but there are texts in the New Testament which were used to justify it.[1]

237. Torture in ancient states. The Egyptians used torture in all ordinary investigations to find out the facts.[2] The Greeks had used torture. It was common in the Periclean age in the courts of Athens. The accused gave his slaves to be tortured " to challenge evidence against himself." [3] Plutarch [4] tells of a barber who heard of the defeat of Nicias in Sicily and ran to tell the magistrates. They tortured him as a maker of trouble by disseminating false news, until the story was confirmed. Philotas was charged with planning to kill Alexander. He was tortured and the desired proof was obtained.[5] Eusebius,[6] describing the persecution under Nerva, says that Simeon, Bishop of Jerusalem, being one hundred and twenty years old, was tortured for several days and then crucified. Torture underwent a special development in the Euphrates valley. The Assyrian stones show frightful tortures which kings sometimes inflicted with their own hands. Maiming, flaying, impaling, blinding, and smothering in hot ashes became usual forms in Persia. They passed to the Turks, and the stories of torture and death inflicted in southeastern Europe, or in modern Persia, show knowledge and inventive skill far beyond what the same peoples have otherwise shown. The motives have been religious contempt, hereditary animosity, and vengeance, as well as political and warlike antagonism.

238. Torture in the Roman empire. The Roman emperors lived in a great fear of supernatural attack. There was a very

---

[1] 1 Cor. v. 1 ; 1 Tim. i. 20; Gal. i. 8.
[2] Maspero, *Peuples de l'Orient*, II, 539.
[3] Mahaffy, *Soc. Life in Greece*, 226.
[4] Nicias, *ad fin.*
[5] Quint. Curt. Rufus, *Alexander*, VI, 11.
[6] *Hist. Eccles.*, III.

great interest for many people in the question : When will the
emperor die ? Many, no doubt, made use of any apparatus of
astrology or sorcery to find out. To the emperor and his adherents this seemed to prove a desire that he should die, and was
interpreted as treasonable. The Christians helped to develop
demonism. They regarded all the heathen gods as demons. As
they gained power in society this notion spread, and there was a
great revival of popular demonism. By the *lex Julia de Majestate*
torture might be applied to persons charged with treason, and the
definition of treason was greatly enlarged. Torture was used to
great excess under Tiberius and Nero. In the fourth century,
after the emperors became Christians, it was feared that persons
who hated them would work them ill by sorcery with the aid of
the demons, formerly heathen gods. Sorcery and treason were
combined and strengthened by a great tide of superstition which
overspread the Roman world.[1] The first capital punishment for
heresy in the Christian church seems to have been the torture
and burning of Priscillian, a Manichæan, at Treves, in 385, with
six of his adherents, by the Emperor Maximus. This act caused
a sensation of truly Christian horror. Of the two bishops who
were responsible, one was expelled from his see ; the other
resigned.[2] In 579 King Chilperic caused ecclesiastics to be tortured for disloyal behavior. About 580 the same king, having
married a servant maid, an act which caused family and political
trouble, upon the death of two of her children, caused a woman
to be tortured who was charged with murdering the children in
the interest of their stepbrother. She confessed, revoked her
confession, and was burned. Three years later another child of
the queen died, and several women were tortured and burned or
broken on the wheel for causing the death by sorcery.[3] Pope
Nicholas I, in 866, opposed the use of torture as barbaric,
and the pseudo-Isidorian Decretals take the same position in
regard to it. Indeed, that was the orthodox Christian view in
the dark ages.

---

[1] Gibbon, Chap. XVII; Hansen, *Zauberwahn*, etc., 108.
[2] Heyer, *Priesterschaft und Inquis.*, 16–18; Lea, *Inquis.*, I, Chap. V.
[3] Hansen, *Zauberwahn, Inquisition, und Hexenprocess im M. A.*, 110, 113.

239. Such was the course of descent by which torture came to the Middle Ages. It was in connection with the revival of the eleventh century that the Roman law of treason was made to apply to heresy by construing it as treason to God.[1] It is, however, of the first importance to notice that it was the masses which first applied death by burning to heretics. The mob lynched heretics long before the church began to persecute.[2] (See, further, sec. 253.)

240. Jewish and Christian universality. Who persecutes whom? The Jews held that their God was the only real God. The gods of other nations were "vanity," that is, nullity. They held that their religion was the only true one. When about the time of the birth of Christ they stepped before the Greco-Roman world with this claim, it cost them great hatred and abuse. In the history of religion it counts as a great fact of advance in religious conceptions. Christianity inherited the idea and applied it to itself. It has always claimed to be absolutely and alone true as a religious system. Every other religion is an invader of its domain. It was this attitude which gave a definition to heresy. Under paganism "speculation was untrammeled. The notion of there being any necessary guilt in erroneous opinion was unknown."[3] When once this notion found acceptance it produced a great number of deductions and corollaries and gave form to a great number of customs, such as they had never had before. The effect on the selection of articles of faith out of the doctrines of warring sects and philosophies is obvious, also the effect on methods of controversy. The effects are important in the fourth and fifth centuries, and the notion became one of the postulates of all thinking. This is the ultimate reason for the wickedness of heresy and for the abomination of all heretics. Certainly Christianity did not, in this matter, improve on the philosophy of paganism. It was this attitude of Christianity and its neglect of the existing political authority which drew upon it the contempt, derision, and hatred of the heathen. The persecution of Christians was popular. It expressed the popular feeling, which was more constantly expressed in the popular comedy and

[1] Lea, *Inquis.*, I, 421. [2] *Ibid.*, 308. [3] Lecky, *Morals*, II, 190.

the improvised popular play.[1] The persecution in Nerva's time was more popular than political.[2] In the following century the Christians denounced heathenism as a worship of demons. "It is not surprising that the populace should have been firmly convinced that every great catastrophe that occurred was due to the presence of the enemies of the gods."[3] "The history of the period of the Antonines continually manifests the desire of the populace to persecute, restrained by the humanity of the rulers."[4] In the third century the Decian persecution was largely due to the "popular fanaticism caused by great calamities, which were ascribed to the anger of the gods at the neglect of their worship."[5] "The most horrible recorded instances of torture were usually inflicted, either by the populace, or in their presence, in the arena."[6] Frightful tortures were inflicted in the attempt to make Christians sacrifice to the heathen gods. This effort was due to the popular apprehension of solidarity in responsibility for the neglect by the Christians of the state gods, to the decline of all social welfare and the implied insult to the state. In the fourth century Christianity became the religion of the state and took up the task of persecuting the heathen. "The only question is : In whose hands is the power to persecute?" That question alone determines who shall persecute whom. Literature was produced which uttered savage hatred against all who were not fully orthodox, and the sects practiced violence and cruelty against each other to the full extent for which they found opportunity. "Never, perhaps, was the infliction of mutilation, and prolonged and agonizing forms of death, more common" than in the seventh and eighth centuries.[7] "Great numbers were deprived of their ears and noses, tortured through several days, and at last burned alive or broken slowly on the wheel."[8] At Byzantium, in the ninth century, a prefect of the palace was burned in the circus for appropriating the property of a widow. It became the custom that capital punishments were executed in the circus.[9]

[1] Reich, *Der Mimus*, I, 90–96.
[2] Lecky, *Morals*, I, 437.
[3] *Ibid.*, 408.
[4] *Ibid.*, 436.   [5] *Ibid.*, 455.
[6] *Ibid.*, 466.
[7] *Ibid.*, II, 238.
[8] *Ibid.*
[9] Reich, *Der Mimus*, I, 192.

All this course of things was due to popular tastes and desires, and it was a course of popular education of the masses in cruelty, love of bloodshed, and gratification of low hatred and other base passions. All the laws, the exhortations of the clergy, and the public acts of torture and execution held out the suggestion that heresy was a thing deserving the extremest horror and abomination. What was heresy? No one knew unless he was an educated theologian, and such were rare. The vagueness of heresy made it more terrible. "The long-continued teaching of the church, that persistent heresy was the one crime for which there could be no pardon or excuse, seemed to deprive even the wisest and purest of all power of reasoning where it was concerned."[1]

241. The ordeal. The doctrines and sentiments of this early age were seed planted to produce an immeasurable crop in the eleventh and twelfth centuries, when they were brought forth again and quoted with the authority of the church fathers. The ordeal is a question addressed to the superior powers in order to learn the truth. The question is always categorical: Is this man guilty or not? The irrationality is that there is a third possibility which cannot be tested; the superior powers may not answer at all. In the early Middle Ages the ordeal was in common use in all civil and ecclesiastical trials. Experience proved the fallacy of it. We are led to believe that the people of the dark ages, not yet being locked in dogmatism, although stupid and ignorant, were better able to learn from experience than those of later times. Innocent III, in 1212, forbade the use of the ordeal, the occasion being its use by the Bishop of Strasburg against heretics.[2] The Lateran Council of 1215 forbade ecclesiastics to take any part in ordeals. It is perhaps true that torture was introduced from the Roman law after the ordeal was ruled out.[3]

242. Irrationality of torture. Torture was far more irrational than the ordeal. The Roman authorities had recorded warnings of its fallacy.[4] Torture destroys nerve power, will, and consciousness. There comes a point at which the victim will assent to anything to escape pain, or to get a quick and easy death.

---

[1] Lea, *Inquis.*, II, 493.
[2] *Ibid.*, I, 306.
[3] *Ibid.*, 421.
[4] Digest, XLVII, 18, espec. sec. 23.

Therefore "confessions" under torture are of no value. Ulpian said of it, *"Res est fragilis et periculosa et quae veritatem fallat."* [1] One of the templars said that if he was tortured further he would confess that he had murdered the Saviour. Another said that he would confess anything if he was tortured further, although he was ready to suffer any death for the Order of Templars. He would confess that he had killed the mother of God.[2] A heretic under torture cried out that Christ, if so treated, would be proved a heretic.[3] Bernard Delicieux declared before King Philip that Peter and Paul could be convicted of heresy by the methods of the inquisitors.[4] Count Frederick von Spee, a Jesuit who opposed the witch persecutions, is quoted as saying, in 1631, "Treat the heads of the church, the judges, or me, as you treat those unhappy ones [accused of witchcraft], subject any of us to the same tortures, and you will discover that we are all sorcerers." [5] He quoted an inquisitor who boasted that if he could get the pope on the rack he would prove him a sorcerer.[6] In the thirteenth century "judges were well convinced of the failure of the procedure with its secret and subjective elements, but they could not in any other way cope with crime." [7]

This means, of course, that by long and manifold suggestion certain selected forms of crime had been stigmatized until the masses regarded them with horror. Then the apparatus of the administration of justice was brought to bear to exterminate all who could be charged with them, and when the process was objected to as horrible, it was defended on grounds of necessity to meet the horrible crime. By this action and reaction a great body of interests was enveloped in a special atmosphere, within which any excess of savagery was possible. The societal selection was prosecuted by murder of all dissenters.

243. Inquisitorial procedure from Roman law. The Roman criminal procedure was, in part, inquisitorial.[8] In the later period

---

[1] Digest, XLVII, 18, espec. sec. 23.
[2] Schotmüller, *Untergang der Templer*, 141, 311, 352.
[3] Flade, *Inquisitionsverfahren in Deutschland*, 84.
[4] Lea, *Inquis.*, II, 87.   [5] Scherr, *Kulturgesch.*, 383.
[6] Janssen, *Gesch. d. Deutschen Volkes*, VIII, 541.
[7] Hansen. *Zauberwahn*, 110.   [8] Mommsen, *Röm. Strafrecht*, 349.

of the republic a private accuser, who must be an injured party, started and conducted the prosecution, but the magistrates could proceed on their own motion, upon denunciation, or by inquisitorial process. The last method became the custom under the empire. Prosecutions for treason were thus carried on, and by the end of the empire sorcerers and heretics, as *hostes publici*, like traitors, were thus tried. All citizens were bound to denounce such criminals. This procedure was taken up into the canon law, so that the Christian church inherited a system of procedure as well as the doctrines above stated.[1]

244. Bishops as inquisitors. In the Carolingian period bishops were instructed to seek out heretics and to secure their conversion, but they rarely distinguished themselves by zeal in this matter. The procedure was that of a grand jury set in motion by common report. Lucius III and Barbarossa, acting together in 1184, prepared a decretal in which the duty of bishops was reaffirmed and an attempt was made to give sharper method to their proceedings. They were to seek out heretics, holders of secret conventicles, or any who " in any way differed, in mode of life, from the faithful in general." Those who refused to be disciplined and to conform were to be abandoned to the secular arm for fitting punishment. All civil officers were to swear to enforce laws against heretics. Here we find the fundamental notions of the later Inquisition, but zealous executioners were wanting. If the decretal had been " obeyed strictly and energetically, it would have established an episcopal instead of a papal Inquisition."

245. Definition of heretic. The definition of a heretic just quoted occurs often and is the only one which could be formulated. A person was as liable to be charged with heresy if better than the crowd as if worse. " In fact, amid the license of the Middle Ages ascetic virtue was apt to be regarded as a sign of heresy. About 1220 a clerk of Spire, whose austerity subsequently led him to join the Franciscans, was only saved by the interposition of Conrad, afterwards Bishop of Hildesheim, from being burned as a heretic, because his preaching led certain women to lay aside their vanities of apparel and behave with

---

[1] Hansen, *Zauberwahn*, etc., 100; Lea, *Inquis.*, I, 311.

humility. . . . I have met with a case, in 1320, in which a poor old woman at Pamiers submitted to the dreadful sentence for heresy simply because she would not take an oath. She answered all interrogations on points of faith in orthodox fashion, but though offered her life if she would swear on the gospels, she refused to burden her soul with the sin, and for this she was condemned as a heretic."[1] "Heretics who were admitted to be patterns of virtue were ruthlessly exterminated in the name of Christ, while in the same holy name the orthodox could purchase absolution for the vilest of crimes for a few coins."[2] There could be no definition of a heretic but one who differed in life and conversation from the masses around him. This might mean strange language, dress, manners, or greater restraint in conduct. Pallor of countenance was a mark of a heretic from the fourth century to the twelfth.[3] In the thirteenth century Franciscans were preëminently orthodox, but when John XXII stigmatized as heretical the assertion that Christ and his Apostles never had any property, they became criminals whom civil officers were bound to send to the stake.[4] John was himself a heretic as to the "beatific vision." He thought that the dead would not enter the presence of God until the judgment day.[5] The Franciscans held that the blood shed by Christ in the Passion lost its divinity, was separated from the Logos, and remained on earth. This was heresy.[6] The Dominicans, with Thomas Aquinas, were heretics as to the immaculate conception.[7] All the disputants on all sides of these questions went into the dispute at the risk of burning or being burned, as the tide should run.

246. The Albigenses. For some reason which is not easy to understand, the Manichæan doctrine took deep root in the Christian church from the fourth century on. To us the doctrine seems ethically bad, but that only shows how little religious dogmas make ethics. The enemies of the Albigenses recognized their high purity of life.[8] They called themselves kathari, or puritans. Popular fanaticism commenced persecution against them in the

---

[1] Lea, *Inquis.*, I, 87. [2] *Ibid.*, III, 641. [3] *Ibid.*, I, 110, 371.
[4] *Ibid.*, 541. [5] *Ibid.*, III, 454, 594. [6] *Ibid.*, II, 171.
[7] *Ibid.*, III, 596. [8] *Ibid.*, I, 101.

eleventh century. They were in antagonism to the hierarchy
and the Catholic system, especially to papal autocracy. "Even
with those abhorred sectaries, the church was wonderfully slow
to proceed to extremities. It hesitated before the unaccustomed
task. It shrank from contradicting its teachings of charity, and
was driven forward by popular fanaticism. The persecution of
Orleans, in 1017, was the work of King Robert, the Pious. The
burning at Milan, soon after, was done by the people against the
will of the archbishop. . . . Even as late as 1144, the church of
Liège congratulated itself on having, by the mercy of God, saved
the greater part of a number of confessed and convicted kathari
from the turbulent mob which strove to burn them. . . . In
1145 the zealous populace seized the kathari and burned them,
despite the resistance of the ecclesiastical authorities." [1] These
cases of lynching are the first cases, in the Middle Ages, of
burning heretics. They show that the masses in the Christian
church thought that the proper treatment of enemies of God,
the church, and all men.

247. Persecution popular. Innocent III began war on the
Albigenses at the beginning of the thirteenth century, as rebels
and heretics. All Catholics approved what he did, and thought that
the Albigenses richly deserved all the treatment they received.
The age was not religious, but it had intense religiosity, and the
whole religiosity was heated to a high pitch by the contest with
the Albigenses. The pride, ambition, and arrogance of the hierarchy and the basest greed and love of plunder of the masses
were enlisted against them. Lea's statement is therefore fully
justified that "the Inquisition was not an organization arbitrarily
devised and imposed upon the judicial system of Christendom by
the ambition or fanaticism of the church. It was rather a natural
— one may almost say an inevitable — evolution of the forces at
work in the thirteenth century, and no one can rightly appreciate
the process of its development and the results of its activity
without a somewhat minute consideration of the factors controlling the minds and souls of men during the ages which laid the
foundation of modern civilization." [2] In the mind of the age

[1] Lea, *Inquis.*, I, 218.   [2] *Ibid.*, iii.

"there was a universal consensus of opinion that there was nothing to do with a heretic but to burn him." This was one of those
wide and popular notions upon which mores grow, because the
folkways are adjusted to it in all departments of life as a rule of
welfare. The courts of Toulouse at first, not recognizing the
forces against the Albigenses, tried to protect their subjects,
but "to the public law of the period [Raymond II of Toulouse]
was an outlaw, without even the right of self-defense against the
first-comer, for his very self-defense was rated among his crimes.
In the popular faith of the age he was an accursed thing, without hope, here or hereafter. The only way of readmission into
human fellowship, the only hope of salvation, lay in reconcilia-
tion with the church through the removal of the awful ban which
had formed half of his inheritance. To obtain this he had repeat-
edly offered to sacrifice his honor and his subjects, and the offer
had been contemptuously spurned. . . . The battle of toleration
against persecution had been fought and lost; nor, with such a
warning as the fate of the two Raymonds, was there risk that
other potentates would disregard the public opinion of Christendom by ill-advised mercy to the heretic." [1]

248. An annalist of Worms is quoted about Dorso's operations
on the upper Rhine in 1231. Dorso burned many persons of
the peasant class. The annalist adds, "The people, when they
saw this, were favorable to the inquisitors and helped them; and
rightly, since those heretics deserved death. Confident in the
approval of the masses, they went on to make arrests in towns
and villages, as they pleased, and then they said to the judges,
without further evidence, 'These are heretics. We withdraw
our hands from them.' The judges were thus compelled to
burn many. That was not according to the sense of the Holy
Scriptures, and the ecclesiastics everywhere were greatly troubled.
Since, however, the people took sides with the unjust judges,
their will was executed everywhere." "The pitiless and incom-
petent judges later saw that they could not maintain their conduct without the help of great men, whom they won by saying
that they would burn rich people, whose goods the great men

[1] Lea, *Inquis.*, I, 207.

should have." "That pleased the great men, who helped them, and called them to their cities and towns." "The people, when they saw this, asked the reason, to which the persecutors answered, 'We would burn a hundred innocent if there was one guilty amongst them.' "[1]

249. It was also true of the persecutions of the philosophers in Mohammedan Spain that they were popular. "The best educated princes allowed themselves to be driven to persecute, in spite of their personal preferences, as a means of winning popularity."[2]

250. Theory of persecution. The public opinion of the ruling classes of Europe demanded that heresy should be exterminated at whatever cost, and yet with the suppression of open resistance the desired end seemed as far off as ever. . . . Trained experts were needed, whose sole business it should be to unearth the offenders and extort a confession of their guilt. . . . Thus to the public of the thirteenth century the organization of the Inquisition and its commitment to the children of Saint Dominic and Saint Francis appeared a perfectly natural or rather inevitable development arising from the admitted necessities of the time and the instrumentalities at hand.[3]

251. Duties laid on the civil authority. The secular authority accepted the functions allotted to it out of the spirit of the age. To fall into disfavor at Rome was, for a prince, to risk the loyalty of his subjects, with whom it was a point of high importance to belong to a "Christian" state, that is, one on good terms with the church. "We are not to imagine, however, from these reduplicated commands that the secular power, as a rule, showed itself in the slightest degree disinclined to perform the duty. The teachings of the church had made too profound an impression for any doubt in the premises to exist. As has been seen above, the laws of all the states of Europe prescribed concremation as the appropriate penalty for heresy, and even the free commonwealths of Italy recognized the Inquisition as the judge whose sentences were to be blindly executed."[4]

[1] Michael, *Gesch. d. Deutschen Volkes*, II, 326.
[2] Renan, *Averroes*, 35.
[3] Lea, *Inquis.*, I, 537.
[4] *Ibid.*, 537.

252. "The practice of burning the heretic alive was thus not the creature of positive law, but arose generally and spontaneously, and its adoption by the legislator was only the recognition of a popular custom."[1] "Confession of heresy became a matter of vital importance, and no effort was deemed too great, no means too repulsive, to secure it. This became the center of the inquisitorial process, and it is deserving of detailed consideration, not only because it formed the basis of procedure in the Holy Office, but also because of the vast and deplorable influence which it exercised for five centuries on the whole judicial system of continental Europe."[2] In the second half of the twelfth century burning had become, by custom, the usual punishment for heretics. The purpose was universally regarded as right and pious, and the means was thought wise and correct. Therefore the whole procedure went forward on a course of direct and consistent development.[3] It was first decreed in positive law in the code of Pedro II, of Aragon, in 1197. In the laws of Frederick II, in 1224, the punishment was death by burning or loss of the tongue. In 1231, in Sicily, burning was made absolute. In 1238 the stake was made the law of the empire against heresy. In 1270 Louis IX made it the law of France.[4] "Dominic and Francis, Bonaventura and Thomas Aquinas, Innocent III and St. Louis, were types, in their several ways, of which humanity, in any age, might well feel proud, and yet they were as unsparing of the heretic as Ezzelino da Romano was of his enemies. With such men it was not hope of gain or lust of blood or pride of opinion or wanton exercise of power, but sense of duty, and they but represented public opinion from the thirteenth to the seventeenth century."[5] That is to say, that the virtues of the individuals were overruled by the vices of the mores of the age.

253. The shares of the church and the masses. The steps of the process by which the Christian church was made an organization to enforce uniformity of confession by bodily pain, that is,

---

[1] Lea, *Inquis.*, I, 222.   [2] *Ibid.*, 410.
[3] Hansen, *Zauberwahn*, etc., 223.
[4] Lea, *Inquis.*, I, 220; Hansen, *Zauberwahn*, etc., 223.
[5] Lea, *Inquis.*, I, 234.

in fact, by murder, demand careful attention. Back of all the popular demands for persecution there was the teaching of the church in antecedent periods and a crude popular logic of detestation and destruction. Then the outbreak of persecution appears as a popular act with lynching executions. At this point the church, by virtue of its teaching and leading functions, ought to have repressed excessive zeal and guided the popular frenzy. It did not do so. It took the lead of the popular movement and encouraged it. This was its greatest crime, but it must be fairly understood that it acted with public opinion and was fully supported by the masses and by the culture classes. The Inquisition was not unpopular and was not disapproved. It was thought to be the proper and necessary means to deal with heresy, just as we now think police courts necessary to deal with petty crimes (see sec. 247). The system of persecution went on to extravagances. The masses disapproved. They could not be held to any responsibility. They turned against the ecclesiastical authorities and threw all the blame on them.

254. The church uses the power for selfish aggrandizement. Things now advanced, therefore, to the second stage. The church authorities accepted the executive duty in respect to the defense of the church and society against heresy. The popular idea was that heresy would bring down the wrath of God on all Christendom, or on the whole of the small group in which it occurred.[1] The church authorities formulated doctrines, planned programmes, and appointed administrative officers. To them the commission laid upon them meant more social power, and they turned it into a measure of selfish aggrandizement. This alienated first all competent judges, and at last the masses.

255. The Inquisition took shape slowly. The Inquisition took shape very gradually through the first half of the thirteenth century. "In the proceedings of this period the rudimentary character of the Inquisition is evident." The mendicant orders furnished the first agents. They were admired and honored by the masses. Gregory IX, in his first bulls (1233), making the

[1] Lea disputes this as to the educated clergy, while admitting it as to the masses, which is the essential point here (Lea, *Inquis.*, I, 237).

Dominicans the official inquisitors, seemed to be uncertain as to the probable attitude which the bishops would adopt to this invasion of their jurisdiction, " while the character of his instructions shows that he had no conception of what the innovation was to lead to." " As yet there was no idea of superseding the episcopal functions." In fact, the mendicant orders supplanted the military orders as papal militia, just as they were later supplanted by the Jesuits, and they very greatly assisted the reorganization of the church into an absolute monarchy under the pope.[1] Frederick II died in 1250. He was the first modern man on a throne. He had aimed to rule all Christendom by despotic methods which he perhaps learned from the Mohammedans. He would have made a monarchy if he had succeeded, which would have anticipated that of Charles V or Philip II by three hundred years.[2] It was the mores of the age which decided between him and the pope. His court was a center of Arabic culture and of religious indifference. There were eunuchs, a harem, astrologers from Bagdad, and Jews richly pensioned by the emperor to translate Arabic works. " All these things were transmuted, in popular belief, into relations with Ashtaroth and Beelzebub." [3] The saying that there had been three great impostors — Moses, Jesus, and Mohammed — was attributed to him, and it appears that his contemporaries generally believed that he first used the statement. The only thing which he left behind was the code of laws which he had made, by way of concession and attempt to buy peace from the popes, by which all civil authorities were made constables and hangmen of the church, to which all dissenters were sacrificed.

256. Formative legislation. In 1252 Innocent IV issued a bull "which should establish machinery for systematic persecution as an integral part of the social edifice in every city and every state." He authorized the torture of witnesses. "These provisions are not the wild imaginings of a nightmare, but sober, matter-of-fact legislation, shrewdly and carefully devised to accomplish a settled policy, and it affords us a valuable insight into

[1] Burckhardt, *Renaissance*, 3.
[2] Jastrow and Winter, *Hohenstaufen*, II, 298.
[3] Renan, *Averroes*, 288.

the public opinion of the day to find that there was no effective resistance to its acceptance." There is evidence, twenty years later, that the Inquisition "had not been universally accepted with alacrity, but the few instances which we find recorded of refusal show how generally it was submitted to." The institution was in full vigor in Italy, but not beyond the Alps, "yet this was scarce necessary so long as public law and the conservative spirit of the ruling class everywhere rendered it the highest duty of the citizen of every degree to aid in every way the business of the inquisitor, and pious monarchs hastened to enforce the obligations of their subjects." "It was not the fault of the church if a bold monarch like Philip the Fair occasionally ventured to incur divine vengeance by protecting his subjects." [1]

257. Dungeons. It is evident that the lust of blood was educated into the mores by public executions with torture, by obscene adjuncts, by inhuman sports, and by public shows. Cruelty and inhumanity in civil cases were as great as under the Inquisition. A person apprehended on any charge was imprisoned in a frightful dungeon, damp, infested by rats and vermin, generally in chains, and he was often forced to lie in a constrained position. This was a part of the policy which prevailed in the administration of justice. It was intended to break the spirit and courage of the accused. Confinement was solitary, and various circumstances besides pain and hunger were brought to bear on the imagination. It was the rule that every accused person must fast for eight or ten hours before torture. The dungeons were often ingenious means of torture. There was one in the Bastille at Paris, the floor of which was conical, with the point downwards so that it was impossible to sit, or lie, or stand in it. In another, in the Châtelet, the floor was all the time covered by water, in which the prisoners must stand. [2]

258. The yellow crosses. One of the penalties inflicted by the Inquisition causes astonishment and at the same time shows how thoroughly the mass of the population were on the side of the Inquisition until the fifteenth century. Persons convicted of

---

[1] Lea, *Inquis.*, I, 224, 309–313, 322, 327–330, 337–342.
[2] Lacroix, *Middle Ages*, I, 407; Flade, *Inquisitionsverfahren*, 86.

heresy, but coerced to penitence, were forced to wear crosses of cloth, generally yellow, three spans long and two wide, sewed on their garments. Thus the symbol of Christian devotion was turned into a badge of shame.[1] It pointed out the wearer as an outcast. However, it depended on the mass of the population to say what it should mean. How did they treat persons thus marked? They boycotted them. The wearers of crosses could not find employment, or human intercourse, or husbands, or wives. They were actually unable to get the relations with other men and women which are essential to existence.[2] If the people had pitied them, or sympathized with them, they would have shown it by kindness, in spite of ecclesiastical orders. In fact, the cross was a badge of infamy and was enforced as such by public action. "The unfortunate penitent was exposed to the ridicule and derision of all whom he met, and was heavily handicapped in every effort to earn a livelihood."[3] It is evident that the way in which the general public treated the cross-wearers can alone account for the weight which those under this penalty attached to it. "It was always considered very shameful." At Augsburg, in 1393, for seventy gold gulden, the wearing of crosses could be escaped.[4]

259. Confiscation. Another penalty of frightful effect was confiscation. As soon as a man was arrested for heresy, his property was sequestrated and inventoried. His family was thrown on the street. It was out of the Roman law that "pope and king drew the weapons which rendered the pursuit of heresy attractive and profitable." "The church cannot escape the responsibility of naturalizing this penalty in European law as a punishment for spiritual transgressions."[5] "It would be difficult to estimate the amount of human misery arising from this source alone." "The threats of coercion which at first were necessary to induce the temporal princes to confiscate the property of their heretical subjects soon became superfluous, and history has few displays of man's eagerness to profit by his fellow's misfortunes more deplorable than that of the vultures which followed in the

---

[1] Lea, *Inquis.*, I, 467.   [3] *Ibid.*, 464, 467–470.   [5] Lea, *Inquis.*, I, 501.
[2] *Ibid.*, 470.   [4] Flade, *Inquisitionsverfahren*, 111.

wake of the Inquisition to batten on the ruin which it wrought."
In Italy the confiscated property was divided into three parts by
the pope's order. One part went to the Inquisition for its expenses, one part to the papal camera, and one part to the civil
authority. Later, the civil authority generally got nothing.
About 1335 a Franciscan bishop of Silva "reproached those of
his brethren who act as inquisitors with their abuse of the funds
accruing to the Holy Office. . . . The inquisitors monopolized
the whole, spent it on themselves, or enriched their kindred at
their pleasure." "Avarice joined hands with fanaticism, and
between them they supplied motive power for a hundred years
of fierce, unremitting, unrelenting persecution which, in the end,
accomplished its main purpose." The confiscations did not concern the populace. They furnished the motive of the great to
support the administration of the Inquisition.[1] "Persecution, as a
steady and continuous policy, rested, after all, upon confiscation.
It was this which supplied the fuel to keep up the fires of zeal,
and when it was lacking the business of defending the faith
languished lamentably. When katharism disappeared under the
brilliant aggressiveness of Bernard Gui, the culminating point of
the Inquisition was passed, and thenceforth it steadily declined,
although still there were occasional confiscated estates over which
king, prelate, and noble quarreled for some years to come."[2] "The
earnest endeavors of the inquisitors were directed much more to
obtaining conversions with confiscations and betrayal of friends
than to provoking martyrdoms. . . . The really effective weapons
of the Holy Office, the real curses with which it afflicted the
people, can be looked for in its dungeons and its confiscations, in
the humiliating penances of the saffron crosses, and in the invisi-
ble police with which it benumbed the heart and soul of every
man who had once fallen into its hands."[3] It is evident that these
means of tormenting and coercing dissenters went much further
to cause them to disappear than autos-de-fe and other executions.
The selection of those who submitted, or played the hypocrite,
was accomplished in the fifteenth century.

[1] Lea, *Inquis.*, I, 511–513, 519–521, 533.
[2] *Ibid.*, 529.   [3] *Ibid.*, 551

260. Operation of the Inquisition. The Inquisition acted effectively. It kept detailed records and pursued its victims to the third generation.[1] It covered Europe with a network of reports which would rival the most developed modern police systems, "putting the authorities on the alert to search for every stranger who wore the air of one differing in life and conversation from the ordinary run of the faithful." "To human apprehension, the papal Inquisition was well-nigh ubiquitous, omniscient, and omnipotent." Inquisitors were set free from all rules which had been found necessary to save judges from judicial error,[2] and the formularies to guide inquisitors inculcated chicane, terrorism, deception, and brow-beating, and an art of entangling the accused in casuistry and dialectics. A new crime was invented for the cases in which confession could not be obtained : suspicion of heresy, which had three degrees, "light," "vehement," and "violent." Even papal decretals which restrained the effort to destroy the accused could be set aside.[3] Thus the Inquisition coöperated with the criminal law. It operated on the society of Christendom for ten or twelve generations a selection of those who would submit and obey, and an elimination of those who dissented.

261. Success of the Inquisition. That the Inquisition succeeded in its purpose is certain. It forced at least external conformity and silence, especially of the masses. The heterodoxy of the Middle Ages "is divisible into two currents, of which one, called the 'eternal gospel,' includes the mystical and communistic sects which, starting from Joachim de Florus, after having filled the twelfth and thirteenth centuries . . . was carried on, in the fourteenth, by the German mystics ; the other, summed up in the blasphemy that there had been three great impostors [Moses, Jesus, and Mohammed], represents materialistic infidelity, due to a study of the Arabs, and skulking under the name of Averroes."[4] Of these two schools of heretics the former was the more popular and tenacious. It is not to be understood that the masses ever recognized their own handiwork in the Inquisition, or the popes of the fifteenth century. On the contrary, the sequence goes on to

[1] Lea, *Inquis.*, I, 366.
[2] *Ibid.*, 405.
[3] *Ibid.*, 364–366, 405, 433, 493; II, 96.
[4] Renan, *Averroes*, 292.

the fourth stage in which the masses, seeing the operation of ambition, venality, and despotism in the officers of the institution created to meet a popular demand, denounce it and turn against it to destroy it.

262. Torture in civil and ecclesiastical trials. (See sec. 237 ff.) In the course of its work the Inquisition had introduced torture into the administration of Christian justice and into the mores. The jurists were all corrupted by it. They supposed that, without torture, no crimes could be detected or punished, and this opinion ruled the administration of justice on the continent until the eighteenth century.[1] Lea finds the earliest instances of legal torture in the Veronese Code of 1228, and in the Sicilian Constitutions of 1231 ; — work of the rationalist emperor, Frederick II, but it was " sparingly and hesitatingly employed." Innocent IV adopted it in 1252, but only secular authorities were to use it. This was to save the sanctity of ecclesiastics. In 1256 Alexander IV, " with characteristic indirection," authorized inquisitors and their associates to absolve each other, and grant dispensations for irregularities. This gave them absolute liberty, and they could inflict or supervise torture.[2] There were other " poses," such as the prohibition to shed blood, i.e. to break the skin, and the rule to ask the civil power, when surrendering the victim to it, not to proceed to extremes, although it was bound to burn the victim. As the system continued in practice its methods, were refined and its experts were trained. Any one who was charged must be convicted if possible. The torture produced permanent crippling or maiming. It would not do to release any one so marked with the investigation and then acquitted. Hence more and more frightful measures became necessary. Nevertheless cases occurred in which the accused held out beyond the power of the persecutors.[3] At Bamberg, in 1614, a woman seventy-four years old endured torture up to the third grade. After three quarters of an hour on the " Bock " she fell dead. The verdict was that she had cleared herself, by enduring the torture, of the " evidence " against her, and would have been freed if she had lived. She was to have Christian burial, and a document attesting this finding was to be given to her husband and children. Some jurists of the sixteenth and seventeenth centuries were led to doubt about torture, but they almost all agreed that it was necessary " in some cases." These were the reformers who were careful not to be extremists. We are told that Peter of Ravenna, in 1511, urged the abolition of torture, and that Louis Vivez, a Spaniard, took the same position a little later. Neither won any attention.[4] In the Carolina, Charles V's law book of 1532, which was in general savage in its penalties, torture was to be applied only

---

[1] Lea, *Inquis.*, I, 560. [2] *Ibid.*, 421.
[3] Cases given by Janssen, *Gesch. d. Deutschen Volkes*, VIII, 629.
[4] Janssen, VIII, 467.

in cases punishable by death or life imprisonment, and only on strong prima facie evidence of guilt. Confession under torture was to have no weight unless confirmed after an interval. These restrictions were not observed in practice.[1] There are very many cases on record in which it was afterwards proved that many persons had suffered torture and cruel execution, upon confession, who were innocent of all crime.[2]

263. The selection accomplished. Thus the apparatus and devices for putting down dissent and enforcing submission to such authority as the great number were willing to recognize had attained a superficial success. Opposition was silenced. Dissent was made so dangerous that no one dared express it, except here and there a hero, and outward conformity to church discipline was almost universal. The mores also underwent influence from a societal power which was great and pervading. The external and artificial character of the conformity was so well known that a name was given to it, — *implicita fides*, — and this was discussed as to its nature and value. The mores are gravely affected by *implicita fides* when it is held by a great number of persons.[3] The selection which had destroyed honest thinkers and sincere churchmen had cultivated a class of smooth hypocrites and submissive cowards. In the fifteenth century the whole of Christendom had accepted the church system with its concepts of welfare and its dictates of duty, and had adopted the ritual means of holiness and salvation which it prescribed. In fact, at no other time were men ever so busy as then with "good works," or so fussy about church ritual. Everybody was anxious not to be a heretic. At the same time the whole mediæval system was falling to pieces, and the inventions and discoveries were disproving all received and approved ideas about the world and welfare in it. Gross sensuality and carnal lust got possession of society, and the church system was an independent system of balancing accounts with the other world. The theater declined into obscenity and coarseness, and the popular pulpit was hardly better.[4] The learned world was returning to classical

---

[1] Scherr, *Kulturgesch. Deutschlands*, 624 ; Janssen, *Gesch. d. Deutschen Volkes*, VIII, 467.   [2] Janssen, VIII, 467.

[3] Harnack, *Dogmengesch.*, III, 453.

[4] Lenient, *La Satire en France*, 309, 315.

paganism. The popes had their children in the Vatican and publicly married them there. Under Sextus IV the courtesans at Rome paid a tax which produced 20,000 ducats per annum. Prelates owned brothels. Innocent VIII tried to stop the scandal. In 1490 his vicar published an edict against all concubinage, but the pope forced him to recall it because all ecclesiastics had concubines. There were 6800 public meretrices at Rome besides private ones and concubines. Concubinage was really tolerated, subject to the payment of an amercement.[1] The proceedings under Alexander VI were only the culmination of the license taken by men who were irresponsible masters of the world, and who showed the insanity of despotism just as the Roman emperors did.[2] The church had broken down under the reaction of its own efforts to rule the world. It had made moral hypocrisy and religious humbug characteristic of Christians, for he who indulges in sensual vice and balances it off by ritual devices is morally subject to the deepest corruption of character. The church system had corrupted the mores by adding casuistry and dialectic smartness to the devices for regulating conduct and satisfying interests. The men of the Renaissance, especially in Italy, acted always from passionate motives and went to great excess. Their only system of conduct was success in what they wanted to do, and so they were often heroes of crime. Yet they all conformed to church ritual and discipline.

264. A great undertaking like the suppression of dissent by force and cruelty cannot be carried out in a great group of states without local differentiation and variation. To close the story, it is worth while to notice these variations in England, Spain, and Venice.

265. Torture in England. The Inquisition cannot be said to have existed in the British Islands or Scandinavia. The laws of Frederick II had no authority there. In England, in 1400, the death penalty for heresy was introduced by the statute *de heretico comburendo*. In 1414 a mixed tribunal of ecclesiastics and laymen was established to search out heretics and punish them. It was employed to suppress Lollardry. Under Edward VI these

---

[1] Burchard, *Diarium*, II, 442.
[2] See Burchard, III, 167, 227.

laws were repealed; under Mary they were renewed. In the first Parliament of Elizabeth they were repealed again, except the statute of 1400, which was repealed in 1676, when Charles II wanted toleration for Roman Catholics. Then the ecclesiastical courts were restricted to ecclesiastical penalties.[1] Torture was never legal in England. The use of it was pushed to the greatest extreme when Clement V and Philip the Fair were seeking evidence against the templars. Then the pope wrote a fatherly letter of expostulation to Edward of England, because of the lack of this engine in his dominions.[2] Cases of torture no doubt occurred. The star chamber had an inquisitorial process in which the rack seems to have been used. Barbaro, a Venetian ambassador in the sixteenth century, reported the non-use of torture as an interesting fact in English mores. He says the English think that it often forces untrue confession, that it " spoils the body and an innocent life ; thinking, moreover, that it is better to release a criminal than to punish an innocent man." [3] From the thirteenth century it was forbidden to keep a prisoner in chains. In other countries this was the rule, and ingenuity was expended to fasten the prisoner in a most uncomfortable position.[4] The last case of the rack in the star chamber was that of Peacham, in 1614.[5] The last execution for heresy in the British Islands was that of a medical student at Edinburgh, eighteen years of age, named Aikenhead, in 1696.[6] The greatest cruelty in England was " pressing " prisoners to compel them to plead because, if they did not plead, the trial could not go on.

It follows that the repressive system of the mediæval church did not produce effects on the mores in England.

266. The Spanish Inquisition. The Spanish Inquisition is an offshoot and development of that of the mediæval church. The latter was started in Aragon and Navarre in 1238.[7] In the latter half of the fourteenth century Eymerich (author of the *Directorium Inquisitorum*) conducted an inquisition in Aragon against Jews and Moors. In Castile, in 1400, an inquisition was in activity.[8] None of these efforts produced a permanent establishment. In the reign of Isabella, Cardinal Mendoza organized the Inquisition as a state institution to establish the throne.[9] The king named the inquisitors, who need not be ecclesiastics. The confiscated property of " heretics " fell to the state. Ecclesiastics were subject to the tribunal. The church long withheld approval from this inquisition, because it was political in origin and purpose, and was created outside the church organization and without church authorization. The populace also opposed it. This union of church and populace forced the grandees to support it.[10] The punishments " implied confiscation of

[1] Lea, *Inquis.*, I, 352.
[2] *Ibid.*, III, 300 ; Schotmüller, *Untergang der Templer*, I, 388.
[3] *Venetian Ambass.*, I, II, 233.
[4] Lea, *Inquis.*, I, 488.
[5] Inderwick, *The King's Peace*, 172.
[6] Lea, *Inquis.*, I, 352.
[7] Hansen, *Zauberwahn*, etc., 338.
[8] *Ibid.*, 338.
[9] Lea, *Inquis. in Spain*, 158.
[10] Heyer, *Priesterschaft und Inquis.*, 42.

property. Thus whole families were orphaned and consigned to penury. Penitence in public carried with it social infamy, loss of civil rights and honors, intolerable conditions of ecclesiastical surveillance, and heavy pecuniary fines. Penitents who had been reconciled returned to society in a far more degraded condition than convicts released on ticket of leave. The stigma attached in perpetuity to the posterity of the condemned, whose names were conspicuously emblazoned upon church walls as foemen to Christ and to the state."[1] When "the Spanish viceroys tried to introduce the Spanish Inquisition at Naples and Milan, the rebellious people received protection and support from the papacy, and the Holy Office, as remodeled in Rome, became a far less awful engine of oppression than that of Seville."[2] The Spanish Inquisition went on to a new form, free from papal and royal control and possessing a "specific organization."[3] "Like the ancient councils of the time of the Goths, the Inquisition is an arm which serves, in the hands of the monarch, to finish the subjugation of the numerous semi-feudal nobles created by the conquest, because before the faith there are no privileged persons, and no one is sheltered from the ire of the terrible tribunal. Its intervention is so absolute, and its dedication to its function so extravagant, that, rendering itself more Catholic than the pope, it usurps his authority and revolts against the orders of the pontiff, giving to the peninsular church the character of a national church, with the king at the head as pontiff, and the inquisitor by his side as chief prelate."[4] The peculiar character of the Spanish Inquisition as a state institution and a civil engine should never be forgotten. It was very different from the papal Inquisition. The creature also ruled its creator, for it controlled the state in the direction of its own institutional character and purposes. The Spanish Inquisition, therefore, offers us the extreme development of the movement which started in the popular tastes, ideas, and wishes of the twelfth century, when it was employed for the selfish purposes of rulers. It presents the extreme case of a positive institution, born from the mores and winning independent power and authority over all interests. It very deeply affected Spanish mores. It had no great effect of societal selection.

267. Inquisition in Venice. The Inquisition in Venice took on a form which was to some extent peculiar. The Venetian political system was secret, suspicious, and despotic. It would not admit any interference from outside. Venice always pretended to hold off church authority. In fact, however, she could not maintain this attitude. The Inquisition won control of many subjects beyond heresy or only constructively heresy.[5] Fra Paolo Sarpi[6] made a collection of Venetian laws which show the jealousy of ecclesiastical interference, or which nullified the ordinances made in Rome. "The position of the republic was indefensible under the public law of the period. It was

---

[1] Symonds, *Catholic Reaction*, I, 185.   [2] *Ibid.*, 199.   [3] *Ibid.*, 179.
[4] Oliveira Martins, *Civilisação Iberica*, 268.
[5] Symonds, *Catholic Reaction*, I, 205.   [6] *Opere*, IV, 7 ff.

so administering its own laws as to afford an asylum to a class universally proscribed, and refusing to allow the church to apply the only remedy deemed appropriate to this crying evil. It therefore yielded to the inevitable, but in a manner to preserve its own autonomy and independence."[1] "The truth is that, in regard both to the Holy Office and the index, Venice was never strong enough to maintain the independence which she voted."[2] In 1573 Paolo Veronese was summoned by the Holy Office to explain and justify his picture of the Supper, now in the Louvre. He had put in a man at arms, a greyhound, and other figures which the inquisitors thought irrelevant and unfit. He was ordered to change the picture within three months. He put Magdalen in the place of the greyhound.[3] It is impossible to make a definite statement of the results of the Venetian effort to resist the church system, but that such an effort was made in Italy is an important historical fact.

268. Use of the Inquisition for political and personal purposes. In spite of the religiosity of the age there were princes and factions which cared more for political power than for theological questions. When the power of the Inquisition was established many ecclesiastical and civil persons desired to employ its agency for their personal or party ends. Boniface VIII, in the bull *Unam Sanctam*, laid down in full force the doctrine of papal supremacy and independence. Any one who resisted the power lodged by God in the church resisted God, unless, like the Manichæans, he believed in two principles, in which case he was a heretic. If the pope errs, he can be judged by God alone. There is no earthly appeal. "We say, declare, define, and pronounce, that it is necessary to salvation that every human creature be subjected to the Roman pontiff." "It was soon perceived that an accusation of heresy was a peculiarly easy and efficient method of attacking a political enemy."[4] John XXII, in his quarrel with Visconti, trumped up charges of heresy which won public opinion away from Visconti, disassociated his friends, and ruined him. Heresy and damnation were used to and fro, as interest dictated, and only for policy.[5] This is the extreme development of the action against dissenters in its third stage, the abuse of power for selfish purposes. "Heretic" became an epithet of immense power in factional quarrels, and the Inquisition was a weapon which any one could use who could seize it. Hence effects on the mores were produced in an age when factions were numerous and their quarrels constant. In these cases, however, the selectional effect was only against the personal enemies of the powerful, and was not a societal effect at all.

269. We have distinguished four stages in the story of the attempt to establish religious uniformity under papal control in

[1] Lea, *Inquis.*, II, 250.   [3] Yriarte, *Patricien de Venise*, 162, 439.
[2] Symonds, *Catholic Reaction*, I, 207.   [4] Lea, *Inquis.*, III, 191–192, 238.
[5] *Ibid.*, 198. Collected cases in Fra Paolo Sarpi, *Della Inquis. de Venezia*, Opere, IV, 24.

the Middle Ages. I. The church taught doctrines and alleged facts about the wickedness of aberrant opinions. II. The masses, accepting these teachings, built deductions upon them, and drew inferences as to the proper treatment of dissenters. They put the inferences in effect by lynching acts. III. The leaders of society accepted the leadership of these popular movements, and the church went on to teach hatred of dissenters and extreme abuse of them. It elevated persecution to a theory of social welfare by the extermination of dissenters, reduced the views and notions of the masses to dogmas, and led in selection by murder. IV. These ideas and practices were then vulgarized by the masses again. Trial by torture, bloody executions, and finally witchcraft persecutions were the results in the next stage. Witchcraft persecutions were not selective. They are well worth study as the greatest illustration of the degree of aberration which the mores may undergo, but they lie aside from the present topic. In savage life alleged witchcraft is punished with great torture and a painful death,[1] but nothing of the kind is found in any of the great religions except Latin Christianity.

[1] Fritsch, *Eingeb. Süd-Afr.*, 99.

CHAPTER VI

SLAVERY

270. Origin and motives. Slavery is a thing in the mores which is not well covered by our definition. Slavery does not arise in the folkways from the unconscious experimentation of individuals who have the same need which they desire to satisfy, and who try in separate acts to do it as well as they can. It is rather due to ill feeling towards members of an out-group, to desire to get something for nothing, to the love of dominion which belongs to vanity, and to hatred of labor. "The simple wish to use the bodily powers of another person, as a means of ministering to one's own ease or pleasure, is doubtless the foundation of slavery, and as old as human nature." [1] "There is an extraordinary power of tyranny invested in the chiefs of tribes and nations of men that so vastly outweighs the analogous power possessed by the leaders of animal herds as to rank as a

---

[1] Maine, *Anc. Law*, 164.

special attribute of human society, eminently conducive to slav-
ishness." [1] The desire to get ease or other good by the labor of
another, and the incidental gratification to vanity, seem to be the
fundamental principles in slavery, when philosophically regarded,
after the rule of one man over others has become established.
The whole group, however, must approve of the custom and
must enforce it ; otherwise it cannot exist. It appears that slavery began historically with the war captive, if he or she was not
put to death, as he was liable to be by the laws of war. Those
laws put the defeated, with his wife, children, and property, at
the mercy of the victors. The defeated might be tortured to
death, as was done amongst the North American Indians, or
they might be saved from death by the women. Then they were
put to help the women and were rated as women. Slavery,
therefore, in its origin, was a humanitarian improvement in the
laws of war, and an alleviation of the status of women. It seems
to be established that it began where the economic system was
such that there was a gain in making a slave of a war captive
instead of killing him. It follows that slavery, wherever it has
existed, has affected all the mores of the society. It promised
great results gratis. It will appear below that it has been
a terrible afrit, a demon which promised service but which
became a master. When adopted into the folkways it has dominated and given tone and color to them all. That is the reason
for giving it a place here.

271. Slavery taught steady labor. It seems to be also right
to understand that slavery proved to be a great schoolmaster to
teach men steady work. If that view is correct, we must understand that no men would do any hard, persistent work if they
could help it. The defeated were forced to it, and learned to
submit to it. Then they helped the whole society up to a higher
status, in which they also shared.[2] Von Götzen gives some
proof of this when he states that he and his troop of carriers sat
by the camp fire evenings and that one after another told his
life. " Nearly all had been, as children, brought from the inner
country to the coast by slave dealers. Now they were proud of

[1] Galton, *Human Faculty*, 79.　　　　[2] Gumplowicz, *Soziologie*, 121.

this slavery, proud of belonging to the 'cultivated' and of not being any longer 'wild' men." [1] In that view slavery is a part of the discipline by which the human race has learned how to carry on the industrial organization. There are some tasks which have been very hard and very disagreeable. Comrades in an in-group have never forced these on each other. It seemed to be good fun, as well as wise policy, to make members of a rival out-group do these tasks, after defeating them in war. For women the grinding of seeds (grain) always was a heavy burden until modern machinery brought natural powers to do it. For men the rowing of boats (galleys) has been a very hard kind of work. [2] After slavery came to exist it was extended to other cases, even to some classes of cases in the in-group. Of these cases the first was that of debt. Amongst the Eveans a debtor who cannot pay is put to death. This, however, is a very exceptional rule. [3] The course of thought is, that a debtor has used another man's product and is bound to replace it. He therefore falls into servitude to his creditor in fact, whether it is so expressed or not. He must live on and work for the creditor. Another case in which slavery was introduced was that of crime. The criminal fell under obligations of restitution of value to an individual or to the whole (chief). Other cases of extension of slavery will appear below. We have many cases of groups exploited by other groups. The former are then inferior and despised groups who are tyrannized over by others who have beaten them in war or easily could do so.

272. Servitude of group to group. Agriculture is a peaceful occupation, the pursuit of which breeds out the physical strength of nomadism. The cases in which nomads rule over tillers belong, in general, under this head, more especially because such a difference in the economy of life produces mutual contempt and hatred. The Israelites entered Canaan as nomads,

---

[1] *Durch Afrika*, 207.

[2] Gumplowicz (*Soziol.*, 118) quotes a seventeenth-century author who said that high wages could get soldiers and sailors for a galley, but not oarsmen, who would allow themselves to be bound by a chain, bastinadoed, etc. Gumplowicz explains that if the galley was to manœuver with exactitude, chains, the bastinado, etc., must be used to regulate the service.

[3] Ratzel, *Völkerkunde*, I, Introd., 83.

and their relation to the Canaanites was that which is here described. Another case is presented by the smiths, who generally appear as the earliest handicraftsmen, but are regarded with doubt and suspicion. They are not slaves, but they are treated as outcasts. Very often, in case of conquest by an invading tribe, the smiths remain under the invaders as a subject and despised caste. The Masarva are descendants of Betchuanas and Bushmen. They stand in a relation of slaves to the Betchuanas, Matabele, and Marutse, in whose land they dwell, except that they may not be sold.[1] The Vaganda are subject to the Vahuma.[2] The latter keep out of sight, being inferior in civilization but greater in power. Von Götzen also met with the Vahuma as rulers over the Vahuta, i.e. "belongers," as they called them.[3] The Arabs hold the negroes of Borku in subjection and rob them of the date harvest.[4] In other parts of the same district a nomad section rules over a settled section of the same population.[5] Nomads hold themselves to be the proper ones to rule.[6] The Hyksos's invasion of Egypt is a case of the subjection of tillers by nomads, attended by all the contempt of men on one grade of civilized effort for those on another.[7] The combination of the two, the nomads forming the ruling caste of military nobles, forms a strong state.[8] The Tuaregs of the Sahara do not allow the inhabitants of Kauar to raise vegetables or grains, but force them to buy the same of them (the Tuaregs), which they bring to them from the Sudan to buy salt, which the Kauar dwellers must have ready.[9] The Akarnanians, in 1350, sold themselves to the barbarians, in a body, in order to escape want.[10] The Masai are another group of warriors and raiders. The Varombutta do their hunting and tilling for them.[11] The Makololo hold the Makalaka in similar serfdom, but the subjection is easy and the servitude light, because the subject individuals can easily run away.[12] The Hupa of California hold their neighbors in similar subjection and in tributary servitude.[13] Other cases are furnished by the Vanyambo, west of the Victoria Nyassa,[14] and the Djur, who long served the Nubians as smiths.[15] It gives us pleasure to learn that, about sixty years ago, the inferior tribes on Uvea (Tai), of the Loyalty group, revolted against the dominant tribe and nearly exterminated it.[16]

[1] Holub, *Maschukalumbe*, I, 477; JAI, X, 9.
[2] Ratzel, I, 477, 481.
[3] *Durch Afrika*, 162.
[4] Nachtigal, *Sahara und Sudan*, II, 110.
[5] *Ibid.*, 104.
[6] *Ibid.*, I, 315.
[7] Ratzel, III, 91.
[8] *Ibid.*, 7.
[9] Rohlfs, *Petermann's Mittlgn, Erg. heft*, XXV, 23.
[10] Cantacuzene, *Hist.*, IV, 20.
[11] JAI, XXI, 380.
[12] Livingstone, *Travels in South Africa*, I, 204.
[13] *Smithson. Rep.*, 1886, Part I, 207.
[14] Stuhlmann, *Mit Emin Pascha*, 242.
[15] Ratzel, III, 143.
[16] *Austral. Assoc. Adv. Sci.* 1892, 634.

273. Slavery and polygamy. Such instances show us the existence in human nature of a tendency of stronger groups to exploit weaker ones in the struggle for existence; in other words, slavery or forced labor is one way in which, in elementary civilization, the survival of the fittest group is brought about. The slavery of individuals has not the same definite result on the competition of life. "We find polygamy and slavery continually at work dissolving the cohesion of old political institutions in the old civilized races of Asia and Africa. In an uncivilized society, like that of Zululand, they prevent such cohesion ever taking place. They help to keep the Kaffir tribes in perpetual unrest and barbarism, by destroying the germs of civilization and preventing its growth."[1] That the two have this effect in common may very probably be true, but in many respects they are antagonistic to each other. Slavery meets the necessity for many laborers which may otherwise be a cause for polygamy. Wherever slavery exists it affords striking illustrations of the tendency of the mores towards consistency with each other, and that means, of course, their tendency to cluster around some one or two leading ones. Africa now furnishes the leading proofs of this. The negro society is one in which physical force is the chief deciding element. The negroes have enslaved each other for thousands of years. Very few of them have ever become slaves to whites without having been previously slaves to other negroes. In 1875 it was reckoned that twenty thousand persons, chiefly women and children whose male relatives had generally been killed, were taken into slavery from around Lake Nyassa. The difficulties and expense of the slave trade in that region became so great that it could not be carried on except by alliance with one tribe which defeated and enslaved another and sold the survivors. The Arabs opened paths for ivory hunting. The slave dealers used these means of communication. They established garrisons in order to exploit the territory, and ended by depopulating it.[2] Junker argues earnestly against the impression which has been established in Europe that Arabs are chiefly to blame for slavery. "There are places in Africa where

[1] JAI, XII, 266. [2] Ratzel, I, 404; III, 145 ff.

three men cannot be sent on a journey together for fear two of them may combine and sell the third." [1]

274. Some men serving others. Freedom and equality. Figurative use of "slavery." Must we infer, then, that there is a social necessity that some men must serve others? In the New Testament it is taught that willing and voluntary service of others is the highest duty and glory of human life. If one man's strength is spent on another man's struggle for existence, the survival of the former in the competition of life is impaired. The men of talent are constantly forced to serve the rest. They make the discoveries and inventions, order the battles, write the books, and produce the works of art. The benefit and enjoyment go to the whole. There are those who joyfully order their own lives so that they may serve the welfare of mankind. The whole problem of mutual service is the great problem of societal organization. Is it a dream, then, that all men should ever be free and equal? It is at least evident that here ethical notions have been interjected into social relations, with the result that we have been taught to think of free and equal units willingly serving each other. That, at least, is an idealistic dream. Yet it no more follows from the fact that slavery has done good work in the history of civilization that slavery should forever endure than it follows from the fact that war has done good work in the history of civilization that war is, in itself, a good thing. Slavery alleviated the status of women; the domestication of beasts of draft and burden alleviated the status of slaves; we shall see below that serfs got freedom when wind, falling water, and steam were loaded with the heavy tasks. Just now the heavy burdens are borne by steam; electricity is just coming into use to help bear them. Steam and electricity at last mean coal, and the amount of coal in the globe is an arithmetical fact. When the coal is used up will slavery once more begin? One thing only can be affirmed with confidence; that is, that as no philosophical dogmas caused slavery to be abolished, so no philosophical dogmas can prevent its reintroduction if economic changes should make it fit and suitable again. As steam has had

[1] JAI, XXII, 103; Junker, *Afrika*, II, 462, 477.

put upon it the hard work of life during the last two hundred years, the men have been emancipated from ancient hard conditions and burdens, and the generalities of the philosophers about liberty have easily won greater and greater faith and currency. However, the mass of mankind, taught to believe that they ought to have easy and pleasant times here, begin to complain again about "wages slavery," "debt slavery," "rent slavery," "sin slavery," "war slavery," "marriage slavery," etc. What men do not like they call "slavery," and so prove that it ought not to be. It appears to be still in their experience that a free man is oppressed by contracts of wages, debt, rent, and marriage, and that the cost of making ready for war and of warding off sin are very heavy. Political institutions readjust and redistribute the burdens of life over a population, and they change the form of the same perhaps, but the burdens are in the conditions of human life. They are always present, and political institutions never can do away with them at all. Therefore slavery, if we mean by it subjection to the conditions of human life, never can be abolished.

275. Ethnographical illustrations of slavery. In Togo male slaves work in the fields where yams are cultivated. Each carries a basket in which he has a chicken, which will live on worms and insects in the field. The slave is soon married. He has two days in the week to work for himself. One of his grown boys can replace him on the other four. He can buy a slave to replace him. Thus they often attain to wealth, freedom, and power. A female slave, if married to a free man, becomes free. This form of slavery is only a mode of service. The slave lives with the family, and enjoys domestic consideration. There is also debt slavery, the whole family being responsible for the debt of a member.[1] Klose, however, describes the ruin wrought by slave raids. "Murder and incendiarism are the orders in this business. Great villages and districts are made deserts and are depopulated by the raids." "It is not in negro nature to subject one's self voluntarily to labor. The negro wants to be compelled to work." The fetich priest gives him a harmless drink, which is to be fatal to him if he tries to run away.[2] The Ngumba in south Kamerun hold their slaves in huts near their own houses. A mishandled slave can leave his master and demand the protection of another. A debtor who cannot pay becomes slave of his creditor until the debt is paid in value, but this does not free

---

[1] *Globus*, LXXXIII, 314.   [2] Klose, *Togo*, 383.

him. He can pay also by his wife or daughter.[1] Amongst the **Ewe**-speaking tribes a woman who is condemned to a fine may sell or pawn her children, if her husband will not give her the amount to be paid. The husbands often hold back until the women pawn the children to them, whereby they obtain complete control of the children.[2] Their slaves are criminals and debtors, or, if foreigners, are victims of war or of kidnapping. They are not regarded with contempt, are well treated, do not have as hard a lot as an English agricultural laborer, and often attain to wealth and honor. The master-owner may not kill a slave.[3] In Bornu the women slaves find favor in the eyes of their masters, and by amiability win affection. If they have children they win a firm position, "for only the most stringent circumstances could compel a Moslem, whose ideas are reasonably correct, to sell the mother of his children."[4] The Somal and Afar do not deal much in slaves. They use women and a pariah class. A Somal is never slave to a Somal, and war captives are not made slaves. Also amongst the Galla it appears that debtor slavery does not exist. Criminal slavery does, however, exist, and is used by the chiefs. It is honorable to treat slaves well. In Kaffa the slaves are lazy and pretentious, because they know that their owners do not look to them for labor, but speculate on their children, whom they will sell.[5] In general, in East Africa, the master-owner has not the power of life and death, and the slave has a right of property. "A headman (of a village) in debt sells first his slaves, then his sisters, then his mother, and lastly his free wives, after which he has nothing left."[6] Stuhlmann[7] says that slaves in Uganda are well treated, as members of the family. Brunache[8] says the same of the Congo tribes so far as they have not been contaminated by contact with whites. This may be regarded as characteristic of African slavery. The Vanika of eastern Africa are herding nomads. They cannot use slaves, and make war only to steal cattle.[9] Bushmen love liberty. They submit to no slavery. They are hunters of a low grade. They hate cattle, as the basis of a life which is different from (higher than) their own. They massacre cattle which they cannot steal or carry away.[10] Mungo Park described free negroes reduced to slavery by famine.[11] In Ashanti a man and a woman discovered in the act in the bush, or in the open air, are slaves of him who discovered them, but they are redeemable by their families.[12] Ashanti slavery is domestic and very mild. The slave marries his master's daughter and plays with the master. He also eats from the same dish.[13] Slavery

[1] *Globus*, LXXXI, 334.
[2] Ellis, *Ewe-speaking Peoples*, 221.
[3] *Ibid.*, 218, 220.
[4] Nachtigal, *Sahara und Sudan*, I, 684 ff.
[5] Paulitschke, *Ethnog. Nordost-Afr.*, I, 260; II, 139.
[6] JAI, XXII, 101.
[7] *Mit Emin Pascha*, 186.
[8] *Cen. Afr.*, 111.
[9] Ratzel, I, 449.
[10] *Ibid.*, 57.
[11] *Pinkerton's Voy.*, XVI, 885.
[12] Ellis, *Tshi-speaking Peoples*, 285.
[13] *Ibid.*, 290.

of this form is never cruel or harsh. Debt slavery is harder, for the services of the pawn count for nothing on the debt.[1] The effect of the abolition of slavery in Algeria was stupor amongst master-owners and grief amongst slaves. The former wondered how it could be wrong to care for persons who would have been eaten by their fellow-countrymen if they had succumbed to the hard struggle for existence at home. The latter saw themselves free — really free — in the desert, with no supply of food, clothing, or other supplies, and no human ties.[2] In all families of well-to-do people little negroes are found. The author saw one who told her that the lady of the house had suckled him.[3] It is reported from eastern Borneo that a white man could hire no natives for wages. They thought it degrading to work for wages, but if he would buy them they would work for him.[4] In spite of what has been said above about slavery on the west coast of Africa it is to be remembered that the master-owner has the power of life and death and that he often uses it. If he is condemned to death for a crime, he can give a slave to be executed in his place.[5] In eastern Angola, if a woman dies in childbirth, her husband has to pay her parents. If he cannot, he becomes their slave.[6] In South Africa Holub found that the fiercest slave chasers were blacks, who had slaves at home and treated them worse than Mohammedans ever did.[7] Formerly a Kaffir would work in the diamond mines for three marks a day until he got money enough to buy cattle and to buy a woman at home, a European suit, a kettle, and a rifle. Then he went home and set up an establishment. Then he would return to earn more and buy more wives, who would support him to his life's end.[8] The stronger Hottentot tribes hold classes of their own population, or mountain Damara and Bushmen, in servitude, although no law defines a "slave." Those people hold the treatment they receive to be due to their origin. Amongst all South African tribes the rich exert their power to subjugate the poor, who hang upon them in a kind of clientage, hoping to receive something. Cruelty and even murder are not punished by the judges.[9]

276. Family slavery. The savage form of slavery in Africa furnishes us one generalization which may be adopted with confidence. Whenever slaves live in a family, sharing in the family

[1] Ellis, *Tshi-speaking Peoples*, 294.
[2] Pommerol, *Une Femme chez les Sahariennes*, 194; cf. Junker, *Afrika*, III, 477.
[3] *Ibid.*, 201.
[4] Ling Roth, *Sarawak*, II, 215.
[5] Kingsley, *Travels in West Africa*, 497; *West Afr. Stud.*, 479.
[6] Serpa Pinto, *Como Eu Atravassei Afr.*, I, 116.
[7] *In's Land der Maschukalumbe*, I, 536.
[8] *Ztsft. f. Ethnol.*, VI, 472.
[9] Fritsch, *Eingeb. Süd-Afr.*, 364.

life and associating freely with the male members of it in work, religion, play, etc., the slavery is of a very light type and implies no hardship for the slave.

277. Slavery in North America among savages. Slavery is believed to have existed amongst the Indians of Virginia. "They made war, not for land or goods, but for women and children, whom they put not to death, but made them do service."[1] The young men and slaves worked in the fields of the Mississippi valley. The latter were not overworked.[2] The Algonquins made slaves of their prisoners, especially of the women and children.[3] The Illinois are represented as an intermediate party who got slaves in the South and sold them in the West.[4] The Wisconsin tribes used to make captives of Pawnees, Osages, Missouris, and Mandans. When Pawnees were such captives (slaves) they were treated with severity.[5] In the Gulf region of North America slavery was common from the earliest times. That slaves might not escape, a sinew in the leg was cut, by the Six Nations.[6] On the northwestern coast of North America slavery was far more developed than east of the Rocky Mountains. In Oregon and Washington slavery was interwoven with the social polity. Slaves were also harshly treated, as property, not within the limits of humanity. For a man to kill a half dozen of his own slaves was a sign of generous magnanimity on his part. One tribe stole captives from its weaker neighbors. Hence the slave trade is an important part of the commerce of all the tribes up to Alaska.[7] In 1841 it was reckoned that one third of the entire population from northern British Columbia to southern Alaska were "slaves of the most helpless and abject description." "The great supply was obtained by trade with the southern Indians, in which the Tsimshian acted as middlemen. They were kidnapped or captured by the southern Indians from their own adjacent tribes and sold to the Tsimshian, who traded them to the northern Thlinkit and interior Tinné tribes for furs." "Slaves did all the drudgery, fished for their owner, strengthened his force in war, were not allowed to hold property or to marry, and when old and worthless were killed. The master's power was unlimited." The slave must commit any crime at the command of the master. The slaves were set free at some ceremonies, but they were put to death at the funerals of chiefs, or as foundation sacrifices, or in reparation for insults or wrongs. The northern Indians were more warlike and would not make good slaves. The Oregon flatheads were docile and industrious.[8] The Chinooks became the wealthiest tribe in the region by acting as middlemen to sell war captives taken inland as far from home

[1] *Smithson. Rep.*, 1891, 524. Cf. Hostmann, *De Beschaving van Negers in Amer.*, I, Chap. IV. [2] *Smithson. Rep.*, 1891, 525.
[3] *Ibid.*, 520. [5] *Bur. Ethnol.*, XIV, 35. [7] *Ibid.*, 1887, Part II, 331.
[4] *Ibid.*, 532. [6] *Smithson. Rep.*, 1891, 528. [8] *U. S. Nat. Mus.*, 1888, 252 ff.

as possible.[1] Amongst the Thlinkits slaves are forbidden to wear the labret, and sex intercourse with a slave woman disgraces a free man.[2] " Amongst the early Central Americans the slave who achieved any feat of valor in war received his liberty and was adopted by the Capulli, or clan."[3] In Mexico there were slaves of three classes, — criminals, war captives, and persons who had voluntarily sold themselves or had been sold by their parents. The captor generally sacrificed a prisoner, but might hold him as a slave. Those who sold themselves did so to get a fund for gambling. There was a public slave mart at Azcapuzalco. The system is described as kind, but slaves might lose their lives through the act of the master at feasts or funerals.[4] " Actual slavery of the Indians in Mexico continued as late as the middle of the seventeenth century."[5] It is evident that slavery existed all over North and Central America, but was more developed on the Pacific coast than in the Mississippi valley. The meat eaters of the buffalo region had less opportunity to use the institution.[6]

278. Slavery in South America. In South America we also meet with at least one case of a tribe, or part of a tribe, which is in clientage to another tribe. This is a subdivision of the third rank of the Mbaya, who voluntarily entered into a relation of clientage to the Mbaya, giving them service under arms, and in house and field, without being their slaves, being protected in return by the powerful and feared tribe.[7] The Guykurus carry on frequent wars to get captives, whom they keep in stringent servitude. " There is, perhaps, no tribe of South American Indians, among whom the state of slavery is so distinctly marked as among them." Slaves and free do not intermarry, lest marriage be profaned. There is no way in which a slave may become free.[8] The Guykurus are the strongest tribe in the valley of the Paraguay. They have horses and were called by the Portuguese Cavalleiros.[9] In Brazil it was thought that the cultivation of the country was impossible unless the Indians were made slaves. The early laws and orders of the kings of Portugal seem to reveal a sincere desire to control greed and cruelty. In 1570 private slave raids were forbidden and slavery was confined to those captured in public and just war. Lisbon, however, became a great slave mart by the law that slaves passing from one colony (Africa) to another (America) must pass through Lisbon and pay a tax there. Peter Martyr is quoted that slavery was necessary for Indians who, if they had no master, would go on with their old customs and idolatry. Slavery killed

---

[1] Strong, *Wakeenah*, 126.
[2] *Bur. Ethnol.*, III, 81.
[5] Brinton, *Nagualism*, 28 note.
[6] See Hamilton, *The Panis, an Histor. Outline of Canadian Indian Slavery in the 18th cent., Proc. Canad. Instit.*, Toronto, 1897, N.S., I, 19–27.
[7] Koch, *Die Guaikuru-Stämme, Globus*, LXXXI, 44.
[8] Koch (p. 45) says that they become free and set up prosperous households.
[9] Spix and Martius, *Brasil.*, II, 73; v. Martius, *Ethnog. Brasiliens*, 71.

[3] Nadaillac, *Prehist. America*, 313.
[4] Bancroft, *Native Races*, II, 217–223.

them, however. It did not make them laborers.[1] In general, in the valley of the Yapura, in the first half of the nineteenth century, slaves were war captives who were very unkindly treated.[2] The aborigines began to sell their war captives to Europeans soon after the latter arrived. They wanted rosewood especially, and they took Indians to Africa as slaves.[8] Boggiani[4] expresses the opinion in regard to the savages of the Chaco, as the meadow region on the Paraguay river is called, that slavery amongst a people of more civilized mores, is, for them, "an incalculable benefit," and that "to hinder slavery, in such circumstances, would be a capital error." "It is necessary to force them to come out of their brutelike condition, and to awaken their intelligence, which is not wanting, if they receive practical and energetic direction." Bridges[5] says that one Fuegian is thrown into clientage to another by their mode of life. "For a young man, with no wife and few relatives, must live with some one who can protect him, and with whom he can live in comfort, whose wife or wives can catch fish for him, etc."

279. Slavery in Polynesia and Melanesia. Polynesia, Melanesia, and the East Indies, especially the last, present us pictures of a society which is old and whose mores have been worn threadbare, while their stage of civilization is still very low. Codrington[6] says: "There is no such thing as slavery, properly so called. In head-hunting expeditions prisoners are made for the sake of their heads, to be used when occasion requires, and such persons live with their captors in a condition very different from that of freedom, but they are not taken or maintained for the purposes of slaves." Ratzel[7] says: "Slavery prevailed everywhere in Melanesia, originating either in war or debt. Sometimes it was hard; sometimes not." Somerville says that "slaves are kept chiefly for their heads, which are demanded whenever any occasion necessitates them, such as the death of the owner." He is speaking of the Solomon Islands.[8] What Finsch says of the Melanesians may be extended to all the inhabitants of the South Sea islands.[9] They will not work because they do not need to. They have few wants. Pfeil wants to make the people of German Melanesia work, in order that they may contribute to the tasks of the human race. The problem presents one of the great reasons for slavery in history.

280. Slavery in the East Indies. The chief of Chittagong[10] wrote to the English governor, in 1774, that slavery in his district was due to the sale of himself by any person who was destitute, and had no friends or position. He and his wife must serve the master and his wife in any desired

---

[1] Varnhagen, *Hist. Geral do Brasil*, I, 115, 178, 181, 269, 273.
[2] v. Martius, 72.
[8] Varnhagen, *Hist. do Brasil*, I, 431; v. Martius, 131.
[4] *Caduvei*, I, 100.
[5] *Voice for South Amer.*, XIII, 201.
[6] *Melanesians*, 346.
[7] *Völkerkunde*, II, 279.
[8] JAI, XXVI, 400.
[9] *Samoafahrten*, 170.
[10] Lewin, *Wild Races of S. E. India*, 85.

way, including services which a free servant would not perform, "through fear of demeaning himself and disgracing his family." Abolition of this slavery would produce complaints by the masters, and would not please the servants who are used to it. "Until lately the universal custom prevailed in the hills of having debtor slaves." The debtor gave one of his children or a female relative to serve as a menial until the debt should be paid. The pawned persons "were treated as members of the creditor's family and never exposed to harsh usage." The effect of interference by the English was that the wives and daughters of the great men suddenly had to do all the housework. "Debtor and creditor lost confidence in each other." [1] "There is a detestable and actual slavery in these hills, which is now only carried on by independent tribes, beyond English jurisdiction. This is the captivity to the bow and spear, — men and women taken prisoners by force in war, and sold from master to master. The origin of this custom was the want of women." [2] In the Chin hills there are slaves who are war captives, or criminals, or debtors, and others who are voluntary slaves, or slaves by birth. The master had full power of life and death, but, in fact, slaves were well treated. The people made raids on the Burmese lowlands and seized captives who were held for ransom. A slave man cohabits with a slave woman and brings up his children with affection "in the same humble, but not necessarily unhappy, position as his own." [3] In Ceylon there were slave persons of all ranks. Those of royal rank were princes who were prisoners or criminals. Any one might obtain slaves by purchase, or accept voluntary slaves who looked to him for good support.[4] A Malay will buy of a chief a number of war captives whom he takes to an island. Then he goes to a Chinaman and tells him that the slaves want to work on that island, but still owe the speaker the cost of transportation. The Chinaman pays this and gives to the slaves, on credit, clothes, etc., including money with which to gamble. Wages are low and interest high. They never can pay their debts and get their freedom again. This kind of slave trade has depopulated northern Nias.[5] On Sumatra, when a debtor is called upon to pay and cannot, or when he dies and does not leave enough property to pay his debts, his children fall into semi-slavery. They can perhaps persuade some one to pay their debts and accept their services. If their master formally three times demands payment of them which they cannot give, they fall into full slavery. Slavery exists in the Malay seaport towns, but not in the rural districts, where life is too simple.[6] In times of famine and want parents sell their children into slavery for a little rice. Children, especially daughters, constitute a large part of the fortune of a house father.[7]

[1] Lewin, *Wild Races of S. E. India*, 86.
[2] *Ibid.*, 91.
[3] Carey and Tuck, *The Chin Hills*, I, 203 ff.
[4] Schmidt, *Ceylon*, 273.
[5] Raap in *Globus*, LXXXIII, 174
[6] Marsden, *Sumatra*, 252.
[7] Wilken in *Bijdragen tot T. L. en V.-kunde*, XL, 175.

At Koetei, on the Mahakkam in Borneo, all well-to-do people have debtors in pawn, whose position is somewhat better than that of slaves. The debtors seem content and submissive. Captives taken on head-hunting expeditions are held as slaves until human sacrifices are wanted.[1] The souls of all those who are put to death at the death of a Dyak rajah become his servants in the other world. In this world the killer can command, as his fetich, the soul of the killed. On the death of a great man his debtor slaves are bound to the carved village post, which indicates the glory of head-hunting, and are tortured to death.[2] "Slavery is greatly practiced" on Timorlaut. A thief, debtor, slanderer, or defamer may become the slave of the one he has wronged. The slave trade is also active between the islands.[3] The slaves of the sea Dyaks adopt their customs and become contented. Sometimes they win affection and are adopted, freed, and married to free women. Slaves and masters eat together the same food in the rural villages.[4] Among the land Dyaks slaves, by destitution and debt, "are just as happy as if perfectly free, enjoying all the liberty of their masters, who never think of ill-using them."[5] In old times one who set a house on fire was liable to become the slave of any one who was burned out.[6] Slaves on Timor do not seem to care for liberty. Their livelihood would not be so certain. There is a kind of slavery to the kingdom, not to any individual, but the slave cannot be sold by the king.[7] In the Barito valley a debtor slave has to do any kind of work. He may be punished by blows, or fines added to his debt, which may also be increased by any breaches of customs, or by the value of broken tools or vessels. A month after a child is born to him ten gulden are added, also expenses of education when the child is ready to go to work. He may be slain at a feast of the dead by his master. The owner can torment the debtor by new fines, and keep up the debt or even increase it.[8] In the Katingan valley there are no debtor slaves, because after three years a debtor who cannot pay becomes an hereditary slave, and cannot get his liberty even if he should get the means to pay his debt.[9] If he ever gets the means to pay and attempts to free himself he is compelled to pay fees, taxes, and customary dues to the "spirits of the house," etc. When he leaves his master's house he must not return to it for a year or two, nor eat anything brought from it — "to prove his independence." Then he gives a feast and becomes free.[10] "Slavery and pawnship are, in the nature of the case, the same."[11] The Dyaks put their Eden on a cloud

[1] Bock, *Reis in Borneo*, 9, 78, 94.
[2] *Ibid.*, 92.
[3] JAI, XIII, 15.
[4] Ling Roth, *Sarawak*, II, 209.
[9] *Ibid.*, II, 149.
[5] *Ibid.*, 209.
[6] *Ibid.*, 213.
[7] JAI, XIII, 417.
[8] Schwaner, *Borneo*, I, 205.
[10] Ling Roth, *Sarawak*, CLXXXV; JAI, XXII, 32.
[11] Perelaer, *Dajaks*, 153.

island. They have a myth that the daughters of the great Being let down seven times seven hundred cords of gold thread in order to lower mortals upon a mountain, but the mortals were overhasty and tried to lower themselves by bamboos and rattans. The god, angry at this, condemned them to slavery. The myth, therefore, accounts for a caste of slaves. Formerly also war captives and criminals who could not pay fines became slaves. Debts cause men to fall into pawnship. Extravagant living, and gambling, lead to this condition. If a man becomes pawn for a debt his whole household goes with him. All have to work very hard to try to satisfy a greedy master. The pawn is entitled to one tenth of the harvest, or of the gain by trade. Free men despise pawns.[1] Wilken [2] says of the Bataks that a slave, by diligence and thrift, can always buy himself. In addition to all the ill chances of gambling, extravagance, making love to another man's wife, etc., by which a man may become a debtor slave, customs exist which are traps for the unwary. Sago and rice are left in the woods, in some islands, until wanted. If a man passes the store, he is supposed to take away the spirit of the goods. If caught, he and all his family become slaves. If a man dies who was wont to fish at a certain place, the place becomes taboo to his ghost. Any one who fishes there becomes a slave to his family. Also, if a district is in mourning, any one who breaks the mourning customs is made a slave.[8] The education of the Chinese in ethical doctrines has made slavery amongst them slight and mild. It is attributed to poverty, which forces parents to sell their daughters.[4] The owners must provide female slaves with husbands, and the law forbids the separation of husband and wife, or of parents and little children.[5] It appears that slavery is forbidden by law, but is tolerated in the case where the parents are poor. Boys once enslaved continue in bondage and their children follow them, but there is no legal possession. Girls become free at marriage.[6]

281. Slavery in Asia. Slavery in Asia is of a kind which puts the slave largely at the mercy of his owner, but the mores have taught the slave owner to use his power with consideration. This is generally, not universally, true. Nivedita says [7] that "slavery in Asia, under the régime of great religious systems, has never meant what Europe and America have made of it. . . . It is a curious consequence of this humanity of custom [or rather, of the judgment in the mores as to the wisest course of conduct in a

[1] Perelaer, *Dajaks*, 155.
[2] *Volkenkunde*, 423.
[8] JAI, XVI, 142.
[4] Williams, *Middle Kingdom*, I, 413.

[5] *Ibid.*, 277.
[6] Medhurst in *China Br.*, RAS, IV, 17
[7] *Web of Indian Life*, 69.

class of cases] that the word 'slave' cannot be made to sting the Asiatic consciousness as it does the European."

282. Slavery in Japan. In Japan slavery was a common punishment, in early times, for crime. Debtors unable to pay became slaves of their creditors, and thieves were made slaves of those whom they had robbed. The attempt to introduce Christianity into Japan and the resistance to it led to the slavery of many Christian converts, if they refused after torture to recant. This was an alternative to death. Slaves were tattooed with marks to show ownership. "Slaves were bought and sold like cattle in early times, or presented as tribute by their owners, — a practice constantly referred to in the ancient records." Their sex unions were not recognized. "In the seventh century, however, private slaves were declared state property, and great numbers were then emancipated, including nearly all, — probably all, who were artisans, or followed useful callings. Gradually a large class of freedmen came into existence, but until modern times the great mass of the common people appear to have remained in a condition analogous to serfdom." [1]

283. Slavery in higher civilization. It appears quite clear that men in savagery and barbarism used each other, if they could, to serve their interests, and slavery resulted. The hardships of life caused it. The rules of war were "Woe to the vanquished!" and "To the victors the spoils." Debt was a relation which might come about between two men from incidents in the struggle for existence, or from loans of money and goods. All mischance might be converted into lack of resources (money and goods), and he who borrowed fell into dependence and servitude. All violations of custom and law led to fines; all need of civil authority made it necessary to pay fees. The debtor pledged his future working time. His relation to his creditor was personal. That he was a borrower proved that he had nothing which could form a property security. The laws of Hammurabi provide that a debtor may give his wife and children as pawn slaves, but only for three years. In the fourth year the creditor was to set them free. The pawn persons were to be well treated. A slave given

[1] Hearn, *Japan*, 256, 258, 353.

in pawn might be sold, but not if it was a female slave with children.[1] To aid or conceal a fugitive slave was a capital offense.[2]
Many Chaldean contracts have been found in which the debtor
bound himself to work for the creditor until he should pay the
debt.[3] It appears that the Babylonian slaves could form a *pecu-
lium* and carry on business with it as a capital, paying their
owners a tax upon it.[4]

284. Slavery amongst Jews. The Jewish law had a provision
like that in the law of Hammurabi, except that the limit was six
years instead of three. A debtor was not to be a slave, but to
give service until the year of jubilee.[5] In 2 Kings iv. 1 the widow
tells Elisha that her husband's creditors will come and take her
two sons to be bondmen. The creditors of some of the Jews
who returned from exile threatened to make them debtor slaves.
Nehemiah appealed to them not to do so.[6] In Matt. xviii. 25
the man who could not pay was to be sold with his wife and
children. Kidnapping was punishable by death.[7] In Job xxxi. 15
we find the ultimate philosophico-religious reason for repudiating
slavery : " Has not He who made me made him [the slave] also
in his mother's womb ? " The laws of the " Book of Covenants "
begin with laws about slaves.[8] A male slave, with his wife, is to
be freed in the seventh year, unless he prefers to remain a slave.
A man may sell his daughter into slavery, i.e. to be a concubine.
There was no difference in principle between a daughter given
to wife and one sold to be a concubine. In Deut. xv. 12 the
female slave is also set free in the seventh year, and persons so
freed are to be given gifts when they depart. The slaves were
war captives, or bought persons, or criminals.[9] The lot of
slaves was not hard. The owners had not the power of life and
death. The slave could acquire property.[10] If the slave was an
Israelite he was protected by especial restrictions on the master
in behalf of fellow-countrymen.[11]

[1] Winckler, *Gesetze Ham.*, 21.   [2] Laws 15 and 16.
[3] Kohler und Peiser, *Aus d. Babyl. Rechtsleben*, IV, 47. Cf. I, 1 and II, 6.
[4] *Ibid.*, I, 1.   [6] Nehem. v. 5.   [8] Exod. xxi.
[5] Levit. xxv. 39.   [7] Exod. xxi. 16.   [9] Exod. xxii. 2.
[10] Levit. xxv. 49; Buhl, *Soc. Verhält. d. Israel.*, 35, 106.
[11] Deut. xv. 12–18; Exod. xxi. 2 ff. ; Levit. xxv. 39–46.

285. Slavery in the classical states. Slavery came to the two great classical states from the antecedent facts of savage and barbaric life. When Aristotle came to study slavery he could not find a time when it was not. We have seen how it had become one of the leading institutions of uncivilized society, and how it had been developed in different forms and degrees. The two great classical states, more especially Rome, built their power on slavery. Both states pursued their interests with little care for the pain they might inflict on others, or the cost in the happiness of others. The Roman state began by subjugating its nearest neighbors. It used its war captives as slaves, increased its power, conquered more, and repeated the process until it used up all the known world. The Phœnicians were merchants, who kidnapped men, women, and children, if they found opportunity, and sold them into slavery far from home. The Ionians, who grew rich by commerce, bought slaves and organized states in which slaves did all the productive work. In both Greece and Rome productive work came to be despised. One is amazed to find how easily any one who went on a journey might fall into slavery, or how recklessly the democracy of one city voted to sell the people of a defeated city into slavery, yet how unhesitatingly everybody accepted and repeated the current opinions about the baseness of slave character. Homer says that a slave has only half the soul of a man.[1] The love stories in the *Scriptores Erotici* very often contain an incident of kidnapping. The story of Eumæus must have been that of many a slave.[2] It is also only rarely and very incidentally that the classical writers show any pity for slaves, although they often speak of the sadness of slavery.[3] If any man, especially a merchant, who went on a journey incurred a great risk of slavery, why was not slavery a familiar danger of every man, and therefore a matter for pity and sympathy? In the great tragedies the woes of slavery, especially the contrasts for princes and princesses, heroes and heroines, are often presented. Polyxena, in Euripides's *Hekuba*, 360, bewails her anticipated lot as a slave. A fierce master will buy her. She will have to

---

[1] *Od.*, XVII, 322.   [2] *Ibid.*, XV, 403.
[3] Buchholz, *Homer. Realien*, II, 63.

knead bread for him, to sweep and weave, leading a miserable life, given as wife to some base slave. She prefers to be sacrificed at Achilles's tomb. When the Greeks were going to kill her, she asked them to keep their hands off. She would submit. Let her die free. " It would be a shame to me, royal, to be called a slave amongst the dead." In the *Trojan Women* the screams of the Trojan women are heard, as they are distributed by lot to their new Greek masters. The play is full of the woes of slavery. At Athens slaves enjoyed great freedom of manners and conduct. They dressed like the poorest freedmen. No one dare misuse the slave of another simply because he was a slave. If the master abused a slave, the latter had an asylum in the temple and could demand to be sold. Slaves could pursue any trade which they knew, paying a stipulated sum to their owners, and could thus buy their manumission. Their happiness, however, depended on the will of another.[1] In the law they were owned as things were, and could be given, lent, sold, and bequeathed. They could not possess property, nor have wives in assured exclusive possession against masters. Their children belonged to their masters. Plato thought that nature had made some to command, others to serve.[2] He thought the soul of a slave base, incapable of good, unworthy of confidence.[3] Aristotle thought that every well-appointed house needs animate and inanimate tools. The animate tools are slaves, who have souls, but not like those of their masters. They lack will. Slaves are like members of the master, ruled by his will. Their virtue is obedience.[4] He says that there were men in his time who said that slavery was an injustice due to violence and established by law.[5]

286. Slavery at Rome. It is in ancient Rome that we find slavery most thoroughly developed. Any civilization which accomplishes any great results must do so by virtue of force which it has at its disposal. The Romans conquered and enslaved their nearest neighbors. By virtue of their increased power they extended their conquests. They repeated this process until they had consumed all the known world. The city of Rome was a center

---

[1] Beloch, *Griech. Gesch.*, I, 469.   [2] *De Repub.*, I, 309.   [3] *De Legibus*, VI, 376.
[4] *Polit.*, I, ii, 7; *Nich. Ethics*, VIII, 10.   [5] *Polit.*, I, 2.

towards which all the wealth of the world was drawn. There was no reverse current of goods. What went out from Rome was government, — peace, order, and security. The provinces probably for a time made a good bargain, although the price was high. In the earliest times slaves were used for housework, but were few in number per household. In 150 B.C. a patrician left to his son only ten. Crassus had more than five hundred. C. Caec. Claudius, in the time of Augustus, had 4116.[1] In the early days a father and his sons cultivated a holding together. Slaves were used when more help was needed. There was one slave to three sons and they lived in constant association of work and play. When conquest rendered slaves numerous and cheap, free laborers disappeared.[2] Ti. Semp. Gracchus, in 177 B.C., after the war in Sardinia, sold so many Sardinian slaves that "cheap as a Sardinian" became a proverb.[3] His son Tiberius is reported to have been led into his agrarian enterprise by noticing that the lands of Etruria were populated only by a few slaves of foreign birth.[4] Bücher [5] puts together the following statistics of persons reduced to slavery about 200 B.C.: after the capture of Tarentum (209 B.C.), 30,000 ; in 207 B.C., 5400 ; in 200 B.C., 15,000.[6] Roman slaves were not allowed to marry until a late date. They were systematically worked as hard as it was possible to make them work, and were sold or exposed to perish when too old to work. Such was the policy taught by the older Cato.[7] The number on the market was always great ; the price was low ; it was more advantageous to work them so hard that they had no time or strength to plot revolts. This is the most cynical refusal to regard slaves as human beings which can be found in history. They were liable to be tortured in their owners' cases in court. They might be given over to the gladiatorial shows and set to fight each other, or wild beasts. Seventy-eight gladiators condemned to fight to the death revolted in 74 B.C. under Spartacus,

---

[1] Drumann, *Arbeiter und Communisten*, 155.
[2] Bender, *Rom*, 150, 159.
[5] *Aufstände d. Unfreien Arbeiter*, 36.
[6] Livy, XXVII, 16; XXVIII, 9; XXXI, 21.
[3] Livy, XLI, 28, 8.
[4] Plutarch, *Ti. Gracchus*, 8.
[7] *De Agri Cultura*, 2, 7; Plutarch, *Cato*, 5; Schmidt, *Société Civile dans le Monde Romain*, 93.

who defeated five armies. Crassus was sent against him with
eight legions. Lucullus was recalled from Thrace and Pompey
from Spain. Spartacus was cut to pieces in his last battle
Crassus crucified six thousand prisoners along the road from
Capua to Rome.[1]

287. Slave revolts. The severity of the Roman system of slavery is
shown by the number of revolts and the severe proceedings in each of them.
There was such a revolt in 499 B.C. The guilty were crucified. The following year there was another.[2] In 416 there was another. The aim always
was to take the citadel and burn the city.[3] Sicily was covered with a swarm
of slaves at the beginning of the second century B.C. They were especially
Syrians, very tough and patient. They were managed under Cato's plan :
" Work or sleep ! " In 196 B.C. the slaves in Etruria revolted and were suppressed with great severity.[4] In 104 those of Sicily revolted. They were
subdued four years later and the last remnant were sent to Rome to fight
beasts. They killed themselves in the arena.[5] The later Roman system was
that the mob of the city put the world in the hands of one or another, and
he gave them bread and games as their part of the plunder. The *frumen-
taria* were the permanent and steady pay of the " world conquerors." They
made herding the best use of Italian land. " Where before industrious
peasants prospered in glad contentment, now unfree herdsmen, in wide
wastes, drove the immense herds of Roman senators and knights." [6] The
Sicilian landowners left their shepherds to steal what they needed, so that
they were educated to brigandage. The greatest sufferer was the small
freeman.[7] There is a story in Diodorus,[8] of Damophilos, an owner of
great *latifundia*, whose slaves came to him to beg clothes. He replied :
" Do the travelers, then, go naked through the country ? Are they not bound
to pay toll to him who needs clothes ? " He caused them to be flogged and
sent them back to work. The misery of the slave population seems to have
reached its acme at Enna where two roads across the island cross each
other. The town lies 3000 feet high. It was a great fortress down into
the Middle Ages.[9] At this place began a slave revolt, led by a Syrian
skilled in sorcery. The slaves took the city and engaged in rapine and
murder. A band was sent to capture Damophilos. The men killed him,
and the women his wife. Their daughter was sent in security to her
relatives.[10] It was ten years before peace was restored to the island.

1 Plutarch, *Crassus*, 9; Appianus, I, c. 120.
2 Dion. Halic., V, 51; X, 16; Livy, III, 15.
3 Livy, IV, 45.
4 *Ibid.*, XXXII, 36.
5 Neumann, *Gesch. Roms*, I, 382.
6 Bücher, *Aufstände d. Unfreien Arbeiter*, 31.

7 *Ibid.*, 45.
8 XXXIV, frag. 2, 8-11
9 Bücher, 52.
10 *Ibid.*, 56.

288. Later Roman slavery. Slaves in the civil wars. Clientage.

Down to about 200 B.C. slavery, although mechanical and cruel, was domestic. The slave was a member of the household, on intimate terms with the master or his children, shared in the religious exercises, and the graves of slaves were under religious protection.[1] In the second century B.C. Roman expansion gained momentum and produced power and wealth. The factions of the city were fighting for control of the booty. Roman character became mechanical and hard. This affected the type of slavery. By 100 B.C. Carthaginians, Greeks, and Romans had developed a system of holding slaves which was cruel and reckless, and slaves had acquired a character of hatred, venom, and desire for revenge. They were malignant, cunning, and hypocritical.[2] In the civil wars each leader sought the help of slaves. Sulla set free 10,000 of them, whom he put in the tribes of the city.[3] After the battle of Cannæ the Romans armed 8000 slaves whom they enfranchised.[4] Æmilius Paulus sold 15,000 Epirotes. Marius made 90,000 Teutons captives at Aquæ Sextiæ and 60,000 Cimbrians at Vercellæ. When Marius offered liberty to slaves only three followed him.[5] Sulla promised liberty to the slaves of the proscribed, if they would bear testimony against their masters. One did so. Sulla freed him, but then put him to death. Thus the slaves were the sport of political factions and leaders. The Roman conquests caused everywhere a certain servile temper. All conquered people were depressed into quasi-slavery. All had to pay a head tax, which was a mark of servitude. The Roman system reduced all to servitude. A late emperor called the senators "slaves in the toga." When all were rendered *nil* under the emperor the slaves gained. They were not in worse case than the rest.[6] During the conquests entire peoples became clients. If any one did not attach himself as client to a great family he was lost. Freed women, for this reason, almost always fell into vice.[7] Clientage became the

[1] Rossbach, *Röm. Ehe*, 23; Plutarch, *Coriolanus*.
[2] Wallon, *L'Esclavage*, I, 406; II, 262.
[5] Plutarch, *Marius*, 35.
[6] Grupp, *Kulturgesch. der Röm. Kaiserzeit*, I, 306.
[3] Plutarch, *Sulla*, 9
[4] Livy, XXII, 57.
[7] *Ibid.*, 271.

refuge of loafers. "Romans did not give anything gratis." All
who were outside the social system had to seek the patronage
of a great man. For his protection he took pay in money or
service. The status was a modified slavery.

289. Manumission. Natural liberty. The slave dealers developed tricks far surpassing those of horse dealers in modern
times.[1] By enfranchisement the owner got rid of the worst
worry of slavery, and tied the freedman to himself by a contract which it was for the interest of the freedman to fulfill.
The owner made a crafty gain.[2] Tacitus[3] says that, in his
time, the Roman people was almost entirely freedmen. If that
is so, we must notice that the "people," under the empire, are
a different set from what they were under the republic. When
the Romans got an educated artisan as a slave they set him to
teach a number of others. When no more outsiders were conquered and enslaved the slaves taught each other. The work
then became gross and ran down.[4] This was another of the
ways in which Rome consumed the products and culture of the
world. Very few instances, real or fictitious, of sympathy with
slaves can be cited. In the story of *Trimalchio*, Encolpius and
his friends beg off a slave who is to be whipped for losing the
garment of another slave in the bath. At a supper at which
Augustus was present a slave broke a vase. His master ordered
him cast to the *murenae* in a tank. The slave begged Augustus
to obtain for him an easier death, which Augustus tried to do.
The master refused. Augustus then gave the slave complete
grace, broke the host's other vases himself, and ordered the
tank filled up.[5] Under Nero, Pedanius having been murdered,
his slaves, four hundred in number, were all condemned to death,
according to law. The populace rose against this sentence, which
was fulfilled, but it shows that there was a popular judgment
which would respond upon occasion.[6] "Not once, in all antiquity,
does a serious thought about the abolition of slavery arise."[7]

---

[1] Dezobry, *Rome au Siècle d'Auguste*, I, 260.
[2] Wallon, *L'Esclavage*, III, Chap. X.
[3] *Annals*, XIII, 26.
[4] Moreau-Christophe, *Droit à l'Oisiveté*, 257.
[5] Seneca, *De Ira*, III, 40.
[6] Tacitus, *Annals*, XIV, 42.
[7] Bücher, *Aufstände*, 17.

It was the basis of the entire social and political order. They were in terror of the slaves and despised them, but could not conceive of a world without them. Probably we could not either, if we had not machines by means of which we make steam and electricity work for us. Individuals were manumitted on account of the gain to the master. The owner said, in the presence of a magistrate, "I will that this man be free, after the manner of the Quirites." The magistrate touched the head of the slave with his rod, the master boxed his ears, and he was a free man.[1] The law provided a writ, "resembling in some respects the writ of *habeas corpus*, to compel any one who detained an alleged freedman to present him before a judge."[2] The Roman lawyers also, if they could find a moment during gestation when the mother had been free, employed legal fiction to assume that the child had been born at that moment.[3] Florentinus defined slavery as "a custom of the law of nations by which one man, contrary to the law of nature, is subjected to the dominion of another."[4] Ulpian likewise said that, "as far as natural law is concerned, all men are equal."[5]

290. Slavery as represented in the inscriptions. "The inscriptions reveal to us a better side of slave life, which is not so prominent in our literary authorities." They show cases of strong conjugal affection between slave spouses, and of affection between master and slave.[6] In the first century the waste of the fortunes won by extortion from the provinces, and the opening of industrial opportunities by commerce, with security, gave great stimulus to free industry. The inscriptions "show the enormous and flourishing development of skilled handicrafts," with minute specialization. "The immense development of the free proletariat, in the time of the early empire, is one of the most striking social phenomena which the study of the inscriptions has brought to light." The time was then past when Roman society depended entirely on slave labor for the supply of all its wants.[7] Dill thinks that "the new class of free

---

[1] Blair, *Slavery amongst the Romans*, 164.
[2] *Ibid.*, 32.
[3] *Ibid.*, 48.
[4] *Digest*, I, 1, 4.
[5] *Ibid.*, L, 17, 32.
[6] Dill, *Nero to M. Aurel.*, 117.
[7] *Ibid.*, 251–252.

artisans and traders had often, so far as we can judge by stone
records, a sound and healthy life, sobered and dignified by
honest toil, and the pride of skill and independence." The
slave acted only under two motives, fear and sensuality. Both
made him cowardly, cringing, cunning, and false, and at the
same time fond of good eating and drinking and of sensual
indulgence. As he was subject to the orders of others, he lacked
character, and this suited his master all the better. The morality
of slaves extended in the society, and the society was guided
by the views of freedmen in its intellectual activity. The
strongest symptom of this was the prevalence of a morality of
tips, which put on the forms of liberality. It was no more
disgrace to take gifts than to give them. Senators took gifts
from the emperor, and all, including the emperor, reckoned on
legacies. Thus the lack of character spread.[2] Slavery proved
a great corrupter of both slaves and owners. It was the chief
cause of the downfall of the state which had been created by
it. It made cowards of both owners and slaves. "The woes
of negro slaves were insignificant, like a drop to an ocean, in
comparison with the sufferings of ancient slaves, for the latter
generally belonged to civilized peoples."[3]

291. Rise of the freedmen in industry. The freedmen were
the ones who were free from the old Roman contempt for productive labor. They seized the chances for industry and commerce and amassed wealth. "Not only are they crowding all the
meaner trades [in the first and second centuries of the Christian
era], from which Roman pride shrank contemptuously, but, by
industry, shrewdness, and speculative daring, they are becoming
great capitalists and landowners on a senatorial scale."[4] "The
plebeian, saturated with Roman prejudice, looking for support to
the granaries of the state or the dole of the wealthy patron,
turned with disdain from the occupations which are in our days
thought innocent, if not honorable."[5] "After all reservations,
the ascent of the freedmen remains a great and beneficent

---

[1] Dill, *Nero to M. Aurel.*, 253.   [4] Dill, *Nero to M. Aurel.*, 100.
[2] Grupp, *Kulturgesch. der Röm. Kaiserzeit*, I, 312–314.
[3] *Ibid.*, 301.   [5] *Ibid.*, 102.

revolution. The very reasons which made Juvenal hate it most
are its best justification to a modern mind. It gave hope of a
future to the slave. By creating a free industrial class it helped
to break down the cramped social ideal of the slave owner and
the soldier. It planted in every municipality a vigorous mer-
cantile class, who were often excellent and generous citizens.
Above all, it asserted the dignity of man." [1] But for the freedmen the society seems to have contained but two classes, — " a
small class of immensely wealthy people, and an almost starving
proletariat." [2]

292. The freedmen in the state. Every despot needs ministers. The history of all despotisms shows that they find those
best suited to their purpose in persons of humble rank. They
can use such ministers against nobles or other great men, and
can command their complete loyalty. Julius Cæsar made some
of his freedmen officers of the mint. It was simply an extension of the usage of aristocratic households. The emperor employed freedmen to write letters and administer the finances of
the empire as he would have used them to manage his private
estate. " Under Caligula, Claudius, and Nero, the imperial
freedmen attained their greatest ascendancy. Callistus, Nar-
cissus, and Pallas rose to the rank of great ministers, and, in
the reign of Claudius, were practically masters of the world.
They accumulated enormous wealth by abusing their power,
and making a traffic in civic rights, in places, or pardons." [3]
The freedmen favorites carried the evil effects of slavery on
character to another stage and were agents of the corruption of
the new form of the state by the inheritance of slavery. " The
women of the freedmen class, for generations, wielded, in their
own way, a power which sometimes rivaled that of the men."
They often had great charms of person and mind. " Their
morals were the result of an uncertain social position, combined
with personal attractions, and education." Some of them did
great mischief. Panthea, mistress of Lucius Verus, is celebrated
as one of the most beautiful women who ever lived. She had a
lovely voice, was fond of music and poetry, and had a very

[1] Dill, *Nero to M. Aurel.*, 105.   [2] *Ibid.*, 94.   [3] *Ibid.*, 106.

superior mind. She "never lost her natural modesty and simple sweetness."[1] In the first century some freedmen married daughters of senatorial houses. They were very able men. No others could have performed the duties of the three great secretaryships, — appeals, petitions, and correspondence. The fortunes of these men were often adventurous in the extreme, like those of the ministers of sultans in the Arabian Nights. A slave, advanced to a higher position in a household, then to a position of confidence, where he proved his ability and devotion, got a great office and became master of the world. Men of this kind have always been refused social status.[2] In the second century the system was changed, and knights became the great officers of administration.

293. Philosophers opponents of slavery. The great neostoics of the first century first denounced slavery and uttered the great humanitarian doctrines. The real question in regard to Roman slavery was this : Is a slave not a man ? If he was one, he was either the victim of misfortune or the inheritor of the misfortune of an ancestor. If he did not thereby lose human status as a member of the race he deserved pity and help. The humanitarian philosophy, therefore, had the simplest task and the most direct application. Dio Chrysostom declared the evil effects of slavery on the masters, sensuality, languor, and dependence. He pointed out the wide difference between personal status and character, — the possible nobility of a slave and the possible servility of a freeman.[3] Seneca especially taught the abstract philosophy of liberalism, kindness, and humanity. He represented a movement in public opinion. Pliny cultivated all the graces of the debonair gentleman. Dill compares him to a " kindly English squire." The inscriptions show that " his household was by no means a rare exception."[4] Slaves had such perquisites and chances that " the slave could easily purchase his own freedom." " The trusted slave was often actually a partner, with a share of the profits of an estate, or he had a commission on the returns."[5] Plutarch's whole philosophy of life is gentle

---

[1] Dill, *Nero to M. Aurel.*, 114–116. [3] *Orat.*, X, 13; XV, 5. [5] *Ibid.*, 117.
[2] *Ibid.*, 112. [4] Dill, *Nero to M. Aurel.*, 182.

and kindly. It is unemotional and nonstimulating. The neostoics had the character of an esoteric sect. We never are sure
that their writings are any more than rhetorical exercises, or
that they act or expect others to act by their precepts. Slavery
was such a fact in the social order that no one could conceive
of the abolition of it, or propose abolition as a thing within the
scope of statesmanship.

294. The industrial colleges. The Romans had a genius for
association and organization. Under the republic artisans began
to unite in colleges. In the last century of the republic the
political leaders took alarm at these unions and forbade them.
Cæsar and Augustus abolished the right of association. In the
second century a certain number of societies existed, in spite of
prohibitions, — miners, salt workers, bakers, and boatmen. Until
Justinian all such unions were carefully watched as dangerous
to public peace and order. In the civil law they were authorized,
and made like natural persons.[1] The fashion of them became
very popular. " The colleges in which the artisans and traders
of the Antonine age grouped themselves are almost innumerable,
even in the records which time has spared. They represent
almost every conceivable branch of industry, or special skill, or
social service." [2] " Men formed themselves into these groups for
the most trivial or whimsical reasons, or for no reason at all,
except that they lived in the same quarter and often met. From
the view which the inscriptions give us of the interior of some
of these clubs, it is clear that their main purpose was social
pleasure." [3] "And yet, many an inscription leaves the impression that these little societies of the old pagan world are
nurseries, in an imperfect way, of gentle charities and brotherli-
ness." [4] They had many honorary members from among the
richer classes. Wandering merchants and military veterans, as
well as young men fond of sport, formed clubs on the same type.
Alexander Severus organized all the industrial colleges and
assigned them *defensores*. In the colleges all were equal, so
that they were educational in effect. " But these instances

[1] *Digest*, III, tit. 4, 1.   [3] *Ibid.*, 254, 266, 268.
[2] Dill, 265.   [4] *Ibid.*, 271.

cannot make us forget the cruel contempt and barbarity of which the slave was still the victim, and which was to be his lot for many generations yet to run. Therefore the improvement in the condition of the slave, or of his poor plebeian brother, by the theoretical equality in the colleges may be easily exaggerated." [1] The statesmen had feared that the artisans might use their organization to interfere in politics. What happened in the fourth century was that the state used the organizations to reduce the artisans to servitude, and to subject them to heavy social obligations by law.

295. Laws changed in favor of slaves. When the conquests ceased and the supply of new slaves was reduced those slaves who were born in the households or on the estates came into gentler relations to their owners. Slaves rose in value and were worth more care. The old plan of Cato became uneconomical. All sentiments were softened in the first century as war became less constant, less important, and more remote. The empire was an assumption by the state of functions and powers which had been family powers and functions, and part of the *patria potestas.* Women, children, and slaves shared in emancipation until the state made laws to execute its jurisdiction over them. Hadrian took from masters the power of life and death over slaves. Antoninus Pius confirmed this, and provided that he who killed his own slave should suffer the same penalty as he who killed the slave of another.[2] This brought the life of every slave into the protection of the state. Under Nero a judge was appointed to hear the complaints of slaves and to punish owners who misused them. Domitian forbade castration. Hadrian forbade the sale of slaves to be gladiators. The right to sell female slaves into brothels was also abolished.[3]

296. Christianity and slavery. In 1853 C. Schmidt published an essay on the " Civil Society of the Roman World and its Transformation by Christianity," in which he thought it right to attribute all the softening of the mores in the first three Christian centuries to Christianity. Lecky, on the other hand, says : " Slavery was distinctly and formally recognized by Christianity,

[1] Dill, 282.   [2] *Instit.*, I, 8 ; *Digest*, I, 6, 2.   [3] Wallon, *L'Esclavage*, III, 51 ff.

and no religion ever labored more to encourage a habit of docility and passive obedience."[1] Schmidt is obliged to take the ground that Christianity received and accepted slavery as a current institution, in which property rights existed, and that it suffered these to stand. If that is true, then Christianity could not exert much influence on civil society. What Christianity did was to counteract to a great extent the sentiment of contempt for slaves and for work. It did this ritually, because in the church, and especially in the Lord's Supper, all participated alike and equally in the rites. The doctrine that Christ died for all alike combined with the philosophical and humanitarian doctrine that men are of the same constitution and physique to produce a state of mind hostile to slavery. In the fourth century the church began to own great possessions, including slaves, and it accepted the standpoint of the property owner.[2] In the Saturnalia of Macrobius (fl. 400 A.D.) Prætextatus reaffirms the old neostoic doctrine about slavery of Seneca and Dio Chrysostom. Dill[3] takes the doctrine to be the expression of the convictions of the best and most thoughtful men of that time. It is not to be found in Jerome, Augustine, or Chrysostom. Nevertheless the church favored manumission and took charge of the ceremony. It especially favored it when the manumitted would become priests or monks. The church came nearest to the realization of its own doctrines when it refused to consider slave birth a barrier to priesthood. In all the penitential discipline of the church also bond and free were on an equality. The intermarriage of slave and free was still forbidden. Constantine ordered that if a free woman had intercourse with her slave she should be executed and he should be burned alive.[4] The pagan law only ordered that she should be reduced to slavery. The manumissions under Constantine were believed, in the sixteenth century, to have caused almshouses and hospitals to

[1] *Eur. Morals*, II, 65.

[2] Muratori (*Dissert. XV*) thinks that all ecclesiastics were bound not to allow the income of their places to be reduced during their tenancy. This duty set their attitude to slavery.

[3] *Roman Society in the Last Century of Rome*, 161.

[4] *Cod. Theod.*, IX, 9.

be built, on account of the great numbers of helpless persons set adrift.[1] Basil the Macedonian († 886) first enacted that slaves might have an ecclesiastical marriage, but the prejudice of centuries made this enactment vain.[2] The abolition of cruci- fixion had special value to the slave class. There was no longer a special and most infamous mode of execution for them. A law of Constantine forbade the separation of members of a family of slaves.[3] These are the most important changes in the law of slavery until the time of the codex of Justinian. Lecky thinks that Justinian advanced the law beyond what his predecessors had done more in regard to slavery than on any other point. His changes touched three points: (1) He abolished all the restrictions on enfranchisement which remained from the old pagan laws, and encouraged it. (2) He abolished the freedmen as an intermediate class, so that there remained only slave and free, and a senator could marry a freed woman, i.e. a slave whom he had already freed. (3) A slave might marry a free woman, if his master consented, and her children, born in slavery, became free if the father was enfranchised. The punish- ment for the rape of a slave woman was made death, the same as for the rape of a free woman.[4] Isidore of Seville († 636) said : " A just God alloted life to men, making some slaves and some lords, that the liberty of ill-doing on the part of slaves might be restrained by the authority of rulers." Still he says that all men are equal before God, and that Christ's redemption has wiped away original sin, which was the cause of slavery.[5]

297. The colonate. At the end of the empire population was declining, land was going out of use and returning to wilderness, the petty grandees in towns were crushed by taxes into poverty, artisans were running away and becoming brigands because the state was immobilizing them, and peasants were changed into colons. The imperial system went on until the man, the emperor, was above all laws, the senate were slaves, and the provinces were the booty of the emperor. The whole system then became

[1] Bodin, *Republic*, Book I, Chap. V.   [3] *Cod. Theod.*, II, 25.
[2] Lecky, *Eur. Morals*, II, 64.   [4] Lecky, *Eur. Morals*, II, 65.
[5] *Sentent.*, lib. III, cap. 47.

immobilized. What the colons were and how they came into existence has been much disputed. They were immobilized peasants. We find them an object of legislation in the *codex Theodosianus* in the fourth century. They were personally free (they could marry, own property, could not be sold), but they were bound to the soil by birth and passed with it. They cultivated the land of a lord, and paid part of the crops or money.[1] Marquardt thinks that they arose from barbarians quartered in the Roman empire.[2] Heisterbergk[3] thinks that there are three possible sources, between which he does not decide, — impoverished freemen, emancipated slaves, barbarian prisoners. Wallon[4] ascribes the colonate to the administration. As society degenerated it became harder and harder to get the revenue, and the state adopted administrative measures to get the property of any one who had any. This system impoverished everybody. To carry it out it was necessary to immobilize everybody, to force each one to accept the conditions of his birth as a status from which he could not escape. What made the colonate, then, was misery.[5] Emancipated slaves and impoverished peasants met in the class of colons, in state servitude. The proprietors were only farmers for the state. The tribute was the due of the state. Laborers were enrolled in the census and held for the state. The interest of the *fiscus* held the colon to the soil.[6] The words " colon " and " slave " are used interchangeably in the *codex Justinianus.*

298. Depopulation. The depopulation of Italy under the empire is amply proved. Vespasian moved population from Umbria and the Sabine territory to the plain of Rome.[7] Marcus Aurelius established the Marcomanni in Italy.[8] Pertinax offered land in Italy and the provinces to any one who would cultivate it.[9] Auelian tried to get land occupied.[10] He sent barbarians to settle in Tuscany.[11] As time went on more and more land

---

[1] Marquardt, *Röm. Staatsverwaltung*, II, 233.
[2] *Ibid.*, 234.
[3] *Entstehung des Colonats*, 11.
[4] *L'Esclavage*, III, 282.
[5] *Ibid.*, 313.
[6] *Ibid.*, 308.
[7] Suetonius, *Vespas.*, 1.
[8] Jul. Capitol., *M. Aurel.*, 22.
[9] Herodianus, II, 4, sec. 12.
[10] *Cod. Just.*, XI, LVIII.
[11] Vopisc., *Aurelian*, 48.

was abandoned and greater efforts were made to secure settlers. Valentinian settled German prisoners in the valley of the Po.[1] In the time of Honorius, in Campania five hundred thousand arpents were discharged from the *fiscus* as deserted and waste. In the third century, if the colon ran away from land which no one would take he was pursued by all the agencies of the law and brought back like a criminal.[2] The colons ran away because the *curiales*, their masters, put on them the taxes which the state levied first on the *curiales*.[3] What was wanted was men. The Roman imperial system had made men scarce by making life hard. Pliny said that the *latifundia* destroyed Italy. The saying has been often quoted in modern times as if it had some unquestionable authority. It is a case of the common error of confusing cause and consequence. The *latifundia* were a consequence and a symptom. Heisterbergk[4] thinks that the *latifundia* were not produced by economic causes, but by vanity and ostentation. The owners did not look to the land for revenue. He asks[5] how a strictly scientific system of grand culture with plenty of labor could ruin any country. Rodbertus[6] thinks that the *latifundia* went from a grand system to a petty system between the times of the elder and the younger Pliny by the operation of the law of rent. He thinks that there must have been garden culture in Italy at the beginning of the empire, and that the colonate arose from big estates with petty industry and from the law of mortgage. He thinks, further, that the colons, until the fourth century, were slaves, and that their status was softened by the legislation of the fourth century. Heisterbergk thinks that the colonate began in the corn provinces, and that it was, at the beginning of the fourth century, on the point of passing away, but the legislation of the fourth century perpetuated it. He thinks that it was injured, as an institution, by the great increase of taxation after Diocletian. Then legislation was necessary to keep the colons on the land.[7]

[1] Am. Marcel., XXVIII, 5.
[2] Moreau-Christophe, *Le Droit à l'Oisiveté*, 274.
[3] Rodbertus, *Hildeb. Ztsft.*, II, 241.
[4] *Colonat*, 67.
[5] *Ibid.*, 63.
[6] *Hildeb. Ztsft.*, 206.
[7] *Colonat*, 143.

299. Summary on Roman slavery. Chrysostom describes the misbehavior of all classes, about 400 A.D.[1] The colons were overburdened. When they could not pay they were tortured. A colon was flogged, chained, and thrown into prison, where he was forgotten. His wife and child were left in misery to support themselves, and get something for him if they could. The Roman system, after consuming all the rest of the world, began to consume itself. The Roman empire at last had only substituted one kind of slaves for another. Artisans and peasants were now slaves of the state. Slavery was at first a means. By it the subjugated countries were organized into a great state. Then it developed its corruption. It was made to furnish gladiators and harlots. Nowhere else do we see how slavery makes cowards of both slaves and owners as we see it at Rome in the days of glory. Slavery rose to control of the mores. The free men who discussed contemporary civilization groaned over the effects of slavery on the family and on private interests, but they did not see any chance of otherwise getting the work done. Then all the other social institutions and arrangements had to conform to slavery. It controlled the mores, prescribed the ethics, and made the character. In the last century of the Western empire the protest against it ceased. It seemed to be accepted as inevitable, and one of the unavoidable ills of life. It ruled society. Scarcely a man represented the old civilization who can command our respect. The social and civic virtues were dead.

300. In all the ancient world we meet with distinct repudiation of slavery only amongst the Therapeuts, a communistic association amongst the Jews in the last century before Christ. They were ascetics, each of whom lived in a cell. We first hear of them through Philo Judæus (*The Contemplative Life*) about the time of the birth of Christ. They had no slaves. They regarded slavery as absolutely contrary to nature. Nature produced all in a state of freedom, but the greed of some had vested some with power over others.[2] The Therapeuts, who included women, did their own work. They carried on no

---

[1] *Hom. on Matthew*, 62; Migne, *Patrol. Graec.*, LVIII, 591.
[2] Cook, *Fathers of Jesus*, II, 25.

productive industry the products of which they could give in exchange. Their system could not endure without an endowment.[1] Bousset[2] thinks that, "if they ever existed, they can never have had more than a limited and ephemeral significance." Their central home was on a hill near lake Marea. Their place of meeting, on the seventh day, was divided by a wall, three or four cubits high, into two compartments, one for the women, the other for the men. They reduced the consumption of food and drink as much as possible. Sometimes they abstained for three or four days. They had a very simple feast on the forty-ninth day, the men and women sitting separately on coarse mattresses.[3]

301. Slavery amongst the Germanic nations. According to the most primary view, the one which we might call natural, a war captive's due fate was to be killed in sacrifice to the god of the victor. During some interval of time before his public execution he was set at work, and the convenience of his services was learned. He was kept alive in order to be employed in the labors which were the most irksome and disagreeable. The joke of letting him live on to perform these tasks was not lost. When, now, we turn our attention to the Germanic invaders of the Roman empire, we are carried back to primitive barbarism. In the heroic age of Scandinavia we find that thralls are sacrificed at Upsala at solemn feasts in honor of the heathen gods. They were thrown from the cliffs, or into a hole in the ground, or tortured and hung up in the clear air, or the spine was broken.[4] In the prehistoric period of German history the unfree were tenderly handled. " A well-born youth, who grew up amongst the same herds and on the same land with an unfree youth, eating and drinking together, and sharing joy and sorrow, could not handle shamefully the comrades of the unfree man." [5] In the Scandinavian *Rigsmal*, Rig, the hero, begets a representative of each of three ranks, — noble, yeoman, laborer, — the first with the mother, the second with the grandmother, and the third with the great-grandmother, as if they had come from later and later

[1] Achelis, *Virg. Subintrod.*, 29–31.   [3] Cook, *Fathers of Jesus*, II, 18–28.
[2] *Relig. des Judent.*, 447.   [4] Estrup, *Skrifter*, I, 261.
[5] Weinhold, *D. F.*, I, 104.

strata of population.[1] Rig slept between man and wife when he
begot the yeoman and thrall, but not when he begot the noble.
The thrall has no marriage ceremony. The food, dwelling, dress,
furniture, occupations, and manners of the three classes are
carefully distinguished, also the physique, as if they were racially
different, and the names of the children are in each case
characteristic epithets. The great-grandfather wears the most
ancient dress; his wife provides an ash-baked loaf, flat, heavy,
mixed with bran. She bore Thrall, who was swarthy, had callous
hands, bent knuckles, thick fingers, an ugly face, a broad back,
long heels. Toddle-shankie also came sunburnt, having scarred
feet, a broken nose, called Theow. Their children were named:
the boys, — Sooty, Cowherd, Clumsy, Clod, Bastard, Mud,
Log, Thickard, Laggard, Grey Coat, Lout, and Stumpy; the
girls, — Loggie, Cloggie, Lumpy [= Leggie], Snub-nosie, Cin-
ders, Bond-maid, Woody [=Peggy], Tatter-coatie, Crane-shankie.
The story seems to present the three classes or ranks as
founded in natural facts. Slaves were such by birth, by sale
of themselves to get maintenance (esteemed the worst of all,
debtors, war captives, perhaps victims of shipwreck), and free
women who committed fornication with slave men.[2] If a debtor
would not pay he was brought into court, and the creditor might
cut off a piece [of his body] above or below.[3] A free man would
not allow his slave to be buried by his side, even if the slave
had lost his life in loyalty to his master. Slaves, criminals, and
outlaws were buried dishonorably in a place by themselves on
one side. They were harnessed to plows when there were no
oxen at hand. When Eisten, king of Opland, wanted to annihilate the Ernds, he gave them their choice of his slave or his dog
for a king. They chose the dog.[4] The sister of King Canute
bought in England most beautiful slave men and women, who
were sent to Denmark, and were sold for use chiefly in vice.[5]
Here we see again the great contempt for slaves. It was a
proverb in Scandinavia: "Put no trust in the friendship of a
thrall,"[6] although in the sagas there are many cases in which

[1] *Corpus Poet. Bor.*, I, 235.
[2] Rothe, *Nordens Staatsvrfssg.*, I, 35.
[3] *Ibid.*, 17.
[4] *Ibid.*, 18.
[5] *Ibid.*, II, 266.
[6] Estrup, *Skrifter*, I, 263.

the heroes profited by trusting them. Yet the sagas are also
full of stories of persons who fell into slavery, e.g. Astrid,
widow of King Trygve Olafson, who was found by a merchant
in the slave market of Esthonia and redeemed.[1] A thrall was
despised because he feared death, and when it impended over
him hid, whimpered, begged, wept, lamented to leave his
swine and good fare, and offered to do the meanest work if he
might live. A hero bore torture bravely and met death laughing.[2] When hero children and thrall children were changed at
birth, the fraud was discovered by the cowardice of the latter
and the courage of the former, when grown.[3] In the heroic age
a conqueror could set a princess to work at the *qvern*. In
Valhalla the hero set thralls to work for his conquered victim,
to give him footbath, light fire, bind dogs, groom horses, and
feed swine Thrall women became concubines. They worked
at the *qvern*, and wove. Love could raise them to pets.
Thralls were obtained in the lands raided, but even after they
became Christians the Scandinavians raided and enslaved each
other. The Roman law system, as the church employed it, and
especially tithes, were means of reducing the masses to servitude.[4] Beggars could be arrested and taken before the *Thing*,
where, if they were not ransomed by their relatives, they were
at the mercy of the captor.[5] Magnus Erikson ascended the
throne of Sweden, Norway, and Skona in 1333. Two years
later he decreed that no one born of Christian parents should
thereafter be, or be called, a thrall.[6]

302. The sale of children. In the Germanic states it remained
lawful until far down in the Middle Ages for a man to sell his
wife or child into servitude, or into adoption in another family
in time of famine or distress. The right fell into disuse.[7]

303. Slavery and the state. The reason why there was little
slavery in the Middle Ages is that slavery needs a great state
to return fugitives or hold slaves to work. The feudal lord was

---

[1] *Heimskringla*, II, 77.   [2] *Corpus Poet. Bor.*, I, 340.   [3] *Ibid.*, 361.
[4] Wachsmuth, *Bauernkriege*, in Raumer, *Taschenbuch*, V.
[5] Gjessing, *Ann. f. Nordiske Oldkyndighed*, 1862, 85 ff.
[6] Geijer, *Svenska Folkets Hist.*, I, 206.
[7] Grimm, *Deutsche Rechtsalterthümer*, 461.

at odds with such a state as existed, and could not get its aid to restore his slaves. Hence the extension of the state made the slaves worse off, e.g. in Russia and parts of Germany.[1] Amongst the Franks "slavery took many forms." The vicissitudes of life produced the strongest contrasts of fortune. Freeman[2] mentions a case in which a boy king reigned, but his mother, formerly a slave woman, reigned as queen in rank and authority, and the power was really exercised by the man who was once her owner. "In the system of a Frankish kingdom a slave-born queen could play, with more of legal sanction, the part often played in Mohammedan courts by the mother of the sultan, son of a slave." The Franks had a peculiar ceremony of manumission. The lord struck a coin from the hand of his slave to the ground, and the slave became free.[3] Philippe le Bel, enfranchising the serfs of Valois, in the interest of the *Fiscus*, uttered a generality which Louis le Hutin reiterated: "Seeing that every human creature who is formed in the image of our Lord, ought, generally speaking, to be free by natural right, — no one ought to be a serf in France." In the eighth and ninth centuries serfs were sold to Jews who sold them to Mohammedans. Montpelier carried on a slave trade with the Saracens. The clergy joined in this trade in the twelfth century, and it is said to have lasted until the fifteenth century.[4] The Romance of Hervis (of about the beginning of the thirteenth century) turns on the story of a youth who ransomed a girl who had been kidnapped by some soldiers. They proposed to take her to Paris and sell her at the fair there. The Parliament of Bordeaux, in 1571, granted liberty to Ethiopians and other slaves, "since France cannot admit any servitude." Still slavery existed in the southern provinces, including persons of every color and nationality.[5] Biot[6] thinks that the slave trade in the Middle Ages was carried on chiefly by pirates, so that slave markets existed on the coast

[1] Vinogradoff, *Vileinage*, 152.
[2] *West. Europe in the Eighth Century*, 11.
[3] Grimm, *Rechtsalt.*, 178.
[4] Bourquelot, *Foires de Champagne, Acad. d. Belles Lettres et Inscrip.*, 1865, 307.
[5] D'Avenel, *Hist. Econ.*, I, 186.
[6] *Abol. de l'Esclav.*, 264.

only, not inland. The Council of Armagh, in 1171, forbade the Irish to hold English slaves and mentions the sale of their children by the English.[1] Thomas Aquinas is led by Aristotle to approve of slavery. Like Aristotle he holds it to be in the order of nature.[2] A society was founded in Spain at the beginning of the thirteenth century to redeem Christian captives from Moorish slavery. The pious made gifts to this society to be used in its work. Christians sold kidnapped persons to the Moors that they might be redeemed again. In 1322 the Council of Valladolid imposed excommunication on the sale of men. In the fourteenth century the Venetians and Genoese were selling young persons from all countries in Egypt.[3] Pope Nicholas V, in 1454, gave Portugal the right to subjugate western Africa, supposed to be lands which belonged to the Saracens, and " to reduce the persons of those lands to perpetual servitude," expressing the hope that the negroes would be thoroughly converted. Margry puts in the year 1444 the first sale of negroes as slaves, under the eyes of Don Enrique of Portugal.[4] As early as 1500 Columbus suggested to the king of Spain to use negroes to work the mines of Hispaniola. The king decreed that only such negroes should be taken to Hispaniola as had been Christianized in Spain. In 1508 the Spaniards took negroes to the mines to work with Indian slaves. The slave trade was authorized by Charles V in 1517.[5] Christian slaves existed in Spain until the seventeenth, perhaps until the eighteenth, century. If blacks and Moors are included, slavery has existed there until the most recent times.[6]

304. Slavery in Europe. Italy in the Middle Ages. Slavery existed in Italy in the thirteenth century, by war, piracy, and religious hatred. The preaching friars, by preaching against all property, helped to break it down, and it began to decline.[7] The religious hatred is illustrated by the act of Clement V († 1314). When he excommunicated the Venetians for seizing Ferrara he ordered that wherever they might be caught they

---

[1] Wilkins, *Conc. Mag. Brit.*, I, 471.   [4] *Navig. Françaises*, 19.
[2] *Opusc.*, XX, ii, 10.   [5] Mason in *Amer. Anthrop.*, IX, 197.
[3] Heyd, *Levanthandel*, II, 442.   [6] Biot. *Abol. de l'Esclav.*, 422.   [7] *Ibid.*, 431.

should be treated as slaves.[1] Not until 1288 was a law passed
at Florence forbidding the sale of serfs away from the land.
Such a law was passed at Bologna in 1256, and renewed in 1283.
Such laws seem to have been democratic measures to lessen the
power of nobles in the rural districts.[2] A man who made a slave
woman a mother must pay damages to her owner. In a contract of 1392 a man in such a case confesses a debt, as for
money borrowed. By a statute of Lucca, in 1539, a man so
offending must buy the woman at twice her cost and pay to the
state a fine of one hundred lire. By a statute of Florence,
1415, it was affirmed that the quality of Christian would not
exempt from slavery.[3] In a contract of sale of a woman at
Venice, 1450, it is specified that the seller sells *purum et
merum dominium*.[4] The Italian cities continued to protect the
slave trade until the middle of the sixteenth century.[5] The
Venetians and Genoese carried on the trade actively, except in
times of great public or general calamity, when they suspended
it to appease the wrath of God.[6] The intimate connection of
the great commercial republics with the Orient, and hatred for
Greek heretics, are charged with causing them to keep up the
trade.[7] Conjugal life at Venice was undermined by the desire
for variety in pleasure, and by the easy opportunity to get beautiful slaves in the markets of the Orient. From the most
ancient times laws, as fierce as inefficacious, punished with
death merchants who traded in men, but the trade did not
cease until the end of the sixteenth century. The national
archives contain contracts from the twelfth century to the sixteenth about slaves. Priests were the notaries in these contracts,
in spite of the state, the popes, and the councils. Slaves were
brought from every country in the Levant, including Circassian
and Georgian girls of twelve and fourteen. Slaves passed
entirely under the will of the buyer.[8] Biot[9] finds evidence of
slavery in Italy until the middle of the seventeenth century.

[1] Libri, *Sciences Mathématiques en Italie*, II, 509.
[2] *Ibid.*, 510.   [4] *Ibid.*, 513.   [6] Cibrario, *Econ. Polit.*, III, 274.
[3] *Ibid.*, 515.   [5] *Ibid.*, 511.   [7] Biot, *Abol. de l'Esclav.*, 426.
[8] Molmenti, *Venezia nella Vita Privata*, I, 280.   [9] *Abol. de l'Esclav.*, 441.

305. Slavery in France. When the Armagnacs captured two men, in 1445, who could not pay ransom, they threatened to sell them to the Spanish Jews.[1] Bodin[2] admits that it is better to hold captives as slaves than to kill them, but his argument is all against slavery. He mentions cases in which it had been decided, apparently on the ground of the dictum of Philippe le Bel, that slaves who set foot in France became free.

306. Slavery in Islam. Islam is more favorable to the emancipation of slaves than Christianity is, as the Visigothic bishops understood it. Mohammed set free his own slaves and ordered that all slaves should have the right to redeem themselves. He taught that it is a good work to emancipate a slave, which will offset many sins.[3] In his last sermon he said : " Know that every Moslem is the brother of every other Moslem. Ye are all a fraternity ; all equal."[4] The law recognizes only two ways in which a human being may become a slave, — (1) by birth, (2) by war. A debtor cannot become a slave, and parents in distress cannot sell their children. Slaves cannot be so sold that a mother and her child under seven years of age are separated. Any slave woman may be made a concubine, but may not be married. Children of slave women are legitimate and free. A woman who has borne her master a child becomes free at the master's death, and may not be sold or pawned by him while he lives. Slaves are in many respects inferior to free persons as to rights and powers. They have no right of property against their owners. They are under milder criminal law than their owners. All this is to be understood of slaves who are Moslems.[5] The Koran often inculcates kindness to slaves.[6] Slaves are goods given to the free by the grace of God. Mohammedans would consider the abolition of slavery a triumph of Christianity over Islam.[7] An unbelieving slave has no guarantees at all against the will of his owner. In the eighth century the serfs in the Asturias rose *en masse* against their Mohammedan lords, and we are told

---

[1] Raumer, *Hist. Taschenbuch*, 2 ser., III, 111.

[2] *Repub.*, Book I, Chap. V.

[3] Dozy, *Musulm. d'Espagne*, II, 43 ; *Koran*, IV, 94 ; V, 91 ; LVIII, 4.

[4] Hauri, *Islam*, 84. [6] Suras II, IV, XXIV.

[5] Juynboll, *Moham. Wet.*, 231. [7] Hauri, *Islam*, 155.

that under the wealth and glory of Grenada the peasants hated the lords with great intensity.[1] In the great days of Abdurrahman III slaves were very numerous. They possessed land and slaves and the sultan charged them with "important military and civil functions, and pursued the policy of all despots in making them his ministers and favorites, in order to humiliate the aristocrats."[2] They were also armed. The late Romans put colons in the army. The Visigoths inherited the usage, although the lords would not give them up. At last the levy arose to one half of the serfs and they became a majority of the army.[3] Schweinfurth[4] says that "wherever Islamism has sway in Africa it appears never to be the fashion for any one to allow himself to be carried." "A strict Mohammedan reckons it an actual sin to employ a man as a vehicle, and such a sentiment is very remarkable in a people who set no limits to their spirit of oppression. It is a known fact that a Mohammedan, though he cannot refuse to recognize a negro, denying the faith, as being *a man*, has not the faintest idea of his being entitled to any rights of humanity." The jurists early set up the doctrine that the life of a Mohammedan slave was worth as much as that of a Mohammedan freeman, but this doctrine rarely was fulfilled in practice, never inside of the harem. The jurists pronounced against the right of life and death on the part of the slave owner, but it was exercised.[5] It is not law, but custom, to emancipate an adult slave after from seven to nine years' service. In most Moslem families slaves are well treated, as members of the household. Their children are educated as those of their masters are.[6] Pischon says that Moslems cannot live without slavery. No free woman will do the menial housework, and no woman may be seen unveiled by a free man.[7] This is a repetition of the opinion of the ancients that slavery was indispensable (sec. 285). If all the women were free, some of them would do the housework. A modern Turk is a tyrant inside his own dwelling. For his wife he has a proverb that she should have "neither mouth nor

---

[1] Dozy, II, 25.   [2] *Ibid.*, III, 61.   [3] *Ibid.*, II, 29.   [4] *Heart of Africa*, I, 374.
[5] Von Kremer, *Kulturgesch. d. Orients*, II, 128.
[6] Pischon, *Einfluss d. Islam*, 25–29.   [7] *Ibid.*, 31.

tongue." The girls are not educated to be such wives. They find some support at home against their husbands. Hence nearly all Turks entertain feelings of dislike and ill will towards their parents-in-law, and prefer slave concubines, whose relatives they welcome, if the wife is pretty, or wins their affection. Great ladies buy promising girls of seven or eight and train them, and sell them again.[1]

307. Review of slavery in Islam. The injunctions of Mohammedanism sound just and humane; the practice of Mohammedans is cruel and heartless. The slave is not a thing or ware; he is a man entitled to treatment worthy of a man. A man may take his slave as a concubine, but he must not sell her to vice. A free man may marry a slave, if she is not his own. A free woman may marry a slave, with the same restriction. If a slave woman bears a child to her master, the child is free, and the mother cannot be sold or given away. At the death of her owner she becomes free. A slave man and woman may marry, with the consent of the owner, to which they have a claim if they have behaved well. A slave man is limited to two wives. Emancipation is a religious and meritorious act on the part of a slave owner.[2] "In general, it must be acknowledged that neither amongst the people of antiquity, nor amongst Christians, have slaves enjoyed such good treatment as amongst Moslems."[3] The provision about a slave woman who becomes a mother by her master is the one to arouse most Christian shame. Still, the Moslems have so many special pleas and technical interpretations by which to set aside troublesome laws that we can never infer that the mores conform to the laws. It is against the law for a Moslem to reduce a Moslem to slavery, but the Turks rob the Kurds and other tribes of their women, or buy them from the barbarous Tcherkess.[4]

308. Slavery in England. Sir Thomas More[5] provided for some of the troubles of life by slavery. Slaves were to do "all laborsome toil," "drudging," and "base business." They were to be persons guilty of debt and breakers of

---

[1] *Globus*, XXX, 127; Vambery, *Sittenbilder aus dem Morgenlande*, 25.
[2] Hauri, *Islam*, 149.   [3] *Ibid.*, 150.   [4] *Ibid.*, 153.   [5] *Utopia*, II, 53.

marriage.[1] Garnier quotes a law of 1547 (I Ed. VI, c. 3), in which a vilein is mentioned as a slave. "Long after this date there are mentioned instances of a slave's emancipation, and such philanthropic writers as Fitzherbert lament the possibility of slavery and its actual existence, as a disgrace both to legislation and religion."[2]

309. Slavery in America. In the Anglo-American colonies which did not have a plantation system for tobacco or indigo the great reason for slavery was to hold the laborer to the place where the owner wanted him to work. In New England the negro slave lived in close intimacy with his owner and the latter's sons. In Connecticut he was allowed to go to the table with the family, "and into the dish goes the black hoof as freely as the white hand."[3] In that colony the creditor might require the debtor, by a law of 1650, to pay by service, and might sell his due service to any one of the English nation. The law remained in force into the nineteenth century.[4]

310. Colonial slavery. France reopened the slave trade by a law of May 20, 1802. One of the reasons for this law submitted by Buonaparte to the legislature was : "The commercial prosperity of France renders it necessary that a certain quantity of the produce of the country, in wine and cereals, should be sent to the Antilles for consumption by the blacks. Now these negroes, were they free, would prefer manioc to wheat, and the juice of the sugar cane to our wines. It is, therefore, indispensable that they should be slaves."[5]

311. Slavery preferred by slaves. It appears, therefore, that the subjection of one man's muscles and nerves to another man's will has been in the mores of all people from the beginning of human societal organization until now. Now it exists, as an institution, only in barbarism and half-civilization. In English North Borneo slavery is traditional. Any slave may be free for £4, "but in most cases they have been brought up as ordinary members of the family, and have no wish to leave

[1] *Utopia*, II, 132, 144, 147.   [3] Mad. Knight's *Journey* (1704).
[2] *Brit. Peasantry*, 71.   [4] Hildreth, *Hist. U. S.*, I, 372.
                [5] Fauriel, *Last Days of the Consulate*, 31.

their home. Cases of unkind treatment are very few and far
between."[1] In fact, the purely sentimental objections to slavery
have reached, in Africa, many people who are on a grade of
civilization where slavery is an advantage to the slave (sec. 275).
Schweinfurth tells us, of the Sudanese, that numbers of them
often "voluntarily attach themselves to the Nubians, and are
highly delighted to get a cotton shirt and a gun of their own.
They will gladly surrender themselves to slavery, being attracted
also by the hope of finding better food in the seribas than their
own native wilderness can produce. The mere offer of these
simple inducements in any part of the Niam-niam lands would
be sufficient to gather a whole host of followers and vassals."[2]
He goes on to show how the mode of grinding durra corn used
in Africa keeps women in slavery. They pound it on a big
stone by means of a little stone. One woman's day's work will
grind enough for five or six men. It has been shown above
(sec. 275) how badly the abolition of slavery has been received
in Algeria and Sahara. Gibson is quoted " that voluntary and
hereditary slavery might well be permitted to continue " in West
Africa.[3] In that region " a slave man could hold property of his
own. If he were a worthy, sensible person, he could inherit."
He could take part in discussions and the palaver, and could
defend himself against abuse. There are now no slaves bought
or sold, but there are "pawns " for debt, who are not free.[4] On
the one hand, the slave trade in Africa has required for its
successful prosecution that the slaves should first be war captives or raid captives of other negroes. This has led to the
wildest and most cruel devastation of the territory. On the
other hand, the question arises whether savages must be left
to occupy and use a continent as they choose, or whether they
may be compelled to come into coöperation with civilized men
to use it so as to carry on the work of the world. Many who
think the latter view sound are arrested by the fact that no
one has ever been found great or good enough to be a slave
owner. On the other hand, a humanitarian doctrine which orders

[1] Cator, *Head-hunters*, 198.
[2] *Heart of Africa*, II, 421.
[3] *N. S., Amer. Anthrop.*, VI, 563.
[4] Nassau, *Fetishism in West Afr.*, 14 ff.

that a slave be turned out of doors, in spite of his own wish, is certainly absurd.

312. Future of slavery. In the eighteenth century, in western Europe, there was a moral revolt against slavery. None of the excuses, or palliatives, were thought to be good. The English, by buying the slaves on their West India islands, took the money loss on themselves, but they threw back the islands to economic decay and uncultivation. When the civilized world sees what its ideas and precepts have made of Hayti, it must be forced to doubt its own philosophy. The same view has spread. Slavery is now considered impossible, socially and politically evil, and so not available for economic gain, even if it could win that. It is the only case in the history of the mores where the so-called moral motive has been made controlling. Whether it will remain in control is a question. The Germans, in the administration of their colonies, sneer at humanitarianism and eighteenth-century social philosophy. They incline to the doctrine that all men must do their share in the world and come into the great modern industrial and commercial organization. They look around for laborers for their islands and seem disposed to seek them in the old way. In South Africa and in our own southern states the question of sanitary and police control is arising to present a new difficulty. Are free men free to endanger peace, order, and health? Is a low and abandoned civilization free to imperil a high civilization, and entitled to freedom to do so? The humanitarians of the nineteenth century did not settle anything. The contact of two races and two civilizations cannot be settled by any dogma. Evidence is presented every day that the problems are not settled and cannot be settled by dogmatic and sentimental generalities. Is not a sentiment made ridiculous when it is offered as a rule of action to a man who does not understand it and does not respond to it? In general, in the whole western Sahara district slaves are as much astonished to be told that their relation to their owners is wrong, and that they ought to break it, as boys amongst us would be to be told that their relation to their fathers was wrong and ought to be broken.

313. Relation of slavery to the mores and to ethics. Inasmuch as slavery springs from greed and vanity, it appeals to primary motives and is at once intertwined with selfishness and other fundamental vices. It is not, therefore, a cause which gradually produces and molds the mores, nor is it an ethical product of folkways and mores. It is characteral. It rises into an interest which overrules everything else. This appears most clearly in the history of Roman slavery (see sec. 288). The due succession of folkways, mores, character, and ethics is here broken. The motive of slavery is base and cruel from the beginning. Later, there are many people of high character who accept it as an inheritance, and are not corrupted by it. The due societal relation of interests and mores is broken, however. It is an evil thing that that relation should be broken. All which is moral (pertaining to mores) or ethical is thrown out of sequence and relation. The interests normally control life. It is not right that ethical generalizations should get dogmatic authority and be made the rule of life. Ethical generalizations are vague and easy. They satisfy loose thinkers, and it is a matter of regret when, in any society, they get the currency of fashion and are cherished by great numbers. Interests ought to control, being checked and verified by ethical principles of approved validity. Slavery is an interest which is sure to break over all restraints and correctives. It therefore becomes mistress of folkways and dictates the life policy. It is a kind of pitfall for civilization. It seems to be self-evident and successful, but it contains a number of forms of evil which are sure to unfold. The Moslems have suffered from the curse of it, although in entirely other ways than the Christians. It intertwines with any other great social evil which may be present. There it has combined with polygamy. It is, in any case, an institution which radically affects the mores, but it is to be noticed that its effect on them is not normal and not such as belongs to the prosperous development of civilization.

CHAPTER VII

ABORTION, INFANTICIDE, KILLING THE OLD

The able-bodied and the burdens. — The advantages and disadvantages of the aged. Respect and contempt for them. — Abortion and infanticide. — Relation of parent and child. — Population policy. — The burden and benefit of children. — Individual and group interest in children. — Abortion in ethnography. — Abortion renounced. — Infanticide in ethnography. — Infanticide renounced. — Ethics of abortion and infanticide. — Christian mores as to abortion and infanticide. — Respect and contempt for the aged. — The aged in ethnography. — Killing the old. — Killing the old in ethnography. — Special exigencies of the civilized. — How the customs of infanticide and killing the old were changed.

314. The competent part of society ; the burdens. The able-bodied and competent part of a society is the adults in the prime of life. These have to bear all the societal burdens, among which are the care of those too young and of those too old to care for themselves. It is certain that at a very early time in the history of human society the burden of bearing and rearing children, and the evils of overpopulation, were perceived as facts, and policies were instinctively adopted to protect the adults. The facts caused pain, and the acts resolved upon to avoid it were very summary, and were adopted with very little reasoning. Abortion and infanticide protected the society, unless its situation with respect to neighbors was such that war and pestilence kept down the numbers and made children valuable for war. The numbers present, therefore, in proportion to the demand for men, constituted one of the life conditions. It is a life condition which is subject to constant variation, and one in regard to which the sanctions of wise action are prompt and severe.

315. The advantages and disadvantages of the aged. Mores of respect and contempt. Those who survive to old age become depositaries of all the wisdom of the group, and they are generally the possessors of power and authority, but they lose physical power, skill, and efficiency in action. In time, they become burdens on the active members of the group. " As a man grows old and weak he loses the only claim to respect which savages understand ; but superstitious fear then comes to his protection. He will die soon and then his ghost can take revenge."[1] That is to say that the mores can interfere to inculcate duties of respect to the old which will avert from them the conclusion that they ought to die. In respect to the aged, therefore, we find two different sets of mores : (a) those in which the aged are treated with arbitrary and conventional respect ; and (b) those in which the doctrine is that those who become burdens must be removed, by their own act or that of their relatives. In abortion, infanticide, and killing the old there is a large element of judgment as to what societal welfare requires, although they are executed generally from immediate personal selfishness. The custom of the group, by which the three classes of acts are approved as right and proper, must contain a judgment that they are conducive, and often necessary, to welfare.

316. Abortion and infanticide. Abortion and infanticide are two customs which have the same character and purpose. The former prevents child bearing ; the latter child rearing. They are folkways which are aggregates of individual acts under individual motives, for an individual might so act without a custom in the group. The acts, however, when practiced by many, and through a long time, change their character. They are no longer individual acts of resistance to pain. They bear witness to uniform experiences, and to uniform reactions against the experiences, in the way of judgments as to what it is expedient to do, and motives of policy. They also suggest to, and teach, the rising generation. They react, in the course of time, on the welfare of the group. They affect its numbers and its quality, as we now believe, although we cannot find that any group has ever been forced by its experience to put these customs under taboo.[2]

317. Relation of parent and child. Children add to the weight of the struggle for existence of their parents. The relation of

[1] Lippert, *Kulturgesch*, I, 229.
[2] Ancient India may be an exception.

parent to child is one of sacrifice. The interests of children and parents are antagonistic. The fact that there are, or may be, compensations does not affect the primary relation between the two. It may well be believed that, if procreation had not been put under the dominion of a great passion, it would have been caused to cease by the burdens it entails. Abortion and infanticide are especially interesting because they show how early in the history of civilization the burden of children became so heavy that parents began to shirk it, and also because they show the rise of a population policy, which is one of the most important programmes of practical expediency which any society ever can adopt.

318. Population policy. At the present moment the most civilized states do not know whether to stimulate or restrict population; whether to encourage immigration or not; whether emigration is an evil or a blessing; whether to tax bachelors or married men. These questions are discussed as if absolute answers to them were possible, independently of differences in life conditions. In France the restriction of population has entered into the mores, and has been accomplished by the people, from motives which lie in the standard of living. In New England the same is true, perhaps to a greater extent. There are many protests against these mores, on the ground that they will produce societal weakness and decay, and ethical condemnation is freely expended upon them by various schools of religious and philosophical ethics. What is certain, however, is that in the popular ethics of the people who practice restriction it is regarded as belonging to elementary common sense. The motives are connected with economy and social ambition. The restriction on the number of children, in all modern civilized society, issues in an improvement of the quality of the children, so far as that can be improved by care, education, travel, and the expenditure of capital (sec. 320). Thus the problem of rearing children has pressed upon mankind from the earliest times until to-day. It is a problem of the last degree of simplicity and reality, — a problem of a task and the strength to perform it, of an expenditure and the means to meet it. For the group, also, population has always presented, as it now does, a problem of policy. That group interests are involved in it is unquestionable. It is one of the matters in regard to which it would be most proper to adopt a careful and well-digested programme of policy. A great many of the projects which are now urged upon society are really applications of population philosophy assumed to be wise without adequate knowledge, or they set population free from all restraints on behalf of certain beneficiaries, while a sound population policy, according to the best knowledge we have, would be the real solution of a number of the most serious evils (alcoholism, sex disease, imbecility, insanity, and infant mortality) which now exhaust the vigor of society.

319. Burden or benefit of children. Abortion and infanticide are, as already stated, the earliest efforts of men to ward off the burden of children and the evils of overpopulation by specific devices of an immediate and brutal character. The weight of the burden of children differs greatly with the life conditions of groups, and with the stage of the arts by which men cope with the struggle for existence. If a territory is underpopulated, an increase in numbers increases the output and the dividend per capita. If it is overpopulated, the food quest is difficult and children cause hardship to the parents. On the other hand, the demand for children will be great, if the group has strong neighbors and needs warriors. The demand may be greater for boys than for girls, or contrariwise. Girls may be needed in order that wives may be obtained in exchange for them, but the greater demand for girls is generally due to the mores which have been established. The demand may be so great as to offset the burden of rearing children and make it a group necessity that that burden shall be endured. From the standpoint of the individual father or mother this means that there are compensations for the toil and cost of rearing children. When girls bring a good bride price to the father, it is evident that he at least receives compensation. As to the mothers, if they receive no compensation, that accords with all the rest of their experience. It is a well-known fact that they often show resentment when a daughter is given (sold) in marriage. That fact has never been adequately explained, but it seems to be anything but strange if the husband sells the girl and takes the bride price, although the wife bore and reared the child. Amongst the Marathas of India, on the contrary, "even to the well-to-do, to have many daughters is a curse." The bride's father has to give a big dowry to the groom. If the fathers have rank, but are poor, the girls often have to marry men who are inferior in age or rank.[1]

320. Individual and group interest. It follows that, in all variations of the life conditions, in all forms of industrial organization, and at all stages of the arts, conjunctures arise in which the value of children fluctuates, and also the relative value of boys and girls turns in favor, now of one, now of the other. In the examination of any case of the customs of abortion and infanticide chief attention should be directed to these conjunctures. On the stage of pastoral-nomadic life, or wherever else horde life existed, it appears that numerous offspring were regarded as a blessing and child rearing, in the horde, was not felt as a burden. It was in the life of the narrower family, whatever its form, that children came to be felt as a burden, so that "progress" caused abortion and infanticide. Further progress has made children more and more expensive, down to our own times, when "neomalthusianism," although unavowed, exists in fact as a compromise between egoism and child rearing. All the folkways which go to make up a population policy seem to imply greater knowledge of the philosophy of population than can be ascribed to uncivilized men. The case is one, however, in which the knowledge is simple and the acts proceed from immediate interest, while the generalization is an unapprehended result. The mothers know the strain of child bearing and child rearing. They refuse to undergo it, for purely egoistic reasons. The consequent adjustment of the population to the food supply comes of itself. It was never foreseen or purposed by anybody. The women would not be allowed by the men to shirk motherhood if the group needed warriors, or if the men wanted daughters to sell

---

[1] *Ethnog. of India*, I, 95.

as wives, so that the egoistic motive of mothers never could alone suffice to make folkways. It would need to be in accord with the interest of the group or the interest of the men. Abortion and infanticide are primary and violent acts of self-defense by the parents against famine, disease, and other calamities of overpopulation, which increase with the number which each man or woman has to provide for. In time, the customs get ghost sanction, but it does not appear that they are in any way directly due to goblinism or to the aleatory element. They become ritual acts and are made sacred whenever they are brought into connection with societal welfare, which implies some reflection. The customs begin in a primary response to pain and the strain of life. Doctrines of right and duty go with the customs and produce a code of conduct in connection with them. Sometimes, if a child lives a specified time, its life must be spared. Sometimes infanticide is practiced only on girls, of whom a smaller number suffices to keep up the tribe. Sometimes it is confined to the imperfect infants, in obedience to a great tribal interest to have able-bodied men, and to spend no strength or capital in rearing others. Sometimes infanticide is executed by exposure, which gives the infant a chance for its life if any one will rescue it. Sometimes the father must express by a ritual act (e.g. taking up the newborn infant from the ground) his decision whether it is to live or not. With these customs must be connected that of selling children into slavery, which, when social hardship is great, is an alternative to infanticide. The Jews abominated infanticide but might sell their children to Jews.[1] Abortion by unmarried women is due to the penalties of husbandless mothers, and is only in form in the same class with abortion by the married. Cases are given below in which abortion is not due to misery, but to the egoistic motive only; also cases in which abortion and infanticide are actually carried to the degree of group suicide. Finally we may mention in this connection superstitious customs or ancient and senseless usages to prevent child bearing, since they bear witness to the dominion of the same ideas and wishes to which abortion and infanticide are due (see sec. 321).

[1] Exod. xxi. 7.

321. Illustrations from ethnography. The Papuans on Geelvink Bay, New Guinea, say that "children are a burden. We become tired of them. They destroy us." The women practice abortion to such an extent that the rate of increase of the population is very small and in some places there is a lack of women.[1] Throughout Dutch New Guinea the women will not rear more than two or three children each.[2] In fact, it is said of the whole island that the people love their children but fear that the food supply will be insufficient, or they seek ease and shirk the trouble of rearing children.[3] In German Melanesia the custom is current. Although many Europeans live with native women, few crossbreeds are to be seen.[4] Codrington[5] gives as reasons: "If a woman did not want the trouble of bringing up a child, desired to appear young, was afraid her husband might think the birth before its time, or wished to spite her husband." Ling Roth[6] quotes Low that the Dyaks never resort to wilful miscarriage, but this statement must be restricted to some of them. Perelaer[7] says that even married women do it and employ harmful means. The Atchinese practice abortion both before marriage and in marriage. It is a matter of course.[8] The women of Central Celebes will not bear children, and use abortion to avoid it, lest the perineum be torn, — "a thing which they consider the greatest shame for a woman."[9] If an unmarried woman of the Djakun, on the peninsula of Malacca, used abortion, she lost all standing in the tribe. Women despised her; no man would marry her, and she might be degraded by a punishment inflicted by her parents. Married women practiced it sometimes to avoid the strain of bearing children, but, if detected, they might be beaten by the husbands, even to death. In the neighboring tribe of the Orang Laut no means of abortion was known. "Such an abomination was not regarded as possible."[10] These tribes on Malacca are very low in grade of civilization. They are aborigines who have been displaced and depressed. The people of Nukuoro are all of good physique, large, and well formed. They have a food supply in excess of their wants and are well nourished. The population has decreased in recent years, by reason of the killing of children before or after birth.[11] On the New Britain islands the women dislike to become mothers soon after marriage. Generally it is from two to four years before a child is born.[12] On the New Hebrides the women employ abortion for egoistic reasons, and miscarriage is often produced by climbing trees and carrying heavy loads.[13] The inhabitants of the New Hebrides

[1] Rosenberg, *Geelvinkbaai*, 91.
[2] Krieger, *Neu-Guinea*, 390.
[3] *Ibid.*, 165.
[4] Pfeil, *Aus der Südsee*, 31.
[5] *Melanesians*, 229.
[6] *Sarawak*, I, 101.
[7] *Dajaks*, 37.
[8] Snouck-Hurgronje, *De Atjehers*, I, 73.
[9] *Bijdragen tot T. L. en V.-kunde*, XXXV, 79.
[10] *Ztsft. f. Ethnol.*, XXVIII, 186.
[11] Kubary, *Nukuoro*, 9, 12, 14.
[12] JAI, XVIII, 291.
[13] *Austral. Assoc. Adv. Sci.*, 1892, 704.

are diminishing in number, especially on the coasts, because they flee inland before the whites. Ten years ago there were at Port Sandwich, on Mallicolo, six hundred souls. To-day there are only half so many. In the last years there have been five births and thirty deaths. Abortion is very common. If a malformed child is born, it and the mother are killed. The nations raid each other to get slaves or cannibal food.[1] These citations seem to represent the general usage throughout the Pacific islands.

322. Oviedo said of the women " of the main land " of South America, when first discovered, that they practiced abortion in order not to spoil their bodies by child bearing.[2] The Kadiveo of Paraguay are perishing largely through abortion by the women, who will not bear more than one child each.[3] They are a subdivision of the Guykurus, who were reported sixty or seventy years ago to be decreasing in number from this cause. The women, " until they are thirty, procure abortion, to free themselves from the privations of pregnancy and the trouble of bringing up children."[4] Martius[5] gave as additional reasons, that the tribe lived largely on horseback, and the women did not want to be hindered by greater difficulties in this life, nor did they want to be left behind by their husbands. The Indians of the plains of North America were driven to similar limitations. " It has long been the custom that a woman should not have a second child until her first is ten years old."[6] Infants interfere very seriously with their mode of life.

Neither abortion nor infanticide is customary in the Horn of Africa unless it be in time of famine.[7] In South Africa abortion is a common custom.[8] Abortion and infanticide are so nearly universal in savage life, either as egoistic policy or group policy, that exceptions to the practice of these vices are noteworthy phenomena.

323. Abortion renounced. In ancient India abortion came to be ranked with the murder of a Brahmin as the greatest crimes.[9] Plato's idea of right was that men over fifty-five, and women over forty, ought not to procreate citizens. By either abortion or infanticide all offspring of such persons should be removed.[10] Aristotle also thought that imperfect children should be put to death, and that the numbers should be limited. If parents exceeded the prescribed number, abortion should be employed.[11] These two philosophers evidently constructed their ideals on the mores already established amongst the Greeks, and their ethical doctrines are only expressions of approval of the mores in which they lived. The Jews,

---

[1] *Globus*, LXXXVIII, 164, after Joly.
[2] *Three First English Books about America*, 237.
[3] *Globus*, LXXXI, 4.
[4] Spix and Martius, *Travels in Brazil*, II, 77.
[5] *Ethnog. Brasil.*, 231.
[6] Grinnell, *Cheyenne Woman Customs*, 15; *N. S. Amer. Anthrop.*, IV, 13.
[7] Paulitschke, *Ethnog. N. O. Afr.*, I, 172.
[8] Fritsch, *Eingeb. Süd-Afr.*, 96.
[9] Zimmer, *Altind. Leben*, 333.
[10] *Republic*, V, 9.
[11] *Politics*, VII, 16.

on the other hand, regarded abortion and infanticide as heathen abominations. Both are forbidden in the " Two Ways," sec. 2. In the laws of the German nations the mother was treated as entitled to decide whether she would bear a child. Abortion produced on her by another was a crime, but not when she produced it on herself. Only in the law of the West Goths was abortion by the mother made criminal, because it was the view that the state was injured.[1] In modern Hungary, at a marriage, the desire to have no children is expressed by a number of ancient and futile usages to prevent child bearing for years, or altogether. Abortion is practiced throughout Hungary by women of all the nationalities. Women rejoice to be barren, and it is not thought creditable to have an infant within two or three years of marriage.[2] Nevertheless the birth rate is very high (thirty-nine per thousand).

324. Illustrations of infanticide.. The Australians practiced infanticide almost universally. A woman could not carry two children. Therefore, if she had one who could not yet march, and bore another, the latter was killed. One or both twins were killed. The native men killed half-white children.[3] Australian life was full of privations on account of limited supplies of food and water. The same conditions made wandering a necessity. If a woman had two infants, she could not accompany her husband.[4] One reporter says that the fate of a child "depended much on the condition the country was in at the time (drought, etc.), and the prospect of the mother's rearing it satisfactorily." [5] Sickly and imperfect children were killed because they would require very great care. The first one was also killed because they thought it immature and not worth preserving.[6] Very generally it was eaten that the mother might recover the strength which she had given to it.[7] If there was an older child, he ate of it, in the belief that he might gain strength. Very rarely were more than four children of one woman allowed to grow up.[8] Curr [9] says that before the whites came women bore, on an average, six children each, and that, as a rule, they reared two boys and a girl, the maximum being ten. All authorities agree that if children were spared at birth they were treated with great affection. On the Andaman Islands infanticide was unknown.[10] It was not common on New Zealand. Boys were wanted as warriors, girls as breeders.[11] A missionary reports a case in New Guinea where the parents of a sickly, peevish child, probably teething, calmly

---

[1] Rudeck, *Oeffentl. Sittlichkeit in Deutschland*, 181.

[2] Temesvary, *Volksbräuche und Aberglauben in der Gebürtshilfe in Ungarn*, 12-14.   [3] Ratzel, *Völkerkunde*, II, 59.

[4] Eyre, *Cent. Aust.*, II, 324; Spencer and Gillen, *Cent. Aust.*, 51, 264.

[5] JAI, XIII, 137.   [8] Dawson, *West Victoria*, 39.

[6] Smyth, *Victoria*, I, 52.   [9] *Austr. Race*, I, 70.

[7] *Novara-Reise*, I, 32.   [10] JAI, XII, 329.

[11] *Ibid.*, XIX, 99.

decided to kill it.[1] In British New Guinea there is more or less infanticide, the father strangling the infant at birth to avoid care and trouble. Daughters are preserved by preference because of the bride price which the father will get for them.[2] On Nukuoro the civil ruler decides long before a birth whether the child is to be allowed to live or not. If the decision is adverse, it is smothered at birth.[3] On the Banks Islands girls are preferred, because the people have the mother family, and because of the marriageable value of girls.[4] On the Murray Islands in Torres Straits all children beyond a prescribed number are put to death, "lest the food supply should become insufficient." "If the children were all of one sex, some were destroyed from shame, it being held proper to have an equal number of boys and girls."[5] On some islands of the Solomon group infanticide is not practiced, except in cases of illegitimate births. On others the coast people kill their own children and buy grown-up children from the bush people of the interior, that being an easier way to get them.[6] There is no infanticide on Samoa. The unmarried employ abortion.[7] Throughout Polynesia infanticide was prevalent for social selection, all of mixed blood or caste being put to death. Only two boys in a family were allowed to live, but any number of girls.[8] In Tahiti they killed girls, who were of no use for war, service of the god, fishing, or navigation.[9] The Malagassans on Madagascar kill all children who are born on unlucky days.[10]

325. The women of the Pima (Arizona) practice infanticide, because, if their husbands die, they will be poor and will have to provide by their own exertions for such children as they have.[11] All Hyperboreans practice infanticide on account of the difficulty of the food supply.[12]

326. The Bondei of West Africa strangle an infant at birth if any of the numerous portents and omens for which they watch are unfavorable. An infant is also killed if its upper teeth come first.[13] Until very recently it was customary in parts of Ahanta for the tenth child born of the same mother to be buried alive.[14] In Kabre (Togo) there is a large population and little food. The people often sell their own children, or kidnap others, which they sell in order to provide for their own.[15] The Vadshagga put to death illegitimate children and those whose upper incisors come first. The latter, if allowed to live, would be parricides.[16] On the Zanzibar coast weak and deformed children are exposed. The Catholic mission

[1] Abel, *New Guinea*, 43.
[2] Krieger, *Neu-Guinea*, 292.
[3] Kubary, *Nukuoro*, 35.
[4] Codrington, *Melanesians*, 229.
[5] JAI, XXVIII, 11.
[6] JAI, XVII, 93.
[7] *Austr. Assoc. Adv. Sci.*, 1892, 621.
[8] Waitz, *Anthrop.*, V, 139.
[9] Ratzel, *Völkerkunde*, II, 126.
[10] Waitz, *Anthrop.*, II, 441.
[11] *Smithson. Rep.*, 1871, 407; quoted, *Bur. Eth.*, I, 99.
[12] Ratzel, II, 769; *Bur. Eth.*, XVIII, 289.
[13] PSM, L, 100.
[14] Ellis, *Tshi-speaking Peoples*, 234.
[15] *Globus*, LXXXIII, 314.
[16] Volkens, *Kilimandscharo*, 252.

saved many, but the natives then exposed more to get rid of them.[1] The Hottentots expose female twins.[2] The Kabyls put to death all children who are illegitimate, incestuous, or adulterine. If the mother should spare the infant she would insure her own death.[3] There is said to be no infanticide in Cambodia.[4] "Widows among the Moghiahs [a criminal tribe of central India] are allowed to remarry. The murder of female infants has, therefore, never prevailed amongst them."[5] The Chinese on Formosa practice female infanticide, "in cases of a succession of girls in a family." "The aborigines, both civilized and savage, looked with horror upon the Chinese for their inhumanity in this respect." They brought the custom from China, where in the overpopulated southeastern provinces it is current custom.[6] The Khonds of India are a poor, isolated hill tribe, who put female infants to death because they regard marriage in the same tribe as incest.[7] All tribes in their status who refuse to practice endogamy have a peculiar problem to deal with. Wilkins[8] says that six sevenths of the population of India have for ages practiced female infanticide. Buddhism is declared to be inhuman and antisocial. It palliates everything which is done to limit population — polygamy and infanticide in China, concubinage in Japan, and prostitution in both. It started and developed in countries which had for generations suffered from overpopulation, with its regular consequences of famine, pestilence, and war.[9]

327. Revolt against infanticide. The ancient Egyptians revolted, in their mores, against infanticide and put an end to it.[10] Strabo[11] thought it a peculiarity of the Egyptians that every child must be reared. The Greeks regarded infanticide as the necessary and simply proper way to deal with a problem which could not be avoided. Dissent was not wanting. At Thebes infanticide was forbidden.[12] Sutherland[13] points out the effect of infanticide to bring the Greek and Latin races to an end. They neglected their own females and begot offspring with foreign and slave women, thus breeding out their own race blood. The Romans do not appear to have had any population policy until the time of the empire, when the social corruption and egoism so restricted reproduction that the policy was directed to the encouragement of marriage and parenthood. Therefore infanticide was disapproved by the jurists and moralists. Ovid, Seneca, Plutarch, Favorinus, and Juvenal speak of abortion as general and notorious, but as criminal.[14] Tacitus praised the Germans because, as he erroneously

[1] Stuhlmann, *Mit Emin Pascha*, 38.
[2] Ratzel, *Völkerkunde*, I, 104.
[3] Hanoteau et Letourneux, *La Kabylie*, III, 220.
[4] PSM, XLIV, 779.
[9] Humbert, *Japan*, 311.
[5] JASB, I, 283.
[10] Lippert, I, 205.
[6] Pickering, *Formosa*, 61.
[11] *Geog.*, VIII, 24.
[7] Hopkins, *Relig. of India*, 531.
[12] Aelian, *Var. Hist.*, II, 7.
[8] *Mod. Hinduism*, 431.
[13] *Moral Instinct*, I, 134, 136.
[14] Cf. Lecky, *Eur. Morals*, II, 20.

asserted,[1] they did not allow infanticide, and he knew that the Jews prohibited it.[2] In the cases of Greece and Rome we have clear instances to
prove the opposite tendencies of the mores, with their attendant philosophies and ethical principles, on the conjuncture of the conditions and
interests. At Rome children were exposed either on account of poverty,
which was the ancient cause, or on account of luxury, egoism, and vice.
" Pagan and Christian authorities are united in speaking of infanticide as
a crying vice of the empire." [3] These protests show that the custom was
not fully protected by the mores. Pliny thought it necessary.[4] Seneca
refers to the killing of defective children as a wise and unquestioned custom which he can use for illustration.[5] For the masses, until the late days
of the empire, infanticide was, at the worst, a venial crime. " What was
demanded on this subject was not any clearer moral teaching, but rather a
stronger enforcement of the condemnation long since passed upon infanticide, and an increased protection for exposed infants. . . . The church
labored to deepen the sense of the enormity of the crime." [6] Evidently
infanticide was a tradition with serious approval from one state of things
to another in which it was harmful and not needed in any view. In 331 A.D.
Constantine gave title to those who rescued exposed children against the
parents of the children.[7] This was in favor of the children, since it increased
the chances that they would be rescued, if we must assume that it was
their interest that their lives should be spared, even if they were reared by
men who speculated on their future value as slaves or prostitutes. As a
corollary of the legislation against infanticide, institutions to care for
foundlings came into existence. Such institutions rank as charitable and
humanitarian. Their history is such as to make infanticide seem kind.
In 374 infanticide was made a crime punishable by death. Justinian
provided that foundlings should be free.[8] Infanticide continued to be
customary. The church worked against it by the introduction of the
mystic religious element. The infants died unbaptized. As the religion
took a more and more ritualistic character this fact affected the minds of
the masses more than the suffering or death of the infants ever had. In a
cold estimate of facts it was also questionable whether the infants suffered
any great harm, and the popular estimate of the crime of extinguishing a
life before any interests had clustered around it was very lenient. " The
criminality of abortion was immeasurably aggravated when it was believed
to involve not only the extinction of a transient life, but also the damnation
of an immortal soul." [9] The religious interest was thus brought to reënforce
the love of children in the struggle against the old custom. The canon

---

[1] Weinhold, *D. F.*, I, 91.

[2] *Germania*, 19 ; *Hist.*, V, 5.

[3] Lecky, *Eur. Morals*, II, 27.

[4] *Nat. Hist.*, IV, 29.

[5] *De Ira*, I, 15.

[6] Lecky, *Eur. Morals*, II, 29.

[7] *Cod. Theod.*, V, 7.

[8] Blair, *Slavery amongst the Romans*, 44.

[9] Lecky, *Eur. Morals*, II, 23.

law also construed it as murder. Through the Middle Ages the sale of children was not common, but the custom of exposure continued.[1] The primitive usages of the Teutons included exposure of infants. The father by taking the child up from the ground ordained that it should live. It was then bathed and named. Rulers exposed infants lest dependent persons should be multiplied. Evil dreams also caused exposure. When the Icelanders accepted Christianity a minority stipulated that they should still be allowed to eat horseflesh and to practice exposure of infants.[2] In old German law infanticide was treated as the murder of a relative. The guilty mother was buried alive in a sack, the law prescribing, with the ingenious fiendishness of the age, that a dog, a cat, a rooster, and a viper should also be placed in the sack.[3] In ancient Arabia the father might kill newborn daughters by burying them alive. The motive of the old custom was anxiety about provision for the child and shame at the disgrace of having become the father of a daughter.[4] In the Koran it is forbidden to kill children for fear of starvation. In modern countries infanticide has been common or rare according to the penalties, in law or the mores, upon husbandless mothers. In the sixteenth century, in Spain, illegitimate births were very common. Infanticide was very uncommon, but abandonment (foundlings) took its place. The foundlings became vagabonds and rogues.[5]

328. Ethics of abortion and infanticide. Abortion and infanticide are at war with the attachment of parents to children, which is a sentiment common, but not universal, amongst animals while the offspring are dependent. It might seem that these customs have been abolished by speculative ethics. In fact, they have not been abolished. They have been modified and have been superseded by milder methods of accomplishing the same purpose. It is evidently a question at what point parental affection begins to attach to the child. We think that we have gained much over savage people in our notion of murder, but it appears that primitive men did not dare to take anything out of nature without giving an equivalent for it, and that they did not dare to kill anything without first sacrificing it to a god, or afterwards conciliating the spirit of the animal or of its species. If it is murder to prevent a life from coming into existence, it

[1] *Polyptique de Irminon*, I, 287.
[2] Weinhold, *D. F.*, I, 93, 96; II, 93.
[3] Rudeck, *Oeffentl. Sittlichkeit*, 182.
[4] Wellhausen, *Ehe bei den Arabern*, 458.
[5] Chandler, *Romances of Roguery in Spain*, 30.

would be a question of casuistry at what point such a crime would ensue. It might be murder to remain unmarried.

329. Christian mores as to abortion and infanticide. The tradition against abortion and infanticide came down into our mores from the Jews. It never got strength in the mores of Christianity until each of those acts was regarded as a high religious crime because the child died unbaptized. The soul was held to belong to it from the moment of conception. In reality nothing has put an end to infanticide but the advance in the arts (increased economic power), by virtue of which parents can provide for children. Neomalthusianism is still practiced and holds the check by which the population is adjusted to the economic power. There is shame in it. No one dare avow it or openly defend it. A " two-child system " is currently referred to in French and German literature as an established family policy, and restriction is certainly a fact in the mores of all civilized people. It is certain that the masses of those people think it right and not wrong. They do not accept guidance from any speculative ethics, but from expediency. Their devotion to their children is greater than a similar virtue ever has been at any previous time, and they prove their willingness to make the utmost sacrifices for them. In fact, very many of them are unwilling to have more children because it would limit what they can do for those they have. In short, the customs and their motives have changed very little since the days of savagery.

330. Mores of respect or contempt for the aged. In the introductory paragraph to this chapter it was observed that there are two sets of mores as to the aged : (a) in one set of mores the teaching and usages inculcate conventional respect for the aged, who are therefore arbitrarily preserved for their wisdom and counsel, perhaps also sometimes out of affection and sympathy ; (b) in the other set of mores the aged are regarded as societal burdens, which waste the strength of the society, already inadequate for its tasks. Therefore they are forced to die, either by their own hands or those of their relatives. It is very far from being true that the first of these policies is practiced by people higher up in civilization than those who practice the second. The people in lower civilization profit more by the wisdom and counsel of the aged than those in higher civilization, and are educated by this experience to respect and value the aged. " The introduction of the father-right won more respect for the aged man." [1] In some cases we can see the two codes in strife. Amongst the ancient Teutons the father could expose or sell his children under age, and the adult son could kill his aged parents.[2] There was no fixed duty of child to parent or of parent to child.

331. Ethnographical illustrations of respect to the aged. " The people of Madagascar pay high honor to age and to parents. The respect to age is even exaggerated." The Hovas always pay formal respect to greater age. If two slaves are carrying a load together, the younger of them will try to carry it all.[3] In West Africa, " all the younger members of society are early trained to show the utmost deference to age. They must never come into the presence of aged persons or pass by their dwellings without taking off their hats and assuming a crouching gait. When seated in their presence it must always be at a 'respectful distance,' — a distance proportioned to the difference in their ages and position in society. If they come near enough to hand an aged man a lighted pipe or a glass of water, the bearer must always fall upon one knee." [4] " Great among the Oromo is the veneration for the old. Failure in respect to age is considered an injury to the customs of the country. The aged always sit in the post of honor, have a voice in public councils, in discussions, and controversies which arise amongst citizens. The young and the women are taught to serve them on all occasions." [5] The Hereros respect the old. Property belongs to an old man even after his son assumes the care of it. Milk pails and joints of meat are brought to him to be blessed.[6] The old are well treated in Australia. Certain foods are reserved for them.[7] Amongst the Lhoosai, on the Chittagong hills of southeastern India, " parents are reverenced and old age honored. When past work the father and mother are cared for by the children." [8] The Nicobarese treat the old kindly and let them live as long as they can.[9] The Andamanese also show great respect to the old and treat them with care and consideration.[10] The tribes in central Australia have no such custom " as doing away with aged or

---

[1] Lippert, *Kulturgesch.*, I, 240.
[2] Grimm, *Deutsche Rechtsalt.*, 461, 487.
[3] Ratzel, *Völkerkunde*, II, 511.
[4] Nassau, *Fetishism in West Afr.*, I 59.
[5] Vannutelli e Citerni, *L'Omo*, 448.

[6] Ratzel, *Hist. of Mankind*, II, 468.
[7] Ratzel, *Völkerkunde*, II, 22.
[8] Lewin, *Wild Races of S. E. India*, 256.
[9] JAI, XVIII, 384.
[10] *Ibid.*, XII, 93.

infirm people ; on the contrary, such are treated with especial kindness, receiving a share of the food which they are unable to procure for themselves." [1] The Jekris, in the Niger Protectorate, "have great respect for their fathers, chiefs, and old age generally. Public opinion is very strong on these points.[2] The Indians on the northwest coast of North America "have great respect for the aged, whose advice in most matters has great weight." [3] "Great is the respect for the aged" amongst the Chavantes, a Ges tribe of Brazil.[4] Cranz [5] says that the Greenland Eskimo take care of their old parents. "The Ossetines [of the Caucasus] have the greatest love and respect for their parents, for old age in general, and for their ancestors. The authority of the head of the family, the grandfather, father, stepfather, uncle, or older brother is unconditionally recognized. The younger men will never sit down in the presence of elders, will not speak loudly, and will never contradict them." [6] "A young Kalmuck never dares show himself before his father or mother when he is not sober. He does not sit down in the presence of old people, drawing his legs under him, which would be a gross familiarity, but he squats on his knees, supporting himself with his heels in the ground. He never shows himself before old people without his girdle. To be without a girdle is extreme negligé." [7] Maine[8] says : "A New Zealand chief, when asked as to the welfare of a fellow-tribesman, replied, 'He gave us so much good advice that we put him mercifully to death.' This gives a good idea of the two views which barbarous men take of the aged. At first they are considered useless and burdensome, and fare accordingly ; later a sense of their wisdom raises them to a place of high honor." It is evident that the statement here made, of the relation in time of the two ways of treating the old, is not correct. The cases above cited are nearly all those of savages and barbarians. The people of higher civilization will be found amongst those of the other mores to be cited below (see sec. 335).

332. "The position of the Roman father assured him respect and obedience as long as he lived. His unlimited power of making a will kept his fate in his own hands." [9] The power in his family which the law gave him was very great, but his sons never paid him affectionate respect. "It is remarkable that we do not hear so often of barbarous treatment of old women as of old men. Could love for mothers have been an effective

[1] Spencer and Gillen, *Native Tribes, Cent. Austr.*, 51.
[2] JAI, XXVIII, 109.
[3] *U. S. Nat. Mus.*, 1888, 240.
[4] Martius, *Ethnog. Brasil.*, 274.
[5] *Hist. von Grönland*, 197.
[6] von Haxthausen, *Transkaukasia*, II, 35.
[7] *Russian Ethnog.* (*Russ.*), II, 445.
[8] *Early Law and Custom*, 23.
[9] Lippert, *Kulturgesch.*, I, 241.

sentiment? Under mother right the relation of child to parent was far stronger, and the relation to the maternal uncle was secondary and derivative with respect to that to the mother." [1]

333. Killing the old. The custom of killing the old, especially one's parents, is very antipathetic to us. The cases will show that, for nomadic people, the custom is necessary. The old drop out by the way and die from exhaustion. To kill them is only equivalent, and perhaps kinder. If an enemy is pursuing, the necessity is more acute.[2] All this enters into the life conditions so primarily that the custom is a part of the life policy; it is so understood and acquiesced in. The old sometimes request it from life weariness, or from devotion to the welfare of the group.

334. Killing the old in ethnography. The "Gallinomero sometimes have two or three cords of wood neatly stacked in ricks about the wigwam. Even then, with the heartless cruelty of the race, they will dispatch an old man to the distant forest with an ax, whence he returns with his white head painfully bowed under a back-load of knaggy limbs, and his bare bronzed bowlegs moving on with that catlike softness and evenness of the Indian, but so slowly that he scarcely seems to get on at all." [3] An old squaw, who had been abandoned by her children because she was blind, was found wandering in the mountains of California.[4] "Filial piety cannot be said to be a distinguishing quality of the Wailakki, or any Indians. No matter how high may be their station, the aged and decrepit are counted a burden. The old man, hero of a hundred battles, when his skill with the bow and arrow is gone, is ignominiously compelled to accompany his sons into the forest, and bear home on his shoulders the game they have killed." [5] Catlin describes his leave-taking of an old Ponca chief who was being deserted by the tribe with a little food and water, a trifling fire, and a few sticks. The tribe were driven on by hunger. The old chief said: "My children, our nation is poor, and it is necessary that you should all go to the country where you can get meat. My eyes are dimmed and my strength is no more. . . . I am a burden to my children. I cannot go. Keep your hearts stout and think not of me. I am no longer good for anything." [6] This is the fullest statement we can quote, attributed to one of the abandoned old men, of the view of the proceeding which could make him acquiesce in it. The victims do not always take this view of the matter. This custom was

[1] Lippert, *Kulturgesch.*, I, 325.
[2] Powers, *Calif. Indians*, 319.
[3] *Ibid.*, 176; Bancroft, *Native Races*, I, 390.
[4] *Ibid.*, 112.
[5] *Ibid.*, 118.
[6] *Smithson. Rep.*, 1885, Part II, 429.

common to all the tribes which roamed the prairies. Every one who lived to decrepitude knew that he must expect it. A more recent authority says that Poncas and Omahas never left the aged and infirm on the prairie. They were left at home, with adequate supplies, until the hunting party returned.[1] That shows that they had a settled home and their cornfields are mentioned in the context. The old watched the cornfields, so that they were of some use. By the law of the Incas the old, who were unfit for other work, drove birds from the fields, and they were kept at public cost, like the disabled.[2] The Hudson's Bay Eskimo strangle the old who are dependent on others for their food, or leave them to perish when the camp is moved. They move in order to get rid of burdensome old people without executing them.[3] The central Eskimo kill the old because all who die by violence go to the happy land; others have not such a happy future.[4] Nansen[5] says that "when people get so old that they cannot take care of themselves, especially women, they are often treated with little consideration" by the Eskimo. Many tribes in Brazil killed the old because they were a burden and because they could no longer enjoy war, hunting, and feasting. The Tupis sometimes killed a sick man and ate the corpse, if the shaman said that he could not get well.[6] The Tobas, a Guy-kuru tribe in Paraguay, bury the old alive. The old, from pain and decrepi-tude, often beg for death. Women execute the homicide.[7] An old woman of the Murray River people, Australia, broke her hip. She was left to die, "as the tribe did not want to be bothered with her." The helpless and infirm are customarily so treated.[8] In West Victoria the old are strangled by a relative deputed for the purpose and the body is burned. One reason given is that, in cases of attack by an enemy, the old would be captured and tortured to death. The victims often beg for delay, but always in vain.[9] The Melanesians buried alive the sick and old. "It is certain that, when this was done, there was generally a kindness intended." Even when the younger hastened the end, for selfish reasons, the sick and aged acquiesced. They often begged to be put out of their misery.[10] On the Easter Islands the aged were treated with little respect. The sick were not kindly treated, unless they were near relatives.[11] The Solomon Islanders are described as "a community where no respect whatever is shown by youth to age."[12] Holub[13] mentions a great cliff from which some South African tribes cast the old when tired of caring for them. Hottentots used to put decrepit old people on pack oxen and take them out into the desert, where they were

[1] *Bur. Eth.*, III, 274.
[2] Martius, *Ethnog. Brasil.*, 126, n.
[3] *Bur. Eth.*, XI, 178, 186.
[4] *Ibid.*, VI, 615.
[5] *Eskimo*, 178.
[6] Martius, *Ethnog. Bras.*, 126.
[7] *Globus*, LXXXI, 108.
[8] Eyre, *Cent. Australia*, I, 321.
[9] Dawson, *West Victoria*, 62.
[10] Codrington, *Melanesians*, 347.
[11] Geiseler, *Oster-inseln*, 31.
[12] Woodford, *Head-hunters*, 25.
[13] *Sieben Jahre in S. Afr.*, I, 409.

left in a little hut prepared for the purpose with a little food. They now
show great heartlessness towards helpless old people.[1] Bushmen abandon
the aged with a little food and water.[2] In the Niger Protectorate the old
and useless are killed. The bodies are smoked and pulverized and the powder is made into little balls with water and corn. The balls are dried and
kept to be used as food.[3] The Somali exploit the old in work to the last
point, and then cast them out to die of hunger.[4] The people of the Arctic
regions generally put the aged to death on account of the hard life conditions. The aged of the Chuckches demand, as a right, to be put to death.[5]
Life is so hard and food so scarce that they are indifferent to death, and
the acquiescence of the victim is described as complete and willing.[6] A case
is also described[7] of an old man of that tribe who was put to death at his
own request by relatives, who thought that they performed a sacred obligation. The Yakuts formerly had a similar custom, the old man begging his
children to dispatch him. They thrust him into a hole in the forest, where
they left him with vessels, tools, and a little food. Sometimes a man and
his wife were buried together. There was no such thing as respect for the
aged or for aged relatives amongst the Yakuts. Younger men plundered,
scolded, and abused the elder.[8]

335. "The custom of putting a violent end to the aged and infirm survived from the primeval period into historic times not infrequently amongst
the Indo-European peoples. It can be authenticated in Vedic antiquity,
amongst the Iranians (Bactrians and Caspian peoples), and amongst the
ancient Germans, Slavs, and Prussians."[9] The Bactrians cast the old and
sick to the dogs.[10] The Massagetæ made a sacrifice of cattle and of an old
man, and ate the whole. This was a happy end. Those who died of disease
were buried and were thought less fortunate.[11] "As far as I know no mention is made among the Aryans of the putting to death of old people in
general (we first meet with it in the migratory period), nor of the putting to
death of parents by their children; but their casting out is mentioned."[12]
The Greeks treated the old with neglect and disrespect.[13] Gomme[14] quotes
a fifteenth-century MS. of a Parsifal episode in which the hero congratu-
lates himself that he is not like the men of Wales, "where sons pull their
fathers out of bed and kill them to save the disgrace of their dying in
bed." He also cites mention of the "holy mawle which (they fancy) hung

[1] Kolben, *Hist. Good Hope*, I, 324; Fritsch, *Eingeb. S. Afr.*, 334.
[2] *Globus*, XVIII, 122.
[3] Kingsley, *West Afr. Studies*, 566.
[4] Paulitschke, *Ethnog. N.O. Afr.*, I, 205.
[5] *N. S. Amer. Anthrop.*, III, 106.
[6] De Windt in *N. Y. Times*, May 10, 1897.
[7] *Russ. Ethnog.* (*russ.*), II, 578.
[8] Sieroshevski, *Yakuty* (*russ.*), 511, 621.
[9] Schrader, *Prehist. Antiq. of the Aryans*, 379; Zimmer, *Altind. Leben*, 327.
[10] Strabo, XI, 517; Spiegel, *Eran. Alterthumskunde*, III, 682.
[11] Herodotus, I, 216.
[12] Ihering, *Evol. of the Aryan*, 33.
[13] Mahaffy, *Soc. Life in Greece*, 229.
[14] *Ethnol. in Folklore*, 136.

behind the church door, which, when the father was seventy, the son might fetch to knock his father on the head as effete and of no more use."[1] Once in Iceland, in time of famine, it was decided by solemn resolution that all the old and unproductive should be killed. That determination was part of a system of legislation by which, in that country, the society was protected against superfluous and dependent members.[2]

336. Special exigencies of the civilized. Civilized men in certain cases find themselves face to face with the primitive circumstances, and experience the primeval necessity, which overrides the sentiments of civilization, whatever may be the strength of the latter. Colonel Fremont, in 1849, in a letter to his wife, tells how in crossing the plains he and his comrades left the weak and dying members of their party, one by one, to die in the snow, after lighting a little fire for him.[3] Many other such cases are known from oral narratives. The question is not one of more or less humanity. It is a question of the struggle for existence when at the limit of one of its conditions. Our civilization ordinarily veils from us the fact that we are rivals and enemies to each other in the competition of life. It is in such cases as the one just mentioned, or in shipwrecks, that this fact becomes the commanding one. The only alternative to the abandonment of one is the loss of all. Abortion, infanticide, and the killing of the old began at times when the competition of life was so direct and pitiless that it left no room for kindly sentiment. The latter is a product of civilization. It could be cultivated only by men for whom the struggle for existence was so easy, and the competition of life so moderate, that the severity was all taken out of them. Then there was a surplus and the conditions of life were easy. The alternative was not murder or suicide. Such a state of ease was reached by migration or by advance in the arts, — in short, by greater command of man over nature. The fundamental elements in the case were altered.

[1] In the national museum at Stockholm is a large collection of flat clubs from all the churches in Sweden, the use of which is described with discretion. That the clubs were kept in the churches denotes that the act was put under religious sanction.

[2] Weinhold, *D. F.*, II, 92.

[3] Thayer, *Marvels of the New West*, 231.

337. How the mores were changed. Abortion, infanticide, and killing the old are primary folkways which respond to hard facts of life in the most direct and primitive manner. They are not blamed when they become ruling customs which everybody observes. They rise into mores more easily than other primitive usages because the superficial reasons for believing that they are conducive to welfare appear so simple and obvious. When a settled life took the place of a wandering life some immediate reasons for these customs were removed. When peace took the place of war with neighboring tribes other causes were set aside. The cases would then become less frequent, especially the cases of infanticide and killing the old. Then, if cases which seemed to call for reëmployment of old customs arose, they could be satisfied only against some repugnance. Men who were not hard pressed by the burden of life might then refrain from infanticide or killing the old. They yielded to the repugnance rather than to the dislike of hardship. Later, when greater power in the struggle for existence was won the infants and the old were spared, and the old customs were forgotten. Then they came to be regarded with horror, and the mores protected the infants and the old. The stories of the French peasantry which come to us nowadays show that the son is often fully ready in mind and will to kill his old father if the mores and the law did not restrain him.

CHAPTER VIII

CANNIBALISM

Cannibalism. — Origin in food supply. — Cannibalism not abominable. — In-group cannibalism. — Population policy. — Judicial cannibalism. — Judicial cannibalism in ethnography. — Out-group cannibalism. — Cannibalism to cure disease. — Reversions to cannibalism. — Cannibalism in famine. — Cannibalism and ghost fear. — Cannibalism in sorcery and human sacrifice. — Cult and cannibalism. — Superstitions about cannibalism. — Food taboos in ethnography. — Expiation for taking life. — Philosophy of cannibalism.

338. Cannibalism. Cannibalism is one of the primordial mores. It dates from the earliest known existence of man on earth. It may reasonably be believed to be a custom which all peoples have practiced.[1] Only on the pastoral stage has it ceased, where the flesh of beasts was common and abundant.[2] It is indeed noticeable that the pygmies of Africa and the Kubus of Sumatra, two of the lowest outcast races, do not practice cannibalism,[3] although their superior neighbors do. Our intense abomination for cannibalism is a food taboo (secs. 353–354), and is perhaps the strongest taboo which we have inherited.

339. Origin in food supply. It is the best opinion that cannibalism originated in the defects of the food supply, more specifically in the lack of meat food. The often repeated objection that New Zealanders and others have practiced cannibalism when they had an abundant supply of meat food is not to the point. The passion for meat food, especially among people who have to live on heavy starch food, is very strong. Hence they eat worms, insects, and offal. It is also asserted that the appetite for human flesh, when eating it has become habitual, becomes a

---

[1] See Andrée, *Anthropophagie;* Steinmetz, *Endokannibalism, Mitt. Anthrop. Ges. in Wien,* XXVI; Schaffhausen in *Archiv für Anthrop.,* IV, 245. Steinmetz gives in tabular form known cases of cannibalism with the motives for it, p. 25.

[2] Lippert, *Kulturgesch.,* II, 275.

[3] Globus, XXVI, 45; Stuhlmann, *Mit Emin Pascha,* 457; JAI, XXVIII, 39.

passion. When salt is not to be had the passion for meat reaches its highest intensity. "When tribes [of Australians] assembled to eat the fruit of the bunya-bunya they were not permitted to kill any game [in the district where the trees grow], and at length the craving for flesh was so intense that they were impelled to kill one of their number, in order that their appetites might be satisfied." [1] It follows that when this custom has become traditional the present food supply may have little effect on it. There are cases at the present time in which the practice of using human flesh for food is customary on a large and systematic scale. On the island of New Britain human flesh is sold in shops as butcher's meat is sold amongst us. [2] In at least some of the Solomon Islands human victims (preferably women) are fattened for a feast, like pigs. [3] Lloyd [4] describes the cannibalism of the Bangwa as an everyday affair, although they eat chiefly enemies, and rarely a woman. The women share the feast, sitting by themselves. He says that it is, no doubt, "a depraved appetite." They are not at all ashamed of it. Physically the men are very fine. "The cannibalism of the Monbutto is unsurpassed by any nation in the world." [5] Amongst them human flesh is sold as if it were a staple article of food. They are "a noble race." They have national pride, intellectual power, and good judgment. They are orderly, friendly, and have a stable national life. [6] Ward [7] describes the cannibalism on the great bend of the Congo as due to a relish for the kind of food. "Originating, apparently, from stress of adverse circumstances, it has become an acquired taste, the indulgence of which has created a peculiar form of mental disorder, with lack of feeling, love of fighting, cruelty, and general human degeneracy, as prominent attributes." An organized traffic in human beings for food exists on the upper waters of the Congo. It is thought that the pygmy tribe of the Wambutti are not cannibals because they are too "low," and because they do not file the lower incisors. The

---

[1] Smyth, *Victoria*, I, xxxviii.
[2] *Aust. Ass. Adv. Sci.*, 1892, 618.
[3] JAI, XVII, 99.
[4] *Dwarf-land*, 345.
[5] Schweinfurth, *Heart of Africa*, II, 94.
[6] Keane, *Ethnology*, 265.
[7] JAI, XXIV, 298.

latter custom goes with cannibalism in the Congo region, and is also characteristic of the more gifted, beautiful, and alert tribes.[1] None of the coast tribes of West Africa eat human flesh, but the interior tribes eat any corpse regardless of the cause of death. Families hesitate to eat their own dead, but they sell or exchange them for the dead of other families.[2] In the whole Congo region the custom exists, especially amongst the warlike tribes, who eat not only war captives but slaves.[3]

It is noteworthy that a fork[4] was invented in Polynesia for this kind of food, long before the fork was used for any other.

340. Cannibalism not abominable. Spix and Martius[5] asked a chief of the Miranhas why his people practiced cannibalism. The chief showed that it was entirely a new fact to him that some people thought it an abominable custom. "You whites," said he, "will not eat crocodiles or apes, although they taste well. If you did not have so many pigs and crabs you would eat crocodiles and apes, for hunger hurts. It is all a matter of habit. When I have killed an enemy it is better to eat him than to let him go to waste. Big game is rare because it does not lay eggs like turtles. The bad thing is not being eaten, but death, if I am slain, whether our tribal enemy eats me or not. I know of no game which tastes better than men. You whites are really too dainty."

341. In-group cannibalism. Cannibalism was so primordial in the mores that it has two forms, one for the in-group, the other for the out-group. It had a theory of affection in the former case and of enmity in the latter. In the in-group it was so far from being an act of hostility, or veiled impropriety, that it was applied to the closest kin. Mothers ate their babies, if the latter died, in order to get back the strength which they had lost in bearing them. Herodotus says that the Massagetæ sacrificed the old of their tribe, boiling the flesh of the men with that of cattle and eating the whole. Those who died of disease before attaining old age were buried, but that they thought a less happy fate. He says that the Padeans, men in the far east of India, put a sick man of their tribe to death and ate him, lest his flesh should be wasted by disease. The women did the same by a sick woman. If any reach old age without falling victims to this custom, they too are then killed

[1] *Globus*, LXXXV, 229.   [3] *Globus*, LXXII, 120; LXXXVII, 237.
[2] Nassau, *Fetishism in West Africa*, 11.   [4] Specimen in the Dresden Museum.
[5] *Brasilien*, 1249.

and eaten. He mentions also the Issidones, in southeastern Russia, who cut up their dead fathers, mingle the flesh with that of sacrificed animals, and make a feast of the whole. The skull is cleaned, gilded, and kept as an emblem, to which they make annual sacrifices. They are accounted a right-eous people. Amongst them women are esteemed equal with men.[1] Strabo[2] says that the Irish thought it praiseworthy to eat their deceased parents. The Birhors of Hazaribag, Hindostan, formerly ate their parents, but "they repudiate the suggestion that they ate any but their own relations" [i.e. each one ate his own relatives and no others?][3]. Reclus[4] says that in that tribe "the parents beg that their corpses may find a refuge in the stomachs of their children rather than be left on the road or in the forest." The Tib-etans, in ancient times, ate their parents, "out of piety, in order to give them no other sepulcher than their own bowels." This custom ceased before 1250 A.D., but the cups made of the skulls of relatives were used as memorials. Tartars and some "bad Christians" killed their fathers when old, burned the corpses, and mingled the ashes with their daily food.[5] In the gulf country of Australia only near relatives partake of the dead, unless the corpse is that of an enemy. A very small bit only is eaten by each. In the case of an enemy the purpose is to win his strength. In the case of a relative the motive is that the survivors may not, by lamentations, become a nuisance in the camp.[6] The Dieyerie have the father family. The father may not eat his own child, but the mother and female relatives must do so, in order to have the dead in their liver, the seat of feeling.[7] The Tuaré of Brazil (2 S. 67 W.) burn their dead. They preserve the ashes in reeds and mix them with their daily meals.[8] The Jumanas, on the head waters of the Amazon, regard the bones as the seat of the soul. They burn the bones of their dead, grind them to powder, mix the powder with intoxicating liquor, and drink it, "that the dead may live again in them."[9] All branches of the Tupis are cannibals. They brought the custom from the interior.[10] The Kobena drink in their *cachiri* the powdered bones of their dead relatives.[11] The Chavantes, on the Uru-guay, eat their dead children to get back the souls. Especially young mothers do this, as they are thought to have given a part of their own souls to their children too soon.[12] In West Victoria "the bodies of relatives who have lost their lives by violence are alone partaken of." Each eats only a bit, and it is eaten "with no desire to gratify or appease the appetite, but only as a symbol of respect and regret for the dead."[13] In Australian cannibalism the eating of relatives has behind it the idea of saving the strength which

[1] Herod., I, 216; III, 99; IV, 26.
[2] IV, 5, 298.
[3] JASB, II, 571.
[4] *Prim. Folk*, 249.
[5] Rubruck, *Eastern Parts*, 81, 151.
[6] JAI, XXIV, 171.
[7] JAI, XVII, 186.
[8] *Globus*, LXXXIII, 137.
[9] Martius, *Ethnog. Bras.*, 485.
[10] Southey, *Brazil*, I, 233.
[11] *Ztsft. f. Ethnol.*, XXXVI, 293.
[12] Andree, *Anthropophagie*, 50.
[13] Dawson, *West Victoria*, 67.

would be lost, or of acquiring the dexterity or wisdom, etc., of the dead. Enemies are eaten to win their strength, dexterity, etc. Only a bit is eaten. There are no great feasts. The fat and soft parts are eaten because they are the residence of the soul. In eating enemies there appears to be ritual significance.[1] It may be the ritual purpose to get rid of the soul of the slain man for fear that it might seek revenge for his death.

342. Some inhabitants of West Australia explained cannibalism (they ate every tenth child born) as "necessary to keep the tribe from increasing beyond the carrying capacity of the territory."[2] Infanticide is a part of population policy. Cannibalism may be added to it either for food supply or goblinism. When children were sacrificed in Mexico their hearts were cooked and eaten, for sorcery.[3]

343. Judicial cannibalism. Another use of cannibalism in the in-group is to annihilate one who has broken an important taboo. The notion is frequently met with, amongst nature peoples, that a ghost can be got rid of by utterly annihilating the corpse, e.g. by fire. Judicial cannibalism destroys it, and the members of the group by this act participate in a ritual, or sacramental cere- mony, by which a criminal is completely annihilated. Perhaps there may also be the idea of collective responsibility for his annihilation. To take the life of a tribe comrade was for a long time an act which needed high motive and authority and required expiation. The ritual of execution was like the ritual of sacrifice. In the Hebrew law some culprits were to be stoned by the whole congregation. Every one must take a share in the great act. The blood guilt, if there was any, must be incurred by all.[4] Primitive taboos are put on acts which offend the ghosts and may, therefore, bring woe on the whole group. Any one who breaks a taboo commits a sin and a crime, and excites the wrath of the superior powers. Therefore he draws on himself the fear and horror of his comrades. They must extrude him by banish- ment or death. They want to dissociate themselves from him. They sacrifice him to the powers which he has offended. When his comrades eat his corpse they perform a duty. They annihi- late him and his soul completely.

[1] Smyth, *Victoria*, I, 245.
[2] Whitmarsh, *The World's Rough Hand*, 178.
[3] *Globus*, LXXXVI, 112.
[4] W. R. Smith, *Religion of the Semites*, 284.

344. Judicial cannibalism in ethnography. " A man found in the harem of
Muato-jamvos was cut in pieces and given, raw and warm, to the people to
be eaten." [1] The Bataks employ judicial cannibalism as a regulated system.
They have no other cannibalism. Adulterers, persons guilty of incest, men
who have had sex intercourse with the widow of a younger brother, traitors,
spies, and war captives taken with arms in their hands are killed and eaten.
The last-mentioned are cut in pieces alive and eaten bit by bit in order to
annihilate them in the most shameful manner.[2] The Tibetans and Chinese
formerly ate all who were executed by civil authority. An Arab traveler of
the ninth century mentions a Chinese governor who rebelled, and who was
killed and eaten. Modern cases of cannibalism are reported from China.
Pith balls stained with the blood of decapitated criminals are used as medicine for consumption. Cases are also mentioned of Tartar rulers who
ordered the flesh of traitors to be mixed with the rulers' own food and that
of their barons. Tartar women begged for the possession of a culprit,
boiled him alive, cut the corpse into mince-meat, and distributed it to the
whole army to be eaten.[3]

345. Out-group cannibalism. Against members of an out-group, e.g.
amongst the Maori, cannibalism " was due to a desire for revenge ; cooking
and eating being the greatest of insults." [4] On Tanna (New Hebrides) to
eat an enemy was the greatest indignity to him, worse than giving up his
corpse to dogs or swine, or mutilating it. It was believed that strength
was obtained by eating a corpse.[5] A negro chief in Yabunda, French Congo,
told Brunache [6] that " it was a very fine thing to enjoy the flesh of a man
whom one hates and whom one has killed in a battle or a duel." Martius
attributes the cannibalism of the Miranhas to the enjoyment of a " rare,
dainty meal, which will satisfy their rude vanity, in some cases also, blood
revenge and superstition." [7] Cannibalism is one in the chain of causes
which keeps this people more savage than their neighbors, most of whom
have now abandoned it. " It is one of the most beastly of all the beastlike
traits in the moral physiognomy of man." It is asserted that cannibalism
has been recently introduced in some places, e.g. Florida (Solomon Islands).
It is also said that on those islands the coast people give it up [they have
fish], but those inland retain it. The notion probably prevails amongst all
that population that, by this kind of food, *mana* is obtained, *mana* being
the name for all power, talent, and capacity by which success is won.[8] The
Melanesians took advantage of a crime, or alleged crime, to offer the culprit
to a spirit, and so get fighting *mana* for the warriors.[9] The Chames of
Cochin China think that the gall of slain enemies, mixed with brandy, is an

---

[1] Oliveira Martins, *Raças Humanas*, II, 67.   [2] Wilken, *Volkenkunde*, 23, 27.
[3] Marco Polo, I, 266 and Yule's note, 275.   [4] JAI, XIX, 108.
[5] *Austral. Ass. Adv. Sci.*, 1892, 649–663.   [6] *Cent. Afr.*, 108.
[7] *Ethnog. Bras.*, 538.   [8] JAI, X, 305.
                    [9] Codrington, *Melanesians*, 134.

excellent means to produce war courage and skill.[1] The Chinese believe that the liver is the seat of life and courage. The gall is the manifestation of the soul. Soldiers drink the gall of slain enemies to increase their own vigor and courage.[2] The mountain tribes of Natal make a paste from powder formed from parts of the body, which the priests administer to the youth.[3] Some South African tribes make a broth of the same kind of powder, which must be swallowed only in the prescribed manner. It " must be lapped up with the hand and thrown into the mouth . . . to give the soldiers courage, perseverance, fortitude, strategy, patience, and wisdom." [4]

346. Cannibalism to cure disease. Notions that the parts of the human body will cure different diseases are only variants of the notion of getting courage and skill by eating the same. Cases are recorded in which a man gave parts of his body to be eaten by the sick out of love and devotion.[5]

347. Reversions to cannibalism. When savage and brutal emotions are stirred, in higher civilization, by war and quarrels, the cannibalistic disposition is developed again. Achilles told Hector that he wished he could eat him. Hekuba expressed a wish that she could devour the liver of Achilles.[6] In 1564 the Turks executed Vishnevitzky, a brave Polish soldier who had made them much trouble. They ate his heart.[7] Dozy [8] mentions a case at Elvira, in 890, in which women cast themselves on the corpse of a chief who had caused the death of their relatives, cut it in pieces, and ate it. The same author relates [9] that Hind, the mother of Moavia, made for herself a necklace and bracelets of the noses and ears of Moslems killed at Ohod, and also that she cut open the corpse of an uncle of Mohammed, tore out the liver, and ate a piece of it. It is related of an Irish chief, of the twelfth century, that when his soldiers brought to him the head of a man whom he hated " he tore the nostrils and lips with his teeth, in a most savage and inhuman manner." [10]

---

[1] *Bijdragen tot. T. L. en V.-kunde*, 1895, 342.

[2] *Globus*, LXXXI, 96.   [4] JAI, XXII, 111; cf. Isaiah lxv. 4.

[3] JAI, XX, 116.   [5] *Intern. Arch. f. Ethnol.*, IX, *Supplem.* 37.

[6] *Iliad*, XXII, 346; XXIV, 212.

[7] Evarnitzky, *Zaporoge Kossacks* (*russ.*), I, 209.

[8] *Mussulm. d'Espagne*, II, 226.

[9] *Ibid.*, I, 47.

[10] Gomme, *Ethnol. in Folklore*, 149.

348. In famine. Reversion to cannibalism under a total lack of other food ought not to be noted. We have some historical cases, however, in which during famine people became so familiarized with cannibalism that their horror of it was overcome. Abdallatif [1] mentions a great famine in Egypt in the year 1200, due to a failure of the inundation of the Nile. Resort was had to cannibalism to escape death. At first the civil authorities burned alive those who were detected, being moved by astonishment and horror. Later, those sentiments were not aroused. " Men were seen to make ordinary meals of human flesh, to use it as a dainty, and to lay up provision of it. . . . The usage, having been introduced, spread to all the provinces. Then it ceased to cause surprise. . . . People talked of it as an ordinary and indifferent thing. This indifference was due to habit and familiarity." This case shows that the horror of cannibalism is due to tradition in the mores. Diodorus says that the ancient Egyptians, during a famine, ate each other rather than any animal which they considered sacred. [2]

349. Cannibalism and ghost fear. Human sacrifice and cannibalism are not necessarily conjoined. Often it seems as if they once were so, but have been separated. [3] Whatever men want ghosts want. If the former are cannibals, the latter will be the same. Often the notion is that the gods eat the souls. In this view, the men eat the flesh of sacrificed beasts and sacrifice the blood, in which is the life or soul, to the gods. This the Jews did. They also burned the kidneys, the fat of the kidneys, and the liver, which they thought to be the seat of life. These they might not eat. [4] When men change, the gods do not. Hence the rites of human sacrifice and cannibalism continue in religion long after they disappear from the mores, in spite of loathing. Loathing is a part of the sacrifice. [5] The self-control and self-subjugation enter into the sacrament. All who participate, in religion, in an act which gravely affects the imagination as

---

[1] *Relation de l'Egypte*, 360.   [2] Diodorus, I, 84.
[3] Ratzel, *Völkerkunde*, II, 124 ; Martius, *Ethnog. Bras.*, 129 ; *Globus*, LXXV, 260.
[4] W. R. Smith, *Relig. of the Semites*, 379.
[5] Lippert, *Kulturgesch.*, II, 292.

horrible and revolting enter into a communion with each other. Every one who desires to participate in the good to be obtained must share in the act. As we have seen above, all must participate that none may be in a position to reproach the rest. Under this view, the cannibal food is reduced to a crumb, or to a drop of blood, which may be mixed with other food. Still later, the cannibal food is only represented, e.g. by cakes in the human form, etc. In the Middle Ages the popular imagination saw a human body in the host, and conjured up operations on the host which were attributed to sorcerers and Jews, which would only be applicable to a human body. Then the New Testament language about the body and blood of Christ took on a realistic sense which was cannibalistic.

350. Cannibalism, sorcery, and human sacrifice. Among the West African tribes sacrificial and ceremonial cannibalism in fetich affairs is almost universal.[1] Serpa Pinto[2] mentions a frequent feast of the chiefs of the Bihe, for which a man and four women of specified occupations are required. The corpses are both washed and boiled with the flesh of an ox. Everything at the feast must be marked with human blood. Cannibalism, in connection with religious festivals and human sacrifice, was extravagantly developed in Mexico, Central America, and British Columbia. The rites show that the human sacrifice was sacramental and vicarious. In one case the prayer of the person who owned the sacrifice is given. It is a prayer for success and prosperity. Flesh was also bitten from the arm of a living person and eaten. A religious idea was cultivated into a mania and the taste for human flesh was developed.[3] Here also we find the usage that shamans ate the flesh of corpses, in connection with fasting and solitude, as means of professional stimulation.[4] Preuss emphasizes the large element of sorcery in the eating of parts of a human sacrifice, as practiced in Mexico.[5] The combination of sorcery, religious ritual, and cannibalism deserves very careful attention. The rites of the festival were cases of dramatic sorcery. At the annual festival of the god of war an image of the god was made of grain, seeds, and vegetables, kneaded with the blood of boys sacrificed for the purpose. This image was broken into crumbs and eaten by males only, "after the manner of our communion."[6] The Peruvians ate sacrificial cakes kneaded with the blood of human victims, "as a mark of alliance with the Inca."[7]

[1] Kingsley, *Travels in W. Afr.*, 287.   [2] *Como Eu Atravassei Afr.*, I, 148.
[3] Bancroft, *Native Races of the Pacific Coast*, I, 170 (III, 150); II, 176, 395, 689, 708; III, 413.   [4] *Ibid.*, III, 152.
[5] *Globus*, LXXXVI, 109, 112.   [6] *Bur. Ethnol.*, IX, 523.
[7] *Ibid.*, 527.

In Guatemala organs of a slain war captive were given to an old prophetess to be eaten. She was then asked to pray to the idol which she served to give them many captives.[1] Human sacrifices and sacramental cannibalism exist amongst the Bella-coola Indians in northwestern British America. Children of the poor are bought from their parents to be made sacrifices. The blood is drunk and the flesh is eaten raw. The souls of the sacrificed go to live in the sun and become birds. When the English government tried to stop these sacrifices the priests dug up corpses and ate them. Several were thus poisoned.[2]

351. Cult and cannibalism. The cases which have been cited show how cult kept up cannibalism, if no beast was substituted. Also, a great number of uses of blood and superstitions about blood appear to be survivals of cannibalism or deductions from it. The same may be said of holiday cakes of special shapes, made by peasants, which have long lost all known sense. In one part of France the last of the harvest which is brought in is made into a loaf in human shape, supposed to represent the spirit of corn or of fertility. It is broken up and distributed amongst all the villagers, who eat it.[3]

A Mogolian lama reported of a tribe, the Lhopa of Sikkim or Bhutan, that they kill and eat the bride's mother at a wedding, if they can catch no wild man.[4]

352. A burglar in West Prussia, in 1865, killed a maid-servant and cut flesh from her body out of which to make a candle for use in later acts of theft. He was caught while committing another burglary. He confessed that he ate a part of the corpse of his first-mentioned victim "in order to appease his conscience."[5]

353. Food taboos. It is most probable that dislike to eat the human body was a product of custom, and grew in the mores after other foods became available in abundance. Unusual foods now cost us an effort. Frogs' legs, for instance, repel most people at first. We eat what we learned from our parents to eat, and other foods are adopted by "acquired taste." Light is thrown on the degree to which all food preferences and taboos

---

[1] Brinton, *Nagualism*, 34.
[2] *Mitt. Berl. Mus.*, 1885, 184.
[3] PSM, XLVIII, 411.

[4] Rockhill, *Mongolia and Thibet*, 144.
[5] PSM, LIV, 217.

are a part of the mores by a comparison of some cases of food taboos. Porphyrius, a Christian of Tyre, who lived in the second half of the second century of the Christian era, says that a Phœnician or an Egyptian would sooner eat man's flesh than cow's flesh.[1] A Jew would not eat swine's flesh. A Zoroastrian could not conceive it possible that any one could eat dog's flesh. We do not eat dog's flesh, probably for the same reason that we do not eat cat's or horse's, because the flesh is tough or insipid and we can get better, but some North American Indians thought dog's flesh the very best food. The Banziris, in the French Congo, reserved dog's flesh for men, and they surround meals of it with a solemn ritual. A man must not touch his wife with his finger for a day after such a feast.[2] The inhabitants of Ponape will eat no eels, which " they hold in the greatest horror." The word used by them for eel means " the dreadful one." [3] Dyaks eat snakes, but reject eels.[4] Some Melanesians will not eat eels because they think that there are ghosts in them.[5] South African Bantus abominate fish.[6] Some Canary Islanders ate no fish.[7] Tasmanians would rather starve than eat fish.[8] The Somali will eat no fish, considering it disgraceful to do so.[9] They also reject game and birds.[10] These people who reject eels and fish renounce a food supply which is abundant in their habitat.

354. Food taboos in ethnography. Some Micronesians eat no fowl.[11] Wild Veddahs reject fowl.[12] Tuaregs eat no fish, birds, or eggs.[13] In eastern Africa many tribes loathe eggs and fowl as food. They are as much disgusted to see a white man eat eggs as a white man is to see savages eat offal.[14] Some Australians will not eat pork.[15] Nagas and their neighbors think roast dog a great delicacy. They will eat anything, even an elephant which has been three days buried, but they abominate milk, and find the smell of tinned lobster too strong.[16] Negroes in the French Congo " have a perfect horror of the idea of drinking milk." [17]

[1] *De Abstinentia*, II, 11.
[2] Brunache, *Cent. Afr.*, 69.
[3] Christian, *Caroline Isl.*, 73.
[4] Perelaer, *Dyaks*, 27.
[5] Codrington, *Melanesians*, 177.
[6] Fritsch, *Eingeb. Südafr.*, 107.
[7] *N. S. Amer. Anthrop.*, II, 454.
[8] Ling Roth, *Tasmanians*, 101.
[9] Paulitschke, *Ethnog. N.O. Afr.*, I, 155.
[10] *Ibid.*, II, 27.
[11] Finsch, *Ethnol. Erfahr.*, III, 53.
[12] *N. S. Ethnol. Soc.*, II, 304.
[13] Duveyrier, *Touaregs du Nord*, 401.
[14] Volkens, *Kilimandscharo*, 244.
[15] Smyth, *Victoria*, I, 237.
[16] JAI, XI, 63; XXII, 245.
[17] Kingsley, *West Afr. Studies*, 451.

355. Expiation for taking life. The most primitive notion we can find as to taking life is that it is wrong to kill any living thing except as a sacrifice to some superior power. This dread of destroying life, as if it was the assumption of a divine prerogative to do so, gives a background for all the usages with regard to sacrifice and food. " In old Israel all slaughter was sacrifice, and a man could never eat beef or mutton except as a religious act." Amongst the Arabs, " even in modern times, when a sheep or camel is slain in honor of a guest, the good old custom is that the host keeps open house for all his neighbors." [1] In modern Hindostan food which is ordinarily tabooed may be eaten if it has been killed in offering to a god. Therefore an image of the god is set up in the butcher's shop. All the animals are slaughtered nominally as an offering to it. This raises the taboo, and the meat is bought and eaten without scruple.[2] Thus it is that the taboo on cannibalism may be raised by religion, or that cannibalism may be made a duty by religion. Amongst the ancient Semites some animals were under a food taboo for a reason which has two aspects at the same time : they were both offensive (ritually unclean) and sacred. What is holy and what is loathsome are in like manner set aside. The Jews said that the Holy Scriptures rendered him who handled them unclean. Holy and unclean have a common element opposed to profane. In the case of both there is devotion or consecration to a higher power. If it is a good power, the thing is holy ; if a bad power, it is unclean. He who touches either falls under a taboo, and needs purification.[3] The tabooed things could only be eaten sacrificially and sacramentally, i.e. as disgusting and unusual they had greater sacrificial force.[4] This idea is to be traced in all ascetic usages, and in many mediæval developments of religious usages which introduced repulsive elements, to heighten the self-discipline of conformity. In the Caroline Islands turtles are sacred to the gods and are eaten only in illness or as sacrifices.[5]

356. Philosophy of cannibalism. If cannibalism began in the interest of the food supply, especially of meat, the wide ramifications of its relations are easily understood. While men were unable to cope with the great beasts cannibalism was a leading feature of social life, around which a great cluster of interests centered. Ideas were cultivated by it, and it became regulative and directive as to what ought to be done. The sentiments of kinship made it seem right and true that the nearest relatives

[1] W. R. Smith, *Relig. of Semites*, 142, 283.
[2] Wilkins, *Mod. Hinduism*, 168.
[3] Bousset, *Relig. des Judenthums*, 124.
[4] W. R. Smith, *Relig. of Semites*, 290; Isaiah lxv. 4; lxvi. 3, 17; swine, dog, and mouse.
[5] Kubary, *Karolinen Archipel*, 168.

should be eaten. Further deductions followed, of which the cases given are illustrations. As to enemies, the contrary sentiments found place in connection with it. It combined directly with ghost fear. The sacramental notion seems born of it. When the chase was sufficiently developed to give better food the taboo on human flesh seemed no more irrational than the other food taboos above mentioned. Swans and peacocks were regarded as great dainties in the Middle Ages. We no longer eat them. Snakes are said to be good eating, but most of us would find it hard to eat them. Yet why should they be more loathsome than frogs or eels? Shipwrecked people, or besieged and famine-stricken people, have overcome the loathing for human flesh rather than die. Others have died because they could not overcome it, and have thus rendered the strongest testimony to the power of the mores. In general, the cases show that if men are hungry enough, or angry enough, they may return to cannibalism now. Our horror of cannibalism is due to a long and broad tradition, broken only by hearsay of some far-distant and extremely savage people who now practice it. Probably the popular opinion about it is that it is wicked. It is not forbidden by the rules of any religion, because it had been thrown out of the mores before any "religion" was founded.

CHAPTER IX

SEX MORES

Meaning of sex mores. — The sex difference. — Sex difference and evolution. — The sex distinction; family institution; marriage in the mores. — Regulation is conventional, not natural. — Egoistic and altruistic elements. — Primary definition of marriage; taboo and conventionalization. — Family, not marriage, is the institution. — Endogamy and exogamy. — Polygamy and polyandry. — Consistency of the mores under polygamy or polyandry. — Mother family and father family. — Change from mother family to father family. — Capture and purchase become ceremonies. — Feminine honor and virtue; jealousy. — Virginity. — Chastity for men. — Love marriage; conjugal affection; wife. — Heroic conjugal devotion. — Hindoo models and ideals. — Slavonic sex mores. — Russian sex mores. — Tribes of the Caucasus. — Mediæval sex mores. — The standard of the "good wife"; pair marriage. — "One flesh." — Pair marriage. — Marriage in modern mores. — Pair marriage, its technical definition. — Ethics of pair marriage. — Pair marriage is monopolistic. — The future of marriage. — The normal type of sex union. — Divorce. — Divorce in ethnography. — Rabbis on divorce. — Divorce at Rome. — Pair marriage and divorce. — Divorce in the Middle Ages. — Refusal of remarriage. — Child marriage. — Child marriage in Hindostan. — Child marriage in Europe. — Cloistering women. — Second marriages; widows. — Burning of widows. — Difficulty of reform of suttee in India. — Widows and remarriage in the Christian church. — Remarriage and other-worldliness. — Free marriage. — The Japanese woman.

357. Meaning of sex mores. The sex mores are one of the greatest and most important divisions of the mores. They cover the relations of men and women to each other before marriage and in marriage, with all the rights and duties of married and unmarried respectively to the rest of the society. The mores determine what marriage shall be, who may enter into it, in what way they may enter into it, divorce, and all details of proper conduct in the family relation. In regard to all these matters it is evident that custom governs and prescribes. When positive institutions and laws are made they always take up, ordain, and regulate what the mores have long previously made facts in the social order. In the administration of law also, especially by juries, domestic relations are controlled by the mores. The decisions rendered by judges utter in dogmatic or sententious form the current notions of truth and right about those relations. Our terms "endogamy," "mother family," "polyandry," etc., are only descriptive terms for a summary of the folkways which have been established in different groups and which are capable of classification.

358. The sex difference. The economy and advantage of sex differentiation are primarily physical. "As structural complexity increases, the female generative system becomes more and more complex. All this involves a great expenditure of energy, and we can clearly see how an ovum-producing organism would benefit by being spared the additional effort required for seeking out and impregnating another organism, and how, on the other hand, organisms whose main reproductive feature is simply the production of spermatozoa would be better fitted for the work of search and impregnation if unhampered by a cumbersome female generative system. Hence the advantage of the sexes being separate." [1] Here we have the reason why the sexes are independent and complementary, but why "equality" can never be predicated of them. Power in the family, in industry, in civil affairs, war, and religion is not the same thing and cannot be. Each sex has more power for one domain, and must have less power for another. Equality is an incongruous predicate. "Under the influence of the law of battle the male has become more courageous, powerful, and pugnacious than the female. . . . So, too, the male has, in the struggle, often acquired great beauty, success on his part depending largely, in many cases, upon the choice of the females who are supposed to select the most beautiful mates. This is thought to be notably the case with birds." [2] In some few cases the female seeks the male, as in certain species of birds. Some male fish look after the eggs, and many cock-birds help to build the nest, hatch the eggs, and tend the young.[3] When the females compete for the males the female is "endowed with all the secondary characters of the polygamous male; she is the more beautiful, the more courageous, the more

[1] Campbell, *Differences in the Nervous Organization of Men and Women*, 29.
[2] *Ibid.*, 43.   [3] *Ibid.*, 34.

pugnacious." This seems to show that the secondary characters are due to sex selection.[1] Men are held to be polygamous by descent and in their "instincts as at present developed." "The instinct for promiscuous intercourse is much stronger among men than women, and unquestionably the husband is much more frequently all in all to the wife than she to him." [2]

359. Sex difference and evolution. According to the current applications of the evolution philosophy it is argued that "inheritable characters peculiar to one sex show a tendency to be inherited chiefly or solely by that sex in the offspring." [3] Women are said to be mentally more adaptable.[4] This is shown in their tact, which is regarded as a product of their desire to adapt themselves to the stronger sex, with whose muscular strength they cannot cope. If a woman should resist her husband she would provoke him, and her life would be endangered. Passive and resigned women would survive. "Here at any rate we may have *one* of the reasons why women are more passive and resigned than men." [5] Their tact is attributed to their quicker perception and to their lack of egoism. "The man, being more self-absorbed than the woman, is often less alive than she to what is going on around." [6] The man has a more stable nervous system than the woman. Combativeness and courage produce that stability; emotional development is antagonistic to it. "In proportion as the emotions are brought under intellectual control, in that proportion, other things being equal, will the nervous system become more stable." [7] Ages of subjection are also said to have produced in women a sense of dependence. Resignation and endurance are two of women's chief characteristics. "They have been educated in her from the remotest times." [8] Throughout the animal kingdom males are more variable than females. Man varies through a wider scale than woman. Dwarfs and giants, geniuses and idiots, are more common amongst men than amongst women.[9] Women use less philosophy; they do not think things out in their relations and analysis as men do.

---

[1] Campbell, *Differences in the Nervous Organization of Men and Women*, 46.
[2] *Ibid.*, 45.   [4] *Ibid.*, 66.   [6] *Ibid.*, 223.   [8] *Ibid.*, 90.
[3] *Ibid.*, 68.   [5] *Ibid.*, 53 f.   [7] *Ibid.*, 84.   [9] *Ibid.*, 133.

Miss Kingsley said that she "had met many African men who were philosophers, thinking in the terms of fetich, but never a woman so doing." [1]

On the facts of observation here enumerated nearly all will agree. The traits are certainly handed down by tradition and education. Whether they are evolutionary is far more doubtful. They are thought to be such by virtue of applications of some generalizations of evolutionary philosophy whose correctness, and whose application to this domain, have never been proved.

360. The sex distinction; family institution; marriage in the mores. The division of the human race into two sexes is the most important of all anthropological facts. The sexes differ so much in structure and function, and consequently in traits of feeling and character, that their interests are antagonistic. At the same time they are, in regard to reproduction, complementary. There is nothing in the sex relation, or in procreation, to bring about any continuing relation between a man and a woman. It is the care and education of children which first calls for such a continuing relation. The continuing relation is not therefore "in nature." It is institutional and conventional. A man and a woman were brought together, probably against their will, by a higher interest in the struggle for existence. The woman with a child needed the union more, and probably she was more unwilling to enter it. It is almost impossible to find a case of a group in which marriage does not exist, and in which the sex relation is one of true promiscuity. We are told that there is no family institution amongst the Bako, dwarfs in Kamerun. They obey animal instincts without restriction.[2] This means that the origin of the family institution lies in the period before any group formations now open to our study, and promiscuity is an inference as to what preceded what we can find. A woman with a child entered into an arrangement with a man, whether the father or not was immaterial, by which they carried on the struggle for existence together. The arrangement must have afforded advantages to both. It was produced by an agreement.

---

[1] *West Afr. Studies,* 375.   [2] *Globus.* LXXXIII, 285.

The family institution resulted and became customary by imitation. Marriage was the form of agreement between the man and the woman by which they entered into the family institution. In the most primitive form of life known to us (Australians and Bushmen) the man roams abroad in search of meat food. His wife or wives stay by the fire at a trysting place, care for the children, and collect plant food. Thus the combination comes under the form of antagonistic coöperation. It presents us the germ of the industrial organization. It is a product of the folkways, being the resultant custom which arises, in time, out of the ways of satisfying interests which separate individuals, or pairs, invent and try. It follows that marriage in all its forms is in the mores of the time and place.

361. Regulation is conventional, not natural. The sex passion affects the weal or woe of human beings far more than hunger, vanity, or ghost fear. It has far more complications with other interests than the other great motives. There is no escaping the good and ill, the pleasure and pain, which inhere in it. It has two opposite extremes, — renunciation and license. In neither one of these can peace and satisfaction be found, or escape from the irritation of antagonistic impulses. There is no ground at all for the opinion that "nature" gave men an appetite the satisfaction of which would be peaceful and satisfactory, but that human laws and institutions have put it under constraints which produce agony.[1] The truth is that license stimulates desire without limit, and ends in impotent agony. Renunciation produces agony of another kind. Somewhere between lies temperance, which seems an easy solution, but there is no definition of temperance which is generally applicable, and, wherever the limit may be set, there, on either side of it, the antagonistic impulses appear again, — one of indulgence, the other of restraint, — producing pitfalls of vice and ruin, and ever renewing the strain and torment of the problem of right and duty. Therefore regulation is imperatively called for by the facts of "nature," and the regulation must come from intelligence and judgment. No determination of what the regulation should

[1] Bebel, *Die Frau*, 73.

be has ever yet been found in law or ethics which does not
bear harshly on great numbers, and in all stages of civilization
numbers are found who violate the regulations and live outside
of them.

362. Egoistic and altruistic elements. Here, then, is the
case : the perpetuation of the species requires the coöperation
of two complementary sexes. The sex relation is antagonistic
to the struggle for existence, and so arouses egoistic sentiments
and motives, while it is itself very egoistic. It is sometimes
said that the struggle for existence is egoistic and reproduction
altruistic, but this view rests upon a very imperfect analysis. It
means that a man who has won food may eat it by himself,
while reproduction assumes the coöperation of others. So far,
well ; but the struggle for existence assumes and demands co-
operation in the food quest and a sharing of the product in
all but a very small class of primitive cases ; and the sex passion
is purely egoistic, except in a very small class of cases of high
refinement, the actuality of which may even be questioned.
The altruistic element in reproduction belongs to the mores,
and is due to life with children, affection for them, with sacrifice and devotion to them, as results produced by experience.
It is clear that a division between the food quest as egoistic
and reproduction as altruistic cannot be made the basis of
ethical constructions. To get the good and avoid the ill there
is required a high play of intelligence, good sense, and of all
altruistic virtues. Under such a play of interests and feelings,
from which no one is exempt, mass phenomena are produced by
the ways of solving the problem which individuals and pairs
hit upon. The wide range and contradictoriness of the folkways
in regard to family life show how helpless and instinctive the
struggle to solve the problem has been. Our own society shows
how far we still are from a thorough understanding of the
problem and from a satisfactory solution of it. It must be added
that the ruling elements in different societies have molded the
folkways to suit their own interests, and thus they have disturbed
and confused the process of making folkways, and have spoiled
the result.

363. Primary definition of marriage ; taboos and conventionalization. The definition of marriage consists in stating what, at any time and place, the mores have imposed as regulations on the relations of a man and woman who are coöperatively carrying on the struggle for existence and the reproduction of the species. The regulations are always a conventionalization which sets the terms, modes, and conditions under which a pair may cohabit. It is, therefore, impossible to formulate a definition of marriage which will cover all forms of it throughout the history of civilization. In all lower civilization it is a tie of a woman to a man for the interests of both (or of the man). It follows that the sex relation has been a great arena for the use and perfection of the mores, since personal experience and reflection never ceased, and a great school for the education of the race in the use of intelligence, the development of sympathetic sentiments, and in a sense of the utility of ethical regulations. The sex taboo is the set of inhibitions which control and restrain the intercourse of the sexes with each other in ordinary life. At the present time, in civilized countries, that intercourse is limited by taboo, not by law. The nature and degree of the taboo are in the mores. Spanish, French, English, and American women, in the order named, are under less and less strict limitations in regard to ordinary social intercourse with men. The sex taboo could, therefore, be easily pursued and described through the whole history of civilization and amongst all nations. It seems to be arbitrary, although no doubt it has always been due, in its origin, to correct or incorrect judgments of conditions and interests. It is always conventional. That it has been and is recognized is the sum of its justification. When Augustine met the objection that Jacob had four wives he replied that that was no crime, because it was under the custom (*mos*) of Jacob's time.[1] This was a complete answer, but it was an appeal to the supreme authority of the mores.

364. Family, not marriage, is the institution. Although we speak of marriage as an institution, it is only an imperfect one. It has no structure. The family is the institution, and it was

[1] *Decret. Gratiani*, II, c. XXXII, qu. iv, c. 7.

antecedent to marriage. Marriage has always been an elastic and variable usage, as it now is. Each pair, or other marital combination, has always chosen its own " ways " of living within the limits set by the mores. In fact the use of language reflects the vagueness of marriage, for we use the word " marriage " for wedding, nuptials, or matrimony (wedlock). Only the last could be an institution. Wedlock has gone through very many phases, and has by no means evolved along lines of harmonious and advancing development. In the earliest forms of the higher civilization, in Chaldea and Egypt, man and wife were, during wedlock, in a relation of rational free coöperation. Out of this two different forms of wedlock have come, the harem system and pair marriage. The historical sequences by which the former has been produced could be traced just as easily as those which have led up to the latter. There is no more necessity in one than in the other. Wedlock is a mode of associated life. It is as variable as circumstances, interests, and character make it within the conditions. No rules or laws can control it. They only affect the condition against which the individuals react. No laws can do more than specify ways of entering into wedlock, and the rights and duties of the parties in wedlock to each other, which the society will enforce. These, however, are but indifferent externals. All the intimate daily play of interests, emotions, character, taste, etc., are beyond the reach of the bystanders, and that play is what makes wedlock what it is for every pair. Nevertheless the relations of the parties are always deeply controlled by the current opinions in the society, the prevalent ethical standards, the approval or condemnation passed by the bystanders on cases between husbands and wives, and by the precepts and traditions of the old. Thus the mores hold control over individual taste and caprice, and individual experience reacts against the control. All the problems of marriage are in the intimate relations. When they affect large numbers they are brought under the solution of the mores. Therefore the history of marriage is to be interpreted by the mores, and its philosophy must be sought in the fact that it is an ever-moving product of the mores.

365. Endogamy and exogamy. Although it seems, at first consideration, that savages could not have perceived the alleged evils of inbreeding, yet a full examination of the facts is convincing that they did do so. In like manner, they were led to try to avert overpopulation by folkways. They acted "instinctively," or automatically, not rationally. Inbreeding preserves a type but weakens the stock. Outbreeding strengthens the stock but loses the type. In our own mores each one is forbidden to marry within a certain circle or outside of another circle. The first is the consanguine group of first cousins and nearer. The latter is the race to which we belong. Royal and noble castes are more strictly limited within the caste. Amongst savage peoples there were two ideas which were in conflict: (1) all the women of a group were regarded as belonging to all the men of that group; (2) a wife conquered abroad was a possession and a trophy. Endogamy and exogamy are forms of the mores in which one of these policies has been adopted to the exclusion of the other. Of that we have an example in civilized society, where royal persons, in order to find fitting mates, marry cousins, or uncles, or nieces, and bring on the family the evils of close inbreeding (Spain); or they take slave women as wives and breed out the blood of their race (Athenians, Arabs). The due adjustment of inbreeding and outbreeding is always a difficult problem of policy for breeders of animals. It is the same for men. The social interests favor inbreeding, by which property is united or saved from dispersion, and close relationship seems to assure acquaintance. At Venice, in the time of glory and luxury, great dowers seemed to threaten to dissipate great family fortunes. It became the custom to contract marriages only between families which could give as much as they got. "This was not the least of the causes of the moral and physical decline of the Venetian aristocracy." [1]

366. Polygamy and polyandry. Polygamy and polyandry are two cases of family organization which are expedient under certain life conditions, and which came into existence or became obsolete according to changes in the life conditions, although

---

[1] Molmenti, *Venezia nella Vita Privata*, 393.

there are also cases of survival, due to persistence of the mores, after the life conditions have so changed that the custom has become harmful. Population, so far as we know, normally contains equal numbers of the two sexes, except that there are periods in which, for some unknown reason, births of one sex greatly preponderate over those of the other.[1] There are also groups in which the food quest, or other duty, of the men is such that many lives are lost and so the adults of the two sexes are unequal in number.[2] Therefore, in a normal population, polygamy would compel many men, and polyandry many women, to remain unmarried. Polyandry might then be supplemented by female infanticide. That any persons in a primitive society should be destined to celibacy is so arbitrary and strange an arrangement that strong motives for it must be found in the life conditions. Two forms of polygamy must be distinguished. (a) In primitive society women are laborers, and the industrial system is often such that there is an economic advantage in having a number of women to one man. In those cases polygamy becomes interwoven with the whole social and political system. Other customs will also affect the expediency of polygamy. Every well-to-do man of the Bassari, in Togo, has three wives, because children are suckled for three years.[3] (b) In higher civilization, with surplus wealth, polygamy is an affair of luxury, sensuality, and ostentation. It is only in the former case that polygamy is socially expedient, and that women welcome more wives to help do the work and do not quarrel with each other. In the latter case, polygamy is an aberration of the mores, due to selfish force. There are very many examples of polygamy in which the two motives are combined. These are transition stages. Polyandry is due to a hard struggle for existence or to a policy of not dividing property. A Spartan who had a land allotment was forced to marry. His younger brothers lived with him and sometimes were also husbands to his wife. Wives were also lent out of friendship or in order to get vigorous offspring.[4]

---

[1] For cases see JAI, XXIII, 364.　　[2] *Globus*, LXXXVII, 179 (Caroline Isl.).
[3] *Globus*, LXXXIII, 312.
[4] Xenophon, *Lacedæmon*, I, 7, 8; Plutarch, *Lycurgus*, 15.

Here state policy or the assumed advantage of physical vigor overrode the motives of monogamy which prevailed in the surrounding civilization. In Plautus's comedy *Stichus* a case is referred to in which two slaves have one woman (wife). Roman epitaphs are cited in which two men jointly celebrate a common wife.[1] These are cases of return to an abandoned usage, under the stress of poverty. An emigrating group must generally have contained more men than women. Polyandry was very sure to occur. It is said that immigrant groups can be found in the United States in which polyandry exists, being produced in this way. Many aboriginal tribes in India, amongst which the Todas are the best known, practice polyandry. Przewalsky says that in Tibet polyandry is attributed to a tax on houses in which there is a married woman.[2] Primarily it is due to poverty and a hard habitat. Two, three, or even four brothers have a wife in common. The Russian traveler adds that rich men have a wife each, or even two, and Cunningham[3] confirms this; that is to say, then, that the number of wives follows directly the economic power of the man. The case only illustrates the close interdependence of capital and marriage which we shall find at every stage. In the days of Venetian glory "often four or five men united to maintain one woman, in whose house they met daily to laugh, eat, and jest, without a shadow of jealousy. If, however, the cleverness of a woman brought a young patrician into a mesalliance, the state promptly dissolved the bond in its own way."[4] The polyandry of the Nairs, on the Malabar coast, has been cited to prove that polyandry is not due to poverty. It is due to the unwillingness to subdivide the property of the family, which is of the modified mother-family form, all the immediate kin holding together and keeping the property undivided. Subdivisions of this people differ as to details of the custom and it is now becoming obsolete. Of course "moral doctrines" have been invented to bring the custom under a broad principle.[5] It appears, however, that the husbands, in the Nair system, are

[1] Pellison, *Roman Life in Pliny's Time*, 100.
[2] *Third Journey* (russ.), 259. [4] Molmenti, *Venezia nella Vita Privata*, 386.
[3] *Ladak*, 306. [5] *Madras Gov. Mus.*, III, 227.

successive, not contemporaneous. The custom is due to the Vedic notion that every virgin contains a demon who leaves her with the nuptial blood, causing some risk to her husband. Hence a maiden was married to a man who was to disappear after a few hours, having incurred the risk.[1] Here, then, we have a case of aberrant mores due to a superstitious explanation of natural facts. Polygamy of the second form above defined is limited by cost. Although polygamy is allowed under Mohammedan law, it is not common for a Mohammedan to have more than one wife, on account of expense and trouble. Lane estimated at not more than one in twenty the number of men in Egypt, in the first half of the nineteenth century, who had more than one wife. If a woman is childless, her husband may take another wife, especially if he likes the first one too well to divorce her.[2] That is to say, polygamy and divorce are alternatives. Other authorities state that polygamy is more common and real amongst Mohammedans than would appear from Lane's statement. In the cities of Arabia more than one wife is the rule, and the Arabs in Jerusalem take three or four wives as soon as they have sufficient means. The poorest have at least two.[3]

367. Consistency of the mores under polygamy or polyandry. When the life conditions, real or imagined, produce polygamy, monogamy, or polyandry, all the mores conform to the one system or the other, and develop it on every side. All the concepts of right and wrong — rights, duties, authority, societal policy, and political interest — are implicit in the mores. They must necessarily all be consistent. A Nair woman is no more likely to overstep the mores of her society than an English woman is to overstep the mores of hers. " The relations between the sexes in Malabar are unusually happy."[4] Tibetan men are said to be courteous to women.[5] Tibetan women like polyandry. They sneer at the dullness and monotony of monogamic life.[6] Thus the ethics follow the customs.

---

[1] Zimmer, *Altind. Leben,* 313; JASB, II, 316, 319; JAI, XII, 291.
[2] Lane, *Modern Egyptians,* I, 274. Cf. Snouck-Hurgronje, *Mekka,* II, 106 ff.
[3] Hauri, *Islam,* 135.   [5] Rockhill in *U. S. Nat. Mus.,* 1893, 677.
[4] *Madras Gov. Mus.,* III, 229.   [6] Bishop, *Among the Thibetans,* 92.

368. Mother family and father family. The ultimate reasons
for the mother family and for a change to the father family are
in the life conditions, industrial arts, war, pressure of population,
etc. In fact, our terms are only names for a group of mores which
cover some set of interests, and we need to be on our guard
against the category fallacy, that is, against arguing from the
contents of the classification which we have made. The term
" matriarchate " encouraged this fallacy and has gone out of use.
By the mother family we mean the system in which descent and
kin are reckoned through women, not through men. In that form
of the family the relation of man and wife is one of contract.
The woman must be thought of as at her home, with her kin,
and the husband comes to her. She has great control of the
terms on which he is accepted, and she and her kin can drive
him away again, if they see fit. The children will be hers and
will remain with her. The property will remain hers, while her
husband must abandon his property when he comes to her. The
next male friend of a woman will be her brother, not her husband, and the next male guardian of a child will be his mother's
brother, not his father. Words of relationship, address, etc.,
must all conform to the fundamental notion which rules the
family. Religion, political control, modes of warfare and alliance,
and education are all constructed to fit the family-form. At
puberty boys are taken into the political organization (tribe) to
which the father belongs and get political status from that. By
birth each one is a member of a blood-kin group (clan) on which
depend blood revenge and other duties and by which marriage is
regulated. All this grows up as a part of the folkways, instinctively, without plan or guidance of intelligent control. Yet it
has been wrought out, along the same logical lines of custom and
rule, all over the world by savage peoples. We meet with many
variations of it in transitional forms, or in combination with later
institutions, but they belong to the time when this arrangement
is breaking down, and passing into the father family. The
mother family system is definite and complete when flourishing
and normal. By the totem device the mother family is made
capable of indefinite extension, and a verification is provided for

its essential facts. The status of women, in the mother family, was strong and independent. Often important societal functions were entrusted to them, and their influence was so high that it produced great results, like the conferring of glory on braves, and the election of war chiefs. In cases, as for instance the ancient Lycians, the men were treated with harshness and abuse. The distribution of social power between the sexes gave opportunity for this, and the opportunity was seized.[1]

369. Change from mother family to father family. It may well be believed that the change from the mother family to the father family is the greatest and most revolutionary in the history of civilization. By changes in the life conditions it becomes possible for the man to get his wife to himself away from her kin, and to become the owner of his children. In the mother family those arrangements could only be suggested to him as modifications of his experience which would be eagerly to be desired, i.e. as objects of idealization. When the life conditions so changed that it became possible, the father family displaced the mother family. All the folkways followed the change. Family arrangements, kin, industry, war, political organization, property, rights, must all conform to the change. The wife is obtained by capture, purchase, or later by contract. By capture or purchase she passes under her husband's dominion, and she may not be a consenting party. She loses status by the change. In the earlier period the man might get a wife by capture. She would be either a work-wife or a love-wife. Now a real status-wife would be obtained by real or fictitious capture and get her status from that fact; that is, she becomes very much at the mercy of her husband. The same is true of a purchased wife. The relation of a wife to her husband is analogous to property. The same is true of the relation of children to their father. The husband gives, sells, or lends wife or daughters as he sees fit, although an interference with his dominion over them without his consent would be a thing to be earnestly resented. Loyalty and fidelity to husband became the highest duties of wives, which the husband enforced by physical penalties. Female honor, for

[1] Herod., I, 173.

wives, consisted in chastity, which meant self-submission to the
limitations which men desired in wives and which the mores had
approved, for the mores teach the women what conduct on their
part is "right," and teach them that it is "right" that they
should be taken as wives by capture or purchase. Female virtue
and honor, therefore, acquire technical definitions out of the
mores, which are not parallel to any definitions of virtue and
honor as applied to males. In Deut. xxi. 10 the case of a man
enamored of a captive woman is considered, and rules are set
for it. The woman may not be sold for money after she has
been "humbled." It is evident that the notions of right and
wrong, and of rights in marriage and the family, are altogether
contingent and relative. In the mores of any form of the family
the ideas of rights, and of right and wrong, will conform to the
theory of the institution, and they may offer us notions of moral
things which are radically divergent or antagonistic.

370. Capture and purchase become ceremonies. As population
increases and tribes are pushed closer together, capture loses
violence and is modified by a compromise, with payment of
money as a composition, and by treaty, until it becomes a ceremony. Then purchase degenerates into a ceremony, partly by
idealization, i.e. the purchase ceremony is necessary, but the
arrangement would seem more honorable if some other construction were put on it. The father, if he takes the customary bride
price but is rich and loves his daughter, so that he wants to
soften for her the lot of a wife as women generally find it, gives
a dowry and by that binds her husband to stipulations as to the
rights and treatment which she shall enjoy. In Homer's time,
no man of rank and wealth gave his daughter without a dowry,
although he took gifts for her, even, if she was in great demand,
to a greater value.[1] What the rich and great do sets the fashion
which others follow as far as they can. In the laws of Manu we
see purchase not yet obsolete, but already regarded as shameful,
if it really is a sale, and so subjected to idealization; that is, they
try to put another construction on it. The ceremonies of purchase and capture lasted for a very long time, because there was

[1] Schoemann, *Griech. Alterthümer*, I, 51.

no other way to indicate the *bond* of wedlock until the promise came into use. That has never furnished a bond of equal reality to that of capture or purchase.

371. Feminine honor and virtue. Jealousy. As the old ceremonies become obsolete the property idea fades out of the marital relation, and the woman's exclusive devotion to her husband is no longer a rational inference from capture or purchase by him, but becomes a sentiment of sex. Idealization comes into play again and sets a standard of female honor and duty which rests on womanhood only, and therefore does not apply to men. It is the lot of every woman to stand beside some man, and to give her strength and life to help him in every way which circumstances offer opportunity for. Out of this relation come her ideas of her honor, duties, and virtue. Jealousy on the part of the husband also changes its sense. He thinks it an abomination to lend, sell, or give his wife. Jealousy is not now the sentiment of a property owner, but it is a masculine sex sentiment which corresponds to the woman's sex honor and duty. What she gives to him alone he accepts on the same basis of exclusiveness.

Darwin[1] argued from the strength of jealousy amongst animals " as well as from the analogy of the lower animals, more particularly of those which come nearest to man," that promiscuity could not have prevailed shortly before man " attained his present rank in the zoölogical scale." Then he refers to the anthropoid apes, which are either monogamous, or pair off for a limited time, or are polygamous in separate families, or still again polygamous but living in a society. The jealousy of the males, and their special weapons for battling with their rivals, make promiscuity in a state of nature extremely improbable. " It does not seem possible for us to apprehend the emotion here called ' jealousy ' when shown by an animal. Amongst uncivilized men the sentiment is that of the property holder. To lend or give a wife is consistent with that sentiment, not a violation of it. Hence it does not prove that jealousy does not exist."[2] The Veddahs are very careful of their wives. They will not allow strangers in their villages, and do not even let their brothers approach their wives or offer them food.[3] They have pure marital customs. Their neighbors, the Singhalese, have not pure marital customs and are not jealous.[4] In the East Indies, not in

[1] *Descent of Man*, 590.
[2] Westermarck, *Marriage*, 130.
[3] Sarasin, *Veddahs*, 462.
[4] Schmidt, *Ceylon*, 277.

all tribes but in many, betrothed persons are separated until their marriage.[1] Kubary says that the jealousy of the Palau Islanders is less a sign of wounded feelings than of care for external propriety.[2] An oa ape (a gibbon) showed jealousy whenever a little Malay girl, his playmate, was taken away from him.[3] Wellhausen [4] says that "the suspicious jealousy, not of the love of their wives, but of their own property rights, is a prominent characteristic of the Arabs, of which they are proud." The blood kin guard their property right in the maiden as jealously as the man guards his property right in his wife. A Papuan kills an adulterer, not on account of his own honor, but to punish an infringement of his property rights. The former idea is foreign to him. He does, however, show jealousy of a handsome young man who captivates the women.[5] In 1898 a pair of wolves were kept as public pets in the Capitol at Rome. The male killed a cub, his own offspring, out of jealousy of the affection of the female for it. Then the female died of grief.[6] These cases show very different forms of jealousy. The jealousy of husband and wife is similar, but not the same as any one of them, and it differs at different stages of civilization. It depends on the exclusiveness and intenseness of devotion which spouses are held to owe each other. Beasts do not manifest an emotion of jealousy so uniform or universal as Darwin assumes in his argument, nor any sentiment like that of a half-civilized man. The latter can always coerce the woman to himself, but jealousy arises when the woman is left free to dispose of her own devotion or attention, and she is supposed to direct it to her husband, out of affection and preference. It is the breach of this affection and preference which constitutes the gravamen.

372. Virginity. We have many examples of peoples amongst whom girls are entirely free until married, on the rational ground that they are under obligations to nobody. They are under no taboo, marriage being the first application of the sex taboo. Farnell [7] says that the first sense of *parthenos* was not "virgin," but unmarried. The Oriental goddess of impure love was parthenos. Artemis was perhaps, at first, a goddess of people who had not yet settled marriage mores, but had the mother family, amongst whom women were powerful. In the development of the father family fathers restricted daughters in order to make

[1] *Bijdragen tot T. L. en V.-kunde*, XXXV, 215.
[2] *Soc. Einrichtungen der Pelauer*, 59.
[3] *Umschau*, VI, 52, after Haeckel, *Aus Insulinde*.
[4] *Ehe bei den Arabern*, 447.
[5] Krieger, *Neu Guinea*, 300, 321.
[6] *London Graphic*, 1902, 534.
[7] *Cults of the Greek States*, 448.

them more valuable as wives. Here comes in the notion of virginity and pre-nuptial chastity. This is really a negative and exclusive notion. It is an appeal to masculine vanity, and is a singular extension of the monopoly principle. His wife is to be his from the cradle, when he did not know her. Here, then, is a new basis for the sex honor of women and the jealousy of men. Chastity for the unmarried meant — no one ; for the married — none but the husband. The mores extended to take in this doctrine, and it has passed into the heart of the mores of all civilized peoples, to whom it seems axiomatic or " natural." It has often been declared absurd that sex honor, especially for women, should be made to depend on a negative. It seems to make an ascetic and arbitrary standard for everyday life. In fact, however, the negation is imposed by the nature of the sex passion and by the conditions of human life. The passion tends to excess. What is " natural " is therefore evil. Negation, restraint, renunciation, are imposed by expediency. Perhaps it is the only case in which man is driven to error and evil by a great force in his nature, and is thus forced, if he would live well, to find a discipline for himself in intelligent self-control and in arbitrary rules. This would justify the current usage of language in which " morals " refers especially to the sex relation.

373. Chastity for men. In modern times there is a new extension of idealization, by which it is attempted to extend to men the same standard of chastity and duty of chastity as to women. Two questions are here confused : (a) whether unmarried men and women are to be bound by the same obligation of chastity ; (b) whether married men and women are to be bound by the same rule of exclusion. The Hindoo lawgivers demand the same fidelity from husband and wife.[1] In the treatise on *Economics* which is ascribed to Aristotle,[2] although there is no dogmatic statement of law or duty, all the prescriptions for the husband and wife are the same, and the man is said to injure the wife by infidelity. Aristotle[3] propounds the rule of taboo on all sex relations except in marriage, which is the doctrine of pair marriage

---

[1] Strange, *Hindu Law*, I, 57.
[2] *Economica*, I, 4.   [3] *Politics*, VII, 16.

(sec. 383). In the *Economicus* of Xenophon [1] the relations of husband and wife are expounded at length in terms of great respect and esteem for a wife. The work seems to be rhetorical and dramatic, not actual, and it is represented as very exceptional and astonishing that such relations should exist between any man and his wife. In Plutarch's *Morals* the tract on " Conjugal Precepts " is written in an elevated tone. It is not specific and seems open to the suspicion of being a " pose." However, the doctrine is that of equal duty for husband and wife, and it may be taken to prove that that was the doctrine of the neostoics. Seneca wrote, " You know that it is a base thing that he who demands chastity of his wife should himself corrupt the wives of others." [2] And again, " Let him know that it will be the worst kind of an injury to his wife for him to have a mistress." [3] Augustine tells a story that Antoninus Pius granted a man a divorce for adultery of his wife, provided the man could show that he had, by his mode of life, maintained fidelity to his wife, and that the emperor added the dictum that " it would be unjust that a man should be able to exact a fidelity which he did not himself observe." [4] Augustine himself maintained the full equality of spouses in rights and duties. Ulpian said that " it seems to be very unjust that a man demands chastity of his wife while he himself does not show an example of it." This dictum got into the *Digest* where the jurists of all succeeding ages could have it before their eyes.[5] It did not often arrest their attention. These utterances, so far as they are sincere expressions of convictions, do not represent the conduct of any school, and perhaps not even that of the men who recorded them. They belong to a period of great corruption of the sex mores of the upper classes, and of rapid extension of such corruption to the lower classes. A character in Plautus's comedy of *The Merchant*[6] complains of the difference in codes for unchaste husbands and unchaste wives. If every woman has to be content with one husband, why should not every man be forced to be content with one wife? Jerome

[1] VII–IX.
[2] *Epist.*, XCIV, 26.
[3] *Ibid.*, XCV, 39.
[4] *Opera* (Paris, 1635), VI, 358.
[5] *Digest*, XLVIII, 13, 5.
[6] Act IV, scene 8.

made the most explicit statement of the Christian rule: "Amongst us [Christians] what is not permitted to women is not permitted to men. The same obligation is held to rest on equal conditions." [1] This is the assertion of a celibate and an ascetic. Perhaps it may be held to apply to pre-marital duty, but it is doubtful whether he had that in mind. All the other statements quoted apply only to the mutuality of conjugal duty. Of all of them it must be said that they are isolated flights of moral enthusiasm, and by no means present the prevailing code or the mores of the time. They do not express the life rules which have ever yet been observed by any but selected and limited classes in any society. The writings of Chrysostom and Augustine show plainly that the Christians of Jerome's time did not practice the doctrine which he uttered. It has never yet been a part of the mores of any society that the same standards of chastity should be enforced against both sexes before marriage. "At the present day, although the standard of morals is far higher than in pagan Rome, it may be questioned whether the inequality of the censure which is bestowed on the two sexes is not as great as in the days of paganism." [2] Conjugal affection has been the great cause of masculine fidelity in marriage. Laertes refused to take Eurykleia lest he should hurt his wife's feelings.[3] Plutarch, in his tract on "Love," dwells upon its controlling power, its exclusiveness, and the devotion it cultivates. Observation and experience of this kind may have produced the modern conviction that a strong affection between spouses is the best guarantee of happiness and truth. This conviction, with the code which belongs with it, have spread further and further, through wider and wider classes, and it is now the accepted moral principle that there ought to be no sex gratification except inside of pair marriage. What that means is that no one could formulate and maintain in public discussion any other rule as more reasonable and expedient to be the guiding principle of the mores, although it has not yet become such. Also, "the fundamental truth that the same act can never be at once venial for a man to demand and infamous for a woman to

---

[1] Migne, *Patrol. Latina*, XXII, 691.   [2] Lecky, *Eur. Morals*, II, 346.
[3] *Od.*, I, 433.

accord, though nobly enforced by the early Christians, has not passed into the popular sentiment of Christendom."[1] Passing by the assertion that the early Christians enforced any such rule, which may well be questioned, we ask: Why are these views not in the mores? Undoubtedly it is because they are dogmatic in form, invented and imposed by theological authority[2] or philosophical speculation. They do not grow out of the experience of life and cannot be verified by it. Woman bears an unequal share of the responsibilities and duties of sex and reproduction just as certainly and justly as man bears an unequal share of the responsibilities and duties of property, war, and politics. The reasons are in ultimate physiological facts by virtue of which one is a woman and the other is a man.

374. Love marriage. Conjugal affection. "Wife." It must be assumed that even in the lowest form of society a man may have preferred one woman to others, but love between a man and a woman is not a phenomenon of uncivilized society. It begins with wealth and luxury. Love stories can be found in very early folklore, legends, and poetry, but they belong to idealization, to romance and unreality. Realistic love stories are now hardly a century old. It is evident that they lead idealization. They put cases and solve them, and every reader forms a judgment whether the case has actuality and whether the solution is correct. Love in half-civilization and in antiquity was erotic only. The Greeks conceived of it as a madness by which a person was afflicted through the caprice or malevolence of some god or goddess. Such a passion is necessarily evanescent. The ancient peoples in general, and the Semites in particular, did not think this passion an honorable or trustworthy basis of marriage. The Kaffirs think that a Christian wife, married for love, is shameful. They compare her to a cat, the only animal which, amongst them, has no value, but is obtained as a gift.[3] The *gandharva* marriage of the Hindoos was a love marriage, and was not honorable. It was free love and became, in practice, an entirely informal union without institutional guarantees.[4] This would be, at best,

---

[1] Lecky, *Eur. Morals*, II, 347.
[2] *Ibid.*, 135.
[3] *Globus*, LXXV, 271.
[4] Wilkins, *Modern Hinduism*, 159.

a conscience marriage, to which a man would adhere from a sense of duty, the strength of which would depend on personal character only.

In all these cases the views entertained were justified, if love meant only erotic passion. On the other hand, we have seen (sec. 362) that conjugal love controls the will by the highest motives. It is based on esteem, confidence, and habit. It presents all varieties and degrees, from exploitation on one side and servility on the other, to good-fellowship on both sides. It depends on the way in which each pair arranges its affairs, develops its sentiments, and forms its habits. Conjugal affection makes great demands on the good sense, spirit of accommodation, and good nature of each. These are very great pre-conditions. It is no wonder that they often fail. In no primitive or half-civilization does the word "wife" bear the connotations which it bears to us. In Levit. xxi. 1 a case may be seen in which a man's blood kin takes precedence of his wife. Arabs, in the time of Mohammed, did not think that the conjugal tie could be as serious and strong as the kin tie, because the former is institutional only ; that is, it is a product of convention and contract.[1] Public demonstrations of love they thought offensive and insulting to the woman. People of rank often admitted no suitors for their daughters. It was thought a disgrace to give a daughter into the power of an outsider. They killed female infants, not, like the poor, because they could not afford to rear them, but from fear of incurring disgrace from them.[2] By veiling the women are excluded from all social intercourse with men and from any share in intellectual interests.[3] They cannot win conjugal affection — certainly not from educated men. Erotic passion fills Mohammedan poetry and is cultivated at home. The few cultivated women of the higher classes emancipate themselves from moral restraints, often without concealment.[4] In Mohammed's last sermon he said : " You have rights against your wives and they have rights against you. They are bound not to violate marital fidelity and to commit no act of public wrong. If they do so, you have the power

---

[1] Wellhausen, *Ehe bei den Arabern*, 450.
[2] *Ibid.*, 432.
[3] Hauri, *Islam*, 124.
[4] *Ibid.*, 131.

to beat them, yet without danger to their lives." [1] Islam is not a field in which conjugal affection could be expected to develop.[2] "A Japanese who should leave his father and mother for his wife would be looked upon as an outcast." Therefore the Bible "is regarded as irreligious and immoral." [3] The notion that a man's wife is the nearest person in the world to him is a relatively modern notion, and one which is restricted to a comparatively small part of the human race.

375. Heroic conjugal devotion. In general, the European analogy for the relation of husband and wife in the rest of the world, now or in past ages, would be rather that of master and servant. The erotic sentiment has generally been thought of as independent of marriage, possible in it, generally outside of it; and it has often been thought of as improper and disgusting between husband and wife. There is a poetical suggestion in Homer that marriages are made in heaven. Zeus is said to select a man's wife with a view to the fate allotted to him.[4] Achilles says that every wise and noble man cherishes his wife.[5] Ulysses says, "Nothing is better or more conducive to prosperity than that husband and wife should live together in concord." [6] Hector and Andromache manifested faultless conjugal affection. Penelope was a type of the devoted wife, a type which must be ranked lower than that of Andromache, because it does not imply equality of the spouses. Valerius Maximus (fl. 25 A.D.) [7] gave a chapter to "Conjugal Love." He found a few cases in which spouses, both male and female, had died for or on account of each other. They do not represent the mores. There is a tragic or heroic element in them all. That is the way in which conjugal love would strike the mind of an ancient man in his most serious moments. Apuleius [8] gives the case of Charites who had intense love for her husband. Her base lover was a victim of erotic passion. Stobæus (fifth or sixth century A.D.) collected and classified passages from Greek authors on various topics. Titles 63

[1] Hauri, *Islam*, 121.
[2] Cf. Snouck-Hurgronje, *Mekka*, II, 110 ff.
[3] *Smithson. Rep.*, 1895, 673.
[4] *Od.*, XVI, 392; XX, 74; XXI, 162.
[5] *Iliad*, IX, 341.
[6] *Od.*, VI, 180.
[7] *Factorum et Dictorum Memorabilium libri novem*, IV, 6.
[8] *Metamor.* VIII.

to 73 are about women and marriage. The views expressed run to both extremes of approval and disapproval. No one of the writers has apparently any notion of conjugal affection. In some cases under the tyrannical Roman emperors of the first century women showed extreme wifely devotion.[1] Roman tombstones (not unimpeachable witnesses) testify to conjugal affection between spouses.[2] In the Icelandic sagas women show heroic devotion to their husbands, although they make their husbands much trouble by self-will and caprice.[3] The barbarian invaders of the Roman empire are reported to have been remarkable for conjugal fidelity. Salvianus excepts the Alemanni.

376. Hindoo models and ideals. In the Mahabharata, the heroic poem of Brahminism dating from about the beginning of the Christian era, much attention is given to beauty and love. Many marriages are made for love, which is regarded as the best motive. A love relation needed the approval of the girl's parents, otherwise it ran down to the *gandharva* form. A hero, who abducted a girl for his brother, released her when she pleaded that she loved another to whom she had given her promise, although her father did not yet know it. The favored lover renounced her on account of the abduction, but she said that she would never choose another. "Whether he lives long or only a short time, whether he is rich in virtue or poor, the husband is chosen once for all. When once the heart has decided and the word has been spoken, let the thing be done." [4] These words are now regarded in Hindostan as the completest and noblest possible expression of marriage and the woman's attitude to it. A model wife in the heroic period was amiable to all, and made herself beloved by politeness and friendliness, and by her virtue and proper behavior. She gave great attention to her parents-in-law. She was reserved in speech and submissive, and she charmed her husband by her grace, wit, and tenderness.[5] The Mahabharata contains episodes of strong devotion of men to their wives and of heroic self-sacrifice of wives for their

---

[1] Pliny, *Letters.*
[2] Friedländer, *Sittengesch.*, II, 410.
[3] E.g. *Burnt Njal*, 238.
[4] Holtzmann, *Ind. Sagen*, I, 253.
[5] *Ibid.*, 256.

husbands. In Hindostan now the relations of husband and wife are not mutual. The man's mother must always be the first to him. "This is in full accordance with the national sentiment which stigmatizes affection which asks for equal return as shop-keeping."[1] "Who talks of vulgar equality," asks the Hindoo wife, "when she may instead have the unspeakable blessed-ness of offering worship."[2]

377. Slavonic sex mores. The southern Slavs and people of the Caucasus have allowed their sex mores to run into some extreme forms which to outsiders seem vicious. Young married women contract a very intimate relation to their bride attendants, of whom two attend a bride on her wedding day. She is but a girl, and is given to a man whom she never saw before, does not like, and never can like ; she comes into a strange house where it is of the first importance for the rest of her life that she shall please her parents-in-law by the greatest humility and submission ; she is forbidden by custom to approach her husband freely ; she scarcely sees him during the day ; yet she may freely converse with his brothers, who were her bride attendants. The elder one, if he is married, and if he is polite to her, becomes her best friend. An Albanian who has been away at work will not bring back a gift for his wife. He shows more attention to the wife of his elder brother. The Servian bride is ashamed of her marital relation, and thinks it indecent to address her husband in public, even after she has borne him children. He remains a stranger to her, and her relation to him is scarcely more than that of sex. Her brother she loves beyond any other. She will mourn for him with the deepest sorrow, but it would be a shame for a woman to mourn for her husband, much more for a bride to mourn for her bridegroom. In former times it was improper for a man to begin conjugal life immediately after marriage. The bride attendants, brothers of the groom, spent the first night by the side of the bride, and for the next three nights the mother or sister of the groom slept with the bride. The groom is reluctant. A Servian woman is derided if she has a child within a year after mar-riage. In some districts sex morality is very high, in others

---

[1] Nivedita, *Web of Indian Life*, 33.   [2] *Ibid.*, 45.

very low. In Carinthia it is worst. There, in the Gurkthal, the illegitimate births are twice as numerous as the legitimate, so that the marriage institution hardly exists. In Slavonic Croatia persons who marry are indifferent to each other's previous conduct with others. Amongst other southern Slavs, at a wedding, the groom must neither talk nor eat, out of shame, and the bride must weep while being dressed. It is reported from Bocca di Cattaro, in the Balkan peninsula, that public contempt is so severe against illicit acts by men before marriage that such acts are very rare amongst those who have any reputation or position to lose.[1]

378. Russian sex mores. A custom widely prevalent through parts of Great Russia and the adjacent Slavonic regions, until the nineteenth century, was that the father married his son, as a boy, to a marriageable young woman, whom the father then took as his own concubine. When the son grew up his wife was advanced in life and the mother of several children. He then did what his father had done. The large house and joint family offered temptation to this custom, and has generally been believed to be to blame for it. Rhamm contradicts that opinion.[2] The same custom existed amongst the Bulgarians.[3] Another motive for it is suggested, that the father wanted to increase the number of laborers in the big house. In 1623, in Poland, the death penalty was provided for a man who should so abuse his daughter-in-law.[4] The same custom is reported from the Tamils of southeast India.[5] In the mountains on the southwestern frontier of Russia there was, in the eighteenth century, an almost entire lack of sex mores. Amongst all the Slavonic peoples females are in a very inferior status and owe formal deference to males. In Bulgaria the wives are from five to ten years older than the husbands, because boys of fourteen begin to make love, but to adult marriageable women.[6] All these facts make it a phenomenon worthy of special mention that the people of the Ukrain are very continent, cherish a high ideal of love between the sexes, and greatly dislike

[1] *Globus*, LXXXII, 104, 187–194, 279.
[2] *Ibid.*, 322.
[3] Strausz, *Die Bulgaren*, 309.
[4] *Globus*, LXXIX, 155.
[5] *Madras Gov. Mus.*, II, 162.
[6] *Globus*, LXXXII, 323.

all improprieties in language and conversation.[1] The popular Russian wedding songs are sad. The bride is addressed as a happy child, free in her father's house, with a sad future before her, of which she is blissfully ignorant.[2] In Karelia "a bride radiant with happiness is an unknown sight. With the betrothal begins the time of tears, which lasts until the marriage feast in the house of the bridegroom. Even if she is happy and contented the mores require that she shall shed tears and affect sadness."[3] The "wailer" is a functionary in a Russian village. She teaches the bride to bewail the loss of her "maiden freedom."[4]

379. Tribes of the Caucasus and Sahara. The Cherkess of the Caucasus live in big houses, in a joint family, under the authority of a patriarch. Wives were bought or captured in common, but so many as the men. Darinsky thinks that those who could, and wanted to, buy separate wives threatened the arrangement. Hence the men, in a body, opposed monogamic unions. Such unions were a crime against the crowd. Hence the customs arose which are now prevalent, — the concealment of all marital relations, the public ignoring of each other by the spouses, and the practical jokes and horseplay at weddings by boys and neighbors. It is a survival of old manifestations of opposition and disapproval.[5] The men of the tribes in Sahara are often absent for days together. This gives the women liberty. The men begrudge this and punish the women for assumed infidelity. Some of the women are famous prostitutes.[6]

380. Mediæval sex mores. The mediæval sex mores were produced out of two opposite currents of thought, — that women were evil and dangerous and to be shunned, and that women were lovely and adorable, and worthy of reverence and worship. Both of these sets of ideas degenerated into folly and vice, and became modes of selfishness and luxury. Elaborate hypocrisy and insincerity became common. Technical definitions of terms were used to obscure their ethical significance. *Minne* came to have a bad meaning and was used for erotic passion. *Courtoisie* became a

[1] *Globus*, LXXXII, 321.
[2] Ralston, *Songs of the Russ. People*, 7.
[3] *Globus*, LXXVI, 316.
[4] Ralston, as above, 65.
[5] *Ztsft. f. vergl. Rechts-wsnsft.*, XIV, 180.
[6] *Ecole d'Anthrop. de Paris*, XIV, 411.

term for base solicitation.[1] Gower, in the *Vox Clamantis* (1382),
tried to distinguish and specify sensual love. He inclines to the
monkish view of women, but he describes good and noble women.
Alanus ab Insulis (+ 1203) in his *De Planctu Naturae*[2] bewailed
the vices of mankind and the vicious relations of men and women.
His aim is to distinguish between good and evil love. He wrote at
the height of the woman cult. In the *Romaunt de la Rose* the thing
discussed seems to be positive vice. It is said that the way to win
women is by lavish gifts. The meretriciousness of women and their
love of luxury are denounced. If a marriage turns out badly, the
men say that God made it, but God is good, and evil is due to man.[3]
In the *Paston Letters* (fifteenth century) marriage appears to be
entirely mercenary.[4] A girl tells her lover what her father will
give with her. If he is not satisfied he must discontinue his suit.[5]
"My master asked mockingly if a man might not beat his own
wife."[6] The one love match in the book is that of Margaret
Paston with a man who was a servant in the family. Margaret's
mother, the most interesting person in the *Letters*, although she
left £20 to her grandson by this marriage, left nothing to her
daughter. Schultz[7] thinks that marriages turned out as well in
the Middle Ages as now, and that adultery was no more frequent ;
also that ecclesiastics were not then more licentious than now.
He quotes freely from Geiler and Murner, who were leading
moral preachers of the fifteenth century. Geiler preached in
Strasburg Cathedral. Murner was a Franciscan. Geiler is incredibly coarse and outspoken. He pretended to state cases
within his knowledge of men who made gain of their wives, and
of wives who entered into arrangements with their husbands to
make gain for both. He preached from these as illustrative cases
and tried to dissuade both men and women from matrimony.[8]
Chateau life was monotonous and stupid, especially for women,
who were moreover partly secluded in special apartments. The
young men and women had very little chance to meet. The

---

[1] Schultz, *Höf. Leben*, I, 581, and the whole of Chap. VII ; Scherr, *D. F. W.*, I, 220.

[2] Migne, *Patrol. Lat.*, Vol. 210.　　　　[5] III, 171.

[3] Line 18,580.　　　　[6] I, 150.

[4] I, 90, 92, 251 ; III, 103, 104 (in spite of　　[7] *D. L.*, 271, 276, 277.
love), 109, 167, 278.　　　　[8] Schultz, *D. L.*, 259, 271–277.

hope of happiness for women was in marriage.[1] Although the woman's consent was necessary, she was controlled by her male relatives, even if a widow, but she had little individuality and generally welcomed a suitor at once.[2] The jongleurs of the twelfth century were vulgar vagabonds. Love, in their conception, is sensual, and women are treated by them with great levity. The women, in their songs, woo the men. In the thirteenth century women are described as more dignified and self-respecting. Siegfried flogged his wife black and blue.[3] Brunhild was also beaten by her husband. The women manifest great devotion to their husbands, especially in adversity, even fighting for them like men.[4] We are constantly shocked at the bad taste of behavior. At Lubeck, if a young widow was married, the crowd made an uproar in front of the house and the bridegroom was forced to stand at show on a certain four-cornered stone in the midst of noisy music "in order to establish the good name of himself and wife."[5] The carnival was an occasion of license for all the grossness and obscenity in the popular taste.[6] The woman cult was a cult of free love and was hostile to honorable marriage. Even in the twelfth century there were complaints of corruption by bad literature. The nobles and knights degenerated in the crusades and in the Italian wars of the Hohenstaufen.[7] "The doctrine of the church appeared to be a support of the family, but it was not such. On the contrary, the bonds of the family were more loosened than strengthened by the ascetic-hierarchical religiosity of the church."[8] Dulaure[9] quotes Gerson and Nicolas de Clemangis that convents in the fifteenth century were places of debauch. Geiler, in a sermon in Strasburg Cathedral, gave a shocking description of convents.[10] A convent is described as a brothel for neighboring nobles.[11] At the end of the fifteenth century the revolt and change in the mores which produced the

---

[1] Lichtenberger, *Poeme des Nibelungen*, 380.
[2] *Ibid.*, 390.
[3] *Nibelungen*, line 837.
[4] Lichtenberger, 368, 375, 391, 400; Uhland, *Dichtung und Sage*, 315.
[5] Barthold, *Hansa*, III, 178.
[6] Schultz, *D. L.*, 414.
[7] Weinhold, *D. F.*, II, 209.
[8] Eicken, *Mittelalt. Weltanschauung*, 467.
[9] *Hist. de Paris*, 268.
[10] Schultz, *D. L.*, 277.
[11] *Ibid.*, 283 ; cf. Janssen, VIII, 391.

Protestant schism caused the social confusion on which Janssen lays such stress in his seventh and eighth volumes. It was a case of revolution. The old mores broke down and new ones were not yet formed. The Protestants of the sixteenth century derided and denounced the Roman Catholics for the contradictions and falsehoods of celibacy, and the Catholics used against the Protestants the looseness as to marriage. Both were right.

381. The standard of the " good wife." Pair marriage. It is safe to believe that if any woman ever entered into a marriage which was not repugnant to her she entered it with a determination to be a "good wife." Her education under the mores of the society around her gave her the notion and standard of a good wife. The modern sentiments of love and conjugal affection have been produced in the middle class. They probably have their roots in the mores of the bourgeoisie of the Middle Ages and in those of the lowest class of free people in the Greco-Roman empire. This middle class is the class which has taken control of modern society, and whose interests are most favored by modern economic developments. They have set aside the old ideas of male dominion and of ascetic purity. In the middle of the nineteenth century the poems of Coventry Patmore and the novels of Anthony Trollope perhaps best expressed the notions of conjugal affection which English-speaking people entertained at that time. It seems that now those notions are thought to be philistine, and there is a reaction towards the old aristocratic standards. The "good husband," as correlative to the good wife, belongs to modern pair marriage. The erotic element has been refined and suppressed, or at least disavowed. The ideals which have been accepted and favored have disciplined and concentrated masculine waywardness, and they have made the sex sentiments more durable. All this has integrated the family more firmly, and the family mores have cultivated and preserved the sentiments. We have seen many cases in which, out of the unconscious and unpremeditated action of the mores, results have been produced which have been most important for the weal or woe of men, but it is one of the most marvelous of these cases that conjugal affection, perhaps the noblest of all sentiments, should have been developed out of the monopolistic tyranny of men over women, and out of the ascetic negation of sex, the common element in which is a prurient and unhealthy sensuality.

382. " One flesh." The notion or figure of " one flesh " is not peculiar to the Jewish or Christian religion. In the Old Testament it clearly refers to carnal union. It has been used to express the ideal that marriage should be the fusion of two lives and interests. It is instructive to notice, in all the discussions of marriage which are to be found in all ages, how few and commonplace are the things which have been said, and how largely refuge has been taken in figures of speech. " One flesh," if not carnal, is only ritual, but ritual conceptions are only conventional conceptions, — good amongst those who agree to repeat the formulas and perform the ritual acts. They are not realities. The problem of marriage is that two human beings try to live together. They are two and not one. Since they are two, their tastes, desires, characters, and wills are two. Ethical philosophers or jurists may be able to define the " one-flesh " idea by translating it into rights and duties, but no state authority can enforce such a definition. Therefore it is nugatory. The idea belongs in an arena beyond state or family, where two make a world. It is beyond the mores also, except so far as the mores have educated the man and woman to a sense of the conduct which is necessary to marital harmony, by the judgments which are current on the hundreds of cases, real or imaginary, which come up for discussion. How then shall two wills be one will? The old way was that one will (the woman's) always was bound to yield. Since that no longer seems right, the modern way is endless discussion, a defeat for one, and all the inevitable consequences in daily experience and effect on character.

383. Pair marriage. Pair marriage is the union of one man and one woman in which all the rights, duties, powers, and privileges are equal and alike for both, the relationship being mutual and reciprocal in all points. It therefore produces a complete fusion of two lives and interests. Pair marriage and all its attendant mores are products of monopoly. Herodotus[1] says of

[1] Herod., IV, 104.

the Agathyrsi that they practiced communalism of women in order that they might all be brethren, without envy or enmity to each other. That is one solution. In it peace and harmony are given a higher place than sex interests. Pair marriage aims at the highest satisfaction of sex interests by monopoly. It sacrifices peace and harmony. Any monopoly exists for the benefit of those who are embraced in it. Its evil effects are to be found by turning to those who fail to get entrance to it. While our mores now require that a man and woman shall come together through love, and therefore make a selection of the most special and exclusive kind, we have no apparatus or intelligent method for making such a selection. The notion that such a selection is necessary, therefore, adds a new difficulty and obstacle. Pair marriage also, partly on account of the intenser sentiment of parenthood and the more integrated family institution, increases expense, and makes the economic conditions of marriage more severe. Pair marriage forces a large fraction of the population to celibacy, and it is they who are the excluded who suffer by that arrangement. This bears chiefly on women. Everything which violates the taboo in the mores is vice, and is disastrous to all who participate in it. The more real pair marriage is, the more disastrous is every illicit relation. The harm is infinitely greater for women than for men. Within the taboo, unmarried women lead aimless existences, or they are absorbed in an effort to earn a living which is harassed by especial obstacles and difficulties. This is the price which has to be paid for all the gain which women get from pair marriage as compared with any other form of sex relation. It assumes that every man and woman can find a mate, which is not true. Very little serious attention is paid to this offset to the advantages of pair marriage. The mores teach unmarried women that it is " right " that things should be so, and that any other arrangement would contain abominations which are not to be thought of. Probably the unmarried women rarely think of themselves as victims of the arrangement by which their married sisters profit. They accept a life career which is destitute of self-realization, except for those few who are so gifted that they can make independent careers in the struggle for existence. Nearly all our discussions of our own social order run upon questions of property. It is under the sex relation that all the great problems really present themselves.

384. Marriage in modern mores. It is very remarkable that marriage amongst us has become the most distinct example there is, and the most widespread, of ritual (what is said in the marriage ceremony, in its rational sense, is of little importance, and people rarely notice it. What force attaches to "obey"?), of religious intervention in private affairs, and of the importance attached to a ceremony. If two people cohabit, the question of right and wrong depends on whether they have passed through a certain ceremony together or not. That determines whether they are "married" or not. The reason is, because if they have passed through the ceremony together, no matter what was said or done, they have expressed their will to come into the status of wedlock, as the mores make it and as the state enforces it, at the time and place. The woman wants to "feel that she is married." Very many women would not feel so in a civil marriage; others want a "fully choral" ceremony; others want the communion with the wedding ceremony. Perhaps the daughter of a great nobleman might not feel married without a marriage settlement. Thus the active effect of the mores may be observed in contemporary custom, and it is seen how completely the notion of being duly married is produced by the mores of the society, or of a class or sect in it.

385. Pair marriage; its technical definition. Polyandry passed over into polygamy when sufficient property was at command.[1] There was a neutral middle point where one man had one wife. It follows that monogamy is not a specific term. It might be monogamy if one man had one wife but also concubines and slaves, or he might have but one wife in fact, although free to have more if he chose. The term "pair marriage" is needed as a technical term for the form of marriage which is as exclusive and permanent for the man as for the woman, which one enters on the same plane of free agreement as the other, and in which all the rights and duties are mutual. In such a union there may

[1] See sec. 366.

be a complete fusion of two lives and interests. In no other form of union is such a fusion possible. This pair marriage is the ideal which guides the marital usages of our time and civilization, gives them their spirit and sense, and furnishes standards for all our discussions, although it is far from being universally realized. The ideal is made an object of "pathos" [1] in our popular literature. Whence did it come? In truth, we can hardly learn. It existed, by necessity of poverty and humble social status, in the classes amongst whom Christianity took root. It found expression in the canon law. It resisted, in the lower classes, the attempt of the church to suppress it in order to aggrandize the corporation. It resisted, in the same classes, the corruption of the Renaissance. It has risen with those classes to wealth and civil power. In modern times "moral" has been used technically for what conforms to the code of pair marriage.

386. Ethics of pair marriage. Pair marriage has excluded every other form of sex relation. To modern people it is hard to understand how different forms of sex relation could exist side by side and all be right. The explanation is in the mores. A concubine may be a woman who has a defined and legally guaranteed relation to one man, if the mores have so determined. Her circumstances have not opened to her the first rank, that of a wife, but she has another which is recognized in the society as honorable. The same may be said of a slave woman, or of a morganatic wife. Amongst the Hebrews, Greeks, and Romans of the empire concubines were a recognized class. A concubine was not a woman who had cast off her own honor until after the thirteenth century,[2] and although her position became doubtful, it was not disreputable for two or three centuries more. Morganatic marriages for princes have continued down to our own time. Whatever is defined and provided for in the mores as a way of solving the problem of life interests is never wrong. Hence the cases of sacral harlotry, of temporary marriage (as in China, Korea, Japan, and ancient Arabia), of royal concubines (since the king was forced to accept a status wife of prescribed rank, etc.), and all the other peculiar arrangements which have,

[1] See sec. 178. [2] Lea, *Sacerd. Celibacy*, 203, note.

existed in history are accounted for. Pair marriage, however, has swept all other forms away. It is the system of the urban-middle-capitalist class. It has gained strength in all the new countries where all men and women were equal within a small margin and the women bore their share of the struggle for existence. The environment, in the new countries, favored the mores of the class from which the emigrants came. In the old countries the mores of the middle class have come into conflict with the mores of peasants and nobles. The former have steadily won. The movement has been the same everywhere, although the dates of the steps in it have been different. As to women, the countries which are at the rear of the modern movement keep the old mores; those which are at the head of it have emancipated women most, and have swept away from their legislation all toleration for anything but pair marriage. Vice, of course, still affects facts, and the growth of wealth and luxurious habits seems to be developing a tendency to take up again some old customs which bear an aristocratic color. It must be expected that when the economic facts which now favor the lower middle classes pass away and new conditions arise the marriage mores will change again. Democracy and pair marriage are now produced by the conditions. Both are contingent and transitory. In aristocratic society a man's family arrangements are his own prerogative. When life becomes harder it will become aristocratic, and concubinage may be expected to arise again.

It seems clear that pair marriage has finally set aside the notion which, in the past, has been so persistently held, — that women are bad by nature, so that one half of the human race is permanently dragging down the other half. The opposite notion seems now to be gaining currency, — that all women are good, and can be permanently employed to raise up the men. These fluctuations only show how each sway of conditions and interests produces its own fallacies.

387. Pair marriage is monopolistic. It has been shown that pair marriage is monopolistic. It produces an exclusive family, and nourishes family pride and ambition. It is interwoven with capital, and we have hardly yet reached the point where we can see what it will become with great wealth, and under the treatment of a plutocratic class. From what has been said it is evidently most important that man and wife should have been educated in the same mores. Pair marriage is also individualistic. It is the barrier against which all socialism breaks into dust. As the cost of a family increases, the connection between family and capital becomes more close and vital. Every socialist who can think is forced to go on to a war on marriage and the family, because he finds that in marriage and the family lie the strongholds of the "individualistic vices" which he cannot overcome. He has to mask this battery, however, because he dare not openly put it forward.

388. The future of marriage. It is idle to imagine that our mores about marriage have reached their final stage. Since marriage is free and individualistic as it exists in our mores, there is little care or pity for those who cannot adapt themselves to it, or it to their circumstances. They are allowed divorce, but not without some feeling of annoyance with them if they use it. It is also idle to imagine that those who are now satisfied will alone control the changes which the future will bring in the mores. It is not difficult to make marriage such that men will refuse it. Women have revolted against it in the past.[1] It is not beyond imagination that they might do so again.

389. Normal type of sex union. It may be, as Lecky says,[2] that "we have ample grounds for maintaining that the lifelong union of one man and one woman should be the normal or dominant type of intercourse between the sexes. We can prove that it is, on the whole, most conducive to the happiness, and also to the moral elevation, of all parties. But beyond this point it would, I conceive, be impossible to advance, except by the assistance of a special revelation. It by no means follows that because this should be the dominant type, it should be the only one, or that the interests of society demand that all connections should be forced into the same die."

390. Divorce. In the mother family the woman could dismiss her husband. This she could also do in all the transition forms

---

[1] JAI, XXIV, 119.　　　　　　　[2] *Eur. Morals*, II, 348.

in which the husband went to live with the wife at her childhood home. In the father family the wife, obtained by capture or purchase, belonged to her husband on the analogy of property. The husband could reject or throw away his property if he saw fit. It is clear that the physical facts attendant on the two customs — one that the man went to live with his wife, the other that he took her to his home — made a great difference in the status of the woman. In the latter case she fell into dependence and subjection to the dominion of her husband. She could not divorce him.

391. In Chaldea a man could divorce his wife by saying, " Thou art not my wife," by repaying her dowry, and giving her a letter to her father. If she said to him, " Thou art not my husband," she was drowned. An adulterous woman was driven into the street clothed only in a loin cloth, at the mercy of the passers.[1] In this view, which ran through the Jewish system and came down into that of Mohammed, a wife has duties, to which her husband has no correlative obligations. She must do her duty or be thrust out. There is no adultery for a man and no divorce for a woman. The most complete negation of divorce is in Hindostan, where a woman (perhaps a child of five or six), if married to a man, is his only, for time and eternity, no matter what may happen. He is hers until she dies, but then he can have another wife. Romulus allowed divorce to the man, if the woman poisoned infants, drank strong wine, falsified keys, or committed adultery.[2] By a law of Numa a man who had as many children as he wanted could cede his wife, temporarily or finally, to another.[3] These laws seem to have been forgotten. If they ever really existed they did not control early Roman society. By the later law a sentence for crime which produced civil death set free the other spouse. In the last century B.C. divorce became very easy and customary. The mores gradually relaxed to allow it. Augustus compelled the husband of Livia to divorce her because he wanted her himself. She was about to become a mother.[4] Cato the younger gave his wife to his friend Hortensius, and took her back after Hortensius's death.[5] Sempronius Sophus divorced his wife because she went to the games without his consent.[6] Women also divorced their husbands in the first century of the Christian era. Juvenal mentions a woman who had eight husbands in five years.[7] Tertullian, writing from the standpoint of a Christian ascetic, said that "divorce is the product of marriage."[8] Jerome knew of a woman who had married her twenty-third husband, she being his twenty-first wife.[9] Seneca said that the

[1] Maspero, *Peuples de l'Orient*, I, 736.
[2] Plutarch, *Romulus*, 22.
[3] Plutarch, *Comp. of Numa and Lykurgus*.
[4] Tacitus, *Annals*, I, 10.
[5] Plutarch, *Cato*.
[6] Valer. Maxim., VI, 3, 12
[7] *Sat.*, VI, 230.
[8] *Apolog.*, 6.
[9] *Epist.*, 2.

women reckoned the years by their husbands, not by the consuls.[1] The women got equality by leveling downwards. "The new woman of Juvenal boldly claims a vicious freedom equal to her husband's."[2] These cases belong to the degeneration of the mores at the period. As they are astonishing, we are in danger of giving them too much force in the notion we form of the mores of that time. All the writers repeat them. "In the *Agricola*, and in Seneca's letters to Marcia and Helvia, we can see that, even at the darkest hour, there were homes with an atmosphere of old Roman self-restraint and sobriety, where good women wielded a powerful influence over their husbands and sons, and where the examples of the old republic were used, as Biblical characters with us, to fortify virtue."[3]

392. Rabbis on divorce. The school of the Rabbi Shammai said, "A man must not repudiate his wife unless he find in her actual immodesty." Rabbi Jochanan said, "Repudiation is an odious thing." Rabbi Eliezer said, "When a first wife is put away the very altar sheds tears."[4]

393. The early Roman mores about marriage were very rigid and pitiless. It was in the family, and therefore under the control of the head of the family. No law forbade divorce, because such a law would have been an invasion of the authority of the male head of the family, but the censors, in the name of public opinion, long prevented any frivolous dissolution of marriage. Few divorces occurred, and then only for weighty reason, after the family council had found them sufficient. There was some stain attaching to a second marriage, after the death of the first spouse. Even men were subject to this stain.[5]

394. Pair marriage and divorce. With the rise of pair marriage came divorce for the woman, upon due reason, as much as for the man. Hence freer divorce goes with pair marriage. Such must inevitably be the case, if it be admitted that any due reason for divorce ever can exist. The more poetical and elevated the ideas are which are clustered around marriage, the more probable it is that experience will produce disappointment. If one spouse enters wedlock with the belief that the other is the most superlative man or woman living, the cases must be very few in which

[1] *Epist.*, 95; *Consolation to his Mother*, 16. [3] *Ibid.*, 188.
[2] Dill, *Nero to M. Aurel.*, 87. [4] Cook, *Fathers of Jesus*, II, 142.
[5] Grupp, *Kulturgesch. der Röm. Kaiserzeit*, 113.

disappointment and disillusion will not result. Moreover, pair marriage, by its exclusiveness, risks the happiness of the parties on a very narrow and specific condition of life. The coercion of this arrangement for many persons must become intolerable.

In the ancient German law there was absolute freedom of divorce by agreement. The pair could end the relation just as they formed it. In the laws of the German nations there was little provision for divorce upon the complaint of the woman. The law of the Langobards allowed it to her for serious bodily injury.[1]

395. Divorce in the Middle Ages. It is pretended that the mediæval church allowed no divorce. This is utterly untrue. Under the influence of asceticism the church put marriage under more and more arbitrary restrictions, going far beyond any rules to be found in the Scriptures, or in the usages of the early church. Divorce was made more and more difficult. These two tendencies contradicted each other, for the greater the restrictions on marriage, the greater the probability that any marriage would be found to have violated one of them, and therefore to be *ab initio* void. This set it aside more absolutely than any divorce *a vinculo* could undo it. Also, when there was an ample apparatus of dispensation by which the rich and great could have their marriages dissolved, by the use of money or political power, the "law of the church" was no law. Still further, the mediæval church, while it had a doctrine of perfection and ideality for marriage, had also a practical system of concession to human weakness, by which it could meet cases of unhappy marriage. In the canon law, divorce and remarriage of the innocent party has been allowed to the man, in case of adultery, physical incapacity, leprosy, desertion, captivity, disappearance, and conspiracy to murder the husband, on the part of the wife ; and to the wife, when the husband's misconduct rendered living with him impossible. However, a dispensation from the ecclesiastical authority was required.[2]

396. The point of this is that no society ever has existed or ever can exist in which no divorce is allowed. In all stages of

---

[1] Heusler, *Deut. Privatrecht*, II, 291. [2] Reichel, *Canon Law*, I, 343.

the father family it has been possible for a man to turn his wife out of doors, and for a wife to run away from her husband. They divorce themselves when they have determined that they want to do so. It would be an easy solution of marriage problems to assert that the society will use its force to compel all spouses who disagree, or for whom the marriage relation has become impossible through the course of events, nevertheless to continue to live in wedlock. Such a rule would produce endless misery, shame, and sin. There are reasons for divorce. Adultery is recognized as such a reason in the New Testament. It is a rational reason, especially under pair marriage. There are other rational reasons. Some of them are modern forms of the reasons allowed in the canon law, as above cited. The exegesis of the New Testament is not simple. It does not produce a simple and consistent doctrine, and therefore inference and deduction have been applied to it. 2 Cor. vi. 14 contradicts 1 Cor. vii. 12. The mores decide at last what causes shall be sufficient. The laws in the United States once went very far in an attempt to satisfy complaining married people. They were no better satisfied at last than at first. Scandalous cases produced a conviction that "we have gone too far," and the present tendency is to revoke certain concessions. The fact that a divorce has been legally obtained does not satisfy some former friends of the divorced so that they will continue social intimacy. A code grows up to fit the facts. Sects help to make such codes. Perhaps they make a code which is too stringent. The members of the sect do not live by it. They seek remarriage in other, less scrupulous sects, or by civil authority, or they change domicile in order to get a divorce. Thus the mores control. When the law of the state or of ecclesiastical bodies goes with the mores it prevails ; when it departs from the mores it fails. The mores are also sure to act in regard to a matter which presents itself in a large class of cases, and which calls for social and ethical judgments. At last, comprehensive popular judgments will be formed and they will get into legislation. They will adjust interests so that people can pursue self-realization with success and satisfaction, under social judgments as to the rules necessary to preserve the institutions of wedlock and the family. The pursuit of happiness, either in the acquisition of property or in the enjoyment of family life, is only possible in submission to laws which define social order, rights, and duties, and against which the individual must react at every point. It is the mores which constantly revise and readjust the laws of social order, and so define the social conditions within which self-realization must go on.

397. Refusal of remarriage. The laws of every State in the United States, except South Carolina, allow marriage by a minister of religion or by magistrates. This does not mean that the legislatures meant to endow ministers of religion with authority to say who may marry and who may not. Ministers who agree not to marry divorced persons assume authority which does not belong to them. In England, with an established church, the fact has recently been ascertained that a clergyman cannot refuse to marry persons who may marry by the civil law as it stands. With us the number of sects and denominations is such that no hardship arises if one sect chooses to adopt stricter laws for the sake of making a demonstration or exercising educational influence, and decides to run the risk of driving its own members to other sects. What the next result of such action will be remains to be learned.

398. Child marriage. Child marriage illustrates a number of points in regard to the mores, especially the possibility of perversity and aberration. Wilutzky[1] thinks that child marriage amongst savages began in the desire of a man to get a wife to himself (monandry) out of the primitive communalism, without violating the customs of ancestors. Girls of ten or twelve years are married to men of twenty-five or thirty on the New Britain Islands. The missionary says, " The result of such an early union, for the girl, has been dreadful."[2] On Malekula girls are married at six or eight.[3] Similar cases are reported from Central and South America where girls of ten are mothers.[4] Rohlfs reports mothers of ten or twelve at Fesan.[5] The Eskimo practice child betrothal,

[1] *Mann und Weib*, 32.
[2] JAI, XVIII, 288.
[3] *Austral. Assoc. Adv. Sci.*, 1892, 704.
[4] Schomburgk, *Brit. Guiana*, I, 122, 164; JAI, XXIV, 205.
[5] *Peterm. Mittlgen, Erg. heft*, XXV, 9.

so that wedlock begins at once at puberty.[1] Schwaner reports,[2] from the Barito Valley, that children are often betrothed and married by the fathers when the latter are intoxicated. The motives of the match are birth, kinship, property, and social position, and the marriage is hastened, lest the parents should see their plans to satisfy these motives frustrated by the children if they should delay. The intimacy of the children is left to chance. Wilken says that child marriage seems to be, in the Dutch East Indies, an exercise of absolute paternal authority, especially seeing that they have marriage by capture. The father wants to secure, in time, the realization of plans which he has made. Especially, the purpose is to make the man take the status-wife appointed for him by the marriage rule, —his mother's brother's daughter. Wilken also explains child betrothal and marriage by the fact that girls have entire liberty until betrothed, and the future husband wants to put an end to this. Girls are often betrothed at birth and married at six, although they remain with their parents. In some parts of the East Indies the custom is declining; in others it is extinct. In some places it continues, although marriage by capture is extinct. Where marriage by capture exists, the reason for child marriage is the fear that the girl may be stolen by another than the desired husband.[3]

399. Child marriage in Hindostan. By the laws of Manu[4] a man may give his daughter in marriage before she is eight years old to a man of twenty-four, or a girl of twelve to a man of thirty, and he loses his dominion over her if he has not found a husband for her by the time that she might be a mother ; yet intercourse before puberty is especially forbidden.[5] The Hindoos, including Mohammedans, practice child marriage and cling to it, in spite of the efforts of the English to dissuade them from it, and in spite of the opinion of their own most enlightened men that it is a harmful custom. It is deeply rooted in their mores. The modern Hindoo father or brother considers it one of the

---

[1] Holm, *Angmagslikerne*, 52; Nelson in *Bur. Eth.*, XVIII, Part i, 292.
[2] *Borneo*, I, 194.
[3] *Bijdragen tot T. L. en V.-kunde*, XXXV, 161, 165; Wilken, *Volkenkunde*, 277.
[4] IX, 88, 93, 94.   [5] XI, 59, 171.

gravest faults he can commit to allow a daughter or sister to arrive at puberty (generally eight years) before a husband has been found for her. It is a disgrace for a family to have in it an unmarried marriageable girl. What is proper is that, from five to sixteen days after puberty, the previously married husband shall beget with her a child in a solemn ceremonial which is one of the twelve (or sixteen) sacraments of Hindoo life.[1] The idea of child marriage was that the woman should be already married to her chosen husband, so that she might be given to him at the proper time.[2] Moreover, " marriage completes, for the man, the regenerating ceremonies, expiatory, as is believed, of the sinful taint which every child is supposed to contract in the mother's womb ; and being, for sudras and for women, the only [ceremony for this purpose] which is allowed, its obligatoriness is, as to the latter, one of the ordinances of the Veda." [3]

400. The wife of the missionary Gehring was present at the marriage of a girl of ten to an adult man amongst the Tamil Mohammedans. The story of the child's shrinking terror is very pathetic. When her veil was withdrawn she fainted from nervousness and excitement. Those present showed no pity for her, but crowded around to enjoy the opportunity of gazing at her. They saw no reason why she was to be pitied.[4]

401. If a girl has had no husband provided for her by her responsible male relative, she may act for herself, but then she forfeits her share in the family property. She may be abducted with impunity. In Manu[5] it is said that three years must elapse before she gets the right of self-disposition. The right is long since a dead letter. The " Law of Manu " can lose its authority where it is favorable to women ! or when it runs counter to the mores, for Hindoo women have no training to take up self-disposition, if the case occurs.[6] Female virtue is rated low, and must be secured by marriage. Independent action by a boy and girl is against the mores and could only lead to inferior forms

---

[1] Jolly, *Recht und Sitte der Indo-Arier*, 54, 58.
[2] Jolly, *Stellung der Frauen bei den alten Indern*, 425.
[3] Strange, *Hindu Law*, I, 35.   [5] IX, 90.
[4] Gehring, *Süd-Indien*, 78, 80.   [6] *Jo. Soc. Comp. Legisl.*, *N. S.*, VIII, 253.

of marriage, by love or capture.[1] Finally, religion bears its share in furnishing motives for child marriage. The souls of ancestors cannot stay in heaven unless there are male descendants to keep up the sacrifices. It is, therefore, impossible to provide male descendants too soon. Among the Tamil-speaking Malaialis of the Kollimallais hills a man takes an adult wife for his little son, and with her he begets a son who will perform this religious duty for himself and his son. This goes on from generation to generation.[2]

402. Nevertheless, it is held to be proved that in ancient India child marriages were unknown and that women were often far beyond puberty before they were married. The human husband was also held to be the fourth. Three gods had preceded him in each case.[3] The custom of child marriage has now spread to the lowest classes, and in the lowlands of the Ganges cohabitation follows at once upon child marriage, with very evil results on the physique of the population.[4]

There was child marriage in Chaldea 2200 years B.C.[5]

403. Child marriage in Europe. The marriage of children was not in the mores of the ancient Germans. The mediæval church allowed child marriage for princes, etc. The motive was political alliance, or family or property interest.[6] The fable was that Joseph was an old man and the Virgin Mary only a girl. This story was invented to make the notion of a virgin wife and mother easier. The marriage was only a child marriage. In England, from the end of the thirteenth to late in the seventeenth century, cases of child marriage occurred, at first in the highest classes, later in all classes, and finally most frequently in the highest and lowest classes. In Scotland premature marriages were so common that, in 1600, they were forbidden, the limits being set at fourteen and twelve years for males and females respectively. The chief motive was to avoid feudal dues on the part of tenants in chief of the crown, if the father should

---

[1] Jolly, *Recht und Sitte*, 54.
[2] *Madras Gov. Mus.*, II, 162.
[3] Monier-Williams, *Brahmanism and Hinduism*, 354.
[4] *Pol.-Anth. Rev.*, III, 711.
[5] Winckler, *Gesetze des Hammurabi*, 22.
[6] Grimm, *Rechts-Alt.*, 436.

die and leave infants who would become wards liable to forced marriages or to mulcts to avoid the same.[1]

404. Child marriage is due, then, to the predominance of worldly considerations in marriage, especially when the interests considered are those of the parents, not of the children; also to abuse of parental authority through vanity and self-will; also to superstitious notions about the other world and the interests of the dead there; also to attempts, in the interest of the children, to avoid the evil consequences of other bad social arrangements.

405. Cloistering. The custom of cloistering women has spread, within historic times, from some point in central Asia. The laws of Hammurabi show that, 2200 years B.C., men and women, in the Euphrates Valley, consorted freely and equally in life. Later, in the Euphrates Valley, we find the custom of cloistering amongst the highest classes. It became more and more vigorous amongst the Persians and spread to the common people. It was not an original custom of the Arabs and was not introduced by the Mohammedan religion. It was learned and assumed from the Persians.[2] Seclusion of women, to a greater or less degree, has prevailed in the mores of many nations. In fact, there is only a question of degree between an excessive harem system and our own code of propriety which lays restraints on women to which men are not subject. The most probable explanation of the customs of veiling and cloistering is that they are due to the superstition of the evil eye. Pretty women attracted admiration, which was dangerous, as all prosperity, glory, and preëminence were dangerous under that notion. When *pretty* women were veiled or secluded, the custom was sure to spread to others. The wives and daughters of the rich and great were secluded in order to shield them from easy approach, and to pet and protect them. This set the fashion which lesser people imitated so far as they could. The tyranny of husbands and fathers also came into play, and another force acting in the same direction was the seduction exerted on women themselves by the flattering sense of being cared for

[1] Furnival, *Child-marriages*, XXVII, XXXIX, XL.
[2] Hauri, *Islam*, 131.

and petted. Lane[1] tells us that "an Egyptian wife who is attached to her husband is apt to think, if he allows her unusual liberty, that he neglects her, and does not sufficiently love her; and to envy those wives who are kept and watched with greater strictness." "They look on the restraint [imposed by husbands] with a degree of pride, as evincing the husband's care for them, and value themselves on being hidden as treasures." Women who earn their own living have to go into the streets and the market and to come in contact with much from which other classes of women are protected. The protected position is aristocratic, and it is consonant with especial feminine tastes. The willingness to fall into it has always greatly affected the status of women.

406. Second marriages. Widows. Second marriages affect very few people beyond those immediately concerned, and they are not connected with any social principle or institution so as to create what is sometimes called a "societal interest," unless there is current in the society some special notion about ghosts and the other world. Nevertheless, the bystanders have, until very recent times, pretended to a right to pass judgment and exert an influence on the remarriage of widows, and less frequently of widowers. The story of the status of widows is one of the saddest in the history of civilization. In uncivilized society a widow is considered dangerous because the ghost of her husband is supposed to cleave to her. Under marriage by capture or purchase she is the property of her husband, and, like his other property, ought to accompany him to the other world. When she is spared she has no rational place in the society; therefore widows were a problem which the mores had to solve. In no other case have societies shown so much indifference to misfortune and innocent misery. If a widow has value for any purpose, she falls to the heir and he may exploit her. On the Fiji Islands a wife was strangled on her husband's grave and buried with him. A god lies in wait on the road to the other world who is implacable to the unmarried. Therefore a man's ghost must be attended by a woman's ghost to pass in safety.[2] Mongol

---

[1] *Modern Egyptians*, I, 268, 466.　　　　[2] JAI, X, 138.

widows could find no second husbands, because they would have to serve their first husbands in the next world. The youngest son inherited the household and was bound to provide for his father's widows. He could take to wife any of them except his own mother, and he did so because he was willing that they should go to his father in the next world.[1] In the laws of Hammurabi the widow was secured a share in her husband's property and was protected against the selfishness of her sons. If she gave up to her sons what she had received from her husband, she could keep what her father gave her and could marry again. In later Chaldea annuities were provided for widows by payments to temples.[2] In the Mahabharata the morning salutation to a woman is, "May you not undergo the lot of a widow."[3]

407. Burning of widows. It appears certain that the primitive Aryans practiced the burning of widows, perhaps by the choice of the widows, and that the custom declined in the Vedic period of India. The burning of widows and the levirate could not exist together.[4] As Manu[5] gives rules for the behavior of widows (not name any man but the deceased husband; not remarry), he assumes that they will live. The custom of suttee was strongest in the lower castes.[6] Akbar, the Mogul emperor, forbade suttee about 1600.[7] He acted from the Mohammedan standpoint. His ordinance had no effect on the usage. The English put an end to the custom in 1830. This did not affect the native states, where the latest instance reported took place in 1880.[8] A man who knows India well says that it was no kindness to widows to put a stop to suttee because, if they live on, their existence is so wretched that death would be better. Wilkins[9] quotes a Hindoo widow's description of the treatment she received, which included physical abuse and moral torture. She was addressed as if she was to blame for the death of her husband. The head of a widow is shaved, although Hindoo women care very much for their hair. She is allowed but one meal a day and must fast frequently.

[1] Rubruck, *Eastern Parts*, 78.
[2] Kohler and Peiser, II, 9.
[3] Holtzmann, *Ind. Sagen*, I, 258.
[4] Zimmer, *Alt-ind. Leben*, 328–331.
[5] V, 157, 161–164.
[6] Jolly, *Stellung der Frauen*, 448.
[7] *Nineteenth Cent.*, XLV, 769.
[8] Wilkins, *Modern Hinduism*, 391.
[9] *Ibid.*, 365.

She is shunned as a creature of ill omen. Inasmuch as girls are married at five or six, all this may happen to a child of ten or twelve, if her husband dies, although she never has lived with him. In 1856 the English made a law by which widows might remarry, but the higher classes very rarely allow it. If they do allow it, the groom is forced to marry a tree or a doll of cotton, so that he too may be widowed. The mores resist any change which is urged, although not enforced, by people of other mores. The reforms proposed in the treatment of widows have no footing at all in the experience and the judgment of Hindoos, if we except a few theists in Calcutta, and they have never taken a united and consistent position. Monier-Williams[1] describes the case of a man who married a widow. He was boycotted so completely that all human fellowship was denied him. He had to go to a distant place and take a position under the government. Among the lower castes of the Bihari Hindoos a widow may marry the younger brother of her deceased husband, to whom her relation is always one of especial intimacy and familiarity.[2]

408. Difficulty of reform. It appears that the difficulty about the remarriage of widows is due to the fact that it runs counter to fundamental religious ideas. The Hindoo reformers are charged with using forms of wedding ceremony which are inconsistent with facts. Some widows are virgins, but there is not always a father or mother to give them away by the formula of " virgin gift." The women all have a notion, taken from the words of a heroine in the Mahabharata, that a woman can be given but once.[3] They cling to the literal formula. By the form of first marriage also a woman passes into the kin of her husband for seven births (generations), the limit of degrees of consanguinity. It is irreligious and impossible to change the kin again, because consequences have been entailed which run seven generations into the future.[4] This is all made to depend, not on the consummation of the marriage, but on the wedding or even betrothal. The census shows that the taboo on the remarriage of widows and the custom of child marriage extend and increase together.[5]

[1] *Brahmanism and Hinduism*, 472.
[2] JASB, VI, 119.   [3] Cf. sec. 376.
[4] JASB, VI, 376.
[5] Jolly, *Recht und Sitte*, 61.

Where husbands are scarce girls are married in childhood in order to secure them, and widows are not allowed to remarry.[1] By the remarriage of widows rajpoots and rajpoot families lose their rank and precedence.[2]   In Homer the remarriage of men is rare, and only one stepmother is mentioned.[3]   The prejudice against second marriages continued amongst the Greeks, even for men, for whom second marriage was restrained, in some parts of Greece by political disabilities, if the man had children. The reason given was that a man who had so little devotion to his family would have little devotion to his country.[4]   In the classical period widows generally married again. Sometimes the dying husband bequeathed his widow.   In later times some widows contracted their own second marriages.[5]   Marcus Aurelius would not take a second wife as a stepmother for his children. He took a concubine. Julian, after the death of his wife, lived in continence.[6]   On Roman tombstones of women the epithet " wife of one husband " was often put as praise.[7]

409. Widows and remarriage in the Christian church. The pagan emperors of Rome encouraged second marriages as they encouraged all marriage, but the Christian emperors of the fourth century took up the ascetic tendency. About 300 the doctrine was, "Every second marriage is essentially adultery."[8]   Augustine, in his tract on "Continence," uttered strong and sound doctrine about self-control and discipline of character. In the tract on the " Benefit of Marriage " he defended marriage, intervening in a controversy between Jerome and Jovinian, in which the former put forth the most extravagant and contradictory assertions about virginity. Augustine's formula is : " Marriage and fornication are not two evils of which the second is worse, but marriage and continence are two goods, of which the second is

---

[1] JAI, XII, 290.

[2] *Ethnol. App. Census of India*, 1901, 74–75.

[3] Keller, *Homeric Society*, 227 ; *Iliad*, XXII, 477; V, 389.

[4] Diodorus Siculus, XII, 12.

[5] Becker-Hermann, *Charikles*, III, 289.

[6] Lecky, *Eur. Morals*, II, 316.

[7] Friedländer, *Sittengesch.*, I, 411.

[8] Athenagoras, *Apolog.*, 28; *Constit. Apost.*, III, 2.

better." Although this statement is very satisfactory rhetoric-ally, it carries no conclusion as to the rational sense of regulation of the sex passion, or as to the limit within which regulation is beneficial. Augustine laid great stress on 1 Cor. vii. 36. In a tract on "Virginity" he glorified that state according to the taste of the period. In a tract on "Widowhood" (chaps. 13 and 14), he repudiated the extreme doctrine about second and subsequent marriages, but he exhorted widows to continence. The church fathers, like the mediæval theologians, had a way of admitting points in the argument without altering their total position in accordance with the admissions or concessions which they had made. The positions taken by Augustine in these tracts about the sex mores cannot be embraced in an intelligible and consistent statement. "At a period of early, although uncertain, date the rule became firmly and irrevocably established, that no *digamus*, or husband of a second wife, was admissible to Holy Orders ; and although there is no reason for supposing that marriage after taking orders was prohibited to a bachelor, it was strictly forbidden to a widower." [1] So it came about that, inasmuch as marriage was, in any case, only a concession and a compromise, and in so far a departure from strict rectitude, a second marriage was regarded with disfavor, and any subsequent ones were regarded with reprobation which increased in a high progression. This has remained the view of the Eastern church, in which a fourth marriage is unlawful. The Western church has not kept the early view, and has set no limit to remarriage, but orthodox and popular mores have frowned upon it after the second or, at most, the third. In Arabia, before the time of Mohammed, widows were forced into seclusion and misery for a year, and they became a class of forlorn, almost vagabond, dependents. It was a shame for a man if his mother contracted a second marriage.[2] In the Middle Ages "popular reprobation was manifested by celebrations which were always grotesque and noisy, and sometimes licentious. They were called *charivaris*. They were enacted in case of the remarriage of widows and

[1] Lea, *Sacerd. Celibacy*, 35.

[2] Wellhausen, *Ehe bei den Arabern*, 433, 455.

sometimes in the case of widowers. They are said to have been a very ancient custom in Provence.[1] This might mean that opposition to second marriages was due to Manichæan doctrines which were widely held in that region. The customs of popular reprobation were, however, very widespread, and nowadays amongst us the neighbors sometimes express in this way their disapproval of any sex relations which are in any way not in accord with the mores. In the Salic law it was provided that any woman who married a second time must do so at night.[2] The other laws of the barbarian nations contain evidence of disapproval.[3] Innocent III ruled, in 1213, that a man did not incur the ecclesiastical disabilities of second marriage, "no matter how many concubines he might have had, either at one time or in succession."[4] The mediæval *coutumes* of northern France are indifferent to second marriages.[5] The ancient German custom approved of the self-immolation of a widow at her husband's death, but did not require it. The remarriage of widows was not approved and the widows did not desire it. This was a consequence of the ancient German notion of marriage, according to which a wife merged her life in that of her husband for time and for eternity.[6] The usage, however, was softened gradually. The widow got more independence, and more authority over her children and property, over the marriage of her daughters, and at last the right to contract a second marriage after a year of mourning.[7] In England, in the eleventh century, a widow's dower could not be taken to pay her husband's taxes, although the exchequer showed little pity for anybody else. The reason given is that "it is the price of her virginity."[8] The later law also exempted a wife's dower from confiscation in the case of any criminal or traitor.[9] In the seventeenth and eighteenth centuries, in France, "a period in which, perhaps, people supported widowhood less willingly than in any other," the actual usages departed from the acknowledged standards of right and

[1] Jolly, *Seconds Mariages*, 194.
[2] *Ibid.*, 177.
[3] *Ibid.*, 193.
[4] Lea, *Sacerd. Celib.*, 283.
[5] Jolly, *Seconds Mariages*, 193.
[6] Tacitus, *Germ.*, 19.
[7] Stammler, *Stellung der Frauen im alten Deutschen Recht*, 37.
[8] *Dialog. of the Exchequer*, B 2, XVIII.
[9] Pike, *Crime in England*, I, 428.

propriety.[1] The same was true in a greater or less degree elsewhere in Europe, and the widowed probably destroyed the prejudice against remarriage by their persistency and courage in violating it. In the American colonies it was by no means rare for a widow or widower to marry again in six or even in three months.

410. Remarriage and other-worldliness. It is evident that the customs in regard to the treatment of widows, second marriages, etc., are largely controlled by other-worldliness. If the other world is thought of as close at hand, and the dead as enjoying a conscious life, with knowledge of all which occurs here, then there is a rational reluctance to form new ties by which the dead may be offended. If the other world and its inhabitants are not so vividly apprehended, the living pursue their own interests, and satisfy their own desires.

411. Tree marriage. In several cases which have been presented, we have seen how the folkways devise means of satisfying interests in spite of existing (inherited) institutions which bear injuriously on interests. A remarkable case of this kind is tree marriage amongst the Brahmins of southern India. The established opinion is that a younger brother ought not to marry before an older one. The latter may be willing. That is immaterial. The device is employed of marrying the older brother to a tree, or (perhaps the idea is) to a spirit which resides in the tree. He is then out of the way and the younger brother may marry.[2]

412. The Japanese woman. The Japanese woman has been formed in an isolated state, of a militant character, with strong and invariable folkways. " Before this ethical creature, criticism should hold its breath; for there is here no single fault, save the fault of a moral charm unsuited to any world of selfishness and struggle. . . . How frequently has it been asserted that, as a moral being, the Japanese woman does not seem to belong to the same race as the Japanese man! . . . Perhaps no such type

[1] Jolly, *Seconds Mariages*, 202.
[2] Jolly, *Recht und Sitte der Indo-Arier*, 59; Hopkins, *Religions of India*, 541; Kohler, *Urgesch. der Ehe*, 28.

of woman will appear again in this world for a hundred thousand years : the conditions of industrial civilization will not admit of her existence. . . . The Japanese woman can be known only in her own country, — the Japanese woman as prepared and perfected by the old-time education for that strange society in which the charm of her moral being, — her delicacy, her supreme unselfishness, her childlike piety and trust, her exquisite tactful perception of all ways and means to make happiness about her, — can be comprehended and valued. . . . Even if she cannot be called handsome according to western standards, the Japanese woman must be confessed pretty, — pretty like a comely child ; and if she be seldom graceful in the occidental sense, she is at least in all her ways incomparably graceful : her every motion, gesture, or expression being, in its own oriental manner, a perfect thing, — an act performed, or a look conferred, in the most easy, the most graceful, the most modest way possible. . . . The old-fashioned education of her sex was directed to the development of every quality essentially feminine, and to the suppression of the opposite quality. Kindliness, docility, sympathy, tenderness, daintiness, — these and other attributes were cultivated into incomparable blossoming. ' Be good, sweet maid, and let who will be clever ; do noble things, not dream them, all day long,' — those words of Kingsley really embody the central idea in her training. Of course the being, formed by such training only, must be protected by society ; and by the old Japanese society she was protected. . . . A being working only for others, thinking only for others, happy only in making pleasure for others, — a being incapable of unkindness, incapable of selfishness, incapable of acting contrary to her own inherited sense of right, — and in spite of this softness and gentleness ready, at any moment, to lay down her life, to sacrifice everything at the call of duty : such was the character of the Japanese woman." [1]

[1] Hearn, *Japan*, 393 ff.

CHAPTER X

THE MARRIAGE INSTITUTION

Mores lead to institutions. — Aleatory interest in marriage and the function of religion. — Chaldean demonism and marriage. — Hebrew marriage before the exile. — Jewish marriage after the exile. — Marriage in the New Testament. — The merit of celibacy. — Marriage in early Christianity. — Marriage in the Roman law. — Roman " free marriage." — Free marriage. — Transition from Roman to Christian marriage. — Ancient German marriage. — Early mediæval usage. — The place of religious ceremony. — The mode of expressing consensus. — Marriage at the church door. — Marriage in Germany, twelfth century. — The canon law. — Mediæval marriage. — Conflict of the mores with the church programme. — Church marriage; concubines. — The church elevated the notion of marriage. — The decrees of Trent about marriage. — Puritan marriage.

413. Mores lead to institutions. We have seen in Chapter IX that the sex mores control and fashion all the relations of the sexes to each other. Marriage, under any of its forms (polygamy, polyandry, etc.), is only a crystallization of a set of these mores into an imperfect institution, because the relation of a woman, or of women, to a husband becomes more or less enduring, and so the mores which constitute the relation get a stability and uniformity of coherence which makes a definable whole, covering a great field of human interest and life policy. It is not a complete specimen of an institution (sec. 63). It lacks structure or material element of any kind, but the parties are held to make good the understandings and coöperative acts which the mores prescribe at all the proper conjunctures, and thus there arises a system of acts and behavior such as every institution requires. In civilized society this cluster of mores, constituting a relationship by which needs are satisfied and sentiments are cherished, is given a positive form by legislation, and the rights and duties which grow out of the relationship get positive definition and adequate guarantees. This case is, therefore, a very favorable one for studying the operation of the mores in the making of institutions, or preparing them for the final work of the lawmaker.

414. Aleatory interest in marriage and the function of religion. The positive history of marriage shows that it has been always made and developed by the mores, that is to say, by the effort of adjustment to conditions in such a way that self-realization may be better effected and that more satisfaction may be won from life. The aleatory element (sec. 6) in marriage is very large. Marriage is an interest of every human being who reaches maturity, and it affects the weal and woe of each in every detail of life. Passing by the forms of the institution in which the wife is under stern discipline and those in which the man can at once exert his will to modify the institution, it may be said of all freer forms that there is no way in which to guarantee the happiness of either party save in reliance on the character of the other. This is a most uncertain guarantee. In the unfolding of life, under ever new vicissitudes, it appears that it is a play of luck, or fate, what will come to any one out of the marital union with another. Women have been more at the sport of this element of luck, but men have cared much more for their smaller risk in it. Therefore, at all stages of civilization, devices to determine luck have been connected with weddings, and in many cases acts of divination have been employed to find out what the future had in store for the pair. Marriage is a domestic and family affair. The wedding is public and invites the coöperation of friends and neighbors. Wedlock is a mode of life which is private and exclusive. The civil authority, after it is differentiated and integrated, takes cognizance and control of the rights of children, legitimacy, inheritance, and property. Religion, in its connection with marriage, takes its function from the aleatory interest. It is not of the essence of marriage. It "blesses" it, or secures the favor of the higher powers who distribute good and bad fortune. In a very few cases amongst savage tribes religious ceremonies "make" a marriage; that is, they give to it (to the authority of the husband) a superstitious sanction which insures permanence and coercion as long as the husband wants permanence and coercion. These cases are rare.

The notion that a religious ceremony makes a marriage, and defines it, had no currency until the sixteenth Christian century.

415. Chaldean demonism and marriage. Chaldean demonism affected wedding ceremonies. The belief was that demons found their opportunities at great crises in life, when interest and excitement ran high. Then the demons rejoiced to exert their malignity on man to produce frustration and disappointment. Cases are not rare in which the consummation of marriage was deferred, in barbarism and half-civilization, to ward off this interference of demons. The Chaldean groom's companions led him to the bride, and he repeated to her the formulas of marriage : " I am the son of a prince. Silver and gold shall fill thy bosom. Thou shalt be my wife and I thy husband. As a tree bears abundant fruit, so great shall be the abundance which I will pour out on this woman." A priest blessed them and said : " All which is bad in this man do ye [gods] put far away, and give him strength. Do thou, man, give thy virility. Let this woman be thy spouse. Do thou, woman, give thy womanhood, and let this man be thy husband." The next morning a ritual was used to drive away evil spirits.[1]

416. Hebrew marriage before the exile. In the canon of the Old Testament we get no information at all about wedding ceremonies, or the marriage institution. The reason for this must be that marriage was altogether a family and domestic affair. It was controlled by very ancient mores, under which marriage and the family were conducted, as beyond question correct. It is in the nature of the case, in all forms of the father family, that a girl until marriage was under the care and authority of her father or nearest male relative. The suitor must ask him to give her, and must induce him to give her by gifts. The transfer was made publicly that it might be known that she was the wife of such an one. The old Hebrew marriage seems to have consisted in this form of giving a daughter, in all its simplicity. We find a taboo on the union of persons related by consanguinity or affinity. Later there was a taboo on exogamic marriage. In the prophets there are metaphors and symbolical acts relating

[1] Maspero, *Peuples de l'Orient,* I, 736.

to marriage, which show a development of the mores in regard to it. The formulas which are attached to the prohibitions in Levit. xviii are in the form of explanations of the prohibitions or reasons for them, but they furnish no real explanations. Their sense is simply: For such is the usage in Israel, or in the Jahveh religion. That was the only and sufficient reason for any prescription. "After the consent of the parents of the bride had been obtained, which was probably attended by a family feast, the bridegroom led the bride to his dwelling and the wedding was at an end. No mention is made anywhere of any function of a priest in connection with it. It is not until after the Babylonian exile, after the Jews had become more fully acquainted with the mores and usages of other civilized peoples of that age, that weddings amongst them were made more solemn and ceremonial. After a betrothal a full year (if the bride was a widow, one month) was allowed the pair, after the captivity, to prepare their outfit, in imitation of the Persian custom (Esther ii. 12)." "At the end of the delay, the bride was led or carried to the house of the groom, in a procession, with dancing and noisy rejoicing, as is now the custom in Arabia and Persia. Ten guests must be present in the groom's house, as witnesses, where prayer formulas were recited and a feast was enjoyed." There were also prayers by all present at a betrothal "in order to give the affair a religious color." The pair retired then to a room where they first made each other's acquaintance. Then two bridesmen led them to the nuptial chamber where they watched over them until after the first conjugal union. This last usage was not universal, and after some experience of its ambiguous character it was abolished. The purpose was that there might be witnesses to the consummation of the marriage, not merely to the wedding ceremony. The whole proceeding was a domestic and family affair, in which no priest or other outsider had any part, except as witness, and there was no religious element in it.[1] The prayer formulas were uttered by the participants and their friends, and they were formulas of invoking blessing, prosperity, and good fortune.

[1] Bergel, *Eheverhält. der Juden*, 19.

417. Jewish marriage after the exile. The Jewish idea of marriage was naïve and primitive. The purpose was procreation. Every man was bound to marry, after the exile, and could be compelled to do so, and to beget at least one son and one daughter. By direct inference sterility made marriage void. It had failed of its purpose. It was the naïveté of this notion of marriage which led to the provision of witnesses for the consummation of the marriage. Marriage meant carnal union under prescribed conditions, and nothing else. In Deut. xxii. 28 f. the rule is laid down that a man who violated a maid must remain her husband. This is another direct inference from the view of marriage. The *ketubah* was the document of a "gift on account of nuptials to be celebrated." It made the bride a wife and not a concubine or maid servant, for the distinction depended on the intention of the bridegroom. In the rabbinical period the betrothal and wedding were united. The wedding was made by a gift (a coin or ring), by a document (*ketubah*), or by the fact of *concubitus*.[1] The man took the woman to wife by the formula: "Be thou consecrated to me," or later, "Be thou consecrated to me by the law of Moses and Israel." These formalities took place in the presence of at least ten witnesses, who pronounced blessings and wishes for good fortune. The third mode of wedding was forbidden in the third century A.D. In the Jewish notions of marriage we see already the beginning of the later casuistry. Procreation being the sense and purpose of marriage, the carnal act was the matter of chief importance. At the same time the Jews thought that copulation and childbirth rendered unclean. They must be rectified by purification and penance. Thus the act had a double character; it was both right and wrong. It was a conjugal duty not to be sensual.[2] All this contributed to the modern notion of pair marriage, for at last no sex indulgence was allowed outside of legal marriage. When the custom of the presence of witnesses in the bride chamber produced dissatisfaction a tent was substituted for the chamber. Later a scarf, ceremoniously spread over the heads of the pair, took the place of the tent. The custom arose that the pair retired to a special room and

---

[1] Deut. xxii. 29.   [2] Freisen, *Gesch. des kanon. Eherechts*, 848.

took a meal together there. "The ceremony had no ecclesiastical character. . . . The blessings only gave publicity to the ceremony. They were not priestly blessings and were not essential to the validity of the marriage."[1] So we see that, even amongst a people so attached to tradition as the Jews, when one of the folkways did not satisfy an interest, or outraged taste, the mores modified it into a form which could give satisfaction.

418. Marriage in the New Testament. According to the New Testament marriage is a compromise between indulgence and renunciation of sex passion. A compromise is always irrational when it bears upon concepts of right and truth, and not on mere expediency of action. The concept of right and truth on either hand may be correct; it is certain that the compromise between them is not correct. The compromise can be maintained only by disregarding its antagonism to the concepts on each side of it. For fifteen hundred years the Christian church fluttered, as in a moral net, in the inconsistencies of the current view of marriage. The procreation of children was recognized as the holiest function and the greatest responsibility of human beings, but it was considered to involve descent into sensuality and degradation. It was the highest right and the deepest wrong to satisfy the sex passion, and the two aspects were reconciled partially in marriage, by a network of intricate moral dogmas which must be inculcated by long and painful education. In the sixteenth century the problem was solved by repudiating the doctrine of celibacy as a meritorious and superior state, and making marriage a rational and institutional regulation of the sex relation, in which the aim is to repress what is harmful, and develop what is beneficial, to human welfare. This change was produced by and out of the mores. The Protestants denounced the falsehood and vice under the pretended respect for celibacy. The new view of marriage could not be at once fully invented and introduced. Therefore the Romanists pointed with scorn to the careless marriage and loose divorce amongst the Protestants (sec. 380).

419. Merit of celibacy. No reasons are ascertainable why Paul should maintain that celibacy is to be preferred to wedlock as a

[1] Freisen, *Gesch. des kanon. Eherechts*, 23, 47, 92–96.

more worthy mode of life. In 1 Cor. vii. 32–34 he argues that the unmarried, being free from domestic cares, can care for the things of God. He speaks often of the degree of certainty he feels that he has with him the Spirit of God. This shows that he often lacked self-confidence in regard to his teachings. He does not seem to hold the ascetic view. In Ephes. v. 22 the marriage institution is accepted and regulated, with some mystical notions, which it is impossible to understand. Marriage and Christ's headship of the church are said to explain each other or to be parallel, but it is not possible to understand which of them is represented as simple and obvious, so that it explains the other. The apostle sometimes seems to lay stress on the vexations and cares of wedlock. If that is his motive, he announces no principle or religious rule, but only a consideration of expediency which is not on a high plane. Tertullian and Jerome (in anticipation of the end of the world) regarded virginity as an end in itself; that is to say, that they thought it noble and pious to renounce the function on which the perpetuation of the species depends. The race (having left out of account the end of the world) cannot commit suicide, and men and women cannot willfully antagonize the mores of existence — economic, social, intellectual, and moral, as well as physical — which are imposed on them by the fact that the human race consists of two complementary sexes. Jerome, in his tracts against Jovinianus, wanders around and around the absurdities of this contradiction. The ascetic side of it became the cardinal idea of religious virtue in the Middle Ages. " Monkish asceticism saw woman only in the distorting mirror of desire suppressed by torture."[1] "Woman" became a phantasm. She was imaginary. She appeared base, sensual, and infinitely enchanting, drawing men down to hell; yet worth it. In truth, there never has been any such creature. In the replies of Gregory to Augustine (601 A.D.)[2] arbitrary rules about marriage and sex are laid down with great elaboration. They are prurient and obscene. The mediæval sophistry about the birth of Christ is the utmost product of human folly in its way. Joseph and Mary were married, but the marriage was never consummated. Yet it was a

---

[1] Lippert, *Kulturgesch.*, II, 520.   [2] Wilkins, *Concilia*, 20.

true marriage and Mary became a mother, but Joseph was not the father. Mary was a virgin, nevertheless. This might all pass, as it does in modern times, as an old tradition which is not worth discussing, but the mediæval people turned it in every possible direction, and were never tired of drawing new deductions from it. At last, it consists in simply affirming two contradictory definitions of the same word at the same time. There are, in the mythologies, many cases of virgin birth. The Scandinavian valkyre was the messenger of the god to the hero and the life attendant of the latter. He loved her, but she, to keep her calling, must remain a virgin. Otherwise she gave up her divine position and deathlessness in order to live and die with him.[1] The notion of merit and power in renunciation is heathen, not Christian, in origin. The most revolting application of it was when two married people renounced conjugal intimacy in order to be holy.

420. Marriage in early Christianity. In the earliest centuries of Christianity very little attention seems to have been paid to marriage by the Christians. It was left to the mores of each national group, omitting the sacrifices to the heathen gods. It is not possible to trace the descent of Christian marriage from Jewish, Greek, or Roman marriage, but the best authorities think that its fundamental idea is Jewish (carnal union), not Roman (jural relations).[2] " The church found the solemn ceremonies for concluding marriage existing [in each nation]. No divine command in regard to this matter is to be found " [in the New Testament].[3] The church, in time, added new ceremonies to suit its own views. Hence there was the same variety at first inside the church as there had been before Christianity. There can, therefore, be no doubt that, throughout the Latin branch of the church, the usages and theories of Roman marriage passed over into the Christian church. Lecky says that at Rome monogamy was from the earliest times strictly enjoined ; and it was one of the greatest benefits that have resulted from the expansion of Roman power, that it made this type dominant in Europe.[4] Although

[1] Wisen, *Qvinnan i Nordens Forntid,* 7.
[2] Freisen, *Gesch. des kanon. Eherechts,* 154

[3] *Ibid.,* 121.
[4] *Eur. Morals,* II, 298.

the Romans had strict monogamy in their early history, they had abandoned it before their expansion began to have effect, and monogamy was the rule, in the civilized world, for those who were not rich and great, quite independently of Roman influence, at the time of Christ. The Roman marriage of the time of the empire, especially in the social class which chiefly became Christians, was "free marriage," consisting in *consensus* and delivery of the bride. Richer people added *instrumenta dotalia* as documents to regulate property rights, and as proofs of the marital affection of the groom by virtue of which he meant to make the bride his wife, not his concubine. The marriage of richer people, therefore, had a guarantee which had no place between those who had no occasion for such documents. Life with a woman of good reputation and honorable life created a presumption of marriage. The church enforced this as a conscience marriage, which it was the man's duty to observe and keep.

421. Marriage in Roman law. In the *corpus juris civilis* there are two passages which deserve especial attention. In Dig., I, xxiii, 2, it is said: "Nuptials are a conjunction of a male and a female and a correlation (*consortium*) of their entire lives; a mutual interchange (*communicatio*) of rights under both human and divine law." In the *Institutes* (sec. I, i, 9) it is said: "Nuptials, or matrimony, is a conjunction of a man and a woman which constitutes a single course of life (*individuam vitae consuetudinem*)." These are formulas for very high conceptions of marriage. They would enter easily into the notion of pair marriage at its best. The former formula never was, amongst the Romans, anything but an enthusiastic outburst. Roman man and wife had no common property; they could make no gifts to each other lest they should despoil each other; their union, in the time of the empire, was dissoluble almost at pleasure; the father and mother had not the same relation to their children; the woman, if detected in adultery, was severely punished; the man, in the same case, was not punished at all. The "correlation of their entire lives" was, therefore, very imperfect. The sense of *individuam vitae consuetudinem* is very uncertain. It could not have meant merely the exclusive conjugal relation of each to the other, although such was the sense given to the words in the church. The law contained no specification of the mutual rights and duties of the spouses. These were set by the mores and varied very greatly in Roman history. *Affectus maritalis* (the disposition of a husband to a wife) and *honore pleno deligere* (to distinguish with complete honor) are alone emphasized as features of marriage which distinguished it from concubinage.[1] Roman jurists took marriage as a fact, for at Rome from the earliest times, it had been a family matter, developed in the folkways. The civil law defined the rights which the state regarded as its business in that connection, and which it would, therefore, enforce.[2]

422. Roman "free marriage." The passages quoted in the last paragraph refer to "free marriage" after the *manus* idea had been lost. They could be applied also to the German notion of marriage after the Germans abandoned the *mund* idea. They also correspond to the Greek view of marriage, for in Greece the authority of the father early became obsolete in its despotic form. From the time of Diocletian the woman who was *sui juris* was a subject of the state without intermediary, just as her brother or husband was, and she enjoyed free disposition of herself. The same view of marriage passed into the Decretals of Gratian and into our modern legislation.[3]

423. Free marriage. At the end of the fourth century A.D. the church set aside the Roman notions of the importance of the *dos* and *donatio propter nuptias*, and made the *consensus* the essential element in marriage. This was an adoption of that form of "free marriage" of the time of the empire which the class from which Christians came had practiced. That is to say, that the church took up the form of marriage which had been in the class mores of the class from which the church was recruited. This is really all that can be said about the origin of "Christian marriage." It is a perpetuation of the mores of the lowest free classes in the Roman world. Justinian reintroduced the *dos* and *donatio* for persons of the higher classes who were, in his time, included in the church. People of the lower class were to utter the *consensus* in a church before three or four clergymen, and a

[1] Cf. Freisen, 26.   [2] Rossbach, *Röm. Ehe.*, 9.   [3] *Ibid.*, 62.

certificate was to be prepared.[1] The lowest classes might still neglect all ceremony. This law aimed to secure publicity, a distinct expression of consent, and a record. There is no reference to any religious blessing or other function of the clergy. They appear as civil functionaries charged to witness and record an act of the parties.[2] In another novel[3] all this was done away with except the written contract about the dower, if there was one.[4]

424. Transition from Roman to Christian marriage. The ideal of marriage which has just been described came into the Christian church out of the Roman world. Roman wedding sacrifices were intended to obtain signs of the approval of the gods on the wedding. They were domestic sacrifices only, since the sacred things of the spouses were at home only. The auspices ceased to be taken at marriages from the time of Cicero. It became customary to declare that nothing unfavorable to the marriage had occurred. There are many relief representations of late Roman marriages on which Juno appears as *pronuba*, a figure of her standing behind the spouses as protectress or patroness. Rossbach[5] thus interprets such a relief : "The bethrothed, with the assistance of Juno, goddess of marriage, solemnly make the covenant of their love, to which Venus and the Graces are favorable, by prayer and sacrifices before the gods. By the aid of Juno love becomes a legitimate marriage." Rossbach mentions exactly similar reliefs in which Christ is the *pronuba*, and the transition to Christianity is distinctly presented. In a similar manner ideas and customs about marriage were brought under Christian symbol or ceremony, and handed down to us as "Christian marriage." The origin of them is in the mores of the classes who accepted Christianity, which were subjected to a grand syncretism in the first centuries of Christianity.

425. Ancient German marriage. No documents were necessary until the time of Justinian (550 A.D.), an oral agreement being sufficient, if probable. There were essential parts of the Roman wedding usages which were independent of paganism and which

---

[1] *Novel.*, LXXIV, c. 4, sec. 1 (537 A.D.).   [3] CXVII, c. 4.
[2] Cf. *Nov.*, XXII, c. 3.   [4] Friedberg, 14-16.
[5] *Röm. Hochzeits und Ehedenkmäler*, 49, 107.

were necessarily performed at home. In the Eastern empire concubinage was abolished at the end of the ninth century. The heathen Germans had two kinds of marriage, one with, the other without, jural consequences. Both were marriage. The difference was that one consisted in betrothal, endowment, and a solemn wedding ceremony; the other lacked these details. Here, again, it is worth while to notice that property and rank would very largely control the question which of these two forms was more suitable. Consequences as to property followed from the former form which were wanting in the latter. If the pair had no property, the latter form was sufficient. In mediæval Christian Germany the canon law obliterated the distinction, but then morganatic marriage was devised, by which a man of higher rank could marry a woman of lower rank without creating rights of property or rank in her or her children. In such a form of marriage the Roman law saw lack of *affectus maritalis* and of *deligere honore pleno ;* hence the union was concubinage, not marriage. The German law held that the intention to marry made marriage, and that property rights were another matter.[1] The ancient mores lasted on and kept control of marriage, and the church, in its efforts to establish its own theories of marriage, property, legitimacy, rank, etc., was at war with the old mores.

426. Early church usage. In the Decretals of Gratian[2] are collected the earliest authorities about marriage in the Christian church, some of which are regarded now as ungenuine. "Nevertheless it is impossible to say that, in the early times of Christianity, there was any church wedding. Weddings were accomplished before witnesses independently of the church, or perhaps in the presence of a priest by the *professiones.*" Then followed the pompous home bringing of the bride. Afterwards the spouses took part in the usual church service and the sacrament and gave oblations.[3] Later special prayers for the newly wedded were introduced into the service. Later still special masses for the newly wedded were introduced. Such existed probably before

---

[1] Freisen, 48, 103 ; Grimm, *D. R. A.*, 420.
[2] II, c. XXX, qu. 5, c. 1.
[3] Pullan, *Hist. Book of Common Prayer*, 217.

the ninth century.[1] The declaration of *consensus* still took place elsewhere than in church, and not until the rituals of the eleventh and twelfth centuries does the priest ask for it, or is it asked for in his presence. In the Greek ritual there has never yet been any declaration of *consensus*.[2]

427. The usage as to religious ceremony. The more pious people were, the more anxious they were to put all their doings under church sanction, and they sought the advice of honored ecclesiastics as to marriage. Such is the sense of Ignatius to Polycarp, chapter 5. Tertullian was a rigorist and extremist, whose utterances do not represent fact. In our own law and usage a common-law marriage is valid, but people of dignified and serious conduct, still more people of religious feeling, do not seek the minimum which the law will enforce. They seek to comply with the usages in their full extent, and to satisfy the whole law of the religious body to which they belong. In like manner, there was a great latitude from the fourth to the sixteenth century, while the Christian church was trying to mold the barbarian mores to its own standards in the usages which were current, but an ecclesiastical function was not necessary to a valid marriage until the Council of Trent. In fact a wedding in church never was an unconditional requirement for a valid marriage among German Roman Catholics until the end of the eighteenth century.[3] Somewhat parallel cases of the addition of religious ceremonies to solemn public acts which had been developed in the mores are the emancipation of a slave, and the making of a knight.[4]

428. Mode of expressing *consensus*. If the consent of the parties is regarded as essential, then the public proceedings must bring out an expression of will. The ancient German usage was that the friends formed a circle in which the persons to be married took their place, and the woman's guardian, later her most distinguished friend, asked them (the woman first) whether it was their will to become man and wife, — these terms being

---

[1] Friedberg, *Recht der Eheschliessung*, 8.
[2] *Ibid.*, 9.
[3] Stammler, *Stellung der Frauen*, 27.
[4] Jenks, *Law and Politics in the Middle Ages*, 251.

defined in the mores. This was a convenient and rational proceeding, of primitive simplicity and adaptation to the purpose. In Scandinavia and Iceland the ancient laws contained exact prescriptions as to the person who might officiate as the conductor of this ceremony. Relatives of the bride, first on her father's side, then on her mother's, were named in a series according to rank.[1] Such a prolocutor is taken for understood in the *Constitutio de Nuptiis* (England).[2] To him the man promises to take the woman to wife " by the law of God and the customs of the world, and that he will keep her as a man ought to keep his wife." Evidently these statements convey no idea of wedlock unless the mores of the time and place are known. They alone could show how a man " ought to keep his wife." The man also promises to show due provision of means of support, and his friends become his sureties. Through the Middle Ages great weight was given to the provision for the woman throughout her life, especially in case of widowhood. In fact, a " wife " differed from a mistress by virtue of this provision for her life. In the *Constitutio de Nuptiis* it is added, " Let a priest be present at the nuptials, who is to unite them of right, with the blessing of God, in full plenitude of felicity."

429. Marriage at the church door. In a French ritual of 700 A.D. the priest goes to the church door and asks the young pair (who appear to be walking and wooing in the street) whether they want to be duly married. The proceedings all concern the marriage gifts, after which there is a benediction at the church door, and then the pair go into the church to the mass. A hundred years later the priest asked for the *consensus*, and statement of the gift from the groom to the bride, and for a gift for the poor. Then the woman was given *by her father* or friends.[3]

430. Marriage in Germany in the early Middle Ages. In the Frank, Suabian, Westphalian, and Bavarian laws "the woman was entitled to her dower when she had put her foot in the bed." The German saying was, "When the coverlet is drawn over

---

[1] Lehmann, *Verlobung und Hochzeit nach den nordgermanischen Rechten des früheren M. A.*, 31.

[2] Wilkins, *Concilia*, I, 216 (644 A.D.).   [3] Friedberg, 61.

their heads the spouses are equally rich," that is, they have all property of either in common.[1] Hence, in German law and custom, *consensus* followed by *concubitus* made marriage. Hence also arose the custom that the witnesses accompanied the spouses to their bedchamber and saw them covered, or visited them later. Important symbolic acts were connected with this visit. The spouses ate and drank together. The guests drove them to bed with blows.[2] The witnesses were not to witness a promise, but a fact. In the Carolingian period, except in forged capitularies, there is very little testimony to the function of priests in weddings.

The custom of the Jews has been mentioned above (sec. 417). Selected witnesses were thought necessary to testify at any time to the consummation of the marriage. In the third century B.C. this custom was modified to a ceremony.[3] In ancient India and at Rome newly wedded spouses were attended by the guests when they retired.[4] The Germans had this custom from the earliest times and they kept it up through the Middle Ages. The jural consequences of marriage began from the moment that both were covered by the coverlet. This was what the witnesses were to testify to. Evidently the higher classes had the most reason to establish the jural consequences. Therefore kings kept up this custom longest, although it degenerated more and more into a mere ceremony.[5] The German Emperor Frederick III met his bride, a Portuguese princess, at Naples. The pair lay down on the bed and were covered by the coverlet for a moment, in the presence of the court. They were fully dressed and rose again. The Portuguese ladies were shocked at the custom.[6] The custom can be traced, in Brandenburg, as late as the beginning of the eighteenth century.[7] English customs of the eighteenth century to seize articles of the bride's dress were more objectionable.

The church ceremony, however, won its way in popular usage. It consisted in blessing the ring and the gifts, and the interest of ecclesiastics began to be centered on the question whether the persons to be married were within the forbidden degrees of relationship.[8] In the *Petri Exceptiones* (between 1050 and 1075)[9]

---

[1] Freisen, 118.   [2] Friedberg, 23.
[3] Freisen, *Kanon. Eherecht*, 92, 96; Bergel, *Eheverhält. der Juden*, 19.
[4] Rossbach, *Röm. Ehe*, 370.   [5] Weinhold, *D. F.*, I, 399.
[6] *Gesch. Fried. III*, by Æneas Silvius, trans. Ilgen, II, 95.
[7] Friedberg, *Recht der Eheschliessung*, 23.   [8] Friedberg, 58.
[9] Savigny, *Gesch. des Röm. Rechts im M. A.*, II, *Append.*

it is expressly stated, amongst other statements of what does *not* make a marriage, that it is not the benediction of the priest, but the mental purpose of the man and woman. Other things only establish testimony and record. Weinhold [1] cites a poem of the eleventh century in which a wedding is described. After the betrothal is agreed upon by the relatives, and property agreements have been made, the groom gives to the bride a ring on a sword hilt, saying, " As the ring firmly incloses thy finger, so do I promise thee firm and constant fidelity. Thou shalt maintain the same to me, or thy life shall be the penalty." She takes the ring, they kiss, and the bystanders sing a wedding song. In a Suabian document of the twelfth century, the bridegroom is the chief actor.[2] He lays down successively seven gloves, the glove being the symbol of the man himself in his individual responsibility and authority. Each glove is a pledge of what he promises according to the prescriptions of the Suabian mores, for which his formula is, " As by right a free Suabian man should do to a free Suabian woman." He enumerates the chief kinds of Suabian property and promises to write out his pledges in a *libellus dotis*, if the bride will provide the scribe. Then the woman's guardian, having received these pledges, delivers her, with a sword (on the hilt of which is a finger ring), a penny, a mantle, and a hat on the sword, and says : " Herewith I transfer my ward to your faithfulness, and to your grace, and I pray you, by the faith with which I yield her to you, that you be her true guardian, and her gracious guardian, and that you do not become her direful guardian." " Then," it is added, " let him take her and have her as his." This must be a very ancient form, of German origin. There is no *consensus* expressed in it and the symbolism is elaborate. The *libellus dotis* is evidently an innovation. It has a Latin name and is a contingent, not a substantive part of the man's acts. The old German form shows that the Latin church usage had not yet overturned the German tradition.

431. The canon law. In the Decretals of Gratian [3] the doctrine of nuptials is that they begin with the public ceremony

---

[1] *Deutsche Frauen*, I, 341. [2] *Rhein. Mus.*, 1829, 281.
[3] II, c. XXVII, qu. 2, and c. XXXIV.

and are completed by *concubitus*. Agreement to cohabit, followed
by cohabitation, constituted marriage by the canon law. This is
the common sense of the case. It was the doctrine of the canon
law and is the widest modern civilized view.

432. Mediæval marriage. In the thirteenth century began
the astonishing movement by which the church remodeled all
the ideas and institutions of the age, and integrated all social
interests into a system of which it made itself the center and
controlling authority. The controlling tendency in the mores of
the age was religiosity, — a desire to construe all social relations
from the church standpoint and to set all interests in a religious
light. Marriage fell under this influence. The priests displaced
the earlier prolocutors, and strove to make marriage an ecclesiastical function and their own share in it essential, although they
did not make the validity of marriage depend on their share in
it.[1] In different places and amongst different classes the custom
of church marriage was introduced at earlier or later times, and
the doctrine of priestly function in connection with marriage
became established with greater or less precision. Friedberg[2]
considers the ordinance of the Synod of Westminster[3] (1175)
the first ordinance which distinctly prescribed church marriage
in England, but from that to the establishment of a custom was
a long way. Pollock and Maitland[4] think that marriage, in England, belonged to the ecclesiastical forum by the middle of the
twelfth century. Rituals of Salisbury and York of the thirteenth
century show the early church customs, only rendered more elaborate and more precise in detail.[5] There is also ritual provision
for an ecclesiastic to bless the bed of the spouses after they are
in it, in order to drive away the evil spirits. In 1240, in the
constitutions of Walter de Cantelupe, marriage is called a sacrament, because it prefigures the sacrament between Christ and the
church. Marriage was to precede *concubitus*. There was to be
no divination or use of devices for luck. By synodal statutes of
1246 it was ordered that priests should teach that betrothal and

[1] Friedberg, 98.
[2] *Ibid.*, 39.
[3] Wilkins, *Concilia*, I, 478.
[4] *Hist. Eng. Law*, I, 109; II, 365.
[5] Surtees Soc., *Man. et Pont. Ecc. Ebor.*, 157, and App. 17.

consummation would constitute irrevocable marriage.[1] If people
treated church ordinances and forms with neglect they were
punished by church discipline, but the marriage was not declared
invalid. Hence the system was elastic and could not be abruptly
changed.

**433. Conflict of mores and church programme. Betrothal and
wedding.** In Germany the popular resistance to a change of the
mores about marriage was more stubborn than elsewhere. Although ecclesiastics were present at marriages, until the thirteenth
century, they sometimes took no part.[2] In the poems, from the
beginning of the twelfth century, mention is made of priestly
benediction ; still it remains uncertain whether this took place
before or after *concubitus*. In the great epics of the thirteenth
century the old custom of the circle of friends and the interroga-
tories by a distinguished relative appears. The couple spend the
night together and on the following morning go to church where
they are blessed.[3] This is the proceeding in Lohengrin. In the
thirteenth century the prolocutor was going out of fashion and
the ecclesiastic got a chance to take his place.[4] Evidently there
was here an ambiguity between the betrothal and the wedding.
It took two or three centuries to eliminate it. When the man
said, " I will take," did he mean," It is my will to take now," or
did he mean, " I will take at a future time " ? Sohm[5] says that
betrothal was the real conclusion of a marriage, and that the wedding was only the confirmation (*Vollzug*) of a marriage already consummated. Friedberg[6] says that the wedding was the conclusion
of a projected marriage and not the consummation of one already
concluded. When there was a solemn public betrothal and then
a wedding after an interval of time, the latter was plainly a repetition which had no significance. What happened finally was that
the betrothal fell into insignificance, or was united with the wedding as in the modern Anglican service, and *concubitus* was allowed
only after the wedding. The wedding then had importance, and
was not merely a blessing on a completed fact. It was then a

---

[1] Wilkins, I, 668, 690.   [4] Weinhold, *D. F.*, I, 373.
[2] Friedberg, 79.   [5] *Trauung und Verlobung*, 37.
[3] *Nibelungen*, 568–597.   [6] *Verlobung und Trauung*, 23.

custom in all classes to try life together before marriage (*Probenächte*). In the fifteenth century, if kings were married by proxy, the proxy slept with the bride, with a sword between, *before* the church ceremony.[1] The custom to celebrate marriages without a priest lasted, amongst the peasants of Germany, until the sixteenth century.[2] "It was, therefore, customary [in the thirteenth century] to have the church blessing, but generally only after consummated marriage. The blessing was not essential, but was considered appropriate and proper, especially in the higher classes. In the fourteenth century the ecclesiastical form won more and more sway over the popular sentiment."[3]

434. Church marriage. Concubines. It is necessary to notice that there is never any question of the status of men. They satisfy their interests as well as they can and the result is the stage of civilization. The status of women is their position with respect to men in a society in which men hold the deciding voice. Men bear power and responsibility. Women are the coadjutors, with more or less esteem, honor, coöperative function, and joint authority. There has never until modern times been a law of the state which forbade a man to take a second wife with the first. A man could not commit adultery because he was not bound, by law or mores, to his wife as she was to him. A man and woman marry themselves and lead conjugal life in a world of their own. Church and state would be equally powerless to marry them. The church may "bless" their union. The state may define and enforce the civil and property rights of themselves or their children. It cannot enforce conjugal rights. Therefore it cannot divorce two spouses. They divorce themselves. The state can say what civil and property right shall be affected by the divorce, and how the force of the state shall enforce the consequences. The marriage relation is domestic and private, where the wills of the individuals prevail and where the police cannot act. The Christian church, about the thirteenth century, introduced a marriage ritual in which the spouses promised exclusive fidelity, the man as much as the woman. As fast and as far

---

[1] Friedberg, 90.   [2] Hagelstange, *Bauernleben im M. A.*, 61.
[3] Friedberg, 85; cf. Weinhold, *D. F.*, I, 378; Grimm, *D. R. A.*, 436.

as church marriage was introduced, the promise set the idea of marriage. If either broke the promise, he or she was liable to church censure and penance. In England the first civil law against bigamy was I James I, chapter 11. Never until 1563 (Council of Trent) was any ecclesiastical act necessary to the validity of a marriage even in the forum of the church. Marriage was in the mores. The blessing of the church was edifying and contributory. It was not essential. Marriage was popular and belonged to the family. In the ancient nations sacrifices were made for good fortune in wedlock. In the Middle Ages Christian priests· blessed marriages which had been concluded by laymen and had already been consummated. The relation of husband and wife varied, at that time, in the villages of Germany or northern France of the same nationality. Until modern times concubinage has existed as a recognized institution. It was an inferior form of marriage, in which the woman did not take the rank of her husband, and her children did not inherit his rank or property, but her status was permanent and defined. Sometimes it was exclusive. Then again slaves have been at the mercy of a master and in ancient times they were always proud to "find favor in his eyes." Thus wives, concubines, and slave women form three recognized ranks of female companions.

435. The church elevated the notion of marriage. In all the ancient civilized states marriage was an affair of property interests and rank. The public ceremony was needed in order to establish rights of property and inheritance, legitimacy, and civil rights. The Christian church of the Middle Ages had to find a ground for its own intervention. This it did by emphasizing the mystic element in marriage, and developing all the symbolism of the Bible which could be applied to this subject and all the biographical details which touched upon it, — Adam and Eve, Tobias, Joseph and Mary, the one-flesh idea, the symbolism of Christ and the church, etc. Thus a sentimental-poetical-mystical conception of marriage was superimposed on the materialistic-sensual conception of it. The church affirmed that marriage was a "sacrament." A half-dozen different explanations of "sacrament" in this connection could be quoted. It is impossible to tell what it means. The church, however, by its policy, contributed greatly to the development of the nobler conception of marriage in modern mores. The materialistic view of it has been left decently covered, and the conception of wedlock as a fusion of two lives and interests into affectionate coöperation, by the sympathy of character and tastes, has become the ideal. The church did much to bring about this change. For an age which attributed a vague and awful efficacy to a "sacrament," and was familiar, in church matters, with such parallelisms as that alleged between marriage and the union of Christ with his church, it is very probable that the church "fostered a feeling that a lifelong union of one man and one woman is, under all circumstances, the single form of intercourse between the sexes which is not illegitimate; and this conviction has acquired the force of a primal moral intuition."[1] What has chiefly aided this effect has been the rise to wealth and civil power of the middle class of the later Middle Ages, in whose mores such views had become fixed without much direct church influence.

436. The decrees of Trent about marriage. It was not until the decrees of Trent (1563) that the church established in its law the sacerdotal theory of marriage in place of the theory of the canon law. The motive at Trent was to prevent clandestine marriages, that is, marriages which were not made by a priest or in church. These marriages were common and they were mischievous because not to be proved. They made descent and inheritance uncertain when the parties belonged to families of property and rank. In form, the decrees of Trent provided for publicity. Marriage was to be celebrated in church, by the parish priest, and before two witnesses. This action was not in pursuance of a change in the mores. It was a specific device of leading churchmen to accomplish an object. In view of the course of the mores, it may be doubted if any effect ought to be attributed to the decrees of Trent for their immediate purpose, but two effects have been produced which the churchmen probably did not foresee. First, it became the law of the church that the consent of a man and a woman, expressed in a church before

---

[1] Lecky, *Eur. Morals*, II, 347.

the parish priest, constituted a marriage without any voluntary participation of the priest. The Huguenots in France, for more than a century, married themselves in this way, a notary being employed to make a record and certificate. Secondly, this law became the great engine of the church to hold its children to their allegiance and prevent mixed marriages. To win the consent of the parish priest to perform the ceremony the parties must conform to church requirements, — confession and communion. The seventeenth and eighteenth centuries were occupied by struggles of living men to regulate their interests in independence of these restraints.

437. Puritan marriage. The Puritan sects made marriage more secular, as the Romish Church made it more ecclesiastical. Although they liked to give a religious tone to all the acts of life, the Puritans took away from marriage all religious character. It was performed by a civil magistrate. Such was the rule in New England until the end of the seventeenth century. However, there was, in this matter, an inconsistency between the ruling ideas and the partisan position, and the latter gave way. There has been a steady movement of the mores throughout the Protestant world in the direction of giving to marriage a religious character and sanction. It has become the rule that marriages shall be performed by ministers of religion, and the custom of celebrating them in religious buildings is extending. The authority and example of the church of Rome have had nothing to do with this tendency. They are not even known. It has been purely a matter of taste, sentiment, and popular judgment as to what is right and proper; also it has been due to the ideas of women in regard to suitable pomp and glory. The mores have once more taken full control of the matter, and the religious ceremony is used to satisfy the interests, and fulfill the faiths, of the population. Such is the effect of civil marriage as established in the nineteenth century. At the present time the ministers of religion seem disposed to use their lawful position as the proper ones to celebrate marriage, that they may impose restrictions on divorce, and on marriage after divorce.

CHAPTER XI

THE SOCIAL CODES

438. Specification of the subject. The ethnographers write of a tribe that the " morality " in it, especially of the women, is low or high, etc. This is the technical use of morality, — as a thing pertaining to the sex relation only or especially, and the ethnographers make their propositions by applying our standards of sex behavior, and our form of the sex taboo, to judge the folkways of all people. All that they can properly say is that they find a great range and variety of usages, ideas, standards, and ideals, which differ greatly from ours. Some of them are far stricter than ours. Those we do not consider nobler than ours. We do not feel that we ought to adopt any ways because they are more strict than our traditional ones. We consider many to be excessive, silly, and harmful. A Roman senator was censured for impropriety because he kissed his wife in the presence of his daughter.[1]

439. Meaning of "immoral." When, therefore, the ethnographers apply condemnatory or depreciatory adjectives to the people whom they study, they beg the most important question which we want to investigate; that is, What are standards, codes, and ideas of chastity, decency, propriety, modesty, etc., and whence do they arise? The ethnographical facts contain the answer to this question, but in order to reach it we want a colorless report of the facts. We shall find proof that "immoral" never means anything but contrary to the mores of the time and place. Therefore the mores and the morality may move together, and there is no permanent or universal standard by which right and truth in regard to these matters can be established and different folkways compared and criticised. Only experience produces judgments of the expediency of some usages. For instance, ancient peoples thought pederasty was harmless and trivial. It has been well proved to be corrupting both to individual and social vigor, and harmful to interests, both individual and collective. Cannibalism, polygamy, incest, harlotry, and other primitive customs have been discarded by a very wide and, in the case of some of them, unanimous judgment that they are harmful. On the other hand, in the *Avesta* spermatorrhea is a crime punished by stripes.[2] The most civilized peoples also maintain, by virtue of their superior position in the arts of life, that they have attained to higher and better judgments and that they may judge the customs of others from their own standpoint. For three or four centuries they have called their own customs "Christian," and have thus claimed for them a religious authority and sanction which they do not possess by any connection with the principles of Christianity. Now, however, the adjective

---

[1] Ammianus Marcellinus, XXVIII, 4.　　[2] Darmstetter, *Zend-Avesta*, I, 100.

seems to be losing its force. The Japanese regard nudity with indifference, but they use dress to conceal the contour of the human form while we use it to enhance, in many ways, the attraction. " Christian " mores have been enforced by the best breechloaders and ironclads, but the Japanese now seem ready to bring superiority in those matters to support their mores. It is now a known and recognized fact that our missionaries have unintentionally and unwittingly done great harm to nature people by inducing them to wear clothes as one of the first details of civilized influence. In the usages of nature peoples there is no correlation at all between dress and sentiments of chastity, modesty, decency, and propriety.[1]

440. Natural functions. The fact that human beings have natural functions the exercise of which is unavoidable but becomes harmful to other human beings, in a rapidly advancing ratio, as greater and greater numbers are collected within close neighborhood to each other, makes it necessary that natural functions shall be regulated by rules and conventions. The passionate nature of the sex appetite, by virtue of which it tends to excess and vice, forces men to connect it with taboos and regulations which also are conventional and institutional. The taboos of chastity, decency, propriety, and modesty, and those on all sex relations are therefore adjustments to facts of human nature and conditions of human life. It is never correct to regard any one of the taboos as an arbitrary invention or burden laid on society by tradition without necessity. Very many of them are due originally to vanity, superstition, or primitive magic, wholly or in part, but they have been sifted for centuries by experience, and those which we have received and accepted are such as experience has proved to be expedient.

441. The current code and character. It follows that, in history and ethnography, the mores and conduct in any group are independent of those of any other group. Those of any group need to be consistent with each other, for if they are not so the conduct will not be easily consistent with the code, and it is when the conduct is not consistent with the code which is current and

[1] Marsden, *Sumatra*, 52.

professed that there is corruption, discord, and decay of character. So long as the customs are simple, naïve, and unconscious, they do not produce evil in character, no matter what they are. If reflection is awakened and the mores cannot satisfy it, then doubt arises; individual character will then be corrupted and the society will degenerate.

442. Definitions of chastity, decency, propriety, etc. Chastity, modesty, and decency are entirely independent of each other. The ethnographic proof of this is complete. Chastity means conformity to the taboo on the sex relation, whatever its terms and limits may be in the group at the time. Therefore, where polyandry is in the mores, women who comply with it are not unchaste. Where there are no laws for the conduct of unmarried women they are not unchaste. It is evidently an incorrect use of language to describe the unmarried women of a tribe as unchaste, unless there is a rule for them. It can only mean that they violate the rule of some other society, and that can be said always about those in any group. There are cases in which women wear nothing but are faithful to a strict sex taboo, and there are cases where they go completely covered but have no sex taboo. Decency has to do with the covering of the body and with the concealment of bodily functions. Modesty is reserve of behavior and sentiment. It is correlative to chastity and decency, but covers a far wider field. It arrests acts, speech, gestures, etc., and repels suggestions at the limit of propriety wherever that may be set by the mores. Propriety is the sum of all the prescriptions in the mores as to right and proper behavior, or as to the limit of degree which prevents excess or vice. It is not dictated in laws. It is a floating notion. From time to time, however, dictates of propriety are enacted into police regulations. Propriety is guaranteed by shame, which is the sense of pain due to incurring disapproval because one has violated the usage which the mores command every one to observe. It is narrated of Italian nuns who had been veiled even from each other for half a lifetime that when turned out of their convents they suffered from exposing their faces the same shame that other women would suffer from far greater exposure. It could not be otherwise Mohammedan women, if surprised when bathing, cover first the face. They are distinguished from non-Mohammedan women by the veil; therefore this covering is to them most important. Chinese women, whose feet have been compressed, consider it indecent to expose them. Within a generation the public latrines in the cities of continental Europe have been made far more secluded and private than they formerly were. Within ten years there has been a great change of standard as to the propriety of spitting. Beyond the domain of propriety lie the domains of politeness, courtesy, good manners, seemliness, breeding, and good form. The definition depends on where the line is drawn. That point is always conventional. It is a matter of tradition and social contact to learn where it lies. It never can be formulated. Habit must form a feeling or taste by which new cases can be decided. There are persons and classes who possess such social prestige that they can alter the line of definition a small distance and get the change taken up into the mores, but it is the mores which always contain and carry on the definitions and standards. Therefore it is to the mores that we must look to find the determining causes or motives, the field of origin, the corrective or corrupting influences, and the educative operations, which account for all the immense and contradictory variety of the folkways, under chastity, decency, modesty, propriety, etc.

443. Chastity. An Australian husband assumes that his wife has been unfaithful to him if she has had opportunity. In most tribes women are not allowed to converse or have any relations whatever with any men but their husbands, even with their own grown-up brothers.[1] Veth[2] thinks that the observance of the sex taboo by Dyak wives has been exaggerated, but that, at least on the west coast, it is better than that of the Malay women. The young unmarried women among the sea Dyaks take great license, and the custom of lending daughters exists, but such customs are unknown on the west coast. On the Andaman Islands there is no sex taboo for the unmarried and they use license. The girls are modest, and when married conform to the taboo of

---

[1] Curr, *Austr. Race,* I, 109.   [2] *Borneo's Wester-Afdeeling,* 251.

marriage. Their husbands "do not fall far short of them." The women will not renew their leaf aprons in the presence of each other.[1] The Yakuts use leather guarantees of their wives and daughters, similar to the mediæval device,[2] which always implies that the wife will make use of any opportunity. The Yakut women wore garments even in bed.[3] The Eskimo of eastern Greenland do not disapprove of a husbandless mother but of a childless wife.[4] Bushmen women observe a stricter taboo than their Kaffir neighbors. They refuse illicit relations with the latter, although the Kaffirs are a superior race.[5] The Zulu women observe a strict taboo with noteworthy fidelity.[6] Madame Pommerol[7] represents the Arab women of the nomadic or semi-nomadic tribes of southern Algiers as destitute of moral training. They have no code of morals or religion. [What she means is that they have no character by education.] They shun men, but handle the veil in a coquettish manner according to artificial and excessive usages. They act only between impulses of desire and fear of fathers or husbands. Fidelity has no sense, since they do not feel the loyalty either of duty or affection. The Mayas of the lowest classes sent out their daughters to earn their own marriage portions.[8] On the Palau Islands mothers train their daughters to make gain of themselves in the local shell money and bring the same to their parents. The girls become *armengols;* that is, they live in the clubhouses which are the residences of the young men, where they do domestic work and win influence. An insult to such a woman is an insult to the club. The origin of the custom was in war; the women were captives. Some are now given in tribute. "The custom is not a pure expression of sensuality." As there is no family life this is the woman's chance to know men and influence them. It is rated as education.[9] Semper[10] quotes native justification of the custom. A man's

---

[1] JAI, XII, 94, 135.
[2] Schultz, *D. L.*, 283.
[3] Sieroshevski, *Yakuty (Polish)*, 342.
[4] Holm, *Angmagslikerne*, 54.
[5] Fritsch, *Eingeb. Süd-Afr.*, 444.
[6] *Amer. Antiq.*, XXIV, 77.
[7] *Une Femme chez les Sahariennes.*
[8] Bancroft, *Races of the Pacific*, I, 123; II, 676.
[9] Kubary, *Soc. Einricht. der Pelauer*, 51, 55, 91.
[10] *Palau*, 65, 324.

young last-wedded wife complained to his older wife that he made her serve the *armengols*. The older wife told her to remember that she had herself enjoyed this life and had been served by the married women. All girls liked to earn the money by which, when they came home, they got husbands. It was ancient custom and must be obeyed. If the married women refused to do their duty, the men would not be served, for a married woman might never show the world that she was on intimate terms with her husband. That would be *mugul*, and when once that word lost its force the whole island would perish. A woman argued to Semper that the custom was a good one because it gave the women a chance to see the other islands, and because they learned to serve and obey the men. It was, she said, their sacred duty. Any girl who did not go abroad as an *armengol* would get the reputation of being stupid and uncultivated, and would get no husband.[1] Cases in which husbands are indifferent to the fidelity of wives to the marriage taboo occur, but they are rare.[2] In some Arabic tribes of Sahara, even those in which the struggle for existence is not severe, fathers expect daughters to ransom themselves from the expense of their rearing by prostitution. The notion of sex honor has not yet overcome the sense of pecuniary loss or gain. The more a woman gains, the more she is sought in marriage afterwards. Tuareg married women enter into relations with men not their husbands like those of women with their lovers in the woman cult of the twelfth and thirteenth centuries in central Europe. These women have decent and becoming manners, with much care for etiquette.[3] A thirteenth-century writer says of the Mongol women that they are "chaste, and nothing is heard amongst them of lewdness, but some of the expressions they use in joking are very shameful and coarse." The same is true now.[4] An Arab author is cited as stating that at Mirbat women went outside the city at night to sport with strange men. Their own husbands

---

[1] Cf. Christian, *Caroline Isl.*, 290.

[2] JAI, XV, 8; *U. S. Nat. Mus.*, 1888, 339.

[3] Duveyrier, *Touaregs du Nord*, 340, 429.

[4] Rubruck, *Eastern Parts*, 79, Rockhill's note.

and male relatives passed them by to seek other women.[1] Amongst the Gowane people in Kordofan (who seem now to be Moslems)[2] a girl cannot marry without her brother's consent. To get this she must give to her brother an infant. She finds the father where she can.[3]

444. Pagan life policy. Very naturally the pagan inference or generalization from the above customs was that a husband must be under continual anxiety about his wife, or he must divorce her, or he must cultivate a high spirit of resignation and indifference. The last was the highest flight of Stoic philosophy about marriage. Plutarch says: "How can you call anything a misfortune which does not damage either your soul or your body, as for example, the low origin of your father, the adultery of your wife, the loss of a crown or seat of honor, none of which affect a man's chances of the highest condition of body and mind."[4]

445. Modesty. Shame. Aristotle[5] hardly rated shame as a virtue. He said that it is only a passing emotion, "an apprehension of dishonor." In his view virtues were habits trained in by education. He deduced them from philosophy and sought to bring them to act on life. He did not regard them as products of life actions. Wundt[6] says that shame is a specific human sentiment, because men alone of animals wear a concealing dress on one part of the body when they wear nothing else. He thinks that men began to cover the body in obedience to the sentiment of decency. The facts here alleged are all incorrect. There are many people who wear something on the body but do not cover the parts referred to (sec. 447). It is certain that pet animals manifest shame when caught doing what they have been taught not to do, — just like children. As to dress, it would be an interesting experiment to let pet dogs play together for a month, dressed in coats and blankets, and then to bring one of them to the meeting without his dress while the others wore theirs. Would he not show shame at not being like the others? A lady made a red jacket for a Javanese ape. He was greatly pleased, buttoned

---

[1] Sprenger, *Geographie Arabiens*, 97.
[2] Probably 31° E. 13½° N.
[3] Wilson and Felkin, *Uganda and Sudan*, II, 309.
[4] *On Tranquil.*, 17.
[5] *Nich. Ethics.*, IV, 9.
[6] *Ethik*, 127.

and unbuttoned the jacket, and showed displeasure when it was taken off. He showed that it aroused his vanity.[1] People who deal with high-bred horses say that they show shame and dissatisfaction if they are in any way inferior to others. It was recently reported in the newspapers that the employés in a menagerie threw some of the beasts into great irritation by laughing in chorus near their cages in such a way that the beasts thought that they were being laughed at. Shame is a product of wounded vanity. It is due to a consciousness, or a fear, of disapproval. It is not limited to exposure of the body, but may be due to disapproval for any reason whatever.

446. The line of decency in dress. The line of decency, for instance in dress, is always paradoxical. No matter where it may be drawn, decency is close to it on one side and indecency on the other. A Moslem woman on the street looks like a bundle of bedclothes. Where all women so look one woman who left off her mantle would seem indecent, and the comparative display of the outlines of the figure would seem shameless. Where low-necked dresses are commonly worn they are not indecent, but they may become so at a point which varies according to custom from place to place and from class to class. The women in modern Jerusalem regard it as very indecent to show themselves *décolletées*. They sit, however, in postures which leave their legs uncovered.[2] A peasant woman could not wear the dress of a lady of fashion. Where men or women wear only a string around the waist, their dress is decent, but it is indecent to leave off the string. The suggestive effect of putting on ornaments and dress at one stage is the same as that of leaving them off at another stage. Barbarians put on dress for festivals, dances, and solemn occasions. Civilized people do the same when they wear robes of office or ceremony. When Hera wanted to stimulate the love of Zeus she made an elaborate toilet and put on extra garments, including a veil.[3] Then taking off the veil was a stimulus. On the other hand, the extremest and most

1 *Umschau*, VI, 52, after Haeckel, *Aus Insulinde.*
2 Goodrich-Frear, *Inner Jerusalem*, 257.
3 *Il.*, XIV, 179; cf. *Od.*, XVI, 416; XVIII, 210.

conventional dress looks elegant and stylish to those who are accustomed to it, as is now the case with ourselves and the current dress, which makes both sexes present an appearance far removed from the natural outline of human beings. Then, at the limit, that is at to-day's fashions, coquetry can be employed again, and a sense stimulus can be exerted again, by simply making variations on the existing fashions at the limit. It is impossible to eliminate the sense stimulus, or to establish a system of societal usage in which indecency shall be impossible. The dresses of Moslem women, nuns, and Quakeresses were invented in order to get rid of any possible question of decency. The attempt fails entirely. A Moslem woman with her veil, a Spanish woman with her mantilla or fan, a Quakeress with her neckerchief, can be as indecent as a barbarian woman with her petticoat of dried grass.

447. Present conventional limits. In our own society decency as to dress, words, gestures, etc., is a constant preoccupation. That is not the case with naked savages or half-naked barbarians. The savages put on ornament to be admired and to exert attraction or produce effect. The same effect is won by words, gestures, dress, etc. Our æsthetic arts all exert the same influence. We expel all these things from our artificial environment down to a limit, in order to restrain and control the stimulus. Then we think that we are decent. That is because we rest at peace in a status which is conventional and accustomed. Variation from it one way is fastidious; the other way is indecent, just as it would be at any other limit whatever. It is the comparison of the mores of different times and peoples which shows the arbitrariness and conventionality. It would be difficult to mention anything in Oriental mores which we regard with such horror as Orientals feel for low-necked dresses and round dances. Orientals use dress to conceal the contour of the form. The waist of a woman is made to disappear by a girdle. To an Oriental a corset, which increases the waist line and the plasticity of the figure, is the extreme of indecency — far worse than nudity. It seems like an application of the art of the courtesan to appeal to sensuality.[1] Perhaps the most instructive case of all is that of the Tuareg

[1] Vambery, *Sittenbilder aus dem Morgenlande*, 49.

men, who keep the mouth always covered. The cloth has a utilitarian purpose, — to prevent thirst by retarding evaporation from the air passages. "They never remove the veil, on a journey, or in repose, not even to eat, much less to sleep." "A Tuareg would think that he committed an impropriety if he should remove his veil, unless it was in extreme intimacy or for a medical investigation." "At Paris I strove in vain to induce three Tuaregs to remove their veils for the purpose of being photographed."[1] No superstitious reason for this veil is known. Madame Pommerol[2] reports that a Tuareg man told her that men keep the mouth covered lest the play of it should expose their feelings to another man. Women, he said, had no such need, since enemies never approach them. Evidently we have here a case of an ancient fact that men are never seen with the mouth uncovered, which has produced a feeling that a man *ought* never to be seen with it uncovered, and rational and utilitarian reasons or explanations have been invented later. Those who paint the body are ashamed to be seen unpainted. In the tribes which are tattooed one would be ashamed who was not tattooed.

448. Decency and vanity. It is another case of shame or offended modesty if the taboo in the mores on acts, words, postures, etc., is broken in one's presence. It is a breach of the respect which one expects, that is, it wounds vanity.

We are ashamed to go barefoot, probably because it is an ordinary evidence of poverty. Von den Steinen has well suggested that some day it may be said that shoes were invented on account of "innate" shame at exposing the feet.[3] In recent years fashion has allowed young people to leave off all head-covering. It could permit them to go barefooted if the whim should take that turn. There is now a "cure" in which men and women walk barefoot in the grass. The cost to their modesty is probably very slight.

449. Modesty the opposite of impudence. Another sense of modesty is the opposite of impudence, shrinking from making demands or otherwise putting one's self forward in a way which

---

[1] Duveyrier, *Les Touaregs du Nord*, 391. [2] *Une Femme chez les Sahariennes*, 310.
[3] *Berl. Mus.*, 1888, 199.

bystanders might think in excess of one's social position or ability. In these cases vanity becomes its own punishment. The Kajans of the Mandalam refrain from injuring private or group interests from fear of public opinion. "Such a sentiment can exist only amongst those who have a feeling of shame strongly developed. Such is the case amongst these people, not only as to punishable offenses, but also in connection with their notions of propriety." [1] "Modesty was an unknown virtue to the bards of Vedic India. They bragged and begged without shame." [2] The same might be said of the troubadours of the Middle Ages.

450. Shame. Shame is felt when one is inferior, or is conscious of being, or of being liable to be, unfavorably regarded. Modesty is the reserve which keeps one from coming into judgment. One of the greatest reasons for covering the body is the conviction that it would not be admired if seen. One of us is ashamed if he is in excellent morning dress when the others wear evening dress, or ungloved when all the rest are gloved. A woman is ashamed to be without a crinoline or a bustle when all the rest wear them. A man, when men wore wigs, could not appear before a lady without his wig. An elderly lady says that when the present queen of England brought in, at her marriage, the fashion of brushing up the hair so as to uncover the ears, which had long been covered, it seemed indecent. No woman now is ashamed to be a woman, but in the first Christian centuries what they heard about their sex might well have made them so. A woman is not ashamed to be a widow in the Occident, but she may well be so in India. A woman may be ashamed to be an old maid, or that she has no children, or has only girls. It depends on the view current in the mores, and on the sensitiveness of the person to unfavorable judgments. "Shame, for Arabs, occupies the place which we ascribe to conscience. 'The tree lives only so long as its bark lives; and the man only so long as he feels shame.' Arabs, however, are not ashamed *in abstracto*, but before father and mother, before relatives, and before common talk. 'Be ashamed before Allah, as an honorable man is ashamed before his own people,' said Mohammed to

[1] Nieuwenhuis, *In Centraal Borneo*, I, 48.   [2] Zimmer, *Altind. Leben*, 196.

a new convert, in order to make clear to him the unknown from the known, and to enlarge the morals of the village to that of the world." [1]

451. The first attachments on the body. Ethnographical studies have established the fact that things were first hung on the body as amulets or trophies, that is, for superstition or vanity, and that the body was painted or tattooed for superstition or in play. The notion of ornament followed. The skull and body have been deformed and mutilated, and the hair has been dressed or removed, in order to vary it and produce effect. Savages lie in ashes, dust, clay, sand, or mud, for warmth, or coolness, or indolence, and they could easily find out the advantage of a coating on the skin to protect them from insects or the sun. Three things resulted which had never been foreseen or intended. (1) It was found that there was great utility in certain attachments to the body which protected it when sitting on the ground or standing in the water. Play seized upon the markings, and the men of a group at last came to use the same markings, from which resulted a group sign. The marks came to be regarded as ornamental. Some attachments had great utility for males in fishing, hunting, fighting, running, and some kinds of work. (2) Goblinism seized upon the custom and gave it new and powerful motives. The group mark became hereditary and maintained group unity with goblinistic sanctions. Some hanging objects were thought to ward off the evil eye. Others were amulets and prevented sorcery. (3) The objects hung on the body might be trophies taken from animals or enemies. These things consciously, and the others unconsciously, acted on vanity. When all wore things attached to the body a man or woman did not look dressed, or "right" without such attachments. He or she looked bare or naked. They were ashamed. This is the shame of nakedness. The connection of dress with warmth and modesty is derived and remote.

452. The fear of sorcery. The reason for retiring to perform bodily functions was the fear of sorcery, if an enemy should get possession of anything which ever was a part of the body.

---

[1] Wellhausen, *Skizzen und Vorarbeiten*, III, 194.

Hence the best plan was to go to running water. Once more, important but unanticipated and even unperceived consequences followed. The customs played the part of sanitary regulations. When it became the custom to retire it became indecent not to retire. Then it became a tradition from ancestors that one always must retire, and the ghosts would be angry if this rule was not observed. It was disrespectful to them, and would offend them to expose the body or not to retire. The Greeks said that it offended the gods. In the books of Moses the sanction for all the rules of decency is, " For it is an abomination unto the Lord." That is only an expression of the disapproval in the mores which God also was supposed to feel.

453. What functions should be concealed? What is the limit of the bodily functions to be concealed? A member of the Jewish sect of the Essenes, who were all celibate men, always wore an apron, even when alone in the bath. The genitals were impure and must not be uncovered to the eye of God. The same sect had elaborate rules like those in Deut. xxiii. 12 ff. When the Medes elected Deioces king he made a rule that no one should laugh or spit in his presence.[1] The Zulu king Chaka punished with death sneezing or clearing the throat in his presence.[2] At Bagdad, in the tenth century, the court of the caliphs had become luxurious, and a very severe and minute etiquette had been introduced. It was forbidden to spit, clear the throat or nose, gape, or sneeze in the presence of the sovereign. The nobles imitated this etiquette and adopted rules to regulate salutations, entrance into company, reception of visitors, table manners, and approach to one's wife. " If any one refused to conform to this etiquette, he exposed himself to universal blame as an eccentric person, or even as an enemy of Islam." [3] In the Italian novel *Niccolo dei Lapi* it is said in honor of the heroine that she never saw herself nude. It was a custom observed by many to wear a garment which covered the whole body even when alone in the bath. Erasmus gives the reason for this. The angels would be shocked at nakedness. He made it a rule for men.

[1] Herodotus, I, 100. [2] Ratzel, *Hist. of Mankind*, II, 444.
[3] Von Kremer, *Kulturgesch. des Orients*, II, 247, 250, 269.

One should never, he says, bare the body more than necessary, even when alone. The angels are everywhere and they like to see decency as the adjunct of modesty.[1] The angels are here evidently the Christian representatives of the ghosts of earlier times. In 1 Cor. xi. 10 it is said : The woman was created for the man. " For this cause ought the woman to have a sign of authority on her head, because of the angels." It seems to be believed that the angels might be led into sin by seeing the women. For this idea there is abundant antecedent in the *Book of Henoch* and the *Book of Jubilees.*

454. Restraint of expression within limits. It is the rule of good breeding everywhere to restrict all bodily functions and to conceal them, such as gaping, sneezing, coughing, clearing the throat and nose, and to restrain all exuberant expressions of joy, pain, triumph, regret, etc., but the limits cannot be defined. They lie in the current practice of the society in which one lives. They are not rational. At the same time they are logical. They are correctly deduced from a broad view of policy. Orientals cover their heads to show respect ; Occidentals bare the head for the same purpose. Each custom has its philosophy of respect. We think it disrespectful to turn the back on any one. Orientals generally think it respectful to pretend not to be able to look another in the face. If ladies are thought to have the right to decide whether to continue acquaintances or not, they salute first. If it is thought unbecoming for them to salute first, then men do it. Which of the great premises is correct it would be impossible to say. The notion of correctness fails, because it implies the existence of a standard outside of and above usage, and no such standard exists. There is an assumed principle which serves as a basis for the usage, and the usage refers back to the principle, but the two are afloat together.

455. Violation of rule. It results from the study of the cases that nakedness is never shameful when it is unconscious.[2] The same is true of everything under the head of decency. It is consciousness of a difference between fact and the rule set by

---

[1] *De Civilit. Morum Pueril.*, I, 3, 9, 10.   [2] Genesis iii. 7.

the mores which makes indecency and produces harm, for that difference, if disregarded, is immorality.

456. The suspensorium. The device known as the suspensorium, represented by von den Steinen,[1] is obviously invented solely for the convenience of males in activity. It is not planned for concealment and does not conceal. By a development of the device it becomes a case, made of leaf, wood, bone, clay, shell, leather, bamboo, cloth, gourd, metal, or reed. It is met with all over the world.[2] Perhaps its existence in ancient Egypt is proved.[3] In almost every case, but not always, there is great disinclination to remove it, or part with it, or to be seen without it. The sentiment attaches only to the part which is covered by the apparatus. To be seen without it would do harm to the man. Women wear a pubic shield, held in place by a string. The conjecture immediately suggests itself that the girdle or string about the loins was anterior to any covering for the genitals. This conjecture is confirmed by the cases in which the girdle is used to cover the umbilicus, while nothing else is covered, for which there is a reason on account of the connection of the umbilicus with birth, life, and ancestry.[4] The primitive notion about the genitals is that they are the seat of involuntary phenomena which are to be referred to superior agents. Hence, more than any other part of the body, they are daimonic and sacred (mystery, passion, reproduction). This notion is an independent cause of rules about the organs, and of superstitious ways in reference to them, including concealment.[5] Waitz recognized in this idea the reason for covering the organ, or the part of it which was believed to be efficient. " Perhaps," he says, " we stand here at the first stage of human clothing," — a suggestion which deserves more attention than it has received.[6]

---

[1] *Berl. Mus.*, 1888, 431; cf. 191, 192, 195; also *Globus*, LXXV, 6; Ratzel, *Völkerkunde*, I, 225, 298; *Berl. Mus.*, II, Plates II, III, XIII, XIV; Hutchinson, *Living Races*, 59; *Jhrb. d. Dtschen Archeolog. Instit.*, 1886, 295.

[2] Waitz (*Anthrop.*, VI, 567 ff.) gives a number of cases from the islands of the Pacific.

[3] *Globus*, LXXIX, 197.   [4] Krieger, *Neu Guinea*, 373.

[5] No ethnographic evidence is known to exist to prove that there is an original sentiment of disgust in regard to the organs (Ellis, " Evolution of Modesty," *Psychol. Rev.*, VI, 134).   [6] *Anthrop.*, VI, 575-576.

457. The girdle and what it conceals. Very many cases can be cited in which a girdle is worn, but nothing for concealment, unless it be of the umbilicus. In the Louvre (S. 962) may be seen a statue of a deformed primitive god of the Egyptians, Bes, who wears a string around the waist and nothing else. A girdle is often used as a pocket, without any reference to decency.[1] Convenience would then lead to the suspensorium arrangement or the pubic shell. Also from the girdle was hung any swinging glittering object to avert the evil eye from the genitals. There was no concealment and could be no motive of modesty. The aborigines of Queensland never cover the genitals except on special public occasions, or when near white settlements. The men wear the case only at corroborees and other public festivals.[2] On Tanna (New Hebrides) it is thought dangerous for a man to see another without any concealment.[3] The Indians on the Shingu show that such covering as they wear has no purpose of concealment, for it conceals nothing.[4] The device of the East Greenland Eskimo is also evidently for utility, not for modesty.[5] In order to escape flies, Brunache and his companions took refuge under a tree which is shunned by flies. It is from this tree that the women pluck the bunches of leaves which they wear dangling before and behind.[6]

458. Modesty and decency not primitive. At the earliest stage of the treatment of the body we find motives of utility and ornament mixed with superstition and vanity and quickly developing connections with magic, kin notions, and goblinism. Modesty and decency are very much later derivatives.

459. What parts of the body are tabooed? Cases may be adduced to prove that the taboo of concealment does not always attach to the parts of the body to which it attaches in our traditions. Hottentot women wear a head cloth of gay European stuff. They will not take this off. The Herero "think it a great cause of shame if a married woman removes this national

[1] Budge, *Gods of the Egyptians*, II, 284.   [3] JAI, XXIII, 368.
[2] Roth, *Queensland Aborig.*, 114.   [4] *Berl. Mus.*, 1888, 173.
   [5] Holm, *Angmagslikerne*, Plates VII, XX, XXII.
   [6] *Afr. Cent.*, 155.

head covering in the presence of strangers." They wear very little else. A woman who stood for her photograph " would more readily have uncovered all the rest of her body than her head."[1] The Guanches thought it immodest for a woman to show her breasts or feet.[2] Yakut women roll cord on the naked thigh in the presence of men who do not belong to the house, and allow themselves to be seen uncovered to the waist, but they are angry if a man stares at their naked feet. In some places the Yakuts attach great importance to the rule that young wives should not let their husband's male relatives see their hair or their feet.[3] In mediæval Germany a respectable woman thought it a great disgrace if a man saw her naked feet.[4] The Indian woman of those tribes of the northwestern coast of North America which wear the labret are as much embarrassed to be seen without it as a white woman would be if very incompletely dressed.[5] The back and navel are sometimes under a special taboo of concealment, especially the navel, which is sacred, as above noticed, on account of its connection with birth. Peschel[6] quotes private information that a woman in the Philippine Islands put a shirt on a boy in order to cover the navel and nothing more. In her view nothing more needed to be covered. Many peoples regard the navel as of erotic interest. Instances occur in the *Arabian Nights.* It is very improper for a Chinese woman who has compressed feet to show them. Thomson[7] gives a picture which shows the feet of a woman, but it was very difficult, he says, to persuade the woman to pose in that way. Chinese people would consider the picture obscene. No European would find the slightest suggestion of that kind in it. An Arab woman, in Egypt, cares more to cover her face than any other part of her body, and she is more careful to cover the top or back of her head than her face.[8] It appears that if any part of the body is put under a concealment taboo for any reason whatever, a consequence is that the opinion grows up that it never ought to be

[1] Fritsch, *Eingeb. Süd-Afr.*, 230, 311, 349.
[2] *N. S. Amer. Anthrop.*, II, 470.
[3] Sieroshevski, *Yakuty (russ.)*, 562, 570.
[4] Weinhold, *D. F.*, I, 164.
[5] *U. S. Nat. Mus.*, 1888, 257.
[6] *Races of Man*, 172.
[7] *Illustrations of China*, II, No. 39.
[8] Lane, *Mod. Egyptians*, I, 69, 266.

exposed. Then interest may attach to it more than to exposed parts, and erotic suggestion may be connected with it. The tradition in which we are educated is one which has a long history, and which has embraced the Aryan race. To us it seems "natural" and "true in itself." It includes some primitive and universal ideas of magic and goblinism which have been held far beyond the Aryan race. Shame and modesty are sentiments which are consequences produced in the minds of men and women by unbroken habits of fact, association, and suggestion in connection with dress and natural functions. It does not seem "decent" to break the habits, or, decency consists in conforming to the habits. However, the whole notion of decency is held within boundaries of habit. Orientals and Moslems now have such different habits from Occidentals that latrines are very differently constructed for them and for Occidentals.

460. Notion of decency lacking. There are cases of groups in which no notions of decency can be found. It is reported of the Kubus of Sumatra that they have acquired a sense of shame within very recent times. "Formerly they knew none and were the derision of the villagers into whose neighborhood they might come."[1] Stevens never saw an Orang-hutan girl blush. Those girls have no feeling about their nakedness which could cause a blush.[2] The Bakairi show no sense of shame as to any part of the body. They are innocent in respect to any reserve[3] [i.e. no taboo of concealment exists amongst them]. A few cases are reported in which the awakening of shame has been observed. A bystander threw a cloth over a nearly naked man on the Chittagong hills. "He was seen to blush, for it was the first time in his life that he realized that he was committing a breach of decency in appearing unclothed."[4] No doubt the more correct explanation is that he felt that in some way he was not approved by the English visitors. Semon tells how he posed a Papuan girl for her photograph, in the midst of a native crowd. She was "proud of the distinction and attention." Suddenly she was convulsed with shame and abandoned the pose, blushing and

[1] JAI, XIV, 123.
[2] Ztsft. für Ethnol., XXVIII, 170.
[3] Berl. Mus., 1888, 65.
[4] Lewin, Wild Races of S. E. India, 87.

refusing.[1] This explanation may not be correct. The feeling of one accustomed to be naked, if his attention is called to it, cannot be paralleled with that of one accustomed to be clothed, if he finds himself unclothed. The Nile negroes and the Masai manifest a "complete absence of any conventional ideas of decency." The men, at least, have no feeling of shame in connection with the pudenda. Complete nudity of males, where it occurs in Africa, seems almost always traceable to Hamitic influence.[2]

461. Dress and decency. If the description of the Tyrrhenians given by Athenæus[3] can be taken as real, they would have to be classed amongst the people who had no notions of decency. Curr says of the Australians[4] that the tribes who wear clothing are more decent than those who are naked. The women of the former retire to bathe and the men respect their privacy. Evidently the dress makes the decency. If there was no dress, there would be no need to retire and no privacy. Wilson and Felkin[5] say of the negroes that their "morals" are inversely as their dress. The Australians practice no indecent dances.[6] The central Australians hold a man in contempt if he shows excessive amorousness.[7] The natives of New Britain are naked, but modest and chaste. "Nudity rather checks than stimulates." The same is observed in English New Guinea. The men wear a bandage which does not conceal, but they attach to this all the importance which we attach to complete dress, and they speak of others who do not wear it as "naked wild men."[8] In the Palau Islands women may punish summarily, even with death, a man who approaches their bathing place, but that place is, therefore, the safest for secret meetings.[9] The Dyaks, except the hill tribes, conceal the body with care, but they do not observe a careful sex taboo.[10] We are told of the Congo tribes, some of whom wear nothing, that there exists "a marked appreciation of the sentiment of decency and shame as applied to private actions."[11] Some

---

[1] *Austral. Bush*, 350.
[2] Johnston, *Uganda Protect.*, 765.
[3] *Deipnosophists*, XII, 14.
[4] *Austral. Race*, 99, 183.
[5] *Uganda and Sudan*, I. 223.
[6] JAI, XIII, 290.
[7] Spencer and Gillen, *Cent. Austral.*, 471.
[8] Finsch, *Ethnol. Erfahr.*, I, 92 ; II, 298.
[9] Semper, *Palau Ins.*, 68.
[10] Ling Roth, *Sarawak*, I, 133.
[11] JAI, XXIV, 292.

of the women repelled the advances of men in Brunache's expedition.[1] Nachtigal[2] found the Somrai in Baghirmi modest and reserved. They proved "the well-known fact that decorum and chastity are independent of dress." On the Uganda railroad, near Lake Victoria, coal-black people are to be seen, of whom both sexes are entirely naked, except ornaments. They are "the most moral people in Uganda." The Nile negroes and Masai are naked. In the midst of them live the Baganda who wear much clothing. The women are covered from the waist to the ankles; the men from the neck to the ankles, except porters and men working in the fields. They provide decent latrines and have good sanitary usages as to the surroundings of their houses. They are very polite and courteous. This character and their dress are accounted for by their long subjection to tyranny. They are "profoundly immoral," have indecent dances, and are dying out on account of the "exhaustion of men and women by premature debauchery."[3] The Kavirondo are naked, but are, "for negroes, a moral race, disliking real indecency and only giving way to lewd actions in their ceremonial dances, where indeed the intention is not immodest, as the pantomime is a kind of ritual."[4]

462. Ornament and simplest dress. The notion of ornament is extremely vague. Things were attached to the body as amulets or trophies. Then the bodies which had nothing of this kind on them seemed bare and naked. Next objects were worn in order to comply with a type, without the character of amulets or trophies. These were ornaments. Hagen[5] noticed, in his own experience, that ornament did away with the appearance of nakedness. The same effect of tattooing may be noticed, even in pictures. The oldest Chinese tradition asserts that dress was originally for ornament.[6] "To the grass-land negroes of North Kamerun dress of any kind is only ornament or protection against severe weather." Their conversation on certain subjects is gross, perhaps because they are entirely unclothed.[7] The Doko women wear a few strings of beads hanging from a girdle, and the girls of the Dime wear one, two, or three ivory cylinders hanging from the waist, but nothing more.[8] The Xosa wear an ornamented girdle, but no apron.[9] The unmarried women in the Temu districts of Togo wear strings of beads but no dress.

[1] *Afr. Cent.*, 55, 264.   [2] *Sahara and Sudan*, II, 590.
[3] Johnston, *Uganda Protect.*, 37, 114, 642, 685.
[4] *Ibid.*, 728, 730.   [7] *Globus*, LXXVI, 306.
[5] *Papuas*, 169.   [8] Vannutelli e Citerni, *L'Omo*, 294, 305.
[6] Puini, *Origine della Civiltà*, 147.   [9] Fritsch, *Eingeb. Süd-Afr.*, 59.

The Moslem women make triangular aprons, worn by men over the suspensorium. The women meet suitors with grace and coquetry, in spite of the lack of clothing.[1] The Mashukalumbe wear no dress, but the women wear little iron bells on a strap around the waist.[2] The women of the Longos near Foweira wear anklets, waistbands, and bracelets of beads, but nothing else.[3] The Herero have a horror of the nudity of adults.[4] The Tasmanians wore no dress but decorated themselves with feathers, flowers, etc.[5] Papuans on the Fly River fasten things through the nose and hang objects around the neck. Some wear a pubic shell, but most have not even that.[6] On the island of New Britain both sexes are unclothed, although tapa cloth in very beautiful patterns is made on the island for other purposes.[7] On the Banks Islands the men wear nothing, although they formerly made very beautiful dresses which were worn in the dance.[8] Some of the Indians on the Shingu wear necklaces and ear pendants, but nothing else.[9]

463. The evolution of dress. The above-mentioned girdle with objects hanging from it turned from an ornament into a garment when it became a kilt of fringed grass or leather. Arab women wore the girdle of thongs with lappets until it was superseded by a kilt of leather cut into a fringe. The primitive apron of the ancient Egyptians was continued underneath the later more elaborate dress. The ancient primitive dress got a sacred character and was worn by everybody, whatever else he wore. It was worn by girls, by women monthly, and also, " it is said, by worshipers at the Caaba." Then the ancient thongs and lappets got the character of amulets.[10] In some Papuan tribes those who had learned all the religious secrets were allowed to wear the girdle as a sign of honor and dignity.[11] Sometimes a skin or mat is worn hanging from the waist behind. It really is worn to be sat upon, upon occasion. Nothing else is worn.[12] In this case, and in some of those mentioned above from Central Africa, a consciousness is sometimes manifested that there is something to conceal, and a posture or mode of walking is adopted which accomplishes the concealment. Amongst the Ja-luo (northeast corner of Lake Victoria) both sexes when unmarried go naked. A man, when he is a father, wears a cape of goatskin " inadequate for decency." Married women wear only a " tail of strings behind." [13] The Nandi wear clothing " only for warmth or

---

[1] *Globus*, LXXXV, 73, 311.   [6] JAI, XXI, 200.

[2] Holub, *Sieben Jahre in Süd-Afr.*, II, 293.   [7] *Berl. Mus.*, 1885, 60.

[3] Wilson and Felkin, *Uganda and Sudan*, II, 53.

[4] Ratzel, *Hist. of Mankind*, II, 469.   [8] Codrington, *Melanesians*, 321.

[5] Ling Roth, *Tasmanians*, 21, 144.   [9] *Berl. Mus.*, 1888, 193.

[10] W. R. Smith, *Relig. of Semites*, 437. Whatever the purpose of the loin cloth of the ancient Egyptians may have been, it cannot have been decency. The monuments show men at work with the loin cloth turned hindside foremost as if to save it from wear (Meyer, *Egypt*, II, 116).

[11] *Globus*, LXXVIII, 5.   [12] Brunache, *Afr. Cent.*, 207.

[13] Johnston, *Uganda Protect.*, 781.

adornment, not for purposes of decency." [1] The Acholi, in Uganda, think it beneath masculine dignity to wear anything.[2] The Vanyoro men are generally clothed in skins. The women, until marriage, wear nothing ; after marriage, bark cloth. The Bari men never wear anything. They think it womanish to do so. The unmarried women wear a pendant of fringe behind and five or six iron bars six inches long, the whole three and a half inches broad, in front. Married women wear a fringe in front and a leather apron behind.[3]

464. Men dressed. Women not. Cases are very numerous in which men wear dress, while women do not.[4] Such is the prevailing fact amongst the Indians of the Upper Amazon [5] and in Central Africa.[6] The women of the Apaporis (0° N., 70° W.) are said to wear nothing, but the men wear long aprons of fine bark string, broad bast girdles, and ornamental strings of teeth and seeds ; also ornaments in the nose and lips, and some tribes below the lower lip.[7] When women wear clothing and men do not the men think it womanish and beneath them to do so.[8] When Livingston remonstrated with a negro for nakedness the latter " laughed with surprise at the thought of being at all indecent. He evidently considered himself above such weak superstition." All thought it a joke when told to wear something when Livingston's family should come.[9]

465. Dress for other purposes than decency. Excessive modesty. The Dyaks wear only a loin cloth of a greater or less number of folds to keep the abdomen warm, " a precaution which all travelers in the tropics must imitate day and night with flannel for fear of dysentery." [10] " The women [of the western side of Torres Straits] frequently wear a kind of full chemise. They do not wear it for the sake of decency, but from luxury and pride, for I often saw a woman take off her garment and content herself with a tuft of grass before and behind." [11] Some Papuan women are mentioned, who wear a petticoat on festival occasions, but they leave the right side of it open to show the tattooing on the hip.[12] Since cotton cloth has become cheap in the Horn of Africa the natives wear a great deal of it out of luxury and ostentation, and also because it is a capital at all times easily realizable.[13] The Rodias, an outcast people on Ceylon, were once compelled by the Kandyan kings to leave the upper part of the body uncovered ; both sexes. The English have tried to reverse the rule, which has become a fixed habit. The Rodia women now wear a neckerchief, the ends of which

[1] Johnston, *Uganda Protect*, 853.   [2] *Ibid.*, 220.
[3] Wilson and Felkin, *Uganda and Sudan*, II, 49, 96.
[4] E.g. JAI, XXIV, 255, 281.
[5] Spix and Martius, *Brasilien*, 1224 ; Martius, *Ethnog. Brasil.*, 388.
[6] Schweinfurth, *Heart of Afr.*, II, 104.   [10] Bock, *Reis in Borneo*, 78.
[7] *Globus*, LXXXVIII, 89.   [11] JAI, XIX, 391.
[8] Schweinfurth, *Heart of Afr.*, I, 152.   [12] JAI, XXVIII, 208.
[9] *South Africa*, II, 590.   [13] Paulitschke, *Ethnog. N. O. Afr.*, I, 80.

cover the breast, when they meet English people, but they have not yet acquired the feeling that it is unseemly to uncover the breast.[1] Mantegazza met women on the Nilgherri hills who covered the breast on meeting him, but did not do so before men of their own race.[2] It is the current idea on the Malabar coast that no respectable woman should cover the breast. Lately, those who have traveled and have learned that other people hold the contrary to be the proper rule feel some shame at the old custom.[3] The Ainos are rated as displaced and outcast aborigines amongst the Japanese. An Aino woman refused to wash in order to be treated for a skin disease, because to wash was against Aino usage.[4] An Aino girl in a mission school who had a curved spine and was lame refused to allow a European physician to examine her with a view to diagnosis and treatment.

466. Contrasted standards of decency. The Japanese do not consider nudity indecent. A Japanese woman pays no heed to the absence of clothing on workmen. European women in Japan are shocked at it, but themselves wear dinner and evening dress which greatly shock Orientals.[5] Schallmeyer[6] saw Japanese policemen note for punishment watermen who approached nearer to the wharf than the law allowed before covering the upper part of the body. The authorities are, therefore, trying to modify the usage. The Japanese regard daily hot baths as a necessity for everybody. Therefore bathing is unavoidable, and is put under the same conventionalization as that which surrounded latrines in the cities of Europe fifty years ago. Every one is expected to ignore what no one can help. Formerly, at least, the sexes were not separated and bathers might walk to and from the bath in a state of complete preparation for it.[7] Before the "reformation" people of the better classes in Japan went to the theater not at all, or secretly. The plays were coarse and outspoken. Japanese education permitted "both sexes indifferently to speak of everything without the slightest periphrasis, or any respect for persons, even children." Hence situations were described and presented on the stage which we should consider too licentious for toleration, although there were no actresses on the stage. This was not due to laxity of morals, but to the fact that they had no taboos on reality. Yet "nothing appears more immoral to the Japanese than our drama." "They permit no intrigue [on the stage] by which the character of a married woman is compromised."[8] The Europeans and Japanese, in contact with each other, find that it is not possible to infer each other's character from each other's folkways. Hearn says: "The ideas of this people are not our ideas; their sentiments are not our sentiments; their ethical life represents for us regions of thought and emotion yet unexplored, or perhaps long forgotten."[9] The two cases in contrast, however, show the

[1] Schmidt, *Ceylon*, 37.
[2] *Gli Amori degli Uomini*, 40.
[3] *Madras Gov. Mus.*, II, 198.
[4] *Ztsft. für Ethnol.*, XIV, (181).
[5] Baelz in *Ztsft. für Ethnol.*, XXXIII, 178.
[6] *Vererbung und Auslese*, 281.
[7] Humbert, *Japan*, 269.
[8] *Ibid.*, 295, 334.
[9] *Japan*, 13.

power of the folkways and their tremendous control. We know as to our own women that there is no conscious or unconscious purpose to stimulate sensuality. They wear what has been and is customary in their society. The Japanese get their customs in the same way and attribute to them the same authority. Neither has any reason to be amazed at or despise the other. Baelz quotes Mrs. Bishop, who after spending twenty years traveling in the East said, " I know now that one can be naked, yet behave like a lady." The above story of the crippled Aino girl gives credibility to Becke's story [1] of a Polynesian woman, wife of a European, who died after child bearing rather than submit to treatment by a physician which would be attended by exposure of her person.

467. Standards of decency as to natural functions, etc. The natives of New Georgia (Solomon Islands) " have the same ideas of what is decent with regard to certain acts and exposures that we ourselves have." They build retiring places over the water, " but their language is quite unlicensed." [2] In Micronesia reserve as to natural functions is lacking.[3] Amongst central African negroes the king alone had a hut for retirement. " The heathen negroes are generally more observant of decorum in this respect than any Mohammedan." [4] In Lhasa, Tibet, there are no latrines either public or private. The street is used.[5] The Andamanese women are modest and very careful about decency of dress and conversation. For the unmarried there is complete license.[6] When Middendorf asked a Tungus girl to sing, she sang a song which was so indecent that he could not translate it.[7] Children of the Eskimo on the eastern coast of Greenland go naked in the house until they are sixteen years old. Then they put on the *natit*, a simple band around the loins, and that is the only thing worn in the house by adults. It is the custom of wearing fur next the skin which compels them to go naked in the house. They are very unwilling, under any circumstances, to lay aside the *natit*. Their songs and games are exceedingly licentious, and their myths are obscene. They do not keep these from the children. A great number live crowded in a little house, as an insurance against accidents or lack of food. This mode of life makes decency impossible and lowers the standard of propriety. Children are married at four or five years of age, but the relationship does not become established until a child is born. In summer, in tent life, two men exchange wives and some property. If one of them wants to keep the other's property, he must keep the wife, too.[8] The Fuegians observe great decorum as to subjects of conversation.[9] The Seminoles of Florida observe a high sex taboo. The women

[1] *Pacific Tales*, 276.
[2] JAI, XXVI, 394.
[3] Finsch, *Ethnol. Erfahr.*, III, 26.
[4] Schweinfurth, *Heart of Afr.*, II, 98.
[5] *Century Mag.*, January, 1904.
[6] JAI, XII, 135.
[7] *Reisen in Siberien*, IV, 1429.
[8] Holm, *Angmagslikerne*, 34, 50–56, 112, 117, 162.
[9] *Scribner's Mag.*, February, 1895.

are virtuous and modest, and no half-breeds with whites exist. The mother of a half-breed would be put to death.[1] The Tehuelches of Patagonia pay great attention to decency. They do not like to see children naked.[2] The Indians of northern Nicaragua think that whites do not bathe enough. They always retire to running water, and are disgusted with whites for not taking that care.[3]

468. Bathing. Customs of nudity. The natives of Rotuma never bathe without the loin cloth. To do so is thought low conduct.[4] The people of Ponape rise early and bathe, the sexes always separating unless married.[5] Bock[6] says that the Dyaks, without hesitation, threw off their garments and bathed in the presence of himself and Malays, the sexes together. The sexes of the Yuroks in California bathe apart and the women never go into the sea without some garment.[7] The women of the Mandans had a bathing place. Armed sentinels were set to prevent men from approaching it.[8] In Hindostan the sexes now bathe together at certain times and places with very little clothing. Wilkins[9] says, "I have never seen the slightest impropriety of gesture on these occasions." Although at an earlier period some clothing was worn in bed, in the fourteenth and fifteenth centuries, in Europe, both sexes slept nude. Better beds and separate bed clothes led to this custom, because it was such a relief to take off woolen and fur worn in the daytime. Then nudity became familiar, and the concealment taboo was broken down.[10] The cities were soon compelled to pass ordinances forbidding any one to appear on the streets nude.[11] In Denmark the historian tells us that people slept naked because linen was dear, and that the custom lasted into the seventeenth century. In the sixteenth century nobles began to wear nightshirts.[12] Upon the entry of kings into cities, until the sixteenth century, mythological subjects were represented in the streets by nude women.[13] From the

[1] *Bur. Ethnol.*, V, 479.
[2] Ratzel, *Völkerkunde*, II, 663.
[3] *Globus*, LXXVIII, 272.
[4] JAI, XXVII, 410.
[9] *Hinduism*, 219.
[5] Pereiro, *La Isla de Ponape*, 112.
[6] *Reis in Borneo*, 39.
[7] Powers, *Calif. Indians*, 55.
[8] *Smithson. Rep.*, 1885, Part II, 86.
[10] Weinhold, *D. F.*, II, 259; Schultz, *Höf. Leben*, II, 168.
[11] Scherr, *D. F. W.*, I, 191.   [12] Lund, *Norges Historie*, II, 246, 380.
[13] Scherr, *D. F. W.*, I, 191.

thirteenth to the fifteenth centuries it was the custom that girls served knights in the bath.[1] Through the Middle Ages the sexes bathed together, and not innocently.[2] The Germans were very fond of bathing and every village had its public bath house. The utility and pleasure of bathing were so great that bathing was forbidden as an ecclesiastical penance.[3] "A practice of men and women bathing together was condemned by Hadrian, and afterwards by Alexander Severus, but was only finally suppressed by Constantine."[4] The Council of Trullanum in 692 forbade the sexes to bathe together.[5] Other councils repeated the prohibition. This shows that Constantine did not suppress the custom, nor did any other civil or ecclesiastical authority do so. The ecclesiastics in Germany, from the eighth century, condemned the custom of the sexes bathing together, but never could control it.[6] Christian men and women bathed together at Tyre in the time of the crusades.[7] All the authorities, beginning with Erasmus (in the Colloquy, *Diversoria*), agree that bathing at a common bath house was abandoned on account of syphilis. Leprosy, which was brought from the East by the crusaders, had had less effect in the same direction. In the sixteenth century there were other epidemics, and wood became dear.[8] The use of body linen and bed linen which could be washed made bathing less essential to comfort and health.[9] The habit of seeing nudity was broken, and as it became unusual it became offensive. Thus a concealment taboo grew up again. Rudeck [10] is convinced by these facts that "it was not modesty which made dress and public decency, but that dress and the decay of objectionable customs made modesty." He seems to be astonished at this conclusion and a little afraid of it. It is undoubtedly correct. The whole history of dress depends on it.

[1] Weinhold, *D. F.*, II, 115.

[2] D'Aussy, *Fabliaux*, IV, passim.

[3] Weinhold, *D. F.*, II, 114.

[4] Lecky, *Eur. Morals*, II, 311.

[5] Hefele, *Conciliengesch.*, III, 310.

[6] Weinhold, *D. F.*, II, 117.

[7] Prutz, *Kulturgesch. der Kreuzzüge*, 528 note.

[8] Zappert in *Arch. für Kunde der Oester. Gesch.-Quellen*, XXI, 41, 82, 132.

[9] The queen of Charles VII of France (1422–1461) said that she owned but two chemises of linen (Clement, *Jacques Cœur*, 246).

[10] *Oeffentl. Sittlichkeit*, 399.

469. Bathing in rivers, springs, and public bath houses. In the fifteenth century it became the custom to bathe in rivers or at mineral springs. Wealth, luxury, fashion, and new forms of vice attended this change.[1] The convents of the fifteenth century are described as places of debauch.[2] An English globe trotter of the beginning of the seventeenth century describes the baths of Baden near Zurich, where the old custom of the sexes bathing together had been modified somewhat, but only for married women.[3] If the custom of bathing together does not still exist throughout Northern Europe, it must have been abolished within a few years. Retzius[4] describes it as existing in Finland in 1878, and many travelers have described the village bath houses of Northern Russia and Scandinavia. Retzius says that the bath house is a kind of sanctuary. Any misdemeanor committed there is considered far more wicked than the same fault elsewhere. Here we see the mores raising a special conventionalization to protect a custom which is expedient, but which transgresses the usual taboo. The fact is that the complete taboo on nudity in Central Europe is not over two centuries old. By itself, nudity was not regarded as shameful or indecent. Therefore in the bath, where it was in order, it was disregarded, just as now a workmen's dress, an athlete's dress, or a bathing dress is disregarded. During the centuries when the ecclesiastical authorities endeavored in vain to stop the sexes from bathing together, it must be that public opinion did not recognize in that usage any serious evil which called for repression. The English now express surprise that the sexes at American watering places go into the sea together, to which Americans attach no importance at all. If Americans bathed in English bathing dresses the sexes would speedily separate.

470. Nudity. In early Christian drama Christ was represented by a naked youth. Then he was represented by a youth who wore a breech cloth only. In the sixteenth century, at Naples, in a representation of the creation of Adam and Eve, the actors

---

[1] Schultz, *D. L.*, 136.
[2] Dulaure, *Hist. de Paris*, 268; Schultz, *D. L.*, 277, 283; cf. Janssen, VIII, 391.
[3] Coryate's *Crudities*, II, 244.   [4] *Finska Kranier*, 118.

had only the privates covered. The stage fell and many were hurt, which was held to show God's displeasure at the show. The flagellants in the theater, in France, were represented naked, as penitents.[1]

471. Alleged motives of concealment taboo. Herodotus says of the Lydians and almost all barbarians that they considered it shameful for one man to be seen by another naked.[2] The Jewish sect, the Essenes, concealed part of the body from the sun, as the "all-seeing eye of God," even in the bath. The Jew might not uncover the body in the face of the temple. The rules of the Essenes for bodily necessities were such that those necessities could not be satisfied on the Sabbath.[3] At Rome "*oppedere, mingere, cacare* towards persons or statues belonged to the grossest marks of contempt, and were so employed more than we think."[4] Patursson[5] bathed with aborigines near the mouth of the Ob. They would not bare the body below the waist and were shocked at his immodesty because he was not so scrupulous.

472. Obscenity. Another topic in this group of subjects, obscenity, is still harder to treat within the limits set by our mores. It offers still more astounding proofs that the folkways can make anything "right," and that our strongest sentiments of approval or abhorrence are given to us by the age and group in which we live. The tabooed parts of the body are not to be seen. It is obscenity when they are exposed to sight. We have already noticed, under the head of decency, a great range of conventions in regard to things and acts which are set aside from all the common activities of life. We have seen that there is no ultimate and rational definition of the things to be tabooed, no universal agreement as to what they are, no philosophical principle by which they are selected; that the customs have had no uniformity or consistency, and that those usages which we might suppose to be referable to a taboo of obscenity have an entirely different motive, while the notion of obscenity does not exist.

---

[1] D'Ancona, *Origine del Teatro in Italia* (1st ed.), I, 213, 218, 280, 375.
[2] Herodotus, I, 10.   [3] Lucius, *Essenismus*, 62, 68.
[4] Grupp, *Kulturgesch. der Röm. Kaiserzeit*, I, 24; cf. sec. 211.
[5] *Siberien i Vore Dage*, 146.

There is no "natural" and universal instinct, by collision with which some things are recognized as obscene. We shall find that the things which we regard as obscene either were not, in other times and places, so regarded, any more than we so regard bared face and hands, or else that, from ancient usage, the exhibition was covered by a convention in protection of what is archaic or holy, or dramatic, or comical. In primitive times goblinism and magic covered especially the things which later became obscene. Facts were accepted with complete naïveté. The fashion of thinking was extremely realistic. The Japanese now cannot understand how facts can be made shameful. They have very exact and authoritative conventions which every one must obey, but the conventions are practical and realistic. They serve purposes ; they do not create an unreal world of convention.[1] This is the extreme view of realism and nature. As has been shown above, however, so soon as objects were attached to the body for any purpose whatever, the conventional view that bodies so distinguished were alone right and beautiful was started, and all the rest of the convention of ornament and dress followed.

473. Obscene representations for magic. The Indians on the Shingu river, Brazil, wear little or no clothing.[2] They have full suits for dancing, but the tabooed organs are represented on the outside of these artificially and of exaggerated size. Evidently it was not the purpose of the dress to conceal organs the sight of which was tabooed.[3] In Central Borneo, in order to drive off evil spirits, rough figures of human beings are cut in wood, the tabooed organs being exaggerated. Those organs are the real amulets which exorcise demons, for they are often cut on the timbers of the houses without the rest of the figure. Then, by further derivation, such representations became purely ornamental on houses, weapons, etc.[4] The Egyptians used representations of what were later tabooed organs as hieroglyphics, and in their conversation admitted no taboo. Pictures in the tombs of the Twentieth Dynasty (1180–1050 B.C.) show the lack of any taboo, and there are inscriptions by them which show an absence of

[1] Hearn, *Japan*, 188–200.
[2] Cf. sec. 462.
[3] *Berl. Mus.*, 1888, 199, 302.
[4] Nieuwenhuis, *Centraal Borneo*, I, 146.

any restriction on realism.[1] This is evidently the naïve realism of children who have not yet learned any conventions. Reproduction and growth have direct connection with food supply, and abundance of reproduction means joy of life and merriment, with good cheer for men. Consequently the most matter-of-fact interest of man was intertwined with all the reproductive energies in nature. The popular and comic *mimus* of the Greeks is traced back to ritual acts of magic, in which the corn demons or growth demons are represented at work, making the reproduction and growth of the crops. The ritual was sympathetic magic, and it was securing the food supply. What was desired was success in agriculture, and the husbandman in his choice of rites, symbols, and emblems was entirely realistic. The growth demons, when they appear in art, are vulgar figures of an exaggerated sensual type. They were meant to suggest reproductive vigor, exuberance, and abundance. The tabooed organs are represented in various ways, but always obtrusively and with exaggeration. The demons wear an artificial phallus outside the dress, which fits the figure tightly.[2] The ritual developed into the Dionysiac rites and orgies, the main idea of which was to rejoice with the reproductive agencies of nature, to present them dramatically to the mind, and to stimulate hope and industry. In Greece these primitive rites of sympathetic magic in agriculture developed into the comic drama, and the demons became stereotyped figures of comedy, always recognizable by their masks (faces of a vulgar type), exaggerated hips, and above all by the phallus. The demon turned into the clown or buffoon, but the phallus was kept as an emblem of his rôle, like the later cap and bells of the fool, until the fifth century of the Christian era in the West, and until the fall of the Byzantine empire. In the Hellenistic period the clown took the rôle of the Olympic god, and wore the phallus. The Phlyakes in lower Italy had the same emblem and it was worn in the atellan plays of the Romans.[3] In the early Christian

[1] Erman, *Aegypten*, I, 223.

[2] *Jhrb. des Dtschen Archaeolog. Instit.*, 1886, 260; *Arch. für Anthrop.*, XXIX, 136.

[3] On the connection of these see Bethe, *Gesch. des Theaters im Alt.*, 299 ff.

centuries the Christian martyr wore the emblem in the comedy, since that rôle was always represented by the simpleton or clown. Ecclesiastical persons also were represented with it, since the buffoon always wore it, whatever his rôle. It also passed to the *karagoz* (shadow play) of the Turks and to the *pantin* puppets of the Javans. In the comedy of Hindostan the phallus disappeared.[1] In Egypt, at least as late as the first half of the nineteenth century, a masked figure marched at the head of the bride's procession at a wedding with the same symbol and indecent gestures.[2]

474. Infibulation. It appears that athletes in Greece bound the organ and tied it up to the girdle in a manner closely resembling the primitive suspensorium. The comedians wore a leathern apron with a large false organ of red leather on the outside. It became a sign of the trade of boxers, athletes, gymnasts, and comedians to bind the organ and tie it up, whereby it was twisted into a horn shape. The purpose was to protect it from injury, and it furnishes suggestion as to the purpose of the primitive suspensorium. The concealment was very imperfect and the notion grew up that the part concealed ought to be concealed, but no more. The Romans thought it indecent to lack the foreskin, and the Jews endeavored to conceal this lack. Infibulation was practiced in two ways, — by a ring through the prepuce or by a bandage around it. It was thought to prevent vice and preserve the voice of prophets, singers, etc. A seventeenth-century traveler, Walter Schultze of Haarlem, is quoted, who describes an ascetic sect in Persia who renounced wine, lived on gifts, and foreswore marriage. They were infibulated with a ring.[3]

475. Was the phallus offensive? For more than two thousand years the most obscene figure we know was used by the clown in popular farce and by athletes as an emblem of their profession. It raised a laugh, but was not otherwise noticed. An interesting question arises whether there ever was any protest against it, or any evidence that anybody thought it offensive.

---

[1] Reich, *Der Mimus*, I, 17, 29, 58, 93, 95, 258, 321, 496, 498, 626, 691, 733.

[2] Burckhardt, *Arabic Proverbs*, 115.

[3] Stieda, *Infibulation*, 23, 25, 36, 40, 44, 56, 66.

The passage in Aristophanes' *Clouds* (530) has been so inter-preted. It appears, however, that in that passage the author is comparing his comedy with that of others. He has admitted, he says, no low tricks appealing to vulgar tastes, no phallus which would make the boys laugh, no lascivious dance, no scurrilous stories, and no "knock-down business." This is not a criticism of the phallus on grounds of obscenity, but on grounds of buffoon-ery. In the *Acharnians* (243 and 259) are matter-of-fact refer-ences to the phallus worn by the actor, as he might have referred to his mantle. Other cases occur which are not so outspoken. In the *Lysistrata* the mention of the phallus in connection with the motive of the play is of the last degree of vulgarity. We cannot find that any Greeks, Romans, or Byzantines protested against these exhibitions of the phallus, which to us are so obscene. The *mimus* was the lowest and most popular kind of theatrical exhibition, and it was in it that the use of the phallus was most constant. Even Christian preachers who denounced the *mimus* as demoralizing, and who specified in detail what they found objectionable in it, never mention the display of obscene things. All people were accustomed to the phallus as the archaic symbol of the servants of Dionysus.[1] Christian preachers would have made no allowance for it on that account, — rather the contrary, — and they would not have refrained from objecting to it on account of the archaic, or artistic, or traditional element, if they had disapproved of it. It must be that everybody was indifferent to it.

The twin pillars which were common in front of Semitic temples and which stood before the temple at Jerusalem are interpreted as phalli.[2]

476. Phallus as amulet. At Rome the phallus was an amulet and was worn by all children. The figure, therefore, cannot have been an obscene one. In the Roman gardens also were ithyphallic figures which appear to bear witness to a survival of the growth-demon idea, or to usages which originated in the growth-demon idea, and were perpetuated traditionally without knowledge of the original meaning. On mediæval churches

---

[1] Reich, 503.   [2] W. R. Smith, *Relig. of the Semites*, 457.

figures were often carved, as an expression of naïve ideas and faiths, and in pure realism, which were frankly obscene. Paintings and stained glass often represented similar objects. In the second half of the sixteenth century such objects were removed, or covered, or modified. It may be that the notion of obscenity developed sooner in respect to literature than in respect to art. Susemihl[1] suggests that the lost tales of Miletus may have been obscene, and also the tales of Paxamos, and that their disappearance may be due to a war on them on this account. Literature would furnish food to the mind. It would not deal with fact. The popular judgment seems long to have refused to admit that facts of structure and function which were universally human could be put under a taboo and made improper to be known and seen. What is familiar tends to remain in our overconsciousness only. The same is true of what offends one's taste and from which one averts attention, although it cannot be caused to cease, like profane language. The cases of toleration of what would now be considered obscene are to be explained in this way.

477. Symbols in Asia. "In ancient times obscene symbols were used without offense to denote sex."[2] Such symbols were very common in western Asia. They are very common now in India. A Chinese woman's foot, an Arab woman's face, a Tuareg man's mouth, is obscene to persons educated in any one of those taboos, because it always is, and ought to be, concealed. It is not obscene to us. On the other hand, the lingam in India is obscene to us, but not to Hindoos who have never learned any taboo in regard to it. An egg or a seed might have been made obscene in some group on account of its connection with reproduction, if that connection had been developed in dogma and usage. An Englishman would never think of the garter as unseemly, but non-English men and women have thought it such. The crucifix shows us how conventionalization and familiarization set aside all the suggestion which an artifact really carries. The figure of a naked man dying in torture is purely horrible and repulsive. No one could get edification from an artistic

---

[1] *Griech. Lit. in der Alexandrinerzeit*, II, 574.

[2] W. R. Smith, *Relig. of the Semites*, 457.

representation of a man hanging on the gallows. Many people overlook so much of the crucifix and add so much in imagination that they get great edification from it. The language used in the communion about eating the body and drinking the blood of Christ refers to nothing in our mores, and appeals to nothing in our experience. It comes down from very remote ages, very possibly from cannibalism.[1] If we heard that the Chinese or Mohammedans had a religious custom in which they used currently the figure of eating the body and drinking the blood of a man (or god), and if we had no such figure of speech in our own use, we should consider it shocking and abominable.

478. The notion of obscenity is modern. It is evident that the notion of obscenity is very modern. It is due to the modern development of the arts of life and the mode of life under steam and machinery. The cheapening and popularization of luxury have made houses larger, plumbing cheaper, and all the apparatus of careful living more accessible to all classes. The consequence is that all the operations and necessities of life can be carried on with greater privacy and more observation of conventional order and decorum. Then the usages and notions grow more strict and refined. It is only in poverty that exposures and collisions occur which violate decency and involve obscenity. Therefore the standards and codes of all classes have risen, and the care about dressing, bathing, and private functions, for the sexes and for children, has been intensified. Out of this has come the notion of what is obscene, as the extreme of indecency and impropriety. What we call obscene was, in ancient times, either a matter of superstition or a free field for jest. The conventionalization in favor of what is amusing must always be recognized. It has always entered into comedy in the theater. A jest will not cover as much now as it once would, but it still goes far. The ancient mythology long covered obscenity in drama. When Hephæstus caught Ares and Aphrodite in his net the gods all enjoyed the joke. The goddesses did not come to see the sight.[2] The difference between the masculine and feminine judgment as to whether a thing is funny or shameful is well drawn. Hera insisted to

[1] *Bull., Soc. d'Anthrop. de Paris*, 1904, 404. [2] *Od.*, VIII, 332.

Zeus that their conjugal familiarity should not be seen.[1] The young women served the men in the bath, but Odysseus feared to anger Nausikaa if he exposed himself to her (although it is not certain that this was on account of his nakedness), and when she walked through the town with him she knew well what would shame her.[2] Odysseus also asked the women to withdraw while he bathed.[3] The mores were in flux and were contradictory. The interpretation of the text is not beyond question. It may not have been nakedness which caused shame, but the dirt and disorder of person produced by shipwreck. Various philosophies claim to have brought in the greater care and refinement of more recent times, but not one of them can show the documentary proof that the men of a time, at that time, showed revolt against the mores of that time in regard to this matter. What has happened is that, in modern times, steam and machinery, with the increase of capital and of power over nature which they have produced, have given social power to the lower middle class, as the representatives of the masses. This has brought into control the mores of those classes, which were simple, unluxurious, philistine, and comparatively pure, because those classes were forced to be frugal, domestic, careful of their children, self-denying, and relatively virtuous, on account of their limited means. The arts of life never can be the same for the poor and the rich. Wealth is often charged with introducing luxury and vice, but that tendency is offset by its giving command over the conditions of life, which makes refined usages possible.

479. Propriety. The rules of propriety apply to all the acts of life, but especially to those which take place in the presence or neighborhood of others; still more especially to those which affect others. A large section of such rules deals with the ordinary intercourse of persons of the two sexes, and regulates details of the sex taboo which are less important. Crawley gives a list of cases [4] in which brother and sister, father and daughter, are separated by the sex taboo. A woman of the Omaha tribe,

---

[1] *Il.*, XIV, 334.
[2] *Od.*, III, 464; IV, 49; VI, 15, 109, 276; Keller, *Hom. Soc.*, 209.
[3] *Od.*, VI, 136.   [4] JAI, XXIV, 444.

whether married or not, if she walked or rode alone would ruin her reputation as a virtuous woman. She may ride or walk only with her husband or near kinsman. In other cases she gets another woman to go with her. Young men are forbidden to speak to girls, if they meet two or more on the road, unless they are akin.[1] A chief never ate with his guests amongst the tribes on the upper Missouri. He sat by and served them, meanwhile preparing the pipe to be smoked afterwards.[2] Junker[3] was warned that, in passing a princess in Buganda, he must not touch her robe of oxhide, for that would be an insult to her. If a woman of the Mongbottu gives coloring matter to a man, that is undue familiarity and will occasion the wrath of an offended husband.[4] An Andaman Islander, if he has occasion to speak to a married woman older than himself, must do it through a third person. He must not touch his younger brother's or cousin's wife, or his wife's sister. Women are restricted in the same way as to the husband's elder brother, or male cousin, or his brother-in-law.[5] The relations of relatives in law are a chapter in propriety.

480. Seclusion of women. In modern Korea women are secluded. It is not proper to ask for them. Women have been put to death by fathers or husbands, or are reported to have committed suicide, when strange men, by accident or design, have touched their hands. A servant woman gave as a reason for not saving her mistress from a fire in the house that she had been touched by a man, in the confusion, and was not worth saving.[6] In China, if a foreigner asks about the ladies, he is taken to refer to the mother, not the wife, of the Chinaman.[7] A young wife is not allowed, amongst the southern Slavs, to address comrades in the great-family house by their names, " out of modesty." She gives them special names, adopted for her intercourse with them. She is guilty of great impropriety if she chats with her husband in the presence of her parents-in-law.[8]

[1] *Bur. Eth.*, III, 365.
[2] *Smithson. Rep.*, 1885, Part II, 457.
[3] *Afrika*, III, 633.
[4] Burrows, *Land of Pygmies*, 85.

[5] JAI, XII, 355.
[6] Bishop, *Korea*, 341.
[7] *Globus*, LXXVIII, 263.
[8] *Ibid.*, LXXXII, 192 ff.

481. Customs of propriety. A native of the Naga Hills told an Englishman that it was not the correct thing to use a poisoned arrow except to shoot it at a woman.[1] On the Palau Islands, and amongst all Moslems,[2] it is an insult to a man to ask him about the health of his wife, and any man may strike with a stick or a stone, not with a cutting weapon, any one who utters the former's wife's name. Women are treated with extreme formality. A man who surprises one bathing is fined. This occurs very rarely, since the men utter cries of warning when approaching the place.[3] In German Melanesia a visitor is at once presented with betel and food, but he immediately gives some of it back to the inmates of the house as security against poison.[4] The Indians of Central America are shocked at the quick actions and loud talking habitual to Europeans, and think them signs of a lack of breeding and of the low level of European culture. Some tribes allow no singing, which they consider a sign of drunkenness.[5] An Ossetin (Caucasus) will never take his child on his arm or caress it in the presence of another, especially of an older person, or his own father or mother. If he did do so, no one would shake hands with him, and any one might with impunity spit in his face. Propriety forbids the Tushins (of the same region) to manifest tenderness, even when old, towards husband or wife, parent or child, in the presence of others; especially is it improper to show tenderness towards sons.[6] An Ossetin man may see his betrothed only in secret and incidentally, or in the house of one of his own relatives. It is a gross insult to ask him about her health, or when the wedding will be. A married woman may not address her husband or male relatives by their names. If she does so, the other women will ridicule her. Other people in the same region have similar excessive rules. An Armenian woman, after marriage, is veiled. She must not talk with any one but her husband, sisters, or little children. She answers her parents-in-law by signs. Her husband ought not to call her by her name before others. A Cherkess wife may talk with her husband only at night. His presence in her room by day is thought improper, and it is improper for man and wife to be seen together outside the house, or to be seen talking together. A newly married woman, among the Grusians, must not speak to her husband's father, mother, or brothers until she has borne a child. A childless wife is not treated with respect by her husband, or his family, or even by outsiders.[7] Darinsky explains that the community used to buy the wives, who were costly, and not equal in number to the men. Now, if a man gets a wife and children of his own, he commits a crime against the old order. He must be well off, and he leaves his poorer brethren in the lurch. They envy and annoy him. To escape this he conceals or ignores his relation to his wife and children.

[1] JAI, XI, 199. [2] Pischon, *Einfluss des Islam*, 17.

[3] Kubary, *Soc. Einrichtungen der Pelauer*, 73, 90.

[4] Pfeil, *Aus der Südsee*, 48, 74. [5] *Globus*, LXXXVII, 129, 130.

[6] Darinsky in *Ztsft. für vergleich. Rechtswssnsft.*, XIV, 189.

[7] *Russ. Ethnog.* (*russ.*), 219, 225, 291, 340, 355, 358.

482. Moslem rules of propriety. To a great extent the legislation of Mohammed consisted in accomplishing reforms and innovations for which the Arabs were almost ready. When he tried to introduce ideas of his own, changing the mores, he failed. He tried many times to put a stop to the usages of mourning which were violent and excessive, — loud outcries, destruction of clothes and furniture, blackening the walls of the house and one's face, and shearing the beard. He did not succeed. These were ancient and popular customs and they were maintained.[1] It is improper for any Moslem, male or female, to uncover the head.[2] They uncover the feet to show respect. This was Semitic and is Oriental.[3] Robertson Smith[4] thinks that the reason was that the shoes could not be washed, unless they were mere linen socks, such as were used in the Phœnician sacred dress. By Moslem rules strangers should never see or hear a man's wives. Physicians may see only the affected parts of a woman. A traveler returning home may not enter his own house at night. Two persons of the same sex must never bare the body between the waist and the knee in presence of each other. The Koran[5] contains elaborate rules for women as to the concealment of parts of the body, and as to movements of the body and gestures as limited by propriety. Neatness, care, and order are religious duties; also devices to preserve and enhance beauty.[6] To an Arab, a blow on the back of the neck is more insulting than one on the face.[7] It is not proper for a man to look any Moslem woman in the face. When Vambery, talking to a lady, raised his eyes to her face she sternly told him to behave with propriety.[8]

483. Hatless women. In contrast with the Moslem rule not to uncover the head is the Christian rule that men should uncover the head in church but that women should cover it. In 1905 Cranstock church in Newquay, Cornwall, England, was closed on account of the "irreverence of numbers of women,

---

[1] Von Kremer, *Kulturgesch. des Orients*, II, 250.

[2] *Ibid.*, 215.

[3] Exod. iii. 5; Josh. v. 15.

[4] *Relig. of the Semites*, 453.

[5] Sura XXIV.

[6] Tornauw, *Mosl. Recht.*, 86.

[7] Burckhardt, *Arabic Proverbs*, I.

[8] *Sittenbilder aus dem Morgenlande*, 16.

who, walking uncovered, presume to enter God's house with no sign of reverence or modesty upon their heads." A rule was adopted at Canterbury, in the same year, that no hatless women should be allowed in the cathedral. A reason or authority for this rule is said to be found in 1 Cor. xi. 4–7 An American church paper said that such a rule would half empty some American churches in the warmer latitudes.[1] A rector at Asbury Park, August 17, 1905, rebuked women for coming to church without hats, and said that the bishop of the diocese had asked the clergy to enforce the rule that "women should not enter the consecrated building with uncovered heads." Russian Jewish women at Jerusalem, being forbidden to wear veils, wear wigs, lest they may "dishonor" their heads by uncovering them.[2]

484. Rules of propriety. The Kabyles of northern Africa are warlike, but have little political organization. Although they are Moslems, they have, by an ingenious use of Moslem law about pious gifts for charitable uses, preserved their own ancient mores about women's property, against the Moslem law. A bride, on leaving her home, is lifted on her mule by a negro, if there is one in the village. There is great rejoicing at the birth of a boy, and the mother is congratulated and decorated. When a girl is born there is silence. A man is fined if he slaughters an animal and eats meat except on a market day, because it would pain his neighbors to see him eat meat when they could not get it.[3] The Kabyles have very strict rules as to sex propriety and decency of language. Any violation of propriety in the presence of a woman, or of a man accompanied by one of his female relatives, calls for especial punishment. The presence of a woman protects her husband from violence by a creditor, and in general imposes peace and decorum.[4] As a mark of respect for a man with whom she is talking, a Tuareg woman will turn her back to him, or draw a fold of her garment over her mouth.[5] The Kalmucks consider that a man without his girdle is in extreme undress. He never shows himself before old people without his girdle.[6]

[1] *The Churchman*, September 2, 1905, 343.

[2] Goodrich-Frear, *Inner Jerusalem*, 57.

[3] This explanation is no doubt a product of later rationalization. The rule is a very ancient Semitic one, due to the old connection between sacrifice and commensality. W. Rob. Smith, *Relig. of the Semites*, 283.

[4] Hanoteau et Letourneux, *La Kabylie*, II, and III, 190, 237, 240.

[5] Duveyrier, *Les Touaregs du Nord*, 430.

[6] *Russ. Ethnog.* (*russ.*), II, 445.

485. Hindoo ritual of the toilet, etc. According to ancient Hindoo custom, younger brothers should in all matters yield to elder brothers.[1] Brahmins use only the left hand for all acts of the bodily toilet. They have a very elaborate ritual for all such acts, and consider their houses defiled by the presence of Europeans who do not observe any such ritual. They remove shoes on entering a house on account of the impurity of leather.[2] It is not good manners amongst them to address the women of the house, or to ask for them. If a woman takes a man's arm in public she is supposed to be his mistress. Gallantry is never displayed. A wife would resent it as disrespectful, fit only for a woman of another grade. Only courtesans, dancers, and harlots are taught to read, sing, or dance. An honest woman would be ashamed to know how to read. Brahmins regard the use of the pocket handkerchief with the same disgust which a European feels for the Hindoo use of the fingers which European laborers practice. Hindoos clean the teeth with a fresh twig every day, and are horrified that Europeans do it with a brush made of the hair of an animal, and do it frequently with the same brush. There are days on which one must not brush the teeth on pain of hell. " Saliva is of all things the most utterly polluting." [3] For a woman to have to part with her hair is one of the greatest of degradations and the most terrible of all trials. Hindoo women never use false hair if they lose their own.[4] Women are safe and are treated with respect in public. The honor of a Hindoo requires that he look no higher than the ankles of a passing woman.[5] He must not touch a woman. If many men and women meet, for instance in traveling, they may lie down side by side to sleep without impropriety.[6] Not one man in a hundred in India ever tasted liquor, " but a Hindoo beggar may not eat bread made with yeast or baked by any but Hindoos of his own or a better caste." [7] The Angharmi of northeastern India consider

---

[1] Holtzmann, *Ind. Sagen*, II, 267.

[2] Monier-Williams, *Brahmanism and Hinduism*, 396.

[3] *Ibid.*, 376. [4] *Ibid.*, 375.

[5] Nivedita, *Web of Indian Life*, 14.

[6] Dubois, *Mœurs de l'Inde* (1825), II, 280, 329, 332, 334, 441, 476, 480.

[7] Nivedita, *Web of Indian Life*, 11.

it a reproach for a woman to bear a child before her hair is long enough to be tied behind. Until marriage the women shave the head. Spouses are therefore separated for a year after marriage.[1]

Modern Egyptians think it improper for a man to "describe the features or person of a female (as that she has a straight nose or large eyes) to one of his own sex, by whom it is unlawful that she should be seen."[2] Modern Sicilian peasants at their balls dance in couples of men and couples of women, "such an idea as a man putting his arm around a woman's waist in a waltz being considered indecent."[3]

486. Greek rules of propriety. Nausikaa disregarded the lack of dress of the shipwrecked when they needed help, but she had a complete code of propriety and good manners with which she compelled them to comply.[4] In the Greek tragedies modest and proper behavior for women is characterized by reserve, retirement, reluctance. They ought not to talk publicly with young men or to expose themselves to the gaze of men. They may not run out into the street with hair and dress disordered, or roam about the country, or run to look at sights. Clytemnestra told Iphigenia to be reserved with Achilles if she could be so and win her point, but to win her point. Iphigenia considered it a cause of shame to her that her proposed marriage was broken off.

487. Erasmus's rules. Erasmus wrote a book of manners for a youth, his pupil. He said that the teeth should be cleaned, but that it was girlish to whiten them with powder. He thought it excessive to rinse the mouth more frequently than once in the morning. He thought it lazy and thieflike to go with one's hands behind one's back. It was not well-mannered to sit or stand with one hand in the other, although some thought it soldierly.[5]

488. Eating. Special occasion for rules of propriety is offered by eating. In Melanesia and Polynesia men and their wives remain in a great measure strangers to each other. They lead separate lives. Women have their lodgings, meals, work, and property separate.[6] Perhaps it is a

---

[1] JAI, XXVII, 27.
[2] Lane, *Mod. Egyptians*, I, 265.
[3] Alec-Tweedie, *Sunny Sicily*, 265.
[4] *Od.*, VI, 285.
[5] *De Civilitate Morum Puerilium*, I, 1, 3, 5, 52, 54.
[6] JAI, XXIV, 231.

consequence that the rule becomes established that men and women should never see each other eat.[1] The Varua of Central Africa put a cloth before the face while drinking, in order not to be seen, especially by any woman.[2] On Tanna (New Hebrides) a woman may not see a man drink *kava*.[3] A man on the Andaman Islands may not eat with any women except those of his own household, until he is old. The unmarried of each sex eat by themselves.[4] Amongst the old Semites it was not the custom for a man to eat with his wife and children. In northern Arabia "no woman will eat before men." Some Southern Arabs "would rather die than accept food at the hands of a woman."[5] There is also a widespread notion that one should not be seen to eat by anybody. The Bakairi are ashamed to see or to be seen eating.[6] In northern Abyssinia people when eating are concealed. At a wedding feast the guests break up into little groups of four to six, who eat separately, each group covered by a sheet.[7] The king of Loango covers his mouth with a garment to eat or drink, in order to keep up an ancient rule that no one may see him eat or drink.[8] The Sudanese think that disease or death would follow if any one should see them take food.[9] No Hindoos like to be looked at while eating. " I never once saw a single Hindoo, except of the lowest caste, either preparing or eating cooked food of any kind."[10] If a man of inferior caste enters the kitchen where food is being prepared all must be thrown away. If food thus contaminated was eaten it would taint the souls as well as the bodies of the eaters, and would cost long and painful expiation. Schwaner[11] reports that the Dyaks withdrew "modestly" when he was about to eat. That the cycle of variation may be complete, we find one case of people (Kafans) who may not take food or drink without the presence of a legal witness, an adult of the same people duly authorized. The chief has a slave who discharges the duty of witness. He must be called at night if the chief has to take medicine. A stranger must conform to the rule. Spouses must eat and drink together, from the same dish or cup. To violate this rule is a reason for divorce.[12] The best explanation of the rules about eating in private is the fear of the evil eye, i.e. the envious or admiring eye of a hungry man, which would bewitch the food.

489. Kissing. Kissing is another occasion for special rules of propriety. In China and Japan kissing is regarded with disgust. It is unknown amongst Polynesians, Malays, negroes, and Indians

---

[1] Crawley gives a list of cases (JAI, XXIV, 435).

[2] *Ibid.*, 433.

[3] *Austral. Assoc. Adv. Sci.*, 1892, 660.

[4] JAI, XII, 344.

[5] W. R. Smith, *Relig. of the Semites*, 279.

[6] *Berl. Mus.*, 1888, 66.

[7] Bent, *Ethiopia*, 32.

[8] Bastian, *Loango-Küste*, I, 262.

[9] Junker, *Afrika*, I, 156.

[10] Monier-Williams, *Brahmanism and Hinduism*, 128.

[11] *Borneo*, II, 168.

[12] Paulitschke, *Ethnog. N.O. Afr.*, I, 248.

of South America.[1] They rub noses, or bite, or smell, instead.
It is said of a Samoan girl, also, that she "looks upon kissing
with disgust."[2] So far apart may human beings be racewise in
their judgment of what is pleasant or disgusting! In Europe,
in the Middle Ages, the custom of kissing was very extended.
Newcomers were saluted with kisses ; also partners in the dance.
A bishop kissed the wife of Rudolf of Hapsburg when receiving
her, but he was banished until Rudolf died.[3] From a fifteenth-
century sermon it is learned that a young lady of rank in France,
at that time, would rise in the midst of divine service, incommod-
ing everybody, in order to kiss on the mouth a cavalier who
entered the church at that time.[4] The custom of kissing became
more general in the fifteenth and sixteenth centuries, but discussion about it shows that there was some doubt whether it
was expedient. "The mores won a victory over philosophy."[5]
In modern times Europeans have taught half-civilized and
barbarian peoples the custom of kissing. The Hottentots, for
instance, in their zeal to imitate Europeans, have adopted this
custom.[6]

490. Politeness, etiquette, manners. Politeness, courtesy, and
good manners are usages, but they rise to the level of the mores
when they become a part of the character of a people, for then
they produce characteristic traits which affect all societal relations.[7]
Uncivilized people often pay punctilious attention to rules of
etiquette about salutations, visits, meetings, the aged, etc. As
all their rules are imperative and admit of no discussion or
exception, they constitute a social ritual which may educate in
certain sentiments, although it is by no means sure to do so. The
functions of politeness and etiquette exist in order to make things
go smoothly in all social contact. Orientals have very thorough
training in this department. They have systems of good manners
which have been practiced for thousands of years. The Chinese

---

[1] Martius, *Ethnog. Brasil.*, 96.   [2] Becke, *Pacific Tales*, 179.
[3] Denecke, *Anstandsgefühl in Deutschland*, VII.
[4] Lenient, *La Satire en France au M. A.*, 310.
[5] De Maulde la Clavière, *Femmes de la Renaissance*, 320.
[6] *Globus*, LXXXV, 80.
[7] See Mallory in *Amer. Anthrop.*, III, 201.

Li-ki ("Ritual of Propriety") dates from the beginning of the Christian era. It is an elaborate text-book of correct conduct in all affairs of life. It is of universal application, except for details of the mode of life in China, and it shows the value of such a code and the use of the habits it inculcates. Chinese and Japanese are well-disciplined people in all the matters of conduct and social contact which are controlled by the mores.

From this point on it will be noticed that the codes to be mentioned are further removed from the sex mores.

491. Good manners. The Andamanese of all classes show great consideration for the very young, weak, aged, or helpless.[1] A white man gave liquor to a native man on the Chittagong hills. The latter insisted on giving some of it to the women first, but they required much urging before they would take it.[2] The Samoans have very polished manners. They had a court language.[3] The Betsileo on Madagascar have a careful etiquette about the houses of their chiefs, about proper conduct in those houses, and about the utensils there; also words are reserved for chiefs which others may not utter.[4] In East Africa any violation of etiquette towards a chief is summarily and severely punished, sometimes by death.[5] Many an A-Sande has lost a finger or his life for an innocent word spoken to the wife of a chief.[6] The Tunguses of Siberia have so much habitual politeness that Wrangell called them "the French of the tundra."[7] The Yakuts think it bad manners to give a big piece of meat to a poor guest and a little piece to a rich one. Good breeding, according to their code, calls for the opposite conduct.[8] A Fuegian husband, giving an order to his wife, out of courtesy tells her to give the order to some one else, although there is no one else.[9] Amongst North American Indians the modes of sitting or squatting for each sex are strictly prescribed.[10] Sapper says of the Central American Indians that when the white man asks a question he often gets

[1] JAI, XII, 93.
[2] Lewin, *Races of S. E. India*, 311.
[3] *Austral. Assoc. Adv. Sci.*, 1892, 630.
[4] JAI, XXI, 223.
[5] *Ibid.*, XXII, 119.
[6] Junker, *Afr.*, II, 481.
[7] Hiekisch, *Tungusen*, 68.
[8] Sieroshevski, *Yakuty*, (*russ.*), I, 440.
[9] *Scribner's Mag.*, February, 1895.
[10] *Globus*, LXXIII, 253.

no answer because he has neglected something required by etiquette. He once on a journey asked a Kekchi Indian to ask the
way of an Indian whom they saw coming. This was improper,
because not any one in the company might ask that question,
according to Kekchi etiquette, but only the leader of the company.[1] Schweinfurth[2] rates the Dinka above Turks and Arabs
in respect to table manners and decorum of eating. All recline
on the ground around a bowl of food, each with a gourd cup in
his hand, but they manage this primitive arrangement with
constant care for propriety.

492. Etiquette of salutation, etc. The modes of expressing
good will and the etiquette of meeting or visiting would be
another large section under this head. What things are possible
is shown by the report that a Tibetan host at a feast "expressed
his respect for us and his appreciation of our remarks by rising
to his feet and extending his tongue at full length." [3]

493. Literature of manners and etiquette. Denecke[4] is able
to trace an indigenous cultivation of good manners by literature
from the eleventh century, when there was taught courtesy to
women, although not the woman cult of a later time. He mentions a series of books down to the nineteenth century, which
inculcated good manners according to the changing notions and
standards of the times. In the second half of the thirteenth century it was taught in von Lichtenstein's *Frauenbuch*, a manual
of manners and morals for women, that a woman should not
salute a knight at his approach lest he infer favor. She was to
be covered like a nun ; she did not share in banquets and did not
kiss guests whom she received ; she shunned outside festivities
and kept a good name. Knights then neglected women because
they cared only for rude pleasures, drink, and hunting. Later,
rules were made for the conduct of men.[5] The history of manners shows that what was inculcated in books never became real
practice. The conquest of the art of eating with propriety was
accomplished by the introduction of forks. Before that the bread

[1] *Globus*, LXXXVII, 128.   [3] *Century Mag.*, January, 1904.
[2] *Heart of Africa*, I, 157.   [4] *Anstandsgefühl in Deutschland.*
                            [5] Denecke, XII.

was a tool with which to eat, and it required cultivated skill to handle it properly. Salt and mustard still presented problems, — knife or fingers? Each one brought his own knife.

494. Honor, seemliness, common sense, conscience. Honor, common sense, seemliness, and conscience seem to belong to the individual domain. They are reactions produced in the individual by the societal environment. Honor is the sentiment of what one owes to one's self. It is an individual prerogative, and an ultimate individual standard. Seemliness is conduct which befits one's character and standards. Common sense, in the current view, is a natural gift and universal outfit. As to honor and seemliness, the popular view seems to be that each one has a fountain of inspiration in himself to furnish him with guidance. Conscience might be added as another natural or supernatural "voice," intuition, and part of the original outfit of all human beings as such. If these notions could be verified, and if they proved true, no discussion of them would be in place here, but as to honor it is a well-known and undisputed fact that societies have set codes of honor and standards of it which were arbitrary, irrational, and both individually and socially inexpedient, as ample experiment has proved. These codes have been and are imperative, and they have been accepted and obeyed by great groups of men who, in their own judgment, did not believe them sound. Those codes came out of the folkways of the time and place. Then comes the question whether it is not always so. Is honor, in any case, anything but the code of one's duty to himself which he has accepted from the group in which he was educated? Family, class, religious sect, school, occupation, enter into the social environment. In every environment there is a standard of honor. When a man thinks that he is acting most independently, on his personal prerogative, he is at best only balancing against each other the different codes in which he has been educated, e.g. that of the trades union against that of the Sunday school, or of the school against that of the family. What we think "natural" and universal, and to which we attribute an objective reality, is the sum of traits whose origin is so remote, and which we share with so many, that we do not know when or how we took them up, and we can remember no rational selection by which we adopted them. The same is true of common sense. It is the stock of ways of looking at things which we acquired unconsciously by suggestion from the environment in which we grew up. Some have more common sense than others, because they are more docile to suggestion, or have been taught to make judgments by people who were strong and wise. Conscience also seems best explained as a sum of principles of action which have in one's character the most original, remote, undisputed, and authoritative position, and to which questions of doubt are habitually referred. If these views are accepted, we have in honor, common sense, and conscience other phenomena of the folkways, and the notions of eternal truths of philosophy or ethics, derived from somewhere outside of men and their struggles to live well under the conditions of earth, must be abandoned as myths.

495. Seemliness. Honor, common sense, and conscience can never be predicated of groups except by a figure of speech. The case with seemliness is different. That also is an individual trait. It is lighter and less definable than honor and propriety. The individual alone must decide what it is fitting for him to do or refuse to do. He will get his standards for this decision from his nearest social environment. Seemliness, however, can be predicated of a society. A civilized state may act in a seemly or unseemly manner, that is, in a way worthy of its history and character, or the contrary. Also the people of a group, in their unorganized acts, can obey unworthy motives and yield to impulses, groupwise, which are beneath the level of culture which they really have obtained, or belong to policies which are narrower than those by which they pretend to act.

496. Cases of unseemliness. The Assyrians were fierce, cruel, bloodthirsty, and pitiless. They have left, cut in the hardest stone, — it must have been by immense labor, — pictures of cruel tortures and executions and of immense slaughters. A king is represented putting out the eyes of prisoners. What the pictures reveal is the lust of conquest, the delights of revenge, and the ecstasy of tyranny. After Assurbanipal took Susa he broke open the tombs of the old heroes of Elam, who had in their day defeated the Assyrians. He desecrated the tombs, insulted the monuments, and carried the bones away to Nineveh. It was believed that the ghosts of these dead heroes would suffer the captivity inflicted on their bones, and sacrifices were made to them just sufficient to prolong their existence and suffering. This policy was pursued with all the ingenious refinements which the dogmas suggested, in order to glut the vengeance of the Assyrian king.[1] The Babylonians were peaceful and industrial, but the Persians combined with great luxury and licentiousness a fiendish ingenuity in torture and painful modes of execution. It is very interesting to notice in Homer criticism of conduct from the standpoint of taste and judgment as to what is seemly.[2] Homer thought it unseemly for Achilles to drag the corpse of Hector behind his chariot. He says that the gods thought so too.[3] He disapproved of the sacrifice of twelve Trojan youths on the pyre of Patroclus.[4] In the poems there are recorded many unseemly acts. Achilles spurned the prayer of Hector that his body might be redeemed, and wished that he could eat part of the body of his conquered foe. The Greeks mutilated the corpse with their weapons.[5] Agamemnon and Ajax Oileus cut off the heads of the slain.[6] Odysseus ordered twelve maidens who had been friends to the suitors to be put to the sword. Telemachus hanged them. Melantheus, who had traitorously taken the suitors' side, was mutilated alive, member by member.[7] Odysseus tells Eurykleia that it is a cruel sin to exult over a dead enemy, but the heroes often did it. This doctrine expresses the better sense of the age, but a doctrine which was beyond their self-control when their passions were aroused. The Olympian household must be taken to represent the society of the time, especially if we throw out the stories of the violations of the sex taboo which were often myths of nature processes or survivals of earlier mores. The Olympian gods show no dignity, magnanimity, or moral

[1] Maspero, *Peuples de l'Orient*, III, 436–439.

[2] Professor Keller calls my attention to a number of words used by Homer to subject conduct to this test of seemliness. It seems to be for him the standard of right.

[3] *Il.*, XXII, 395; XXIV, 51.

[4] *Ibid.*, XXIII, 164.

[5] *Ibid.*, XXII, 338.

[6] *Ibid.*, XI, 147; XIII, 102.

[7] *Od.*, XXII, 441, 447.

earnestness. They entertain mean sentiments of jealousy, envy, offended vanity, resentment, and rancor. They are divided by enmities and feuds. The females are frivolous and shallow; their fathers and husbands are often angry with them for levity, folly, disobedience, and self-will; but they have to remember that the goddesses are females and make the best of it with a groan and a laugh. The gods have great weakness for feminine grace and charm. They make allowances for the women, pet them, and despise them. There is some recognition of a possibly nobler relation of men to women, but it is only a transitory ideal. The goddesses get into difficulties by their intrigues and follies, but they avail themselves to the utmost of their feminine privileges to escape the penalties. They fool the gods. It reminds us of a modern French novel. We meet with the same sentiments, maxims, and philosophy. What were the gods for? They were superfluous and useless, or mischievous, but theology taught that they kept the whole thing going. They dealt meanly with men. Athena took the form of Deïphobus in order to persuade Hector to meet Achilles and be killed.[1] They sent dreams to men to mislead them. What can men do against that? They mixed in the fights of men, but availed themselves of their godship, if things went against them, and especially in order to get revenge for defeat. There was no chivalry or nobility of mind or behavior. It is plain that the gods are not idealized men. They are worse than the men. Von der March[2] has collected evidence that the heroes were savage, cruel, cowardly, venal, rancorous, vain, and lacking in fortitude, when compared with German epic heroes. It is far more important to notice that this evidence proves that the Greeks did not have, and therefore could not ascribe to the gods, a standard of seemliness above what these traits of the picture disclose. Since that is so, it follows that the standard of what is fit, seemly, becoming, good form, is a function of the folkways, or rather of class ways, since it is only selected classes who cultivate seemliness. Seemliness is a light, remote, and less important form of propriety. It is a matter of taste, and taste is cultivated by the folkways.

[1] *Il.*, XXII, 226.   [2] *Völkerideale*, I, Chap. I.

497. Greek tragedies and notions of seemliness. We think it unseemly to criticise the ways of Divine Providence, and we refrain from it, whatever we may think. Since Christianity is no longer imposed by pains and penalties, we think it unseemly to assail Christianity in the interest of a negative or destructive philosophy. The Greeks of the fifth century B.C. had not these notions. They upbraided the gods for their ways to men and for their vices. The antagonisms of the mores were antagonisms of gods. In the *Eumenides* the most tragic consequences follow from the antagonism of the mores of the mother and father family. The Furies do not insist on the duty of Orestes to kill his mother, in blood revenge for the murder of his father, because they belong to the old system, in which the son was of the mother's blood ; but Apollo, the god of the new system, orders it. A new doctrine of procreation has to be promulgated. "The mother does not procreate the son ; she only bears and cherishes the awakened life." [Here we see how the doctrines are invented afterwards to fit the exigencies of new folkways.] Orestes obeys Apollo and is a victim. Since the command comes from a god, how shall the man not obey ? To us it is a simple case of a common tragedy, that an individual is the victim of a great social movement. In the *Herakleidæ*, Alcmena urges that a war captive be slain. The king of Athens forbids that any one be slain who was taken alive. The former prevailed. The Athenian doctrine was new and high and not yet current. In the *Ion* Ion tells Zeus and Poseidon that if they paid the penalties of all their adulteries they would empty their temple treasuries. They act wrongly when they do not observe due measure in their pursuit of pleasure. It is not fair to call men wicked when they imitate the gods. Let the evil examples be blamed. In the *Andromache* horror is expressed of the folkways of the barbarians, in which incest is not prevented. In the *Medea* Jason, who is a scoundrel and a cur, prates to Medea about her gain in coming to Greece : "Thou hast learned what justice means, and how to live by law, not by the dictates of brute force." She had not learned it at all — quite the contrary. In the *Hekuba* it is said to be a disgrace to murder guests in Greece, and in *Iphigenia amongst the Taurians* the same doctrine is stated when Greeks are to be the victims of the contrary rule. "Barbarian" was a cultural category. To be Greek was to have city life with market place, gymnastic training, and a share in the games.[1] These were arbitrary marks of superiority such as the members of an esoteric corporation always love, but the time came when the Greek history contained so many shameful things that the Greeks ceased to talk of the contrast with barbarians. It was proposed to Pausanias that he should repay on the corpse of Mardonius the insults inflicted by Xerxes on the body of Leonidas. He indignantly refused.[2] The old laws of war put the life and property of the vanquished, and their wives and children, at the mercy of the conquerors, but the Greeks, when the Peloponnesian war began, felt the shame of this law as between Greeks. Therefore they sinned against their own better feeling when in that war they enslaved and slaughtered the vanquished. That they knew better is shown by the conduct of the Athenians towards Mytilene, in 427. At first all adult males were sentenced to death, and the women and children to slavery, but later this sentence was revoked. Cases also occurred in which the law of war was not followed, but the conquered were spared. By retaliation they inflamed their own passions and went on from bad to worse until there was a revulsion of pure shame. Lysander put to death three thousand Athenians, captives, after the battle of Ægospotami, as reprisals for the barbarities executed by the Athenians against Sparta and her allies. The allies wanted to exercise war law on Athens, but Sparta would not consent. To her then belongs the honor of fixing a new precedent. It was her duty to do so after the act of Lysander. Beloch thinks that science made the greater humanity of the fourth century.[3] It is more probable that it was due to a perception of the horror and shame of the other course. The parties in the cities, in the later centuries, were also guilty of excess, rancorous passion, revenge, and oppression. These cases come under the head of unseemliness in so far as they show a lack of sense of where to stop. That sense, especially in the political acts of democracies, must be a

[1] Burckhardt, *Griech. Kulturgesch.*, I, 314.   [2] Herodotus, IX, 78.
[3] Beloch, *Griech. Kulturgesch.*, I, 470, 594; II, 103, 107, 364, 441.

resultant, in the minds of men of the most numerous classes, from the spirit and temper of the folkways.

498. Seemliness in the Middle Ages. In the Middle Ages very great attention was given to seemliness in the private conduct of individuals. Moderation especially was to be cultivated. Women were put under minute rules of dress, posture, walk, language, tone of voice, and attitude. The guiding spirit of the regulations was restraint and limit.[1] Public life, however, was characterized by great unseemliness, and the examples of it are especially valuable because they show how necessary a sense of seemliness is to prevent great evils, although the virtue itself is vague and refined, and entirely beyond the field of positive cultivation by education or law. When the crusaders captured Mohammedan cities they showed savage ferocity. A case is recorded of a quarrel between a man of rank and a cook. The former proceeded to very extreme measures, and the cook, since he was a cook, could get no redress or attention.[2] In the fifteenth century a rage for indecent conduct arose. The type which the Germans call the *Grobian* was affected. Rudeness of manners in eating, dancing, etc., was cultivated as a pose. This fashion lasted for more than a century. In 1570 a society was formed of twenty-seven members, who swore to be nasty, not to wash or pray, and to practice blasphemy, etc. When drunk such persons committed great breaches of order, decency, etc.[3]

499. Unseemly debate. The folkways of the Middle Ages were fantastic and extravagant. The people had their chief interest in the future world, about which there could be no reality. They lived in a world of phantasms. The phantasms were dictated to them upon authority in the shape of dogmas of world philosophy and precepts of conduct. In discussing the world philosophy and its application they attained to extremes of animosity and ferocity. Whether Jesus and his apostles lived in voluntary beggary; whether any part of the blood of Jesus remained on earth; whether the dead went at once, or only at the judgment day, into the presence of God, — are specimens of the questions they

---

[1] Weinhold, *D. F.*, I, 159–168.   [2] Schultz, *Höf. Leben*, II, 448.
[3] Denecke, *Anstandsgefühl in Deutschland*, XXI.

debated. The unseemliness was in the mode of discussion, not in the absurdity of the subject. They all went into the debate understanding that the defeated or weaker party was to be burned. That was the rule of the game. All the strife of sects and parties was carried on in unseemly ways and with scandalous incidents. The lack of control, measure, due limit, was due to the lack of reality. Torture, persecution, violent measures, would all have been impossible if there had been a sense of seemliness. The punishments, executions, and public amusements grossly outraged any human and civilized taste. The treatment of the Templars, although it was no doubt good statecraft to abolish the order, was a scandalous outrage. In the face of Christendom torture was used to extort the evidence which was wanted to destroy the order, without regard to truth and justice.[1] The crusades were extravagant and fantastic, and were attended by incidents of shameful excess, gross selfishness, venality, and bad faith. It is one of the most amazing facts about witch persecutions in the sixteenth and seventeenth centuries that jurists did not see the unseemliness of their acts compared with the civilization of the period and the character claimed by their states. How was it possible for grave, learned, and honest men to go on torturing and burning miserable old women ? It is not until the end of the seventeenth century that we hear of sheriffs in England who refused to burn witches. One of the most unseemly incidents in history is the execution of Damiens for attempting to kill Louis XV. The authorities of the first state in Christendom multiplied tortures of the extremest kind, and caused them to be executed in public on the culprit. The treatment of the Tories in the American Revolution was unseemly. It left a deep stain on our history.

500. Unseemliness of lynching, torture, etc. It is an unseemly thing and unworthy of our age and civilization that persons should be lynched for alleged crime, without the trial and proof which our institutions provide for. The arguments in defense of lynching (except on the frontier, where civil institutions do not

[1] Lea, *Inquis.*, III, 238, 260, 319; Schotmüller, *Der Untergang des Templer-Ordens*, I, 625.

yet exist) never touch on this point. It is unseemly that any one should be burned at the stake in a modern civilized state. It is nothing to the purpose to show what a wicked wretch the victim was. Burning alive has long been thrown out of the folkways of our ancestors. The objection to reviving it is not an apology for the bad men or a denial of their wickedness : it is the goodness of the lynchers. They fall below what they owe to themselves. Torture has also long been thrown out of our folkways. It might have been believed a few years ago that torture could not be employed under the jurisdiction of the United States, and that, if it was employed, there would be a unanimous outburst of indignant reprobation against those who had so disgraced us. When torture was employed in the Philippines no such outburst occurred. The facts and the judgment upon them were easily suppressed. The recognition of Panama was unseemly. It was unworthy of the United States. It was defended and justified by the argument that we got something which we very earnestly wanted.

501. Good taste. Finally we may notice here also the matter of taste. Good taste is the most subtle of all the codes of judgment which are cultivated by the mores. What we now consider good taste was violated in the dramas of the Greeks and Romans. This is entirely aside from obscenity or vulgarity. For instance, it does not appear that the author of the *Medea* appreciated the dastardly conduct of Jason. De Julleville [1] says that in the thirteenth century no one knew the distinction between good and bad taste. The assertion is fully justified. The mediæval people may have had good taste in architecture, stained glass, and hammered iron (as we are told), but their literature, administration of justice, and politics show that they lacked good taste, and also the case shows what a high protection against folly and error good taste is. This last office it shares with the sense of humor. The sports of that age were cruel. People found fun in the sufferings of the weak under derision and abuse. " The Middle Ages did not shrink from presenting as funny situations which were painful or atrocious, the horror of which we to-day could not endure." Although the age was

[1] *Comédie en France au M. A.,* 21.

full of religiosity, the extravagances of which ought to have been restrained by good taste, if it had existed, there was, on the other hand, no true reverence for what were "sacred things." The churches were put to uses which would to-day be considered improper. Parodies and caricatures of ecclesiastical persons, institutions, and ritual called out no remonstrance. Mock sermons were a favorite form of monologue in a theatrical entertainment. In a morality produced late in the fifteenth century, called *Les Blasphémateurs*, the actors tortured and wounded the figure on a crucifix. The Virgin and two angels came down to catch in a cup the blood which miraculously flowed from the body, but the actors kept on. "The hideous scene is interminable." Personalities were employed beyond all decent toleration, not only in theological disputes, but in political conflicts of all kinds. Of course the fanaticism of the age accounts for the extravagance of the acts and doctrines, and good taste seems to be only a trivial defense against fanaticism, but good taste consists largely in a sense of due limits, and if there had been a good code of social usage tempered by taste, it would have prevented many of the greatest scandals in the history, especially the church history, of the period. Buffoons had a share in the great "moralities," although they did not have a rôle in the action. Their function was to interject comical comments from time to time. The comments aimed to be witty, but were generally gross, coarse, and obscene. Late in the fifteenth century, in France, a buffoon recited a prelude containing licentious jests to an edifying morality called *Charity*.[1]

502. Whence good taste is derived. Good taste is a more delicate and refined philosophy of action than any which have been mentioned above. It would escape from any attempt to formulate it, more completely than propriety or politeness. It floats in the ways of the group, and is absorbed by those who grow up in it. It is a product of breeding. We have a well-worn saying that there is no disputing about it. That is true, but for equal reason there is no disputing about decency, propriety, obscenity, or sex taboo. Good taste is a product of the group. It is

[1] De Julleville, 21, 74, 86, 89, 107, 304.

absorbed from the group. Like honor, however, it calls for an individual reaction of assent and dissent, and becomes an individual trait or possession in the form which it ultimately takes.

503. The great variety in the codes. All the topics which have been treated in this chapter are branches or outreachings of the social code. They show how deep is the interest of human beings in the sex taboo, and in the self-perpetuation of society. Men have always tried, and are trying still, to solve the problem of well living in this respect. The men, the women, the children, and the society have joint and several interests, and the complication is great. At the present time population, race, marriage, childbirth, and the education of children present us our greatest problems and most unfathomable mysteries. All the contradictory usages of chastity, decency, propriety, etc., have their sense in some assumed relation to the welfare of society. To some extent they have come out of caprice, but chiefly they have issued from experience of good and ill, and are due to efforts to live well. Thus we may discern in them policies and philosophies, but they never proceed to form any such generalities as do rationally adopted motives. There is logic in the folkways, but never rationality. Given the premises, in a notion of kin, for instance, and the deductions are made directly and generally correctly, but the premises could never be verified, and they were oftener false than true. Each group took its own way, making its own assumptions, and following its own logic. So there was great variety and discord in their policies and philosophies, but within the area of a custom, during its dominion, its authority is absolute; and hence, although the usages are infinitely various, directly contradictory, and mutually abominable, they are, within their area of dominion, of equal value and force, and they are the standards of what is true and right. The groups have often tried to convert each other by argument and reason. They have never succeeded. Each one's reasons are the tradition which it has received from its ancestors. That does not admit of argument. Each tries to convince the other by going outside of the tradition to some philosophic standard of truth. Then the tradition is left in full force. Shocking as it must be to any group

to be told that there is no rational ground for any one of them
to convert another group to its mores (because this seems to
imply, although it does not, that their folkways are not better
than those of other groups), yet this must be said, for it is true.
By experience and science the nations which by name are Christian have reached ways which are better fitted, on the whole,
for well living than those of the Mohammedan nations, although
this superiority is not by any means so complete and sweeping
as current opinion in Christian countries believes. If Christians
and Mohammedans come together and argue, they never make
the slightest impression on each other. During the crusades, in
Andalusia, and in cities of the near East where they live side by
side, they have come to peace, mutual respect, and mutual influence. Syncretism begins. There is giving and taking. In Egypt
at present the Moslems see the power of the English to carry
on industry, commerce, and government, and this observation
produces effect on the folkways. That is the chief way in which
folkways are modified or borrowed. It was by this process that
Greeks and Romans influenced the folkways of barbarians, and
that white men have influenced those of negroes, Indians, Polynesians, Japanese, etc.

504. Morals and deportment. Different groups and different
ages have differed much in the place in the social codes in which
certain subjects have been placed; that is, for instance, as to
whether the treatment of women by men should be put under
morals, or under manners, or under good taste; whether public
exhibitions deserved more attention than deportment, etc. For
instance: "There is hardly a word, in the instructions of Plutarch, upon schools and schooling, but he alludes casually to the
strange scenes which boys were allowed to witness, — criminals
dressed up with robes and crowns, and presently stripped and
publicly tortured; paintings of subjects so objectionable that
we should carefully explain to the child the distinction between
art as such and art as a vehicle of morals. On the other hand,
deportment was strictly watched: for example, it was the rule
not to use the left hand unless it were to hold bread at dinner,
while other food was taken with the right; to walk in the street

without looking up ; to touch salt fish with one finger ; fresh fish, bread, and meat, with two ; to scratch yourself thus ; to fold your cloak thus." [1]

505. The relation of the social codes to philosophy and religion. Amongst the widest differences of opinion would be that on the question whether the social codes issue out of and are enthused by philosophy or religion. We are told that "for most men, actions stand in no necessary connection with any theoretical convictions of theirs, but are, on the contrary, independent of the same, and are dominated by inherited and acquired motives." [2] Why is this not true ? Also, " the antagonism between the principles of our religion and our actual behavior, even of the faithful, as well as the great difference in the ethical views of different peoples who profess the same religion, sufficiently proves that the motives of our acts, and our judgments on the acts of others, proceed primarily from practical life [i.e. from the current mores], and that what we believe has comparatively little influence on our acts and judgments." [3] Religion and philosophy are components of the mores, but not by any means sources or regulators of them.

506. Rudeck's conclusions. A recent German writer on the history of public morality [4] says of the moral development of the German people that one cannot bear to contemplate it, because the people face the facts with absolute indifference. There is not a trace of moral initiative or of moral consciousness. Existing morality presents itself to us as a purely accidental product of forces which act without sense or intelligence. We can find all kinds of forces in history except ethical forces. Those are entirely wanting. There is no development, for development means the unfolding and growth of a germ according to the elements which it contains. The people allow all kinds of mores to be forced on them by the work of their own hands, that is, by the economic and political arrangements which they have

[1] Mahaffy, *The Greek World under Roman Sway*, 324.
[2] Schultze-Gävernitz in Ammon, *Gesellschaftsordnung*, 117.
[3] Schallmeyer, *Vererbung und Auslese*, 231.
[4] Rudeck, *Gesch. der Oeffentl. Sittlichkeit in Deutschland*, 422.

adopted. The German people has no subjective notion of public morality and no ethical ideal for public morality. They distinguish only between good and bad mores (*Sitten und Unsitten*), without regard to their origin.

507. Rudeck's book is really a chapter in the history of the mores. The above are the conclusions which seem to be forced upon him, but he recoils from them in dismay. The conclusions are unquestionably correct. They are exactly what the history teaches. They ought to be accepted and used for profit. The fact that people are indifferent to the history of their own mores is a primary fact. We can only accept it and learn from it. It shows us the immense error of that current social discussion which consists in bringing " ethical " notions to the criticism of facts. The ethical notions are figments of speculation. Criticism of the mores is like criticising one's ancestors for the physique one has inherited, or one's children for being, in body and mind, one's children. If it is true of the German people that there is no moral initiative or consciousness in their tone and attitude towards their mores, they are to be congratulated, for they have kept out one great influx of subjective and dogmatic mischief. Other nations have a " nonconformist conscience " or a party of "great moral ideas," which can be caught by a phrase, or stampeded by a catching watchword with a "moral" suggestion. " Existing morality *does* present itself as a purely accidental [i.e. not to be investigated] product of forces which act without sense or intelligence," but the product is in no true sense accidental. It is true that there are no ethical forces in history. Let us recognize the fact and its consequences. Some philosophers make great efforts to interpret ethical forces into history, but they play with words. There is no development of the mores along any lines of logical or other sequence. The mores shift in endless readjustment of the modes of behavior, effort, and thinking, so as to reach the greatest advantage under the conditions. " The people allow all kinds of mores to be forced on them by the work of their own hands," that is, by the economic and political arrangements which have been unconsciously forced on them by their instinctive efforts to live well. That is just what they do, and that is the way in which mores come to be. " The German people has no subjective notion of public morality and no ethical ideal for public morality." Nor has any other people. A people sometimes adopts an ideal of national vanity, which includes ambition, but an ethical ideal no group ever has. If it pretended to have one it would be a humbug. That is why the introduction of " moral ideas " into politics serves the most immoral purposes and plays into the hands of the most immoral men. All ethics grow out of the mores and are a part of them. That is why the ethics never can be antecedent to the mores, and cannot be in a causal or productive relation to them. " The German people distinguishes only between customs and abuses [*Sitten und Unsitten*] without regard to their origin." They are quite right to do so, because the origin is only a matter for historians. For the masses the mores are facts. They use them and they testify that they are conducive to well living (*Sitten*), or the contrary (*Unsitten*). The men, women, and children who compose a society at any time are the unconscious depositaries and transmitters of the mores. They inherited them without knowing it; they are molding them unconsciously; they will transmit them involuntarily. The people cannot make the mores. They are made by them. Yet the group is at once makers and made. Each one may put into the group life as much as he can, but the group will give back to him order and determination from which he cannot escape. The mores grow as they must grow under the conditions. They are products of the effort of each to live as well as he can, and they are coercions which hold and control each in his efforts to live well. It is idle to try to get outside of this operation in order to tell which part of it comes first and makes the other. " Our age presents us the incredible spectacle that the dependence of the higher social culture on the economic development is not only clearly recognized by social science, but is proclaimed as the ideal." Social science does not proclaim this as an ideal. It does not deal in ideals. It accepts the dependence of culture on economic development as a fact. In fact, Rudeck is not justified in saying (p. 426) that " culture is the unity of the moral will in all the life phenomena of a people," and that "that people alone is a culture people which sets before itself, as the purpose of its entire existence, the production of the greatest possible amount of specified moral qualities." These are notions of culture and of a culture people which an ethical philosopher might think it fine should be. Rudeck has just found that no such things ever have existed in Germany; yet Germany possesses culture and the Germans are a culture people. He is really complaining that these fine ethical notions have never had any place in history. Such being the case, the true inference would be that they are unrealities and ought to be discarded altogether. Rudeck can find, in the eighteenth century, only one act of the state which had an improving effect on "external morals." That was the abolition of obscene playing cards, and this improving effect was not won intentionally, but as an incidental consequence of a tax which was imposed for revenue. The case is interesting and instructive. It is thus alone that the state acts. It needs revenue and lays a tax. Other consequences follow. Sometimes "moral" consequences follow. The Methuen treaty caused Englishmen to drink port instead of claret for a hundred and fifty years, to the great increase of gout and drunkenness. The statesman might well be appalled if he should realize that he probably never can lay a tax without effects on industry, health, education, morals, and religion which he cannot foresee and cannot control. In the case of the cards, the consequence was favorable to good morals. That consequence was the purest accident. The state went on its way and got its revenue. The people met the effect through the mores and made the best of it, just as they did with the effects of the Methuen treaty. The cases are useful for a statesman to consider, when he needs to get revenue and the question by what taxes to get it is yet in his mind and *before* him. When he has decided and acted it remains only to take the consequences, for, through the mores, they will enter into the web of life which the people are weaving and must endure. That web contains all the follies and errors, just as well as all the wisdom and all the achievements, of the past. The whole inheritance passes on together, including all the luck.

CHAPTER XII

INCEST

Definition. — Incest notion was produced from the folkways. — The notion that inbreeding is harmful. — Status-wife, work-wife, love-wife. — The abomination of incest. — The incest taboo is strongest in the strongest groups. — Incest in ethnography. — Incest in civilized states. — Where the line is drawn, and why. — Human self-selection. — Restriction by biological doctrine not sufficiently warranted. — Summary of the matter now.

508. Definition of incest. Incest is the marital union of a man and a woman who are akin within the limits of a prohibition current at the time in the laws or mores of the group. The primitive notion of kinship did not divide kinship into grades of remoteness as we do. Very often it was counted by classes or age strata. In the totem system all the women of his mother's totem were tabooed to a man, although their cousinship to himself might be very remote. At the same time, he could marry his father's sister's daughter, or his mother's brother's daughter, unless his father and his uncle had married women of the same totem. Inasmuch as a man and his wife must have different totems and the children took the totem of their mother, a man might marry his own daughter. Generally this was forbidden by supplementary rules, but in Buka and North Bougainville it occurs not infrequently.[1] The varieties of the consanguinity taboo are very numerous. They are entirely different in theory under the mother family and the father family. They are now very different in different states of our Union.[2] If the taboo on marriage is not defined in terms of " blood " or assumed kinship, violation of it is not incest. For instance, in the mediæval church, two persons who had been sponsors in baptism to the same child might not marry. Also, if two persons are debarred

---

[1] Parkinson, *Ethnog. d. Nordwestl. Salomo Ins.*, 6.
[2] Snyder, *Geog. of Marriage.*

by affinity, violation is not incest. In England a man may not marry his deceased wife's sister. If he does it, his marriage is unlawful, but it is not incest. The definition of incest must include the notion of a blood connection as blood connection is understood in that group at the time. Other prohibitions may be expedient, or may seem required by propriety (e.g. the marriage of a man with his father's widow), but they do not come under incest.

Restrictions on marriage by kinship, as the people in question construed kinship, go back to the most primitive society. Some very primitive people have intricate restrictions, and they maintain them by the severest social sanctions.

509. Incest notion produced from the folkways. It is evident that primitive people must have received a suggestion or impression of some important interest at stake in this matter. They adopted taboos and established folkways to protect interests. In time these taboos and folkways won very great force and high religious sanction; also a sense of abomination was produced which seemed to be a "natural" feeling. There certainly is no natural feeling. The abomination is conventional and traditional. The Pharaohs, Ptolemies, and Incas, also the Zoroastrians, are sufficient to show that there is no reason for the abomination in any absolute or universal facts. The sanctions by which savage people sustained the taboo were the strongest possible, — exile and death. Here we have, therefore, a social limitation of the greatest force, sanctioned by religion and group consent and growing into an abomination which has come down to us and which we all feel, but which is a product of the most primitive folkways; and yet we do not know the motive for it in the minds of primitive men. In the matter of cannibalism we saw (Chapter VIII) that with advancing civilization a taboo has been set up against a food custom which appears to have been universal amongst primitive men; that is, we have reversed and hold in abomination what they did. In regard to incest we have accepted and fully ratified their taboo.

510. Notion that inbreeding is harmful. This taboo and the reasons for it are a complete enigma unless the primitive people had observed the evils of close inbreeding. Inbreeding maintains the excellence of a breed at the expense of its vigor. Outbreeding (unless too far out) develops vigor at the expense of the characteristic traits. It is very probable, but not absolutely certain, that inbreeding is harmful. Any marriage between persons who have the same faults of inheritance causes the offspring to accumulate faults and to degenerate. Close kinship creates a probable danger that faults will be accumulated. This is a logical deduction. Embryology, at present, seems to teach that there is a combination and extrusion of germ units of such a kind that the physiological process conforms only in a measure to this logical deduction, and the historical-statistical verification of the harm of inbreeding remains very imperfect. It is possible that at first, and within limits, inbreeding is not harmful, but becomes such if repeated often. Is it possible that the lowest savages can have perceived this and built a policy on it ? Morgan[1] thinks that it is possible. Westermarck[2] thinks it beyond the mental power of the lowest races. He thinks that, by natural selection, those groups which practiced inbreeding for any reason died out or were displaced by those who followed the other policy. He goes on to propose a theory that persons who grew up, or who now grow up, in intimacy develop an instinctive antipathy to sex relations with each other.[3] While it is true that primitive savages do not observe and reflect, it is also true that, in their own blundering way, when their interests are sharply at stake, they do observe, and they change their ways accordingly. Therefore they appear to us at one time hopelessly brutish ; at another time we are amazed at their ingenuity and their mental activity (myths, legends, proverbs, maxims). If the loss or pain is great enough, the savage man is capable of astounding cleverness to escape it. After animal breeding began men had ample opportunity to observe the effects of close inbreeding. There is more doubt now about the penalties of inbreeding than there is about the power of savage men to perceive them and try to escape them, if they exist.

511. Status-wife, work-wife, love-wife. In the primitive horde it appears that there was a prescribed wife for each man, or the

---

[1] *Anc. Soc.*, 424.   [2] *Marriage*, 317.   [3] *Ibid.*, 319, 334, 352.

classification was such that his choice was restricted to a very small number. The prescribed wife was a status-wife. She alone could hold the position of a true "wife." The man might also capture a woman abroad who would be a worker, or work-wife, and she might win the man, so that she became a love-wife. There would often be a comparison between the children of the status-wife and the children of a work-wife or love-wife, in which the latter would appear the more vigorous. If so, there would be a school in which the advantages of outbreeding would appear as a fact, although not explained.

512. Abomination of incest. The taboos in the mores contain prescriptions as to the allowable consanguinity of spouses. There is a great horror of violating them. This sentiment is met with amongst people who have scarcely any other notion of crime, or of right and wrong. The rules are enforced by death or banishment as penalties of violation. The notion of harm in inbreeding has spread all over the earth. It has come down to ourselves. In the form in which it was held by savage people it was mistaken to such a degree that they might, in spite of it, practice close inbreeding. Our study of the mores teaches us that there must have been, antecedent to this state of the mores in regard to this matter, a long development of interests, folkways, rites, and superstitions.[1] It is believed, not without reason, that the horde life would tend to run into grooves in which the prescribed wife would be a close relative, in the final case a sister. Experience of this might produce the rules of prohibition. The captured wife was also a trophy, and the play of this fact on vanity would always tend to disintegrate the system of endogamy. There are many reasons why endogamy seems more primitive than exogamy, and it required force of interest, superstition, or vanity to carry a society over from the former to the latter. A calamity might come to reënforce the interest,[2] but can hardly be postulated to explain a custom so widespread. All the ultimate causes of the law of incest, therefore, lie beyond our investigation. They are open only to conjecture and speculation. The case is very

[1] Durkheim in *L'Année Sociologique*, I, 59–65.
[2] Starcke, *Prim. Fam.*, 230.

important, however, to show the operation of the mores on facts erroneously assumed, and their power to work out their effects, as an independent societal operation, without regard to error in the material to which they are applied.

513. Incest taboo strongest in the strongest groups. We shall see, in the cases to be presented, that incest has a wider definition and a stricter compulsion in great tribes, and in prosperity or wealth, than in small groups and poverty. The definiteness of this taboo, and the strictness with which it is enforced, seem to be correlative with the energy of the tribal discipline in general and the vigor of the collective life of the group. Wives can be got abroad, either by capture or contract, only by those who command respect for their power or who use power. On the other hand, endogamy is both cause and effect of weakness and proceeds with decline. Some cases will be given below in which incestuous marriages occur where the parties are unable to obtain any other wives. Neglect of the incest taboo is rather a symptom than a cause of group decline.

514. Incest in ethnography. Martius says of the tribes on the upper Amazon, in general, that incest in all grades is frequent amongst them. In the more southern regions the taboo is stricter and better observed. Amongst the former it is shameful for a man to marry his sister or his brother's daughter. The usages are the more strict the larger the tribe is. In small isolated groups it frequently happens that a man lives with his sister. He heard of two tribes, the Coërunas and the Uainumus, who observed little rule on the subject. They were dying out.[1] "Not seldom an Indian is father and brother of his son." [2] Effertz writes that, amongst the Indians of the Sierra Madre, Mexico, incest between father and daughter "is of daily occurrence," although incest between brother and sister is entirely unknown. The former unions are due to economic interest. The Indian tills small bits of land scattered in the hills. He cannot exist without a woman to grind corn for him. When he goes to a distant patch of land he takes his daughter with him. He has but one blanket and the nights are cold. If he has no daughter he must take another woman, but then he must share his crop with her.[3]

515. The tribes of South Australia are "forbidden to have intercourse with mothers, sisters, and first or second cousins. This religious law is strictly carried out and adhered to under penalty of death." The most

---

[1] *Ethnog. Brasil.*, 115.   [2] *Ibid.*, 334 note.   [3] *Umschau*, VIII, 496.

opprobrious epithet for an opponent in a quarrel is one which means a person who has sex intercourse with kin nearer than second cousins.[1] Some Dyaks are indifferent to the conduct of their wives, and both sexes practice sex vice, but they insist on drowning any one who violates the taboo of incest.[2] Other Dyaks (the Ot Danom) have no notion of incest. The former are on the coast, the latter inland. Hence it seems probable that the notion of incest came to the Dyaks from outside.[3] The Khonds practice female infanticide, from a feeling that marriage in the same tribe is incest.[4] Cucis are allowed to marry without regard to relationship of blood, except mother and son.[5] The Veddahs think marriage with an older sister abominable, but marriage with a younger sister is prescribed as the best. Sometimes a father marries his daughter; in other subdivisions a first cousin (daughter of the father's sister or mother's brother) is the prescribed wife.[6] Mantegazza reports that father and daughter, mother and son, are not rarely united amongst the Anamites and that Cambodian brothers and sisters marry.[7] Amongst the Kalongs on Java sons live with mothers, and luck and prosperity are thought to be connected with such unions. Not long ago, on Minahasa in the Tonsawang district, the closest blood relatives united in marriage; also on Timorlaut. The Balinese had a usage that twins of different sex, in the highest castes, were united in marriage. They could have no notion of incest at all.[8] The Bataks have a tradition that marriage between a man and his father's sister's daughter was formerly allowed, but that calamities occurred which forced a change of custom.[9]

516. The people of Teita, in East Africa, who are very dirty and low, marry mothers and sisters because they cannot afford to buy wives. They have been in touch with whites for fifty years.[10] The chiefs of the Niam Niam take their daughters to wife.[11] The Sakalava, on Madagascar, allow brother and sister to marry, but before such a marriage the bride is sprinkled with consecrated water and prayers are recited for her happiness and fecundity, as if there were fears that the union was not pleasing to the higher powers, and as if there was especial fear that there might be no offspring. Such marriages are contracted by chiefs who cannot find other brides of due rank.[12]

517. The Ossetes think a marriage with a mother's sister right, but marriage with a father's sister is severely punished. They have the strictest father family. Marriage with a father's relative to the remotest cousinship

[1] JAI, XXIV, 169.
[2] Perelaer, *Dyaks*, 59.
[5] Lewin, *Wild Races of S. E. India*, 276.
[6] *N. S. Ethnol. Soc.*, London, II, 311; Sarasin, *Veddahs*, 466.
[7] *Gli Amori degli Uomini*, 272.
[8] *Bijdragen tot T. L. en V.-kunde*, XXXV, 151.
[9] *Ibid.*, XLI, 203.
[10] JAI, XXI, 361.
[3] Wilken, *Volkenkunde*, 267.
[4] Hopkins, *Relig. of India*, 531.
[11] Junker, *Afrika*, III, 291.
[12] Sibree, *Great Afr. Island*, 252.

is forbidden, but consanguinity through the mother they do not notice at all.[1] The Ostiaks also have strict father family, and allow marriage with any relative on the female side, but with none on the male side. It is an especially fortunate marriage to take two sisters together.[2]

518. Amongst the Tinneh, men sometimes marry their mothers, sisters, or daughters, but this is not approved by public opinion.[3] As the Yakuts had no word for uterine brother and sister but only for tribal brother and sister, the statements about the taboo lack precision, but they care nothing for incest, and it occurs. They laugh at the Russian horror of it. They formerly had endogamy, and it is stated that brothers and sisters married. Now they have exogamy between subdivisions of the nation, but a girl's brothers never let her depart as a virgin, lest she take away their luck.[4] A Hudson Bay Eskimo took his mother to wife, but public opinion forced him to discard her.[5] Marriages of brothers and sisters appear to have been allowed formerly amongst the Mordvin, in central Russia. A case is mentioned of a girl who was sent from home for a time, and on her return given to her brother as his wife.[6] Langsdorff[7] reported of the Aleuts on the island of Kodiak, at the beginning of the nineteenth century, that parents and children, brothers and sisters, cohabited there.

519. Incest in civilized states. The ancient kings of Teneriffe, if they could not find mates of equal rank, married their sisters to prevent the admixture of plebeian blood.[8] In the Egyptian mythology Isis and Osiris were sister and brother as well as wife and husband. The kings of ancient Egypt married their sisters and daughters. The doctrine of royal essence was very exaggerated, and was applied with quantitative exactitude. A princess could not be allowed to transmit any of it away from the possessor of the throne. There is said to be evidence that Ramses II married two of his own daughters and that Psammetik I married his daughter. Artaxerxes married two of his daughters.[9] The Ptolemies adopted this practice. The family married in and in for generations, especially brothers and sisters, although sometimes of the half-blood. "Indicating the Ptolemies by numbers according to the order of their succession, II married his niece and afterwards his sister; IV his sister; VI and VII were

[1] von Haxthausen, *Transkaukasia*, II, 27.
[2] Pallas, *Voyages* (*French*), IV, 69.
[3] *Smithson. Rep.*, 1866, 310.
[4] Sieroshevski, *Yakuty* (*russ.*), I, 560.
[5] *Bur. Eth.*, XI, 180.
[6] Abercromby, *Finns*, I, 182.
[7] *Voyages and Travels*, 358.
[8] *N. S. Amer. Anthrop.*, II, 478.
[9] Maspero, *Peuples de l'Orient*, I, 50.

brothers and they consecutively married the same sister; VII also subsequently married his niece; VIII married two of his own sisters consecutively; XII and XIII were brothers and consecutively married their sister, the famous Cleopatra." "The line of descent was untouched by these intermarriages, except in the two cases of III and VIII." The close intermarriages were sterile. The line was continued by others.[1] The Peruvian Incas, but not other Peruvians, married their sisters.[2] In the Vedic mythology the first man and king of the dead, Yama, had his sister, Yami, to wife. In a hymn these two are represented as discussing the propriety of marriage between brother and sister. This shows the revolt of later mores against what once was not tabooed.[3] The scholars think that Herodotus (III, 31), by his story of the question whether Cambyses could marry his sister, shows that such marriages were not allowed amongst the ancient Persians. They are mentioned as a usage of the magi. In the Avesta they are prescribed as holy and meritorious. They are enjoined by religion. They were practiced by the Sassanids,[4] although in the Dinkart version of the law they are apologized for and to some extent disavowed.[5] After the time of Cambyses such marriages occurred, especially in the royal family. They now occur amongst the Persians.[6]

520. In the Chaldean religion the gods and goddesses were fathers, sons, brothers, sisters, and mothers, as well as husbands and wives, to each other. The notions of "son of god" and "mother of god" were very current. Marduk is son of Ea and intercessor for men with him.[7] In the laws of Hammurabi, if a man consorts with his mother after the death of his father, both are to be burned. Incest with a daughter is punished only by banishment. This light punishment may be only a concession to public opinion, since the culprits injured no interest but their own.[8]

[1] Galton, *Hered. Genius*, 151.   [2] Prescott, *Peru*, I, 117.
[3] Hopkins, *Relig. of India*, 131; Zimmer, *Altind. Leben*, 333.
[4] Darmstetter, *Zend-Avesta*, Introd., xlv.
[5] Justi, *Persien*, 225.   [6] Geiger, *Ost-Iran. Kultur*, 245–247.
[7] Tiele, *Gesch. der Relig. im Alterthum*, I, 174.
[8] Müller, *Hammurabi*, 129.

521. In the Old Testament Abraham married his half-sister by the same father. In 2 Sam. xiii. 13 it is shown that such a marriage was allowable in David's time, but Ezek. xxii. 11 refers to such a marriage as an abomination. Nahor's wife was his niece by his brother. Jacob married two sisters at the same time, both his cousins. Esau married his cousin. Judah took to wife his son's widow, but disapproval of that is expressed. Amram, the father of Moses, married his paternal aunt. These unions were all in contravention of the Levitical law. There are statements of the law which differ : Levit. xviii and xx; Deut. xxi. 20; xxvii. 20–23. In Ezek. xxii. 10 and 11 incest is charged as a special sin of the Jews. In the post-exilic and rabbinical periods the law varied from the old law. In general it was extended to include under the taboo more distant relatives.[1]

Marriages between brothers and sisters were allowed in Phœnicia, but were contracted probably only when the woman had inherited something in which her brother had no share.[2]

522. In Homer Zeus and Hera are brother and sister. Union of mother and son is regarded as shocking, but not that of brother and sister.[3] Arete was niece and wife of Alcinous, and was especially respected.[4] In the case of Œdipus the union of mother and son, by error, was terribly punished.[5] In the tragedy of *Andromache* marriages between mother and son, father and daughter, brother and sister, are mentioned as characteristic of barbarians. Dionysius of Syracuse, having lost his wife, married Doris and Aristomache on the same day. With Doris he had three children and with Aristomache four. His son by Doris, Dionysius, married Sophrosyne, his daughter by Aristomache. Dion, the brother of Aristomache, married a daughter of Aristomache.[6] Whether these marriages were extraordinary in Sicily we do not know. They may not represent the current mores as to marriage, but only the shamelessness possible to a Sicilian tyrant. At Athens the only limitations were on the ascending

---

[1] *Jewish Encyc.*, s.v. "Incest," VI, 571.   [2] Pietschmann, *Phoenizier*, 237.

[3] *Il.*, IV, 58; XIV, 296; XI, 223; *Od.*, X, 7; cf. VIII, 267; XI, 271; VIII, 306; VII, 65.

[4] *Od.*, XII, 338; XIII, 57.   [5] Keller, *Homer. Soc.*, 205, 232.

[6] Burckhardt, *Griech. Kulturgesch.*, I, 197.

and descending relationships, but it appears that in later times marriages between brother and sister were disapproved.[1]

523. The term "incest" was applied at Rome to the case of a man present at the purification of women, on the feast of the *Bona Dea*, May 1.[2] The sense of the word is, then, nearly equal to "profane." The emperor Claudius married his niece Agrippina and made such marriages lawful. Gaius[3] restricted this precedent to its exact form, marriage of a brother's daughter, not sister's daughter, and further restricted it, if the brother's daughter was in any forbidden degree of affinity.

524. In the Ynglinga saga Niord takes his sister to wife, because the law of Van-land allowed it, although that of the Ases did not.[4] Other cases in the *Edda* go to show that the taboo on such marriages was not in the ancient mores of Scandinavia.[5] In the German poems of the twelfth century it belongs to the description of the heathen kings that they are fierce and suspicious towards all who woo their daughters, and that they sometimes intend to marry their own daughters after the death of their queens.[6]

525. Those Arabs of Arabia Felix who practiced fraternal polyandry also formed unions with their mothers.[7] Robertson Smith thinks that this means their fathers' wives.[8] The Arabs were convinced of the evil of marriage between cousins.[9]

526. A mediæval traveler reports of the Mongols that they paid no heed to affinity in marriage. They took two sisters at once or in succession. The only limitation was that they must not marry mothers, daughters, or sisters by the same mother.[10] In Burma and Siam, at least until very recent times, in the royal families of the different subdivisions brothers and sisters married.[11]

527. In Russia, in the seventeenth century, men in the government service who were often sent out on duty and had no homes,

[1] Becker-Hermann, *Charikles*, III, 288.
[2] Rossbach, *Röm. Ehe*, 266.
[3] *Instit.*, I, 62.
[4] Laing, *Sagas of the Norse Kings*, I, 273.
[5] Weinhold, *D. F.*, I, 235.
[6] Lichtenberger, *Nibelungen*, 334.
[7] Strabo, XVI, 4, 25, or 783.
[8] *Jo. Philol.*, IX, 86.
[9] Wellhausen, *Ehe bei den Arabern*, 441.
[10] Rubruck, *Eastern Parts*, 77.
[11] Yule, *Court of Ava*, 86.

and whose incomes were small, were reproached by an ecclesiastic with the fact that they lived in vice with their mothers, sisters, and daughters.[1] Marriages between persons related by blood are frequent in Corsica and are considered the most auspicious marriages.[2]

528. The Kabyles stone to death those who voluntarily commit incest and the children born of incestuous unions. The taboo, in their usage, includes parents and children-in-law, brothers and sisters-in-law, and foster brothers and sisters.[3]

529. In 1459 there died at Arras a canon, eighty years old, who had committed incest with his daughters and with a granddaughter whom he had had by one of them.[4]

530. Where the line is drawn, and why. The instances show that the notion of incest is by no means universal or uniform, or attended by the same intensity of repugnance. It is not by any means traceable to a constant cause. Plutarch[5] discussed the question why marriages between relatives were forbidden by the traditional mores of his time. He conjectured various explanations. Fear of physical degeneration is not one of them. We must infer that such consequences had not then been noticed or affirmed. We have found cases in which no taboo existed and cases in which close intermarriages are especially approved. An operation of syncretism, when different usages and ideas have been brought together by conquest and state combinations, must be allowed for. In some cases a great interest was thought to be at stake; in other cases no importance was attached to the matter. The mores developed under the notions which got control by accident or superstition. There was no rational ground for the taboo, and none even blindly connected with truth of fact, until the opinion gained a footing that close intermarriage was unfavorable to the number or vigor of the offspring. Unless that opinion is accepted as correct there is no reason for the taboo now.[6] Incest is, for us,

---

[1] Kostomarow, *Dom. Life and Customs of Great Russia* (*russ.*), 154.
[2] Gubernatis, *Usi Nuziali*, 273. [4] Lea, *Inquis.*, III, 639.
[3] Hanoteau et Letourneux, *Les Kabyles*, III, 206. [5] *Quaest. Rom.*, 108.
[6] Starcke, *Prim. Fam.*, 211.

a thing so repugnant that we consider the feeling "natural." We may test the feeling by our feeling as to the marriage of first cousins. First cousins are very commonly married in England. Such marriages are under no civil or ecclesiastical prohibition, and although many persons disapprove of them on grounds of expediency, and parents might refuse to consent to them, they do not come under the abomination of incest. In many states of the United States marriages of first cousins are illegal. In Kansas they are put under heavy penalties. We hear no preaching against close in-marriage. The matter is not discussed. The limitations are set in the current mores and are accepted without dispute. Evidently the only question is where the line should be drawn. If it was proposed to forbid the marriage of first cousins some discussion might be aroused. If it was decided wise to forbid such marriages, it would take long for such a sentiment of repugnance to be developed in regard to them as we now feel in regard to the marriage of sisters, or even of aunts and nieces. In history the movement must have been in the other direction. The repugnance arose first and then became a ground for the rules.

531. Human self-selection by taboo and other-worldliness. Laws against incest and all caste rules which arbitrarily limit the number of persons whom a given individual may marry may be regarded as blind attempts of mankind to practice some kind of self-selection. Sex selection inside the human race is the highest requirement which life now addresses to man as an intelligent being, and the very highest result which our sciences could produce would be to give us trustworthy guidance in a policy of sex selection. It is not possible for some persons to dispose of the life determination of others, as breeders control the union of beasts. What is needed is that individuals, in making their own decisions for their own self-realization, shall understand the whole range of interests which are involved, and shall do what it is expedient or necessary to do to satisfy them all. In times past men and women have thus limited themselves by rules about incest, group and class marriage, rank or caste, religion, wealth, and other considerations. In every society there are traits which are approved and others which are disapproved in each sex. In marrying, people are influenced by these appreciations and they select for or against them. Thus marriage is controlled by a complicated selection according to a number of standards which prevail at the time and place. At present the popular view seems to be that all standards are false, and that the limitations ought to be trampled on as representing abandoned ideals. It is thought that the whole matter ought to be left to the control of an unintelligent impulse, which is capable of any caprice, but whose authority is imperative. Perverse as the old restrictions often were, they had in them a notion of self-selection such as is needed now, if only the criteria and standards which are correct can be ascertained. The old restrictions contained a notion of breeding up, a notion which is by no means false, if we can get a rational idea of what is "up." No marriage ought now to be contracted without full application of all we know about heredity and selection. If, in any society, marriages were thus contracted, the effect would be most favorable on posterity, and on the power in action and the perpetuity of the group, for the net result would be that those who are least fit to propagate the race would be the ones who would be left unmarried or would marry each other. In the latter case their posterity would soon disappear, and the evil factors would be eliminated. A father now refuses his daughter to a drunkard, a criminal, a pauper, a bankrupt, an inefficient man, one who has no income, etc. Some men refuse their daughters to irreligious men, or to men who are not of their own sect or subsect. Some allow inherited wealth, or talent, or high character, etc., to outweigh disadvantages. In short, we already have selection. It always has existed. The law of incest was an instinctive effort in the same direction. The problem is the same now as it always has been, — to refine and correct the standards and to determine their relative importance.

532. Restrictions by biological facts as yet too uncertain. As yet, undoubtedly, the great reason why people are reluctant to construct a policy of marriage and population on biological doctrines is that those doctrines are too uncertain. The reluctance is well justified. Hasty action, based on shifting views of fact

and law, would simply add new confusion and trouble to that produced by the customs and legislative enactments which we have
inherited from the past and which were based on transcendental
doctrines. So long as we do not know whether acquired modifications are inheritable or not, we are not prepared to elaborate a
policy of marriage which can be dogmatically taught or civilly
enforced. This much, however, is certain, — the interests of
society are more at stake in these things than in anything else.
All other projects of reform and amelioration are trivial compared
with the interests which lie in the propagation of the species, if
those can be so treated as to breed out predispositions to evils of
body and mind, and to breed in vigor of mind and body. It even
seems sometimes as if the primitive people were working along
better lines of effort in this matter than we are, when we allow
marriage to be controlled by "love" or property; when our organs
of public instruction taboo all which pertains to reproduction as
improper; and when public authority, ready enough to interfere
with personal liberty everywhere else, feels bound to act as if
there was no societal interest at stake in the begetting of the
next generation.

533. It is self-evident that there ought to be no restriction
on marriage except such as is necessary to protect some interest
of the parties, their children, or the society. The necessity must
also be real and not traditional or superstitious. The evils of
inbreeding are so probable as to justify strong prejudice against
consanguine marriages. If primitive men set up the taboo on
incest without knowing this, they acted more wisely than they
knew. We who have inherited the taboo now have knowledge
which gives a rational and expedient reason for it. The mores,
therefore, still have a field of useful action to strengthen and
reaffirm the taboo. There is also a practical question still
unsettled, — whether the marriage of first cousins should be
included in the taboo.

CHAPTER XIII

KINSHIP, BLOOD REVENGE, PRIMITIVE JUSTICE, PEACE UNIONS

Kinship. — Forms of kinship. — Family education. — Kinds of kinship. — How family mores are formed. — Family and marriage. — Goblinism and kinship; blood revenge. — Procreation; forms of the family. — Notions about procreation and share in it. — Blood revenge and the in-group — Institutional ties replace the blood tie. — Peace in the in-group. — Parties to blood revenge. — Blood revenge in ethnography. — Blood revenge in Israel. — Peace units and peace pacts. — The instability of great peace unions. — The Arabs. — The development of the philosophy of blood revenge. — Alleviations of blood revenge. — The king's peace. — The origin of criminal law.

534. Kinship. Kinship is a fact which, in the forms of heredity and race, is second to none in importance to the interests of men. It is a fact which was concealed by ignorance from primitive men. It is yet veiled in much mystery from us. Nevertheless the notion of kinship was one of the very first notions formed by primitive men as a bond of association, and they based folkways upon their ideas about it. They deduced the chief inferences and handed the whole down to succeeding generations. Therefore the assumed knowledge of the facts of kinship was used as the basis of a whole series of societal conventions. The first construction was the family, which was a complete institution. Of course marriage was a relationship which was controlled and adjusted by the family ideas. From the folkways as to kinship all the simplest conceptions of societal rights and duties were derived, societal institutions were constructed, and societal organization has grown up.

535. Forms of kinship. That a certain child was born of a certain woman, after having been for some time in physical connection with her body, is an historical and physical fact. That

493

another child was born of the same mother is another fact, of the same order. It may be believed that these facts produce permanent life relations between the mother and children, and between the children, or it may be believed that the facts have no importance for duties, interests, or sympathies. The relations, if recognized, may be defined and construed in many different ways and degrees. They could also be carried further by including more generations, or wider collateral branches, until kinship would include a sib, or family in the widest sense, — those related within some limit of descent and cousinship on a system decided on (mother family, father family, etc.) and traditional. Kinship is purely matter of fact and history, and therefore rational. There is no "natural affection." There is habit and familiarity, and the example and exhortations of parents may inculcate notions of duty. Sentiments and sympathies will then be produced out of familiarity in life, or out of use and wont. The construction and limits of kinship in any society are products of the folkways, or — inasmuch as the system is built up with notions of welfare and rights and duties — of the mores. In fact, since the folkways in regard to this matter begin at a very primitive stage of human life, run up to the highest civilization, and are interwoven with the most tender sympathies and ethical convictions at all stages, kinship is one of the most important products of the folkways and mores. It is, in fact, the most important societal concept which the primitive man thought out, and it would be such even if we were now compelled to reject it as erroneous.

536. Family education. No doubt the folkways about kinship are produced in connection with views about interests, and in connection with faiths about procreation, and impressions produced by experience. The mother and children live in constant contact and intimacy. The family grows into an institution which takes its nature from the traditional and habitual behavior of its members to each other in daily life. Use and wont have here a great field for their constructive operation. Each family (mother and children) is independent and makes its own world, in which nearly all its interests are enfolded. There are constantly recurring occasions for acts of a reciprocal character, and such acts especially build up institutions. The family is also an arena in which sympathies are cultivated, which does not mean that they are always nourished and developed. Habits are formed and discipline is enforced. Rules are accepted from custom and enforced by authority and force. Rights and duties are enforced as facts long before they are apprehended as concepts.

537. Kinds of kinship. The sib, or large family, including all those who are known to be related at all, is a group of very varying importance in different societies. In some societies the common bond is strong and produces important social consequences. In other cases no heed is paid to relationship beyond first and second cousins. Although the Yakuts keep up the *rod*, or great family, for some purposes, we are told that often "nothing unites the members of the rod but a vague tradition of common descent."[1] Whether individuals can break the ties of kin, by voluntary act, is answered differently in different societies. The Salic Franks allowed a man to do it by breaking his staff (which was his personal symbol) in a ceremonial act.[2] If kinship depends on connection of the body of the child with that of the mother, his nourishment by her milk is another ground of kinship. The Arabs recognize this tie of a child to its foster mother. Later the child is nourished by food shared with commensals. Hence the tie of commensality forms a basis of social union like kinship.[3]

538. How mores are formed. The family groups which are in local neighborhood have, in general, the same folkways as an inheritance, but variations occur from varieties of character and circumstances. The variations are life experiments, in fact, and they lead to selection. In the community as a whole the mores of family life are selected, approved, and established, and then handed down by tradition. It may be believed that there is a common interest of the entire larger group in the education and treatment of children, and that all the adults recognize that interest more or less completely. The big group, therefore, molds

---

[1] Sieroshevski, *Yakuty* (*Polish version*), 248.
[2] Clement, *Das Recht der Salischen Franken*, 243.
[3] W. R. Smith, *Relig. of the Semites*, 274.

notions of consanguinity, and the sanctions of tribal authority and public opinion coerce all to observe the modes of family life which the ruling authority thinks most expedient for the group interests.

539. Family and marriage. The family institution must have preceded marriage. In fact, marriage appears, in ethnography and history, as the way of founding a family and as molded by the family mores existing in the society.

540. Goblinism and kinship. Blood revenge. Integration of kin relations was produced by goblinism. This furnished an interest which impelled to development of the kin idea. If a man was murdered, his ghost would seek revenge, just as a man while alive would have sought revenge for a smaller injury. The ghost was dangerous to two persons or classes of persons, the murderer and those near the corpse. The latter would be, almost always, his kinsmen. It behooved the latter, therefore, if they wanted to appease the ghost and save themselves, to find the murderer and to punish him. Hence the custom of blood revenge. It was not due to kin notions, but to goblinistic notions. Kin only defined those who came under the obligation. In this way kin became a tie of mutual offense, defense, and assistance, and kin groups were formed into societies, — we-groups or in-groups, — inside of which there was comradeship, peace, law, and order, while the relation to all out-groups was one of suspicion, hostility, plunder, and subjugation if possible. The primary notion of kin was embodied in formulæ about blood, — which were only figures of speech, — which have come down to us, so that propositions about blood are used now to express our notions of kinship, heredity, etc. In fact, according to modern embryology, not a drop of blood passes from either parent to the offspring. Superstitions about blood (seat of the soul or life, etc.) helped to develop the notion of kin. The primitive idea is that the ghost of a murdered man can be appeased only by blood. The blood of Abel cried unto God from the ground. Some peoples go out to kill anything, in order that blood may be shed and so the ghost may be satisfied.

541. Procreation. Forms of the family. The notion of kin was so elastic that various conceptions of procreation have been grafted upon it, and various ways of organizing the family, or of reckoning kinship, have been connected with it. Mores grow upon the notions of kinship. They dictate modes of behavior and ideas of right and duty, and train all members of the society in the same. The relation of father and child is known to few persons, perhaps only to two. Kinship through the father, therefore, seems to uncivilized people far less important than kinship through the mother. When the father relationship is regarded as the real tie and is made the norm of kin groups, great changes are produced in the mores of the mother family.

542. Notions about procreation and share in it. It is difficult to see how savage men could have got any idea of procreation. The ethnographical evidence is that they have no idea, or only a most vague and incorrect idea, of the functions of the parents. The Australians think that an ancient spirit enters into a baby at birth, enlivens it, and is its fate. This notion interferes with ideas of sexual conception. So we are told that the Dieyerie women do not admit that a child has only one father, and say that they do not know whether the husband or the *pirauru* is the father.[1] The highest tribes in Australia say that " the daughter emanates from her father solely, being only nurtured by her mother." [2] The father, however, is always known or assumed. How else could the father move up one grade in tribal position when the boy is initiated ? [3] Amongst several tribes of central Australia it is believed that " the child is not the direct result of intercourse, that it may come without this, which merely, as it were, prepares the mother for the reception and birth of an already formed spirit child who inhabits one of the local totem centers." [4] Melanesian women feel severely the strain of child rearing. They seem to have less love for the children than the fathers have. They often kill the babes. If an unmarried girl becomes pregnant, she says that some man who hates her got the help of spirits, who caused her situation.[5] The Indians in British Columbia think that a woman conceives by eating, and this belief is introduced into their folk tales.[6] The rules about the food of women are often connected with notions about sex relations and procreation. The Seri of California thought that fire is bestial, not physical, and is produced similarly to sexual reproduction.[7] In ancient Greece " the inferiority of women to men was strongly asserted, and it was illustrated and defended by a very curious physiological notion that the generative power belonged exclusively to men, women having only a very subordinate part in

---

[1] JAI, XX, 53.
[2] *Ibid.*, XIV, 352.
[3] Cunow, *Verwandtschafts-organization der Austral.*, 126.
[4] Spencer and Gillen, *Cent. Austral.*, 265.
[5] Pfeil, *Aus der Südsee*, 18, 143.
[6] *U. S. Nat. Mus.*, 1888, 379.
[7] *Bur. Eth.*, XVII, Part I, 199.*

the production of their children."[1] This notion is expressed in the *Eumenides*, where it is said to lessen the crime of Orestes. His mother did not generate him. She received and nursed the germ. In Islam this same opinion prevails. It is a father family doctrine, exactly opposite to that of the mother family, where the function of the mother was thought far more important.[2] It is a good example of the way in which the philosophy follows the view taken in the mores of the leading interest.

543. Blood revenge and the in-group. Blood revenge is out of place in the in-group. It would mean self-extermination of the group. It would serve the interests of the enemies in the out-groups. Hence the double interest of harmony and coöperation in the in-group and war strength against the out-groups forces the invention of devices by which to supersede blood revenge in the in-group. Chiefs and priests administered group interests, especially war and other collisions with neighbors, and they imposed restraints, arbitration, or compensation in internal quarrels. Cities of refuge and sanctuaries secured investigation and deliberation to prove guilt and determine compensations. The chiefs and priests thus modified or set aside kin law by inchoate civil forms. Then criminal law and penalty took the place of retaliation. Between groups blood revenge was only a detail of the normal relations of hostility and violence. Out-groups, however, sometimes made agreements with each other to limit blood revenge and vendetta. White men have had trouble with red men and black men because their customs as to relationship were not on the same level. The whites in New York and Pennsylvania colonies could not understand why the Indians were indifferent to their demands for the surrender of an Indian who, in time of peace, had killed a white man. According to Indian ideas the bloodshedding did not concern the civil body (tribe), but the kin group (clan).[3] A wife was not included in blood revenge. Her relation to her husband was not one of "blood." It was institutional. Therefore it was not so strong as the tie of sister to brother by the same mother.

544. Institutional ties replace the blood tie. In the history of civilization several institutional ties have become stronger than

[1] Lecky, *Eur. Morals*, II, 280.   [2] Wilutzky, *Mann und Weib*, 121.
[3] *Smithson. Rep.*, 1893, 595.

the blood tie, but the primitive man, who has not yet accepted any tie as equal to the blood tie, always resists this change. Kinship was lost by separation, and fire superseded it as a bond of association. Fire being kept and lent became a unifying force, because, in effect, all united in a common effort to get and keep it.[1] Common religion (sacrifices) also became a bond of union. The common sacrifices at Upsala held the scattered Swedes in unity, and served also as a peace bond, although not a sufficient one.[2] It is said also of the Brahuis, in Baluchistan, that the two bonds which unite the confederacy are common land and common good and ill, "which is another name for common blood feud."[3] Changes in the numbers in the group, or in life conditions, make some other element more important than kin. Then that element becomes the societal bond. Then the folkways, ideas, and sentiments change to adapt themselves to the new center of interest. Throughout the Occident the institutional tie of man and wife is rated higher than any tie of kinship.

545. Peace in the in-group. Government, law, order, peace, and institutions were developed in the in-group. So far as sympathy was developed at all, it was in the in-group, between comrades. The custom of blood revenge was a protection to all who were in a group of kinsmen. It knit them all together and served their common interest against all outsiders. Therefore it was a societalizing custom and institution. Inside the kin-group adjudication, administration of justice by precedents and customs, composition for wrongs by payments or penalties, amercements by authority for breach of orders or violations of petty taboo, and exile took the place of retaliation. In the in-group it was the murderer who had to fear the ghost of the murdered. Religious rites absolved the murderer from the ghosts or gods and delivered him from the furies, who demanded revenge. The Hebrew law provided cities of refuge for those who were guilty of accidental homicide.[4] The manslayer could go home at the death of the high priest.[5] In 2 Sam. iii and iv are cases of blood revenge

[1] Lippert, *Kulturgesch.*, I, 265. [3] Risley, *Ethnog. of India*, I, 67.
[2] Geijer, *Svenska Folkets Hist.*, I, 112. [4] Deut. xix ; Josh. xx.
[5] Num. xxxv.

and of efforts to suppress it. The homicide in chapter iv is not a case of blood revenge but of partisan murder.

546. Parties to blood revenge. It was a very serious modification of blood revenge when it was extended so that any kinsman of the murdered man was bound to kill any kinsman of the murderer. Hagen [1] says: "No regulated societal common life is possible where blood revenge is in full operation; not even on the primitive stage of the Bogjadim state," a village in German New Guinea. This is true if blood revenge is allowed in the in-group, or if the in-group has very low integration, for blood revenge sets every man against his neighbor and makes society impossible. Krieger [2] says of the same people: "The comradeship of clansmen with each other in respect to their attitude towards out-groups is most definite in blood revenge during the stage between the kin-group organization and the lowest state organization." If a nation stops in that stage, or even degenerates a little, blood revenge becomes a symptom of a state of societal disease. It becomes firmly fixed, is elaborated, continues beyond the stage of other things at which it can be useful, and, as an institution, becomes a caricature. What is lacking is an authority which can impose commands on the in-group and extrude blood revenge from it. The Naga, in northeastern India, fifty years ago lived in villages in which, if two men quarreled, all the others took sides with one or the other and civil war ensued. The experience of these quarrels and of blood revenge produced "a reluctance to enter into quarrels which entailed consequences so disastrous, and hence a society living in general peace and honesty." The situation, however, was unstable, and once or twice a year they had grand fights in which the entire village participated by way of clearing off all old scores. Evidently they had no adequate government or administration of justice. Revenge is still, in case of a murder, "a sacred duty, never to be neglected or forgotten," although English rule has modified the old usages and may bring those people into a better political organization. Revenge is still a kin affair, not a civil affair. It is handed down from generation to generation,

[1] *Unter den Papuas*, 256. [2] *Neu Guinea*, 199.

including innocent victims, women and children, and devastating whole villages. It becomes fanatical and men will sacrifice their most serious interests to it. If the male kinsmen die out or are unable to keep up the feud, others may be hired to fulfill the duty.[1]

547. Blood revenge in ethnography. The Eskimo have no civil organization outside of the family. All justice depends on the immediate coercion of wrongdoers by force. Hence death often results. Retaliation is the sacred duty of every kinsman.[2] That the deceased was in the wrong is quite immaterial. Blood revenge was almost universal amongst the American aborigines. In some tribes the stage had been reached where it was set aside by compensation.[3] Amongst the Brazilian tribes it was a question to be decided in each case whether retaliation should be executed against the wrongdoer only or against all his kin.[4] The Arawaks practiced blood revenge, like nature peoples, as late as 1830. Generally the cases were those of jealousy and adultery.[5] The Australians of Victoria kill the elder brother of a murderer or his father. If these are not living they kill him. He is not allowed to defend himself. In some tribes the nearest relative of the murdered must take the life of a tribesman of the murderer. All deaths are attributed to human agency, and it is ascertained by divination to what tribe the murderer belonged. Public opinion enforces the duty of blood revenge. Any one who should neglect it would be despised.[6] The Dyaks keep an account current of the number of lives which one tribe " owes " to another. The hill Dyaks, whose wars are constant and bloody, are very scrupulous about this account of heads due. They are more so than the sea Dyaks, who have perhaps been influenced by contact with outside peoples.[7] Amongst the Ewe-speaking peoples of West Africa [8] a family is collectively responsible for crimes and wrongs of which any one of its members is guilty, and each one is assessed for his share of the composition to be paid. Each member of a family also gets his share of any payment paid to it for wrongs to its members. Ellis says that formerly the village was the collective unit for paying or receiving compensation. This is noteworthy because, in general, composition by payment is later than the custom of equal retaliation, while civil units come later than kin units as the collective units which are responsible. The Somali attribute the duty of blood

[1] JAI, XI, 67; XXVI, 174; XXVII, 25, 36.
[2] *Bur. Eth.*, VI, 582; XI, 186; XVIII, Part I, 292.
[3] Powers, *Calif. Indians*, 21.
[4] Martius, *Ethnog. Brasil.*, 127.
[5] *Ibid.*, 693; Schomburgk, *Brit. Guiana*, II, 460.
[6] Smyth, *Aborig. of Vict.*, I, 129; II, 229.
[7] Veth, *Borneo's Wester Afdeeling*, II, 283.
[8] Ellis, *Ewe-speaking Peoples*, 208.

revenge to the kin, not to the tribe. They have a tariff for bodily injuries less than murder, and for age and sex. The blood money goes to the kin. Blood revenge is executed against any kinsman of the murderer. The Galla do not accept compensation for blood guilt, "no doubt on account of the density of population."[1] In the *Eumenides* of Æschylus it is said (line 520), "Not all the wealth of the great earth can do away with blood guilt." In Japan blood revenge continued until very recently. The person who meant to seek it had to give notice in writing to the criminal court. He was then free to execute his purpose, but he must not make a riot. The Japanese father family is a religious corporation, and the family bond is that of a cult.[2] The Japanese view is the half-civilized view, where the kin sentiment is highly developed and the civil interest is only imperfectly apprehended. In Scandinavia the feeling that it is base to take compensation for blood continued until a late time. We find in the saga of Grettir the Strong[3] that banishment is used instead of blood revenge. This was thought to be a letting down of honor. Life and honor as well as property were under the protection of kin. Blood revenge was a holy duty. The son could not take his inheritance until he had avenged his father. Attempts were made to introduce the weregild. The fine for killing an old man or a woman was twice as much as for an able-bodied man. The slayer with twelve of his kin must swear that he would be content with the payment if the case were his, and the friends of the deceased must swear to let the matter drop.[4] Amongst the tribes of the Caucasus, who live by custom, blood revenge is now a living institution. The Ossetes have the father family in its extremest development. The surname is the mark of kinship, and the duty of blood revenge falls on those with the same surname to the hundredth cousin. One's mother's brother is not in one's kin, and there is no duty of blood revenge for him. Sometimes blood revenge is superseded by the arbitration of a tribunal which is voluntarily accepted.[5]

548. Blood revenge in Israel. The law of Israel was, "Ye shall take no ransom for the life of a manslayer, which is guilty of death; but he shall surely be put to death."[6] This law upheld blood revenge by forbidding the first and most obvious alleviation of it, but verses 22 and 23 distinguished accidental from intentional homicide and verse 27 provided that the avenger of blood should not be guilty of blood. This arrested any feud. The institution of cities of refuge was derived from the Canaanites and developed in Israel.[7] Blood revenge was a duty of the whole family and was originally directed against the entire family of the slayer.[8] This the later law forbade.[1] At first also every beast or inanimate object which caused

[1] Paulitschke, *Ethnog. N.O. Afrikas*, I, 262; II, 151, 156.
[2] Hearn, *Japan*, 321.
[3] P. 250.
[4] Geijer, *Svenska Folkets Hist.*, I, 300.
[5] von Haxthausen, *Transkaukasia*, 26, 29, 50.
[6] Num. xxxv. 31.
[7] Maurer, *Völkerkunde, Bibel, und Christenthum*, I, 164.
[8] 2 Sam. xiv. 7.

death was guilty. In Deut. xxi provision is made for the case of a murdered man whose corpse is found, with customs of wide range for performing rites of purification, and washing hands to put away guilt or suspicion.

549. Peace units and peace pacts. The in-group when it is merged in a state by conquest and compounding becomes a peace unit. All in the same civil body are united by a peace pact. If the central authority cannot suppress local war and private war, it is inadequate, and the state is liable to disruption. The Roman empire was a peace unit of high integration and complete efficiency. It could not, however, maintain itself, and broke up by internal strife which the central authority could not suppress. The Roman law was the peace pact of that peace unit. It was so good a solution of the collisions of human interests that it has been borrowed, or used by modern states as a model. The Romish church in the Middle Ages tried to rule the world, not by force but by dogmas like catholicity. Catholicity was an attempt to build a peace pact on ideals, and big ideas, and sympathies. Islam also tries to serve as a peace pact, but Moslem states have freely fought with each other. Islam does not contain an adequate philosophy. Its theories of society are theocratic and do not meet the actual facts and problems. If a union of two or more states is made, even for the purpose of aggregating more force for war, it will necessarily be a peace union when regarded from within. A confederation is the highest organization yet invented for the purpose of making a great peace union without interfering with domestic autonomy. Norway and Sweden, Austria and Hungary, are states united in couples under a rational peace pact. The former couple has been disrupted; the latter is convulsed by quarrels between its members. The United States is a great peace unit, with a rational peace pact as a bond of union. It has gone through one great convulsion, from which it issued with the peace pact greatly strengthened. It tends to become a consolidated empire. This can be seen in the propositions to turn over various subjects of domestic importance to the federal authority. Happiness and prosperity have been

---

[1] Deut. xxiv. 16; 2 Kings xiv. 6; Ezek. xviii. 19.

due to the peace pact, valid over a continent, with immunity from powerful neighbors. We now think that we will renounce all this and go out after world power and glory so as to be like the other nations.

550. The instability of great peace unions. Now that we have the laws of Hammurabi we can see that the Euphrates valley was organized into a peace unit with a very complete and highly finished peace pact twenty-five hundred years before Christ. All the ordinary cases of discord and diverse interest were provided for under an elaborate system of laws as good as that of a modern European state. The later states of western Asia were involved in war by conflicting interests, ambition, and jealousy until the time of Alexander the Great. The smaller states were at last all submerged in the Roman empire. All the constructive work has been overthrown again and again. Only within a century or two has a structure been set up which has more stability, but it is all in jeopardy now. A union of the existing groups could not be brought about but by conquest, and that would mean very great wars, yet all are ready, by virtue of their institutions and ideas, to merge in a confederation in which peace would reign and incalculable blessings would result.

551. The Arabs. The Arabs in the time of Mohammed were a nation inhabiting a territory which kept them from feeling any national sentiment of unity.[1] The tribe and kin group were their strongest societal units. At the time of Mohammed's birth blood revenge between the kin groups was so destructive that all were instinctively struggling towards devices which might supersede it. In the century preceding Mohammed's birth the nation had been agitated by social movements in which the old was falling and the new was pushing out to acceptance and establishment. "It seemed as if the persons were too big for the circumstances."[2] If a tribe ever was a peace group amongst the Arabs, we have no proof of it. Islam was an attempt to unite the whole nation into a peace group by religion. The attempt succeeded, and the nation, in the élan of its new unity and energy, set out to conquer its neighbors. It had no state organization. The caliph was

[1] Wellhausen, *Skizzen und Vorarbeiten*, III, 182. [2] *Ibid.*, 196.

theological as well as civil head. The Arabs had no political experience. The leaders in the kin groups were the only chiefs they had, and they established a kind of aristocracy in Persia, but the first caliphs were pure despots, like negro heads of states. The Arabs plundered the conquered states. The greatest duty known to the Arabs was blood revenge. It was their only social engine by which to restrain crime and secure some measure of order. Blood was, in their view, more holy than anything else. It put religion in the background. The kin group was the realized ideal. The gods were comparatively insignificant.[1] In old Arabia a man engaged in a blood feud must abstain from women, wine, and unguents.[2] Within the kin group there was no blood revenge, but a guilty person was held personally responsible. A guest friend ("stranger within thy gates") was not liable to blood revenge with his own kin. His status was in the tribe in which he was a guest, by which he must be defended against his tribe of origin, if the case arose.[3] The Arabs thought it dishonorable to take money for blood guilt. It was, they thought, like selling the blood of one's kin. Bedouin tribes in the nineteenth century refused to settle blood feuds by payments. Arbitration was admitted in the time of Mohammed, at Medina, where old blood feuds had become intolerable by their consequences.[4] In Egypt, in the first half of the nineteenth century, blood revenge was still observed. Third cousins of the murderer and his victim were the limits of responsibility on either side.[5]

552. Development of the philosophy of blood revenge. Blood revenge was nothing but an exercise of revenge and it had all the limitations of revenge. It produced a rude fear of consequences and had some of the effects of the administration of justice. However, it had no process of proof, no due notion of guilt, no means of following up responsibility. Therefore it could not infuse fear into the hearts of the guilty. It was

---

[1] Wellhausen, *Skizzen und Vorarbeiten*, III, 194.

[2] W. R. Smith, *Relig. of the Semites*, 482.

[3] The Hebrew law was, "The stranger that sojourneth with you shall be unto you as the home-born among you" (Levit. xix. 34).

[4] Proksch, *Blutrache bei den Arabern*, 18, 30, 33, 36, 51, 54.

[5] Lane, *Mod. Egypt.*, I, 295.

entirely irrational. Therefore it ran into extravagance without due connection of guilt and punishment, and it cost very many lives of the innocent. In primitive society injuries consist in the invasion of a man's interests through his property, his wife, and his children, or by maiming or killing himself. Each one, when he considers himself injured, tries to redress himself. If he is not able to do it he falls back on others for aid. The kin group is the only body which has ties of sympathy and obligation to him. The kin group may be bound to give help without any regard to the justness of the quarrel, or it gets the function of a jury. Evidently the latter case is more reasonable and civilized than the former. In the original institution of blood revenge the individual was called on to sacrifice himself for others. He was a bad man if he began an inquiry into the conduct of the man who called for the sacrifice. He ought to obey the call whether it came from one who had done right or wrong.[1] Evidently, in this view, the institution was a case of social duty, not of goblinistic service to the dead. It was a further application of rationalism and justice when the behavior of the deceased was weighed before decreeing blood revenge. If the kin group decides that the injury is real and that it is properly called on to interfere, routine of method of investigation will be developed, rights will be defined, the duty of blood revenge will be defined and limited, and proceedings of redress will be invented. All this work is done in the folkways and by the methods of folkways. The steps lie along the line of advancing civilization. The notion that a man who had committed a murder and had been killed for it had got what he deserved is a very recent and civilized notion. That would not keep his ghost from demanding to be laid by blood atonement. This was the root idea out of which the custom of blood revenge arose. Blood atonement was a notion in goblinism. It was one of the very earliest cases we can find in which there was a notion of duty and social obligation. The kin were those on whom the duty fell. The strong sympathy of men of the same kin was a consequence, not a cause, but it superseded, later, the original cause. At first, the play of revenge gave satisfaction

[1] Wellhausen, *Skizzen und Vorarbeiten*, III, 194.

to wounded vanity, but that could only last while the case was personal and close, not when the cases and the obligations were remote and institutional. Another remoter, and perhaps unforeseen, consequence was the deterrent effect on crime. The law of retaliation also, "an eye for an eye," was a *law*. It had a primitive and crude justice in it. It has come down to our own time in "reprisals" as practiced in international quarrels, which include also the solidarity of responsibility of all in a group for the torts of each member of it. By producing a solidarity of interest on both sides blood revenge helped to produce a social philosophy. It also made each interest group a peace group inside, because only by being a peace group could it conserve all its force. Thus the war interest against outsiders and the interest of concord inside worked together to produce order, government, law, and rights.

553. Alleviations of blood revenge. The Arabs, in their efforts to supersede blood revenge, tried compurgation, tribunals, payments in composition, banishment, and arbitration. Many tribes which have adopted Mohammedanism still practice blood revenge.[1] Amongst the Kabyles a man falls under it if he kills another by accident, or by the fault of the victim, or in preventing a crime.[2]

554. The king's peace. In the history of civilization the devices to do away with blood revenge are those which have been incidentally mentioned. The last means of suppressing all forms of private war was the king's peace. In modern states due respect to the king required that there should be no quarreling or fighting in his presence. His presence was interpreted to mean in or near his residence, his court, and his environs. Then his peace was interpreted to cover his highroads, and his jurisdiction was presently held to go as far as his peace, because he must have authority to enforce his peace. When small states were united into big ones the peace bond had to be extended over the larger unit. Gradually all petty jurisdictions were absorbed, all justice and redress came from the king or in his name, and

[1] Proksch, *Blutrache bei den Arabern.*
[2] Hanoteau et Letourneux, *La Kabylie.*

private redress was forbidden. For a long time it seemed that the freeman's prerogative was being taken from him. As long as the duel survives the movement is incomplete.

555. Origin of criminal law. When the state took control of injuries and acts of violence and undertook to revenge them on behalf of the victims, as well as in vindication of public authority and order, injuries became crimes and revenge became punishment. Crimes were injuries which could be compensated for, and also violations of the king's peace, that is, of public welfare. In the latter point of view they brought the king's vanity into play. The German emperor Frederick II, by his ferocity against rebels, showed how potent wounded vanity is, as a motive, even in an able man. The crime of treason or rebellion always excites the vanity and fierce revenge of civil authority. It is beyond question that the state in its penalties simply took over the usages of kin groups in inflicting retaliation or gratifying revenge. It did not philosophize. It assumed functions, and with them it took the methods of procedure and the instrumentalities which it found in use for those functions. Criminal law, therefore, and criminal administration were developed out of blood revenge when it was rendered rational and its traditional processes were subjected to criticism.

CHAPTER XIV

UNCLEANNESS AND THE EVIL EYE

Demonism and the aleatory interest. — Universality of primitive demonism. — Uncleanness. — Female uncleanness. — Uncleanness in ethnography. — Uncleanness in higher religions. — Uncleanness amongst Jews. —
Uncleanness amongst Greeks. — These customs produced modesty and the
subordination of women. — Uncleanness, holiness, devotedness. — The evil
eye; *jettatura*. — The evil eye in ethnography. — Amulets against the evil
eye. — Devices against the evil eye. — Insult and vituperation against the
evil eye. — Interaction of the mores and the evil eye.

556. Demonism and the aleatory interest. Uncleanness and
the evil eye are dogmatic notions, products of demonism. The
dogmas are arbitrary. A corpse is unclean and makes any one
unclean who touches it. A baby is not unclean. The evil eye
brings bad luck, not pain or disease. Uncleanness and the evil eye
have each a field. Neither is of universal application. The mores,
starting out from primitive demonism, produced these two dogmas
as an adjustment of experience and observation to demonism.
Uncleanness is a very rude and primary expression of the unsan-
itary and contagious. It undoubtedly often happens that calamity
befalls in the hour of success and rejoicing. A number of people
were trodden to death on the Brooklyn bridge when it was opened.
A few centuries ago, and in all ancient times, such an incident
would have been accepted as the obvious chastisement of the
superior powers on the overweening pride of men. The same
might be said of the death of Mr. Huskisson at the opening of the
first railroad. The sum of such incidents stands in some relation
to fundamental superstitions about demons, if such are believed.
The incidents can be fitted into the doctrines very easily. The
whole aleatory interest is a field for this kind of general dogmas
of the application of fundamental principles to classes of cases.
The folkways, deeply concerned in the aleatory interest, work out
the applications.

557. Universality of primitive demonism. Demonism is the broadest and most primitive form of religion. All the higher religions show a tendency to degenerate back to it. Brahminism, Buddhism, Zoroastrianism, Mohammedanism, and mediæval Christianity show this tendency. Greek religion is most remarkable because we find in Homer very little demonism. It appears, therefore, that in his time primitive demonism had been overcome. In the fifth century B.C. we find it coming in again, and in the fourth century it became the ruling form of popular religion. It predominated in late Greek religion, mixed with demonism from western Asia and Egypt, and passed to Rome, where it entered into primitive Christianity, combining with highly developed demonism from rabbinical Judaism. Religion always arises out of the mores. Changes in religion are produced by changes in the mores. Religious ideas, however, in the next stage, are brought back to the mores as controlling dogmas. The product of the first stage becomes the seed in the second. Goblinism and demonism have great effect on the mores, probably because demonism is so original and universal in all religions, and so popular in its hold on the minds of all. Demonism furnishes devices of magic, sorcery, sortilege, divination, augury, oracles, etc., by which it is believed that men can get from the superior powers (spirits, demons, etc.) what they want, and can learn what is to be in the future. It therefore has the greatest apparatus by which to satisfy human needs, as they appear under the demonistic interpretation of the world and human life.

The most important immediate and direct consequences of demonism in the second stage, when it is brought back to the work of life as a normative system, are the notions of uncleanness and of the evil eye.

558. Uncleanness. The notion of uncleanness is ritual. It is not entirely irrational. Contagious diseases and diseases which are the result of ignorance and neglect of sanitation give sense to the notion. The interpretation of those phenomena as due to the intervention of superior powers is like the interpretation of other diseases as due to demons. In fact, uncleanness is a step towards a rational view of disease, because it brings in secondary causes, and puts the action of demons one step further off. The effect of uncleanness was that it made the affected person unfit and unable to perform ritual acts on which human welfare was supposed to depend. The affected person became dangerous to others, and was forced to banish himself from societal contact with them. He was also cut off from access to the superior powers. It was therefore indispensable that he should recover cleanness in order to carry on his life. The recovery was accomplished through ritual acts and devices, and chiefly through the intervention of shamans, who were experts in the rites and devices required.

559. Female uncleanness. The ritual notion of uncleanness, being a product of deduction from demonistic world philosophy, was arbitrary, and was capable of indefinite extension. It was not a disease, was not held to facts by symptoms of pain, etc. Women were held to be unclean, and causes of uncleanness by contact, at marriage, menstruation, and childbirth. They were always possessed by demons, which accounted for their special functions as mothers. The periods mentioned were periods of special activity of the demonistic function. The belief was common in the Orient that a woman was dangerous to her husband at marriage. A demon left her at that time in the nuptial bloodshed. At menstruation women were dangerous to men. The ritual idea of uncleanness was so extended that women were put under a kind of imprisonment for a time, especially in the Zoroastrian system (sec. 561), in order to remove them from social contact. At child bearing also they were forced into retirement for a specified period.[1] Corpses also were unclean and made all those unclean who came into contact with them. There are numerous other and comparatively trifling causes of ritual uncleanness.[2]

560. Uncleanness in ethnography. The Macusi of British Guiana forbid women to bathe during the period, and also forbid them to go into the forest, for they would risk bites from enamored snakes.[3] If a woman of the Ngumba, in Kamerun, bears a dead child, the uncleanness is double. She

---

[1] Levit. xii.   [2] *Ibid.*, xiii, xiv, xv.

[3] Schomburgk, *Brit. Guiana*, II, 316.

may not touch the hand of a man until she is unwell again.[1] In Madagascar no one who had been at a funeral might enter the palace, or approach the sovereign, for a month, and no corpse might be buried in the capital city. The mourners washed their dresses, or dipped a portion of them in running water, as a ritual purification.[2] The Tshi peoples of West Africa cause women to retire, at the period, to huts prepared for the purpose in the bush, because they are at that time offensive to the deities.[3] The Ewe-speaking peoples think a mother and baby unclean for forty days after childbirth.[4] The Bechuanas, when they have touched a corpse, dug a grave, or are near relatives of a deceased person, — the ritual uncleanness being thus extended to a wider circle of those in any way concerned in a burial, — purify themselves by prescribed ritualistic washings, put on new garments and cut their hair, or purify themselves with the smoke of a fire into which magic-working materials have been cast. On returning from battle they ceremonially wash themselves and their weapons.[5] The Karoks of California think that if a menstruating woman approaches any medicine which is about to be given to a sick man she will cause his death.[6] The Tamils think that saliva renders ritually unclean whatever it touches. Therefore, in drinking, they pour the liquid down the throat without touching the cup to the lips.[7] The Romans held that nothing else had such marvelous efficacy as, or more deadly qualities than, the menstrual flow.[8] Here we find that which is, in one view, evil and contemptible, regarded, in another view, as powerful and worthy of respect. The Arabs thought that "a great variety of natural powers" attached themselves to a woman during the period.[9] The gum of the acacia was thought to be a clot of menstrual blood. Therefore it was an amulet. The tree is a woman.[10] At the great feast of the dead amongst the Eskimo on Bering Straits the feast makers make wiping motions, stamp, and slap the thighs, in order to "cast off all uncleanness that might be offensive to the shades," and thus to render their sacrifices acceptable.[11] The spirits amongst the Kwakiutl, Chinooks, and their neighbors kill an unclean man. These people have fastings and washings for purification.[12]

561. Uncleanness in higher religions. In the higher religions the same notions of ritual cleanness were retained and developed. Pious Zoroastrians could not travel by sea without great inconvenience, because they could not help defiling the natural element water, which they were forbidden to do.[13] They were forbidden to blow a fire with the breath, lest they should

[1] *Globus*, LXXXI, 337.
[2] Sibree, *Great Afr. Island*, 290.
[3] Ellis, *Tshi-speaking Peoples*, 94.
[4] Ellis, *Ewe-speaking Peoples*, 153.
[5] Fritsch, *Eingeb. Süd-Afr.*, 201.
[6] Powers, *Calif. Indians*, 31.
[7] Gehring, *Süd-Indien*, 96.
[8] Pliny, *Hist. Nat.*, VII, 64.
[9] W. R. Smith, *Relig. of the Semites*, 448.
[10] *Ibid.*, 133.
[11] *Bur. Eth.*, XVIII, Part I, 371.
[12] *U. S. Nat. Mus.*, 1895, 393.
[13] Darmsteter, *Zend-Avesta*, I, xxxiv.

defile the element fire, and they wore a covering over the mouth when they approached the fire for any purpose. Parings of the nails and cuttings of the hair were unclean. They would be weapons for demons if they were not covered by rites and spells. The menses of women were caused by the evil god Ahriman. A woman, during the period, was "unclean and possessed by the demon. She must be kept confined and apart from the faithful, whom her touch would defile, and from the fire, which her very look would injure. She was not allowed to eat as much as she wanted, as the strength which she might acquire would accrue to the fiends. Her food was not given to her from hand to hand, but passed to her from a distance in a long leaden spoon." At childbirth, the mother was unclean, in spite of the logic of the religion, according to which she should be pure because she has increased life. "The strength of old instincts overcame the drift of new principles." [The old mores were too strong for the new religion.] A woman who bears a dead child is a grave, and must be ritually purified as such. Only to save her from death can she drink water, which she would defile, and if it is given to her she must undergo a penalty. These views go back to the notion that she has been near death and has had the death fiend in her. A great fire is lighted to drive off the demons.[1] At this day there is in the house of a Parsee a room for the monthly seclusion of women. It is bare of all comforts and from it neither sun, moon, stars, fire, water, or sacred implements, nor any human being, can be seen. The first ceremony performed on a newborn child is washing its hands, to purify it, since it also is unclean.[2]

562. Uncleanness amongst the Jews. Ritual uncleanness is represented in the Old Testament as due to contact with carcasses of unclean cattle and other unclean things;[3] to contact with a woman in childbirth, with a longer period if the infant is a girl than a boy.[4] Care about clean and unclean things was praised as a high religious virtue,[5] and the prophets used the distinction for the difference between virtue and vice.[6] The food taboo is expressed by declaring forbidden animals unclean.[7] Plague and leprosy are cases of ritual uncleanness, also issues.[8] Distinctions of this kind (cleanness and uncleanness), enforced by ritual, depend on clear facts of observation and prescribe simple acts. They include no dogmas. They prescribe things to be done. They produce notions and habits. They enter so deeply into ways of living that it takes long counter-education to eradicate them. The strength of the adherence to this distinction, in the rabbinical period, is well shown in the New Testament.

563. Uncleanness amongst Greeks. The Greeks had similar conceptions of uncleanness. Marriage was surrounded by rites of purification and

[1] Darmsteter, *Zend-Avesta*, xcii.
[2] Geiger, *Ostiran. Kultur*, 236, 259.
[3] Levit. v. 2; xi. 26.
[4] *Ibid.* xii.
[5] *Ibid.* x. 10; xi. 47.
[6] Isaiah vi. 5; Ezek. xxxiii. 17.
[7] Levit. xi.
[8] *Ibid.* xiv, xv.

precaution, the marriage bath being one of the most essential acts in the wedding rites.[1] Death and the dead produced uncleanness, and purification by water, fire, or smoke was required.[2]

564. These mores produced modesty and subordination of women. Two things of great social importance in respect to women are traceable to these mores: (*a*) The sex modesty of women. The usages of Zoroastrianism are cruel. They treat women as base, not on the same plane with men, affected by a natural inferiority, and therefore as having something to be ashamed of. Inasmuch as these usages were all in the mores, the women accepted them as true and right, and probably never rebelled against them even in thought. The mores therefore taught them sex modesty, and especial shame of the sex function. (*b*) The subordination of women. They never were subordinated because they are weaker, because in savagery and barbarism they often are not so, but because of their feminine disabilities and the correlative inferiorities. They accepted the facts and the interpretation which the mores put on them. Then they acquiesced in the treatment they received which was reasonable upon that state of facts.

565. Uncleanness, holiness, devotedness. Uncleanness was an application of taboo. It had a double aspect. It was at once repelling and protective. If corpses were unclean they were put out of contact with the living as far as possible, and this was done to protect the living. The things which were excluded by taboo because they were bad came into parallelism with the things which were tabooed because they were holy and were not to be treated carelessly as common and insignificant. The holy things were in contrast with the profane things; unclean things were in contrast with all which concerned the cult.[3] Nelson says of the Eskimo that at a feast the " wiping motion followed by the stamping and the slapping on the thighs indicated that the feast-makers thus cast off all uncleanness that might be offensive to the shades, and thus render their offerings

[1] Rohde, *Psyche*, II, 72.
[2] Guhl und Koner, *Leben der Griechen und Römer*, 367.
[3] Maurer, *Völkerkunde, Bibel, und Christenthum*, I, 105.

acceptable." [1] This purification was ritual and produced ritual or cult cleanness. Any one who touched a holy thing was raised to a disagreeable amount of holiness, which he must maintain or undergo the ritual uncleanness of a profaned holy thing. Special offerings and atonements were necessary to remove the danger from being holy, which might prove fatal.[2] The Jewish Scriptures which were canonical were distinguished as "those which defile the hands." This shows the original identity of "unclean" and "holy." Both are under taboo, devoted to higher powers. Whatever touches the devoted thing becomes likewise devoted. The high priest has to wash, on the day of atonement, after he has worn the holy vestment.[3] The Sadducees scoffed at the saying of the Pharisees that the Holy Scriptures defile the hands.[4]

566. The evil eye. *Jettatura*. Another direct and immediate product of primitive demonism is the notion of the evil eye. This is a concrete dogma and a primary inference from demonism. It is often confounded with the *jettatura* of the Italians. The evil eye is an affliction which befalls the fortunate and prosperous in their prosperity. It is the demons who are irritated by human luck and prosperity who inflict calamity, pain, and loss, at the height of good luck. The *jettatura* is a spell of evil cast either voluntarily or involuntarily by persons who have the gift of the evil eye and can cast evil spells, perhaps unconsciously and involuntarily. It follows from the notion of the evil eye that men should never admire, praise, congratulate, or encourage those who are rich, successful, prosperous, and lucky. The right thing to do is to vituperate and scoff at them in their prosperity. That may offset their good luck, check their pride, and humble them a little. Then the envy of the superior powers may not be excited against them to the point of harming them. It is the most probable explanation of the cloistering and veiling of women that it was intended to protect them, especially if they were beautiful, from the evil eye. The admiration which they would attract would be fatal to them. The notion of the evil eye led to covering some parts of the body and so led to

---

[1] *Bur. Ethnol.*, XVIII, Part I, 371.   [3] Levit. xvi. 4, 24.
[2] Hastings, *Dict. Bible*, "Relig. of Israel." [4] Bousset, *Relig. des Judenthums*, 124.

notions of decency (sec. 459). It is assumed that demons envy human success and prosperity and so inflict loss and harm on the successful. Hence admiration and applause excite their malignity.

567. Ethnographical illustrations. Of the following cases many are cases of jettatura. In the Malagasy language many proper names of persons are coarse and insulting because a pleasant-sounding name might cause envy.[1] In Bornu when a horse is sold, if it is a fine one, it is delivered by night, for fear of the evil eye (covetous and envious eyes) of bystanders.[2] Schweinfurth[3] tells an incident of a man who, going through a Nubian village, noticed that the limb of a tree was rotten and ready to fall. He warned some people who were standing under it. Immediately afterwards it did fall, but the fall was attributed to the evil eye of the person who first noticed the danger. The Dinka are mentioned as free from this superstition.[4] In the Sudan food is usually covered by a conical straw cover to prevent the evil eye [viz. of the hungry people who might admire and long for it].[5] Customs of eating and drinking in private, and of covering the mouth when eating or drinking, belong here. All along the north coast of Africa the belief in the evil eye prevails. A hen's-egg shell upon which three small leaden horseshoes have been riveted is an amulet against it.[6] At Katanga, Central Africa, only the initiated may watch the smelting of copper, for fear of the evil eye, which would spoil the process.[7] In the Caroline Islands a canoe, while being built, is enclosed in a building for fear of the evil eye.[8] This represents a class of cases in which a high and refined art is being practiced. In parts of Melanesia, and often elsewhere, a shell or leaf is fastened on the end of the masculine organ to ward off the evil eye. The same is the purpose of hanging strips of leather, etc., which catch attention, to divert it from the organ which is sensitive to the evil eye. Hence arose the taboo on parts of the body. In some groups in India, at weddings, women of the bride's and bridegroom's parties sing songs, each deriding and decrying the other. This is for luck. "Praise is risky; abuse and blame are safe."[9] In Behar, on a certain day, sisters abuse brothers, in the belief that this will cause them long life and good luck.[10] In the Horn of Africa magicians who want to get rid of a man stupefy him with drugs and sell him into slavery as having the evil eye (jettatura).[11] Amongst the Kabyles a husband left alone with his bride first strikes her three light blows on the shoulder

---

[1] Sibree, *Great Afr. Island*, 167.
[2] Nachtigal, *Sahara und Sudan*, I, 607.
[3] *Heart of Africa*, II, 406.
[4] *Ibid.*, I, 157.
[5] Junker, *Afrika*, I, 69.
[6] *Globus*, LXXV, 19.
[7] *Ibid.*, LXXII, 164.
[8] Kubary, *Karolinenarchipel.*, 292.
[9] JASB, IV, 63.
[10] *Ibid.*, II, 598.
[11] Paulitschke, *Ethnog. N.O. Afr.*, II, 140.

with the back of his knife to ward off from her the evil eye.[1] In India a small object of iron is hung on a cradle because iron wards off the evil eye.[2] The jettatura belongs to persons born at certain periods in the year, or a woman's behavior during pregnancy may cause her child to have it.[3] People are held to be in danger of the evil eye in prosperity and on festive occasions when they put on fine dress and ornaments. Witches, beggars, and people of the lowest class have the evil eye. Diseases of decline are attributed to the jettatura. Cattle cease to give milk and trees lose leaves on account of it. Flowers and fruit wither untimely. Gems break or lose brilliancy.[4]

568. Amulets against the evil eye. In the Dutch East Indies the phallus, or the symbol of it, is a charm against the evil eye which is cast in quarrels.[5] Roman boys wore a symbol of this kind. Obscene gestures were supposed to ward off the evil eye.[6] In some parts of India a tiger's tooth or claw is an amulet for the same purpose, also obscene symbols or strings of cowries. Whatever dangles and flutters attracts attention to itself and away from the thing to be protected.[7] Hindoo parents give their children ugly and inauspicious names, especially if they have lost some children.[8] The notion of the evil eye was very strong amongst the Arabs, with the notion that beauty attracted it.[9] Mohammed himself believed in the evil eye. The superstition came down from the heathen period when rags and dirty things were hung on children to protect them from the evil eye.[10] The veiling of women amongst the Arabs was probably due to it. Beautiful women also painted black spots on their cheeks.[11] Children, horses, and asses are now disfigured amongst Moslems to protect them from the risk they would run if beautiful. To save a child from the evil eye they say " God be good to thee " and spit in its face.[12] Amongst the Bedouins, whenever one utters praises he must add : " Mashallah," that is, God avert ill ! The only other way to avert ill is to give the praised object to him who praised it.[13] Glittering and waving objects are much used by Moslems on dress and horse caparisons to distract attention. They put texts of the Koran on streamers on their houses for the same purpose.

569. Devices against the evil eye. Homer has the idea that the gods curb the pride of prosperity and are jealous of it. His heroes are taught as a life policy to avert envy. Self-disparagement is an approved pose.[14] Plutarch [15]

---

[1] Hanoteau et Letourneux, *La Kabylie*, II, 219.

[2] JASB, II, 170.

[5] Wilken in *Bijdragen tot T. L. en V.-kunde*, XXXV, 399.

[6] *Jewish Encyc.*, s.v. " Evil Eye."

[7] Monier-Williams, *Brahmanism and Hinduism*, 254. [8] *Ibid.*, 371.

[9] Lane, *Arabian Nights*, I, 67.

[10] W. R. Smith, *Relig. of the Semites*, 448.

[11] Von Kremer, *Kulturgesch. des Orients*, II, 212, 253.

[12] Pischon, *Einfluss des Islam*, 110.

[13] *Globus*, LXXV, 193.

[3] *Ibid.*, I, 120.

[4] *Ibid.*

[14] Keller, *Hom. Soc.*, 114.

[15] *Symposium*, V, 9.

explains the efficiency of objects set up to avert witchcraft on the theory that by their oddity they draw the evil eye from persons and objects. Fescennine verses of the Romans, which were used at weddings and triumphs, were intended to ward off ill luck. Soldiers followed the chariot of the triumphing general and shouted to him derisive and sarcastic verses to avert the ill to which he was then most liable. The Greeks used coarse jests at festivals for the same purpose.[1] Modern Egyptians have inherited this superstition. Mothers leave their children ragged and dirty, especially when they take them out of doors, for fear of admiration and envy. Boys are greatly envied. They are kept long in the harem and dressed in girl's clothes for the same protection.[2] Amongst the richer classes at Cairo chandeliers are hung before a bridegroom's house. If a crowd collects to look at a fine chandelier, a jar is purposely broken to distract attention from it, lest an envious eye should cause it to fall.[3] When the Pasha gave up his monopoly of meat, butchers hung up carcasses in full view on the street. This was complained of, since every beggar could see the meat and envy it, "and one might, therefore, as well eat poison as such meat." [4] An antidote is to burn a bit of alum, with the recital of the first and the last three chapters of the Koran.[5] The Jews of Southern Russia do not allow their children to be admired or caressed. If it is done, the mother will order the child to "make a fig gesture" behind the back of the one who did it.[6]

The evil eye is mentioned in Proverbs xxiii. 6 and xxviii. 22, and perhaps in Matt. xx. 15. The emphasis in Proverbs seems to be on envy and covetousness, not on magical evil.

In China children are often named "dog," "hog," "flea," etc., to ward off the evil eye.[7]

570. Insult and vituperation for luck and against evil eye. Amongst the southern Slavs the evil eye acts by bringing evil spirits into action as the agents, and they "decry" the person or thing. No doubt this mode of operation is to be generally understood when not mentioned. The beautiful suffer most. One may unwittingly do the harm by admiration. One should never say, "What a beautiful child!" but "What an ugly child!" if one admires it. The language has become inverted by this usage.[8] The superstition is popular in Hungary. A child is never to be praised or admired. If one looks at a child for a while in admiration, he should then spit on it three times.[9] Possibly the custom of throwing an old shoe after a bride is to be traced to the same superstition. It is a contemptible and derisory gift for luck, like vituperative outcries. The fear of the evil eye and the *jettatura* is now very strong in southern Italy.[10]

[1] Smith, *Antiq.*, I, 839; II, 831.   [3] *Ibid.*, 384.   [5] *Ibid.*, 381.
[2] Lane, *Mod. Egypt.*, I, 77.   [4] *Ibid.*, 385.   [6] *Globus*, LXXXIII, 316.
[7] Williams, *Middle Kingdom*, I, 797.
[8] Krauss, *Volksglaube der Südslaven*, 41–43.
[9] Temesvary, *Aberglaube in der Geburtshilfe*, 75.   [10] *Bur. Ethnol.*, III, 297.

571. Interaction of the mores and the evil eye. The doctrine of the evil eye is plainly an immediate deduction from demonism. If the atmosphere is full of demons, surrounding us all, agents of all things which happen and affect our interests, human welfare depends either on their uncontrollable caprice, or on devices by which they can be controlled. In the former case human beings need to have omens, oracles, rites of divination, etc., to find out what is to be. In the latter case all devices of magic and sorcery are of the highest value to men. This is why magic is so ultimate and original in the history of civilization. It teaches men *not* to look for any rational causation in the order of things, and to believe in the efficacy of ritual proceedings which contain no rational relation of means to ends. Then it costs no effort to believe that one person can bewitch another, and do it unconsciously. Any relation of responsibility can be invented and believed, since there are no tests of agency. It follows that a new function is opened for the mores. They have to select and establish those relations of agency and responsibility which are to be believed in; that is, they define crimes and criminal responsibility. Ordeals as tests fall in with the same system. They touch no actual relations and therefore prove nothing. It is the mores which establish faith in them and give them the sanction of the society. As to the evil eye, as the evil result of envy and of prosperity, it is an *a posteriori* inference from observed facts, exaggerated into a dogma. Cases of disaster in the hour of triumph occur, both as consequences of overweening self-confidence and by pure chance (Cæsar, Cæsar Borgia, Napoleon). The aleatory interest always averages up, but the successful, who have enjoyed good fortune for a time, believe that it must last for them, and forget that the balance requires bad luck. The lookers-on, however, form their philosophy from what they see. They believe in Nemesis, or other doctrine of offsets, and try by vituperation to make artificial offsets which will avert greater and more real calamities. In all steps of these doctrines and acts the mores are called into play. They are the only limits to the applications of the doctrines. They are of little use. They are afloat in and with the faiths and doctrines. They never can make definitions or set limits. They only enthuse customs, which may change from day to day in their definitions and limits and carry the mores with them. No doubt primitive religion here had excellent effect, for as it arose out of demonism it brought in authority and fixed dogma, which, although erroneous and in itself bad, was a great deal better than the floating superstitions of demonism.

CHAPTER XV

THE MORES CAN MAKE ANYTHING RIGHT AND PREVENT CONDEMNATION OF ANYTHING

572. Mores define the limits which make anything right. At every turn we find new evidence that the mores can make anything right. What they do is that they cover a usage in dress, language, behavior, manners, etc., with the mantle of current custom, and give it regulation and limits within which it becomes unquestionable. The limit is generally a limit of toleration. Literature, pictures, exhibitions, celebrations, and festivals are controlled by some undefined, and probably undefinable, standard of decency and propriety, which sets a limit of toleration on the appeals to fun, sensuality, and various prejudices. In regard to all social customs, the mores sanction them by defining them and giving them form. Such regulated customs are etiquette. The regulation by the mores always gives order and form, and thus surrounds life with limits within which we may and beyond which we may not pursue our interests (e.g. property and marriage). Horseplay and practical jokes have been tolerated, at various times and places, at weddings. They require good-natured toleration, but soon run to excess and may become unendurable. The mores set the limits or define the disapproval. The wedding journey was invented to escape the "jokes." The rice and old shoes will soon be tabooed. The mores fluctuate in their prescriptions. If the limits are too narrow, there is an overflow into vice and abuse, as was proved by seventeenth-century puritanism in England. If the limit is too remote, there is no discipline, and the regulation fails of its purpose. Then a corruption of manners ensues. In the cases now to be given we shall see the power of the mores to give validity to various customs. The cases are all such that we may see in them sanction and currency given to things which seem to us contrary to simple and self-evident rules of right; that is, they are contrary to the views now inculcated in us by our own mores as axiomatic and beyond the need of proof.[1]

573. Punishments for crime. Mediæval punishments for criminals, leaving out of account heretics and witches, bore witness to the grossness, obscenity, inhumanity, and ferocity of the mores of that age. The punishments were not thought wrong or questionable. There was no revolt against them in any one's mind. They were judged right, wise, and necessary, by full public opinion. They were not on the outer boundary of the mores, but in the core of them. Schultz[2] says that the romancers have not exaggerated the horrors of mediæval dungeons. Many of them still remain and are shown to horrified tourists. There was no arrangement for having them cleaned by anybody, so that in time they were sure to become horribly dangerous to health. They were small, dark, damp, cold, and infested by vermin, rats, snakes, etc.[3] Several dungeons in the Bastille were so constructed that the prisoners could neither sit, stand, nor lie, in comfort.[4] Fiendish ingenuity was expended on the invention of refinements of suffering, and executions offered public exhibitions in which the worst vices in the mores of the time were fed and strengthened. Many punishments were not only cruel, but obscene, the cruelty and obscenity being destitute of moral or civil motive and only serving to gratify malignant passion. A case is mentioned of a law in which it was provided that if a criminal had no property, his wife should be violated by a public official as a penalty.[5] In the later Middle Ages, after torture was introduced into civil proceedings, ingenuity

---

[1] See secs. 184–188, on Fashion.
[2] *Höf. Leben*, I, 37.
[3] Scherr, *Kulturgesch.*, 377.
[4] Lacroix, *Moyen Age*, I, 430.
[5] Schultz, *D. L.*, 160.

and "artistic skill" were manifested in inventing instruments of torture.[1] A case is given of extravagant cruelty and tyranny on the part of a man of rank towards a cook who had displeased him. It was impossible to obtain protection or redress. The standpoint of the age was that a man of rank must be allowed full discretion in dealing with a cook.[2] In many cases details were added to punishments, which were intended to reach the affections, mental states, faiths, etc., of the accused, and add mental agony to physical pain. "Use and wont" exercised their influence on people who saw or heard of these acts of the authorities until cruelties and horrors became commonplace and familiar, and the lust of cruelty was a characteristic of the age.

574. Prisons in England in the time of Queen Anne. The prisons of England, in Queen Anne's time, were sinks of misery, disease, cruelty, and extortion, from which debtors suffered most, on account of their poverty. Women contributed to the total loathsomeness and suffered from it. The Marshalsea prison was "an infected pest house all the year long." There were customs by which jailers and chaplains extorted fees from the miserable prisoners. In the country the prisons were worse than in London. Pictures are said to exist in which debtor prisoners are shown catching mice for food, dying of starvation and malaria, covered with boils and blains, assaulted by jailers, imprisoned in underground dungeons, living with hogs, with clogs on their legs, tortured with thumbscrews, etc. "Nobody ever seems to have bothered their heads about it. It was not their business." In 1702 the House of Commons ordered a bill to be brought in for regulating the king's bench and fleet prisons, "but nobody took sufficient interest in it, and it never became an act." [3] If the grade and kind of humanity which the case required did not exist in the mores of the time, there would be no response. It was on the humanitarian wave of the latter half of the century that Howard succeeded in bringing about a reform. The prisons in the American colonies were of the same kind as those in the old country. The Tories, in the revolution, suffered most from

---

[1] Lecky, *Rationalism*, I, 332.   [2] Schultz, *Höf. Leben*, II, 448.
[3] Ashton, *Social Life in the Reign of Queen Anne.*

their badness. It is not known that personal abuse was perpetrated in them.

575. Wars of factions. Penalties of defeat. Political factions and religious sects have always far surpassed the criminal law in the ferocity of their penalties against each other. Neither the offenses nor the penalties are defined in advance. As Lea says,[1] the treatment of Alberico, brother of Ezzelino da Romano, and his family (1259) shows the ferocity of the age. Ezzelino showed the same in many cases, and the hatred heaped up against him is easily understood, but the gratification of it was beastly and demonic.[2] Great persons, after winning positions of power, used all their resources to crush old rivals or opponents (Clement V, John XXII) and to exult over the suffering they could inflict.[3] In the case of Wullenweber, at Lubeck,[4] burgesses of cities manifested the same ferocity in faction fights. The history of city after city contains similar episodes. At Ghent, in 1530, the handicraftsmen got the upper hand for a time and used it like savages.[5] All parties fought out social antagonisms without reserve on the doctrine: To the victors the spoils; to the vanquished the woe! If two parties got into a controversy about such a question as whether Christ and his apostles lived by beggary, they understood that the victorious party in the controversy would burn the defeated party. That was the rule of the game and they went into it on that understanding.

In all these matters the mores of the time set the notions of what was right, or those limits within which conduct must always be kept. No one blamed the conduct on general grounds of wrong and excess, or of broad social inexpediency. The mores of the time were absolutely imperative as to some matters (e.g. duties of church ritual), but did not give any guidance as to the matters here mentioned. In fact, the mores prevented any unfavorable criticism of those matters or any independent judgment about them.

[1] *Inquis.*, II, 228.
[2] *Rerum Ital. Script.*, IX, 134.
[3] Lea, *Inquis.*, II, 452.
[4] Barthold, *Hansa*, III, 291.
[5] Räumer, *Hist. Taschenbuch*, 2 ser., III, 413.

576. Bundling. One of the most extraordinary instances of what the mores can do to legitimize a custom which, when rationally judged, seems inconsistent with the most elementary requirements of the sex taboo, is bundling. In Latin Europe generally, especially amongst the upper classes, it is not allowed that a young man and a young woman shall be alone together even by day, and the freer usage in England, and still more in the United States, is regarded as improper and contrary to good manners. In the latter countries two young people, if alone together, do not think of transgressing the rules of propriety as set by custom in the society. Such was the case also with night visits. Although the custom was free, and although better taste and judgment have abolished it, yet it was *defined* and regulated, and was never a proof of licentious manners. It is found amongst uncivilized people, but is hardly to be regarded as a survival in higher civilization. Christians, in the third and fourth centuries,[1] practiced it, even without the limiting conditions which were set in the Middle Ages. Having determined to renounce sex, as an evil, they sought to test themselves by extreme temptation. It was a test or proof of the power of moral rule over natural impulse.[2] "It was a widely spread custom in both the east and the west of the Roman empire to live with virgins. Distinguished persons, including one of the greatest bishops of the empire, who was also one of the greatest theologians, joined in the custom. Public opinion in the church judged them lightly, although unfavorably."[3] "After the church took on the episcopal constitution, it persecuted and drove out the *subintroductae*. They were regarded as a survival from the old church which was disapproved. The custom that virgins dwelt in the house with men arose in the oldest period of the Christian church."[4] "They did not think of any evil as to be apprehended." "In fact, we have only a little clear evidence that the living together did not correspond in the long run to the assumptions on which

---

[1] Achelis, *Virgines Subintroductae*, 4.

[2] Harnack, *Pseudo-Clement. Briefe de Virginitate ;* Cyprian, *Epist. IV ad Pompon* (c. 250 A.D. ; Achelis, *Virgines Subintroductae ;* Julicher in *Archiv für Religionswssnsft.*, VII, 372.　　[3] Achelis, 12.　　[4] *Ibid.*, 74.

it was based." [1] The custom was abolished in the sixth
century. [2] "Spiritual marriage" was connected with the monastic
profession and both were due to the ascetic tendency of the
time. "From the time when we can clearly find monastic
associations in existence, we find hermits living in comradeship
with nuns." [3] We are led back to Jewish associations. The
custom is older than Christianity. The custom at Corinth [4] was
but imitation of Jewish "God worshipers" or "Praying
women." [5] The Therapeuts had such companions. Their houses
of worship were arranged to separate the sexes. Their dances
sometimes lasted all night. [6] In the Middle Ages several sects
who renounced marriage introduced tests of great temptation. [7]
Individuals also, believing that they were carrying on the war
between "the flesh" and "the spirit" subjected themselves to
similar tests. [8] These are not properly cases in the mores, but
they illustrate the intervention of sectarian doctrines or views
to traverse the efforts to satisfy interests, and so to disturb the
mores.

577. Two forms of bundling. Two cases are to be distinguished: (1) night visits as a mode of wooing; [9] (2) extreme
intimacy between two persons who are under the sex taboo (one
or both being married, or one or both vowed to celibacy), and
who nevertheless observe the taboo.

578. Mediæval bundling. The custom in the second form
became common in the woman cult of the twelfth century and it
spread all over Europe. [10] As the vassal attended his lord to his
bedchamber, so the knight his lady. The woman cult was an
aggregation of poses and pretenses to enact a comedy of love, but
not to satisfy erotic passion. The custom spread to the peasant
classes in later centuries, and it extended to the Netherlands,

---

[1] Achelis, 67.   [3] *Ibid.*, 47.   [5] Achelis, 32.
[2] *Ibid.*, 58.   [4] 1 Cor. vii. 36–40.   [6] *Ibid.*, 31.
[7] Lea, *Inquis.*, II, 357; III, 109; *Sacerd. Celibacy*, 167.
[8] Todd, *Life of St. Patrick*, 91.
[9] This custom existed amongst uncivilized people. Fritsch, *Eingeb. Süd.-Afr.*,
140; Gomme, *Folklore*, 220; Ling Roth, *Sarawak*, I, 109; JAI, XXI, 120; *Globus*,
LXXVIII, 228; La Hontan, *Voyages dans l'Amer.*, II, 133; Masson, *Balochistan*,
III, 287.   [10] Weinhold, *D. F.*, I, 260, ff.

Scandinavia, Switzerland, England, Scotland, and Wales, but it took rather the first form in the lower classes and in the process of time. In building houses in Holland the windows were built conveniently for this custom. "In 1666–1667 every house on the island of Texel had an opening under the window where the lover could enter so as to sit on the bed and spend the night making love to the daughter of the house." The custom was called *queesten.* Parents encouraged it. A girl who had no *queester* was not esteemed. Rarely did any harm occur. If so, the man was mobbed and wounded or killed. The custom can be traced in North Holland down to the eighteenth century.[1] This was the customary mode of wooing in the low countries and Scandinavia. In spite of the disapproval of both civil and ecclesiastical authorities, the custom continued just as round dances continue now, in spite of the disapproval of many parents, because a girl who should refuse to conform to current usage would be left out of the social movement. The lover was always one who would be accepted as a husband. If he exceeded the limits set by custom he was very hardly dealt with by the people of the village.[2] The custom is reported from the Schwarzwald as late as 1780. It was there the regular method of wooing for classes who had to work all day. The lover was required to enter by the dormer window. Even still the custom is said to exist amongst the peasants of Germany, but it is restricted to one night in the month or in the year.[3] Krasinski[4] describes kissing games customary amongst the Unitarians of the Ukrain. He says that they are a Greek custom and he connects them with bundling.

579. Poverty and wooing. Amongst peasants there was little opportunity for the young people to become acquainted. When the cold season came they could not woo out of doors. The young women could not be protected by careful rules which would prevent wooing. They had to take risks and to take care

---

[1] Wilken in *Bijdragen tot T. L. en V.-Kunde,* XXXV, 205.

[2] Scheltema, *Frijen en Trouwen,* 59; Schotel, *Het Oud-Holland. Huisgezin,* 228; *Globus,* LXXXII, 324.

[3] Rudeck, *Gesch. der Sittlichkeit,* 146, 404.   [4] *Cossacks of the Ukrain,* 281.

of themselves.   Poverty was the explanation of this custom in all civilized countries, although there was always in it an element of frolic and fun.

580. Night wooing in North American colonies.   All the emigrants to North America were familiar with the custom.   In the seventeenth century, in the colonies, the houses were small, poorly warmed, and inconvenient, allowing little privacy.   No doubt this is the reason why the custom took new life in the colonies. Burnaby [1] says that it was the custom amongst the lower classes of Massachusetts that a pair who contemplated marriage spent the night together in bed partly dressed.   If they did not like each other they might not marry, unless the woman became pregnant. The custom was called " tarrying."   It was due to poverty again. Modern inhabitants of tenement houses are constrained in their customs by the same limitation, and the effect is seen in their folkways.   The custom of bundling had a wide range of variety. Two people sitting side by side might cover themselves with the same robe, or lie on the bed together for warmth.   Peters [2] defended the custom, which, he said, "prevails amongst all classes to the great honor of the country, its religion, and ladies." The older women resented the attempts of the ministers to preach against the custom.   Sofas were introduced as an alternative.   The country people thought the sofa less proper.   In the middle of the eighteenth century the decline in social manners, which was attributed to the wars, caused the custom to produce more evil results.[3]   Also the greater wealth, larger houses, and better social arrangements changed the conditions and there was less need for the custom.   It fell under social disapproval and was thrown out of the folkways.   Stiles [4] says that " it died hard " after the revolution.   In 1788 a ballad in an almanac brought the custom into popular ridicule.   Stiles quotes the case of Seger *vs.* Slingerland, in which the judge, in a case of seduction, held that parents who allowed bundling, although it was the custom, could not recover.[5]

---

[1] *Travels in the Middle Settlements of N. Amer.* (1759–1760), 144.
[2] *Hist. of Connecticut*, 325.   [4] *Bundling*, 75.
[3] Stiles, *Bundling*, 80.   [5] Stiles, *Bundling*, 112.

581. Reasons for bundling. A witness before the Royal Commission on the Marriage Laws, 1868,[1] testified that night visiting was still common amongst the laboring classes in some parts of Scotland. " They have no other means of intercourse." It was against custom for a lover to visit his sweetheart by day. As to the parents, " Their daughters must have husbands and there is no other way of courting." This statement sums up the reasons for this custom which, not being a public custom, must have varied very much according to the character of individuals who used it. Attempts were always made to control it by sanctions in public opinion.

582. Public lupanars. Perhaps the most incredible case to illustrate the power of the mores to extend toleration and sanction to an evil thing remains to be mentioned, — the lupanars which were supported by the mediæval cities. Athenæus[2] says that Solon caused female slaves to be bought by the city and exposed in order to save other women from assaults on their virtue. In later times prostitution was accepted as inevitable, but it was not organized by the city. Salvianus (fifth century, A.D.) represents the brothels as tolerated by the Roman law in order to prevent adultery.[3] Lupanars continued to exist from Roman times until the Middle Ages. Those in southern Europe were recruited from the female pilgrims from the north who set out for Rome or Palestine and whose means failed them.[4] It is another social phenomenon due to poverty and to a specious argument of protection to women in a good position. This argument came down by tradition with the institution. The city council of Nuremberg stated, as a reason for establishing a lupanar, that the church allowed harlots in order to prevent greater evils.[5] This statement, no doubt, refers to a passage in Augustine, *De Ordine :*[6] "What is more base, empty of worth, and full of vileness than harlots and other such pests ? Take away harlots from human society and you will have tainted everything with lust. Let them be with the matrons and you will produce

[1] Page 172.
[2] *Deipnosophists*, XIII, 25.
[3] *De Gubernat. Dei*, VII, 99.
[4] Weinhold, *D. F.*, II, 22.
[5] Schultz, *D. L.*, 73.
[6] Migne, *Patrol. Latina*, XXXII, 1000.

contamination and disgrace. So this class of persons, on account
of their morals, of a most shameless life, fills a most vile function
under the laws of order." The bishop had laid down the proposition that evil things in human society, under the great orderly
scheme of things which he was trying to expound, are overruled
to produce good. He then sought illustrations to prove this.
The passage quoted is one of his illustrations. Everywhere else
in his writings where he mentions harlots he expresses the
greatest abomination of them. His general proposition is fallacious and extravagant. and he had to strain the cases which he
alleged as illustrations, but he was a church father, and five hundred years later no one dared criticise or dissent from anything
which he had said. It went far beyond the incidental use of an
illustration made by him, to cite the passage, with his authority,
for a doctrine that cities might wisely establish lupanars in order
to prevent sex vice, especially in the interest of virtuous women.[1]
Such houses were maintained without secrecy or shame. Queen
Joanna of Naples made ordinances for a lupanar at Avignon, in
1347, when it was the papal residence. Generally the house
was rented to a "host" under stipulations as to the food, dress,
and treatment of the inmates, and regulations as to order, gambling, etc.[2] The inmates, like the public executioners, were
required to wear a distinctive dress. Frequenters did not need
to practice secrecy. The houses were free to persons of rank,
and were especially prepared by the city when it had to entertain great persons. Women who were natives of the city were
not admitted. This is the only feature which is not entirely
cynical and shameless.[3] In 1501 a rich citizen of Frankfurt am
Main bequeathed to the city a sum of money with which to build
a large house into which all the great number of harlots could
be collected,[4] for the number increased greatly. They appeared
at all great concourses of men, and were sent out to the Hansa
stations.[5] In fact, the people of the time accepted certain social

---

[1] Scherr, *Deutsches Frauenleben*, I, 275.

[2] Jaeger, *Ulms Leben im M. A.*, 544.

[3] Rudeck, *Oeffentl. Sittlichkeit*, 26–35.

[4] Westerhout, *Geslachtsleven onzer Voorouders*, 198.

[5] Scherr, *Kulturgesch.*, 223.

phenomena as "natural" and inevitable, and they made their arrangements accordingly, uninterfered with by "moral sense." In Wickliffe's time the bishop of Winchester obtained a handsome rent from the stews of Southwark.[1] Probably he and his contemporaries thought no harm. Never until the nineteenth century was it in the mores of any society to feel that the sacrifice of the mortal welfare of one human being to the happiness of another was a thing which civil institutions could not tolerate. It could not enter into the minds of men of the fifteenth century that harlots, serfs, and other miserable classes had personal rights which were outraged by the customs and institutions of that time.

583. The end of the lupanars. All the authorities agree that the thing which put an end to the city lupanars was syphilis.[2] It was not due to any moral or religious revolt, although there had been individuals who had criticised the institution of harlots, and some pious persons had founded convents, in the thirteenth and fourteenth centuries, for repentant harlots. Protestants and Catholics tried, to some extent, to throw the blame of the lupanars on each other. Luther urged the abolition of them in 1520. They reached their greatest development in the fifteenth century.[3] The mere existence of an article so degrading to both husband and wife as the girdle[4] is significant of the mores of the period, and shows how far the mores can go to make anything "right," or properly customary.

584. Judgment is beclouded by the atmosphere formed by the mores. Education. Witch persecutions are another case of the extent to which familiarity with the customs prevents any rational judgment of phenomena of experience and observation. How was it possible that men did not see the baseness and folly of their acts? The answer is that the ideas of demonism were a

---

[1] Trevelyan, *England in the Age of Wickliffe*, 280.

[2] The origin of this disease being unknown, it has been suggested that it was due to vice and excess in the Middle Ages (*Umschau*, VII, 71).

[3] See *Cambridge Hist. of Mod. Europe*, I, especially Lea's chapter; Janssen, *Deutsches Volk*, VIII; Schultz, *Höf. Leben*, I, 452; same author, *Deutsch. Leben*, 254, 257, 277, 283; Du Laure, *Paris*, 268; Scherr, *Kulturgesch.*, 222, on the fifteenth century.   [4] Schultz, *D. L.*, 283.

part of the mental outfit of the period. The laws were traditions from generations which had drawn deductions from the doctrines of demonism and had applied them in criminal practice. The legal procedure was familiar and corresponded to the horror of crimes and criminals, of which witchcraft and witches were the worst. The mores formed a moral and civil atmosphere through which everything was seen, and rational judgment was made impossible. It cannot be doubted that, at any time, all ethical judgments are made through the atmosphere of the mores of the time. It is they which tell us what is right. It is only by high mental discipline that we can be trained to rise above that atmosphere and form rational judgments on current cases. This mental independence and ethical power are the highest products of education. They are also perilous. Our worst cranks are those who get the independence and power, but cannot stand alone and form correct judgments outside of the mores of the time and place. It must be remembered that the mores sometimes becloud the judgment, but they more often guide it.

CHAPTER XVI

SACRAL HARLOTRY. CHILD SACRIFICE

Men's clubhouses. — Consecrated women. — Relation of sacral harlotry and child sacrifice. — Reproduction and food supply. — The Gilgamesh epic. — The Adonis myth. — Religious ritual, religious drama, and harlotry. — The Babylonian custom ; its relation to religion. — Religion and the mores. — Cases of sacral harlotry. — The same customs in the Old Testament. — The antagonism of abundance and excess. — Survivals of sacral harlotry ; analogous customs in Hindostan. — Lingam and yoni. — Conventionalization. — Criticism of the mores of Hindostan. — Mexican mores ; drunkenness. — Japanese mores. — Chinese religion and mores. — Philosophy of the interest in reproduction ; incest. — The archaic is sacred. — Child sacrifice. — Beast sacrifice substituted for child sacrifice. — Mexican doctrine of greater power through death. — Motives of child sacrifice. — Dedication by vows. — Degeneration of the custom of consecrating women. — Our traditions come from Israel. — How the Jewish view of sensuality prevailed.

The topics treated in this chapter are further illustrations of the power of the mores to make anything right, and to protect anything from condemnation. See also Chapter XVII.

585. Men's clubhouses. It is a very common custom in barbaric society that the men have a clubhouse in which they spend much of their time together and in which the unmarried men sleep. Such houses are centers of intrigue, enterprise, amusement, and vice. The men work there, carry on shamanistic rites, hold dances, entertain guests, and listen to narratives by the elders. Women are excluded altogether or at times. In the Caroline Islands such houses are institutions of social and religious importance. While the women of the place may not enter them, those from a neighboring place live in them for a time in license, but return home with payment which is used partly for religious purposes and partly for themselves.[1]

[1] Snouck-Hurgronje, *De Atjehers*, I, 64–66; *Bur. Eth.*, XVIII, 285; *Amer. Anthrop.*, XI, 56; Codrington, *Melanesians*, 102, 299; Serpa Pinto, *Como eu Atravassei Africa*, I, 82; Kubary, *Karolinenarchipel.*, 47, 226, 244; Powers, *Calif. Indians*, 24.

586. Consecrated women. It may even be said to be the current view of uncivilized peoples, up to the full development of the father family, that women have free control of their own persons until they are married, when they pass under a taboo which they are bound to observe. Therefore before marriage they may accumulate a dowry. Very many cases also occur of men-women and women-men, persons of either sex who assume the functions and mode of life of the other. Cases also occur in barbarism of women consecrated to the gods. Among the Ewe-speaking peoples of West Africa[1] girls of ten or twelve are received and educated for three years in the chants and dances of worship, serving the priests. At the end of the time they become public women, but are under no reproach, because they are regarded as married to the god and acting under his direction. Properly they should be restricted to the worshipers at the temple, but they are not. Probably such was the original taboo which is now relaxed and decayed. Children whom such women bear belong to the god. The institution "is essentially religious in its origin and is intimately connected with phallic worship."

587. Sacral harlotry and child sacrifice. These observations may serve to introduce a study of the phenomena, so incomprehensible to us, of sacral prostitution and child sacrifice. That study is calculated to show us that the mores define right and wrong. It would be a great mistake to regard the above cases as mere aberrations of sex appetite. The usages had their origin in interests. Sacral harlotry was a substitute for the child sacrifice of females. The other incidental interests found advantage in it. It was an attempt to solve problems of life. It was regarded as conducive to welfare, and was connected with religion. It was kept up by the conservatism and pertinacity of religious usage until a later time and another set of conditions, when it became vicious.

588. Reproduction and food supply. The operations of nature by which plants and animals reproduce are of great interest and importance to man, because on them depends the abundance of

[1] Ellis, *Ewe-speaking Peoples*, 141.

his food supply. It is impossible to tell when this interest would "begin," but it would become intense whenever the number of men was great in proportion to the food supply. Hence the rainfall, the course of the seasons, the prevalence of winds, the conjunction of astronomical phenomena with spawning or fruit seasons, and the habits of plants and animals caught the feeble attention of savage man and taught him facts of nature, through his eagerness to get signs of coming plenty or suggestions as to his own plans and efforts. Attention has been called to a very interesting fact about the fructification of the domesticated date palm wherever oasis cultivation prevailed in western Asia.[1] The fructification must be artificial. Men carry the pollen to the female plant and adopt devices to distribute it on the wind or by artificial contact. At the present time this is done by attaching a bunch of the male seed on a branch to windward.[2] Tylor first suggested that certain ancient pictorial representations are meant to depict the work of artificial fructification as carried on by mythological persons, — cherubim, who represent the winds.[3] The function of the wind distributing the seed is divine work. The tree is of such supreme value[4] that the well living of men depends on this operation. The sex conjunction therefore was the most important and beneficent operation in nature, and correct knowledge of it was the prime condition of getting an abundant food supply. Man followed the operation with all the interest of the food supply and all the awe of religion. It is certain that his interest in it was "innocent." He began to mythologize about it on account of the grand elements of welfare, risk, and skill which were in it. A parallel case is furnished by the treatment accorded to rice by the Javanese. It is to them the great article of food supply. They endow it with a soul and ascribe to it sex passion. They have ceremonies by which to awaken this passion in the rice as a means of increasing their own food supply. The ceremonies consist in sympathetic magic by men and women at night.[5]

[1] Barton, *Semitic Origins*, 78.
[2] Wellsted, *Arabia*, II, 12.
[3] *Proc. Soc. Bibl. Archæol.*, 1890, XII, 383.
[4] Herodotus, I, 193.
[5] Wilken, *Volkenkunde*, 550.

589. The Gilgamesh epic. The Gilgamesh epic which originated in the Euphrates valley more than 2000 years B.C.[1]
consists of a number of episodes which were later collected and
coördinated into a single work like other great epics. Jastrow[2]
construes it as a variation of the story of Adam and Eve.
Gilgamesh is a hero admired by all women. The elders of
Uruk beg his mother, the mother-goddess Aruru (a form of
Ishtar), to restrain him. In order to comply she makes of clay
Eabani, a satyr-like, hairy wild man, with a tail and horns, who
lives with the beasts. Jastrow thinks that this means that he
consorted with female beasts, having as yet no female of his
own species. No one could capture him, so the god Shamash
assailed him by lust, sending to him a priestess of Ishtar who
won him to herself (woman) away from beasts. She said to him :
" Thou shalt be like a god. Why dost thou lie with beasts ? "
" She revealed his soul to Eabani." She was, therefore, a culture
heroine, and the myth means that, with the knowledge of sex,
awoke consciousness, intelligence, and civilization. Eabani followed the priestess to Uruk, where he and Gilgamesh became
comrades, — heroes of war and slayers of monsters. Ishtar fell
in love with Gilgamesh, but he refused her because all men and
beasts whom she loved she reduced to misery. Her vengeance
for this rejection brings woe and death on the two friends. The
Mexicans had a similar myth that the sun god and the maize
goddess produced life in vegetation by their sex activity. The
sun god contracted venereal disease so that they probably connected syphilis with sexual excess.[3] In the worship of Ishtar at
Uruk there were three grades of harlot priestesses, and there
the temple consecration of women was practiced in recognition
of the connection between the service of Ishtar and civilization.
At first the goddesses of life and of love were the same. The
Venus of reproduction and the Venus of carnal lust were later
distinguished. At some periods the distinction was sharply
maintained. At other times the former Venus was only an

[1] Maspero, *Peuples de l'Orient*, I, 576, 589.
[2] *Amer. Jo. Semit. Lang. and Lit.*, XV, 201.
[3] *Archiv f. Anthrop.*, XXIX, 156.

intermediary to lead to the latter. The Mexicans had two goddesses, — one of chaste, the other of impure, love. The festivals
of the former were celebrated with obscene rites ; those of the
latter with the self-immolation of harlots, with excessive language
and acts. The goddess was thought to be rejuvenated by the death
of the harlots. The obscene rites were at war with the current
mores of the people at the time. The demons of license became
the guardians of good morals. They concealed the phallus.
Sins of license were confessed to the gods of license.[1] Teteoinnan, the maize-mother, also became a harlot through the work
of furthering growth, but in the service of the state she punished transgressions of the sex taboo.[2] This is as if the need of
the taboo having been learned by the consequences of license
and excess, the goddess of the latter became the guardian of
the former. In the Semitic religions the beginning and end of
life were attributed to supernatural agencies dangerous to man.[3]
The usages to be mentioned below show that this was not an
abstract dogma, but was accepted as the direct teaching of
experience.

590. The Adonis myth. There was in the worship of Ishtar
wailing for Tammuz (Adonis). He was either the son or the
husband of Ishtar. She went to Hades to rescue him. His
death was a myth for the decay of vegetation, and his resurrection
was a myth for its revival. The former was celebrated with
lamentations ; the latter with extravagant rejoicings and sex
license.[4] This legend, which under local modifications and much
syncretism existed until long after Christianity was introduced
in the Greco-Roman world, coincides with the laws of Hammurabi as to harlot priestesses.

591. Sacral harlotry. Three things which later reached strong
independent development are here united, — religious ritual, religious drama (with symbols, pantomime, and mysteries which
later came to be considered indecent), and harlotry. Sacral
harlotry was the only harlotry. It was normal and was not a
subject of ethical misgiving. It was a part of the religious and

---

[1] *Archiv f. Anthrop.*, XXIX, 150.   [2] *Ibid.*, 183.
[3] W. R. Smith, *Relig. of the Semites*, 447.   [4] Lucian, *De Syria Dea*, 6.

social system. When, later, prostitution became an independent social fact and was adjudged bad, sacral harlotry long continued under the conventionalization and persistence of religious usage (sec. 74), but then the disapproval of prostitution in the mores produced an ethical war which resulted in the abolition of harlotry. Sacral harlotry, while it lasted, was practiced for one of two purposes, — to collect a dowry for the women or to collect money for the temple.

592. The Babylonian custom ; its relation to religion. Herodotus [1] states that the women of the Lydians and of some peoples on the island of Cyprus collected a dowry by freedom before marriage ; that a woman chosen by the god from the whole nation remained in the little cell on top of the eight-storied tower at Babylon, and was said by the priests to share the couch of the god ; that the Thebans in Egypt tell a similar story of their god ; that at Patara, in Lycia, the priestess who gave the oracle consorted with the god ; and that at Babylon every woman was compelled once to sacrifice herself to the first comer in the temple of Mylitta. The last statement was long considered so monstrous that it was not believed. That incredulity arose from modern mores, in which religion and sex license are so strongly antagonized that religion seems to us an independent force, of " divine origin," which is sent into the world with an inherent character of antisensuality, or as a revelation of the harm and wickedness of certain sex acts. That notion, however, is a part of our Jewish inheritance. The fact stated by Herodotus is no longer doubted. It is only one in a series of parallel cases, all of which must have originated in similar ideas and have been regarded as contributing in the same way to human welfare. Preuss [2] attempts to explain it. " It is only to be understood if men earlier, in order to make natural objects prosper, had practiced sex usages of a kind which later, according to the mores of daily life, seemed to them to be prostitution. From this development came the fact that the Germans called the Corn-mother the ' Great Harlot.' " We know that men have sacrificed their children and other human beings, the selected

[1] Herodotus, I, 93, 181, 199. [2] *Globus*, LXXXVI, 360.

being the bravest or most beautiful; that they have mutilated themselves in all ways from the slightest to the most serious; that they have celebrated the most extravagant orgies; and that they have acted against their own most important interests, — all in the name of religion. There is nothing in religion itself which antagonizes sensuality, cruelty, and other base elements in human nature. Religion has its independent origin in supposed interests, and makes its own demands on men. The demands of religion are sacrifices and ritual observances. The whole religious system is evolved within the circle of interests, ideas, and mores which the society possesses at the time. Religion also finds adjustment and consistency with all other interests and tastes of the group at the time. A father of many daughters would use the temple service as a way to provide for one of them.[1] Religion is also extremely persistent. Therefore it holds and carries over to later ages customs which once were beneficial, but which at the later time are authoritative but harmful. If parents threw their children into the furnace to Molech, why should they not devote their daughters to Ishtar? If they once practiced sympathetic magic to make rice grow, religion might carry the customs over to a time when they would be shocking and abominable. Although the survival of these customs became sensual and corrupting, it is certain that it was not their original purpose to serve sensuality. They were not devices to cultivate or gratify licentiousness. We know of no case of a primitive custom with such a purpose. The provisions in the laws of Hammurabi are as simple and matter-of-fact as possible. They are provisions for actual interests which, it seemed, ought to be provided for. Another proof of the innocence of the customs is that in independent cases the same customs were established. The customs were responses of men to the great agents who (as they thought they perceived) wrought things in nature. The methods and means used by the agents were revered. They could not be despised or disapproved by men. Therefore reproduction was religious and sex was consecrated. The whole realm was one of

---

[1] Maurer, *Völkerkunde, Bibel, und Christenthum*, 95.

mystery and wonder. Men became as gods by knowledge of it. From that knowledge they acquired power to make things grow and so got food and escaped want. The interest in sex, and the customs connected with it, was revivified in connection with agriculture. The mode of fructifying the date palm was a very great discovery in natural science. Primitive men would turn it into a religious fact and rule. The inference that women should be consecrated to the goddess of life and that in her service reproduction should be their sacred duty was in the logic of primitive people. Ishtar was polyandrous, but she turned into Astarte, the wife of the chief Baal, or else she became androgyne and then masculine. There is a virgin mother and a mother of the gods. The idea of the latter continued with invincible persistency. She may be unmarried, choosing her partners at will, or " queen, head, and first born of all gods." [1] In these changes we see the religious notions and the mores adjusting themselves to each other. As long as the underlying notions were true and sincere and the logic was honest, the usages were harmless. When the original notions were lost, or the logic became an artificial cover for a real ethical inconsistency, and the customs were kept up, perhaps to give gain to priests, the usages served licentiousness.

593. Religion and the mores. Religion never has been an independent force acting from outside creatively to mold the mores or the ideas of men. Evidently such an idea is the extreme form of the world philosophy in which another (spiritual) world is conceived of as impinging upon this one from "above," to give it laws and guidance. The mores grow out of the life as a whole. They change with the life conditions, density of population, and life experience. Then they become strange or hostile to traditional religion. In our own experience our mores have reached views about ritual practices, polygamy, slavery, celibacy, etc., which are strange or hostile to those in the Bible. Since the sixteenth century we have reconstructed our religion to fit our modern ideas and mores. Every religious reform in history has come about in this way. All religious doctrines and ritual

[1] W. R. Smith, *Relig. of the Semites*, 56-59.

acts are held immutable by strong interests and notions of religious duty. Therefore they fall out of consistency with the mores, which are in constant change, being acted on by all the observation or experience of life. Sacral harlotry is a case, the ethical horror of which is very great and very obvious to us, of old religious ideas and customs preserved by the religion into times of greatly changed moral (i.e. of the mores) and social codes.

594. Cases of sacral harlotry. Survivals of sacral harlotry are found in historic Egypt. Even under the Cæsars the most beautiful girl of the noble families of Thebes was chosen to be consecrated in the temple of Ammon. She gained honor and profit by the life of a courtesan, and always found a grand marriage when she retired on account of age. In all the temples there were women attached to the service of the gods. They were of different grades and ranks and were supposed to entertain the god as harem women entertained princes. In the temples of goddesses women were the functionaries and obtained great honor and power.[1] Constantine demolished the temples of impure cult in Phœnicia and Egypt and caused the priests to be scattered by soldiers. Farnell[2] thinks that the Babylonian custom (especially because it was required that the man should be a stranger) was due to fear of harm from the nuptial blood. The attendants in the temples are known as " hierodules." Otto[3] says that the hierodules were not temple slaves, or harlots, but he finds evidence that the temples had income from temple harlots. The Phœnicians who settled Carthage took the religion of western Asia with them. Perhaps there was an element of sensuality in the antecedent religion of north Africa which united with that of the imported religion. This would account for the cultus at Sicca, in Numidia. There was there a temple of Astarte or Tanith in which women lived who never went forth except to collect a dowry by harlotry.[4] At Byblos (Gebal), in Phœnicia, there was

[1] Maspero, *Peuples de l'Orient*, I, 50, 126.
[2] *Archiv f. Religionsgesch.*, VII, 88.
[3] *Priester und Tempel im Hellen. Aeg.*, I, 316.
[4] Valer. Max., II, 6, 15.

a great temple of the same goddess at which there were elaborate celebrations of the Adonis myth. There was sacral harlotry for strangers only, the money going as a sacrifice to the goddess. Every woman must have her head shaved in mourning for Adonis, or sacrifice herself under this custom.[1] Tanith has been identified with Artemis, and the later cults of Punic Africa give great prominence to the "celestial virgin," or "virginal *numen.*" "The identification of the mother-of-the-gods with the heavenly virgin, that is, the unmarried goddess, is confirmed, if not absolutely demanded, by Augustine.[2] At Carthage she seems also to be identical with Dido."[3] "The Arabian Lat was worshiped by the Nabatæans as mother-of-the-gods and must be identified with the virgin-mother whose worship at Petra is described by Epiphanius."[4] In the worship of Anaitis in Armenia male and female slaves were dedicated to the goddess, but men of rank also consecrated their daughters. After long service they married, no one considering them degraded. They were not mercenary, being well provided for by their families. Therefore they received only their social equals.[5] Baal Peor seems also to have been a case of sacral harlotry.[6] The strongest reason for thinking so is Hosea ix. 10. Rosenbaum[7] interprets the pestilence as venereal. The *kedeshim* (male prostitutes) were expelled from Judah by Asa.[8] They had been there since Rehoboam.[9] They are heard of again.[10] They were under vows and brought their earnings to Jahveh[11] Farnell[12] interprets a fragment of Pindar as proof of sacral harlotry at Corinth. At a temple of the Epizephyrian Locri it was practiced in fulfillment of a vow made by the people, under some ancient insult, to consecrate their daughters if the goddess would help them.[13] Farnell also[14] directs attention to a case in Sicily where the connection is with the Carthaginian Eryx. In

[1] Lucian, *De Syria Dea*, 6; Pietschmann, *Phoenizier*, 229.
[2] *De Civit. Dei*, II, 4.
[3] W. R. Smith, *Relig. of the Semites*, 56.
[4] *Ibid.*
[5] Strabo, XI, 14, 16.
[6] Num. xxiii. 28; xxv. 1; Josh. xxii. 17.
[7] *Die Lustseuche im Alterthum*, 77.
[8] 1 Kings xv. 12.
[9] 1 Kings xiv. 24.
[10] 1 Kings xxii. 46; 2 Kings xxiii. 7.
[11] Deut. xxiii. 18.
[12] *Cults of the Greek States*, 635.
[13] Athenæus, XII, 11.
[14] *Cults of the Greek States*, 641.

the *Cistellaria* of Plautus the usage is referred to as Tuscan.[1] Augustus rebuilt Carthage and it appears that the old usages had survived the interval of one hundred and fifty years. The temple of Tanith was rebuilt and called that of the celestial virgin. The Romans forbade sacral harlotry, which was in strong antagonism to their sex mores. Hahn has called attention[2] to a passage which proves the existence of sacral harlotry in Scandinavia just before the introduction of Christianity in the tenth century. The hero remains through the winter with the woman who was the consecrated attendant of the god Frey and who traveled about with his wooden image. The people take the hero to be the god, and rejoice when the priestess becomes a mother by him.[3] The Mexicans, with the same interests, under like conditions evolved the same customs and similar ideas. Mayas of the lowest classes sent out their daughters to earn their own marriage portions.[4]

595. The same customs in the Old Testament. In 1 Sam. i Hannah vowed that if God would give her a son she would devote him to the Lord, in sign of which no razor should touch him. She gave him to be an *ædituus*, who lived in the temple awaiting divine instructions and commissions. In Josh. ix. 23, 27 we have a case of war captives condemned to menial service in the temple. In Ezek. xliv. 8, 9, the people are blamed for putting heathen in the temple service instead of doing it themselves. The *kedeshim*, temple prostitutes of both sexes, are frequently mentioned in the Old Testament, especially at every reformation of the religion. They seem to become objects of condemnation within the period of the history.

596. Antagonism of abundance and excess. The Germans had a Corn-mother, a goddess of agricultural growth and fertility. The Mexicans also had a mother-of-the-gods, Teteoinnan. The former became a harlot. The latter, by her sex activity, brought about growth and abundant reproduction, and became a goddess of lewdness.[5] Thus wherever the agricultural interest controls

---

[1] II, 3, 20.   [2] *Globus*, LXXV, 286.

[3] *Scripta Hist. Islandorum*, II, 67.

[4] Bancroft, *Native Races of the Pacific Coast*, I, 123; II, 676.

[5] *Archiv f. Anthrop.*, XXIX, 138, 150.

this set of ideas we see the struggle between the idea that unre-strained sex indulgence produces abundance and the idea that it produces excess, lewdness, and harm. We can still trace to the metaphorical use of "mother," "father," and "son," and also to the use of the same words to express the possession of a quality in a high degree, or a tie of destiny, some of the most important concepts of our own religion.

597. Survivals of sacral harlotry. Analogous customs in Hindostan. The early Portuguese travelers to the East found sacral harlotry in Cochin China. All virgins of noble birth were bound by vows from infancy. Otherwise no honorable man would marry them.[1] Modern Egyptian dancing girls, Ghowazy or Barmeky, had a tradition that they belonged to a race by themselves. They kept up isolation and peculiar customs. Each was compelled to surrender to a stranger and then to marry a man of her own group.[2] "Probably Heaven and Earth are the most ancient of all Vedic gods, and from their fancied union, as husband and wife, the other deities and the whole universe were at first supposed to spring." "The whole world is embodied in the woman. . . . Women are gods. Women are vitality," say the Vedic Scriptures. In Manu[3] "the self-existent god is described as dividing his own substance and becoming half male and half female."[4] A competent author, who wrote at the beginning of the nineteenth century, says that the women attached to the temples in Hindostan sang and danced twice a day, the songs being about mythological subjects and indecent according to the current mores of everyday life. Vows play a very important part in the Hindoo system of sacral harlotry. A woman, with the consent of her husband, vowed her unborn child, if a girl, to the temple, in order to get an easy confinement. It was no dis-grace to a family to have a daughter living this life. Barren women visited remote temples, under a vow of self-devotion, in order to bear children. They were victimized by the priests. At festivals of Vishnu priests tried to enlist girls in the attendant

[1] Oliveira Martins, *As Raças Humanas*, II, 181.
[2] Burckhardt, *Arabic Proverbs*, 145. [3] *Laws*, I, 5.
[4] Monier-Williams, *Brahmanism and Hinduism*, 181–183.

multitude. The line between the sacral usage and licentiousness was broken down at some remote resorts, but in the great
temples the conduct of the women was not at all shameless,
although they were trained to please. They observed perfect
decorum. No one could venture on any impropriety with them.
The bystanders would not allow it, and the proceedings were all
controlled by strict rules. The Brahmins propounded a doctrine
that intercourse with the consecrated women would free from
sin.[1] The vows show us the motive which maintained this usage,
and these statements clearly show the conventionalization which
enveloped the whole. Although the practices in the temples
have undergone some modification, they still exist. There are
secret mysteries, and dramatic representations of mythological
incidents, which seem like survivals of the ancient usages above
mentioned.[2] There are courtesans at the temples near which
pilgrims congregate, and they pay part of their earnings to the
temple.[3] The holy festival of Jugganatha, at Puri, which is a
spring festival of Vedic origin, is a kind of Saturnalia, in which
the bonds of social order are loosened and the standards of
decency are laid aside. There are rites in which " words are
uttered by persons who, on other occasions, would think themselves disgraced by the use of them." [4] The Phalgun festival in
northern India commemorates Krishna's voluptuous amusements. The rites are indecent.[5] The mythological stories about
the gods have to be converted by interpretation or special pleas
into something which modern mores can tolerate.[6] Songs, dances,
pantomimes, and mythological dramas are represented in front
of the image of a deity by men, but in the presence of a general
company of men and women.[7] The Sakta worshipers are a sect
who worship Sakta, the mighty, mysterious, feminine force
recognized in nature, and which they personify as the Mother of
the Universe, like the ancient Mother-goddess. This goddess is
manifested, for Hindoos, in natural appetites, in highly developed

---

[1] Dubois, *Mœurs de l'Inde*, I, 434–439; 478–480; II, 353, 366, 370, 377.

[2] Wilkins, *Modern Hinduism*, 94, 216, 290; Monier-Williams, *Brahmanism and Hinduism*, 451.

[3] Wilkins, 242.

[4] *Jo. Roy. As. Soc.*, 1841, 239; Wilkins, 286.

[5] Wilkins, 235.

[6] *Ibid.*, 317.

[7] *Ibid.*, 216.

faculties by which one exalts one's self and defeats one's enemies. The rites of the sect are horrible and obscene, and have for their purpose to violate and outrage the restrictions in the mores. By those rites men and women obtain union with the Supreme Being. The members of the sect call themselves "perfect ones" and all others "beasts." They use mystic texts and secret orgies, at which they drink strong drinks, eat meat and fish, and practice sex license. They recognize no caste.[1] There are also other sects which have inverted all conceptions of decency, propriety, and expediency. They practice self-torture, crime, and uncleanliness, and use loathsome food, etc. In all these matters they show great ingenuity of invention. They are dying out.[2] There are also sects which are cannibal, incestuous, and practicers of secret license and obscenity.[3] In some parts of the Madras presidency, girls are made *basivis* by a vow of the parents, in order to give them the privileges of males. This custom may be derived from the institution of the " appointed daughter," that is, a daughter selected in order that her son may perform the rites for her father (who had no son) and may carry on the line. Modern *basivis* " live in their father's house. They do not marry, yet they bear children, the father of whom they may choose at pleasure, and the children inherit their family name." It is a device to insure male descendants, and is so regulated by religious consecration and rules that it is recognized in the mores. If a *basivi* breaks the rules she falls to a status which is very different. Men are also dedicated and wear female dress, if they are born imperfect or malformed.[4]

598. Lingam and yoni. The lingam symbol is to be seen all over India, alone or with the yoni. In some parts of India the lingam is worn as an amulet.[5] The word "lingam" is said to mean "symbol."[6] To Europeans the object seems indecent and obscene

---

[1] Monier-Williams, 185, 190.

[2] JASB, I, 477; III, 200; JAI, XXVI, 341; Monier-Williams, 87; Hopkins, *Relig. of India*, 491.

[3] Hopkins, *Relig. of India*, 456; JASB, I, 477, 492; III, 201.

[4] JASB, II, 322, 349; cf. JASB, I, 502.

[5] Monier-Williams, 254.

[6] Nivedita, *Web of Indian Life*, 212.

If it is of phallic origin, "the Hindus are no more conscious of the fact than we of the similar origin of the maypole."[1] It is no more erotic than an egg or a seed. It is a symbol of Siva, the eternal reproductive power of nature, reintegrating after disintegration. One form of Siva is androgyne. The dualism of the male, spirit, and the female, matter, is essential to all creation. "To one imbued with these dualistic conceptions the lingam and the yoni are suggestive of no improper ideas."[2]

599. Conventionalization. In all these cases it is evident that the mores extend their protection over archaic and sacred things, and preserve them instead of forbidding them. The great means of preserving them is by conventionalization. They are put under a conventional understanding, different from the everyday usages.with their ethics, and are judged by an arbitrary standard. In the English translation of the Bible words and phrases are used which are archaic and now under taboo in everyday life Our children have to be taught that "that is in the Bible," that is, they have to learn the conventionalization by which the archaic forms are covered. The words in the Bible are not subject to criticism, and they cannot be cited to justify similar usage in common life.

600. Mores of Hindostan. The phenomena which. are presented in Hindostan, when studied from our standpoint, show how completely different may be the estimate of things according to use and wont. The phenomena are very different in character. Some of them are cases of degeneracy and aberration of customs, after they have been discarded by the mores, have become vicious, and have fallen into the hands of abandoned persons who have given up all position inside the mores. Others of these customs show how old usages, when brought in question, lose innocence. Consciousness and reflection produce doubt and then shame. Sometimes things which are private or secret by convention come in contact with things which are secret by vice. All the phenomena in Hindostan show how completely the moral effect depends on the integrity or decay of conventionalization. The conventionalization is still so strong

---

[1] Nivedita, 212.   [2] Monier-Williams, 78, 183, 224.

that the effects on public morals which we might expect are not produced. Public manners are marked by decency and propriety and the society is not vicious.[1] Things which exist under conventionalization never furnish grounds for an ethical judgment on the group which practices them.

601. Mexican mores. Drunkenness. In Mexico also there were goddesses of erotic passion to whom men and women were consecrated. Courtesans sometimes immolated themselves in the service of the goddess. The notion of virtue in resistance to passion existed, but the goddess, like the Greek Venus, resented any effort to escape her sway and exerted herself to defeat it.[2] The Mayas did not maintain a severe form of sex taboo and they had festivals at which that taboo was entirely suspended.[3] Pederasty also existed under the sanction of religion. Young men in the training house, which was a house of lamentation and penance, were allowed license which was contrary to the current mores of the society, but was an old privilege of soldiers. The dances which they performed daily were obscene. The persons in the dance represented vegetation demons, and the dances helped to get good crops.[4] The notion was not to employ sympathetic magic, but the men, by parallel operations, were supposed to help in the work of fructification which the demons were accomplishing in the plant. Hence a great drama of human coöperation was carried on in the dances. Snakes and frogs were eaten because they were demons of rain and growth. The obscene dances were " not consequences of sex desire, but, on account of their antiquity, they were accepted as a matter of course." [5] At the time of the Spanish conquest public opinion about the dances was not fixed, but they lasted on through the force of ancient religious tradition. We may be sure that the case of Mexico throws light on the ancient usages of sacral harlotry. In comparatively recent times there were cases in Russia of sex license on the eve of great Christian festivals.[6] There is a parallel also, amongst the Mexicans, in

[1] Dubois, I, 439. [2] Bancroft, *Native Races of the Pacific Coast*, II, 336; III, 377.
[3] *Ibid.*, II, 676. [4] *Archiv f. Anthrop.*, XXIX, 153, 158, 164.
[5] *Ibid.*, 173. [6] Petri, *Anthropology (russ.)*, 435.

the case of drunkenness. Religion controlled and forbade drunkenness, but then again allowed it on specified occasions. To drink *pulque* was forbidden, under penalty of death, except to prescribed persons at certain festivals, but on the festival of the fire god all intoxicated themselves by custom and tradition.[1] Kings in Central America were expressly allowed to intoxicate themselves at festivals, and functionaries were appointed to perform their duties while they were incapacitated. It is nowadays considered not dishonorable to become intoxicated during festivals, and "it may be observed that Indians now thank God for the gift of drunkenness."[2] That is a case of the persistence of ideas born of old mores long after another religion and social system have displaced the folkways themselves.

602. Japanese mores. In Japan the government formerly bought girls of fourteen from their parents and caused them to be educated in feminine accomplishments. For ten years they lived as courtesans to the profit of the state. They were then discharged with a sum of money. The number of them at one time was twenty thousand. They furnished at the tea houses afternoon entertainments at which families were present, but men alone remained later.[3] When a people, through acquaintance with mores different from its own, is led to philosophize about the latter, or is made conscious of them and uncertain about them, then the old mores of that people lose their innocence. The Japanese have had much experience of this within fifty years.

603. Chinese religion and mores. For contrast it may be worth while to notice the evidence collected by Schallmeyer[4] that the specifically Chinese religions are free from all immoral notions and usages. Indeed the Chinese religions are said to be hostile to indecency. Meadows is quoted as saying that any sentence of the canonical writings of China could be read in any English family without offense, and that there is nothing in Chinese religious rites resembling the immoral rites which are met with elsewhere. Chinese lyric poetry is said to be pure.

---

[1] *Archiv f. Anthrop.*, XXIX, 16   [3] Oliphant, *China and Japan*, II, 494.
[2] *Globus*, LXXXVII, 130.   [4] *Vererbung und Auslese*, 200.

604. Philosophy of interest in reproduction. Incest. Some
reserve in regard to the interpretation of myths is proper and
necessary, but the absorbing interest of sex production for man,
after he begins to depend upon it and coöperate with it for his
food supply, is a product of the study of myths which may be
accepted with confidence. That interest was no more sensual
than interest in the rainfall, and the mythologizing about it was
no more depraved than mythologizing about creation or language.
Men were sure to apply all which they learned about reproduction in food plants and animals to their own reproduction. If
Chaldean civilization goes back five or six thousand years before
Christ, then the Chaldeans had had ample time, even before
Hammurabi, to experience the evils of overpopulation and of
sex vice. In the Chaldean mythology Ishtar, goddess of all sex
attraction and repulsion, destroyed all the lovers whom she
selected. She had the double character, which appears in all
myths and philosophy, of sex license and sex renunciation
together. She was a goddess of the mother family and polyan-
dric.[1] The two policies, sex license and sex renunciation, were
both advocated at the same time in the early centuries of the
Christian era and in the Middle Ages. Men found out that the
problem of reproduction for them was far more complicated than
the multiplication of dates to the utmost limit. At this point of
knowledge instinctive or intelligent regulations had to be put
on physical appetites. For primitive men the reproductive
function is as simple a function as eating or sleeping. It is not
in itself wicked or base. It is naïve until knowledge comes.
Then it is found that rules must be made to regulate the interest.
If there are rules, there is the sense of wrongdoing in the
breach of them. A thing which is tabooed becomes interesting
and more or less awful. The numbers of the sexes are never
exactly equal, and the proportion is further disturbed by polygamy. Therefore experience of evil and inconvenience forced
some reflection and some judgments as to life policy. Regulations were devised behind which there was a philosophy of the
satisfaction of interests ; that is to say, mores were developed

[1] Tiele-Gehrich, *Relig. in Alterthume*, I, 169.

to cover the case. There seems also to be some connection between sacral harlotry and the prevention of incest. The poorest who cannot marry or buy slaves have always practiced incest (sec. 516). Sacral harlotry won another religious sanction from these cases. In the laws of Hammurabi we find two classes of women attached to the temple. If the interpretations of the specialists may be trusted, the arrangement was in one class of cases in the nature of a life annuity, and those who had no husband had the god for a husband, — an idea which, with one or another new coloring, has come down to our own time. That any one should renounce the sex function was not within the mental horizon of early times. When the women lived in the temple that fact established conventionalization about them and gave to their life that regulation which has made decency and order in all ages. Their case was defined and sanctioned in the mores. The couples retired outside the temple.[1] When marriage was accompanied by very easy divorce and could not be defined except as a form of property right of the husband, when there were concubines who were not wives only because they had no property, and slaves who had no defined relation to the household until they had borne children to the head of it, the women in the temple might be surrounded by other special forms of taboo which would give them a status within the mores. They were "holy" by virtue of their consecration to the goddess.[2] So far as we know, their lives were not spent in dissipation. The accounts in Herodotus and Baruch vi. 43, of the later usage at Babylon show that there was method and decorum in the institution, and that it was carried on with conventional dignity. It is our custom to think out the consistency of all our doctrines and usages. It is certain that ancient peoples did not do that, just as the masses now do not. They accepted and lived in unquestioned usage. Therefore we know of cases in classic society in which maidens and matrons on special occasions shared in functions which seem totally repugnant to their character. The explanation lies in conventionalization within

---

[1] Herod., I, 199; Hosea iv. 14; W. R. Smith, *Relig. of the Semites*, 454.

[2] W. R. Smith, *Relig. of the Semites*, 141.

the mores for an occasion or under a conjuncture of circum
stances. It is unquestionably possible that in that way lewdness
can be set aside and thus corrupting effect on character can be
prevented.

605. The archaic is sacred. In the minds of primitive people
all which is archaic is sacred and all which is novel is questionable. Therefore religion holds and consecrates whatever is
archaic and traditional. The appetites of men were anterior to
any mores regulative of them, and the goddess Ishtar, Astarte,
Aphrodite, or Venus is a goddess of erotic passion and reproduction. The folkways devised to prevent experienced ills are
an invasion of her domain and a rebellion against her sway. The
regulations cannot be made absolute for a long time. There
must be a compromise. Some females must be given to the
goddess as devotees, at least under conditions, or there must be
set times and places within which her sway shall be unhampered
by human rules. The conditions establish conventionalization
around an institution. It is by this process and by changing
the conditions that marriage has been made what it now is.
Concubinage, slave women, harlotry, and all other forms but the
prescribed one have been put under taboo. It is very possible
that some future generation will look back in wonder at our
self-complacency, which feels no care or responsibility for the
women who are forced, in our system, to renounce sex. It is
safe to say that the Chaldeans of 2500 B.C. would have been as
much shocked at the inhumanity of our arrangement as we can
be at the lewdness of theirs.

606. Child sacrifice. The temple consecration of women must
be connected with child sacrifice. The latter is logically anterior.
Their historical relation we do not know. To dedicate a girl to
the goddess would be an alternative to the sacrifice of her. All
forms of child sacrifice and sacral suicide go back to the pangs
and terrors of men under loss and calamity. Something must be
found which would wring pity and concession from the awful
superior powers who afflict mankind. Every one born under this
human lot must perish if he is not redeemed. His first vicarious
sacrifice is his firstborn, but if he can get a war captive from a

foreign group this substitute may be accepted. The Mexican human sacrifices were of this kind. The people stood around assenting and rejoicing, because the rite meant salvation to themselves and their children. A man who took a captive in war gave him to the priest to be sacrificed, and he might not eat of the flesh, "since the victim was in a sense his son," that is, took the place of his son as a vicarious sacrifice for himself. They also sacrificed their own infants.[1] Child sacrifice expresses the deepest horror and suffering produced by experience of the human lot. Men must do it. Their interests demanded it, however much it might pain them. Human sacrifices may be said to have been universal. They lasted down to the half-civilized stage of all nations and sporadically even later,[2] and they have barely ceased amongst the present half-civilized peoples.[3] They are not primarily religious. They are a reaction of men under the experience of the ills of life, inventing a world philosophy and putting agents behind it, in order to have something, if it be only a delusion, to which hope of escape can attach. Human sacrifices are based on an inference or deduction. There is behind them an assumption as to the character and logic of the superior powers who rule the aleatory interest. It is not until skepticism arises as to this assumption that the usage can be given up.

607. Beast sacrifice substituted for human sacrifice. In the case of Abraham and Isaac, the former was "tried" by God, apparently meaning that he underwent some doubt whether he ought not to sacrifice his son as other west Semites did theirs, and whether a beast would not suffice (Gen. xxii. 7). For his descendants the legend fixed the usage and doctrine (verse 13), different from that of the other west Semites, that a beast was a due substitute. The Chaldees followed the same reasoning.[4] According to the mythology of the Egyptians there was a great destruction of men in the reign of the god Ra, but when he mounted to the sky he replaced the sacrifice of men by that of

---

[1] Bancroft, *Native Races of the Pacific Coast*, II, 305, 308–309.

[2] Schrader, *Prehist. Antiq. of the Aryans*, 422.

[3] Hopkins, *Relig. of India*, 363, 450.

[4] Maspero, *Peuples de l'Orient*, I, 680.

beasts.[1] In the tragedy of *Iphigenia*, Iphigenia is not slain. Artemis snatches her away and puts a hind in her place. Robertson Smith [2] thinks that the notion of the ancients that the sacrifice of human beings was anterior to that of beasts, and that the latter were substitutes, was a "false inference from traditional forms of ritual that had ceased to be understood." At Hierapolis sacrificed children were called oxen.[3] All the Baals demanded human sacrifices.[4] In every case in which the mores had overcome the terror which made human sacrifices, the mythology invented explanations. It was forbidden to the Jews to make their children "pass through the fire" to Molech.[5] They often did it. This shows that their mores had not yet outgrown it, but that religious teachers were trying to forbid it.[6] They held the same doctrine as the neighboring nations, that the firstborn belonged to God.[7] The firstborn must be sacrificed or redeemed.[8] They had doctrines of ransom by beasts, as above, or by money,[9] or by circumcision, if the incoherent text is rightly interpreted.[10] Nevertheless, they never were sure enough of their position before the captivity to *hold to it* against the faith and usage of neighboring nations.[11] The doctrine in Micah vi. 6–8, as early as the end of the eighth century B.C., raised the real issue about the sense and utility of all sacrifices in its widest form, but that doctrine was much too far beyond the mores of the time to have any effect.

608. Mexican doctrine of greater power through death. Preuss says: "In the ancient Mexican cultus I recognized, to my astonishment, that really spirits were killed in the sacrificed men, in order that they [the spirits] might thus be rendered capable of being born again, and rendering greater services to men." [12]

---

[1] Maspero, *Peuples de l'Orient*, I, 123. [3] *Ibid.*, 366, 375.

[2] *Relig. of the Semites*, 365. [4] Cf. Deut. xviii. 10; 2 Kings xvi. 3; xxi. 6.

[5] Levit. xviii. 21; Deut. xviii. 10. Molech is a false word. It has the consonants of the word for "king" and the vowels of the word for "shameful thing" (W. R. Smith, *Relig. of the Semites*, 67).

[6] 2 Kings xvi. 3; xvii. 7; xxi. 6; xxiii. 10. [7] Ex. xxii. 29.

[8] Ex. xxxiv. 20. [9] Num. xviii. 15. [10] Ex. iv. 24.

[11] Jer. xxxii. 35; Ezek. xx. 26, 31. According to 2 Chron. xxviii. 3, Ahaz offered his son in the stress of war (Hastings, Dict. of the Bible, *Relig. of Israel*).

[12] *Globus*, LXXXVI, 321.

Death was believed to enhance the power of the spirits who ruled meteorological phenomena. The notion was that insects caused meteorological phenomena; then they were gods; the insects and beasts gave to the gods the magic power which they (insects and beasts) once had over rainfall, etc. The humming bird which hibernates and wakes again in spring was thought to cause the heat of summer. Therefore it was taken to be an envelope of the war god. Free flow of blood lets loose magic power. Hence the great bloodshedding in the Mexican cultus. "Human sacrifice is in Mexico the same in sense as beast sacrifice. In both cases, magic powers, magic beasts and spirits, are killed." By death new birth with greater magic power becomes possible.[1]

609. Motives of child sacrifice. The Semites adopted the world philosophy which lies back of human sacrifice and incorporated it with their religion, which thereby became gloomy and ferocious. What a man must sacrifice was what he loved most, and that was his firstborn child. It was rationalizing to argue that a beast could be substituted with equal effect, and we often find that people who had advanced to that point of philosophy, when face to face with a great calamity showed that they did not believe that the effect was equal. They went back to child sacrifice.[2] The Hebrews in the seventh century thought that they felt the wrath of God and they tried to avert it in this way.[3] Tiele thinks that there is no evidence of child sacrifice or of the temple consecration of women in the Euphrates valley in historical times, but in Syria and Arabia child sacrifice lasted on in spite of the culture of the Aramæans and Phœnicians. In old Arabia fathers burned their little daughters as sacrifices to the goddess.[4] Human sacrifices were used for auguries before any important enterprise, and as thank offerings for victory or success. Every year a number of children of the foremost families were sacrificed as an expiation for the sins of the nation, "while fiendish music drowned their cries and the lamentations of their mothers."[5]

[1] *Globus*, LXXXVI, 117–119.

[2] Possibly 2 Kings iii. 27; 2 Chron. xxviii. 3; Pietschmann, *Phoenizier*, 167.

[3] W. R. Smith, *Relig. of the Semites*, 465.   [4] *Ibid.*, 370.

[5] Tiele-Gehrich, *Relig. im Alterthum*, I, 212, 240; Maspero, *Peuples de l'Orient*, I, 680; Sanchuniathon apud Euseb., *Prep. Evang.*, I, 10.

The Carthaginians kept up the custom. The leading families were bound to furnish the sacrifice as representatives of the commonwealth. The children to be sacrificed were selected by lot from those who were liable. Children were exchanged in order to be saved. The parents might not lament, for to do so would deprive the sacrifice of its efficacy.[1] The custom was an abomination to the Romans, but it was so firmly fixed in the mores of the Carthaginians that the conquerors could not stop it. The proconsul Tiberius put an end to it by hanging the priests of the cult to the trees of their own temple grove.[2] As Tertullian says that soldiers who executed this order were still living when he wrote, the order of Tiberius must have been issued about the middle of the second century A.D. or a little later.

610. Dedication by vows. The connection between child sacrifice and the temple consecration of girls is in the substitution of the latter for the former, as a ransom. The girl devoted to death belonged to the goddess in one way, if not in the other. Vows made in illness sometimes included such substitution. In the historic period, after child sacrifice had ceased in the Euphrates valley, many variations occurred. Barren women made vows. Children were vowed to the goddess for life or for a time. They were redeemed by money which they earned in the temple life. The accumulation of a dowry was only a variation.[3] In later times (second century A.D.) we find the sacrifice of a woman's hair as a substitute for herself.[4] Men were also dedicated in sex perversion.

611. Degeneration of the customs of consecrating women. Evidently vicarious sacrifice and expiatory sacrifice are very ancient heathen ideas. They contain deductions and assumptions about the nature of the deity which are of the first theological importance. The cases of custom which have been described also show the power and persistency of theological dogma to override for centuries the strongest interests and sentiments. Evidently the variations in the custom marked the breaking down of the boundaries which held it firm in the religious

[1] Pietschmann, *Phoenizier*, 229.
[2] Tertullian, *Apol.*, 9.
[3] Pietschmann, *Phoenizier*, 222.
[4] Lucian, *De Syria Dea*, 6.

mores. The Babylonian custom described by Herodotus seems to be a variation by which every woman was held bound to the goddess. Then sensuality, priestcraft, greed, and frivolity easily used such a custom until it became a root of corruption. This is what happened, and forms of the custom which had no sense but the gratification of licentiousness spread around the Mediterranean. The old female sex mores were very simple and austere, but they were corrupted after the middle of the second century B.C. Those of Roman Carthage, if we can trust Salvianus, became more corrupt than those of Punic Carthage ever had been. They were less ferocious and more frankly voluptuous. Salvianus's description of southern Gaul makes it as bad as Africa. According to him the Vandals were pure-minded, and their mores were so pure and firm that they successfully resisted the Roman corruption and put the sex relation back again on the basis of the "law of God."[1]

612. Our traditions from Israel. If now we turn back to the Israelites we can see the stream by which our own mores have come down to us. There arose amongst the Israelites, in the tenth century B.C., an opposition to the religion which was common to the west Semites. It was like the reform of the Iranian religion by the magi, who produced a religion which was too severe and exacting for any but priests to live by it. There have also been many attempts to reform Islam from within. They have taken the form of throwing off later additions and returning to primitive purity, that is, to the mode of life of Arabs in Mohammed's time. In some cases (e.g. the Wahabees of the nineteenth century) the reforms have originated with people who were on a lower grade of life than the mass of Moslems. Present-day scholars find the origin of the resistance of Israelitish prophets to the prevailing religion of western Asia in the hostility of a rustic population, with a primitive mode of life and archaic mores, to the luxury of Tyre and Sidon, wealthy cities of commerce and industry.[2] The conflict was between two sets of mores. The biblical scholars now tell us that Jahveh

---

[1] *De Gubernat. Dei*, VII, 72–77; cf. VII, 15–16, 27, 86, 97–100.
[2] Barton, *Semitic Origins*, 300.

was a Baal amongst other Palestinian Baals until this antagonism arose. Then he was made the god in whose name the ancient mores of Israel were defended against the introduction ot luxury and licentiousness. The antagonism was between simple, rustic, largely pastoral modes of life and the ways of cities with wealth, culture, and luxury. This is a permanent social antagonism, but it carried with it the antagonism of simplicity to sensuality, materialism, formal manners, and luxury. For four or five centuries a succession of " prophets " developed the antagonism between the Jahveh religion and heathenism. They maintained that Jahveh was not only the single god of the Hebrews but the sole God of all the earth. Other gods were nullities. The prophets condemned idolatry, and all sensuality, licentiousness, and bestiality, with which they connected all sorcery and divination. They insisted on a broad and firm sex taboo and denounced sacral harlotry and child sacrifice together. It must be remembered that the peoples of that age generally regarded sex usages which seem to us the most abominable as trivial, unworthy of notice, matters of personal liberty and choice. Brahmins, a century ago, held that view of pederasty.[1] The prophets also set in opposition to their own traditional ritual religion a doctrine of righteousness, by which religion was made ethical. It was a marvelous product for an insignificant hill people. It is, however, to be noticed that in the *Zend-Avesta* there was also a great revolt against sex vice.[2]

613. How the Jewish view of sensuality came to prevail. The religious system of the Jewish prophets never has become the actual popular religion of any people. The Old Testament contains the story of the protests and failures of the prophets. Their work did not issue from the mores of the Jewish nation, and did not influence the mores before the captivity. The prophets were trying to introduce a new world philosophy by virtue of its ethical value and by interpretations of current political history. In Jer. xliv we see the latter argument turned against the prophet. The people cite their own experience. When they served the Queen of Heaven they fared well.

[1] Dubois, *Mœurs de l'Inde*, 439.   [2] Darmstetter, *Zend-Avesta*, I, 100, 102.

In the rabbinical period the Jews emphasized everything which could differentiate them from heathen, and in the New Testament we find that idolatry and sensuality are presented as the two great heathen characteristics which Christians are to avoid. It is impossible for us to know to what extent the mores of the masses, in the western Roman empire, were marked by the ancient Roman austerity in the sex mores. It is, however, reasonable to believe that the ancient mores prevailed most in the class amongst whom Christian converts were found. Salvianus also gives to the German nations very remarkable testimony as to their freedom from sensuality and sex vice. The experience of societies also went to prove that such vice can corrupt the finest brain and the most cultivated character; also that, if it becomes current in a society, as pederasty and prostitution did in the Greco-Roman world, it will eat out all manly virtues, all coöperative devotion, the love of children, the energy of invention and production, of an entire population. Thus by the syncretism of the mores of the nations, and by experience, the conviction was produced that the view of sensuality and sex vice which the Jewish prophets taught was true, and that that view was the most important part of the mores and of religion for the welfare of mankind.

CHAPTER XVII

POPULAR SPORTS, EXHIBITIONS, AND DRAMA

Limits. The cases of public amusement and entertainment which shall here be mentioned are such as were within the limits of usage and accepted propriety at the time. They are not cases of vice or of disputed propriety at the time. Drunkenness, gambling, bull baiting, cockfighting, and prize fighting are amusements which have entered into the mores of groups and subgroups, as bullfighting still does in Spain, but they were limited to classes or groups, or they were important on account of the excess, or they were disapproved by great numbers or by the ecclesiastical authorities. They would, therefore, lie outside the mores, to which the cases to be noticed belonged. The theater in England in Charles II's time testified to a depraved taste and a low standard of morals, but it was temporary and indeed limited in time. In different groups also the moral standards are unequal at the same time, and the mores are on different levels. There is a wider limit now for romances and dramas in France than in English-speaking countries. The cases which now interest us are those of long and wide currency, which the mores have firmly established according to current standards, even though moralists may have inveighed against them sometimes, as the same class now sometimes denounces all dancing.

The cases here to be noticed are further illustrations of the fact that the mores can make anything right, and can protect anything from condemnation, in addition to those in the last two chapters.

614. Literature and drama in ethology. Poetry, drama, and literary fiction are useful to ethology in one or the other of two ways: (1) they reveal facts of the mores; (2) they show the longings and ideals of the group, — in short, what the people like and wish for. The second division includes mythology, fairy tales, and extravaganzas. The taste for them, if it exists, is a feature of the mores, but in fact such a taste is hardly ever popular. It is a product of culture. Myths, legends, proverbs, fables, riddles, etc., are popular products.

615. Public amusements of the uncivilized. Reversion to archaic, "natural" ways. We find in savage life, almost universally unless the group has been crushed by conquest or misfortune, festivals, games, dances, and orgies, which are often celebrated with masks and dramatic action. The motives are fidelity to the traditions of ancestors, entertainment, sex excitement, war enthusiasm, and occult influence in aid of the food quest. The dramatic representation of sex attraction and of the ways of animals is often intensely graphic, and it gives great pleasure to the spectators. An occult effect, to bring about what is desired in war or the chase by enacting it in a dance or play, involves demonism, the existing form of religion. Therefore religion, dramatic dances, music, songs, emotional suggestion, and sex stimulation are intertwined from low barbarism or savagery. Experience of the perils and pains of sexual excess and overpopulation force the development of folkways of restraint, which are customary and conventional regulations of primary natural impulses. At the recurring points of time at which the festivals are held there is often a reversion from the moral status created by the later mores to the ancient " natural " ways, because the later ways are a reflection on the ancestors who were " uncultivated." Their ghosts will be displeased at the new ways and will inflict ill fortune on the group. The festival is not a time at which to emphasize the novelty, but to set it aside and revert to old ways. How far back shall the reversion go? What is " natural "? As no one ever has known from what depths of beastliness, rendered more acute by some intelligence, man came, no one has ever known what " nature " would be. Men reverted actually to some ancient custom of their ancestors beyond which they knew nothing, and which therefore to them seemed primitive and original. The festivals were always outside of the routine of regular life. We, for a holiday frolic, relax, for ourselves and our children, the discipline of ordinary life ; for instance, on the Fourth of July. In the theater we make allowances for what we would not tolerate in the street or parlor. That a thing is in jest is, and always has been, an excuse for what is a little beyond the limit otherwise observed. It was a favorite Arab jest to fasten the train of a woman's dress, while she was sitting, to the waist of it, so that when she arose her dress would be disordered.[1] She must learn to guard herself.

616. Chaldean and Mexican myths of reproduction dramatically represented. In the mythical period of Chaldea the worship of the Great Mother Ishtar (the patroness of sex attraction, but a goddess whose love was a calamity to all her husbands,[2] perhaps a mythical representation of the perils and pains of sex) was a setting loose of sex passion from the later societal (" moral ") regulations,

[1] Wellhausen, *Skizzen und Vorarbeiten*, III, 85.
[2] Maspero, *Peuples de l'Orient*, I, 580.

in favor of the original passionate impulse of sex and reproduction. The festival was, therefore, a period of license. The seat of the licentious rites, and of sacral prostitution, was Uruk, the city of the dead (i.e. of ancestors), where men liked to be buried (in order to join their ancestors).[1] The Tammuz (Adonis) worship was connected with the worship of Ishtar, the relation between the god and the goddess being different in different myths. The Tammuz worship was a dramatic enactment of the death and resurrection of the god (connected with the decay and renewal of the world of vegetation), with corresponding lamentations and rejoicings of the worshipers.[2] In Mexico we find a parallel pantomime of the nature process at a religious harvest festival, the pantomime being used for occult magic, in order to get good crops in the next season. Obscene figures and rites were used. There is a maize goddess who is the "Mother of the Gods." The union of the sun god with the earth gives fertility, so that the food supply is at stake in these rites and notions.[3] This most absorbing interest of mankind drove men's minds along the same lines of world philosophy. The "Mother of the Gods," by her sex activity, brought about growth on earth and became goddess of lewdness and filth, just as the German Corn-mother became a harlot. So the goddess by whose activity the earth bears flowers was honored at a festival at which boys and girls nine or ten years old became senselessly drunk and perpetrated sex vice. This was at a *religious* festival.[4] Here then we find reversion to more primitive sex mores, and dramatic representation of a myth, conjoined in religion, on the very threshold of the higher civilization. The reversion to primitive sex mores to satisfy notions of duty to religion and ancestors comes to us as an incomprehensible violation of "primary instincts," which we have inferred from ideas that we can trace back beyond any known origin, which we suppose to be universally accepted, and which seem to us axiomatic as to social welfare. The only way to understand the case is to take the standpoint of the mores of that time. The mores contained the answer to the questions: How far back shall

[1] Tiele-Gehrich, *Relig. im Altert.*, I, 160.
[2] Barton, *Semitic Origins*, 85.
[3] *Archiv für Anthrop.*, XXIX, 129.
[4] *Ibid.*, 138, 150.

we go ? What shall be the degree of license at the festival ? At the limit fixed by custom the mores extend their sanction over the function and make it "right." Another source of barbaric festivals may be noticed. Men won victories over the elements and over beasts before they won victories over each other. This is true of remote antiquity and of primitive society. It is also true of the Middle Ages. The destruction of great beasts, demons, and other monsters led to dramatic and religious festivals. Magnin [1] thinks that he could make a cycle of beasts, of which Reineke Fuchs would be the last link, anterior to the cycles of Arthur and Charlemagne.

617. Limit of toleration for propriety in exhibitions. Therefore : What shall be the limit of toleration in theatrical and other exhibitions with respect to dress, language, gesture, etc., in order to define propriety, is altogether a matter of the mores. It is not conceivable that the *Lysistrata* of Aristophanes could be presented on any public stage in Christendom. The whole play is beyond the toleration of modern mores. We meet with jugglers in Homer,[2] also mountebanks and tumblers.[3] The *kubisteteres* spun around on the perpendicular axis of the body, and are compared to the wheel of the potter. Then they pitched down headforemost, like plungers or tumblers turning somersaults. Some archæologs have thought that the play of these persons had some analogy with that of the cubic stones which were so prominent in the cult of the Phrygian Cybele. If that analogy is accepted, then the pyramidal dance must be regarded as originally hieratic and consecrated to Cybele. That dance was at first aristocratic, but speedily became popular and descended to the mountebanks.[4]

618. Origin of Athenian drama. The theater originated in the Dionysiac mysteries of the Greeks, in which dramatic action and responsive choruses were employed. Sex symbols were used without reserve. Intoxication and ecstasy belonged to due performance. In later mysteries dramatic action was employed to present myths and legends, or religious doctrines, in order to get

---

[1] *Origines du Théâtre Moderne,* 60. [3] *Il.,* XVIII, 601.

[2] *Il.,* XVI, 750; XVIII, 604.   [4] Magnin, *Origines du Théâtre Moderne,* 178.

the powerful effects in suggestion which dramatic action exerts. Many myths presented acts such as later mores could not tolerate. Allowance had to be made for the representations, as we now make allowances for Bible stories and Shakespeare. We know that the mysteries were often in bad repute for their indecency and realism, even in an age of low standards. Anybody who is not in the convention can scoff at it, however low his own code may be. The Greeks described the Phrygian mysteries as abominable and immoral, while they praised and admired the Eleusinian. "The former were introduced by slaves and foreigners, and participated in by the superstitious and ignorant. They were celebrated for money by strolling priests, and any one who paid a fee was initiated without preparation, except some ritual acts. There was no solemnity in the surroundings, and no dignity in the ceremonial, but all was vulgar and sordid."[1] The Athenian drama, in the fifth century B.C., went through an amazing development and reached high perfection. The art of the theater was especially cultivated. As to the effect of the dramas on the character of the spectators, it is to be noticed that they were presented only once in the year, at the greater festival of Dionysus in the spring, and that then a large number of plays were represented. The spectators, at Athens, were a very mixed assemblage and included the populace, "who remained populace in spite of any beautiful verses which they might chance to hear." They cared only to be amused, "just like modern audiences."[2]

619. Dramatic taste and usage in worship. Customs derived from the mysteries. About the time of Christ, by syncretism all the religions took on a dramatic form in their ritual, with liturgies and responses, on account of the attractiveness of that form for worshipers. The Christian year was built up as a drama of the life of Christ. The ceremony of the mass was produced by an application of modes of worship which, so far as we can learn, were devised and used in the mysteries. "There is unmistakable evidence that a marriage ceremony of a religious nature existed, and that this ceremony stood in close relation to

[1] Ramsay, *Relig. of Greece and Asia Minor*, Hastings's Dict., Addit. vol., 120.
[2] Beloch, *Griech. Gesch.*, I, 579, 592.

a part of the ritual of the mysteries. In fact, the marriage was, as it were, a reproduction by the bride and bridegroom of a scene from the divine life, i.e. from the mystic drama. The formula, 'I escaped evil: I found better,' was repeated by the celebrant who was initiated in the Phrygian mysteries; and the same formula was pronounced as part of the Athenian marriage ceremony. Another formula, 'I have drunk from the *kymbalon*,' was pronounced by the initiated; and drinking from the same cup has been proved to have formed part of a ceremony performed in the temple by the betrothed pair." "It is an extremely important fact that the human marriage ceremony was thus celebrated by forms taken from the mysteries; and the conclusion must be that the human pair repeat the action in the way in which the god and goddess first performed and consecrated it, and that, in fact, they play the parts of the god and goddess in the sacred drama. This single example is, as we may be sure, typical of a whole series of actions."[1]

620. The word "god." "That man when he dies becomes a god was considered already in the fourth century B.C. to be part of the teaching conveyed in the mysteries."[2] This meant no more than the earlier notion that when a man died he became a ghost. The word "god" was used in senses very strange to our ears,[3] and to quote an expression of any writer of the beginning of the Christian era in which he uses the word "god," and to give to that word our sense of it, is to be led into great error. The age was one which put all its religion in dramatic form and acted it out. It was an age with a gift for manufacturing rites and liturgies.

621. Kin yields to religion as social tie. This was due to a great ethnological change which was then coming to its culmination. The kin tie, which had been the primitive mode of association and coherence of groups, began to break down in the sixth century B.C. in Greece. It was superseded by the social tie of a common religious faith and ritual. The Pythagorean and Orphic sects developed this tie. They had a revelation of the

---

[1] Ramsay in Hastings's Dict., Addit. vol., 129–130. [2] *Ibid.*, 125.
[3] Boissier, *Religion Romaine*, I, 132.

other world, a system of mystic and cathartic rites, which cleared men of ritual uncleanness, purified them, and "saved" them. The cathartic rites were a means of warding off evil spirits and did the work of the old shamans.[1] The sectarian brotherhood of the initated, the "church," the faith, the contrast of ordinary life with the ecstatic emotions of the mysteries, the consequent antagonism of the "flesh" or the "world," and the "spirit," were easy deductions from the teaching and ritual of the sects.[2] It was all concentrated in the godlikeness, divinity, or immortality of the human soul, with the mystic notions of union between the soul and God. "Mysticism, as doctrine and theory, grew up from the soil of a more ancient practice in worship." "The worship of Dionysus must have furnished the first germ of the belief in the immortality of the soul."[3] The idea of the Orphic mysteries was that humanity is suffering and sinful, and must be initiated in order to wash away its stains and be redeemed from its sins. Initiation puts a man in communication with the divinity. The soul is raised by ecstasy to feel its own divinity, which is the deepest element in all mystic religion. In all this compound of rites and notions the great antecedent philosophy was not the same as ours. It was demonism, superstitious anxiety about the world of demons, who floated around men and stretched their hands out of the surrounding darkness to seize them. It was from these that men wanted to be "saved." Atonement was to be made to the chthonic gods, for they were displeased at ritual uncleanness, and the chthonic cults had the other world in view.[4] The uncleanness was ritual, and hence it came from anything far out of the regular order, either by abomination or holiness. The rabbis held that the handling of the Scriptures defiled the hands and called for ceremonial washing (Num. xix. 8, 10).[5]

622. Combination of religion and drama. Syncretism. The interest of all this for our present purpose is the combination of religious ideas with dramatic representation. Processions of all kinds easily turn into such representations. Rites and ceremonies

---

[1] Rohde, *Psyche*, II, 70.   [2] *Ibid.*, 34.   [3] *Ibid.*, 3.
[4] Wobbermin, *Beeinflussung des Urchristenthums durch das Mysterienwesen*, 21
[5] W. R. Smith, *Relig. of the Semites*, 426. See sec. 565.

are but a form of drama. Symbols and emblems have the same character. The old religions were subjected to criticism, which means that they had lost their authority. They did not verify when the attempt was made to use them for societal needs. Slaves, merchants, soldiers, etc., afloat in the world, associated from choice and contributed traditions from the whole known world. Then syncretism began, and a body of sectarian notions was formed. There was a new totemism, a breaking down of national religion, a spirit of propaganda, and a setting forth of the whole in all dramatic forms.[1] In the sects women were admitted, a fact of double significance. It was an emancipation for the women and a peril for the sect. The doubt with which the mysteries are now regarded is due to the uncertainty as to the relations of the sexes in them. The word "orgy" originally meant worship, or rites, then secret rites, that is, mysteries. The sense in which the word has come down to us shows the notion about secret meetings which became commonly accepted.

The customs which had grown out of religious interest had reached the desire for entertainment and pleasure. They satisfied it and stimulated it, and the religious element might be forgotten.

623. Beginnings of the theater at Rome. The Floralia were instituted at Rome in 240 B.C. They were celebrated by courtesans with processions, lascivious pantomimes, etc. They are said to have come from Greece.[2] In the same year Livius Andronicus presented at Rome the first play translated from the Greek. In 154 the first permanent theater was established there against great opposition. In 146 the first theater outside the circus, with seats, was provided.[3] All mimic actions were foreign to the austere mores of the early Romans, but in the second century B.C. the mores changed through the growth of wealth and contact with other nations. Young Romans learned from actors to sing and dance, acts which their ancestors thought unworthy of free persons. The earliest plays were called *saturae*, because they were

---

[1] W. R. Smith, *Relig. of the Semites*, 357–359.
[2] Wissowa, *Relig. of the Romans*, 163.
[3] Magnin, *Origines du Théâtre Moderne*, 324, 463.

mixed dialogues, music, and dances. The sense of the word was closely that of "farce" in the Middle Ages,[1] i.e. an episode or intermezzo of a comic character interjected into a drama. The *saturae* contained an Etruscan element, but atellans were entirely Etruscan. They were comic and grotesque, and got their name from Atella (i.e. Aversa or Santo Arpino) in Campania. They could be played by persons who did not on that account lose their places in their tribes or their right to serve in the legion. No personalities at all were allowed on the Roman stage. Cynicism and obscenity characterized the Oscan style.[2] In 55 B.C. the younger Cato was present at the Floralia. The populace hesitated to call, in his presence, for the stripping of the *mimae*. He left in order not to hinder the celebration from taking its usual course.[3] Valerius Maximus[4] says that the pantomime was brought to Rome from Etruria, the Etruscans having brought it from their old home in Lydia. We see from the epigrams in the first book of Martial that at the Roman theater in the first century of the Christian era incidents of the Roman mythology were made into dramas and represented in pantomime.

624. Gladiatorial exhibitions. The gladiatorial exhibitions are supposed to have been of Etruscan origin in the form of funeral games. Games to rejoice the ghosts, sacrifices of prisoners, a chance given to a prisoner to fight for his life, are steps of a development of which we find many examples. The Romans showed the pitilessness and inhumanity of their mores in the development they gave to the gladiatorial exhibitions. "Campanian hosts used to entertain their guests at dinner with them in the days before the Second Punic War. It was in Campanian towns that in the first century was displayed most glaringly the not unusual combination of cruelty and voluptuousness."[5] Some murmurs of dissent arose from the philosophers of the first and second centuries of the Christian era, — Plutarch, Seneca, Marcus Aurelius,[6] — but at that time the popular sentiment had not

---

[1] Magnin, *Origines*, 304.
[2] *Ibid.*, 304–317.
[3] Val. Max., II, x, 8.
[4] II, IV, 7.

[5] Dill, *Nero to M. Aurel.*, 236.
[6] Cf. Lecky, *Eur. Morals*, I, 285; Dill, *Nero to M. Aurel.*, 235.

faltered at all in its love and zeal for the gladiatorial shows and beast contests on account of any doubt whether the exhibitions were "right." Tertullian, at the end of the second century, wrote a tract, *Ad Nationes*, in which he criticised the theater, and also another, *De Spectaculis*, against the public entertainments. Although the latter is chiefly controversial against heathen and heathenism, it contains direct and noble arguments against the games of the arena on account of their inhumanity. He says that the games were at first connected with funerals, and that the theater was a temple of Venus, under cover of which the games won a footing. That would mean, then, that they were at first under a convention of time, place, occasion, and religion. Correctly understood, therefore, what happened at Rome was that the convention was broken over and the exceptional rite was made the everyday usage, the religious sentiment being disregarded and the sensual entertainment alone being valued. When we have reached this point we can understand the original place of the games within the intellectual horizon of the nation, and also the deep demoralization which they caused in later times. They were consonant with early Roman mores which were warlike. Cicero thought them an excellent school to teach contempt for pain and death. He cited gladiators as examples of bodily exercise, courage, and discipline. He seems to have known that some disapproved of the exhibitions, and he was disposed to agree with them if the gladiators were others than criminals condemned to death.[1] A usage which is consonant with the tastes, mores, and world philosophy of a people need work no corruption on them, for it is under taboos and conventions; but if all the restraints are taken away it enters into their life for just what it is in its character, — sensual, cruel, bloody, obscene, etc. What had been savage and bloodthirsty when the Romans were warriors became base and cowardly when they never risked their own blood in any way. Condemned criminals were compelled to take rôles in which they suffered torture and a frightful death, in order to entertain the Roman crowd. Such rôles were Prometheus, Dædalus, Orpheus, Hercules, and Attys; Pasiphae and the bull.

[1] *Tusc. Disp.*, II, 17.

and Leda and the swan were also enacted. In Martial's *Epigrams*, Book I, the cases are mentioned where a woman fought with a lion ; Laureolus, a robber, was crucified and torn, as he hung on the cross, by a bear ; Dædalus, when his wing broke, was precipitated amongst bears who tore him to pieces ; and Orpheus was torn by a bear. These exhibitions were recognized as indecencies.[1] Later the exhibitions had no limit.[2] " From father to son, for nearly seven centuries, the Roman character became more and more indurated under the influence of licensed cruelty. The spectacle was also surrounded by the emperors, even the greatest and best, for politic reasons, with ever growing splendor." [3] " It is a grave deduction from the admiring judgment of the glory of the Antonine age, that its most splendid remains are the stately buildings within whose enclosure for centuries the populace were regaled with the sufferings and the blood of the noblest creatures of the wild animal world and of gallant men. The deserts and forests of Africa and the remotest East contributed their elephants and panthers and lions to these scenes." [4]

625. Spread of gladiatorial exhibitions. The Romans carried gladiatorial exhibitions wherever their conquests extended. " The Teutonic regions of the North and Greece were almost the only provinces in which the bloody games were not popular. The one Greek town where the taste for them was fully developed was the mongrel city of Corinth, which was a Roman colony. In the novel of Apuleius we meet a high Corinthian magistrate traveling through Thessaly to collect the most famous gladiators for his shows. Plutarch urges public men to banish or to restrain these exhibitions in their cities. When the Athenians, from an ambition to rival the splendor of Corinth, were meditating the establishment of a gladiatorial show, the gentle Demonax bade them first to overturn their altar of Pity. The apostles of Hellenism, — Dion, Plutarch, and Lucian, — were unanimous in condemning an institution which sacrificed the bravest men to the brutal passions of the mob." [5] At Byzantium the lack of any

---

[1] Martial, II, Introd.
[2] Scherr, *Kult. Gesch.*, 181.
[3] Dill, *Nero to M. Aurel.*, 235.
[4] *Ibid.*, 238.
[5] *Ibid.*, 240.

standard of decency and propriety in the exhibitions was even more complete, and they lasted indefinitely.[1] Constantine in 325 A.D. absolutely forbade gladiatorial exhibitions, because bloody shows were unfit for a time of peace. He forbade the condemnation of criminals to be gladiators. His laws, however, failed of effect.[2] At the end of the fourth century Symmachus, "who was regarded as one of the most estimable pagans of his age," collected some prisoners to fight in honor of his son. They committed suicide to escape the destiny for which he designed them. He lamented the misfortune which had befallen him from their "impious hands," but endeavored to calm his feelings by recalling the patience of Socrates and the precepts of philosophy. He will not, he says, use such people any more, but Libyan lions, more docile than men.[3] He serves to point a moral on the mores of his age.

626. The folk drama. The culture classes pass by the sports of the "vulgar" with contempt; but the student of the mores cannot do so. The tastes of the crowd are manifested in them. We read the great dramas which have become a part of the world literature, and we form from them our ideas of the current intellectual interest of the time of their origin and of the society in which they were produced. Such inferences need to be corrected. They are certainly erroneous. The Greeks were not all of them, nor any of them all the time, on a plane of classical severity and correctness. Far from it. They were realistic, egoistic, cold, cruel, and fond of sensual pleasure.[4] The great dramas, epics, etc., were enjoyed only by the real upper strata of the society, just as is the case in regard to Shakespeare amongst us. The great populace of no society has ever found its amusement in purely intellectual suggestions. With us popular amusement is found in the circus, negro minstrels, the variety show, opera bouffe, the spectacle, and ballet, and it attaches to parody and burlesque, "knock-down business," buffoonery, and broad

---

[1] Gibbon, Chap. XL, i.

[2] Schmidt, *La Société Civile dans le Monde Romain et sa Transformation par le Christianisme*, 469.

[3] *Ep.*, II, 46; Migne, *Patrol. Latina*, XVIII, 190.   [4] Reich, *Der Mimus*, 32.

allusion. Stupidity is always funny. Everything which breaks over the social taboo is funny. A violation of propriety, accidental disorder of the dress, grotesque postures, vulgar gestures of derision or defiance, blows, painful accidents and mishaps,—if not too serious, — deformations of the body (humpbacks), epithets and nicknames, slang and other abuses of language (like mispronunciation by foreigners), vituperation, caricature and burlesque of respectable types like the pedant, dandy, Puritan, imbecile, or the rich and great, always raise a laugh in the crowd and are relished by the crowd. They are constant elements of farce and fun. They have been so for three thousand years. Jugglery and feats of strength and skill excite wonder until they become familiar. They are proofs of individual capacity. They do not give amusement like the points which have just been mentioned and which have been repeated to generation after generation The crowd always delights in any degradation of the things which the selected classes prefer and try to impose on all. They rejoice to see the restrictions trampled upon which they hear preached as the rules of life. In opera bouffe classical heroes, gods of the classical mythology, royalty, nobles of the mediæval type, feudalism, dominies, are turned to ridicule. The crowd worships its heroes fanatically while they are in fashion, but it likes to turn about and roll them in the mud of satire, in order to teach them who made them and how easily it can unmake them. Aristophanes derided all which was serious in the Athenian social system. Long before Don Quixote was written chivalry was treated with derision. Satire is a reversal of respect and admiration.

627. The popular taste. Realism. Conventionality. Satire. That which is realistic and graphic appeals to the popular and uneducated taste, not that which is conventional, regulated, and refined according to rule and standard. That which is realistic reproduces all the facts of life. If the mirror is held up to nature it will show some nasty things. The social taboos began in superstitious fear, but they formed a series of conventional folkways under which some acts and facts of life were veiled from sight, knowledge, speech, and publicity. Other lesser conventions were grafted on these, and produced the great mass of usages within which our lives are passed. That which is artistic is the highest form of conventional refinement. Realism antagonizes and breaks through all these conventions and taboos, which are always a strain upon those who are not brought up in them from infancy. Therefore we hear demands for realism and naturalness from those who weary of the strain and do not want to submit to it. The conventionalities define respectability, and respectability has always been sneered at. In all comedy it is made ridiculous. The husband was possessed of conventional rights in which he was protected by society so that he had a secured and uneventful status. In comedy his rights have been violated and his security has been broken. The crowd has always enjoyed this. It rejoiced to see the wife deceive the husband, and the adulterer fool him. The latter represented freedom and cleverness at war with philistinism. On the other hand, all the taboos and conventions which have penetrated the masses and become familiar to them from infancy are fiercely defended by them (e.g. female dress and the taboo on man's dress for females). The popular magazines and the " great moral shows " religiously respect the standards of the crowd. That which is broad is funny, but there is always a limit of toleration. What is prudish, puritanical, fastidious, affected, pharisaical, etc.? These adjectives are in use, and they apply to things which are beyond a line which is undefined and indefinable. It depends on the codes and standards of the group. Realism presents everyday experience, no humbug, the world as it is. It must, therefore, be cynical and ruthless to all conventions. It shows the meanness of greatness, the other side of virtue, the weakness of heroes. No doubt it is great fun to pour scorn and ridicule on all who assume to be better than we are, and to look down on us. The easiest way to do it is to show up their weaknesses, follies, and sins. Here is another task for the satirists. Satire in comedy may be a gratification of envy. The rôle of Pierrot is dangerous to him who exercises it. In fact no man is fit for it. Where does any one get a charter to be censor of all the rest? He will certainly become proud, arrogant, self-seeking, and tyrannical. Each one satirizes follies which are not to his taste, or sins to which he is not tempted. Satire to be artistic and permanently effective must be marked by light and shade. It always exaggerates what it wants to impress on the attention, but to do this artistically it must subdue other elements. This is very difficult to accomplish when for popular effect it must use big brushes and glaring colors.

628. Popular exhibitions. From the time of Homer we can trace popular exhibitions which accompanied the theatrical forms above described as an inferior class of the same species. The popular exhibitions were marked by the features which have been described (sec. 626), to which we may add bloodshed and cruel rites.

629. Ancient popular festivals. The *thargelia* were ancient sanguinary festivals celebrated in Greece in honor of Apollo and Diana. Two men, or a man and a woman, were immolated in Attica, to expiate the sins of the people. " The circular dances of the Greeks around the victims, or later around the altar, can only be compared with the songs and furious dances of the Iroquois and Brazilians around their prisoners." [1] At Athens also the *kronia* were festivals of Saturn. The notion that there was a period of original liberty and equality " at the beginning " was entertained at that time, and this festival was held to represent it. Also on Crete there were festivals of Mercury. In Thessaly the *peloria* were a festival, the name of which was derived from Pelor, the man that brought news that an earthquake had drained the valley of Tempe. The *sacea* were a festival at Babylon similar to the *saturnalia*. A slave in each house, including the palace of the king, ruled as a house sovereign for five days. The leading idea was to reverse or invert everything in ordinary life. The *kordax* was an ancient dance of the old comedy, with indecent gestures, in which the human figure was caricatured according to all the deformations which it underwent by vice or sensuality. All the effects of gluttony and Bacchic excess were caricatured in the figure of Silenus. The old woman fond of wine lost all modesty under the influence of wine.[2] The leaders of the choruses, in a

[1] Magnin, *Origines du Théâtre Moderne*, 30.   [2] *Ibid.*, 51.

later time at Athens, offered reminders of primitive barbarism and of the immolation of human beings, and a representation of savage nudity, but they presented no image which was ridiculous or base. Tragedy had a long struggle to become separate from lyric forms, but Æschylus at last accomplished the separation. This was really the separation of the high literary drama from the popular *mimus*. After ten centuries of glory in Greece tragedy was lost again under the lyric form.[1] The popular drama, however, lasted on until to-day, and it has never changed its characteristic elements.

630. The *mimus*. The essence of the *mimus* is in pantomime as the name denotes. It imitates facts of life and behavior and is, therefore, essentially realistic. It may well be derived from the mimetic dances of nature peoples, in which beasts, warriors, and lovers are imitated, with jest and satirical exaggeration of characteristic traits. In the folk drama in its simplest forms nothing has ever been written. The actor assumed a rôle and improvised all which he had to say in trying to act it out. His responsibility for the rôle was far greater than that of an actor in a culture drama. The actor, by repeating a rôle, produced a representation of it which was personal to himself and which he perfected. The most interesting and marked characters became fixed. A large number of them are now established in literature and have become known all over the world. The latest instance of such a type is, perhaps, Lord Dundreary. The word *mimus* appears in Greece in the fifth century B.C. The *mimus* was a picture of life or, more exactly, an unwritten parody of life. It was divided into grades and the actors into castes. Women had previously appeared as jugglers and mountebanks. They now appeared amongst the actors of the popular drama. This made the exhibitions questionable according to Greek standards. The exhibitions were given by wandering companies. While actors of the culture drama always wore masks, those of the *mimus* were the first to appear unmasked;[2] later others imitated them. At the present day the theatrical exhibitions which may be seen on the outskirts of a fair in central Europe well represent the ancient *mimus*.

[1] Magnin, *Origines*, 33, 38-40.   [2] Reich, *Der Mimus*, 527.

The marionettes were an early offshoot of the *mimus*, and the modern Punch-and-Judy show is a descendant in part of both. For the mores the *mimus* and the marionette theater are a thousandfold more important than the great tragedies, but the former have left no mark on history. They never were written down; the actors are dead; their reputation is forgotten. The mores contain the effect as a fact but no explanation of it. From the time of Alexander the Great that which is common, popular, realistic prevailed in politics and literature. The heroic and ideal-poetic declined and was made an object of satire in the *mimus*. " The trivial, prosaic, and libertine taste of the Macedonian princes of Egypt and Syria at last reigned alone in enslaved Greece." Then, under different forms and names, nothing remained but mimes, realistic representation of common life.[1] The Olympian gods and Homeric heroes were burlesqued for fun. The *mimus* won acceptance at courts and in higher circles. It was developed into the so-called " hypothesis " and won a place on the stage. The most distinguished maker of hypotheses was Philistion,[2] who lived at the beginning of the Christian era. They became popular throughout the Greco-Roman world in the first centuries of the Christian era.[3] The emperor Tiberius caused actors to be expelled from Italy as disturbers of the peace, and because the old Oscan farce, once amusement for the common people, had become indecent.[4] Out of the common origin of all dramatic exhibitions (sec. 616) the *mimus* kept the corn demons, or growth demons, which always commanded the interest of husbandmen. The actors of this rôle wore masks in which the features of a low and sensual countenance were greatly exaggerated. An artificial phallus (sec. 473) was worn outside of the dress, and the entire region of the hips was enlarged so as to produce a conventional, extravagant, and stereotyped figure, like the modern clown, punch, or Mephisto, being, in fact, in some measure, their ancestor.[5] Greek vases represent these

---

[1] Magnin, *Origines*, 161.   [3] *Ibid.*, 27–29.

[2] Reich, *Der Mimus*, 12.   [4] Tacitus, *Annales*, IV, 14.

[5] Preuss (*Archiv für Anthrop.*, XXIX, 182) suggests that Falstaff's fatness may be a survival of one of the physical features of the stereotyped buffoon.

figures. The same set of ideas and course of thought has been traced in Mexico in connection with crop interests and growth demons.[1] There also the public rites at festivals passed by imperceptible steps into dramatic representations with dogmatic meaning or magical significance.

631. Modern analogies. The end man of the negro minstrel troupe is a modern creation like the Greek *phlyax*, for he is a buffoon of the plantation-negro type, with every feature exaggerated to the utmost, so that he is unreal and a caricature; but the exaggerations direct attention to familiar facts and display characteristic features which are a cause of merriment. The rise, development, and decline of negro ministrelsy illustrate, within our observation, many features in the history of popular comedy. It originated in fun making by the imitation of a foreign group, whose peculiar ways appeared to be ridiculous antics. Then the negro was used to burlesque and satirize the weaknesses, follies, and affectations of whites. The negro plantation hand is a type which is disappearing and interest in him is declining. He is no longer available for direct study or derived satire.

632. Biologs and ethologs. The Greek *phlyax* (the play) passed to southern Italy in the fourth century B.C., whence it was transmitted to Rome and confused with the atellan. It became very popular, and lasted until the fifth century A.D.[2] Reich divides the mimes into two classes: (1) biologs, i.e. those who represent individual types, e.g. an unfaithful wife, an imbecile husband, a fatuous nobleman, a physician, etc.; (2) ethologs, i.e. those who impersonate some feature in the mores of the time and satirize it, e.g. faith in miracles, fondness for drink or gambling, sycophancy to the rich, or "getting on in the world." This is a very important distinction and one which illuminates the connection between the drama and the mores. Socrates was an etholog, although not an actor. He spent sarcasm, irony, and humor on the ways of the Athenians of his time.[3] Aristophanes was another, Rabelais was another, Erasmus was an inferior one. In his *Colloquies* and *Praise of Folly* he is more of a preacher, but

---

[1] *Archiv für Anthrop.*, XXIX, 133.   [2] Reich, *Der Mimus*, 679, 682.
[3] *Ibid.*, 360.

his aim is to influence by graphic satirical description. In our day the comic papers attempt the task of the etholog. They try to satirize manners and men. A comic paper owned or subsidized by a political party is the sorriest representative of Pierrot that the world has yet seen. The biolog personates an individual type, like an aberration of human nature, which may be found anywhere and at any time. The etholog personates a specimen of a class which helps to characterize a period. Dandies exist at all times, but vary in detail. The fatuity and vanity of all dandies are features for the etholog; the follies of the dandy of a period belong to the biolog. Beau Brummel would be a model for a biolog. The etholog is apt to overlook his best subjects. He cannot himself escape from his own times enough to recognize them. He never satirizes the reigning features. The American etholog never satirizes democracy, or the politician, or the newspaper. The etholog wants a big party or a strong sentiment behind him. It is not until after skepticism about a ruling "way" has formed in the minds of a large section of the masses that the etholog makes himself the mouthpiece of it. We have no satire yet on militarism, or imperialism, or the Monroe doctrine. A protective tariff is a grand object for satire, but so long as the masses believe in it satire is powerless. The same is true of any folkway so long as it is not yet doubted. Satire is then blasphemy. While a way is prevalent there is pathos about it (sec. 178), as there is now amongst us about democracy, but there never can be satire and pathos at the same time, in the same society, about the same thing. One might have believed that nothing need be sacred to the theaters of Paris, but a few years ago a play was written which set the French Revolution in a different light from the now consecrated commonplace in regard to it. It was found impossible to produce it. A marionette player and his wife made fun of Père Duchesne on the boulevard during the Revolution. Both were guillotined.[1] These facts limit very much the high moral function sometimes ascribed to satire. It never gets into action until the mischief is done. It never squelches a folly at its commencement. That

[1] Magnin, *Marionettes*, 188.

function belongs to educated reason, but educated reason is not in the masses.

633. Dickens as a biolog. Charles Dickens was a biolog. His novels contain very little evidence of the manners and customs of his time, and what they do contain is forced and untrue. He invented characters whose names have become common nouns and adjectives for individual types which are found in all societies at all times (Pecksniff, Micawber, Turveydrop, Uriah Heep, etc.), but which may, at a time, be especially common and produce fine specimens.

634. Early Jewish plays. Ezekiel (an Alexandrian Jew, fl. c. 200 B.C.) is said to have written a play on the exodus from Egypt, with the same motive as the mystery plays, — the edification of the faithful. Herod Atticus († c. 180 A.D.), having caused the death of his wife, Regilla, was not satisfied with the expiations in the usual funeral rites. He built, as a monument to her, a theater with a roof.[1] Ezekiel's play on the exodus was presented in Herod's theater. Nicholas of Damascus (b. 74 B.C.) is said to have written a play on the story of Susanna.[2]

635. Roman *mimus*. The *mimus*, in the Greco-Roman empire, stereotyped its figures for a period, since of course they did not change suddenly or greatly. In the Roman *mimus* the recurring features were the pursuit of legacies, the impotency of men, the stupidity of the clown, blows and other physical violence. The fixed types were: old women as drunkards, sorceresses, go-betweens, peddlers, and panders; men as *scholasticus* (the pedant and learned imbecile), Ardalio (a character introduced by Philistion), the fatuous, fussy old man, and then the Christian, a type which was kept up for several centuries.[3] These personages, remaining unchanged in character, were put in various assumed positions and conjunctures. The actors had to invent the dialogue and work out the situation. The characters have come down to us as Punch, Harlequin, Pantaloon, etc.[4]

---

[1] Lucian, *Demonax*, 33.
[2] D'Ancona, *Origine del Teatro in Italia*, I, 15.
[3] Reich, *Der Mimus*, 58, 436, 470, 505.
[4] Magnin, *Origines du Théâtre Moderne*, 321.

Punch (=Pulcino, Pulcinella) is only a Neapolitan rendering of Maccus, a character in the atellans. "Maccus," in Etruscan, meant a little cock.[1] Christian antiphonal singing, like the Greek mystery acts of Dionysus, helped to develop the drama.[2] In the first centuries of the Christian era "obscenity dominated the theater." "It was no longer a school of patriotism, recalling the heroes of the early ages or criticising the misdoings of contemporaries. It was a scene of vice and corruption for actors and spectators. There was nothing represented but the adventures of deceived husbands, adulteries, intrigues of libertines, incidents in lupanars. The only characters represented were shameless women and effeminate men. The most shameful things were exhibited. Everything which ought to be respected was there degraded. Virtue was mocked and the gods were derided. The actor caused the taste for evil things to penetrate the mind of the spectator; he stimulated ignoble and criminal passions, and, familiar as he was with vice, he blushed sometimes at the shameful rôle which he was forced to play before the crowd."[3]

636. "The Suffering Christ." "Pseudo-Querolus." In the fourth century the Christians tried to use the theater for their purposes. The drama *The Suffering Christ* is attributed to Gregory of Nazianz. It represents the passion of Jesus as understood by the Nicene theologians. It consists of twelve hundred and seventy-three verses taken more or less exactly from the tragedies of Euripides and patched together. Lintilhac[4] says it is now the accepted opinion that it cannot be of remoter origin than the eleventh century, so that the most noteworthy fact about it would be that it is a Greek liturgical play of even date with the earliest western plays of that class. In it the Virgin Mary is a pagan woman, who uses verses of Hecuba and Medea, and thinks of suicide.[5] Another play of the fourth century, which is mentioned as important in the history of the drama, is the *Pseudo-Querolus*. It is an imitation of Plautus. Querolus

---

[1] Magnin, *Origines*, 47.   [2] D'Ancona, I, 45.
[3] Schmidt, *La Société Civile dans le Monde Romain*, 98.
[4] *Théâtre Serieux du M. A.*, 13 note.   [5] D'Ancona, I, 372.

is the forerunner of Molière's Misanthrope and so a biolog, — a permanent type of person.[1] Dramas representing martyrdom and other Christian incidents were presented with very great realism.[2]

637. The *mimus* and Christianity. The *mimus* opened war on Christianity. The religion was unpopular and hated. It set itself against the mores of the society at the time. It was scoffed at just as Puritans, Quakers, Mormons, and Christian Scientists have been scoffed at since and for the same reasons. It shared the unpopularity of the Jews, who came before the heathen world claiming the isolation of superiority, exclusive favor of God, ascendancy by rights over all the world. To the pagans the Christians seemed to make a great fuss about nothing. The *mimus* seized the popular sentiment and gave it expression. The Christian became the clown and simpleton. Christian rites were parodied and ridiculed. Martyrdoms were represented on the stage, the martyr being the buffoon. The heathen gods were taken under the protection of the *mimus*, instead of being burlesqued as they had been for several centuries. This mockery ran through the Roman empire until the end of the fourth century, when the church got the protection of the state against public insult, but Christianity fell under the dominion of heathen mores. The great ecclesiastics of the fifth century preached fiercely against the theater, not because of the insults of the theater against the church, for they were silenced, but on account of the action of the theater upon Christian mores. Chrysostom denounced the theater on account of the manners of actresses in the *mimus*, on account of false hair, paint, exposed bodies, uncovered heads, melodies, gross language, gestures, strife, representations of adultery and other sex vice, and because it was the school of intrigue and seduction. This became the attitude of the church towards the theater.[3]

638. Popular phantasms. Although the crowd likes to see realistic representations of life, and also likes to see in the drama that ridicule of the cultured classes which seems like a victory

---

[1] Klein, *Gesch. des Dramas*, III, 599, 638.   [2] D'Ancona, I, 372.
[3] Reich, 80, 93, 95, 107, 117.

over them, yet it also loves fantastic scenes, and acts in which the limitations of reality are left behind and imaginary luck and joy are represented, — such as magical transformations, fairy tales, and realms of bliss. Extremes of realism and phantasm meet in the folk drama. After the fifth century the sense of societal decline and loss was strong in the popular mind. It was felt that the world was failing. There was a contempt for life.[1] Pagan society was ennuyé. "It wanted to laugh. It wanted games and dances to make gay the last hours which separated it from its fall."[2] Salvianus says that the Roman world died laughing.[3]

639. Effects of vicious amusements. Vicious amusements provoke all kinds of vicious passions. Excitement, sensuality, frivolity, and meanness go together. Lecky[4] points out the contrast between the conduct of the Romans of the time of Marius, who refused to plunder the houses of the opposing faction when Marius threw them open, and that of the Romans of the time of Vespasian, who enjoyed the fun and plunder of his war with Vitellius in the streets of Rome. "The moral condition of the empire is, indeed, in some respects one of the most appalling pictures on record."

640. Gladiatorial games. The mores of the Romans of the third century B.C. (sec. 624) seized upon the gladiatorial contests as something suited to the genius of the Roman people, and, as the Romans gained wealth and power by conquest and plunder, with numerous war captives, they developed the sport of the arena to a very high point. Then the sport reacted on the mores and made them more cruel, licentious, and cowardly. It required more and more extravagant inventions to produce the former degree of pleasure. The Romans were fond of all torture and showed great invention in connection with it, both for beasts and men. Children amused themselves by torturing beasts and insects, making them draw loads, and making fowls and birds fight. They loved the sight of pain and bloodshed

---

[1] Schmidt, *La Société Civile dans le Monde Romain*, 113.
[2] *Ibid.*, 101.　　　　　　　[3] *De Gubernat. Dei.*, VII.
[4] *Eur. Morals*, I, 264.

and found their greatest pleasure in it.[1] Under Nero women fought in the arena. This was forbidden under Severus. A law, probably of the time of Nero, forbade masters to give their slaves to fight beasts. Hadrian forbade the sale of slaves to be gladiators. Marcus Aurelius forbade the condemnation of criminals to be gladiators, and he tried to limit the gladiatorial exhibitions. They were far too popular.[2] It is thus that amusements and mores react on each other to produce social degeneration. The whole social standard of "right" moves down with the moral degeneracy, and at no stage is there a sense of shame or wrongdoing in the public mind in connection with what is customary and traditional at the time. There is no contrast between facts and standards. The great Christian ecclesiastics of the fourth and fifth centuries denounced the public amusements and tried to keep the Christians away from them. They tried to convert actors. They pointed out the subtle corruption of character produced by feigning vice. Gladiators were not admitted to baptism unless they repented and renounced their profession.[3] In 325 Constantine forbade gladiatorial combats as unfit for a time of peace. He forbade the use of condemned criminals in the arena. These laws were powerless.[4]

641. Compromise between church and customs. The *maiuma* (mock sea fight on the Tiber in May) was forbidden, probably under Constance, a prohibition which was repeated by Theodosius. Arcadius tried to allow it again, under conditions that propriety be observed, but it was impossible, and he forbade all immodest exhibitions. Theodosius forbade magistrates to be present at exhibitions after midday, when the most obscene and bloody were presented, except on the anniversaries of his own birth and accession. He also forbade actresses to use fine clothes and jewels, and forbade Christians to be actors. Leo I († 461) forbade that any Christian woman, free or slave, should be compelled to be an actress or meretrix.[5] Salvianus describes,[6]

---

[1] Grupp, *Kulturgesch. der röm. Kaiserzeit*, I, 200.

[2] Magnin, *Origines*, 435.

[3] Schmidt, 251–253.

[4] *Ibid.*, 469.

[5] *Ibid.*, 451, 466, 477.

[6] *De Gubernat. Dei*, VI, 10, 15, 38, 44–55.

in very emphatic but general terms, the public exhibitions in
Gaul and Africa in the second half of the fifth century. There
was, he says, scarcely a crime or outrage which was not represented on the stage, and the spectators enjoyed seeing a man
killed or cruelly lacerated. All the earth was ransacked for
beasts. All the senses were outraged by indecencies. Nevertheless, on any day on which performances occurred the churches
were empty. The Christians, as we see, lived in the mores of
their age, and all these things had centuries of tradition behind
them. Salvianus and other ecclesiastics were not heeded because
they derived their standards from Christian dogmas, and those
standards were far removed from the current mores. The
church was forced to compromise. It allowed feasts, fairs, and
games near the churches. It converted heathen festivals, with
processions, lights, and garlands, into Christian festivals and
usages. It borrowed the attractions of the worship of Isis,
Mithra, and Cybele, and adopted all the means of suggestion
employed in their rites. The great ecclesiastics were divided as
to this policy. Augustine put an end, so far as his jurisdiction
went, to the feasts in the churches in honor of martyrs, with
singing, dancing, and drinking, although they were very popular.[1] He complained earnestly of the indecency of the exhibitions
of his time.[2] " Especially at the festivals in honor of the heathen
gods, and in civil celebrations, the ancient religious practices
were renewed, not infrequently degenerating into shameless
immorality, yet protecting civil usages. The patriot, the philosopher, the skeptic, and the pious man had to make a capitula-
tion with those ancient religious practices, for they were not,
in truth, emancipated from them at heart, and they did not
know of anything better to replace what those practices did for
society."[3] So the philosopher, patriot, skeptic, and pious man
always have to compromise with the ancient and existing mores.
Salvianus[4] says that poverty caused the great exhibitions to
cease. It was advancing poverty and misery which put an end
to all the old forms of amusement. It was not the church or

---

[1] McCabe, *St. Aug.*, 238.
[2] *De Civit. Dei*, II, 27.
[3] Harnack, *Dogmengesch.*, I, 116.
[4] *De Gubernat. Dei*, VI, 42.

Christianity. The Christian rites and festivals alone remained. Modern Spanish bullfights appear to be a survival of the old sports of the arena. Bullfights were introduced into Italy in the fourteenth century. They were general in the fifteenth century. The Aragonese brought them to Naples and the Borgias to Rome.[1] We hear of a kind of gladiatorial exhibition at some festivals in India early in the nineteenth century.[2] There were gladiators also in Japan [3] and in Mexico.[4]

642. The *cantica*. Roman drama ran down to pantomime with explanatory recitation, that is, *cantica*. From the seventh to the tenth century few dramas were produced with dialogue. Some biblical narratives, legends of saints, and profane compositions from .that time exist, which are probably *cantica*, to be accompanied by pantomime at fairs or in church porches.

643. Passion for the games. It certainly was not on account of any decline in the taste for amusement that the games declined. In the fifth century, when the Vandals were besieging Carthage, "the church of Carthage was crazy for the games," and the cries of those dying in battle were confused with those of the applauding spectators at the games. The leading men of Treves were gratifying their love of feasting when the barbarians entered their city.[5] The people of Antioch were in the theater when the Persians surprised them, about 265 A.D.[6]

644. German sports. Amongst the Germanic nations, from a very early period, popular amusements consisted in pantomimes, mummery with animal masks, horseplay by clowns, etc. The feast of Holda, or Berchta, during the first twelve days of January, was an especial period for those sports. From the sixth century there was also a pantomime of the strife of winter and spring.[7]

645. The *mimus* from the third to the eighth century. As the culture drama fell into neglect the *mimus* was left in possession of the field. The culture drama, as we have seen, was built

[1] Gregorovius, *Lucret. Borgia*, 220.   [2] Dubois, *Mœurs de l'Inde*, II, 331.
[3] JAI, XII, 222.
[4] Bancroft, *Native Races of the Pacific Coast*, II, 305.
[5] Salvianus, *De Gubernat. Dei*, VI, 69, 71, 77.
[6] Ammianus Marcel., XXIII, v, 3.   [7] Grimm, *Deutsche Mythol.*, 166, 440.

upon and above the *mimus*, and has the character of a high product which could be maintained only in a peaceful and prosperous society whose other literary and artistic products were of a high grade. With a failure of societal power the highest products disappeared first, but the low and vulgar *mimus*, which had been disregarded but had amused the crowd during prosperity, continued to exist. In the third, fourth, and fifth centuries the *mimus* existed throughout the Roman world and was very popular. In the fifth century it flourished at Ravenna, and perhaps it continued later in the same form as in the East. It can be traced in Italy in the sixth century, after which its existence is doubtful. In the seventh century the theater was a thing of the past, but the *mimus* still existed. The ascetics of Charlemagne's time disapproved of it and got legislation against it, but the laws were of no avail. The ecclesiastics were fond of the *mimus*. It was in the hands of strolling players of the humblest kind. It coarsened with the general decay. All court festivals needed the *mimus* for the festivities.[1]

646. Drama in the Orient. There is no drama in Mohammedan literature and it appears that there is no original drama in the Orient.[2] The *mimus* declined in the West in the disaster of the fifth century, but in the Byzantine empire it lasted until the Turkish conquest, so that it appears that if there is any historical connection between modern and ancient drama it must be through Byzantium.[3] The actors at Byzantium kept a certain traditional license in the face of the emperor and court which was not without social and political value.[4]

647. Marionettes. Marionettes are mentioned in Xenophon's *Symposium*. They were of more ancient origin. The puppet play was used as a means of burlesquing the legitimate theater and drama. It passed to the Turks as the puppet shadow play, in which the hero Karagöz is the same as Punch in figure, character, and acts. This puppet play spread all over the Eastern world. Lane[5] says of it in Egypt, in the first half of the nineteenth century, that it was very indecent. Reich[6] describes

[1] Reich, *Der Mimus*, 785–810.   [3] *Ibid.*, 48, 133.   [5] *Mod. Egypt*, II, 125.

[2] *Ibid.*, 622.   [4] *Ibid.*, 191.   [6] *Der Mimus*, 656.

an indecent shadow play. A special form of it was developed in Java, the *wajang-poerva*, with figures of the *pantin* type, operated by strings and levers. This amusement is very popular in Java and very representative of the mores. Whether these oriental forms of the *mimus* were derived from the Greco-Roman world is uncertain. The *mimus* is so original and of such spontaneous growth that it does not need to be borrowed.

648. The drama in India. In India, at the beginning of the Christian era, there was a development of drama of a high character. The one called the *Clay-waggon* (a child's toy) is described as of very great literary merit, — realistic, graphic, and Shakespearean in its artistic representation of life.[1] Every drama which has that character must be in and of the mores. In the *Clay-waggon* the story is that of a Brahmin of the noblest character, who marries a courtesan, she having great love for him. The courtesan gives to the Brahmin's son a toy wagon of gold for his own made of clay. The name of the play comes from this trivial incident in it. A wicked, vain, and shallow-pated prince intervenes and is taken as a biolog, or standing type of person. Modern Hindoo dramas require a whole night for the representation. They represent the loves and quarrels of the gods and other mythological stories. "The actors are dressed and painted in imitation of the deities they represent, and frequently the conversations are rendered attractive by sensual and obscene allusions, whilst in the interludes boys dressed in women's clothes dance with the most indecent gestures. The worst dances that I have ever seen have been in front of an image and as a part of the rejoicings of a religious festival. Crowds of men, women, and children sit to watch them the whole night through."[2] The history of Ram is also enacted in pantomime in northern India. The text of the *Ramayana* is read and days are spent in acting it, by a great crowd, which moves from place to place, and naïvely plans to act city incidents in cities, forest incidents in forests, boat episodes on ponds, and war episodes or battles on great fields.[3]

---

[1] Klein, *Gesch. des Dramas*, III, 84.   [2] Wilkins, *Modern Hinduism*, 225.
[3] *Globus*, LXXXVII, 60.

649. Punch in the West. Punch was brought to Italy in the fifteenth century.[1] Polichinelle, as developed in France, is distinctly French. The model is Henri IV. The hump is an immemorial sign of the French *badin-ès-farces*. " Polichinelle seems to me to be a purely national (French) type, and one of the most spontaneous and vivacious creations of French fantasy."[2] The puppet play of Punch and Judy has enjoyed immense popularity in western Europe. The Faust legend has been developed by the puppets.[3] With the improvements in the arts people became more sophisticated. The puppets were left to children and to the simplest rural population, not because the mores improved, but because people were treated to more elaborate entertainments and the puppets became trivial. Punch is now a blackguard and criminal, who is conventionally tolerated on account of his antiquity. He is not in modern mores and is almost unknown in the United States. He is generally popular in southern Europe. To the Sicilians " a puppet play is a book, a picture, a poem, and a theater all in one. It teaches and amuses at the same time."[4] Then it still is what it has been for three thousand years.

650. Resistance of the church to the drama. The council in the palace of Trullo, at Constantinople in 692,[5] adopted canons forbidding clerics to attend horse races or theatrical exhibitions, or to stay at weddings after play began, also pantomimes, beast combats, and theatrical dances, also heathen festivals, vows to Pan, bacchanal rites, public dances by women, the appearance of men dressed as women, or of women dressed as men, and the use of comic, tragic, or satyric masks. All the Dionysiac rites had been forbidden long before. These canons prove that those rites were still observed. These clerical rules and canons do not represent the mores and they never overruled the mores at Constantinople. They only bear witness to what existed in the mores late in the seventh century, and

---

[1] Reich, *Der Mimus*, 669, 673, 676.
[2] Magnin, *Marionettes*, 121–122. [3] *Ibid.*, 343.
[4] Alec-Tweedie, *Sunny Sicily*, 173, and Chap. XI.
[5] Hefele, *Conciliengesch.*, III, 304.

they were an attempt to purify the usages which had been taken over by compromise from heathenism. In the sixth century in the West dances in church were often forbidden. The only stock of ideas in the eighth and ninth centuries were fantastic notions of nature, heaven and hell, history, supernatural agents, etc., which notions the ecclesiastics had an interest to teach. Dramatic representation was a means of teaching. The external action corresponded closely with the mental concept or story. From the time of Charlemagne pantomimes, tableaux, etc., set forth incidents of biblical stories and the resurrection, ascension, etc. The mores of the age seized on these modes of representation and gave method and color to them. All the grossness, superstition, and bad taste of the age were put into them. Satan and his demons were realistically represented, and the mass was travestied by ecclesiastics in a manner which we should think would be deeply offensive to them.[1] It was another case of conventionality for a limited time and place. Some of the clergy no doubt enjoyed the fun; others had to tolerate what was old and traditional. The folk drama reawakened as burlesque, parody, satire. The evil characters in the Scripture stories (Pharaoh, Judas, Caiaphas, the Jews) all fed this interest. All persons and institutions which pretended to be great and good and were not such provoked satire (clergy, nobles, warriors, women). The drama, introduced to show forth religious notions, served also to set forth others (social, political, city rivalry, class antagonisms). The "mass of fools" was a complete parody of the mass, with mock music and vestments and burlesque ceremony. In the "mass of innocents" children took the place of adults and carried out the ceremony as a parody. At the "feast of the ass" an ass was led into church and treated with mock respect. This last degenerated into obscenity, indecency, and disorder. Bulls and edicts against it were long vain. It was popular as a relief from restraint.[2] It continued the function of the Saturnalia, which had been a grand frolic

[1] Scherr, *D. F. W.*, I, 245.
[2] Lenient, *La Satire en France au M.A.*, 422; Du Cange, s. v. "Festum Asinorum."

and relaxation. The ecclesiastics tolerated these outbursts, perhaps because they saw that the lines could not be drawn very tightly without such relaxation. From the eleventh century the ecclesiastics opposed any automatic figure. They construed the making of such a figure as an attempt to call the saints, etc., to life again. The skill employed also seemed to them like sorcery.[1] " There was not an ecumenic, national, or diocesan council in whose canons may not be found severe and peremptory reproofs of all sorts and qualities of drama, of actors, and of those who run to see plays." [2] This became the orthodox attitude of the church to the theater. There were complaints of the attendance of clerics and people at theatrical exhibitions until the tenth century. Then they cease because the church ceremonies were more interesting and better done.[3] The Christian drama reached the height of its hieratic development between the ninth and twelfth centuries.[4]

651. Hrotsvitha. Klein [5] puts as the next important literary work of dramatic composition after the *Pseudo-Querolus* the works of the nun Hrotsvitha. In the tenth century she wrote six comedies in Latin, in imitation of Terence, her purpose being to show the superiority of the conventual conception of love to the worldly theory, and of religious passion to erotic passion. In the introduction she apologizes for her realistic descriptions of erotic passion, which she says was necessary for the argument implicit in her plays. She introduces God as a character, and miracles as a means of bringing about the dénouement at which she wants to arrive. It became the custom in mediæval drama to reach, by introducing a miracle, the moral result which current dogma required.[6] The situations and intrigue are generally very unedifying. To our taste the plays seem very unfit to be acted by nuns before nuns.

652. Jongleurs. Processions. In the eleventh century abbeys and cathedrals were built. At the beginning of the century the

---

[1] Magnin, *Marionettes*, 58.
[2] D'Ancona, *Origini del teatro in Italia*, I, 12.
[3] *Ibid.*, I, 49.   [4] Magnin, *Origines du Théâtre Moderne*, XXV
[5] *Gesch. des Dramas*, III, 646.   [6] Magnin, *Théâtre de Hrotsvitha*.

basilicas of the churches were repaired throughout Latin Christendom.[1] The Jongleurs of the twelfth century were the popular minstrels. " Poet, mountebank, musician, physician, beast showman, and to some extent diviner and sorcerer, the jongleur is also the orator of the public market place, the man adored by the crowd to whom he offers his songs and his couplets. Questions of morals and politics, toothache, pious legends, scandalous tales about priests, noble ladies, and cavaliers, gossip of grog shops, and news from the Holy Land were all in his domain." [2] In the second third of the twelfth century the vulgar language began to displace the Latin in church, especially in dramas.[3] Processions were in the taste and usage of the Middle Ages and Renaissance for both civil and religious pomp and display. The dresses, banners, arches, etc., contributed to the spectacle, and all took on a dramatic character for, on a saint's day or other occasion, the exhibition had a second sense of reference to the story of the saint, or the success in war of the king or potentate. The latter sense might be dramatically set forth, and generally was at least suggested. Tableaux and dramatic pantomime in the streets were combined with the processions. Mythological subjects as well as incidents of Christian history were so represented. All classes coöperated in these functions. Poets and artists of the first rank assisted. The contribution of these functions to the development of the drama is obvious. In modern times the taste for processions is lost, and the cultivated classes refuse to participate, but when the whole population of a city took part in setting forth something they all cared for, the social effect was great, and the whole proceeding nourished dramatic taste and power. In Italy the pantomime with song and dance, or ballet, had its origin in the procession.[4] In the churches arrangements were made, with elaborate machinery, for exhibiting representations of Scripture incidents. Godfrey, Abbot of St. Albans († 1146) wrote a play on the life of St. Catharine " such as was afterwards called

---

[1] Lintilhac, *Théâtre Sérieux du M. A.*, 18.
[2] Lenient, *La Satire*, 23.
[3] Lintilhac, *Théâtre Sérieux du M. A.*, 34.
[4] Burckhardt, *Renaissance*, 401.

a miracle." The Annunciation was represented in St. Mark's, Venice, in 1267. In Germany the mysteries were partly in German from the end of the thirteenth century.[1]

653. Adam de la Halle. De Julleville [2] puts Adam de la Halle as the first comic writer in France, in point of time. He wrote the *Jeu de la Feuillée* about 1262. It is described as a "scenic satire rather than a comedy." It is local, personal, and satirical, and includes miracles and capricious inventions without much regard to probability. It stands by itself and is not the first of a series. The notion of a connection between comedy and bodily deformity was now so firmly established that Adam was called the "Humpback of Arras," although he was not humpbacked at all.[3] Association of acts and ideas is always very important in all folkways and popular mores. At Florence, in 1304, on boats on the Arno, devils were represented at work. The bridge on which the spectators stood broke down under the crowd, and it was said that "many went to the real hell to find out about it."[4] At Paris, in 1313, at the celebration of the knighting of the sons of Philippe le Bel, devils were represented tormenting souls.[5]

654. Flagellants. The flagellants exerted some of the suggestions of the processions, and they used dramatic devices to set forth their ideas, to say nothing of the dramatic element in the self-scourging. They were outside of the church system, and acted on their own conception of sin and discipline, like modern revivalists. They reappeared from time to time through the fourteenth and fifteenth centuries. They meant to declare that the asserted correlation between goodness and blessing did not verify, and they were at a loss for a doctrine to replace it. Their antiphonal singing turned into dialogue, and then became drama at the end of the thirteenth century.[6]

655. Use of churches for dramatic exhibitions. The mediæval plays were presented in churches or on the open spaces on the streets in front of them, at Florence. Later this became

---

[1] D'Ancona, I, 62, 78, 86.

[2] *La Comédie en France au M. A.*, 19.

[3] Magnin, *Marionettes*, 121.

[4] D'Ancona, I, 88.

[5] *Ibid.*, 89.

[6] *Ibid.*, 98–107.

customary in all cities.[1] The old idea had been that churches
were common public property, a universal rendezvous for every
common interest. Dedications of churches and feasts of martyrs
had been general merrymakings. D'Ancona collects dicta of
councils and popes condemning dramatic actions in churches, and
the singing of lewd songs and dancing by women.[2] The language
used implies that the songs, gestures, acts, and suggestions connected with the performances in the churches were lewd and
indecent. The populace, while using the license, well perceived
its incongruity and impropriety, and this stimulated the satire,
which was so strong a feature of the late Middle Ages and which
produced the farce. The mysteries and moralities for a time
gave entertainment, but they became tedious. The farce was at
first " stuffing," put in to break up the dullness by fun making
of some kind and to give spice to the entertainment, just as meats
were *farcies* to give them more savor. It grew until it surpassed
and superseded the sober drama. The populace did not want
more preaching and instruction, but fun and frolic, relief from
labor, thought, and care. The take-off, caricature, burlesque,
parody, discerns and sets forth the truth against current humbug,
and the pretenses of the successful classes. The fool comes
into prominence again, not by inheritance but by rational
utility. The fifteenth century offered him plenty of material.
As a fool he escaped responsibility. This rôle, — that of the
badin in France, the *gracioso* in Spain, *arlèquino* in Italy, *Hanswurst* in Germany, — becomes fixed like the buffoon (*maccus*)
in the classical comedy. In France, from the beginning of the
fourteenth century, the *basochiens* were young clerks and advocates who were studying law and who made fun of law proceedings. They met with only limited toleration. Their satire was
not relished by the legal great men. In the fourteenth century
they took up moralities overweighted with allegory but broken
up by farces. In the fifteenth century the *Enfans sans Souci*
were another variety of *comédiens*. Their emblem was the
cap with two horns or ass's ears.[3] The life of St. Louis was

---

[1] D'Ancona, *Origine del Teatro in Italia*, I, 344.   [2] *Ibid.*, I, 47.
[3] Lenient, *La Satire en France au M. A.*, 324–340.

represented in tableaux at Marseilles in 1517.[1] The Passion was represented in the Coliseum until 1539, when Paul III forbade it. Riots against the Jews had been provoked by the exhibition.[2]

656. Protest against misuse of churches. It may be said that there was never wanting a dissenting opinion and protest amongst the ecclesiastics about the folk drama in the churches. In 1210 Innocent III forbade such exhibitions by ecclesiastics. Then the fraternities began to represent them on public market places. The "festival of fools" at Christmas time was originally invented to turn the heathen festivals into ridicule. When there were no more heathen it degenerated into extreme popular farce. Thomas Aquinas consented to the *mimus*, if it was not indecent.[3] The synod of Worms, in 1316, forbade plays in churches. Such plays seem to have reached their highest perfection in the fourteenth century.[4] Plays of this type gave way in the fifteenth century to "moralities," with allegorical characters, which prevailed for a long time, the taste for allegory marking the mental fashion of the time. The council of Basle forbade plays in churches (1440).[5]

657. Toleration of jests by the ecclesiastics. The ecclesiastical authorities were very patient with the folk theater for its satires on the clergy, the church, and religion. They heeded only attacks on "the faith." "We are astonished to meet, in a time which we always think of as crushed under authority, with such incredibly bold expressions against the papacy, the episcopate, chivalry, and the most revered doctrines of religion such as paradise, hell, etc."[6] Lenient suggests as reasons the divisons and factions in church and state and the current contempt for popular poetry. In the fifteenth century, in France, the popular drama expressed the class envy of the poor against the rich. In the mystery play *Job* (1478) the "Pasteur" says: "The great lords have all the goods. The poor people have nothing but pain and adversity. Who would not be irritated [at such a state of things]?" The passion plays of the Rhine valley followed

[1] Scherr, *D. F. W.*, II, 124.
[2] D'Ancona, I, 282.
[3] Summa, II, 2, qu. 168, art. 3.
[4] von Schack, *Gesch. der Dramat. Lit.*, I, 35.
[5] Session XXI, sec. 11.
[6] Lenient, *La Satire en France au M. A.*, 29.

those of France. Those of the fourteenth century lacked the rude jests and ghoulish interest of those of France in the fifteenth. The street public never tired of the horrors of executions, or of the low gaiety of funerals, etc. The "sot" first appeared in the *Passion de Troyes* at the end of the fifteenth century. He was long popular.[1]

658. Fictitious literature. Fictitious literature, after printing became common, was greatly increased, especially in Italy and Spain. Through the dialogued story it led up to the drama. At the end of the fifteenth century F. de Rojas wrote a dialogued story, *Calisto e Melibœa*, about two distressed lovers. The heroine is Celestina, a bawd who helped them out of their troubles. The book is generally named after her, and she became a fixed character in drama and fiction. The noble bawd, however, is an artificial creation of literature and never could be a biolog. It is not true enough. The Spaniards also developed a new form of the mystery play, — the *autos sacramentales*. These plays represented some Scriptural incident, but the rôles were taken by allegorical figures. They were regularly represented on the festival of Corpus Christi, in the afternoon, on the public square. They satisfied the taste of the people for religiosity, if not religion. Machiavelli (1469–1527) wrote a story, *Mandragore*, which in its day enjoyed great popularity. A man in Paris heard of the beauty of a lady at Florence. He went to the latter place to see her and fell in love with her. Her husband was an imbecile who greatly desired a child. He persuaded his wife to receive the stranger. She and the lover contracted an enduring relation. Cardinal Bibbiena wrote a comedy at the beginning of the sixteenth century, *Calandra*, which was esteemed as a great work. The intrigue consists of *quiproquos* produced by twins, a male and a female, who exchange dress. Many classical stories are introduced. Lope de Vega (1562–1635) wrote autos and comedies. He wrote eighteen hundred comedies, four hundred autos, and a great number of other pieces, — in all, it is said, twenty-one million verses.[2] Calderon (1600–

---

[1] Lintilhac, *Théâtre Serieux du Moyen Age*, 106, 123, 133, 167.
[2] Zarate, *Liter. Españ.*, II, 308, 423, 451.

1681) continued on the same lines. The servant-buffoon was the time form of the buffoon. All these productions furnished models and material for the poets and dramatists of other countries. The comedies are always long and wordy and generally tedious. They run in fixed molds, and have unyielding conventions to obey. Rarely have they ethological value.

659. Romances of roguery. The " romances of roguery" were closely akin to the popular drama as exponents of popular tastes and standards. It is very possible that the romances were derived from the tastes.[1] The clever hero has been a very popular type in all ages and countries. He easily degenerates into the clever rogue. The rogue is an anti-hero to offset the epic hero. There was in France, in the thirteenth century, "a bold rogue, Eustache le Moine, who became the central hero of a *roman*, which set forth his life and deeds as thief and pirate."[2] In Germany Till Eulenspiegel was a rascal who lived in the first part of the fourteenth century and around whose name anecdotes clustered until he became an anti-hero. There were in Germany popular tales which were picaresque novels in embryo. Those about Eulenspiegel were first reduced to a coherent narrative in 1519. Hemmerlein was an ugly and sarcastic buffoon of the fourteenth century. Hanswurst was a fat glutton of the fifteenth century who aimed to be clever but made blunders. Pickelhering, in Holland, was of the same type.[3] In England, in the sixteenth century, Punch began to degenerate. He took away the rôle of "Old Vice," and became more and more depraved, — a popular Don Juan, a type of physical and moral deformity.[4] The play was popular. The marionettes, being only dolls and sexless, escaped the onslaught of the Puritans.[5]

660. Picaresque novels. The picaresque novels do not deal with love, but with intrigues for material gain in the widest sense. *Lazarillo de Tormes* is counted as the first of these. It is attributed to Diego Hurtado de Mendoza and is thought to have been produced about 1500. The best known of the class is *Gil Blas*. The hero lives by his wits, has many vicissitudes,

---

[1] Chandler, *Romances of Roguery*, 191. [2] *Ibid.*, 9.
[3] Magnin, *Marionettes*, 298. [4] *Ibid.*, 255-265. [5] *Ibid.*, 233.

and plays and suffers many cruel practical jokes. The Spanish stories of Quevedo and Perez are coarse but never obscene. The view of women, however, is low. They are fickle, shallow, vain, and cunning. The church is " gingerly handled," but the clergy are derided for immorality, hypocrisy, and trickiness.

661. Books of beggars. A variety of the picaresque species was the " books of beggars." An English specimen of this variety is Audley's *Fraternity of Vagabonds* (1561). Mediæval social ways produced armies of vagabonds, beggars, and outcasts, who practiced vice and evil ways and cultivated criminal cleverness. The picaresque stories illustrate their ways.

662. At the beginning of the sixteenth century. Isabella d'Este describes a play at Ferrara, in 1503, in which the Annunciation was represented, angels descending from heaven by concealed machinery, etc. There was also a *moresca*, a ballet or pantomime dance, with clowns and beasts, and blows and other clown tricks. Another very noteworthy incident is the enactment, at Urbino in 1504, of a " comedy," in which the recent history of that city was represented, including the marriage of Lucrezia Borgia, the conquest of Urbino by Cesar Borgia, the death of Alexander VI, and the return of the Duke of Urbino. This application of the dramatic method to their own recent history, which had been indeed dramatic, shows the high development of graphic and artistic power, which is also shown by the other arts of the time. Ladies did not then abdicate their prerogative to judge and condemn the propriety of artistic products offered to them. Isabella declared the *Cassaria* " lascivious and, immoral beyond words," and forbade her ladies to attend the performance of it at the marriage of Lucrezia Borgia to her (Isabella's) brother.[1] In France, in the sixteenth century, imitations of classical dramas held the stage. The Protestants sought to use the drama for effect on the populace.[2] St. Charles Borromeo (1538–1584), as Archbishop of Milan, carried on a war against exhibitions of all kinds. He maintained that they were indecent.[3]

[1] Gregorovius, *Isabella d'Este*, 212, 251, 255, 264; Burckhardt, *Renaissance*, 316.
[2] De Julleville, *La Comédie en France au M. A.*, 183, 331.
[3] Scherillo, *La Commedia del Arte*, Chap. VI.

663. The theater at Venice. The first tragedy produced in
Italy was written by Albertino Mussato, a Paduan, early in the
fourteenth century in imitation of Latin dramas. The subject
was the conflicts of Padua with Ezzelino da Romano. Albertino's
work was not imitated, for the mysteries held the stage until the
end of the fifteenth century. They were represented on stages
erected in public places of the cities. At Venice were invented
momaria, in which there was no theatrical illusion, but *brio*,
joviality, and irony. They began at weddings, where after the
wedding feast some one, impersonating an heroic personage, narrated the great deeds of the ancestors of the spouses, with num-
berless exaggerations and jest, from which the name *momaria*, or
bombaria, was derived. The companies of the *calza* figured in
all gay assemblies at Venice from 1400 to the end of the sixteenth century. They renewed the Latin comedies and "carried
festivity and good taste even into the churches." Theatrical
exhibitions became the favorite amusement of the Venetians,
and were presented not only in private houses but also in
monasteries, although secular persons were not present.[1]

664. Dancing. Public sports. From the early Middle Ages the
ecclesiastical authorities disapproved of dancing, but the people
were very fond of it and never gave it up. The poems and
romances are full of it.[2] Some usages of dancing in Germany
were very gross. The man swung his partner off the floor as
far as he could. If any woman refused to dance with any man,
it occurred sometimes that he slapped her face, but it was disputed whether this was not beyond the limit.[3] The usages at the
carnival were very gross and obscene.[4] All popular sports were
coarse and cruel. It seemed to be considered good fun to torment
the weak and to watch their helpless struggles. Birds were shot,
and beasts baited, in a way to give pain and prolong it. At
Nuremberg the "cat knight" fought with a cat hung about his
own neck, which he must bite to death in order to be knighted

[1] Molmenti, *Venezia nella Vita Privata*, 297–299.
[2] Lacroix, *Manners, Customs, and Dress of M. A.*, 241.
[3] Angerstein, *Volkstänze*, 30.
[4] Schultz, *D. L.*, 414.

by the *bürgermeister*. Blind people were shut in an inclosed
space in the market place with a pig as a prize, which they were
to beat with sticks. The fun was greatest when they struck
each other. This amusement is reported from many places in
central Europe.[1] "Nothing amused our ancestors more than
these blind encounters. Even kings took part at these burlesque
representations." At Paris they were presented every year at
mid-lent.[2]

665. Women in the theater and on the stage. No young
women were allowed to be present at the *commedia del arte* in
the first times of the principate at Florence. Masi[3] says that
this was true in general of all Italy. Later they were addressed
in the prologue, which became customary, and so they must have
been present. Popular opinion still held that they ought to stay
at home, as of old. They were never on the stage. De Julleville
says[4] that women in France in the Middle Ages were present
at the freest farces. In the middle of the sixteenth century, in
Italy, wandering players began to employ women for female
parts. The Italian comedians, when they went to Paris, continued this custom there.[5] Philip II of Spain forbade women on
the stage.[6] French actresses appeared at London in 1629;
they were allowed in 1659.[7] Innocent XI, in 1676, forbade the
employment of women on the stage.[8]

666. The "commedia del arte." In Italy the *commedia del
arte* was the continuation or revival of the *mimus*. The speeches
were impromptu; the characters and rôles were stereotyped.
The action and speeches must have grown by the contributions
of talented men who played the parts from generation to generation. The characters have become traditional and universal.[9]
Such were Maccus (later Polichinella) of Naples, Manducus or

[1] Barthold, *Hansa*, III, 177.

[2] Lacroix, *Manners, Customs, and Dress of M. A.*, 220; Schultz, *D. L.*, 409;
Scherr, *Kult. Gesch.*, 623.   [5] Scherillo, *La Commedia del Arte*, 72.

[3] *Teatro Ital. nel Sec. XVIII*, 232.   [6] Chandler, *Romances of Roguery*, 159.

[4] *Comédie en France au M. A.*, 23.   [7] Magnin, *Marionettes*, 233.

[8] D'Ancona, *Origine del Teatro in Italia*, I, 341.

[9] Burckhardt *Die Renaissance*, 318. In Gozzi's *Memoirs* (ed. Symonds) may
be seen good colored plates representing these fixed characters of the *commedia
del arte*.

the French Croquemitaine, Bucco, a half-stupid, half-sarcastic buffoon, Pappus (the later Venetian Pantalon) the fussy old man, and Casnar, the French Cassandre. Scaramucca or Fracassa was added to satirize the Spanish soldier. He was recognized as the Miles Gloriosus of Plautus.[1] The Spanish trooper was a boastful coward. He called himself the son of the earthquake and lightning, cousin of death, or friend of Beelzebub.[2] At the marriage of Alphonso d'Este comedies of Plautus were acted for effect and conventional pretense, but they were considered tiresome, and interludes of pantomime, ballet, clown tricks, peasant farce, mythology, and fireworks were introduced to furnish entertainment.[3]

667. Jest books. Italian comedy at Paris. In the sixteenth century the theater became entirely secular, and amusement and religion were separated as a consequence of the general movement of the Renaissance. In the Middle Ages serious men collected jests and published jest books, which were collections of the jokes made by the *mimus*, just as modern jests have been made by negro minstrels, circus clowns, and variety actors.[4] At the end of the sixteenth century the Italians, "suffocated by Spanish etiquette, and poisoned by Jesuitical hypocrisy, sought to expand healthy lungs in free spaces of open air, indulging in dialectical niceties, and immortalizing street jokes by the genius of masked comedy."[5] The *commedia del arte* took this course. It was open to every chance of political and social influence. It became the recognized Italian comedy and was transported to the north as such. In each province of Italy the fixed characters were independently developed, so that variations were produced. The type of play reached a climax in the middle of the seventeenth century. Then it declined for lack of competent actors. It was the realism of everyday life. It tended always back again to the mountebanks, jugglers, rope dancers, etc.[6] The *lazzi* were "business" which gave the actors time to improvise. In the

[1] Scherillo, *La Commedia del Arte*, 90, 114.
[2] *Ibid.*, 95. [4] Reich, *Der Mimus*, 473.
[3] Burckhardt, 316. [5] Symonds, *Catholic Reaction*, I, 55.
[6] Masi, *Teatro Ital. nel Sec.*, XVIII, 229.

sixteenth century Italian comedians began to play at Paris in Italian. The Italian actresses undressed on the stage much and often, so that "Italian comedy" came to mean vulgar and licentious comedy. The Parlement of Paris held that the plays were immoral. Many of them are said to have been obscene.[1] Madame de Maintenon having heard that they were immoral, they were forbidden in 1697.[2] The Italian comedy struggled on, however. For a long time no women visited it, but in the eighteenth century a comedy called *Arlequin, Empereur dans la Lune* became celebrated. It was a satire on the France of the time. Women ignored the grossness for the sake of the satire.[3] The plays of the Italians were all either farces for pure fun or satires on the mores of the time. "Many were satires on women." In one of these last, the saying was ascribed to Aristotle, upon seeing a tree from the limbs of which four women were hanging, "How happy men would be, if all trees bore that fruit." Women were currently represented as empty-headed, vain, fond of pleasure, frivolous, and fickle. Lawyers were also a favorite object of satire.[4] In the Italian theater *écriteaux* were hung up, on which the speeches were written and the audience joined in singing the couplets.[5]

668. "Commedia del arte" in Italy. In Italy the *commedia del arte* went through many vicissitudes. At Venice, late in the eighteenth century, Gozzi undertook to revive it by composing what he called "fables." They were fairy extravaganzas, based on Mother Goose stories or fairy tales. They were in part improvised, but in part written, either in prose or verse, in order to make sure of the essential points of the action. The older custom had been to prepare only a *scenario*, in which the story was told in brief outline, with the allotment of parts in the production.[6] Pantaleone, in the *commedia del arte*, is sad, — an imbecile, dissolute old man. Gozzi gave him *brio* and *bonarietà*, with cordiality and humor. Goldoni, who got into a war with

---

[1] Bernardin, *Comédie Ital. en France,* 9, 12, 13.
[2] *Ibid.*, 52.
[3] Bernardin, *Com. Ital. en France,* 27.
[4] *Ibid.*, 42.
[5] *Ibid.*, 90.
[6] Gozzi's *Memoirs* (*Symond's trans.*).

Gozzi, made Pantaleone a philistine, who used good sense against the follies of fashion. No women were present at these comedies at Venice at this time.[1]

Scherillo[2] quotes Perucci, that at the end of the seventeenth century the folk theater was obscene in word and act beyond the ancient comedies. If that is true, it is only a detail of the degeneracy of Italy from the middle of the sixteenth century.

669. Summary and review. It is evident that amusement and relaxation are needs of men. The fondness for exhibitions and theatrical representations can be traced through history. The suggestion is direct and forcible. It can be made to play upon harmful tastes as well as upon good ones. There is nothing to guide it or decide its form and direction except the mores, — the consenting opinion of the masses as to what is beneficial or harmful. The leading classes try to mold this opinion. The history shows that the mores can make anything right, and protect any violation of the sex taboo or of ordinary propriety. There is no subject in regard to which the mores need more careful criticism than in regard to amusements. The standard and the usage degenerate together unless there is control by an active and well-trained taste and sense. The popular taste and sense are products of inherited mores. It is this reflex action of habitual acts and experiences which makes the subject difficult. All the primary facts and the secondary or remoter reflections are intertwined as in an organic growth, and all go together. The facts exert constant education, and every positive effort to interfere with the course of things by primitive education must be content to exert slight effects for a long time. Wealth and luxury exert their evil effects through amusement. Poverty cuts down these products of wealth and brings societies back to simplicity and virtue. Men renounce when they cannot get. The periods of economic and social decay have cut off the development of forms of amusement, arrested vice, and forced new beginnings.

670. Amusements need the control of educated judgment and will. The history shows that amusements are a pitfall in which

[1] Masi, *Teatro Ital.*, 89, 232, 264.　　[2] *La Commedia del Arte*, 50.

good mores may be lost and evil ones produced. They require conventional control and good judgment to guide them. This requirement cannot be set aside. Amusements always present a necessity for moral education and moral will. This fact has impressed itself on men in all ages, and all religions have produced Puritan and ascetic sects who sought welfare, not in satisfying but in counteracting the desire for amusement and pleasure. Their efforts have proved that there is no solution in that direction. There must be an educated judgment at work all the time, and it must form correct judgments to be made real by a cultivated will, or the whole societal interest may be lost without the evil tendency being perceived.

671. Amusements do not satisfy the current notions of progress. It is clear from the history that amusements have gone through waves upward and downward, but that the amplitude of the waves is very small. It is true that the shows of the late Roman empire were very base, and that the great drama has gone very high by comparison, but the oscillation between the two entirely destroys anything like a steady advance in dramatic composition or dramatic art. This is a very instructive fact. It entirely negatives the current notion of progress as a sort of function of time which is to be expected to realize itself in a steady improvement and advance to better and better. The useful arts do show an advance. The fine arts do not. They return to the starting point, or near it, again and again. The dramatic art is partly literary and partly practical handicraft. Theater buildings improve; the machinery, lights, scenery, and manipulation improve. The literary products are like other artistic products: they have periods of glory and periods of decay. It is the literary products which are nearest to the mores. They lack all progress, or advance only temporarily from worse to better literary forms.

CHAPTER XVIII

ASCETICISM

The exaggeration of opposite policies. — Failure of the mores and revolt against expediency. — Luck and welfare; self-discipline to influence the superior powers. — Asceticism in Japan. — Development of the arts; luxury; sensuality. — The ascetic philosophy. — Asceticism is an aberration. — The definitions depend on the limits. — Asceticism in India and Greece; Orphic doctrines. — Ascetic features in the philosophic sects. — Hebrew asceticism. — Nazarites, Rechabites, Essenes. — Roman asceticism. — Christian asceticism. — Three traditions united in Christianity. — Asceticism in the early church. — Asceticism in Islam. — Virginity. — Mediæval asceticism. — Asceticism in Christian mores. — Renunciation of property; beggary. — Ascetic standards. — The Mendicant Friars. — The Franciscans. — Whether poverty is a good. — Clerical celibacy. — How Christian asceticism ended.

672. The exaggeration of opposite policies. It is not to be expected that all the men in a society will react in the same way against the same experiences and observations. If they draw unanimously the same conclusions from the same facts, that is such an unusual occurrence that their unanimity gives great weight to their opinion. In almost all cases they are thrown into parties by their different inferences from the same experiences and observations. There is nothing about which they differ more than about amusement, pleasure, and happiness, and as to the degree in which pleasure is worth pursuing. Those who feel deceived by pleasure and duped by the pursuit of happiness revolt from it and denounce it. Inasmuch as others not yet disillusioned still pursue pleasure as the most obviously desirable good, there are two great parties who divide on fundamental notions of life policy. Two such parties, face to face, tend to exaggerate their distinctive doctrines and practices. Each party goes to extremes and excess. We have seen in the last chapter (secs. 624 ff.) that at the beginning of the Christian era moral restraints were thrown aside and that all living men seemed to plunge into vice, luxury, and pleasure, so far as their means would allow. There were, however, a number of sects and religions in the Greco-Roman world that held extremely pessimistic views as to the worth of human life and of those things which men care for most. They renounced the ordinary standards of welfare and happiness, and sought welfare and happiness in merely denying the popular standards. The old world philosophies no longer commanded faith, and they seemed to be rejected with active hatred, not with mere indifferent unbelief. The poor and those who were forced to live by self-denial joined these sects of philosophy or religion. The age which saw extremes of luxury and vicious excess was also the age which saw great phenomena of ascetic philosophy and practice. Each school or tendency developed its own mores to treat the problems of life in its own way. An ascetic policy never is a primary product of the "ways" in which unreflecting men meet the facts of life. It is reflective and derived. It is a secondary stage of faith built on experience and reflection. It is, therefore, dogmatic. It must be sustained by faith in the fundamental pessimistic conviction. It never can be verified by experience. It purposely runs counter to all the sanctions which are possible in experience. If any one declares evil good and pain pleasure, he cannot find proof of it in any experiment. The mores produced out of asceticism are therefore peculiar and in many ways instructive.

673. Failure of the mores and revolt against expediency. We have seen that the mores are the results of the efforts of men to find out how to live under the conditions of human life so as to satisfy interests and secure welfare. The efforts have been only very imperfectly successful. The task, in fact, never can be finished, for the conditions change and the problem contains different elements from time to time. Moreover, dogmas interfere. They dictate "duty" and "right" by authority and as virtue, quite independently of any verification by experience and expediency. All the primitive taboos express the convictions of men that there are things which must not be done, or must not be done beyond some limited degree, if the men would live well.

Such convictions came either from experience or from dogma. The former class of cases were those things which were connected with food and the sex relation. The latter class of cases were those things which were connected with the doctrine of ghosts. There are also a great many primitive customs for coercing or conciliating superior powers, — either men or spirits, — which consist in renunciation, self-torture, obscenity, bloodshedding, filthiness, and the performance of repugnant acts or even suicide. These customs all imply that the superior powers are indifferent, or angry and malevolent, or justly displeased, and that the pain of men pleases, or appeases and conciliates, or coerces them, or wins their attention. Thus we meet with a fundamental philosophy of life in which it is not the satisfaction of needs, appetites, and desires, but the opposite theory which is thought to lead to welfare. Renounce what you want; do what you do not want to do; pursue what is repugnant; in short, invert the relations of pleasure and pain, and act by your will against their sanctions, so as to seek pain and flee pleasure. A doctrine of due measure and limit upon the rational satisfaction of needs and desires is turned into an absolute rule of well-being. Within narrower limits the same philosophy inculcates acts of labor, pain, and renunciation, which produce no results in the satisfaction of wants but are regarded as beneficial or meritorious in themselves, as a kind of gymnastic in self-control and self-denial. It is not to be denied that such a gymnastic has value in education, especially in the midst of luxury and self-indulgence, if it is controlled by common sense and limited within reason. Nearly all men, however, are sure to meet with as much necessity for self-control and self-denial as is necessary to their training, without arbitrarily subjecting themselves to artificial discipline of that kind.

674. Luck and welfare. Self-discipline to influence the superior powers. The notion of welfare through acts which upon their face are against welfare is directly referable to experience of the impossibility of establishing sure relations between positive efforts and satisfactions. The lowest civilization is full of sacrifices, renunciation, self-discipline, etc. It is the effect of the aleatory element and of the explanation of the same by goblinism (secs. 6, 9). The acts of renunciation or self-discipline have no rational connection with the interests which they aim to serve. Those acts can affect interests only by influencing the ghosts or demons who always interfere between efforts and results and make luck. Soldiers, fishermen, hunters, traders, agriculturists, etc., are bidden to practice continence before undertaking any of their enterprises. Hence arises the notion of a "state of grace," not the state produced by work in the workday world, but a state produced by abstinence from work, from enjoyment, and from the experience of good and ill. Abstention from wine, meat, other luxuries of food and drink, and from women gives power which is magical, because it has no real causal connection with desired results in war or industry. Uncivilized people almost always have some such notion of reaching a higher plane of power, or more especially of luck, by self-discipline. Acts of self-discipline, e.g. fasting, gashing, mutilating one's self, also enter into mourning. In some tribes parents who expect a child engage in acts of the same kind.[1] Asceticism in higher civilization is a survival of the life philosophy of an earlier stage, in which the pain of men was believed to be pleasant to the superior powers. The same sentiment revives now in times of decline or calamity, when the wrath of God is recognized or apprehended. We appoint a fast when we are face to face with calamity. The same sentiment is at work in sects and individuals when they desire "holiness," or a "higher life," or mystic communion with higher powers, or "purity" (in the ritual sense), or relief from "sin," or escape from the terror of ghosts and demons, or power to arise to some high moral standard by crushing out the natural appetites which according to that standard are base and wicked.

675. Asceticism in Japan. The Shinto religion of the Japanese "is not an essentially ascetic religion ; it offers flesh and wine to its gods ; and it prescribes only such forms of self-denial as ancient custom and decency require. Nevertheless, some of its votaries perform extraordinary austerities on special occasions, —

[1] Spix and Martius, *Brasil*, 1318.

austerities which always include much cold-water bathing. But the most curious phase of this Shinto ascetism is represented by a custom still prevalent in remote districts. According to this custom a community yearly appoints one of its citizens to devote himself wholly to the gods on behalf of the rest. During the term of his consecration this communal representative must separate from his family, must not approach women, must avoid all places of amusement, must eat only food cooked with sacred fire, must abstain from wine, must bathe in fresh cold water several times a day, must repeat particular prayers at certain hours, and must keep vigil upon certain nights. When he has performed these duties of abstinence and purification for the specified time he becomes religiously free, and another man is then elected to take his place. The prosperity of the settlement is supposed to depend upon the exact observance by its representative of the duties prescribed; should any public misfortune occur, he would be suspected of having broken his vows. Anciently, in the case of a common misfortune, the representative was put to death." [1]

676. Development of the arts. Luxury. Sensuality. In the development of the arts there has been an increase of luxury in the ways of living. This has seemed to be a good. It has seemed like successful accomplishment of what man must do to win and enjoy power over nature. Luxury, however, has brought vice and ill, and has wrought decay and ruin. It is the twin sister of sensuality, which is corruption. Is luxury a good or not? Men have lost faith in it, and have declared that the triumphs of the arts were delusions, "snares to the soul," corruption of the individual and society. They have turned back to the "old simple ways," and have renounced the enjoyments which were within their reach by the power of the arts. Such renunciation has always been popular. The crowd has always admired it. It is certainly a noteworthy feature in the history of civilization that there has always been present in it a reaction, a movement of fear and doubt about the innovations of every kind by which it is attended, which has caused sects of philosophers and

---

[1] Hearn, *Japan*, 165.

religious persons to refuse to go on, to renounce luxurious novelties, and to prefer the older and inferior ways.

677. The ascetic philosophy. Here then we have a life philosophy, or a life standpoint, from which the things to be done are presented inverted. It is ill luck, loss, calamity, etc., which have inverted human nature. The element of luck crossed and cut off the relations between effort and satisfaction, and disturbed all the lessons of industry. All effort would be vain if the ghosts who control luck were not propitiated. If they were friendly, labor was of no importance. Self-discipline, therefore, entered into everything. This is asceticism. It is always irrational or magical, addressed directly or remotely to the superior powers, as an appeal to their will and favor, their mystical friendship, and a prayer for the transcendental communications which they give. Pater[1] says that asceticism is a sacrifice of one part of human nature to another, that the latter may survive; or a harmonious development of all parts to realize an ideal of culture. If the first sentence of this statement could be accepted as a fair definition, the second cannot. Asceticism does not aim at a harmonious development and never could produce it. It selects purposes and pushes towards their accomplishment. The selection has often been made with the purpose to attain to holiness, or a higher realization of religious ideals. The ideals are necessarily arbitrary and are very sure to be extravagant. They do not have good effect on character, and they produce moral distortion. They are, however, an outflow of honest religious emotion.

678. Asceticism is only an aberration. The great viewpoints and the great world philosophies are found logically at the end of a long study of life, if anywhere. If one is found or adopted, it furnishes leading for the notions of ways to be employed in all details of life. This is equally true if it is reached on a slight, superficial, or superstitious view of life. The ascetic philosophy produces contradiction and confusion in the acts of men, because some of them work for expediency and others for inexpediency at the same time. Therefore also the mores, if they are affected by

[1] *Marius the Epicurean*, 357.

asceticism, are inconsistent and contradictory. Nevertheless asceticism is only an aberration which starts from a highly virtuous motive. We must do what is right and virtuous because it is so. It is right and virtuous to fight sensuality in personal character and social action. The fight will often consist in acts which have no further relation to interests. By zeal the work of this fight absorbs more and more of life, and it may engage a large number associatively. It becomes the great purpose by which mores are built. Then the notion of pleasing superior powers by self-inflicted pain is thrown out, and all the primitive superstition is eliminated. We find a vast network of mores, which may characterize a generation or a society, which are due to the revolt against sensuality, either in the original purity of the revolt (which is very rare) or in some of its thousands of variations and combinations.

679. The definitions depend on the limit. Especially in connection with food, drink, and sex the asceticism of one age becomes the virtue of another. The ideas of temperance and moderation of one age are often clearly produced by previous ascetic usages. The definitions are all made by the limit. A stricter observance than the current custom is ascetic, but it may become the custom and set the limit. Then it is only temperance. It is often impossible to distinguish sharply between taboos which only impose respect for gods, temples, etc. (cleanliness, quiet, good clothing), and those which are ascetic. When the ascetic temper and philosophy assumes control it easily degenerates into a mania. Acts are regarded as meritorious in proportion as they are painful, and they are pushed to greater and greater extravagances because what becomes familiar loses the subjective force from which the ascetic person wins self-satisfaction. Asceticism then becomes a mental aberration and a practical negation of the instinct of self-preservation. It leads to insanity.[1] If it takes a course against other persons, it explains the conduct of great inquisitors like Conrad of Marburg.[2]

680. Asceticism in India and Greece. Orphic doctrines. In India ascetic acts were supposed to produce not only holiness

---

[1] Galton, *Hered. Genius*, 239.   [2] Lea, *Inquisition*, II, 330.

but also power, which might arise to superhuman degrees or even avail to overcome gods. Rohde [1] finds that the theological ascetic morality of the later history of Greece, which was not a determination of the will in a given direction but a mode of defending the soul from an external evil influence which threatened to soil it, had its first impulse in the notion of the antagonism between soul and body, because that notion would cause the body to be regarded as a base constraint from which the soul would need to be "purified." The notion of the pure soul imprisoned in a material sensual body, and stained by the base appetites of the latter, was current amongst the Greeks for five centuries before Christ. Hence the antagonism between the soul and the "body," the "flesh," or the "world." The soul passed from one body to another, according to the Orphic sects, with intervals in which it underwent purification. In each incarnation it underwent punishment for the misdeeds of the last previous existence. The soul is immortal. The soul of the bad man goes on forever in reincarnations from which it cannot escape. The soul which is purified by the Orphic rites and Orphic mode of life is redeemed from this eternal round and returns to God. Orpheus gives salvation by his rites, but it is a work of grace by the redeeming gods. Orpheus provides by his revelations and intercessions the way to salvation, and he who would walk in this way must carefully obey his ordinances. This is a life which must be lived. It is not ritual only. Here asceticism comes in, for the thing to be renounced is not the errors and faults of earthly life, but earthly life itself (worldliness). The man must turn away from everything which would entangle him in the interests of mortal life and the appetites of the body. Renunciation of meat food was one of the leading forms of this asceticism ; sex restraint was another. The rites do not free men from the touch of demons. They purify the soul from the unclean contact with the body and from the dominion of death. Mysticism is conjoined with this doctrine of purification. The soul came from God and seeks to return to him. It is released by the rites and practices from everything on earth, including

[1] *Psyche*, II, 101.

morals, which are only petty attempts to deal with details, and therefore are of no interest to a soul which is released. The dead are led to the place of the dead. The Orphic priests described this " intermediate state " with graphic distinctness, surpassing that of the Eleusinian mysteries. Probably this was the most popular, although not the most original, part of their teaching. The doctrine was not a folk notion ; it was "holy doctrine" that there would be in Hades a judgment and a retribution. Then woe to him who had not been purified in the Orphic orgies! The Orphic sects also had a doctrine that the living, by the rites, could act upon the fate of deceased relatives in the other world.[1] These sects began in the second half of the sixth century before Christ. We do not know the course or mode by which they spread. They formed close associations or conventicles to practice the cult of Dionysus.[2]

681. Ascetic features in the philosophic sects. The Pythagoreans also formed, in the sixth century, at Crotona, an association to practice moderation and simplicity. The use of meat food was limited, and by some it was renounced entirely.[3] Our knowledge of this sect is very slight and vague, although the tradition of its doctrines was certainly very strong in later times. It is believed that there was included in its teachings disapproval of prenuptial unchastity by men.[4] This would not be considered ascetic by us, but it appeared so to ancient Greeks. The Cynics were ascetics. They renounced the elegances and luxuries of life, and their asceticism became more and more the essence of their sectarianism. Some Greek priests were married, but others were bound to be chaste for life or while engaged in priestly duties. Sometimes some foods were forbidden to them, and this taboo might be extended to all who entered the temple. All must be clean in body and dress.[5] In the tragedies we find mention of the ascetic notion of virginity.[6] In the *Elektra* (250–270) the heroine lays great stress on the fact that her

---

[1] Rohde, *Psyche*, II, 121–130.   [3] Ueberweg, *Hist. Philos.*, I, 45.
[2] *Ibid.*, 104.   [4] Lecky, *Eur. Morals*, II, 314.
[5] Stengel, *Griech. Kultusalterthümer*, 35.
[6] Euripides, *Hippolytus*, 1300 ; *Trojan Women*, 38, 975.

peasant husband has never taken conjugal rights. Orestes asks whether the husband has taken a vow of chastity, so that a vow of chastity was not an unknown thing. The notion of virginity was very foreign to the mores of the Greeks, but it existed amongst them. It gained ground in the later centuries. At the time of Christ it is certain that a wave of asceticism was running through the Hellenistic world.[1] It may have been due to the sense of decline and loss in comparison with the earlier times. It seems to bear witness to a feeling that the world was on a wrong path, in spite of Roman glory and luxury. If they could not correct the course of things, they could at least renounce the luxury. That seemed like an effort to stem the tide. More commonly the sentiment was less defined and less morally vigorous. It was only world sickness. Cases occurred of individuals who renounced marriage, or lived in it without conjugal intimacy.[2] The Stoics, Cynics, Neopythagoreans, and Neoplatonists all had ascetic elements in their doctrines. The wandering preachers of these sects were rarely men of any earnest purpose, and their speeches were empty rhetorical exercises, but they popularized the doctrines of the sects. Simon Stylites only continued a pagan custom. There were in front of the temple at Hierapolis two columns one hundred and eighty feet high. Twice a year a man climbed one of these and remained on top of it for seven days to pray and commune with the gods, or in memory of Deukalion and the flood. He drew up supplies with a rope. People brought him gifts of money and he prayed for them, swinging a brazen instrument which made a screaming sound.[3]

682. Hebrew asceticism. The Jewish tradition was that at Sinai all the people were ordered to refrain from women for the time, but that for Moses this injunction was unlimited (Exod. xix. 15). In the rabbinical period it was established doctrine that any one who desired to receive a revelation from God must refrain from women.[4] Other cases in the Old Testament show that persons who were under a renunciation of this kind were in

[1] Mahaffy, *The Grecian World under Roman Sway*, 180.
[2] Lecky, *Eur. Morals*, II, 315.
[3] Lucian, *De Syria Dea*, sec. 28.
[4] *Jewish Encyc.*, V, 226.

a state of grace. The ritual of uncleanness was ascetic and it enforced ascetic views of sex and marriage.[1]

683. Nazarites, Rechabites, Essenes. The Nazarites were Hebrew ascetics by temporary vow (Num. vi.). They did not cut their hair or drink wine, and never touched a corpse.[2] The Rechabites were a Jewish ascetic association of the ninth century B.C. They renounced the civilized life of the nation at that time and reverted to the pre-Canaanite life. They adopted wild dress and coarse food, and renounced wine. They lived in tents and cultivated Bedouin mores. The Essenes of the last century before Christ were an ascetic community with puritan and rigoristic tenets and practices. The laws of Antiochus Epiphanes that unclean animals might be brought to Jerusalem opened a chance that faithful Jews might eat of such. The attempt to guard one's self was made easier if a number had meals in common. This may be the origin of the custom of the Essenes to have common meals.[3] The company cultivated holiness by set rules of life, ritual, washings, etc. Their philosophy was that fate controls all which affects man.[4] They performed no sacrifices in the temple, but had rites of their own which seemed to connect them with the Pythagoreans. They were "the best of men," and "employed themselves in agriculture." They thought evil of all women, and educated children whom they adopted. All who joined the society gave their property to it and all property was held in common.[5] They used rites of worship to the sun. Their asceticism was derived from their doctrine of the soul's preexistence and its warfare with the body.[6] They were stricter than the Pharisees. They rejected wealth, oaths, sensual enjoyment, and slavery.[7] They renounced all occupations which excite greed and injustice, such as inn keeping, commerce, weapon making.[8] Sex intercourse was so restricted that they could not fulfill the primary duties which the law laid on every

---

[1] Levit. xv. 16, 18. Deut. xxiii. 11; Josephus, *Cont. Ap.*, II, 24.
[2] Judges xiii. 4–14; Amos ii. 11.
[3] Lucius, *Essenismus*, 102.
[4] Josephus, *Antiq.*, XIII, 5, 9.

[5] Cook, *Fathers of Jesus*, II, 30, 38.
[6] Hastings, Dict. Bib., *Devel. of Doct. in Apoc. Period;* Supp. Vol. 292, a.
[7] Lucius, *Essenismus*, 54, 59, 68.
[8] *Ibid.*, 52.

man to beget children. Often they were persons who entered the society after having fulfilled this duty.[1] They had extreme rules of Sabbath keeping, food taboo, purification, and extreme doctrines of renunciation of luxury and pleasure. They either died out or coalesced with Christians.[2]

684. Roman asceticism. The primitive Roman mores were very austere, not ascetic, and the institutions of the family and sex were strictly controlled by the mores. The Vestal Virgins might be cited as a proof that virginity was considered a qualification for high religious functions, so that it seemed meritorious and pure and a nobler estate than marriage.

685. Christian asceticism. Christianity is ascetic in its attitude towards wealth, luxury, and pleasure. It inherited from Judaism hostility to sensuality, which was thought by the Jews to be a mark of heathenism and an especial concomitant of idolatry. We distinguish between luxury and pleasure on the one side and sensuality on the other, and repress the last for rational, not ascetic, reasons.

686. Three traditions united in Christianity. The three streams of tradition which entered into Christianity brought down ascetic notions and temper. The antagonism of flesh and spirit is expressed, Galat. v. 16, and the evil of the flesh, Romans vii. 18, 25; Eph. v. 29. Yet ascetics are denounced, I Tim. iv. 3, "forbidding to marry, and commanding to abstain from meats, which God created to be received with thanksgiving by them that believe and know the truth." In I Tim. iii. 2 and Titus i. 6 it is expressly stated that a priest or bishop is to be the husband of one wife. In Revelation xiv. 4 a group are described as "they who were not defiled with women, for they are virgins." The notion that procreation is "impure" and that renunciation of it is "purity" is present here. Cf. Levit. xv. 16–18. In I Cor. vii the doctrine is that renunciation of marriage is best; that marriage is a concession to human frailty; that all sex relation outside of marriage is sin. If there is a

---

[1] *Jewish Encyc.*, V, s. v. "Essenes."
[2] Cook, *Fathers of Jesus*, II, 48; Lucius, *Essenismus*, 131; Graetz, *Gesch. der Juden*, III, 92 ff.

technical definition of sin, virtue, purity, etc., it can only be satisfied by arbitrary acts which are ascetic in character. The definitions also produce grades of goodness and merit beyond duty and right. The "religious" become a technical class, who cultivate holiness beyond what is required of simple Christians. Saints are heroes of the same development. In general, the methods of attaining to holiness and saintliness must be arbitrary and ascetic,— fasting, self-torture, loathsome acts, excessive ritual, etc.

687. Asceticism in the early church. It has been sufficiently shown that the Greco-Roman world, at the birth of Christ, was penetrated by ascetic ideas and streams of ascetic usage. In the postapostolic period there was a specific class of ecclesiastical ascetics. There were many different fields of origin for such a class in the different provinces.[1] Epictetus (b. 60 A.D.) had a spirit and temper which have always been recognized as closely Christian. He thought the aim should not be to endure pain and calamity with fortitude, but to suppress evil desires and to cultivate discipline. There were congregations in the earliest days of Christianity which were composed of persons who wanted to lead a purer life than was common amongst Christians. They adopted rules, as "counsels of perfection," such as renunciation of marriage and of eating meat.[2] The ascetic tendency got strong sway in the church in the second half of the second century, but the practices were voluntary, suggested by the religious impulses of the individual, and the leaders tried to hold the ruling tendency in reason. They held it to be absurd that self-inflicted pain could please God.[3] The tendency, however, could not be arrested. It was in the age. All the philosophies except Epicureanism, and all the sects in the mysteries, had encouraged it. The Christians had doctrines which were not hostile to it. It therefore flourished amongst them. In the second century there was a deep desire for a moral reformation, and to further it moral discipline was formulated in rules and made a system. The individual was taught to endure hardships,

---

[1] Harnack, *Pseudoclement. Briefe de Virg.*, 3.
[2] Hatch, *Griechenthum und Christenthum*, 121.   [3] Lea, *Sacer. Celib.*, 29.

to drink water rather than wine, to sleep on the ground oftener than on a bed. In some cases they submitted to corporal cruelty, being scourged and loaded with chains. The converse error here appeared, for they made a display of their powers of endurance.[1] The moral gymnastics could be best practiced in solitary life. Many philosophers urged their disciples to leave home and to practice elsewhere, — in another town or in loneliness.[2] At the end of the third century the ascetic party, in spite of the withdrawal of the puritans, was very powerful. The ascetic sentiment was stimulated and was spreading on account of the ideas of neoplatonism, the increasing confusion in the Christian body, the excitement and anxiety of a period of social decline, and finally on account of the need to provide other means of expending the passionate love of God which had formerly driven Christians to martyrdom. When the church became a religion recognized by the state there was no more martyrdom. A similar tendency marked the sects of philosophy at the same time. The author of the *Letters on Virginity* ascribed to Clement (about 300 A.D.) is a strong admirer of celibacy. He has heard of shameless Christian men and women who consort, eat, drink, gossip, slander, and visit each other, although unmarried persons. The ascetics were forced to separate themselves entirely from the rest. They wandered, praying and preaching and casting out devils, having no means. The motives of asceticism were the apprehension of the end of the world, enthusiasm, dualistic philosophy, fear of sensuality, and gnostic doctrines. In 300 A.D. the ascetics were corrupt and venal and needed more complete isolation (monasticism).[3] In the fourth century an ascetic life, instead of a form of life for Christians inside the church, came to be thought of as an independent form of life. It was thought of as a " philosophy," most closely related to Cynicism. In externals Cynics and Christian ascetics were alike. The coarse garments and uncut hair gave them the same appearance.[4] In the fourth century the ethics of Paul were abandoned by Christians. The average Christians

---

[1] Hatch, *Griechenthum und Christenthum*, 108. [2] *Ibid.*, 109.
[3] Harnack, *Pseudo-Clement. Briefe de Virg.*, 19, 21, 22. [4] Hatch, 122.

were average citizens. They held the current ethical ideas of the society. The intellectual scaffolding built by current culture was stronger than the new ideas which were accepted. The mores held sway against the new influences. In place of the notions of justice and holiness the old notion of "virtue" prevailed. Instead of the law "Love thy neighbour as thyself," the old enumeration of virtues constituted ethical reflection. At the end of the fourth century this transformation was recognized by the leaders of the church.[1] The Manichæan sects practiced asceticism even more zealously than the orthodox. Renunciation of "the world" was selfish. The period was one of turmoil. The burdens of the state were excessive. It was an evil that the best men renounced the duties of the state and civil society. Virginity was praised as Christlike and taught in opposition to society and the family. Marriage was not forbidden, but a special mystery attached to it, to explain how it might be honored, although it was so depreciated. The body of that soul which desired to be the bride of Christ must be virgin.[2] If any one turned to a home and family he must understand that he descended to something inferior and doubtful. The Roman state had been trying for three hundred years to stimulate marriage and increase population. Constantine repealed all the laws against celibacy. Later emperors liberated ecclesiastics from the "municipal burdens which were eating out the heart of the empire." All were eager to become clerics, and as the number of settled priests was limited, they became monks. The wealth of the church also attracted them.[3] The situation produced hypocrites, false ascetics, and vicious clerics. After the middle of the fourth century the church began to legislate that those who took vows must keep them. The penalty of death was to be inflicted on any man who should marry a sacred virgin. Pope Siricius, in 384, described the shameless license of both sexes in violation of vows.[4] In part this was due to another logical product of the conception of purity as negation, especially of sex. Men and women exposed themselves

---

[1] Hatch, 123.
[2] Harnack, *Dogmengesch.*, I, 747.
[3] *Ibid.*, 59.
[4] *Ibid.*, 60.

to temptation and risk by sensual excitement, holding themselves innocent if they were not criminal.[1] These tricks of the human mind upon itself are familiar now in the history of scores of sects, and in the phenomena of revivalism. Ritual asceticism is consistent with sensual indulgence. The sophistry necessary to reconcile the two is easily spun.

688. Asceticism in Islam. Islam, at the beginning, had an ascetic tendency, which it soon lost. Mohammed and his comrades practiced night watches with prayer.[2] Jackson found in the modern Yezidi community a "sort of ascetic order of women," *fakiriah*, corresponding to fakirs amongst men.[3] The dervishes are the technically religious Moslems, and in the history of Islam there have been frequent temporary appearances of sects and groups which regarded pain as meritorious.

689. Virginity. Virginity is negative and may be a renunciation. It then falls in with the ascetic way of thinking, and the notion that virginity, as renunciation, is meritorious is a prompt deduction. Christian ecclesiastics made this deduction and pushed it to great extremes. The renunciation was thought to be more meritorious if practiced in the face of opportunity and temptation. The ascetics therefore created opportunity in order to put themselves in the midst of the war of sense and duty.[4]

690. Mediæval asceticism. In the eleventh and twelfth centuries the ascetic temper underwent a revival which was like an intellectual storm. It was nourished by reading the church fathers of the fourth and fifth centuries. It entered into mediæval mores. It was in the popular taste, and the church encouraged and developed it. It was connected with demonism and fetichism which had taken possession of the Christian church in the ninth and tenth centuries. Relics were fetiches. The Holy Sepulcher and the Holy Land were fetiches; that is, they were

---

[1] Such perversions have been very frequent. See Todd, *Life of St. Patrick*, 91, for a case; also, Lea, *Inquisition*, III, 109. Sometimes the test was to show that the temptation was powerless. Lea, *Inquis.*, II, 357; *Sacerd. Celib.*, 167.

[2] Wellhausen, *Skizzen und Vorarbeiten*, III, 210.

[3] *Hist. of Religions*, section of the *Amer. Orient. Soc.*, VII, 22.

[4] Achelis, *Virgines Subintroductae*. The author thinks that the relationship was one of Platonic comradeship.

thought to have magical power on account of the spirits of the great dead in them. Transubstantiation was the application of magic and fetich ideas to the ceremony of the mass. All the mediæval religiosity ran to forms of which asceticism and magic were the core. Cathedral building was a popular mania of ascetic religion. Pilgrimages had the same character. We may now regard it as ascertained fact that asceticism, cruelty to dissenters, fanaticism, and sex frenzy are so interlaced in the depths of human nature that they produce joint or interdependent phenomena. That an ascetic who despises pain, or even thinks it a good, should torture others is not hard to understand. That the same age should produce a wild outburst of sex passion and a mania of sex renunciation is only another case of contradictory products of the same cause of which human society offers many. That the same age should produce sensual worldlings and fanatical ecclesiastics is no paradox.

691. Asceticism in Christian mores. The ascetic standards and doctrines passed into the mores of Christianity and so into the mores of Christendom, both religious and civil. In the popular notion it was the taboos which constituted Christianity, and those were the best Christians who construed the taboos on wealth, luxury, pleasure, and sex most extremely, and observed them most strictly. Such persons were supposed to be able to perform miracles. In the Middle Ages the casuists and theologians seemed never to tire of multiplying distinctions and antitheses about sex.[1] In fact their constant preoccupation with it was the worst departure from the reserve and dignity which are the first requirements in respect to it. A document of the extremest doctrine is *Hali Meidenhad*,[2] of the thirteenth century. The aim of the book is to persuade women to renounce marriage. Marriage is servitude. God did not institute it. Adam and Eve introduced it by sin. Our flesh is our foe. Virginity is heaven on earth. Happy wedlock is rare. Motherhood is painful. Family life is full of trials and quarrels. Virginity is not God's command but his counsel. Marriage is only a concession (1 Cor. vii.). This was the orthodox doctrine of the

[1] See Peter Lombard, *Sentent.*, IV, 31.   [2] *Early Eng. Text Soc.*, 1866.

time. Among the religious heroes of the age not a few were irresponsible from lack of food, lack of sleep, and the nervous exaltation which they forced upon themselves by ascetic practices.[1]

692. Renunciation of property. Beggary. Those who did not practice asceticism accepted its standards and applied them. A special case and one of the most important was the admiration which was rendered in the thirteenth century to the renunciation of property and the consequent high merit attributed to beggary for the two following centuries. The social consequences were so great that this view of poverty and beggary is perhaps the most important consequence in the history of the mores which go with the ascetic philosophy of life.

693. Ascetic standards. All who were indifferent or hostile to the church and religion maintained the ascetic standards for ecclesiastics in their extremest form. All the literature of the Middle Ages contains scoffing at priests, monks, and friars. In part, they were scoffed at because they did not fulfill that measure of asceticism which the scoffers chose to require, and which the clerics taught and seemed bound to practice.

694. The mendicant friars. The notion that poverty is meritorious and a good in itself was widely entertained but unformulated at the beginning of the thirteenth century. Jacques de Vitry, who was in Italy in 1216, and who left a journal of his journey,[2] met with an association in Lombardy, the Umiliati, who held the doctrines of the later Franciscans. The ideas which were current at that time about the primitive church were entirely fantastic. They had no foundation in fact. They were in fact deductions from ascetic ideals. The church of the thirteenth century was the opposite in all respects of what the primitive church was supposed to have been. Francis of Assisi and a few friends determined (1208) to live by the principles of the primitive church as they supposed that it had been. It is certain that they were only one group, which found favorable

---

[1] Cf. Lea, *Inquis.*, II, 214, about Peter Martyr.
[2] *Nouveaux Mem. de l'Acad. des Sciences, lettres et beaux arts de Belgique*, XXIII, 30.

conditions of growth, but that there were many such groups at the time. De Vitry was filled with sadness by what he saw at the papal court. All were busy with secular affairs, kings and kingdoms, quarrels and lawsuits, so that it was almost impossible to speak about spiritual matters. He greatly admired the Franciscans, who were trying to live like the early Christians and to save souls, and who shamed the prelates, who were "dogs who do not bark." The strongest contrasts between the gospel ideals and the church of that time were presented by wealth and the hierarchy. Francis renounced all property. Poverty was idealized and allegorized. Since he would not produce or own things, he had to beg or borrow them from others who were therefore obliged to sin for him. The first corollary from the admiration of poverty was the glorification of beggary and its exaltation above productive labor.[1] There is a rhapsody on poverty in the *Roman de la Rose*. If it is base and corrupting to admire wealth, it is insane to admire poverty. It never can be anything more than a pose or affectation. The count of Chiusi gave to Francis the mountain La Verna as a place of retirement and meditation. Armed men were necessary to take possession of this place on account of beasts and robbers.[2] Here, then, we have all the crime, selfishness, and violence of "property." The legendary story of Francis is fabulous. It is a product of the popular notions of the time. He was said to perform miracles. Crowds flocked to him. His order spread with great rapidity and without much effort on his part. Evidently it just met the temper, longings, and ideals of the time. Its strength was that it suited the current mores. Unlimited money and property were given to it. Francis died in 1226 and was canonized in 1228. Dominic (1170–1221) aimed to found an order of preachers in order to oppose the Albigenses and other heretics. He wanted to found a learned and scholarly order which should be able to preach and teach. He made it a mendicant order in order to preserve it from the corruptions to

[1] The ideas of Francis had been promulgated by the Timotheists in the fifth century. They were then declared heretical (Lea, *Sacerd. Celib.*, 377).

[2] Carmichael, *In Tuscany*, 224.

which the conventual life was exposed. The two orders of friars became fierce enemies to each other and fought upon all occasions.[1] In their theory and doctrines they exactly satisfied the notions of the time as to what the church ought to be, and "they restored to the church much of the popular veneration which had become almost hopelessly alienated from it."[2] The age cherished ideals and phantasms on which it dwelt in thought, developing them. Suffering was esteemed as a good, and self-denial with suffering made saintliness. Francis and his comrades cherished all these ideals and had all these ways of thinking. Francis became the ideal man of his time.[3]

695. The Franciscans. Other mendicant orders prove the dominant ideas of the time. These were the Augustinian hermits (1256), the Carmelites (1245), and the Servites, or Servants of Mary (c. 1275). The mendicants did not live up to their doctrine for a single generation. In the middle of the century Bonaventura had to reprove the Franciscans for their greed of property, their litigation and efforts to grasp legacies, and for the splendor and luxury of their buildings.[4] The two great orders of friars became an available power by virtue of their hold on the tastes and faiths of the people. They became the militia of the pope and helped to establish papal absolutism. They "were perfectly adapted to the world conditions of the time."[5] The doctrines of poverty were at war with the character, aims, and ambitions of the church. The Franciscans, in order to establish the primitive character of their system, asserted that Christ and his disciples lived by beggary in absolute renunciation of property. This was a Scriptural and historical doctrine

---

[1] Lea, *Inquis.*, I, 302. [2] Lea, *Sacerd. Celib.*, 377.

[3] Little, *St. Francis of Assisi*, 138. Carmichael (*In Tuscany*, 228) is satisfied that Francis received the stigmata. He says: "No serious person any longer seeks to dispute the fact." The stigmata were imparted by an angel and consisted in "long nails of a black, hard, fleshy substance. The round heads of the nails showed close against the palms, and from out the backs of the hands came the points of the nails, bent back as if they had pierced through wood and then been clinched." The wounds caused pain so great that Francis could not walk. Little does not reject all the fabulous details in the life of the saint as the legends have brought it down. [4] Lea, *Inquis.*, III, 29.

[5] Michael, *Gesch. des Deutschen Volkes*, II, 78.

and question of fact, on which fierce controversy arose. It divided the order into two schools, the conventuals and the spirituals. In 1275 the spirituals, who clung to the original ideals and rules of Francis, were treated as heretics and persecuted. They rated Francis as another Christ, and the rule as a new revelation. They always were liable to fall into sympathy with enthusiastic sects which were rated as heretical.[1] The Franciscans also, in their origin, were somewhat independent of hierarchical authority and of established discipline. It was necessary that the order should be brought into the existing ecclesiastical system. The popes of the thirteenth century until Boniface VIII accepted the standards of the age and approved of the mendicant friars. In 1279, in the bull *Exiit qui seminat*, the Franciscan rule was ascribed to revelation by the Holy Ghost, and the renunciation of property was approved. The use of property was right, but the ownership was wrong.[2] Boniface was of another school. He was a practical man who meant to increase the power of the hierarchy. Absurd as was the notion of non-property, it was at least germane to the doctrine of Christianity that Christians ought to renounce the pomps and vanities of wealth and the struggle for power, and to live in frugality, simplicity, and mutual service. The papal hierarchy was in pursuit of pomp and luxury and, above all, of power and dominion. Boniface ordered the spiritual Franciscans to conform to the rule of the conventuals. Some would not obey and became heretics and martyrs. Their zeal for the ideas and rule of Francis was so great that they welcomed martyrdom for their adherence.[3] The most distinguished of the martyrs of the spirituals was Bernard Delicieux, who found himself at war with the Inquisition and the pope, and who, after a trial in which all the arts of browbeating and torture were exhausted, died a prisoner, in chains, on bread and water.[4] The other party also had its martyrs, who were willing to die for the doctrine that Christ and his apostles did not live by beggary.[5] Any doctrine that the apostles lived in poverty, by begging, was a criticism of the hierarchy as it then

---

[1] Lea, *Inquis.*, III, 33. [2] *Ibid.*, 30. [3] *Ibid.*, 51.
[4] *Ibid.*, II, 75, 99 [5] *Ibid.*, 59.

was. John XXII, another non-sentimental pope, declared that the doctrine that Christ and his apostles lived in negation of property was a heresy. Then Francis of Assisi and all who had held the same opinions as he became heretics.[1] In 1368 the strict Franciscans split off and formed the order of the Observantines, and in 1487 the Recollects, another order of strict observers of the rule, was founded in Spain, with the authorization of Innocent VIII. The stricter orders were always more enthusiastically devoted to the service of the papacy.[2]

696. Whether poverty is a good. The history of the mendicant orders is an almost incomprehensible story of wrongheadedness. That poverty is a good is an inversion of common sense. That men do not want what they must have to live is a denial of all philosophy. The mendicants did not invent these dogmas. They were in the mores, and they made the mendicants. That the mendicants at once became greedy, avaricious, and luxurious, emissaries of tyranny and executioners of cruelty, was only an instance of the extravagances of human nature.

697. Clerical celibacy. If according to Christian standards virginity was the sole right rule and marriage was only a concession, it might justly be argued that the clergy ought to live up to the real standard, not the conventional concession. This was the best argument for sacerdotal celibacy. It was well understood, and not disputed, that celibacy was a rule of the church, and not an ordinance of Christ or the Gospel. It was an ascetic practice which was enjoined and enforced on the clergy. They never obeyed it. The rule produced sin and vice, and introduced moral discord and turpitude into the lives of thousands of the best men of the Middle Ages. In the baser days of the fourteenth and fifteenth centuries the current practice was a recognized violation of professed duty and virtue, under money penalties or penances. Yet the notion of celibacy for the clergy had been so established by discipline in the usage of priests and the mores of Christendom that a married priest was a disgusting and intolerable idea. At the same time usage had familiarized everybody with the concubinage of priests and prelates, and all Christendom

[1] Lea, *Inquis.*, I, 541.   [2] *Ibid.*, III, 172, 179.

knew that popes had their bastards living with them in the Vatican, where they were married and dowered by their fathers as openly as might be done by princes in their palaces. The falsehood and hypocrisy caused deep moral corruption, aside from any judgment as to what constituted the error or its remedy. Pope Pius II was convinced that there were better reasons for revoking the celibacy of the clergy than there ever had been for imposing it,[1] but he was not a man to put his convictions into effect. The effect on character of violation of an ascetic rule, acknowledged and professed, was the same as that of the violation of one of the Ten Commandments.

698. How Christian asceticism ended. By the beginning of the sixteenth century the ascetic views and tastes were all gone, overwhelmed by the ideas and tastes of a period of commerce, wealth, productive power, materialism, and enjoyment. In the new age the pagan joy in living was revived. Objects of desire were wealth, luxury, beauty, pleasure, — all of which the ascetics scorned and cursed. The reaction was favorable to a development of sensuality and materialism; also of art. Modern times have been made what they are by industry on rational lines of effort, with faith in the direct relation of effort to result. The aleatory element still remains, and it is still irrational, but the attitude of men towards it is changed. All the ground for asceticism is taken away. We work for what we want with courage, hope, and faith, and we enjoy the product as a right. If the luck goes against us, we try again. We are very much disinclined to any increase of pain or of fruitless labor. There is a great change in the mores of the entire modern society about the aleatory element. That change accounts for a great deal of the modern change of feeling about religion.

[1] Burckhardt, *Renaissance in Italien*, 465.

CHAPTER XIX

EDUCATION, HISTORY

The superstition of education. — The loss from education; "missionary-made men." — Schools make persons all on one pattern; orthodoxy. — Criticism. — Reactions of the mores and education on each other. — The limitations of the historian. — Overvaluation of history. — Success and the favor of God. — Philosophic faiths and the study of history. — Democracy and history. — The study of history and the study of the mores. — The most essential element of education. — The history of the mores is needed.

Introduction. The one thing which justifies popular education for all children is the immense value of men of genius to the society. We have no means of discerning and recognizing, in their early childhood, the ones who have genius. If we could do so it would be a good bargain to pay great sums for them, and to educate them at public expense. Our popular education may be justly regarded as a system of selecting them. The pupils retire from the schools when they think that "they do not want any more schooling." Of course thousands withdraw for one who keeps on. It is a very expensive system, and the expense all falls on the taxpayers. The beneficiaries are left entirely free to spend their lives wherever they please. If the system is sound and just it must be so by virtue of some common interest of all the people of the United States in the social services of men of talent and genius in any part of the United States.

699. The superstition of education. Popular education and certain faiths about popular education are in the mores of our time. We regard illiteracy as an abomination. We ascribe to elementary book learning power to form character, make good citizens, keep family mores pure, elevate morals, establish individual character, civilize barbarians, and cure social vice and disease. We apply schooling as a remedy for every social phenomenon which we do not like. The information given by schools and colleges, the attendant drill in manners, the ritual of the mores practiced in schools, and the mental dexterity produced by school exercises fit individuals to carry on the struggle for existence better. A literate man can produce wealth better than an illiterate man. Avenues are also opened by school work through which influences may be brought to bear on the reason and conscience which will mold character. Not even the increased production of wealth, much less the improvement of character, are assured results. Our faith in the power of book learning is excessive and unfounded. It is a superstition of the age. The education which forms character and produces faith in sound principles of life comes through personal influence and example. It is borne on the mores. It is taken in from the habits and atmosphere of a school, not from the school text-books. School work opens an opportunity that a thing may be, but the probability that it will be depends on the persons, and it may be *nil* or contrary to what is desired. High attainments in school enhance the power obtained, but the ethical value of it all depends on how it is used. These facts are often misused or exaggerated in modern educational controversies, but their reality cannot be denied. Book learning is addressed to the intellect, not to the feelings, but the feelings are the spring of action.

700. The loss from education. Missionary-made men. Education has always been recognized as a means of individual success and group strength. In barbarism the children are educated by their elders, especially the little boys by the big ones, but the whole mental outfit possessed by the group is transmitted to the children, and all the mores pass by this tradition. It is to be noticed, therefore, that in our modern education the sense of the term has been much narrowed, since we mean by it book learning or schooling. Teachers are not wanting who teach manners and mores out of zeal and ambition, and families and churches can be found which duly supplement the work of schools, but the institutions follow no set plan of coöperation, and one or another of them fails in its part. The modern superstition of education contains a great error. It is forgotten that there is always a loss and offset from education in its narrow sense. Petrie, speaking from observation and experience of Egyptian peasants, says: "The harm is that you manufacture idiots. Some of the peasantry are taught to read and write, and the result of this burden, which their fathers bore not, is that they become fools. I cannot say this too plainly: An Egyptian who has had reading and writing thrust on him is, in every case that I have met with, half-witted, silly, or incapable of taking care of himself. His intellect and his health have been undermined by the forcing of education."[1] Petrie's doctrine is that each generation of men of low civilization can be advanced beyond the preceding one only by a very small percentage. He does not lay stress on the stimulation of vanity and false pride. If he is right, his doctrine explains the complaints of "missionary-made men" which we hear from Miss Kingsley and others, and such social results as are described by Becke.[2] Amongst ourselves also the increase of insanity, nervous diseases, crime, and suicide must be ascribed in part to the constant and more intense brain strain, especially in youth. Women also, as they participate more in the competition of life, have to get more education, and they fall under the diseases also. The cases of child suicide are the most startling product of our ways of education. These personal and social diseases are a part of the price we pay for "higher civilization." They are an offset to education and they go with it. It would be great ignorance of the course of effort in societal matters not to know that such diseased reactions must always be expected.

701. Schools make persons all on one pattern. Orthodoxy. School education, unless it is regulated by the best knowledge and good sense, will produce men and women who are all of one pattern, as if turned in a lathe. When priests managed schools it was their intention to reach just this result. They carried in their heads ideals of the Christian man and woman, and they wanted to educate all to this model. Public schools in a democracy may work in the same way. Any institution which runs for years in the same hands will produce a type. The examination

---

[1] *Smithson. Rep.*, 1895, 596. [2] *Pacific Tales.*

papers show the pet ideas of the examiners. It must not be forgotten that the scholars set about the making of folkways for themselves, just as members of a grown society do. In time they adopt codes, standards, preferred types, and fashions. They select their own leaders, whom they follow with enthusiasm. They have their pet heroes and fashion themselves upon the same. Their traditions become stereotyped and authoritative. The type of product becomes fixed. It makes some kind of compromise with the set purposes of the teachers and administrators, and the persons who issue from the schools become recognizable by the characteristics of the type. It is said that the graduates of Jesuit colleges on the continent of Europe are thus recognizable. In England the graduates of Oxford and Cambridge are easily to be distinguished from other Englishmen. In the continental schools and barracks, in newspapers, books, etc., what is developed by education is dynastic sentiment, national sentiment, soldierly sentiment; still again, under the same and other opportunities, religious and ecclesiastical sentiments, and by other influences, also class and rank sentiments.[1] In a democracy there is always a tendency towards big results on a pattern. An orthodoxy is produced in regard to all the great doctrines of life. It consists of the most worn and commonplace opinions which are current in the masses. It may be found in newspapers and popular literature. It is intensely provincial and philistine. It does not extend to those things on which the masses have not pronounced, and by its freedom and elasticity in regard to these it often produces erroneous judgments as to its general character. The popular opinions always contain broad fallacies, half-truths, and glib generalizations of fifty years before. If a teacher is to be displaced by a board of trustees because he is a free-trader, or a gold man, or a silver man, or disapproves of a war in which the ruling clique has involved the country, or because he thinks that Hamilton was a great statesman and Jefferson an insignificant one, or because he says that he has found some proof that alcohol is not always bad for the system, we might as well go back to the dominion in education of the

[1] Schallmeyer, *Vererbung und Auslese*, 265.

theologians. They were strenuous about theology, but they let other things alone. The boards of trustees are almost always made up of "practical men," and if their faiths, ideas, and prejudices are to make the norm of education, the schools will turn out boys and girls compressed to that pattern. There is no wickedness in any disinterested and sincere opinion. That is what we all pretend to admit, but there are very few of us who really act by it. We seem likely to have orthodox history (especially of our own country), political science, political economy, and sociology before long.[1] It will be defined by school boards who are party politicians. As fast as physics, chemistry, geology, biology, bookkeeping, and the rest come into conflict with interests, and put forth results which have a pecuniary effect (which is sure to happen in the not remote future), then the popular orthodoxy will be extended to them, and it will be enforced as "democratic." The reason is because there will be a desire that children shall be taught just that one thing which is "right" in the view and interest of those in control, and nothing else. That is exactly the view which the ecclesiastics formerly took when they had control. Mathematics is the only discipline which could be taught under that rule. As to other subjects we do not know the "right answers," speaking universally and for all time. We only know how things look now on our best study, and that is all we can teach. In fact, this is the reason why the orthodox answers of the school boards and trustees are mischievous. They teach that there are absolute and universal facts of knowledge, whereas we ought to teach that all our knowledge is subject to unlimited verification and revision. The men turned out under the former system, and the latter, will be very different agents in the face of all questions of philosophy, citizenship, finance, and industry.

702. Criticism. Criticism is the examination and test of propositions of any kind which are offered for acceptance, in order to find out whether they correspond to reality or not. The

---

[1] According to a German newspaper the parliament of Bavaria, in 1897, expressed a wish that the government of that state would not appoint any more Darwinians to chairs in the universities of the kingdom.

critical faculty is a product of education and training. It is a mental habit and power. It is a prime condition of human welfare that men and women should be trained in it. It is our only guarantee against delusion, deception, superstition, and misapprehension of ourselves and our earthly circumstances. It is a faculty which will protect us against all harmful suggestion. "We are all critical against the results reached by others and uncritical against our own results." [1] To act by suggestion or autosuggestion is to act by impulse. Education teaches us to act by judgment. Our education is good just so far as it produces well-developed critical faculty. The thirteenth century had no critical faculty. It wandered in the dark, multiplying errors, and starting movements which produced loss and misery for centuries, because it dealt with fantasies, and did not know the truth about men or their position in the world. The nineteenth century was characterized by the acquisition and use of the critical faculty. A religious catechism never can train children to criticism. "Patriotic" history and dithyrambic literature never can do it. A teacher of any subject who insists on accuracy and a rational control of all processes and methods, and who holds everything open to unlimited verification and revision is cultivating that method as a habit in the pupils. In current language this method is called " science," or " scientific." The critical habit of thought, if usual in a society, will pervade all its mores, because it is a way of taking up the problems of life. Men educated in it cannot be stampeded by stump orators and are never deceived by dithyrambic oratory. They are slow to believe. They can hold things as possible or probable in all degrees, without certainty and without pain. They can wait for evidence and weigh evidence, uninfluenced by the emphasis or confidence with which assertions are made on one side or the other. They can resist appeals to their dearest prejudices and all kinds of cajolery. Education in the critical faculty is the only education of which it can be truly said that it makes good citizens. The operation of the governmental system and existing laws is always "educating" the citizens, and very often it is

[1] Friedmann, *Wahnideen im Völkerleben*, 219.

making bad ones. The existing system may teach the citizens to war with the government, or to use it in order to get advantages over each other. The laws may organize a big "steal" of the few from the many, and they may educate the people to believe that the way to get rich is to "get into the steal." "Graft" is a reaction of the mores on the burdens and opportunities offered by the laws, and graft is a great education. It educates faster and deeper than all the schools. The people who believe that there is a big steal, and that they must either get into it or be plundered by it, have nothing to learn from political economy or political science.

703. Reactions of the mores and education on each other. Every one admits that education properly means much more than schooling or book learning. It means a development and training of all useful powers which the pupil possesses, and repression of all bad prepossessions which he has inherited. The terms "useful" and "bad" in this proposition never can mean anything but the currently approved and disapproved traits and powers; that is, what is encouraged or discouraged by the mores. The good citizen, good husband and father, good business man, etc., are only types which are in fashion at the time. In New England they are not the same now as fifty years ago. The mores and the education react on each other They are not as likely to settle into grooves in a new country as in old countries. In Spain and Portugal, and to a less extent in Italy and Russia, the mores have taken rigid form, and they control schools and universities so that the types of educated men vary little from generation to generation. When the schools are not too rigidly stereotyped they become seats of new thought, of criticism of what is traditional, and of new ideas which remold the mores. The young men are only too ready to find fault with what they find existing and traditional, and the students of all countries have been eager revolutionists. Of course they make mistakes and do harm, but the alternative is the reign of old abuse and consecrated error. The folkways need constant rejuvenation and refreshment if they are to be well fitted to present cases, and it is far better that they be revolutionized than that they be subjected to traditional change-lessness. In the organization of modern society the schools are the institutional apparatus by which the inheritance of experience and knowledge, — the whole mental outfit of the race, — is trans-mitted to the young. Through these institutions, therefore, the mores and morality which men have accepted and approved are handed down. The transmission ought to be faithful, but not without criticism. The reaction of free judgment and taste will keep the mores fresh and active, and the schools are undoubtedly the place where they should be renewed through an intelligent study of their operation in the past.

704. The limitations on the historian. If the schools are to prosecute this study, history is the chief field for it. No historian ever gets out of the mores of his own society of origin. He may adopt a party in church, politics, or social philosophy. If he does, his standpoint will be set for him, and it is sure to be sectarian. Even if he rises above the limitations of party, he does not get outside of the patriotic and ethical horizon in which he has been educated, especially when he deals with the history of other countries and other times than his own. Each historian regards his own nation as the torchbearer of civilization; its mores give him his ethical standards by which he estimates whatever he learns of other peoples. All our histories of antiquity or the classical nations show that they are written by modern scholars. In modern Russian literature may be found passages about the "civilizing mission" of Russia which might be trans-lated, *mutatis mutandis*, from passages in English, French, or German literature about the civilizing mission of England, France, or Germany. Probably the same is true of Turkish, Hindoo, or Chinese literature. The patriotism of the historian rules his judgment, especially as to excuses and apologies for things done in the past, and most of all as to the edifying omissions, — a very important part of the task of the historian. A modern Protestant and a Roman Catholic, or an American and a European, cannot reach the same view of the Middle Ages, no matter how unbiased and objective each may aim to be. There is a compulsion on the historian to act in this way, for if he wrote otherwise, his fellow-countrymen would ignore his work. It follows that a complete and unbiased history hardly exists. It may be a moral impossibility. Every student during his academic period ought to get up one bit of history thoroughly from the ultimate sources, in order to convince himself what history is not. Any one who ever lived through a crisis in the history of a university must have learned how impossible it is to establish in memory and record a correct literary narrative of what took place, the forces at work, the participation of individuals, etc. Monuments, festivals, mottoes, oratory, and poetry may enter largely into the mores. They never help history; they obscure it. They protect errors and sanctify prejudices. The same is true of literary commonplaces which gain currency. It is commonly believed in the United States that at some time in the past Russia showed sympathy and extended aid to the United States when sympathy and aid were sorely needed. This is entirely untrue. No specification of the time and circumstances can be made which will stand examination. Nevertheless the popular belief cannot be corrected.

705. Overvaluation of history. Never was history studied as it is now. Amongst scholars there is a disposition to overvalue it, and to develop out of it something which must be called "historyism." Jurisprudence has passed through the dominion of this tendency. Political economy is now lost in it. When has anybody ever been governed by "the teachings of history" when he was philosophizing or legislating? The teachings of history can always be set aside, if they are a hindrance, by alleging that the times have changed and that new conditions exist. This allegation may be true, and the possibility that it is true must always be taken into account. No two cases in history ever are alike.

706. Success and the favor of God. Sects and parties have claimed God's favor and power. They have boldly declared that they would accept success or failure as proof of his approval on their doctrines and programme. No one of them ever stood by the test. There were some in the crusades who argued that the Moslems must be right on account of their successes. The

Templars were charged with making this deduction when grounds for burning them were sought. It was a heresy. If the Christians had any success, the deduction might be made against the Moslems, but not contrariwise. All nations have treated in this way the deductions about the approval of the superior powers. If there are any superior powers which meddle with history, it is certain that men have never yet found out how their ways and human ways react on each other, nor any means of interpreting their ways.

707. Philosophic faiths and the study of history. In a similar manner other philosophic faiths interfere with the study of history. The mores impose the faiths on the historian, and the faiths spoil his work. " It is not difficult to understand how a people imbued with the idea that the world is an illusion should have neglected all historical investigations. No such thing as genuine history or biography exists in Sanskrit literature. Historical researches are, to a Hindoo, simple foolishness." [1]

708. Democracy and history. Democracy is almost equally indifferent to history, and the dogmas of democracy make history unimportant. If "the people" always know what is right and wise, then we have the supreme oracle always with us and always up to date. In the report of a civil-service examination which got into the newspapers, it was said that one candidate for a position on the police answered the question, Who was Abraham Lincoln ? by saying that he was a distinguished general on the Southern side in the Civil War. Nevertheless, if appointed, he might have made an excellent policeman. His ludicrous ignorance of American biography proved nothing to the contrary. The question brought into doubt the intelligence of the examiners. If all policemen were examined on American history, it is fair to believe that incredible ignorance and errors would be displayed. No amount of study of American history would make them better policemen. The same may be said of the masses as a whole. A knowledge of history is a fine accomplishment, but ignorance of it does not hinder the success of men in their own lines of industry. They do not, therefore, care about

---

[1] Monier-Williams, *Brahmanism and Hinduism*, 39.

history or appreciate it. Its rank in school studies is an inheritance of European tradition. Popular opinion does not recognize
its position as fit and just. Its effect on the minds and mores
of the pupils is almost *nil*, unless the history deals directly
with the mores.

709. The study of history and the study of the mores. There
is, therefore, great need for a clearer understanding of the relation between the study of history and the study of the mores.
Abraham Lincoln's career illustrated in many ways the mores
of his time, and the knowledge of some of the facts about the
mores would have been by no means idle or irrelevant for a
policeman. In like manner it may well be that other branches
of study pursued in our schools contain valuable instruction or
discipline, but it does not lie on the surface, and it is an art to
get it out and bring it to the attention of the scholar.

710. The most essential element in education. A man's education never stops as long as he lives. All the experience of
life is educating him. In school days he is undergoing education
by the contact of life, and by what he does or suffers. This
education is transferring to him the mores. He learns what
conduct is approved or disapproved; what kind of man is
admired most; how he ought to behave in all kinds of cases;
and what he ought to believe or reject. This education goes on
by minute steps, often repeated. The influences make the man.
All this constitutes evidently the most essential and important
education. If we understand what the mores are, and that the
contact with one's fellows is all the time transmitting them, we
can better understand, and perhaps regulate to some extent,
this education.

711. The history of the mores is needed. The modern historians turn with some disdain away from the wars, intrigues, and
royal marriages which the old-fashioned historians considered
their chief interest, and many of them have undertaken to write
the history of the "people." Evidently they have perceived
that what is wanted is a history of the mores. If they can get
that they can extract from the history what is most universal
and permanent in its interest.

CHAPTER XX

LIFE POLICY. VIRTUE vs. SUCCESS

Life policy. — Oaths; truthfulness vs. success. — The clever hero. — Odysseus, Rother, Njal. — Clever heroes in German epics. — Lack of historic sense amongst Christians. — Success policy in the Italian Renaissance. — Divergence between convictions and conduct. — Classical learning a fad. — The humanists. — Individualism. — Perverted use of words. — Extravagance of passions and acts. — The sex relation and the position of women. — The cult of success. — Literature on the mores. — Moral anarchy.

712. Life policy. Some primitive or savage groups are very truthful, both in narrative and in regard to their promises or pledged word. Other groups are marked by complete neglect of truthfulness. Falsehood and deceit are regarded as devices by which to attain success in regard to interests. The North American Indians generally regarded deceit by which an enemy was outwitted as praiseworthy; in fact it was a part of the art of war. It is still so regarded in modern civilized warfare. It is, however, limited by rules of morality. There was question whether the deception by which Aguinaldo was captured was within the limit. In sport also, which is a sort of mimic warfare, deception and "jockeying" are more or less recognized as legitimate. Samoan children are taught that it is "unsamoan" to tell the truth. It is stupid, because it sacrifices one's interest.[1] It does not appear that the experience of life teaches truthfulness on any of the lower stages. The truthful peoples are generally the isolated, unwarlike, and simple. Warfare and strength produce cunning and craft. It is only at the highest stage of civilization that deceit is regarded with contempt, and is thought not to pay. That honesty is the best policy is current doctrine, but not established practice now. It is a part of a virtue policy, which is inculcated as right and necessary, but whether it is a success policy is not a closed question.

[1] *Globus*, LXXXIII, 374.

713. Oaths. Truthfulness vs. success. It is evident that truthfulness or untruthfulness, when either is a group character-istic, is due to a conviction that societal welfare is served by one or the other Truthfulness is, therefore, primary in the mores. It does not proceed from the religion, but the religion furnishes a sanction for the view which prevails in the mores. Oaths and imprecations are primitive means of invoking the religious sanction in promises and contracts. They always implied that the superior powers would act in the affairs of men in a proposed way, if the oath maker should break his word. This implication failed so regularly that faith in oaths never could be maintained. Since they have fallen into partial disuse the expediency of truthfulness has been perceived, and the value of a reputation for it has been recognized. Thus it has become a question whether a true success policy is to be based on truth or falsehood. The mores of groups contain their answer, which they inculcate on the young.

714. The clever hero. Krishna. The wily and clever hero, who knows what to do to get out of a difficulty, or to accomplish a purpose, is a very popular character in the great epics. In the *Mahabharata* Krishna is such a hero, who invents stratagems and policies for the Panduings in their strife with the Kuruings. The king of the latter, when dying, declares that the Panduings have always been dishonorable and tricky, while he and his party have always adhered to honorable methods. However, he is dying and his party is almost annihilated. The victors are somewhat affected by his taunts, which refer to Krishna's inventions and suggestions, but Krishna shows them the booty and says : " But for my stratagems you would have had none of these fine things. What do you care that you got them by tricks ? Do you not want them ? " They applaud and praise him. Then the surviving Kuruings, weary of virtue and defeat, surprise and murder the Panduings in the night, an act which was contrary to the code of honorable war. The antagonism of a virtue policy and a success policy could not be more strongly presented [1] In

---

[1] Holtzmann, *Indische Sagen*, I, 170.

the same poem Samarishta says that five lies are allowed when one's life or property is in danger. The wicked lie is one uttered before witnesses in reply to a serious question, and the only real lie is one uttered of set purpose for selfish gain. Yayati, however, says, "I may not be false, even though I should be in direst peril."[1] The heroes fear to falsify, and the Vedas are quoted that a lie is the greatest sin.[2] The clever hero has remained the popular hero. At the present day we are told that Ganesa, or Gana-pati, son of Siva, really represents "a complex personification of sagacity, shrewdness, patience, and self-reliance, — of all those qualities, in short, which overcome hindrances and difficulties, whether in performing religious acts, writing books, building houses, making journeys, or undertaking anything. He is before all things the typical embodiment of success in life, with its usual accompaniments of good living, plenteousness, prosperity, and peace."[3] The Persians, from the most ancient times, have been noted liars. They used truth and falsehood as instruments of success. The relation of king and subject and of husband and wife amongst them were false. They were invented and maintained for a purpose.[4]

715. Odysseus. The Greeks admired cunning and successful stratagem. Odysseus was wily. He was a clever hero. His maternal grandfather Autolykos was, by endowment of Hermes (a god of lying and stealing), a liar and thief beyond all men.[5]

716. Clever hero in German epics. In the German poems of the twelfth century Rother is a king who accomplishes his ends by craft. In the *Nibelungen*, Hagen is the efficient man, who, in any crisis, knows what to do and can accomplish it by craft and strength combined. The heroes are noteworthy for tricks, stratagems, ruses, and perfidy.[6] In all the epic poems the princes have by their side mentors who are crafty, fertile in resource, and clever in action.[7] In the Icelandic saga of

---

[1] Holtzmann, *Indische Sagen*, I, 105.
[2] *Ibid.*, 23, 37, 119.
[3] Monier-Williams, *Brahmanism and Hinduism*, 216.
[4] Hartmann, *Ztsft. d. V. f. Volkskunde*, XI, 247.
[5] *Od.*, XIX, 394.
[6] Lichtenberger, *Nibelungen*, 334, 354.
[7] Uhland, *Dichtung und Sage*, 232.

Burnt Njal, Njal is the knowing man, peaceful and friendly. His crafty devices are chiefly due to his knowledge of the law, which was full of chicane and known to few. These clever heroes, developed out of the mores of one period and fixed in the epics, became standards and guides for the mores of later times, in which they were admired as types of what every one would like to be.

717. **Lack of historic sense amongst Christians.** In the first centuries of the Christian era no school of religion or philosophy thought that it was an inadmissible proceeding to concoct edifying writings and attribute them to some great authority of earlier centuries, or to invent historical documents to advance a cause or support the claims of a sect. This view came down to the Middle Ages. The lack of historic feeling is well shown by the crusaders who, after Antioch was taken, in the next few days and on the spot, began to write narratives of the deeds of their respective commanders which were not true, but were exaggerated, romantic, and imaginary. They were not derived from observation of facts, but were fashioned upon the romances of chivalry.[1] This was not myth making. It was conscious reveling in poetic creation according to the prevailing literary type. It was not falsehood, but it showed an entire absence of the sense of historic truth. In the case of the canon law, " the decretals were intended to furnish a documentary title, running back to apostolic times, for the divine institution of the primacy of the pope, and for the teaching office of bishops ; a title which in truth did not exist." [2] There was probably lacking in the minds of the men who invented the decretals all consciousness of antagonism between fact and their literary work. If they could have been confronted with the ethical question, they would probably have said that they knew that the doctrines in question were true, and that if the fathers had had occasion to speak of them they would have said such things as were put in their mouths. Mediæval history writing was not subject to canons of truth or taste. It included what was edifying, to the glory of

[1] Kugler, *Kreuzzüge*, 52.
[2] Eicken, *Mittelalterl. Weltanschauung*, 656.

God and the church. Legends and history were of equal value, since both were used for edification. The truth of either was unimportant.

718. Success policy in the Italian Renaissance. The historical period in which the success policy was pursued most openly and unreservedly was the Italian Renaissance. The effect on all virtue, especially on truthfulness of speech and character, was destructive, and all the mores of the period were marked by the choice of the code of conduct which disregards truth. The most deep-lying and far-reaching cause of societal change was the accumulation of capital and the development of a capitalistic class. New developments in the arts awakened hope and enterprise, and produced a " boundless passion for discovery " in every direction.[1] The mediæval church system did not contain as much obscurantism in Italy as in some other countries, and the interests of the Italians were intertwined with the hierarchical interests of Rome in many ways. It flattered Italian pride and served Italian interests that Rome should be the center of the Christian world. Every person had ties with the church establishment either directly or by relatives. In spite of philosophic freedom of thought or moral contempt for the clergy, "it was a point of good society and refined taste to support the church." " It was easy for Germans and Englishmen to reason calmly about dethroning the papal hierarchy. Italians, however they might loathe the temporal power, could not willingly forego the spiritual primacy of the civilized world." Thus the Renaissance pursued its aims, which were distinctly worldly, with a superficial good-fellowship towards the church institution.[2] " The attitude of the upper and middle classes of Italy towards the church, at the height of the Renaissance, is a combination of deep and contemptuous dislike with accommodation towards the hierarchy as a body deeply interwoven with actual life, and with a feeling of dependence on sacraments and ritual. All this was crossed, too, by the influence of great and holy preachers." [3]

[1] Symonds, *Renaissance*, III, 320.   [2] *Ibid.*, I, 390–405.
[3] Burckhardt, *Renaissance*, 458.

719. Divergence between convictions and conduct. This means that faith in Christian doctrine was gone, but that the ecclesiastical system was a tolerated humbug which served many interests. Burckhardt quotes [1] a passage from Guicciardini in which the latter says that he had held positions under many popes, which compelled him to wish for their greatness, on account of his own advantage. Otherwise he would have loved Martin Luther, not in order to escape the restraints of the current church doctrine, but in order to see the corrupt crew brought to order, so that they must have learned to live either without power or without vices. Thus the conduct of men was separated from their most serious convictions by considerations of interest and expediency, and a moral inconsistency was developed in character. Churches were built and foundations were multiplied, so that the masses seemed more zealous than the popes, but at the beginning of the sixteenth century there were bitter complaints of the decline of worship and the neglect of the churches. [2] We have all the phenomena of a grand breaking up of old mores and the beginning of new ones. " It required the unbelief of the fifteenth century to give free rein to the rising commercial energies, and the craving for material improvement, that paved the way for the overthrow of ascetic sacerdotalism." [3] The new class of burghers with capital produced a new idea of liberty to be set against the feudal idea of liberty of nobles and ecclesiastics, and that new class became the founders of the modern state.

720. Classical learning a fad. Whatever may have been the origin of the zeal for classical study of the late Middle Ages, it was a remarkable example of a fad which became the fashion and very strongly influenced the mores. It was strengthened by the revolt against the authority of the church, and the humanism which it produced took the place of the mental stock which the church had offered. " Humanism effected the emancipation of intellect by culture. It called attention to the beauty and delightfulness of nature, restored man to a sense of his dignity, and freed him from theological authority. But in Italy,

---

[1] Burckhardt, *Renaissance*, 465.
[2] *Ibid.*, 490.   [3] Lea, *Sacerd. Celibacy*, 364.

at any rate, it left his conscience, his religion, his sociological ideas, the deeper problems which concern his relation to the universe, the subtler secrets of the world in which he lives, untouched." [1] That means that it was a fad and was insincere. There were men who were great scholars within the standards of humanism, but the enthusiasm for art, the zeal for Latin and Greek literature, the coöperative struggle for exhumations and specimens, were features of a reigning fad. The Renaissance was an affair of the upper and middle classes. It never could spread to the masses. Classical learning came to be valued as a caste mark. Then it became still more truly an affectation, and was tainted with untruth. The masses were superior in the sincerity and truthfulness of their mores by the contrast. The humanists were pagan and profane, but did not follow their doctrines into a reformation of the church. They exaggerated the knowledge of the ancients and the prestige of classical opinion until it seemed to them that anything ancient must be true and authoritative. They transferred to what was ancient the irrational reverence which had been paid to the doctrines of the church, and paid to the great classical authors the respect which had been paid to saints. [2] In the sixteenth century they fell into discredit for their haughtiness, their shameful dissipation, and for their unbelief. [3]

721. The humanists. The humanists of Italy are a class by themselves, without historical relations. They had no trade or profession and could make no recognized career. Their controversies had a large personal element. They sought to exterminate each other. Three excuses have been suggested for them. The excessive petting and spoiling they met with when luck favored them; the lack of a guarantee for their physical circumstances, which depended on the caprice of patrons and the malice of rivals; and the delusive influence of antiquity, or of their notions about it. The last destroyed their Christian morality without giving them a substitute. Their careers were such generally that only the strongest moral natures could

---

[1] Symonds, *Catholic Reaction*, II, 137.
[2] Burckhardt, 184. [3] *Ibid.*, 267.

endure them without harm. They plunged into changeful and wearing life, in which exhaustive study, the duties of a household tutor, a secretary, or a professor, service near a prince, deadly hostility and danger, enthusiastic admiration and extravagant scorn, excess and poverty, followed each other in confusion. The humanist needed to know how to carry a great erudition and to endure a succession of various positions and occupations. To these were added on occasion stupefying and disorderly enjoyment, and when the basest demands were made on him he had to be indifferent to all morals. Haughtiness was a certain consequence in character. The humanists needed it to sustain themselves, and the alternation of flattery and hatred strengthened them in it. They were victims of subjectiveness. The admiration of classical antiquity was so extravagant and mistaken that all the humanists were subject to excessive suggestion which destroyed their judgment.[1]

722. "Individualism." Recent writers on the period have emphasized the individualism which was produced. By this is meant the emancipation of men of talent from traditional morality, and the notion that any man might do anything which would win success for his purposes. There was no grinding of men down to an average.[2] This code was very widely applied in statecraft and social struggles. A smattering knowledge of Plutarch, Plato, and Virgil furnished heroic examples which could justify anything.[3] Machiavelli's *Prince* was only a text-book of this school of action for statesmen. Given the existing conditions in Italy, he assumed a man of ability and asked how he should best act. " He said that, to such a man, undertaking such a task, moral considerations were of subsidiary importance, and success was the one criterion by which he was to be judged. The conception was one forced on him by the actual facts of Italian history in his own time. The methods which he codified were those which he saw being actually employed." [4] Gobineau [5]

[1] Burckhardt, *Renaissance*, 268–271.
[2] Symonds, *Renaissance*, I, 423.
[3] Gauthiez, *Lorenzaccio*, 71.
[4] Creighton, *Hist. Essays and Reviews*, 336.
[5] *La Renaissance*, 377.

supposes a dialogue between Michael Angelo, Machiavelli, and Granacci about Francis I, Henry VIII, Charles V, and Leo X, in which the speakers attempt to foresee the development of events. They do not rightly estimate the royal personages, do not foresee the Reformation, and do not at all correctly judge the future. It was impossible that any one could do the last at a time when great historical movements and efforts of personal vanity and desire were mixing in gigantic struggles to control the world's history. Italy offered a narrower arena for personal ambition. Creighton[1] describes Gismondo Malatesta of Rimini. He "thoroughly mastered the lesson that to man all things are possible. He trusted to himself, and to himself only. He pursued his desires, whatever they might be. His appetites, his ambition, his love of culture, swayed his mind in turns, and each was allowed full scope. He was at once a ferocious scoundrel, a clear-headed general, an adventurous politician, a careful administrator, a man of letters and of refined taste. No one could be more entirely emancipated, more free from prejudice, than he. He was a typical Italian of the Renaissance, combining the brutality of the Middle Ages, the political capacity which Italy early developed, and the emancipation brought by the new learning." This might serve as a description of any one of the great secular men of the period. "Capacity might raise the meanest monk to the chair of St. Peter, the meanest soldier to the duchy of Milan. Audacity, vigor, unscrupulous crime, were the chief requisites of success."[2] "In Italy itself, where there existed no time-honored hierarchy of classes and no fountain of nobility in the person of a sovereign, one man was a match for another, provided he knew how to assert himself. . . . In the contest for power, and in the maintenance of an illegal authority, the picked athletes came to the front."[3]

723. Perverted use of words. Many words were given a peculiar and technical meaning in the use of the period. *Tristezza* often meant wickedness. It was a duty to be cheerful and gay.[4] "Terribleness was a word which came into vogue to describe

---

[1] *Hist. Essays and Reviews*, 138.
[2] Symonds, *Renaissance*, I, 52.
[3] *Ibid.*, 53.
[4] Gauthiez, *Lorenzaccio*, 92.

Michael Angelo's grand manner. It implied audacity of imagination, dashing draughtsmanship, colossal scale, something demonic
and decisive in execution."[1] *Virtù* meant the ability to win
success. Machiavelli used it for force, cunning, courage, ability,
and virility. "It was not incompatible with craft and dis-
simulation, or with the indulgence of sensual vices."[2] Cellini
used *virtuoso* to denote genius, artistic ability, and masculine
force.[3] "The Italian *onore* consisted partly of the credit attaching to public distinction and partly of a reputation for *virtù*"
in the above sense.[4] It was objective, — "an addition conferred from without, in the shape of reputation, glory, titles
of distinction, or offices of trust."[5] "The *onesta* of a married
woman is compatible with secret infidelity, provided she does not
expose herself to ridicule and censure by letting her amour be
known."[6] A *virago* meant a bluestocking, but was a term
of respect for a learned woman. Modesty was "the natural
grace of a gifted woman increased by education and association."[7]
The tendency of words to special uses is an index of the character of the mores of a period. The development of equality,
when the restraints of traditional morality are removed, ought
not to be passed without notice.

724. Extravagance of passions and acts. It followed from the
"ways" of the period that the human race "was bastardized"
"by the physical calamities, the perpetual pestilences, the constant wars, the moral miseries, the religious conflicts, and the
invasion of ancient ideas only half understood." The men died
young in years, old in vice, decrepit and falling to pieces when
not beyond the years of youth.[8] The emancipation of men with
inordinate ambition and lust meant a grand chance of crime.
Pope Paul III (Farnese) said that men like Cellini, "unique in
their profession, are not bound by the laws." Cellini had committed a murder. He committed several others, to say nothing
of minor crimes. After he escaped from St. Angelo, he was in

---

[1] Symonds, *Catholic Reaction*, II, 392.
[2] Symonds, *Renaissance*, I, 416.
[3] Symonds, *Autobiog.*, I, 74.
[4] Symonds, *Renaissance*, I, 416.
[5] *Ibid.*, 420.
[6] *Ibid.*, 420.
[7] Gregorovius, *Lucretia Borgia*, 28.
[8] Gauthiez, *Lorenzaccio*, 230.

the hands and under the protection of Cardinal Cornaro. The pope, Clement VII, wanted to get possession of him and Cornaro wanted a bishopric for a friend, so the pope and cardinal made a bargain and Cellini was surrendered.[1] " Italian society admired the bravo almost as much as imperial Rome admired the gladiator. It also assumed that genius combined with force of character released men from the shackles of ordinary morality." [2] Cellini was a specimen man of his age. He kept religion and morality far separated from each other.[3] Varchi wrote a sonnet on him which is false in fact and in form, and displays the technical and conventional insincerity of the age.[4] The augmentative form of the name Lorenzaccio expresses the notion that he was great, awful, and wicked.[5] His biographer says that he was a " mattoid." [6] He missed success because his antagonists were stronger than he, but his career was typical of the age. He was in part a victim of the classical suggestion. He expected to be glorified as a tyrannicide. This taste for the imaginative element was an important feature in the Italian Renaissance and helped to make it theatrical and untrue. " In gratifying his thirst for vengeance [the Italian] was never contented with mere murder. To obtain a personal triumph at the expense of his enemy by the display of superior cunning, by rendering him ridiculous, by exposing him to mental as well as physical anguish, by wounding him through his affections or his sense of honor, was the end which he pursued." [7] " However profligate the people might have been, they were not contented with grossness unless seasoned with wit. The same excitement of the fancy rendered the exercise of ingenuity, or the avoidance of peril, an enhancement of pleasure to the Italians. This is perhaps the reason why all the imaginative compositions of the Renaissance, especially the *novellae*, turn upon adultery." [8] The false standards, aims, codes, and doctrines required this play of the fantasy to make them seem worth while. The fantastic

[1] Symonds, *Renaissance*, III, 467.

[2] Symonds, *Autobiog. of Cellini*, I, XI, 196.

[3] *Ibid.*, XIV.

[4] *Ibid.*, 227.

[5] Gauthiez, *Lorenzaccio*, 104.

[6] *Ibid.*, 79.

[7] Symonds, *Renaissance*, I, 413.

[8] *Ibid.*, 410.

element gave all the zest. When the mediæval imaginative element failed the classical learning furnished a new one with suggestions, examples for imitation, and unlimited maxims and doctrines. Hence the passions become violent and upon occasion criminal,[1] that is to say, they violated the code recognized by all men in all ages. "Force, which had been substituted for Law in government, became, as it were, the mainspring of society. Murders, poisoning, rapes, and treasons were common incidents of private as of public life. In cities like Naples blood guilt could be atoned for at an inconceivably low rate A man's life was worth scarcely more than that of a horse. The palaces of the nobles swarmed with professional cutthroats, and the great ecclesiastics claimed for their abodes the right of sanctuary. Popes sold absolution for the most horrible excesses, and granted indulgences beforehand for the commission of crimes of lust and violence. Success was the standard by which acts were judged ; and the man who could help his friends, intimidate his enemies, and carve a way to fortune for himself by any means he chose was regarded as a hero."[2] If we should follow the manners and morals of the age into detail we should find that they were all characterized by the same fiction and conventional affectation, and by the same unrestrainedness of passion. Caterina Sforza avenged the murder of her lover with such atrocities that she shocked the Borgia pope.[3] The artists of the late Renaissance were absorbed in admiration of carnal beauty. There was vulgarity and coarseness on their finest work. Cellini's work is marked by "blank animalism."[4] There was a great lack of all sentiment. "Parents and children made a virtue of repressing their emotions." "No period ever exhibited a more marked aversion from the emotional or the pathetic."[5] There was no shame at perfidy or inconsistency, and very little notion of loyalty. It shocks modern taste that Isabella d'Este should have bought eagerly the art treasures of her dearest friend when they had been stolen and put on the market, and that after

---

[1] Burckhardt, 175, 432, 445.
[2] Symonds, *Renaissance*, I, 101.
[3] Creighton, *Essays*, 344.
[4] Symonds, *Renaissance*, III, 453–455.
[5] Müntz, *Leonardo da Vinci*, I, 12.

warm adherence to her brother-in-law, Ludovico il Moro, until
he was ruined, she should have turned to court the victor.[1]
It is not strange that the age became marked by complete
depravity of public and private morals, that the great men are
enigmas as to character and purpose, and that they are demonic
in action. The sack of Rome put an end to the epoch by a
catastrophe which was great enough to strike any soul with
horror, however hardened it might be.[2] That event seems to
show how the ways of the time would be when practiced by
brutal soldiers.

725. The sex relation and position of women. In such a
period the sex relation is sure to be degraded and the position
of woman is sure to be compromised. They can only be defined
by the restraints which are observed or enforced. When all
restraints are set aside sensuality is set free. Women were
not suppressed. They took their place by the men and only
demanded for themselves a liberty equal to that assumed by the
men. The opinion has been expressed that Isabella d'Este
" may be regarded as the most splendid realization of the Renaissance ideal of woman." [3] Vittoria Colonna has been more
generally accorded that position. She is doubly interesting for
her Platonic relation to Michael Angelo, who was fifteen years her
senior,[4] and for her personal character. The title " bastard " was
often worn with pride. In royal houses it happened often that
the illegitimate branch took the throne on the failure of the other,
so that the existence of the former was a recognized and useful
fact, not a shameful one.[5] Although it was true that woman
" occupied a place by the side of man, contended with him for
intellectual prizes, and took part in every spirited movement,"
although many of them became celebrated for humanistic attainments, and were intrusted with the government of states,[6] yet it
was not possible that they could maintain womanly honor and

---

[1] Cartwright, *Isabella d'Este*, I, 145.
[2] Geiger, *Renaissance*, 318.
[3] Opdyke, trans. of Castiglione, *Courtier*, 398.
[4] Lannau-Rolland, *Michel Ange et Vittoria Colonna*, Chap. VI.
[5] Heyck, *Die Mediceer*, 70; Symonds, *Renaissance*, I, 37.
[6] Gregorovius, *Lucretia Borgia*, 27.

dignity side by side with the concubines and bastards of their husbands. The love of men for men was a current vice which was hardly concealed and which degraded the sex relation.[1] The individualism of the period is interpreted as a motive for making love to the wife of another, that is, to another fully developed individual.[2] Adultery also appealed to the love of intrigue and the appreciation of the imaginative element. Lewd stories and dramas were produced in great numbers in which the cunning and deception of adultery were developed in all imaginable combinations of circumstances. In real life a woman's relatives showed great ferocity in enforcing against her all the current conventions about her conduct. That was because she might bring disgrace and ridicule on them by marrying beneath her, or by a liaison which was known and avenged by her husband. The assassination of the husband in such cases was only a trifling necessity which might be called for.[3] A physician having married a widowed duchess, born a princess of Aragon, her brothers murdered her and her children and caused the physician to be assassinated by hired bravos.[4] In the comedies marriage was derided and marital honor treated with contempt. Downright obscenity was not rare. Some of the comedies would not now be tolerated anywhere before an audience of men only.[5] It seems trifling that objection was made to the nakedness of some figures in Michael Angelo's "Last Judgment." "As society became more vicious, it grew nice."[6]

726. The cult of success. This deep depravation of all social interests by the elevation of success to a motive which justified itself has the character of an experiment. Amongst ourselves now, in politics, finance, and industry, we see the man-who-can-do-things elevated to a social hero whose success overrides all other considerations. Where that code is adopted it calls for arbitrary definitions, false conventions, and untruthful character.

727. Literature. There were several books published in the Renaissance period which aimed to influence the mores. In the

[1] Gauthiez, *Lorenzaccio*, 65.
[2] Burckhardt, *Renaissance*, 455.
[3] *Ibid.*, 441.
[4] *Ibid.*, 442.
[5] Gregorovius, *Lucretia Borgia*, 96.
[6] Symonds, *Renaissance*, III, 425.

middle of the fifteenth century was written Pandolfini's *Governo della Famiglia*. An old man advises his two sons and three grandsons on the philosophy and policy of life. He urges thrift and advises to stay far removed from public life. It is, he says, a "life of insults, hatreds, misrepresentations, and suspicions." He advises not to come into the intimacy of great nobles and not to lend them money. He has a low opinion of all women and would not trust a wife with secrets. Della Casa, in the first half of the sixteenth century, wrote *Il Galateo*, a treatise on manners and etiquette. He lays great stress on cleanliness of person and house, and he forbids all impropriety, for which he has a very positive code. Castiglione's *Courtier* inculcates what the age considered sound ideas on all social relations, rights, and duties. In the dialogue different views are put forward and discussed, from which it results that the views to be regarded as correct often lack point and definiteness. Symonds thinks that the type presented with approval differs little from the modern gentleman.[1] Cornaro wrote at the age of eighty-three a book called *Discorsi della Vita sobria*, which is said to set forth especially the diet by which the writer overcame physical weakness and reached a hale old age. When ninety-five he wrote another book to boast of the success of the first. He died in 1565, over a hundred years old.[2]

728. Moral anarchy. The antagonism between a virtue policy and a success policy is a constant ethical problem. The Renaissance in Italy shows that although moral traditions may be narrow and mistaken, any morality is better than moral anarchy. Moral traditions are guides which no one can afford to neglect. They are in the mores and they are lost in every great revolution of the mores. Then the men are morally lost. Their notions, desires, purposes, and means become false, and even the notion of crime is arbitrary and untrue. If all try the policy of dishonesty, the result will be the firmest conviction that honesty is the best policy. The mores aim always to arrive at correct notions of virtue. In so far as they reach correct results the virtue policy proves to be the only success policy.

[1] *Renaissance*, I, 118.   [2] Burckhardt, 335, 338.

LIST OF BOOKS CITED

Full titles of all books cited are given below in the alphabetical order of the authors' names or of the leading word of the title. Numbers after the title are the pages in the present volume on which the book is cited or used as an authority.

Aarbøger for Nordisk Oldkyndighed, 130

Abdallatif, Relation de l' Egypte (trad. de Sacy) (Paris, 1810), 336

Abel, C. W., Savage Life in New Guinea (London, 1902), 317

Abercromby, J., The Pre- and Proto-historic Finns, Eastern and Western, with Magic Songs of the West Finns (2 vols. London, 1898), 485

Achelis, H., Virgines Subintroductae (1 Cor. vii) (Leipzig, 1902), 295, 525, 526, 620

Achelis, T., Die Ekstase in ihrer kulturellen Bedeutung (Berlin, 1902), 210

Aelian, Variae Historiae, 318

Aeneas Silvius. See Piccolomini

Alanus ab Insulis, De Planctu Naturae (Migne, Patrol. Lat., V, 210), 369

Alberi, E., Relazione degli Ambasciatori Veneti al Senato (Firenze, 1840): Letter of D. Barbaro, sent to England for the Accession of Edward VI (Series I, Tome II, 230), 257

Alec-Tweedie, Mrs., Sunny Sicily (New York, no date), 458, 589

Am Urquell, 137

Ameer Ali, The Influence of Woman in Islam (Nineteenth Century, XLV, 755)

American Anthropologist, 17, 121, 142, 149, 305, 315, 326, 339, 460, 485, 533

American Journal of Semitic Languages and Literature, 536

American Journal of Sociology, 112

Ammianus Marcellinus, Rerum Gestarum (libri 18, out of 31), 418, 586

Ammon, O., Die Gesellschaftsordnung und ihre natürlichen Grundlagen (Jena, 1896), 39, 475, 541

d'Ancona, A., Le Origini del Teatro in Italia (2 tomes. Firenze, 1877 e 1891), 227, 445, 580–582, 591–595

Andree, R., Die Anthropophagie (Leipzig, 1887), 329, 332

Andree, R., Ethnographische Parallele und Vergleiche (2 Folgen. Leipzig, 1889), 326

Angerstein, W., Volkstänze im Deutschen Mittelalter (2te Aufl. Berlin, 1874), 599

l'Année Sociologique, 482. See Durkheim

l'Anthropologie, 130, 146. See Bulletins

Apostolic Constitutions. Die Syrischen Didaskalia übersetzt und erklärt von A. Achelis und J. Fleming (Leipzig, 1904) contains the "Two Ways," 316

Appianus, Historia Romana, 281

Apuleius, Metamorphoses, 364, 571

Arabian Nights, 287, 434. See Lane

Archiv für Anthropologie, 329, 447, 536–537, 543, 548–549, 563, 577–578

Archiv für Kunde der Œsterreichischen Geschichtsquellen, 443

Archiv für Religionswissenschaft, 525

Ashton, J., Social Life in the Reign of Queen Anne (London, 1883), 523

Athenæus, Deipnosophistorum libri 15, 436, 529, 542

Athenagoras, Apologia (on the resurrection of the dead), 390

Augustine, Opera (Paris, 1635), 290, 348, 360–361, 390–391, 529, 542, 585

d'Aussy. See Legrand

Australian Association for the Advancement of Science : Fourth Meeting, at Hobart, Tasmania, January, 1892 (Sydney, 1892), 187, 204, 264, 314, 317, 330, 334, 382, 459, 461

d'Avenel, G., Histoire Économique de la Propriété, des Salaires, des Denrées, et de tous les Prix en général, depuis l'an 1200 jusqu'en l'an 1800 (2 tomes. Paris, 1894–1898), 165–166, 298

Burckhardt, J., Griechische Kulturge-schichte (3 Bände. 2te Aufl. Stutt-gart, 1898), 105–107, 109–110, 468, 487

Burckhardt, J., Die Kultur der Renais-sance in Italien (Basel, 1860), 22, 249, 592, 598, 601, 627, 643–645, 650, 652–653

Burckhardt, J. L., Arabic Proverbs (Lon-don, 1830), 448, 455, 544

Bureau of Ethnology, Washington, Annual Reports, 14, 17, 25, 125, 127, 129–130, 139, 152, 186, 270–271, 317, 325, 337, 383, 442, 453, 485, 497, 501, 512, 515, 518, 533

Burnaby, A., Travels through the Mid-dle Settlements of North America in 1759 and 1760 (London, 1775), 528

Burrows, G., The Land of the Pigmies (London, 1898), 453

Büttner, C. G., Das Hinterland von Walfischbai und Angra Pequena (Heidelberg, 1884), 188

Cambridge History of Modern Europe, (ed. by A. W. Ward and G. W. Prothero) (New York, 1902, etc.), 531

Cameron, V. L., Across Africa (2 vols. London, 1877)), 145

Campbell, H., Differences in the Nervous Organization of Man and Woman (London, 1891), 343–344

Cantacuzene, J., Romana Historia (Bonn, 1832), 264

Carey, B. S., and Tuck, H. N., The Chin Hills (Rangoon, 1896), 186, 273

Carmichael, M., In Tuscany (3d ed. New York, 1902), 216, 623–624

Cartwright, J., Isabella d'Este, Mar-chioness of Mantua, 1474–1539 (2 vols. New York, 1903), 598, 650–651

Castiglione, B., The Book of the Courtier [1528] (trans. by L. E. Opdyke) (New York, 1903), 651, 653

Cato Major, De Agri Cultura, 280–281, 289

Cator, Dorothy, Everyday Life among the Head-hunters (New York, 1905), 305

Cayley-Webster, H., Through New Guinea and the Cannibal Countries (London, 1898), 150

Cellini. See Symonds
Celestina. See Mabbe
Century Magazine, 193, 441, 462

Ch. Br. R. A. S. = China Branch, Royal Asiatic Society

Chandler, F. W., Romance of Roguery : I. The Picaresque Novel in Spain (New York, 1899), 320, 597

Charles, R. H., The Book of Enoch (trans.) (Oxford, 1893), 431

Charles, R. H., The Book of Jubilees or the Little Genesis (trans.) (Lon-don, 1902), 431

Christian, F. W., The Caroline Islands (London, 1899), 139, 151, 423

Chrysostom, Opera (Migne, Patrol. Graeca, XLVII–LXIV. Homily on Matthew in LVIII, 591), 294

Churchman, The, 456

Cibrario, G. A. L., Della Politica Eco-nomia del Medio Evo (2ᵃ ed. 3 tomes) (Torino, 1841–1842), 300

Cicero, Orations, 405 ; Tusculan Dispu-tations, 570

Clement, K. J., Das Recht der Salischen Franken (Berlin, 1876), 495

Clement, P., Jacques Cœur et Charles VII, France au XV siècle (Paris, 1853), 443

Cockayne, O., Hali Maidenhad (Early English Text Society, London, 1866), 621

Codrington, R. H., The Melanesians (Oxford, 1891), 149, 272, 314, 317, 325, 334, 339, 438, 533

Cook, K. R., The Fathers of Jesus : a Study of the Lineage of the Christian Doctrines and Traditions (2 vols. London, 1886), 294–295, 379, 615–616

Corpus Juris Canonici (Colon. Munat., 1717), 348, 404, 406, 410

Corpus Juris Civilis (Lipsiae, 1858), 403

Corpus Poeticum Boreale, the Poetry of the Old Northern Tongue (Oxford, 1883), 296–297

Coryate, T., Crudities (New York, 1905), 444

Cranz, D., Historie von Grönland bis 1779 (Leipzig, 1780), 323

Crawford, J., History of the Indian Archipelago (2 vols. London, 1820) 149

Crawley, A. E., Sexual Taboo (JAI, XXIV, 116, 219), 116, 219, 430, 452, 459

Creighton, M., Historical Essays and Reviews (New York, 1902), 647, 650

Cunningham, A., Ladak (London, 1854), 352

von Langsdorff, G. H., Voyages and Travels in Various Parts of the World, 1803-1807 (Carlisle, 1817), 485

Lazarus (in Zeitschrift für Völkerpsychologie, I), 4, 60

Lea, H. C., A History of the Inquisition of the Middle Ages (3 vols. New York, 1888), 213-218, 237-238, 240-241, 243-244, 245-248, 250-259, 470, 489, 524, 526, 611, 622

Lea, H. C., Sacerdotal Celibacy (Philadelphia, 1867), 225-229, 375, 391-392, 526, 617, 620, 623-624, 644

Lecky, W. E. H., History of European Morals from Augustus to Charlemagne (3 ed. New York, 1877), 47, 208, 218-219, 225, 235, 238-239, 291, 318-319, 361-362, 377, 390, 402, 415, 443, 498, 569, 583, 613-614

Lecky, W. E. H., History of Rationalism in Europe (New York), 523

Lefèvre, Les Phénomènes de Suggestion et d'Autosuggestion (Paris, 1903), 21

Lefèvre, A., Race and Language (New York, 1894), 137-138

Legrand d'Aussy, P. J., Fabliaux ou Contes Fables et Romans du XIIme et du XIIIme Siècle (Paris, 1829), 441

Lehmann, K., Verlobung und Hochzeit (München, 1882), 408

Leland, C. G., and Prince, J. D. Kuloskap the Master (New York, 1902), 11

Lenient, C., La Satire en France au Moyen Age (Paris, 1883), 233, 255, 460, 590, 592, 594-595

Lewin, T. H., Wild Races of Southeastern India (London, 1870), 272-273, 322, 435, 461, 484

Libri-Carrucci, G. B., Sciences Mathematiques en Italie depuis la Renaissance (Paris, 1835), 300

Lichtenberger, H., Le Poème et la Légende des Nibelungen (Paris, 1891), 370, 488, 641

Lichtenstein, H., Reisen im Südlichen Afrika, 1803-1806 (2 Bände. Berlin, 1811-1812), 25

Ling Roth. See Roth

Lintilhac, E., Théâtre Sérieux du Moyen Age (Paris, no date), 581, 592, 596

Lippert, J., Kulturgeschichte der Menschheit (2 Bände. Stuttgart, 1887), 131, 186, 309, 318, 322-323, 324, 329, 336, 401, 499.

Little, W. J. K., St. Francis of Assisi (New York, 1897), 624

Livingstone, D., Travels in South Africa (2 vols. New York, 1858), 112, 188, 264, 439

Livy, 280-282

Lloyd, A. B., In Dwarf Land and Cannibal Country (New York, 1899), 330

Lope de Vega, 596

Lorris, G. de, and Meung, J. de, The Romant de la Rose (trans. by F. S. Ellis) (London, 1900), 623

Lubbock, J., Prehistoric Times (London, 1872), 126-127

Lucian, De Dea Syria, 537, 542, 556, 614

Lucian, Demonax, 580

Lucianus Samosatensis (Rostok, 1860) [I, Part II, 68, "End of the Wanderer"]

Lucius, P. E., Der Essenismus (Strassburg, 1881), 445, 615-616

Lumholtz on the Tarahumari (Scribner's Magazine, October, 1894), 120

Lund, T., Norges Historie (Kjobenhavn, 1885), 442

Mabbe, J., Celestina, or the Tragicke-Comedy of Calisto and Melibe, englished from the Spanish of Fernando de Rojas (London, 1894), 596

Machiavelli, Mandragore, 646. See Rousseau

Macrobius, Saturnalia, 290

Madras Government Museum, 352-353, 367, 385, 440

Magnin, C., Histoire des Marionettes (Paris, 1862), 589, 593, 597

Magnin, C., Les Origines du Théâtre Moderne (Paris, 1838), 564, 568-569, 575-581, 584, 591

Magnin, C., Théâtre de Hrotsvitha (Paris, 1845), 591

Mahaffy, J. P., Egypt under the Ptolemaic Dynasty (London, 1899)

Mahaffy, J. P., Social Life in Greece (London, 1874), 236, 326

Mahaffy, J. P., The Greek World under Roman Sway (New York, 1890), 475, 614

Maine, Sir H. S., Ancient Law (New York, 1871), 261

Maine, Sir H. S., Early Law and Custom (New York, 1883), 323

Mantegazza, P., Gli Amori degli Uomini (Milano, 1886), 440, 484

Nelson on the Eskimo (Bureau of Ethnology, XVIII, Part I), 383
Neumann, K., Geschichte Roms während des Verfalls der Republik (2 Bände. Breslau, 1881–1884), 281
Nieuwenhuis, A. W., In Centraal Borneo (2 tomes. Leiden, 1900), 428, 446
Nilsson, B., Les Habitants Primitifs de la Scandinavie (Paris, 1868), 122
Nineteenth Century, 388
Nivedita (Margaret E. Noble), Web of Indian Life (New York, 1904), 22, 73, 91, 275, 366, 457, 546–547
Novara Reise. See Wüllestorff

Oliphant, L., The Earl of Elgin's Mission to China and Japan (London, 1859), 549
Opdyke. See Castiglione
Otto, W., Priester und Tempel im Hellenischen Aegypten (Leipzig, 1905), 541

Pallas, P. S., Voyages en Russie (5 tomes. Paris, 1793), 485
Pandolfini, A., Trattato del Governo della Famiglia (Milano, 1902), 653
Parkinson, R., Die Ethnographie der nordwestlichen Salomo Inseln (Museum zu Dresden), 150, 479
Pater, W. H., Marius the Epicurean (London, 1885), 610
Patrick, Psychology of Language (Expletives) (Psychological Review, VIII, 113), 196
Patursson, S. O., Sibirien i vore Dage (Kjøbenhavn, 1901), 445
Paulitschke, P., Ethnographie Nordost Afrikas (2 Bände. Berlin, 1896), 145, 268, 315, 326, 339, 439, 459, 502, 516
Peel, C. V. A., Somaliland (London, 1900), 147
Pellison, M., Roman Life in Pliny's Time (trans.) (Meadville, Pennsylvania, 1897), 352
Pereiro, A. C., La Isla de Ponape (Manila, 1895), 442
Perelaer, M. T. H., Ethnographische Beschrijving der Dyaks (Zaltbommel, 1870), 274–275, 314, 339, 484
Peschel, O., The Races of Man (New York, 1876), 434
Petermann's Mittheilungen, 382
[Peters, S.], A History of Connecticut (London, 1781), 528

Petri, E., Anthropologie (in Russ.) (St. Petersburg, 1890), 548
Petri, E., Exceptiones Legum Romanorum (in Appendix to Vol. II of Savigny, F. C., Röm. Recht im Mittelalter, Heidelberg, 1834), 409
Petrie, W. M. Flinders, Race and Civilization (Smithson. Report, 1895), 189, 630
Pfeil, J., Studien aus der Südsee (Braunschweig, 1899), 127, 152, 272, 314, 454, 497
Philo Judæus, The Contemplative Life, 294
Philology, The Journal of (Cambridge, England), 488
Piccolomini, Æneas Silvius (Pope Pius II), Die Geschichte Kaiser Friedrichs des Dritten (übersetzt von Ilgen) (Leipzig, 1899), 409
Pickering, W. A., Formosa (London, 1898), 318
Pietschmann, R., Die Phönizier (Berlin, 1899), 9, 10, 224, 487, 542, 555–556
Pike, L. O., Crime in England (London, 1873–1876), 392
Pinkerton, J., Collection of Voyages (17 vols. 1808–1814), 268
Pischon, C. N., Der Einfluss des Islam auf das Leben seiner Bekenner (Leipzig, 1881), 204, 260, 302, 454, 517
Pliny, Naturalis Historia, 104, 175, 199, 208, 319, 365, 512
Plutarch, Lives of Illustrious Men, 378
Pöhlmann, R., Die Uebervölkerung der Antiquen Grossstädte (Leipzig, 1884), 103
Politisch-Anthropologische Revue, 385
Pollock, Sir F., and Maitland, F. W., English Law (Cambridge, 1895), 411
Polyptique de l'Abbé Irminon (ed. Guerard) (Paris, 1844), 320
Pommerol, J., Une Femme chez les Sahariennes (Paris), 189, 269, 422, 427
Porphyrius, De Abstinentia, 26, 339
Portman, L., Vacation Studies (New York, 1902), 113
Powers, S., The Tribes of California (Washington, 1877), 120, 129, 152–153, 324, 442, 501, 512, 533
Prescott, W. H., The Conquest of Peru (Philadelphia, no date), 486
Preuss, Die Feuergötter (Mitt. der Anthrop. Gesellschaft in Wien, XXXIII, 156), 135, 337, 538, 554, 577

Rubruck. See Rockhill

Rudeck, W., Geschichte der oeffentlichen Sittlichkeit in Deutschland (Jena, 1897), 184, 316, 320, 443, 475–478, 527, 530

Russian Ethnography : The Peoples of Russia (published by the Journal "Nations and Peoples," St. Petersburg, 1878) (in Russ.), 323, 326, 454, 456

de Saint Genois, J., Sur des Lettres Inédites de Jacques de Vitry écrites en 1216 (in Nouv. Mém. de l'Acad. Roy. de Belgique, XXIII, 1849), 215–216, 622–623

Salviani Opera Omnia (Vindobonae, 1883) (Corpus Script. Ecclesiast., VIII), 365, 529, 557, 559, 583–586

Sarassin, P. and F., Die Weddahs (Wiesbaden, 1893), 357, 484

Sarpi, Fra Paolo, Della Inquisizione di Venezia (in Vol. IV of his Opere), 230, 258–259

Savigny. See Petri

Schaafhausen, Menschenfresserei und das Menschenopfer (Archiv für Anthropologie, IV, 245), 329

von Schack, A. F., Dramatische Literatur und Kunst in Spanien (Frankfurt, 1854), 595

Schallmeyer, W., Vererbung und Auslese (Jena, 1903), 91, 440, 475, 549, 631

Scheltema, J., Volksgebruiken der Nederlanders bij het Vrijen en Trouwen (Utrecht, 1832), 527

Scherillo, M., La Commedia dell' Arte in Italia (Torino, 1884), 598, 601, 603

Scherr, J., Deutsche Frauenwelt (Leipzig, 1898), 196, 369, 442, 530, 590, 595

Scherr, J., Deutsche Kultur- und Sittengeschichte (Leipzig, 1879), 82, 184, 222, 255, 522, 530–531, 571

Schmidt, C., La Société Civile dans le Monde Romain et sa Transformation par le Christianisme (Strassbourg, 1853), 280, 289, 290, 572, 581, 583–584

Schmidt, E., Ceylon (Berlin, 1897), 273, 357, 440

Schoemann, G. F., Griechische Alterthümer (Berlin, 1897), 356

Schomburgk, R., Britisch Guiana in 1840–1844 (Leipzig, 1847), 131, 139, 182, 382, 501

Schotel, G. D. J., Het Oud-Hollandsch Huisgezin der Zeventiende Eeuw (Haarlem, 1867), 527

Schotmüller, K., Untergang des Templer-Ordens (Berlin, 1887), 23, 241, 257, 470

Schrader, E., The Prehistoric Antiquities of the Aryan Peoples (trans.) (London, 1890), 326, 553

Schultz, A., Das Höfische Leben zur Zeit der Minnesinger (Leipzig, 1879–1880), 369, 442, 469, 522–523, 531

Schultz, A., Deutsches Leben in XIVten und XVten Jahrhundert (Cited D. L.) (Leipzig, 1892), 184, 369–370, 422, 444, 599

Schultze, Psychologie der Naturvölker, 136, 140

Schurz, H., Entstehungsgeschichte des Geldes (Deutsche Geographische Blätter, XX, Bremen, 1897), 14', 144–154

Schwaner, C. A. L. M., Borneo (Amsterdam, 1853), 188, 274, 383, 459

Schweinfurth, G., The Heart of Africa (trans.) (New York, 1874), 147, 188, 302, 305, 439, 441, 462, 516

Scientific American, 130

Scribner's Magazine, 142, 441, 461

Scripta Historica Islandorum : II. Historiae Olavi Trygvii (Hafniae, 1827), 543

Seeck, G., Untergang der antiquen Welt (Berlin, 1895), 103–107

Selenka, E., Der Schmuck des Menschen (Berlin, 1900)

Semon, R., In the Australian Bush (New York, 1899), 435–436

Semper, K., Die Palau Inseln (Leipzig, 1873), 143, 151–152, 422–423, 436

Seneca, De Ira, 283, 319; Letters, 360, 379; Opera, 319

Serpa Pinto, Como eu atravassei Africa (London, 1881), 269, 337, 533

Seuberlich. See Nekrassow

Sibree, J., jr., The Great African Island (London, 1880), 448, 512, 516

Sieroshevski, V. L., Jakuty (in Russ.) (St. Petersburg, 1896), 326, 434, 461, 485

Sieroshevski, V. L., Twelve Years in the Country of the Yakuts (Polish version of the last with revision and additions) (Warsaw, 1900), 422, 495

Simkhovitsch, W. G., Die Feldgemeinschaft in Russland (Jena, 1898), 89

595; also Opuscula Omnia (Paris, 1534), 299
Thomson, J., Illustrations of China (London, 1873), 434
Tiele, C. P., Geschichte der Religion im Alterthume (Gotha, 1896), 81, 486, 550, 555, 563
Times, The New York, 208, 218, 235, 326
Todd, J. H., Life of St. Patrick (Dublin, 1864), 526, 620
Tornauw, Das Moslimische Recht (Leipzig, 1855), 455
Trevelyan, G. M., England in the Age of Wycliffe (New York, 1899), 531
Two Ways, The, 316. See Apostolic Constitutions
Tylor, E. B., Anthropology (New York, 1881), 120, 187
Tylor, E. B., Early History of Mankind (London, 1865), 125

Ueberweg, F., History of Philosophy (trans.) (New York, 1873), 613
Uhland, Geschichte der Dichtung und Sage (Stuttgart, 1865), 204, 370, 641
Umschau, Die, 91, 189, 358, 425, 483, 531

Valerius Maximus, Factorum et Dictorum Memorabilium libri novem, 364, 378, 541, 569
Vambery, H., Sittenbilder aus dem Morgenlande (Berlin, 1877), 303, 426, 455
Vanutelli, L., e Citerni, C., L'Omo (Milano, 1899), 145, 303, 322, 437
de Varnhagen, F. A., Historia Geral do Brazil (Rio de Janeiro, 1854–1857), 272
Venetian Ambassadors. See Alberi
Veth, P. J., Borneo's Wester-Afdeeling (Zaltbommel, 1856), 421, 501
Vinogradoff, P. G., Villainage in England (Oxford, 1892), 298
Vissering, W., On Chinese Currency (Leiden, 1877), 153
Vitry. See Saint Genois
Volkens, G., Der Kilimandscharo (Berlin, 1897), 148, 317, 339

Wachsmuth, Bauernkriege (Räumer, Hist. Taschenbuch, V), 83, 297
Waitz, F. T., Anthropologie (1859–1872), 139, 317, 432
Wallon, H. A., L'Esclavage dans l'Antiquité (Paris, 1847), 282–283, 289, 292

Weinhold, K., Die Deutschen Frauen in dem Mittelalter (Wien, 1882), 154, 204, 295, 319–320, 327, 370, 409–410, 412–413, 434, 442–443, 469, 488, 526, 529
Wellhausen, J., Die Ehe bei den Arabern (Göttingen, 1893), 320, 358, 363, 391, 488
Wellhausen, J., Skizzen und Vorarbeiten (Berlin, 1887), 429, 504–506, 562, 620
Wellsted, J. R., Travels in Arabia (London, 1837), 535
Westerhout, R. A., Het Geslachtsleven onzer Voorouders in de Middeleeuwen (Amsterdam, no date), 530
Westermarck, E., Human Marriage (London, 1891), 357, 481
Whitmarsh, H. P., The World's Rough Hand (New York, 1898), 333
Whitney, W. D., Language and the Study of Language (New York, 1867), 134–136, 139
Wiklund, K. B., Om Lapparna i Sverige (Stockholm, 1899), 14
Wilken, G. A., Huwelijks- en Erfrecht bei de Volken van Zuid Sumatra (Bijdragen tot T. L. en V. kunde van Indie, XL), 273
Wilken, G. A., Volkenkunde van Nederl. Indie (Leiden, 1893), 25, 273, 275, 318, 334, 383, 484, 535
Wilkins, D., Concilia Magnae Britanniae et Hiberniae, 446–1717 (London, 1737), 299, 401, 408, 411–412
Wilkins, W. J., Modern Hinduism (London, 1887), 27, 62, 69, 224, 318, 340, 388, 442, 545, 588
Williams, S. W., The Middle Kingdom (New York, 1883), 275, 518
Wilson, C. T., and Felkin, R. W., Uganda and the Egyptian Sudan (London, 1882), 424, 436, 438–439
Wilutsky, P., Mann und Weib (Breslau, 1903), 382, 498
Winckler, H., Die Gesetze Hammurabis (Leipzig, 1902), 234, 277, 385
Winter, E. See Jastrow, J.
Wisen, T., Om Qvinnan i Nordens Forntid (Lund, 1870), 402
Wissowa, G., Religion und Kultus der Römer (München, 1892), 568
Wobbermin, G., Beeinflussung des Urchristenthums durch das Mysterienwesen (Berlin 1896), 567

INDEX

A CATALOG OF SELECTED
DOVER BOOKS
IN ALL FIELDS OF INTEREST

A CATALOG OF SELECTED DOVER
BOOKS IN ALL FIELDS OF INTEREST

CONCERNING THE SPIRITUAL IN ART, Wassily Kandinsky. Pioneering work by father of abstract art. Thoughts on color theory, nature of art. Analysis of earlier masters. 12 illustrations. 80pp. of text. 5⅜ x 8½. 23411-8

ANIMALS: 1,419 Copyright-Free Illustrations of Mammals, Birds, Fish, Insects, etc., Jim Harter (ed.). Clear wood engravings present, in extremely lifelike poses, over 1,000 species of animals. One of the most extensive pictorial sourcebooks of its kind. Captions. Index. 284pp. 9 x 12. 23766-4

CELTIC ART: The Methods of Construction, George Bain. Simple geometric techniques for making Celtic interlacements, spirals, Kells-type initials, animals, humans, etc. Over 500 illustrations. 160pp. 9 x 12. (Available in U.S. only.) 22923-8

AN ATLAS OF ANATOMY FOR ARTISTS, Fritz Schider. Most thorough reference work on art anatomy in the world. Hundreds of illustrations, including selections from works by Vesalius, Leonardo, Goya, Ingres, Michelangelo, others. 593 illustrations. 192pp. 7⅛ x 10¼. 20241-0

CELTIC HAND STROKE-BY-STROKE (Irish Half-Uncial from "The Book of Kells"): An Arthur Baker Calligraphy Manual, Arthur Baker. Complete guide to creating each letter of the alphabet in distinctive Celtic manner. Covers hand position, strokes, pens, inks, paper, more. Illustrated. 48pp. 8¼ x 11. 24336-2

EASY ORIGAMI, John Montroll. Charming collection of 32 projects (hat, cup, pelican, piano, swan, many more) specially designed for the novice origami hobbyist. Clearly illustrated easy-to-follow instructions insure that even beginning papercrafters will achieve successful results. 48pp. 8¼ x 11. 27298-2

THE COMPLETE BOOK OF BIRDHOUSE CONSTRUCTION FOR WOOD-WORKERS, Scott D. Campbell. Detailed instructions, illustrations, tables. Also data on bird habitat and instinct patterns. Bibliography. 3 tables. 63 illustrations in 15 figures. 48pp. 5¼ x 8½. 24407-5

BLOOMINGDALE'S ILLUSTRATED 1886 CATALOG: Fashions, Dry Goods and Housewares, Bloomingdale Brothers. Famed merchants' extremely rare catalog depicting about 1,700 products: clothing, housewares, firearms, dry goods, jewelry, more. Invaluable for dating, identifying vintage items. Also, copyright-free graphics for artists, designers. Co-published with Henry Ford Museum & Greenfield Village. 160pp. 8¼ x 11. 25780-0

HISTORIC COSTUME IN PICTURES, Braun & Schneider. Over 1,450 costumed figures in clearly detailed engravings–from dawn of civilization to end of 19th century. Captions. Many folk costumes. 256pp. 8⅜ x 11¾. 23150-X

STICKLEY CRAFTSMAN FURNITURE CATALOGS, Gustav Stickley and L. & J. G. Stickley. Beautiful, functional furniture in two authentic catalogs from 1910. 594 illustrations, including 277 photos, show settles, rockers, armchairs, reclining chairs, bookcases, desks, tables. 183pp. 6½ x 9¼. 23838-5

AMERICAN LOCOMOTIVES IN HISTORIC PHOTOGRAPHS: 1858 to 1949, Ron Ziel (ed.). A rare collection of 126 meticulously detailed official photographs, called "builder portraits," of American locomotives that majestically chronicle the rise of steam locomotive power in America. Introduction. Detailed captions. xi+ 129pp. 9 x 12. 27393-8

AMERICA'S LIGHTHOUSES: An Illustrated History, Francis Ross Holland, Jr. Delightfully written, profusely illustrated fact-filled survey of over 200 American light-houses since 1716. History, anecdotes, technological advances, more. 240pp. 8 x 10¾. 25576-X

TOWARDS A NEW ARCHITECTURE, Le Corbusier. Pioneering manifesto by founder of "International School." Technical and aesthetic theories, views of industry, economics, relation of form to function, "mass-production split" and much more. Profusely illustrated. 320pp. 6⅛ x 9¼. (Available in U.S. only.) 25023-7

HOW THE OTHER HALF LIVES, Jacob Riis. Famous journalistic record, exposing poverty and degradation of New York slums around 1900, by major social reformer. 100 striking and influential photographs. 233pp. 10 x 7⅞. 22012-5

FRUIT KEY AND TWIG KEY TO TREES AND SHRUBS, William M. Harlow. One of the handiest and most widely used identification aids. Fruit key covers 120 deciduous and evergreen species; twig key 160 deciduous species. Easily used. Over 300 photographs. 126pp. 5⅜ x 8½. 20511-8

COMMON BIRD SONGS, Dr. Donald J. Borror. Songs of 60 most common U.S. birds: robins, sparrows, cardinals, bluejays, finches, more–arranged in order of increasing complexity. Up to 9 variations of songs of each species.
Cassette and manual 99911-4

ORCHIDS AS HOUSE PLANTS, Rebecca Tyson Northen. Grow cattleyas and many other kinds of orchids–in a window, in a case, or under artificial light. 63 illustrations. 148pp. 5⅜ x 8½. 23261-1

MONSTER MAZES, Dave Phillips. Masterful mazes at four levels of difficulty. Avoid deadly perils and evil creatures to find magical treasures. Solutions for all 32 exciting illustrated puzzles. 48pp. 8¼ x 11. 26005-4

MOZART'S DON GIOVANNI (DOVER OPERA LIBRETTO SERIES), Wolfgang Amadeus Mozart. Introduced and translated by Ellen H. Bleiler. Standard Italian libretto, with complete English translation. Convenient and thoroughly portable–an ideal companion for reading along with a recording or the performance itself. Introduction. List of characters. Plot summary. 121pp. 5¼ x 8½. 24944-1

TECHNICAL MANUAL AND DICTIONARY OF CLASSICAL BALLET, Gail Grant. Defines, explains, comments on steps, movements, poses and concepts. 15-page pictorial section. Basic book for student, viewer. 127pp. 5⅜ x 8½. 21843-0

THE CLARINET AND CLARINET PLAYING, David Pino. Lively, comprehensive work features suggestions about technique, musicianship, and musical interpretation, as well as guidelines for teaching, making your own reeds, and preparing for public performance. Includes an intriguing look at clarinet history. "A godsend," *The Clarinet,* Journal of the International Clarinet Society. Appendixes. 7 illus. 320pp. 5⅜ x 8½. 40270-3

HOLLYWOOD GLAMOR PORTRAITS, John Kobal (ed.). 145 photos from 1926-49. Harlow, Gable, Bogart, Bacall; 94 stars in all. Full background on photographers, technical aspects. 160pp. 8⅜ x 11¼. 23352-9

THE ANNOTATED CASEY AT THE BAT: A Collection of Ballads about the Mighty Casey/Third, Revised Edition, Martin Gardner (ed.). Amusing sequels and parodies of one of America's best-loved poems: Casey's Revenge, Why Casey Whiffed, Casey's Sister at the Bat, others. 256pp. 5⅜ x 8½. 28598-7

THE RAVEN AND OTHER FAVORITE POEMS, Edgar Allan Poe. Over 40 of the author's most memorable poems: "The Bells," "Ulalume," "Israfel," "To Helen," "The Conqueror Worm," "Eldorado," "Annabel Lee," many more. Alphabetic lists of titles and first lines. 64pp. 5³⁄₁₆ x 8¼. 26685-0

PERSONAL MEMOIRS OF U. S. GRANT, Ulysses Simpson Grant. Intelligent, deeply moving firsthand account of Civil War campaigns, considered by many the finest military memoirs ever written. Includes letters, historic photographs, maps and more. 528pp. 6⅛ x 9¼. 28587-1

ANCIENT EGYPTIAN MATERIALS AND INDUSTRIES, A. Lucas and J. Harris. Fascinating, comprehensive, thoroughly documented text describes this ancient civilization's vast resources and the processes that incorporated them in daily life, including the use of animal products, building materials, cosmetics, perfumes and incense, fibers, glazed ware, glass and its manufacture, materials used in the mummification process, and much more. 544pp. 6⅛ x 9¼. (Available in U.S. only.) 40446-3

RUSSIAN STORIES/RUSSKIE RASSKAZY: A Dual-Language Book, edited by Gleb Struve. Twelve tales by such masters as Chekhov, Tolstoy, Dostoevsky, Pushkin, others. Excellent word-for-word English translations on facing pages, plus teaching and study aids, Russian/English vocabulary, biographical/critical introductions, more. 416pp. 5⅜ x 8½. 26244-8

PHILADELPHIA THEN AND NOW: 60 Sites Photographed in the Past and Present, Kenneth Finkel and Susan Oyama. Rare photographs of City Hall, Logan Square, Independence Hall, Betsy Ross House, other landmarks juxtaposed with contemporary views. Captures changing face of historic city. Introduction. Captions. 128pp. 8¼ x 11. 25790-8

AIA ARCHITECTURAL GUIDE TO NASSAU AND SUFFOLK COUNTIES, LONG ISLAND, The American Institute of Architects, Long Island Chapter, and the Society for the Preservation of Long Island Antiquities. Comprehensive, well-researched and generously illustrated volume brings to life over three centuries of Long Island's great architectural heritage. More than 240 photographs with authoritative, extensively detailed captions. 176pp. 8¼ x 11. 26946-9

NORTH AMERICAN INDIAN LIFE: Customs and Traditions of 23 Tribes, Elsie Clews Parsons (ed.). 27 fictionalized essays by noted anthropologists examine religion, customs, government, additional facets of life among the Winnebago, Crow, Zuni, Eskimo, other tribes. 480pp. 6⅛ x 9¼. 27377-6

FRANK LLOYD WRIGHT'S DANA HOUSE, Donald Hoffmann. Pictorial essay of residential masterpiece with over 160 interior and exterior photos, plans, elevations, sketches and studies. 128pp. 9¼ x 10¾.   29120-0

THE MALE AND FEMALE FIGURE IN MOTION: 60 Classic Photographic Sequences, Eadweard Muybridge. 60 true-action photographs of men and women walking, running, climbing, bending, turning, etc., reproduced from rare 19th-century masterpiece. vi + 121pp. 9 x 12.   24745-7

1001 QUESTIONS ANSWERED ABOUT THE SEASHORE, N. J. Berrill and Jacquelyn Berrill. Queries answered about dolphins, sea snails, sponges, starfish, fishes, shore birds, many others. Covers appearance, breeding, growth, feeding, much more. 305pp. 5¼ x 8¼.   23366-9

ATTRACTING BIRDS TO YOUR YARD, William J. Weber. Easy-to-follow guide offers advice on how to attract the greatest diversity of birds: birdhouses, feeders, water and waterers, much more. 96pp. 5³⁄₁₆ x 8¼.   28927-3

MEDICINAL AND OTHER USES OF NORTH AMERICAN PLANTS: A Historical Survey with Special Reference to the Eastern Indian Tribes, Charlotte Erichsen-Brown. Chronological historical citations document 500 years of usage of plants, trees, shrubs native to eastern Canada, northeastern U.S. Also complete identifying information. 343 illustrations. 544pp. 6½ x 9¼.   25951-X

STORYBOOK MAZES, Dave Phillips. 23 stories and mazes on two-page spreads: Wizard of Oz, Treasure Island, Robin Hood, etc. Solutions. 64pp. 8¼ x 11.   23628-5

AMERICAN NEGRO SONGS: 230 Folk Songs and Spirituals, Religious and Secular, John W. Work. This authoritative study traces the African influences of songs sung and played by black Americans at work, in church, and as entertainment. The author discusses the lyric significance of such songs as "Swing Low, Sweet Chariot," "John Henry," and others and offers the words and music for 230 songs. Bibliography. Index of Song Titles. 272pp. 6½ x 9¼.   40271-1

MOVIE-STAR PORTRAITS OF THE FORTIES, John Kobal (ed.). 163 glamor, studio photos of 106 stars of the 1940s: Rita Hayworth, Ava Gardner, Marlon Brando, Clark Gable, many more. 176pp. 8⅜ x 11¼.   23546-7

BENCHLEY LOST AND FOUND, Robert Benchley. Finest humor from early 30s, about pet peeves, child psychologists, post office and others. Mostly unavailable elsewhere. 73 illustrations by Peter Arno and others. 183pp. 5⅜ x 8½.   22410-4

YEKL and THE IMPORTED BRIDEGROOM AND OTHER STORIES OF YIDDISH NEW YORK, Abraham Cahan. Film Hester Street based on *Yekl* (1896). Novel, other stories among first about Jewish immigrants on N.Y.'s East Side. 240pp. 5⅜ x 8½.   22427-9

SELECTED POEMS, Walt Whitman. Generous sampling from *Leaves of Grass*. Twenty-four poems include "I Hear America Singing," "Song of the Open Road," "I Sing the Body Electric," "When Lilacs Last in the Dooryard Bloom'd," "O Captain! My Captain!"—all reprinted from an authoritative edition. Lists of titles and first lines. 128pp. 5³⁄₁₆ x 8¼.   26878-0

THE BEST TALES OF HOFFMANN, E. T. A. Hoffmann. 10 of Hoffmann's most important stories: "Nutcracker and the King of Mice," "The Golden Flowerpot," etc. 458pp. 5⅜ x 8½. 21793-0

FROM FETISH TO GOD IN ANCIENT EGYPT, E. A. Wallis Budge. Rich detailed survey of Egyptian conception of "God" and gods, magic, cult of animals, Osiris, more. Also, superb English translations of hymns and legends. 240 illustrations. 545pp. 5⅜ x 8½. 25803-3

FRENCH STORIES/CONTES FRANÇAIS: A Dual-Language Book, Wallace Fowlie. Ten stories by French masters, Voltaire to Camus: "Micromegas" by Voltaire; "The Atheist's Mass" by Balzac; "Minuet" by de Maupassant; "The Guest" by Camus, six more. Excellent English translations on facing pages. Also French-English vocabulary list, exercises, more. 352pp. 5⅜ x 8½. 26443-2

CHICAGO AT THE TURN OF THE CENTURY IN PHOTOGRAPHS: 122 Historic Views from the Collections of the Chicago Historical Society, Larry A. Viskochil. Rare large-format prints offer detailed views of City Hall, State Street, the Loop, Hull House, Union Station, many other landmarks, circa 1904-1913. Introduction. Captions. Maps. 144pp. 9⅜ x 12¼. 24656-6

OLD BROOKLYN IN EARLY PHOTOGRAPHS, 1865-1929, William Lee Younger. Luna Park, Gravesend race track, construction of Grand Army Plaza, moving of Hotel Brighton, etc. 157 previously unpublished photographs. 165pp. 8⅞ x 11¾. 23587-4

THE MYTHS OF THE NORTH AMERICAN INDIANS, Lewis Spence. Rich anthology of the myths and legends of the Algonquins, Iroquois, Pawnees and Sioux, prefaced by an extensive historical and ethnological commentary. 36 illustrations. 480pp. 5⅜ x 8½. 25967-6

AN ENCYCLOPEDIA OF BATTLES: Accounts of Over 1,560 Battles from 1479 B.C. to the Present, David Eggenberger. Essential details of every major battle in recorded history from the first battle of Megiddo in 1479 B.C. to Grenada in 1984. List of Battle Maps. New Appendix covering the years 1967-1984. Index. 99 illustrations. 544pp. 6½ x 9¼. 24913-1

SAILING ALONE AROUND THE WORLD, Captain Joshua Slocum. First man to sail around the world, alone, in small boat. One of great feats of seamanship told in delightful manner. 67 illustrations. 294pp. 5⅜ x 8½. 20326-3

ANARCHISM AND OTHER ESSAYS, Emma Goldman. Powerful, penetrating, prophetic essays on direct action, role of minorities, prison reform, puritan hypocrisy, violence, etc. 271pp. 5⅜ x 8½. 22484-8

MYTHS OF THE HINDUS AND BUDDHISTS, Ananda K. Coomaraswamy and Sister Nivedita. Great stories of the epics; deeds of Krishna, Shiva, taken from puranas, Vedas, folk tales; etc. 32 illustrations. 400pp. 5⅜ x 8½. 21759-0

THE TRAUMA OF BIRTH, Otto Rank. Rank's controversial thesis that anxiety neurosis is caused by profound psychological trauma which occurs at birth. 256pp. 5⅜ x 8½. 27974-X

A THEOLOGICO-POLITICAL TREATISE, Benedict Spinoza. Also contains unfinished Political Treatise. Great classic on religious liberty, theory of government on common consent. R. Elwes translation. Total of 421pp. 5⅜ x 8½. 20249-6

MY BONDAGE AND MY FREEDOM, Frederick Douglass. Born a slave, Douglass became outspoken force in antislavery movement. The best of Douglass' autobiographies. Graphic description of slave life. 464pp. 5⅜ x 8½. 22457-0

FOLLOWING THE EQUATOR: A Journey Around the World, Mark Twain. Fascinating humorous account of 1897 voyage to Hawaii, Australia, India, New Zealand, etc. Ironic, bemused reports on peoples, customs, climate, flora and fauna, politics, much more. 197 illustrations. 720pp. 5⅜ x 8½. 26113-1

THE PEOPLE CALLED SHAKERS, Edward D. Andrews. Definitive study of Shakers: origins, beliefs, practices, dances, social organization, furniture and crafts, etc. 33 illustrations. 351pp. 5⅜ x 8½. 21081-2

THE MYTHS OF GREECE AND ROME, H. A. Guerber. A classic of mythology, generously illustrated, long prized for its simple, graphic, accurate retelling of the principal myths of Greece and Rome, and for its commentary on their origins and significance. With 64 illustrations by Michelangelo, Raphael, Titian, Rubens, Canova, Bernini and others. 480pp. 5⅜ x 8½. 27584-1

PSYCHOLOGY OF MUSIC, Carl E. Seashore. Classic work discusses music as a medium from psychological viewpoint. Clear treatment of physical acoustics, auditory apparatus, sound perception, development of musical skills, nature of musical feeling, host of other topics. 88 figures. 408pp. 5⅜ x 8½. 21851-1

THE PHILOSOPHY OF HISTORY, Georg W. Hegel. Great classic of Western thought develops concept that history is not chance but rational process, the evolution of freedom. 457pp. 5⅜ x 8½. 20112-0

THE BOOK OF TEA, Kakuzo Okakura. Minor classic of the Orient: entertaining, charming explanation, interpretation of traditional Japanese culture in terms of tea ceremony. 94pp. 5⅜ x 8½. 20070-1

LIFE IN ANCIENT EGYPT, Adolf Erman. Fullest, most thorough, detailed older account with much not in more recent books, domestic life, religion, magic, medicine, commerce, much more. Many illustrations reproduce tomb paintings, carvings, hieroglyphs, etc. 597pp. 5⅜ x 8½. 22632-8

SUNDIALS, Their Theory and Construction, Albert Waugh. Far and away the best, most thorough coverage of ideas, mathematics concerned, types, construction, adjusting anywhere. Simple, nontechnical treatment allows even children to build several of these dials. Over 100 illustrations. 230pp. 5⅜ x 8½. 22947-5

THEORETICAL HYDRODYNAMICS, L. M. Milne-Thomson. Classic exposition of the mathematical theory of fluid motion, applicable to both hydrodynamics and aerodynamics. Over 600 exercises. 768pp. 6⅛ x 9¼. 68970-0

SONGS OF EXPERIENCE: Facsimile Reproduction with 26 Plates in Full Color, William Blake. 26 full-color plates from a rare 1826 edition. Includes "The Tyger," "London," "Holy Thursday," and other poems. Printed text of poems. 48pp. 5¼ x 7. 24636-1

OLD-TIME VIGNETTES IN FULL COLOR, Carol Belanger Grafton (ed.). Over 390 charming, often sentimental illustrations, selected from archives of Victorian graphics—pretty women posing, children playing, food, flowers, kittens and puppies, smiling cherubs, birds and butterflies, much more. All copyright-free. 48pp. 9¼ x 12¼. 27269-9

PERSPECTIVE FOR ARTISTS, Rex Vicat Cole. Depth, perspective of sky and sea, shadows, much more, not usually covered. 391 diagrams, 81 reproductions of drawings and paintings. 279pp. 5⅜ x 8½. 22487-2

DRAWING THE LIVING FIGURE, Joseph Sheppard. Innovative approach to artistic anatomy focuses on specifics of surface anatomy, rather than muscles and bones. Over 170 drawings of live models in front, back and side views, and in widely varying poses. Accompanying diagrams. 177 illustrations. Introduction. Index. 144pp. 8⅜ x11¼. 26723-7

GOTHIC AND OLD ENGLISH ALPHABETS: 100 Complete Fonts, Dan X. Solo. Add power, elegance to posters, signs, other graphics with 100 stunning copyright-free alphabets: Blackstone, Dolbey, Germania, 97 more–including many lower-case, numerals, punctuation marks. 104pp. 8⅛ x 11. 24695-7

HOW TO DO BEADWORK, Mary White. Fundamental book on craft from simple projects to five-bead chains and woven works. 106 illustrations. 142pp. 5⅜ x 8. 20697-1

THE BOOK OF WOOD CARVING, Charles Marshall Sayers. Finest book for beginners discusses fundamentals and offers 34 designs. "Absolutely first rate . . . well thought out and well executed."–E. J. Tangerman. 118pp. 7¾ x 10⅝. 23654-4

ILLUSTRATED CATALOG OF CIVIL WAR MILITARY GOODS: Union Army Weapons, Insignia, Uniform Accessories, and Other Equipment, Schuyler, Hartley, and Graham. Rare, profusely illustrated 1846 catalog includes Union Army uniform and dress regulations, arms and ammunition, coats, insignia, flags, swords, rifles, etc. 226 illustrations. 160pp. 9 x 12. 24939-5

WOMEN'S FASHIONS OF THE EARLY 1900s: An Unabridged Republication of "New York Fashions, 1909," National Cloak & Suit Co. Rare catalog of mail-order fashions documents women's and children's clothing styles shortly after the turn of the century. Captions offer full descriptions, prices. Invaluable resource for fashion, costume historians. Approximately 725 illustrations. 128pp. 8⅜ x 11¼. 27276-1

THE 1912 AND 1915 GUSTAV STICKLEY FURNITURE CATALOGS, Gustav Stickley. With over 200 detailed illustrations and descriptions, these two catalogs are essential reading and reference materials and identification guides for Stickley furniture. Captions cite materials, dimensions and prices. 112pp. 6½ x 9¼. 26676-1

EARLY AMERICAN LOCOMOTIVES, John H. White, Jr. Finest locomotive engravings from early 19th century: historical (1804–74), main-line (after 1870), special, foreign, etc. 147 plates. 142pp. 11⅜ x 8¼. 22772-3

THE TALL SHIPS OF TODAY IN PHOTOGRAPHS, Frank O. Braynard. Lavishly illustrated tribute to nearly 100 majestic contemporary sailing vessels: Amerigo Vespucci, Clearwater, Constitution, Eagle, Mayflower, Sea Cloud, Victory, many more. Authoritative captions provide statistics, background on each ship. 190 black-and-white photographs and illustrations. Introduction. 128pp. 8⅞ x 11¾. 27163-3

LITTLE BOOK OF EARLY AMERICAN CRAFTS AND TRADES, Peter Stockham (ed.). 1807 children's book explains crafts and trades: baker, hatter, cooper, potter, and many others. 23 copperplate illustrations. 140pp. 4⅝ x 6.   23336-7

VICTORIAN FASHIONS AND COSTUMES FROM HARPER'S BAZAR, 1867–1898, Stella Blum (ed.). Day costumes, evening wear, sports clothes, shoes, hats, other accessories in over 1,000 detailed engravings. 320pp. 9⅜ x 12¼.   22990-4

GUSTAV STICKLEY, THE CRAFTSMAN, Mary Ann Smith. Superb study surveys broad scope of Stickley's achievement, especially in architecture. Design philosophy, rise and fall of the Craftsman empire, descriptions and floor plans for many Craftsman houses, more. 86 black-and-white halftones. 31 line illustrations. Introduction 208pp. 6½ x 9¼.   27210-9

THE LONG ISLAND RAIL ROAD IN EARLY PHOTOGRAPHS, Ron Ziel. Over 220 rare photos, informative text document origin (1844) and development of rail service on Long Island. Vintage views of early trains, locomotives, stations, passengers, crews, much more. Captions. 8⅞ x 11¾.   26301-0

VOYAGE OF THE LIBERDADE, Joshua Slocum. Great 19th-century mariner's thrilling, first-hand account of the wreck of his ship off South America, the 35-foot boat he built from the wreckage, and its remarkable voyage home. 128pp. 5⅜ x 8½.
40022-0

TEN BOOKS ON ARCHITECTURE, Vitruvius. The most important book ever written on architecture. Early Roman aesthetics, technology, classical orders, site selection, all other aspects. Morgan translation. 331pp. 5⅜ x 8½.   20645-9

THE HUMAN FIGURE IN MOTION, Eadweard Muybridge. More than 4,500 stopped-action photos, in action series, showing undraped men, women, children jumping, lying down, throwing, sitting, wrestling, carrying, etc. 390pp. 7⅞ x 10⅝.
20204-6 Clothbd.

TREES OF THE EASTERN AND CENTRAL UNITED STATES AND CANADA, William M. Harlow. Best one-volume guide to 140 trees. Full descriptions, woodlore, range, etc. Over 600 illustrations. Handy size. 288pp. 4½ x 6⅜.   20395-6

SONGS OF WESTERN BIRDS, Dr. Donald J. Borror. Complete song and call repertoire of 60 western species, including flycatchers, juncoes, cactus wrens, many more–includes fully illustrated booklet.   Cassette and manual 99913-0

GROWING AND USING HERBS AND SPICES, Milo Miloradovich. Versatile handbook provides all the information needed for cultivation and use of all the herbs and spices available in North America. 4 illustrations. Index. Glossary. 236pp. 5⅜ x 8½.
25058-X

BIG BOOK OF MAZES AND LABYRINTHS, Walter Shepherd. 50 mazes and labyrinths in all–classical, solid, ripple, and more–in one great volume. Perfect inexpensive puzzler for clever youngsters. Full solutions. 112pp. 8⅛ x 11.   22951-3

PIANO TUNING, J. Cree Fischer. Clearest, best book for beginner, amateur. Simple repairs, raising dropped notes, tuning by easy method of flattened fifths. No previous skills needed. 4 illustrations. 201pp. 5⅜ x 8½.   23267-0

HINTS TO SINGERS, Lillian Nordica. Selecting the right teacher, developing confidence, overcoming stage fright, and many other important skills receive thoughtful discussion in this indispensible guide, written by a world-famous diva of four decades' experience. 96pp. 5⅜ x 8½.   40094-8

THE COMPLETE NONSENSE OF EDWARD LEAR, Edward Lear. All nonsense limericks, zany alphabets, Owl and Pussycat, songs, nonsense botany, etc., illustrated by Lear. Total of 320pp. 5⅜ x 8½. (Available in U.S. only.)   20167-8

VICTORIAN PARLOUR POETRY: An Annotated Anthology, Michael R. Turner. 117 gems by Longfellow, Tennyson, Browning, many lesser-known poets. "The Village Blacksmith," "Curfew Must Not Ring Tonight," "Only a Baby Small," dozens more, often difficult to find elsewhere. Index of poets, titles, first lines. xxiii + 325pp. 5⅜ x 8¼.   27044-0

DUBLINERS, James Joyce. Fifteen stories offer vivid, tightly focused observations of the lives of Dublin's poorer classes. At least one, "The Dead," is considered a masterpiece. Reprinted complete and unabridged from standard edition. 160pp. 5³⁄₁₆ x 8¼.
26870-5

GREAT WEIRD TALES: 14 Stories by Lovecraft, Blackwood, Machen and Others, S. T. Joshi (ed.). 14 spellbinding tales, including "The Sin Eater," by Fiona McLeod, "The Eye Above the Mantel," by Frank Belknap Long, as well as renowned works by R. H. Barlow, Lord Dunsany, Arthur Machen, W. C. Morrow and eight other masters of the genre. 256pp. 5⅜ x 8½. (Available in U.S. only.)   40436-6

THE BOOK OF THE SACRED MAGIC OF ABRAMELIN THE MAGE, translated by S. MacGregor Mathers. Medieval manuscript of ceremonial magic. Basic document in Aleister Crowley, Golden Dawn groups. 268pp. 5⅜ x 8½.   23211-5

NEW RUSSIAN-ENGLISH AND ENGLISH-RUSSIAN DICTIONARY, M. A. O'Brien. This is a remarkably handy Russian dictionary, containing a surprising amount of information, including over 70,000 entries. 366pp. 4½ x 6⅛.   20208-9

HISTORIC HOMES OF THE AMERICAN PRESIDENTS, Second, Revised Edition, Irvin Haas. A traveler's guide to American Presidential homes, most open to the public, depicting and describing homes occupied by every American President from George Washington to George Bush. With visiting hours, admission charges, travel routes. 175 photographs. Index. 160pp. 8¼ x 11.   26751-2

NEW YORK IN THE FORTIES, Andreas Feininger. 162 brilliant photographs by the well-known photographer, formerly with *Life* magazine. Commuters, shoppers, Times Square at night, much else from city at its peak. Captions by John von Hartz. 181pp. 9¼ x 10¾.   23585-8

INDIAN SIGN LANGUAGE, William Tomkins. Over 525 signs developed by Sioux and other tribes. Written instructions and diagrams. Also 290 pictographs. 111pp. 6⅛ x 9¼.   22029-X

ANATOMY: A Complete Guide for Artists, Joseph Sheppard. A master of figure drawing shows artists how to render human anatomy convincingly. Over 460 illustrations. 224pp. 8⅜ x 11¼. 27279-6

MEDIEVAL CALLIGRAPHY: Its History and Technique, Marc Drogin. Spirited history, comprehensive instruction manual covers 13 styles (ca. 4th century through 15th). Excellent photographs; directions for duplicating medieval techniques with modern tools. 224pp. 8⅜ x 11¼. 26142-5

DRIED FLOWERS: How to Prepare Them, Sarah Whitlock and Martha Rankin. Complete instructions on how to use silica gel, meal and borax, perlite aggregate, sand and borax, glycerine and water to create attractive permanent flower arrangements. 12 illustrations. 32pp. 5⅜ x 8½. 21802-3

EASY-TO-MAKE BIRD FEEDERS FOR WOODWORKERS, Scott D. Campbell. Detailed, simple-to-use guide for designing, constructing, caring for and using feeders. Text, illustrations for 12 classic and contemporary designs. 96pp. 5⅜ x 8½. 25847-5

SCOTTISH WONDER TALES FROM MYTH AND LEGEND, Donald A. Mackenzie. 16 lively tales tell of giants rumbling down mountainsides, of a magic wand that turns stone pillars into warriors, of gods and goddesses, evil hags, powerful forces and more. 240pp. 5⅜ x 8½. 29677-6

THE HISTORY OF UNDERCLOTHES, C. Willett Cunnington and Phyllis Cunnington. Fascinating, well-documented survey covering six centuries of English undergarments, enhanced with over 100 illustrations: 12th-century laced-up bodice, footed long drawers (1795), 19th-century bustles, 19th-century corsets for men, Victorian "bust improvers," much more. 272pp. 5⅜ x 8¼. 27124-2

ARTS AND CRAFTS FURNITURE: The Complete Brooks Catalog of 1912, Brooks Manufacturing Co. Photos and detailed descriptions of more than 150 now very collectible furniture designs from the Arts and Crafts movement depict davenports, settees, buffets, desks, tables, chairs, bedsteads, dressers and more, all built of solid, quarter-sawed oak. Invaluable for students and enthusiasts of antiques, Americana and the decorative arts. 80pp. 6½ x 9¼. 27471-3

WILBUR AND ORVILLE: A Biography of the Wright Brothers, Fred Howard. Definitive, crisply written study tells the full story of the brothers' lives and work. A vividly written biography, unparalleled in scope and color, that also captures the spirit of an extraordinary era. 560pp. 6⅛ x 9¼. 40297-5

THE ARTS OF THE SAILOR: Knotting, Splicing and Ropework, Hervey Garrett Smith. Indispensable shipboard reference covers tools, basic knots and useful hitches; handsewing and canvas work, more. Over 100 illustrations. Delightful reading for sea lovers. 256pp. 5⅜ x 8½. 26440-8

FRANK LLOYD WRIGHT'S FALLINGWATER: The House and Its History, Second, Revised Edition, Donald Hoffmann. A total revision–both in text and illustrations–of the standard document on Fallingwater, the boldest, most personal architectural statement of Wright's mature years, updated with valuable new material from the recently opened Frank Lloyd Wright Archives. "Fascinating"–*The New York Times*. 116 illustrations. 128pp. 9¼ x 10¾. 27430-6

PHOTOGRAPHIC SKETCHBOOK OF THE CIVIL WAR, Alexander Gardner. 100 photos taken on field during the Civil War. Famous shots of Manassas Harper's Ferry, Lincoln, Richmond, slave pens, etc. 244pp. 10⅝ x 8¼. 22731-6

FIVE ACRES AND INDEPENDENCE, Maurice G. Kains. Great back-to-the-land classic explains basics of self-sufficient farming. The one book to get. 95 illustrations. 397pp. 5⅜ x 8½. 20974-1

SONGS OF EASTERN BIRDS, Dr. Donald J. Borror. Songs and calls of 60 species most common to eastern U.S.: warblers, woodpeckers, flycatchers, thrushes, larks, many more in high-quality recording. Cassette and manual 99912-2

A MODERN HERBAL, Margaret Grieve. Much the fullest, most exact, most useful compilation of herbal material. Gigantic alphabetical encyclopedia, from aconite to zedoary, gives botanical information, medical properties, folklore, economic uses, much else. Indispensable to serious reader. 161 illustrations. 888pp. 6½ x 9¼. 2-vol. set. (Available in U.S. only.) Vol. I: 22798-7
Vol. II: 22799-5

HIDDEN TREASURE MAZE BOOK, Dave Phillips. Solve 34 challenging mazes accompanied by heroic tales of adventure. Evil dragons, people-eating plants, blood-thirsty giants, many more dangerous adversaries lurk at every twist and turn. 34 mazes, stories, solutions. 48pp. 8¼ x 11. 24566-7

LETTERS OF W. A. MOZART, Wolfgang A. Mozart. Remarkable letters show bawdy wit, humor, imagination, musical insights, contemporary musical world; includes some letters from Leopold Mozart. 276pp. 5⅜ x 8½. 22859-2

BASIC PRINCIPLES OF CLASSICAL BALLET, Agrippina Vaganova. Great Russian theoretician, teacher explains methods for teaching classical ballet. 118 illustrations. 175pp. 5⅜ x 8½. 22036-2

THE JUMPING FROG, Mark Twain. Revenge edition. The original story of The Celebrated Jumping Frog of Calaveras County, a hapless French translation, and Twain's hilarious "retranslation" from the French. 12 illustrations. 66pp. 5⅜ x 8½. 22686-7

BEST REMEMBERED POEMS, Martin Gardner (ed.). The 126 poems in this superb collection of 19th- and 20th-century British and American verse range from Shelley's "To a Skylark" to the impassioned "Renascence" of Edna St. Vincent Millay and to Edward Lear's whimsical "The Owl and the Pussycat." 224pp. 5⅜ x 8½. 27165-X

COMPLETE SONNETS, William Shakespeare. Over 150 exquisite poems deal with love, friendship, the tyranny of time, beauty's evanescence, death and other themes in language of remarkable power, precision and beauty. Glossary of archaic terms. 80pp. 5³⁄₁₆ x 8¼. 26686-9

THE BATTLES THAT CHANGED HISTORY, Fletcher Pratt. Eminent historian profiles 16 crucial conflicts, ancient to modern, that changed the course of civilization. 352pp. 5⅜ x 8½. 41129-X

THE WIT AND HUMOR OF OSCAR WILDE, Alvin Redman (ed.). More than 1,000 ripostes, paradoxes, wisecracks: Work is the curse of the drinking classes; I can resist everything except temptation; etc. 258pp. 5⅜ x 8½. 20602-5

SHAKESPEARE LEXICON AND QUOTATION DICTIONARY, Alexander Schmidt. Full definitions, locations, shades of meaning in every word in plays and poems. More than 50,000 exact quotations. 1,485pp. 6½ x 9¼. 2-vol. set.
Vol. 1: 22726-X
Vol. 2: 22727-8

SELECTED POEMS, Emily Dickinson. Over 100 best-known, best-loved poems by one of America's foremost poets, reprinted from authoritative early editions. No comparable edition at this price. Index of first lines. 64pp. 5³⁄₁₆ x 8¼. 26466-1

THE INSIDIOUS DR. FU-MANCHU, Sax Rohmer. The first of the popular mystery series introduces a pair of English detectives to their archnemesis, the diabolical Dr. Fu-Manchu. Flavorful atmosphere, fast-paced action, and colorful characters enliven this classic of the genre. 208pp. 5³⁄₁₆ x 8¼. 29898-1

THE MALLEUS MALEFICARUM OF KRAMER AND SPRENGER, translated by Montague Summers. Full text of most important witchhunter's "bible," used by both Catholics and Protestants. 278pp. 6⅝ x 10. 22802-9

SPANISH STORIES/CUENTOS ESPAÑOLES: A Dual-Language Book, Angel Flores (ed.). Unique format offers 13 great stories in Spanish by Cervantes, Borges, others. Faithful English translations on facing pages. 352pp. 5⅜ x 8½. 25399-6

GARDEN CITY, LONG ISLAND, IN EARLY PHOTOGRAPHS, 1869–1919, Mildred H. Smith. Handsome treasury of 118 vintage pictures, accompanied by carefully researched captions, document the Garden City Hotel fire (1899), the Vanderbilt Cup Race (1908), the first airmail flight departing from the Nassau Boulevard Aerodrome (1911), and much more. 96pp. 8⅞ x 11¾. 40669-5

OLD QUEENS, N.Y., IN EARLY PHOTOGRAPHS, Vincent F. Seyfried and William Asadorian. Over 160 rare photographs of Maspeth, Jamaica, Jackson Heights, and other areas. Vintage views of DeWitt Clinton mansion, 1939 World's Fair and more. Captions. 192pp. 8⅞ x 11. 26358-4

CAPTURED BY THE INDIANS: 15 Firsthand Accounts, 1750-1870, Frederick Drimmer. Astounding true historical accounts of grisly torture, bloody conflicts, relentless pursuits, miraculous escapes and more, by people who lived to tell the tale. 384pp. 5⅜ x 8½. 24901-8

THE WORLD'S GREAT SPEECHES (Fourth Enlarged Edition), Lewis Copeland, Lawrence W. Lamm, and Stephen J. McKenna. Nearly 300 speeches provide public speakers with a wealth of updated quotes and inspiration–from Pericles' funeral oration and William Jennings Bryan's "Cross of Gold Speech" to Malcolm X's powerful words on the Black Revolution and Earl of Spenser's tribute to his sister, Diana, Princess of Wales. 944pp. 5⅜ x 8⅜. 40903-1

THE BOOK OF THE SWORD, Sir Richard F. Burton. Great Victorian scholar/adventurer's eloquent, erudite history of the "queen of weapons"–from prehistory to early Roman Empire. Evolution and development of early swords, variations (sabre, broadsword, cutlass, scimitar, etc.), much more. 336pp. 6⅛ x 9¼. 25434-8

AUTOBIOGRAPHY: The Story of My Experiments with Truth, Mohandas K. Gandhi. Boyhood, legal studies, purification, the growth of the Satyagraha (nonviolent protest) movement. Critical, inspiring work of the man responsible for the freedom of India. 480pp. 5⅜ x 8½. (Available in U.S. only.)   24593-4

CELTIC MYTHS AND LEGENDS, T. W. Rolleston. Masterful retelling of Irish and Welsh stories and tales. Cuchulain, King Arthur, Deirdre, the Grail, many more. First paperback edition. 58 full-page illustrations. 512pp. 5⅜ x 8½.   26507-2

THE PRINCIPLES OF PSYCHOLOGY, William James. Famous long course complete, unabridged. Stream of thought, time perception, memory, experimental methods; great work decades ahead of its time. 94 figures. 1,391pp. 5⅜ x 8½. 2-vol. set.
Vol. I: 20381-6   Vol. II: 20382-4

THE WORLD AS WILL AND REPRESENTATION, Arthur Schopenhauer. Definitive English translation of Schopenhauer's life work, correcting more than 1,000 errors, omissions in earlier translations. Translated by E. F. J. Payne. Total of 1,269pp. 5⅜ x 8½. 2-vol. set.   Vol. 1: 21761-2   Vol. 2: 21762-0

MAGIC AND MYSTERY IN TIBET, Madame Alexandra David-Neel. Experiences among lamas, magicians, sages, sorcerers, Bonpa wizards. A true psychic discovery. 32 illustrations. 321pp. 5⅜ x 8½. (Available in U.S. only.)   22682-4

THE EGYPTIAN BOOK OF THE DEAD, E. A. Wallis Budge. Complete reproduction of Ani's papyrus, finest ever found. Full hieroglyphic text, interlinear transliteration, word-for-word translation, smooth translation. 533pp. 6½ x 9¼.   21866-X

MATHEMATICS FOR THE NONMATHEMATICIAN, Morris Kline. Detailed, college-level treatment of mathematics in cultural and historical context, with numerous exercises. Recommended Reading Lists. Tables. Numerous figures. 641pp. 5⅜ x 8½.
24823-2

PROBABILISTIC METHODS IN THE THEORY OF STRUCTURES, Isaac Elishakoff. Well-written introduction covers the elements of the theory of probability from two or more random variables, the reliability of such multivariable structures, the theory of random function, Monte Carlo methods of treating problems incapable of exact solution, and more. Examples. 502pp. 5⅜ x 8½.   40691-1

THE RIME OF THE ANCIENT MARINER, Gustave Doré, S. T. Coleridge. Doré's finest work; 34 plates capture moods, subtleties of poem. Flawless full-size reproductions printed on facing pages with authoritative text of poem. "Beautiful. Simply beautiful."–Publisher's Weekly. 77pp. 9¼ x 12.   22305-1

NORTH AMERICAN INDIAN DESIGNS FOR ARTISTS AND CRAFTSPEOPLE, Eva Wilson. Over 360 authentic copyright-free designs adapted from Navajo blankets, Hopi pottery, Sioux buffalo hides, more. Geometrics, symbolic figures, plant and animal motifs, etc. 128pp. 8⅜ x 11. (Not for sale in the United Kingdom.)   25341-4

SCULPTURE: Principles and Practice, Louis Slobodkin. Step-by-step approach to clay, plaster, metals, stone; classical and modern. 253 drawings, photos. 255pp. 8⅛ x 11.
22960-2

THE INFLUENCE OF SEA POWER UPON HISTORY, 1660–1783, A. T. Mahan. Influential classic of naval history and tactics still used as text in war colleges. First paperback edition. 4 maps. 24 battle plans. 640pp. 5⅜ x 8½.   25509-3

THE STORY OF THE TITANIC AS TOLD BY ITS SURVIVORS, Jack Winocour (ed.). What it was really like. Panic, despair, shocking inefficiency, and a little heroism. More thrilling than any fictional account. 26 illustrations. 320pp. 5⅜ x 8½. 20610-6

FAIRY AND FOLK TALES OF THE IRISH PEASANTRY, William Butler Yeats (ed.). Treasury of 64 tales from the twilight world of Celtic myth and legend: "The Soul Cages," "The Kildare Pooka," "King O'Toole and his Goose," many more. Introduction and Notes by W. B. Yeats. 352pp. 5⅜ x 8½. 26941-8

BUDDHIST MAHAYANA TEXTS, E. B. Cowell and others (eds.). Superb, accurate translations of basic documents in Mahayana Buddhism, highly important in history of religions. The Buddha-karita of Asvaghosha, Larger Sukhavativyuha, more. 448pp. 5⅜ x 8½. 25552-2

ONE TWO THREE . . . INFINITY: Facts and Speculations of Science, George Gamow. Great physicist's fascinating, readable overview of contemporary science: number theory, relativity, fourth dimension, entropy, genes, atomic structure, much more. 128 illustrations. Index. 352pp. 5⅜ x 8½. 25664-2

EXPERIMENTATION AND MEASUREMENT, W. J. Youden. Introductory manual explains laws of measurement in simple terms and offers tips for achieving accuracy and minimizing errors. Mathematics of measurement, use of instruments, experimenting with machines. 1994 edition. Foreword. Preface. Introduction. Epilogue. Selected Readings. Glossary. Index. Tables and figures. 128pp. 5⅜ x 8½. 40451-X

DALÍ ON MODERN ART: The Cuckolds of Antiquated Modern Art, Salvador Dalí. Influential painter skewers modern art and its practitioners. Outrageous evaluations of Picasso, Cézanne, Turner, more. 15 renderings of paintings discussed. 44 calligraphic decorations by Dalí. 96pp. 5⅜ x 8½. (Available in U.S. only.) 29220-7

ANTIQUE PLAYING CARDS: A Pictorial History, Henry René D'Allemagne. Over 900 elaborate, decorative images from rare playing cards (14th–20th centuries): Bacchus, death, dancing dogs, hunting scenes, royal coats of arms, players cheating, much more. 96pp. 9¼ x 12¼. 29265-7

MAKING FURNITURE MASTERPIECES: 30 Projects with Measured Drawings, Franklin H. Gottshall. Step-by-step instructions, illustrations for constructing handsome, useful pieces, among them a Sheraton desk, Chippendale chair, Spanish desk, Queen Anne table and a William and Mary dressing mirror. 224pp. 8⅛ x 11¼. 29338-6

THE FOSSIL BOOK: A Record of Prehistoric Life, Patricia V. Rich et al. Profusely illustrated definitive guide covers everything from single-celled organisms and dinosaurs to birds and mammals and the interplay between climate and man. Over 1,500 illustrations. 760pp. 7½ x 10⅛. 29371-8

Paperbound unless otherwise indicated. Available at your book dealer, online at **www.doverpublications.com**, or by writing to Dept. GI, Dover Publications, Inc., 31 East 2nd Street, Mineola, NY 11501. For current price information or for free catalogues (please indicate field of interest), write to Dover Publications or log on to **www.doverpublications.com** and see every Dover book in print. Dover publishes more than 500 books each year on science, elementary and advanced mathematics, biology, music, art, literary history, social sciences, and other areas.